INSIDE ORA
DESIGNER/2000

Albert Lulushi

To join a Prentice Hall PTR internet mailing list, point to:
http://www.prenhall.com/mail_lists/

Prentice Hall PTR
Upper Saddle River, New Jersey 07458

ISBN 0-13-849753-2

90000

9 780138 497538

Library of Congress Cataloging-in-Publication Data

Lulushi, Albert.
    Inside oracle designer/2000 / Albert Lulushi.
      p. cm.
    Includes index.
    ISBN 0-13-849753-2 (alk. paper)
    1. Software engineering. 2. Designer/2000.
  QA76.758.L85 1997
  005.2'76—dc21   97-44451
                              CIP

Acquisitions editor: Mark L. Taub
Editorial assistant: Tara Ruggiero
Cover designer: Anthony Gemmellaro
Cover photo: Courtesy of Panoramic Images

Cover design director: Jerry Votta
Manufacturing manager: Alexis R. Heydt
Marketing manager: Dan Rush
Composition: Pine Tree Composition, Inc.

©1998 by Prentice Hall PTR
Prentice-Hall, Inc.
A Simon & Schuster Company
Upper Saddle River, New Jersey 07458

Prentice Hall books are widely used by corporations and government agencies for training, marketing, and resale.
The publisher offers discounts on this book when ordered in bulk quantities. For more information, contact Corporate Sales Department, Phone: 800-382-3419; FAX: 201-236-7141;
E-mail: corpsales@prenhall.com
Or write: Prentice Hall PTR, Corporate Sales Dept., One Lake Street, Upper Saddle River, NJ 07458.

Oracle, Designer/2000, Developer/2000, and PL/SQL are registered trademarks or trademarks of Oracle Corporation. Windows, Windows NT, and Windows 95 are registered trademarks or trademarks of Microsoft Corporation. ScreenCam is a registered trademark of Lotus Development Corp. Java is a trademark of Sun Microsystems, Inc. The American Software Club (TASC) is a fictional company used for illustration purposes. Any resemblance to any company in real life is purely coincidental. All other products or company names mentioned may be registered trademarks or trademarks of their respective owners.

Printed in the United States of America
10 9 8 7 6 5 4 3 2 1

ISBN: 0-13-849753-2

Prentice-Hall International (UK) Limited, *London*
Prentice-Hall of Australia Pty. Limited, *Sydney*
Prentice-Hall Canada Inc., *Toronto*
Prentice-Hall Hispanoamericana, S.A., *Mexico*
Prentice-Hall of India Private Limited, *New Delhi*
Prentice-Hall of Japan, Inc., *Tokyo*
Simon & Schuster Asia Pte. Ltd., *Singapore*
Editora Prentice-Hall do Brasil, Ltda., *Rio de Janeiro*

In memory of my father, Reshat Lulushi, and

to my mother, Seadet Lulushi.

CONTENTS

Preface   xxv
Acknowledgments   xxxv

PART I   INTRODUCTION TO DESIGNER/2000   **1**

1   Analyzing the Requirements   **3**

   1.1   **Creating a New Application System   4**
        1.1.1   Introducing Designer/2000 Launch Pad   4
        1.1.2   Introducing the ORDERS Application   7
        1.1.3   Repository Object Navigator   7

   1.2   **Data Modeling   11**
        1.2.1   Data Requirements of the ORDERS Application   11
        1.2.2   OLTP and OLAP Applications   13
        1.2.3   Introducing the Entity Relationship Diagrammer   13
        1.2.4   Creating Entities and Relationships   15
        1.2.5   Creating Attributes   16
        1.2.6   Defining Unique Identifiers for Entities   17
        1.2.7   Defining Text Information for Entities   18

   1.3   **Function Modeling   20**
        1.3.1   Functional Requirements of the ORDERS Application   22
        1.3.2   Creating the Function Hierarchy of the System   23
        1.3.3   Maintaining Properties of Functions   26

   1.4   **Summary   31**

2   Designing and Generating Database Objects   **32**

   2.1   **Database Design Transformer   33**

2.1.1 Purpose and Use 33
2.1.2 Populating the Run Set 34
2.1.3 Running the Transformer 36

2.2 Designing the Physical Database 36
2.2.1 Starting the Design Editor 37
2.2.2 Creating the ORDERS Database 38
2.2.3 Creating a Database User 40
2.2.4 Recovering the Design of Existing Database Objects 40

2.3 Enhancing the Data Design 44
2.3.1 Creating and Maintaining Data Diagrams 45
2.3.2 Creating Table Implementations 47
2.3.3 Maintaining Column Properties 50
2.3.4 Maintaining Constraint Properties 52
2.3.5 Implementing Business Rules with Check
      Constraints 56
2.3.6 Performing Data Derivation 58
2.3.7 Maintaining Index Properties 59

2.4 Generating Database Objects 60

2.5 Summary 64

3 Designing and Generating Software Modules   **65**

3.1 Generating the Initial Module Design 66
3.1.1 Application Design Transformer 66
3.1.2 Accepting Candidate Modules 67

3.2 Enhancing the Design of User Interface Modules 69
3.2.1 Module Diagrams 70
3.2.2 Views and Elements of the Module Diagram 70
3.2.3 Arranging the Layout of Module Diagrams 73
3.2.4 Adding Links to Module Diagrams 73
3.2.5 Maintaining Properties of Module Elements 74

3.3 Expanding Modules with Unbound and Action Items 78
3.3.1 Formula Unbound Items 79
3.3.2 Derivation Unbound Items 81
3.3.3 Action Items 82

3.4 Designing and Programming PL/SQL Modules 83
3.4.1 Creating a PL/SQL Function 84
3.4.2 The Logic Editor 87
3.4.3 Programming the Body of PL/SQL Program Units 88
3.4.4 Creating an Application Logic Program Unit 89

3.5 Generating the Application Modules 91
3.5.1 Generating and Installing PL/SQL Modules 92
3.5.2 Overview of Designer/2000 Front-End Generators 93

3.5.3   Generating Developer/2000 Forms Modules   94

3.5.4   Generating Developer/2000 Reports Modules   98

3.6   What Next?   100

3.7   Summary   101

4   Understanding the Designer/2000 Architecture   **103**

4.1   Overview of Designer/2000   104

4.1.1   Software Engineering and Tools   104

4.1.2   Components of Designer/2000   106

4.1.3   Characteristics of Designer/2000   107

4.1.4   Installing and Configuring the Designer/2000 Client Software   110

4.2   Designer/2000 Repository Model   112

4.2.1   Elements   113

4.2.2   Associations   114

4.2.3   Topological Information about Diagrams   114

4.2.4   Rules   115

4.3   Repository Administration Utility   116

4.3.1   Understanding the Physical Layout of the Repository   116

4.3.2   Preparing for the Creation of the Repository   118

4.3.3   Creating the Designer/2000 Repository   119

4.3.4   Maintaining the Designer/2000 Repository   123

4.3.5   Diagnosing and Optimizing the Repository   125

4.3.6   Creating and Maintaining Repository Users   129

4.4   Extending and Customizing the Repository   132

4.4.1   Ways to Extend the Designer/2000 Repository   132

4.4.2   Steps to Extend the Designer/2000 Repository   133

4.4.3   Extending Properties of Existing Objects   134

4.4.4   Creating New Element Types   134

4.4.5   Creating New Association Types   137

4.4.6   Creating New Text Types   138

4.4.7   Extracting and Loading User Extensions   140

4.5   Summary   141

5   Maintaining Application Systems   **142**

5.1   Creating and Maintaining Application Systems   143

5.1.1   Creating Application Systems   143

5.1.2   Saving Application Systems   146

5.1.3   Opening Application Systems   146

5.1.4   Filtering Groups of Objects   146

5.1.5   Closing Application Systems   147

5.1.6   Renaming Application Systems   148

5.1.7   Freezing and Unfreezing Application Systems   148
5.1.8   Creating Multiple Versions of Application Systems   149
5.1.9   Copying Application Systems   151
5.1.10   Deleting Application Systems   152
5.1.11   Managing User Access   154
5.1.12   Transferring the Ownership of Application
         Systems   157
5.1.13   Archiving Application Systems   158
5.1.14   Restoring Application Systems   160

5.2   Creating and Maintaining Application Objects   162
5.2.1   Sharing and Unsharing Objects   163
5.2.2   Transferring Ownership of Objects   165
5.2.3   Copying Objects   166
5.2.4   Refining the Granularity of Share and Copy
         Operations   168
5.2.5   Deleting Objects   170

5.3   User-Defined Object Sets   172
5.3.1   Creating and Populating Object Sets   172
5.3.2   Locking and Unlocking User-Defined Sets   173
5.3.3   Checking In and Checking Out Objects   174
5.3.4   Sample Designer/2000 Configuration Management
         Scenario   177
5.3.5   Loading and Unloading Objects   179

5.4   Summary   180

6   Object Navigators in Designer/2000   182

6.1   Components of Object Navigators   183
6.1.1   Navigator Window   183
6.1.2   Property Palette   186

6.2   Working with Navigator Windows   188
6.2.1   Expanding and Collapsing Object Trees   188
6.2.2   Navigating, Searching, and Selecting Objects   189
6.2.3   Searching Repository Objects   190
6.2.4   Managing Filters of Repository Objects   193
6.2.5   Marking Objects   195
6.2.6   Creating Objects in the Repository Object Navigator   196
6.2.7   Deleting Objects in the Repository Object Navigator   198
6.2.8   Requerying Objects in the Navigator Window   198

6.3   Working with Property Palettes   200
6.3.1   Setting Properties of Objects   201
6.3.2   Reverting Changes of Properties   201
6.3.3   Copying and Pasting Properties of Objects   201

6.3.4   Pinning Property Palettes   203
6.3.5   Managing Properties of Multiple Objects   203
6.3.6   Customizing the Property Palette Options   205

6.4   Summary   206

7   Diagrammers in Designer/2000   207

7.1   Diagrams and Diagrammers   208
7.1.1   Diagrams   209
7.1.2   Designer/2000 Diagrammers   210

7.2   Components of Diagrammers   211
7.2.1   Multiple Document Interface Applications   211
7.2.2   Menu   212
7.2.3   Toolbar   214

7.3   Working with Diagrams   214
7.3.1   Creating Diagrams   215
7.3.2   Opening Diagrams   215
7.3.3   Closing Diagrams   216
7.3.4   Saving Diagrams   217
7.3.5   Deleting Diagrams   218
7.3.6   Maintaining Summary Information of Diagrams   219
7.3.7   Printing Diagrams   220
7.3.8   Changing Connection and Application System   221
7.3.9   Changing Zooming Levels of Diagrams   221
7.3.10 Maintaining the Layout of Diagrams   222
7.3.11 Maintaining the Layout of Function Hierarchy
        Diagrams   224
7.3.12 Expanding and Collapsing Function Hierarchy
        Diagrams   226

7.4   Working with Objects in Diagrams   227
7.4.1   Creating Objects   227
7.4.2   Selecting Objects   228
7.4.3   Moving and Resizing Objects   229
7.4.4   Reverting Changes to Diagrams   230
7.4.5   Deleting Objects   230
7.4.6   Cutting, Copying, and Pasting Objects   230
7.4.7   Maintaining Visual Properties of Objects   231
7.4.8   Editing Objects   233

7.5   Customizing Diagrammer Preferences   235
7.6   Enhancing Diagrams with OLE Technology   237
7.6.1   Inserting OLE Objects in Diagrams   237
7.6.2   Editing OLE Objects in Diagrams   238
7.6.3   Maintaining Links to OLE Objects   239

7.7   **The Matrix Diagrammer   240**
 7.7.1 Creating and Maintaining
    Documents   241
 7.7.2 Creating and Maintaining Objects   245
7.8   **Summary   247**

PART II   STRATEGIC PLANNING AND BUSINESS AREA ANALYSIS   249

8   Modeling the Business Direction of the Enterprise   251

8.1   **Setting the Scene   252**
 8.1.1 The American Software Club   252
 8.1.2 Your Assignment   253
8.2   **The Enterprise Model   255**
8.3   **Business Units   256**
 8.3.1 Creating and Maintaining Business Units   256
 8.3.2 Creating and Maintaining Locations   259
 8.3.3 Creating and Maintaining Planning Items   261
 8.3.4 Creating and Maintaining Executives   265
8.4   **Goals and Objectives   267**
 8.4.1 Characteristics of Goals   267
 8.4.2 Objectives   269
 8.4.3 Mission Statement   269
 8.4.4 Planning Horizon, Hierarchies, and
    Priorities   269
 8.4.5 Goals and Objectives in Designer/2000   270
 8.4.6 Associating Business Units with Goals   271
8.5   **Problems   273**
 8.5.1 Entering Problems in the Repository   274
 8.5.2 Associating Problems with Business Units   275
8.6   **Critical Success Factors   276**
8.7   **Key Performance Indicators   279**
8.8   **Assumptions   281**
8.9   **Summary   282**

9   The Enterprise Functional and Information Models   284

9.1   **Defining the Functional Model of the Enterprise   285**
 9.1.1 Functional Areas of the Enterprise   285
 9.1.2 Functions and Functional Hierarchies   286
 9.1.3 Creating Functions in the Function Hierarchy
    Diagrammer   287
 9.1.4 Types of Functions   290

9.1.5 Maintaining Functions in the Function Hierarchy Diagrammer 292

9.1.6 Associating Functions with Other Repository Objects 294

9.2 Defining the Information Model of the Enterprise 296

9.2.1 Data Subjects, Entities, and Attributes 296

9.2.2 Creating Entities in the Entity Relationship Diagrammer 298

9.2.3 Maintaining Entities in the Entity Relationship Diagrammer 300

9.2.4 Relationships 303

9.2.5 Types of Relationships 305

9.2.6 Creating Relationships in the Entity Relationship Diagrammer 308

9.2.7 Maintaining Relationships in the Entity Relationship Diagrammer 310

9.3 Modeling Mutual Exclusivity of Data and Relationships 310

9.3.1 Supertype and Subtype Entities 311

9.3.2 Arcs 314

9.4 Associating Entities with Other Repository Objects 316

9.4.1 Associating Entities with Business Functions 316

9.4.2 Associating Entities with Business Units 318

9.5 Summary 320

10 Modeling Business Processes 321

10.1 What Are Business Processes? 322

10.2 Why Model Business Processes? 323

10.3 Creating the Process Model of the Enterprise 326

10.3.1 Criteria for Defining High-Level Processes 326

10.3.2 TASC's High-Level Processes 327

10.4 Creating Processes in the Process Modeller 328

10.4.1 Creating a New Root Process 330

10.4.2 Creating Organization Units 331

10.4.3 Creating Process Steps 337

10.4.4 Creating Process Inputs and Outputs 337

10.4.5 Creating Process Flows 338

10.5 Modeling the Customer 341

10.5.1 Gathering Information for the Customer Model 341

10.5.2 TASC's Pre-Sales Process Model 344

10.5.3 TASC's After-Sales Process Model 349

10.6 Analyzing the Business Areas of the Enterprise 352

10.6.1 Defining Business Areas 353

10.6.2 Prioritizing Business Areas 353

10.7 Summary 354

11   Business Area Analysis   **356**

   11.1   Defining Business Area Processes   357
      11.1.1   Input and Output of the Business Area   357
      11.1.2   States of Orders   359
      11.1.3   Entering Business Area Processes in the Repository   360

   11.2   Analyzing Processes in Detail   363
      11.2.1   How Approve Orders Works   363
      11.2.2   Roles   365
      11.2.3   Process Steps   367
      11.2.4   Events   370
      11.2.5   Stores   372
      11.2.6   Flows   373
      11.2.7   Naming Conventions   376

   11.3   Animation and Multimedia   377
      11.3.1   Multimedia Properties   377
      11.3.2   Animating the Process Diagrams   380
      11.3.3   Configuring the Process Modeller for
              Multimedia Files   382
      11.3.4   Using Multimedia Files   384
      11.3.5   Setting Icons for Process Step Approve
              Order   385

   11.4   Synthesizing the Business Area   385
      11.4.1   Identifying Value-Adding Processes   387
      11.4.2   Benchmarking   389
      11.4.3   Activity-Based Costing   390
      11.4.4   Critical Path Analysis   394

   11.5   Summary   397

12   Business Process Reengineering   **399**

   12.1   Symptoms of Aching Processes   400
   12.2   Prescriptions for Aching Processes   403
   12.3   Preparing for Reengineering Business Processes   406
      12.3.1   Why Reengineer?   406
      12.3.2   Prerequisites to Reengineering   407

   12.4   Reengineering   409
      12.4.1   Prepare for Reengineering   410
      12.4.2   Choose the Process to Reengineer   410
      12.4.3   Envision the New Process   411
      12.4.4   Design the New Process   412
      12.4.5   Implement the Design   412
      12.4.6   Constantly Improve the Reengineered
              Process   413

12.5   Reengineering TASC   414
 12.5.1   Breaking Old Assumptions   414
 12.5.2   Reorganizing the Business Units   415
 12.5.3   Reorganizing the Relationships with Customers and
    Business Partners   416
 12.5.4   The Reengineered Order Fulfillment Process   420
 12.5.5   Defining Information Systems to Implement the New
    Process   421

12.6   Summary   423

PART III   SYSTEMS REQUIREMENTS DEFINITION AND ANALYSIS   425

13   Requirements Analysis   427

 13.1   Business Requirements and System Requirements   428
  13.1.1   User Interface Requirements   429
  13.1.2   Data Requirements   430
  13.1.3   Functional Requirements   430
  13.1.4   Security Requirements   431
  13.1.5   Intersystem Interface Requirements   432
  13.1.6   Documentation Requirements   432
  13.1.7   Physical Environment and Resources Requirements   433
  13.1.8   Reliability, Availability, and Serviceability
     Requirements   434

 13.2   Using Designer/2000 in Requirements Analysis   434

 13.3   Building the High-Level System Model   436
  13.3.1   Defining the First Decomposition of the System   436
  13.3.2   Defining the User Roles   437
  13.3.3   Defining the Subsystems   438
  13.3.4   Defining the Major System Data Entities and Flows   438

 13.4   Documenting the High-Level System Design   439

 13.5   Defining the User Interface Requirements   441
  13.5.1   Defining the Hierarchy   442
  13.5.2   Identifying Elementary Functions   444

 13.6   Summary   445

14   Data Modeling   446

 14.1   Techniques and Approaches to Data Modeling   447

 14.2   Entity Modeling   447
  14.2.1   Collecting Data about Data   448
  14.2.2   Creating and Maintaining Entities   449
  14.2.3   Creating and Maintaining Attributes   450

14.2.4 Maintaining Detailed Properties for Attributes   452
14.2.5 Specifying Allowable Values for Attributes   455

14.3 Domains in Designer/2000   457
14.3.1 Creating Domains   457
14.3.2 Maintaining Properties of Domains   459
14.3.3 Allowed Values of a Domain   460
14.3.4 Maintaining Domains in the Design Editor   461
14.3.5 Updating Properties Inherited from Domains   463

14.4 Relationship Modeling   463
14.4.1 Resolving Many-to-Many Relationships   464
14.4.2 Including Relationships in Unique Identifiers   466

14.5 Normalization and Denormalization of Data   468
14.5.1 Unnormalized Data   468
14.5.2 First Normal Form   470
14.5.3 Second Normal Form   471
14.5.4 Third Normal Form   473
14.5.5 Denormalization   475

14.6 Data Modeling for Data Warehouses   477
14.6.1 Defining the Questions   478
14.6.2 Defining the Measures and Facts   479
14.6.3 Defining the Dimensions   480
14.6.4 Organizing Dimensions in Hierarchies   481

14.7 Maintaining Multiple Data Models   482

14.8 Summary   484

15 Business Rules Modeling   485

15.1 Function Data Usages   486
15.1.1 Creating and Maintaining Data Usages in the Function
          Hierarchy Diagrammer   486
15.1.2 Creating and Maintaining Data Usages in the Matrix
          Diagrammer   489

15.2 Business Rules   491
15.2.1 Separating Business Rules from Interface
          Requirements   491
15.2.2 Categories of Business Rules   493

15.3 Data Definition Rules   494
15.3.1 Attribute Rules   495
15.3.2 Inter-Attribute Rules   496
15.3.3 Entity Rules   498
15.3.4 Inter-Entity Rules   500

15.4 Data Manipulation Rules   501
15.4.1 Create Rules   502

15.4.2 Update Rules 502

15.4.3 Delete Rules 504

15.4.4 Events and Triggers 508

15.5 Access Privilege Rules 509

15.5.1 User Group Rules 510

15.5.2 Function Access Rules 510

15.5.3 Data Access Rules 511

15.6 Summary 511

16 Quality Assurance of the System Requirements 513

16.1 Organizing the Diagrams 514

16.1.1 Establishing and Maintaining Diagramming Conventions 515

16.1.2 Using Multiple Diagrams 515

16.1.3 Planning the Layout of Diagrams 516

16.1.4 Minimizing Layout Changes 518

16.1.5 Using Visual Aids to Add Clarity to Diagrams 518

16.1.6 Associating Diagrams with Legends 518

16.2 Verifying and Reporting the Data Model 519

16.2.1 Removing Uncommon Relationships 520

16.2.2 Checking the Quality of Data Model 521

16.2.3 Data Model Reports 522

16.3 Verifying and Reporting the Functional Model 525

16.4 Summary 526

PART IV SYSTEM DESIGN 529

17 Creating the Initial Logical Database Design 531

17.1 Database Design Transformer Interface 533

17.2 Creating the Logical Database Design 535

17.2.1 Populating the Transformer's Run set 536

17.2.2 Setting the Scope of the Transformer 538

17.3 Controlling the Settings of the Transformer 539

17.3.1 Creating Database Implementation Objects 539

17.3.2 Controlling the Commit Frequency of the Transformer 540

17.3.3 Setting Properties for Key Constraints 541

17.3.4 Setting Miscellaneous Properties 543

17.4 How the Transformer Creates the Database Design 544

17.4.1 Creating Tables 545

17.4.2 Creating Columns 545

17.4.3 Creating Primary and Unique Keys 548

17.4.4 Creating Foreign Key Constraints 549

17.5 Maintaining the Logical Database Design 551

17.5.1 Maintaining Column Mappings 551

17.5.2 Maintaining Mappings of Key Constraints 553

17.5.3 Creating Indexes for Foreign Keys 553

17.5.4 Setting the Scope of the Transformer 554

17.6 Mapping Supertype and Subtype Entities to Tables 555

17.6.1 Supertype Implementation 556

17.6.2 Explicit Subtype Implementation 558

17.6.3 Implicit Subtype Implementation 559

17.6.4 Arc Implementation 561

17.7 Summary 563

18 Enhancing the Logical Database Design   **564**

18.1 Maintaining Data Diagrams 565

18.1.1 Including Objects in Data Diagrams 565

18.1.2 Creating Objects in Data Diagrams 568

18.1.3 Maintaining the Layout of Data Diagrams 569

18.2 Maintaining Tables 571

18.2.1 Name Properties 571

18.2.2 Column Definition Properties 572

18.2.3 Display Properties 577

18.2.4 GUI Control Properties 579

18.2.5 User Interface Properties 581

18.3 Providing for Data Auditing and Journaling 582

18.4 Creating and Maintaining Indexes 586

18.5 Maintaining Views 587

18.5.1 Implementing Business Views of Data 588

18.5.2 Enforcing Data Access and Security Rules 588

18.5.3 Setting Properties of Views 589

18.6 Maintaining Snapshots 593

18.7 Creating and Maintaining Sequences 597

18.8 Using the Database Object Guide 599

18.9 Summary 603

19 Implementing the Physical Database Design   **604**

19.1 Documenting the System's Foundations 605

19.1.1 Nodes 606

19.1.2 Databases 608

19.1.3 Communities 610

19.2   **Defining Database Components 611**
     19.2.1   Files 612
     19.2.2   Storage Definition 613
     19.2.3   Setting Storage Parameters to Avoid Fragmentation 614
     19.2.4   Tablespaces 616
     19.2.5   Rollback Segments 618

19.3   **Defining Database Users 620**
     19.3.1   Database Roles 620
     19.3.2   Database Users 622
     19.3.3   Database Profiles 624

19.4   **Implementing Logical Design Objects in a Database Schema 625**
     19.4.1   Creating Implementation Objects 626
     19.4.2   Maintaining Table Implementations 626
     19.4.3   Maintaining View Implementations 631
     19.4.4   Maintaining Snapshot Implementations 632
     19.4.5   Maintaining Sequence Implementations 635

19.5   **Using the Database Administrator Guide 637**

19.6   **Preserving the Physical Database Design Flexibility 640**
     19.6.1   Parametrizing Properties of Database Objects 640
     19.6.2   Preparing Different Database Sizing Models 643

19.7   **Summary 646**

20   Implementing Business Rules with Constraints   647

20.1   **Business Rules Reviewed 648**
     20.1.1   Data Definition Rules 648
     20.1.2   Data Manipulation Rules 649
     20.1.3   Access Privilege Rules 649

20.2   **Implementing Business Rules 650**
     20.2.1   Methods for Implementing Business Rules 650
     20.2.2   Attribute Rules 651
     20.2.3   Tuple Rules 655
     20.2.4   Entity Rules 655
     20.2.5   Inter-Entity Rules 656
     20.2.6   Data Manipulation Rules 657
     20.2.7   Access Privilege Rules 657

20.3   **Creating and Maintaining Constraints 658**
     20.3.1   Creating Constraints 658
     20.3.2   Editing Constraints 659
     20.3.3   Setting Validation Properties of Constraints 660
     20.3.4   Handling Failures of Constraints 662

20.4   **Primary and Unique Key Constraints 663**

20.5   **Foreign Key Constraint Properties 665**

20.6   Check Constraint Properties   668

20.7   Deriving Column Values in Front-End Applications   670

20.8   Summary   671

21   Creating the Application Design   673

21.1   The Purpose of the Application Design Transformer   674

21.2   Generating Presentation Layer Modules   674

    21.2.1   Steps of the Module Creation Process   675

    21.2.2   How the Application Design Transformer Creates Modules   677

    21.2.3   How the Application Design Transformer Merges Functions   679

    21.2.4   How the Transformer Creates Module Elements   681

21.3   Accepting and Rejecting Candidate Modules   682

21.4   Generating Menu Modules   684

    21.4.1   Steps of the Menu Creation Process   684

    21.4.2   How the Application Design Transformer Creates Menus   685

21.5   Summary   686

22   Maintaining Modules in the Design Editor   687

22.1   Modules in Designer/2000   688

    22.1.1   Types of Modules   688

    22.1.2   Populating the Repository with Modules   689

22.2   Structure of Modules   693

    22.2.1   The Data View of a Module   693

    22.2.2   The Display View of a Module   695

    22.2.3   Module Application Logic   697

22.3   Working with Modules   697

    22.3.1   The Module Application Guide   698

    22.3.2   Creating and Maintaining Modules   701

    22.3.3   Maintaining Help Contents   702

    22.3.4   Creating and Maintaining Module Associations   702

    22.3.5   Maintaining Module Arguments   704

    22.3.6   Copying Modules   705

    22.3.7   Developer/2000 Module Security   707

22.4   Creating and Maintaining Module Elements   708

    22.4.1   Displaying Modules in Diagrams   709

    22.4.2   Creating Module Elements   709

    22.4.3   Maintaining Module Components   711

22.4.4 Maintaining Table Usages 713
22.4.5 Maintaining Bound Items 715
22.4.6 Maintaining Unbound Items 718
22.4.7 Maintaining Item Groups 720
22.4.8 Maintaining Windows 720

22.5 Module Wizards 721
22.5.1 The Module Component Data Wizard 723
22.5.2 The Module Component Display Wizard 725
22.5.3 The Chart Wizard 726

22.6 Reusable Components 727

22.7 Summary 729

23 PL/SQL in Designer/2000 **731**

23.1 Overview of PL/SQL 732
23.1.1 Brief History of the PL/SQL Language 732
23.1.2 Functionality of PL/SQL Engines 733
23.1.3 Structural Elements of PL/SQL Blocks 735
23.1.4 Manipulating Data in PL/SQL Blocks 736

23.2 Procedural Constructs of PL/SQL 738
23.2.1 IF Statement 738
23.2.2 Looping Statements 740
23.2.3 Unconditional Branching 741

23.3 Data Types and Variables 741
23.3.1 PL/SQL Data Types 741
23.3.2 PL/SQL Variables 742
23.3.3 PL/SQL Constants 743
23.3.4 PL/SQL Records 744
23.3.5 PL/SQL Tables 745

23.4 Cursors in PL/SQL 748
23.4.1 Declaring Explicit Cursors 749
23.4.2 Methods and Attributes of Explicit Cursors 750
23.4.3 Using the FOR Loop with Explicit
Cursors 753
23.4.4 Cursor Variables 754
23.4.5 Implicit Cursors 756

23.5 PL/SQL Program Units 757
23.5.1 Components of Program Units 757
23.5.2 Arguments in Program Units 759
23.5.3 PL/SQL Packages 760
23.5.4 Benefits of Packages 761
23.5.5 PL/SQL Libraries 763
23.5.6 Database Triggers 763

23.6 Exception Handling 765
    23.6.1 Internal Exceptions 765
    23.6.2 User-Defined Exceptions 767
    23.6.3 Error-Reporting Functions 768
    23.6.4 Propagation of Exceptions 768
23.7 Summary 770

24 Maintaining PL/SQL Objects in Designer/2000   772

24.1 Maintaining Server Side PL/SQL Objects 773
    24.1.1 Creating PL/SQL Definitions 773
    24.1.2 Defining PL/SQL Objects with the Operating System File
          Method 774
    24.1.3 Defining PL/SQL Objects Using the Free Format
          Method 775
    24.1.4 Defining PL/SQL Objects Using the Declarative
          Method 777
    24.1.5 Advantages of the Declarative Method 779
    24.1.6 Implementing PL/SQL Objects 781
    24.1.7 Database Triggers 782
24.2 Understanding and Maintaining the Server API 784
    24.2.1 Table API 785
    24.2.2 Database Triggers 788
    24.2.3 Module Component API 790
24.3 Maintaining Application Logic Objects 790
    24.3.1 Events 791
    24.3.2 Named Routines 792
    24.3.3 Library Modules 793
24.4 The Logic Editor 794
    24.4.1 The Outline Pane 795
    24.4.2 The Editor Pane 797
    24.4.3 Selection Tree Window 798
24.5 Working with the Logic Editor 801
    24.5.1 Checking the Syntax of PL/SQL Objects 801
    24.5.2 Importing and Exporting the Contents of PL/SQL
          Objects 802
24.6 Summary 803

PART V SOFTWARE GENERATION AND DEVELOPMENT   805

25 Generating Database Server Objects   807

25.1 Preparing for Generation 808

25.1.1   Checking the Quality of Generated Objects   808
25.1.2   Preparing the Target Database   810

25.2   Designer/2000 Server Generator   810
25.2.1   Purpose of the Server Generator   810
25.2.2   Generating the Database Structure Objects   811
25.2.3   Generating Database Objects   813
25.2.4   The Output of the Server Generator   815
25.2.5   Generating Table API and Module API   816
25.2.6   Generating Code Control and Reference Code
Tables   816

25.3   Post-Generation Tasks   818
25.3.1   Reviewing the Generated DDL Statements   818
25.3.2   Deploying the Generated Objects   819
25.3.3   Testing the Deployed Objects   819

25.4   Different Scenarios of Using the Server Generator   820
25.4.1   Generating the Same Database Schema for Different
Environments   820
25.4.2   Implementing Database Upgrades   822
25.4.3   Generating Database Schemas for Multiple
Sites   824

25.5   Recovering the Design of Databases   825
25.5.1   The Recover Database Design Utility   826
25.5.2   The Table to Entity Retrofit Utility   829

25.6   Summary   831

26   Generating Front-End Software Modules   833

26.1   Repository-Based Software Development   834
26.2   Maintaining Preferences   835
26.2.1   The Generator Preferences   836
26.2.2   Managing the Generator Preferences   837
26.2.3   Working with Preferences   838
26.2.4   Creating and Maintaining Named Preference
Sets   839
26.2.5   Implementing Preferences Security   840

26.3   Object Class Libraries   842
26.3.1   Subclassing, Objects, and Object Libraries   842
26.3.2   Types of Objects in an Object Library   842
26.3.3   Object Libraries Shipped with Designer/2000   844
26.3.4   Using Object Libraries during Generation   846

26.4   Generator Templates   847
26.4.1   Purpose and Use of Templates   847
26.4.2   Types of Template Objects   848

26.4.3   Templates Supplied by Designer/2000   850
26.4.4   Creating Customized Templates   851

26.5   Designer/2000 Front-End Generators   852
26.5.1   Invoking and Using Front-End Generators   852
26.5.2   Developer/2000 Forms Generator   854
26.5.3   Developer/2000 Reports Generator   861
26.5.4   Developer/2000 Graphics Generator   863
26.5.5   Oracle WebServer Generator   864
26.5.6   Visual Basic Generator   865
26.5.7   Microsoft Help Generator   866

26.6   Summary   869

27   Introduction to Generating Developer/2000 Forms Modules   871

27.1   Preparing for Generation   872
27.1.1   Overview of the Sample Application System   872
27.1.2   Creating the Database Administration Objects   873
27.1.3   Creating the Database Objects   875

27.2   Enforcing Application-wide GUI Standards   876

27.3   Implementing a Flexible Messaging Strategy   880
27.3.1   Hard Coding and Soft Coding Messages   880
27.3.2   Customizing the CG$ERRORS Package   881
27.3.3   Externalizing Application-Specific Messages   883
27.3.4   Externalizing Designer/2000 Forms Generator
         Messages   885
27.3.5   Handling Messages Raised by Stored Program Units   885

27.4   Generating Developer/2000 Forms Modules   888
27.4.1   Generating Modules with a Single-Record Form
         Layout   888
27.4.2   Generating Modules with a Multi-Record Tabular
         Layout   892
27.4.3   Adding a Current Record Indicator to Tabular Blocks   893

27.5   Summary   895

28   Advanced Developer/2000 Forms Generation   897

28.1   Generating Forms with Multiple Table Usages   898
28.1.1   Rearranging the Module Layout   898
28.1.2   Defining the Layout of the Product Information
         Window   899
28.1.3   Defining the Layout of the Product Items Window   902

28.2   Item Lookups and Lists of Values   904
28.2.1   Features of List of Values Controls   905
28.2.2   Using Lists of Values to Restrict Data Access   906

28.2.3   Adding a List of Values Button   906
28.2.4   Using a List of Values for Data Entry and Validation   907

28.3   Adding GUI Controls to Modules   909
28.3.1   Overview of the Module   909
28.3.2   Adding Push Buttons   910
28.3.3   Adding Check Boxes   910
28.3.4   Adding Radio Groups   911
28.3.5   Adding List Controls   912

28.4   Adding Calendar Controls to Developer/2000 Forms Modules   915

28.5   Summary   917

29   C++ Object Layer Generator   918

29.1   The Purpose of the C++ Object Layer Generator   919

29.2   Preparing for C++ Generation   923
29.2.1   C++ Generator Class Sets   923
29.2.2   Checking the Properties of Entities in the Class Set   924

29.3   Using the C++ Object Layer Generator   927
29.3.1   Launching the C++ Object Layer Generator   928
29.3.2   Loading C++ Class Sets   928
29.3.3   Removing Anomalies from a C++ Class Set   928
29.3.4   Define the Classes to Be Generated   930
29.3.5   Distributing the Generated Code to Files   930
29.3.6   Setting Generation Options   934
29.3.7   Browsing the Generated Classes   936
29.3.8   Generating the C++ Classes   938

29.4   Understanding the Output of the C++ Object Layer Generator   938
29.4.1   Mapping Class   939
29.4.2   Classes That Reference Object Instances   940
29.4.3   Classes That Related Objects Use to Reference the Object Instance   941

29.5   Summary   942

Index   943

PREFACE

Inside Oracle Designer/2000 is a complete reference for Designer/2000, the Oracle Corporation's suite of business modeling, system design, and software development tools. The book offers extensive coverage of each tool and addresses all the important concepts that software engineers working with Designer/2000 must master.

WHAT THIS BOOK IS ABOUT

The following is a list of the top ten things this book covers:

1. Methodology
2. Business process modeling
3. Business Process Reengineering (BPR)
4. Information Systems analysis
5. Data modeling
6. Application design
7. Business rule definition and implementation
8. Web-based (thin client) application development
9. Database design and implementation
10. Software modules design and generation

Through examples and software provided with it, the book will show you how to use Designer/2000 for each of the topics listed above. The section "Organization of the Book" further ahead provides additional information on these and other topics discussed in the book.

WHAT BENEFITS THE BOOK PROVIDES

The following is a list of the top ten benefits you will get from reading *Inside Oracle Designer/2000*:

1. A complete reference for Designer/2000 version 2 tools.

2. A guide through the rapid design and development of an application within the first three chapters, to introduce Designer/2000 and highlight the principal activities you perform with it.

3. Presentation of concepts and activities in an iterative fashion to allow you to build gradually your knowledge, confidence, and comfort level with Designer/2000.

4. Concrete examples for each important concept encountered during design and development activities.

5. Step-by-step instructions on how to perform each activity in Designer/2000.

6. A guide through the process of designing and implementing an On-Line Transaction Processing system.

7. Information on how to use Designer/2000 to model and design a data ware-house.

8. A companion CD-ROM, which you can install and use in your environment and which contains all the application systems discussed and built in the book.

9. Over 170 Lotus ScreenCam® movies, which you can play back to see how each important activity or task is performed.

10. A number of tips and techniques to organize and manage the Designer/2000 repository and tools.

ORGANIZATION OF THE BOOK

Inside Oracle Designer/2000 is organized into five parts. The following paragraphs summarize the contents of these parts.

❑ **Part One.** This part introduces you to the tools, features and ways of working with Designer/2000. If you are new to Designer/2000, read carefully the first three chapters, which walk you step by step through the process of creating a Developer/2000- and Oracle-based application system. If you are familiar with previous versions of Designer/2000, these chapters will be very helpful as an introduction to the major features and enhancements of Designer/2000, version 2. The remaining four chapters of this part present the architecture of Designer/2000 and the tasks related to the creation and maintenance of application systems in the Repository. They also discuss patterns of working with two interface components of Designer/2000: object navigators and diagrammers.

❑ **Part Two.** This part focuses on the use of Designer/2000 as a set of tools that facilitate strategic planning and business area analysis of the enterprise. Chapters in this part show you how to model the business direction of the enterprise by recording critical information, such as business units, goals, objectives, problems, and critical success factors. They also discuss the Designer/2000 tools used to document and maintain the enterprise high-level business, functional, and data models. A major theme of this part is the use of the Process Modeller to facilitate the analysis and reengineering of business processes in the enterprise.

❑ **Part Three.** This part covers the use of Designer/2000 tools, such as the Function Hierarchy Diagrammer and the Entity Relationship Diagrammer, to define, analyze, and record the requirements of an information system. Its primary focus is techniques and methods used during requirement analysis, data modeling, and business rule modeling activities. It also describes several Repository reports provided by Designer/2000 to help you ensure the quality of the system requirements you have identified in the application system.

❑ **Part Four.** This part is dedicated to the transition from the requirements of a system to the database and module design, as well as to the enhancements of these designs in preparation for the generation of software modules. Separate chapters in this part discuss the Database Design Transformer and the Application Design Transformer—the two Designer/2000 components that allow you to convert the information captured during the requirement analysis into logical database structures and software module designs. Other chapters cover the use of the Design Editor—a component of critical importance among all the Designer/2000 tools—to enhance the logical data model, create a physical implementation of it in one of several target databases supported by Designer/2000, and implement a number of business rules using constraints. The maintenance and enhancement of software modules in the Design Editor is also discussed in detail in its own separate chapter. PL/SQL, the procedural extension of SQL by Oracle Corporation, is a very important part of any Oracle-based information system. It is the programming language for the Oracle Server, Developer/2000, and Oracle WebServer; therefore Designer/2000 fully supports it. Two chapters in Part IV discuss PL/SQL. One of them presents an overview of the language and provides examples of its most important syntactic structures and concepts. The other discusses the creation and maintenance of PL/SQL objects in the Designer/2000 Repository.

❑ **Part Five.** This part discusses the use of the Design Editor to generate the database server objects and the front-end modules that are part of an application system. Separate chapters in this part discuss the Server Generator component and the front-end generators of multiple flavors. Two chapters are dedicated to the enhancement and generation of Developer/2000 Form modules. They are organized as workshops with instructions you can follow and examples you can try yourself. The last chapter of this part describes the C++ Object Layer Generator, the Designer/2000 tool that allows you to create a layer of C++ classes that encapsulate and hide the complexity of the relational model of the database from object-oriented programming environments.

AUDIENCE

Designer/2000 is a suite of tools with a broad functionality that can be used throughout the Information Technology (IT) spectrum. Since *Inside Oracle Designer/2000* covers each of these tools, people in a number of areas will benefit from it. In particular, you will find the book helpful if your job requires you to play one of the following roles:

❑ **Business process modeler.** People interested in modeling business processes of the enterprise and BPR will learn how Designer/2000 supports these activities in the Process Modeller tool.

❑ **Data modeler.** IT professionals who perform data analysis will learn how to model entities, relationships, and data-related business rules with the Entity Relationship Diagrammer and other Designer/2000 tools.

❑ **System modeler.** The book shows an efficient way to capture the functional requirements of the system using the Function Hierarchy Diagrammer, and the benefits of separating user interface requirements from business rules that the system will implement.

❑ **Database architect.** Database architects will see how the Database Design Transformer helps translate the logical data model into a complete database schema and how data-related business rules are implemented and stored declaratively using the Design Editor.

❑ **System architect.** System architects will learn to use the Application Design Transformer to generate the initial modules and components of the system. They will see how the Design Editor helps them manage the complex relationships between system components, and maintain the properties of each module.

❑ **Database developer.** Database developers will learn the basics of PL/SQL, the Oracle Server programming language, and how to use the Design Editor to design and implement stored PL/SQL program units and database triggers. In addition, they will learn to use the Server Generator to create and install the database objects in a physical database.

❑ **Application developer.** Oracle application developers will see how the Design Editor helps them define the layout and functionality of screen and report modules and how to generate software applications for different environments, such as Developer/2000 and Oracle WebServer. Microsoft Windows developers will learn how to generate a set of C++ objects that can be used to develop Visual C++ applications, and how to generate Visual Basic applications from the Designer/2000 repository.

THE COMPANION CD-ROM

Inside Oracle Designer/2000 is first and foremost a hands-on guide to the use of Designer/2000 tools, and you should read it as such. I strongly urge you to follow the discussion of different topics in the book by performing the activities with one or more application systems in your environment. In order to help you with these activities, I have provided a CD-ROM that contains a number of application systems that you can load in your Repository, as well as Lotus ScreenCam movies you can play. Designer/2000 version 2.0.8 (Beta) was used to produce the application systems and record the movies. I discuss the contents of the CD-ROM in the following two sections. The last page in this book shows you how to use the CD-ROM.

SOFTWARE

To help you understand the topics discussed in *Inside Oracle Designer/2000*, the companion CD-ROM contains sample applications discussed throughout the book. The intention of the provided software is to allow you to perform in your environment the most important activities discussed in this book. This software is organized by application systems covered in the book. A list of these applications follows:

❑ **Introductory ORDERS Application.** This is the application system ORDERS discussed in Chapters 1, 2, and 3.

❑ **Enterprise Strategic Analysis.** This is the application system STRATEGIC ANALYSIS discussed in Chapters 8, 9, and 10.

❑ **Process Order Model.** This is the application system PROCESS ORDERS discussed in Chapter 11.

❏ **Reengineered Process Order Model.** This is the application system REENG PROC ORD discussed in Chapter 12.

❏ **Order Management System Requirements.** This is the application system TASC OMS (REQ) discussed in Chapters 13, 14, and 15.

❏ **TASC 3NF Data Model.** This is the application system TASC 3NF discussed in Chapter 14. It contains the data model for TASC's order management business area in the Third Normal Form.

❏ **Sales Analysis System Data Model.** This is the application system TASC SAS discussed in Chapter 14. It contains the data model for TASC's Sales Analysis System.

❏ **Order Management System Design.** This is the application system discussed in Chapters 17 through 25.

❏ **Order Management System Development.** This is the application system discussed in Chapters 27 and 28.

LOTUS SCREENCAM MOVIES

To help you understand the topics discussed in *Inside Oracle Designer/2000*, I provide the most important actions you will encounter in the form of Lotus Screen-Cam movies. You will find over 170 of these movies for a total duration of over 3 hours. To help you access them more easily, the movies are organized by parts and chapters of the book. The movies provided on the CD-ROM are not recorded with sound. However, a script describes the most important activities that occur during the movie.

In order to view the movies, you need to download from the CD-ROM the ScreenCam Player application and store it in a folder on your PC. Versions of ScreenCam Player for Windows 95 and for Windows NT are available. You need to use the one that matches your environment. For the latest version of the ScreenCam Player application, visit the Web site of Lotus Development Corporation at www.lotus.com.

After you download the ScreenCam Player, launch it and open any of the movies provided on the CD-ROM. While the movie is playing, you may press the space bar to pause it. Pressing the space bar again resumes the movie. You can view the movies provided with *Inside Oracle Designer/2000* two ways. The most traditional one is to browse the movie directory until you find the movie you want to view. Using the Web browser, save the movie file to your PC and view it using ScreenCam Player.

The easiest way is to configure ScreenCam Player as a helper application for your Web browser that is launched each time you click one of the movie hyperlinks. The following are the actions you need to perform with Netscape Navigator:

1. Select Options | General Preferences.
2. Click the Helpers tab in the Preferences dialog box.
3. Click New Type.... Enter *'application'* in the Mime Type field, *'ScreenCam'* in the Mime SubType field, and click OK.
4. Enter *'scm'* in the File Extensions field.
5. Select the radio button Launch the Application and provide the full path of the ScreenCam Player executable in the text box.
6. Click OK to close the Preferences dialog box.

The following are the steps required to achieve the same thing in Microsoft Internet Explorer:

1. Select View | Options ... and click the Programs tab.
2. Click the button File Types ... in the group Viewers.
3. Click New Type ... in the dialog box File Types to display the dialog box Add New File Type.
4. Enter *'scm'* in the field Associated extension.
5. Type *'application/ScreenCam'* in the field Content Type (MIME).
6. Click New to add an action.
7. Type *'open'* in the Action field.
8. Provide the full path of the ScreenCam Player executable in the text box.
9. Click OK until all the dialog boxes are closed.

TYPOGRAPHIC CONVENTIONS

This book uses the following typographic conventions to make your reading and understanding of the material easier:

❏ Selection from menu items is presented in the following format:

File | Open, File | Save As ..., or Edit | Copy.

❏ Everything you should type in order to set a property is shown enclosed in single quotes and in italics. Example:

Set the text field Hint to *'Total cost of the order.'*

❏ Any code used in Designer/2000 tools is shown in Courier font, as in the following example:

```
BEGIN
  SELECT order_date
  INTO v_order_date
  FROM ORDERS
  WHERE
    order_number = v_order_number;
END;
```

❏ Tips offered throughout the book appear in boxes like the following one:

 Tips are hints or suggestions you may follow to enhance the way you work with Designer/2000

❏ Warnings raised throughout the book appear in boxes like the following one:

 Warnings are situations about which you need to be careful. They may potentially turn into problematic situations.

❏ Cautions discussed throughout the book appear in boxes like the following one:

 These are situations that may have catastrophic consequences for your environment. Avoid them at any cost.

❑ Lotus ScreenCam movies provided on the CD-ROM are referenced in the book using a characteristic icon with the movie number. The position of the icon indicates the beginning of the movie. These icons are similar to the one shown below:

QUESTIONS AND COMMENTS

I welcome any questions or comments you may have about *Inside Oracle Designer/2000*. You can send them directly to my Compuserve email account 102630.2211@compuserve.com. I strongly suggest that you periodically visit my Web home page at www.alulushi.com. There you will find answers to the most frequently asked questions about *Inside Oracle Designer/2000*, as well as a list of updated software assets of the CD as they become available.

ACKNOWLEDGMENTS

Putting together a hefty tome like the one you are holding in your hands is not a one-person job. Several people believed in the success of this project and helped me make it a reality. In the following paragraphs, I wish to extend the warmest thanks to all of them.

First and foremost, without the support, encouragement, and advice from my wife, Enit Kaduku, this book would have remained just an idea. Thanks to her, I was able to materialize the idea and complete the project, albeit at the cost of several beautiful weekends gone by. Her advice was crucial in finalizing the content, organization, and layout of the book.

Thanks to Corinne Gregory for the careful technical editing of the book. Her critique and comments played an important role in making the book more compact and more focused.

Special thanks to Ian Fisher, Vice-President, Designer/2000 Product Management at the Oracle Corporation, who made it possible for me to obtain the Designer/2000 Release 2 Beta software on time to incorporate the many improvements and added features of this release in the book.

The staff at Prentice Hall deserve my deepest appreciation for standing by me throughout the duration of the project. Thanks to Mark Taub, Executive Editor, who offered his support and guidance from the beginning; to my production editor, Jane Bonnell, who conducted diligently all the activities related to the production of the book under a very tight schedule; and to Christa J. Carroll, who added consistency and uniformity to the manuscript with her sharp copyediting skill.

Thanks also to my friend and mentor, Regis Scheithauer, who reminded me to pause and smell the roses.

Last but not least, many thanks to the old man Johann Sebastian Bach (1685–1750), who almost three hundred years ago wrote music that lifted my spirits up and helped me carry on during the long nights of work with the book.

Albert Lulushi

Part I

INTRODUCTION TO DESIGNER/2000

Chapter 1. Analyzing the Requirements

Chapter 2. Designing and Generating Database Objects

Chapter 3. Designing and Generating Software Modules

Chapter 4. Understanding the Designer/2000 Architecture

Chapter 5. Maintaining Application Systems

Chapter 6. Object Navigators in Designer/2000

Chapter 7. Diagrammers in Designer/2000

ANALYZING THE REQUIREMENTS

- Creating a New Application System
- Data Modeling
- Function Modeling
- Summary

In this chapter, you will analyze the requirements of a small system that will be ultimately composed of two tables in the database, a Developer/2000 form to create and manipulate data in these tables, and a Developer/2000 report to retrieve these data. The complexity of the system is purposely kept to a minimum in order to allow you to become familiar with the different concepts and tools used to analyze and document the requirements of a system in Designer/2000. This chapter assumes that you have access to a Designer/2000 Repository already installed and configured with privileges to create application systems. If you need to create the Repository and the user account yourself, read the instructions presented in Chapter 4 before proceeding with the rest of this chapter and the following two chapters.

1.1   CREATING A NEW APPLICATION SYSTEM

The work in Designer/2000 is organized around application systems. An application system is a set of objects, associations, and diagrams stored in the Designer/2000 Repository. The Repository may contain multiple application systems, each with a different purpose and role in the process of business or system modeling activities. In the following sections, you will learn how to create a new application system in Designer/2000.

1.1.1   INTRODUCING DESIGNER/2000 LAUNCH PAD

Designer/2000 is not a monolithic application but a suite of tools and utilities that are used at different stages of a database system's life cycle. The purpose of some of these tools may be revealed fairly clearly by their names. You can easily realize, for example, that the Entity Relationship Diagrammer is the tool to model the entities and relationships in your system, or that Repository Reports provides a series of canned reports to display the data you have entered in your Repository. However, when a dozen or more tools are involved, as in this case, keeping track of which of them to use at any given point in time is difficult. To help you think about these tools in an organized fashion, Designer/2000 provides a launch pad application that you can use to start each of its components. To invoke the launch pad application in a Windows 95 environment (or something visually similar) follow these steps:

1. Click the Start button.
2. Select Start | Programs | Oracle Designer 2000 | Oracle Designer 2000. The Connect dialog box shown in Figure 1.1 appears.
3. Provide the user name and password required to access the Designer/2000

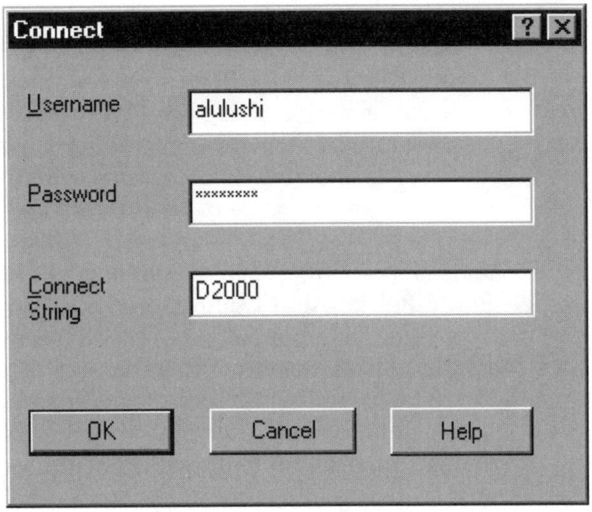

FIGURE 1.1 Connect dialog box.

Repository. If the Repository is located in a remote database server, enter the connect string for that server as defined in your SQL*Net configuration file TNSNAMES.ORA.

4. Click OK to connect to the Repository.

If the connection to the Repository is established, you will be presented with the Application System dialog box shown in Figure 1.2. The list box at the center of this dialog box allows you to select one of the applications you can access and

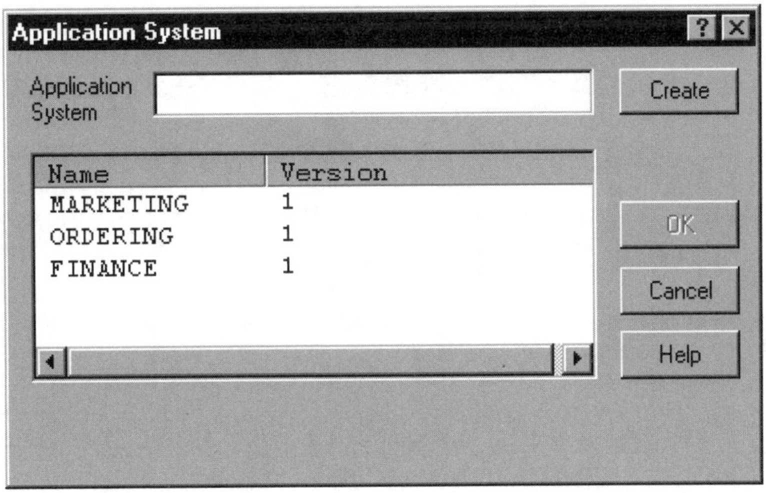

FIGURE 1.2 Application System dialog box.

to initialize the Designer/2000 launch pad. You can also create a new application system by entering the name in the text field Application System and clicking Create. Because you will create a new application system in the next sections, just click Cancel in this dialog box.

At this point, the Designer/2000 launch pad is displayed. Conceptually, this launch pad is like a toolbar, except that the iconic buttons that invoke different tools are organized in groups, according to the logical architecture of Designer/2000. The first group contains tools used to model business processes and information system requirements. These tools are the Process Modeller, the Entity Relationship Diagrammer, the Function Hierarchy Diagrammer, and the Data Flow Diagrammer. The second group contains two tools used to create preliminary database and system designs from the requirements of the application. These tools are the Database Transformer and the Application Transformer. The initial design created by the transformers can be refined and enhanced in the Design Editor, a unified environment used to design and generate database objects, database administration objects, and software modules. A number of tools are used throughout the design and development of a database system. These tools are listed as utilities to the left of the launch pad. The most important among these tools is the Repository Object Navigator, from which you can access every other tool and utility of Designer/2000. Figure 1.3 shows the Designer/2000 launch pad.

The Designer/2000 launch pad is a way to present all the components of Designer/2000 in an organized way that helps inexperienced analysts identify the tool they need for a particular task during the design and development of systems. The truth is that at different stages in the life cycle of a system a combination of tools from different groups is used.

By default, the Designer/2000 launch pad is presented in panel view, as shown in Figure 1.3. This view is helpful especially if you are new to Designer/2000. When you reach the level in which the meaning and purpose of each tool is clear in your mind, you may want to display the launch pad as a tool palette. Clicking the icon allows you to toggle the display mode of the Designer/2000 launch pad between panel and tool palette.

Furthermore, you may want to start each of these applications directly, bypassing the launch pad altogether. Chapter 4 shows how you can achieve this by creating shortcuts to each of these tools.

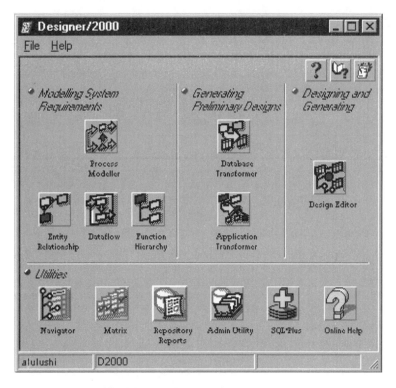

FIGURE 1.3   Designer/2000 launch pad.

1.1.2   INTRODUCING THE ORDERS APPLICATION

The application you will develop in this and the following two chapters will allow your users to enter simple ordering information into a database, retrieve and maintain the orders on the screen, and report the data related to these orders. Figure 1.4 shows a typical order that you will be able to support by the end of Chapter 3.

Section 1.2 in this chapter will analyze the requirements of such an application, and Section 1.3 will identify the components of the user interface and the business rules that the application will implement.

1.1.3   REPOSITORY OBJECT NAVIGATOR

The Repository Object Navigator is used to create and manage the properties of every object that can be stored in the Designer/2000 Repository. Other tools implement friendlier and more graphical interfaces to one or more categories of such objects, but the Repository Object Navigator is the catch-all tool. This Navigator is also used to create and maintain application systems. Assuming that you

ORDER NUMBER	ORDER DATE
123	9/16/97

CUSTOMER	DELIVERY DATE
Robert Johsnon	23 October 1997

ITEM NUMBER	PRODUCT	QUANTITY	UNIT PRICE	ITEM COST
1	Microsoft Win95	2	$ 39.99	$ 79.98
2	Personal Oracle	4	$ 99.99	$ 399.96
				$ 0.00
				$ 0.00
				$ 0.00
			ORDER TOTAL	$ 479.94

INSTRUCTIONS

Personal Oracle should be version 7.3.2 or higher.

FIGURE 1.4 A typical order that will be handled by the application system you will develop by the end of Chapter 3.

have started the Designer/2000 launch pad as explained in the previous paragraph, you can start the Repository Object Navigator by clicking its icon ▓ in the Utilities group of tools.

Initially, you will see the dialog box Welcome To The Repository Object Navigator, shown in Figure 1.5. This dialog box is displayed each time you start the Navigator and the context of the Designer/2000 is not associated with an application system. Among other things, it allows you to create a new application in the Repository or open an existing one.

 If you do not want to see the dialog box Welcome To The Repository Object Navigator in the future, clear the check box in the lower left-hand corner of the dialog box.

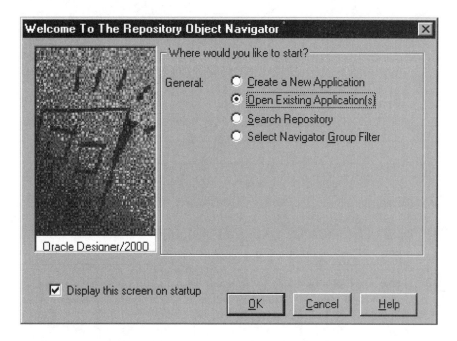

FIGURE 1.5 The Welcome To The Repository Object Navigator dialog box.

To create the new application system, follow these steps:

1. Select the radio button Create a New Application in the dialog box Welcome To The Repository Object Navigator.
2. Click OK.

At this point, the dialog box is closed and two windows are displayed. The one to the left contains an entry in which the cursor is placed, waiting for your input. This node represents the new application system you are about to create. The window is where you can browse all the objects within the new application. The objects are displayed hierarchically using the familiar Windows Explorer metaphor. This window is known as the Object Navigator window. Each application system is displayed in its own Object Navigator and there can be multiple applications open in the Repository Object Navigator at any time. The second window displays the properties of the object currently selected in the Object Navigator. This window is called the Property Palette. By looking carefully at the properties in this window, you notice three different colors to represent them. Conventionally, the burgundy colored properties are those for which you are required to specify a value. *Name* is one such property. The properties displayed in green are for read-only use. They are populated with values internally when the object is created or modified; you cannot set them directly. Properties like *Version* and *Version Date* fall in this group. Finally, you see the properties displayed in the regular font color. These are properties for which you may, but are not required to, specify a value. Such properties include *Title, Status,* and *Comment.*

3. Type 'ORDERS' as the name of the new application system.
4. Click the Save button 🖫 in the Navigator's toolbar to complete the process of saving the new application.

Notice when you save the application how Designer/2000 populates the read-only properties. Notice also that the label of the application in the Object Navigator becomes ORDERS 1 to indicate that this is the first version of this application system. The objects that may be defined for this application are under its name in nodes like Reference Data Definition, Enterprise Modelling, and Entity/Relationship Modelling. By double-clicking the name of a node, you can expand the node. The list of nodes that appears represents types of objects that a Designer/2000 application system may contain. In the rest of this chapter and in the following two chapters, you will create objects from several of these types using a number of Designer/2000 tools. The Repository Object Navigator will not be used for the rest of this chapter; therefore you may exit the tool. Figure 1.6 shows the Repository Object Navigator for the ORDERS application system.

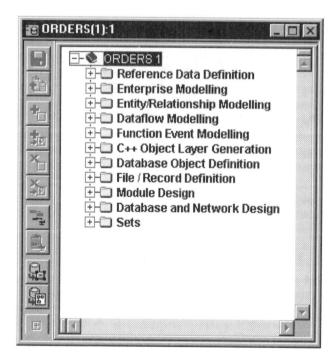

FIGURE 1.6 Repository Object Navigator for the ORDERS application system.

1.2   DATA MODELING

Two levels of data modeling for a system exist. The first one aims at discovering and identifying the entities that the system will support, their attributes, and the relationships that exist among them. In addition, this effort also discovers the data-related business rules that will be implemented by the system. The outcome of this level of data modeling is the logical data model of the system. The second level of data modeling maps the logical data model into a particular database schema. The outcome of this effort is the physical data model of the system. In Designer/2000, the Entity Relationship Diagrammer is used to create the logical data model of a system; the Database Transformer creates an initial physical model based on the logical model; the Design Editor is used to enhance and maintain the physical data model and generate the SQL scripts to implement the data model in a physical database schema. The rest of this section will build the logical data model for ORDERS and will introduce you to the Entity Relationship Diagrammer. Chapter 2 will discuss issues related to the physical model as well as the other tools mentioned above.

1.2.1   DATA REQUIREMENTS OF THE ORDERS APPLICATION

The ORDERS application will allow you to record and maintain information about orders placed by customers for one or more products. By looking at Figure 1.4, you can see that the data that this system will support may be grouped in the following two entities:

❑   **Order.** An order is a request for one or more products to be delivered by a date indicated by the customer, for which the customer agrees to pay the total amount associated with the order. An order is uniquely identified by an order number. An order may be composed of zero or more line items.

❑   **Line Item.** A line item represents a product ordered by a customer in a given order. For each line item, the customer may request one or more instances of the product. Each line item is uniquely identified by the order number and a unique item number within the order. A line item must be part of one and only one order.

Figure 1.7 represents the attributes of the entity ORDER and some of their properties. Note that these attributes are derived from the data elements of the order form shown in Figure 1.4. However, not every order-related item from that form is identified as an attribute of the entity. No ORDER TOTAL attribute exists, for example, although a need exists to know what the amount of goods for each order is. According to a well-known database design principle, avoid as much as possible storing data that can be computed from other data. Therefore, although no ORDER TOTAL attribute exists, you still need to store the method to compute

ATTRIBUTE NAME	DATA TYPE, LENGTH, AND PRECISION	OPTIONAL?	COMMENT
ORDER NUMBER	INTEGER	No	The unique identifier for the order.
CUSTOMER	VARCHAR2(100)	No	The name of the customer placing the order.
ORDER DATE	DATE	No	The date when order was placed.
DELIVERY DATE	DATE	Yes	The date by which the order must be delivered.
DESCRIPTION	VARCHAR2(240)	Yes	Instructions and other information about the order.

FIGURE 1.7 Attributes of entity ORDER.

it in the form of a data-related business rule. To complete the description of this entity, consider the following two rules with which orders must comply:

❑ If the delivery date of an order is specified, it must be after the date when the order was placed.

❑ The total amount charged to a customer for an order is the sum of item costs for all the line items in that order.

Figure 1.8 represents the attributes of the entity LINE ITEM and their properties. One business rule that instances of this entity must satisfy is the following: The cost of a line item is the product of the unit cost of merchandise times the quantity of the product ordered under the line item.

ATTRIBUTE NAME	DATA TYPE, LENGTH, AND PRECISION	OPTIONAL?	COMMENT
ITEM NUMBER	INTEGER	No	The unique item number within an order.
PRODUCT	VARCHAR2(100)	No	The name of the product ordered under the line item.
QUANTITY	INTEGER	Yes	The quantity of products ordered under the line item.
UNIT COST	NUMBER(8,2)	Yes	The cost of a product unit.
ITEM COST	NUMBER (8,2)	Yes	The cost for this line item.

FIGURE 1.8 Attributes of entity LINE ITEM.

1.2.2 OLTP AND OLAP APPLICATIONS

By looking at the attributes of the entity LINE ITEM, you notice a deviation from the principle that data that can be derived from other attributes should not be stored separately. The cost of an item can be computed based on the unit cost and the quantity of products ordered, and therefore it should not be maintained separately. Nevertheless, the attribute ITEM COST is identified as an attribute of LINE ITEM. In an apparently similar situation in the entity ORDER, the opposite decision was made. Although the cost of an order can be computed by other data, it is not identified independently.

When deciding what to store separately in the database, take into account the usage and purpose of the system. In a typical order entry application, a line item is rarely modified after its creation. Therefore, you will rarely need to recalculate the cost of the item. Even when you have to do so, everything occurs within the same UPDATE operation against the table that stores LINE ITEM data. The total cost of an order, on the other hand, depends on the cost of each individual line item within the order. Each time you add, delete, or modify the cost of a line item, you need to recalculate the total cost of the order, which will correspond to an extra UPDATE operation against the orders table. Applications used to create and maintain data, such as the one you are creating in these chapters, are called on-line transaction processing (OLTP) applications. For these applications, you want to minimize the amount of redundant data that they generate or maintain.

Another class of applications exists, which are used mainly to analyze and understand data. The data for these applications is loaded in cycles, usually during non-operational hours, and queried by a number of sophisticated users to mine the data and discover trends and interesting features contained in them. These applications, called on-line analytical processing (OLAP) applications, require very fast query response time, which can be achieved only by storing redundant and pre-calculated data. If you were to model the entities ORDER and LINE ITEM for an OLAP application, for example, you would store not only the total cost of the order, but also other data elements, such as the total amount of orders for a given period of time (day, week, month, and so on), for a given product, and for a given customer.

1.2.3 INTRODUCING THE ENTITY RELATIONSHIP DIAGRAMMER

The Entity Relationship Diagrammer is the tool used to enter information about entities, attributes, and relationships like the ones described in the previous section. To start this diagrammer, click the icon Entity Relationship 🖼 in the Designer/2000 launch pad. Assuming that you did not initialize the launch pad to a particular system, you will be prompted with the Application System dialog box. You can pick the application ORDERS created in Section 1.1.3 and click OK. This action will also initialize the launch pad to this application. From now on,

A visual indicator of the context of the Designer/2000 launch pad is the name and version number of the application displayed in the lower right-hand corner of the status bar. This bar also displays the Repository user name and the database connection string specified in the Connect dialog box when the launch pad is initially started.

every tool you start from here will be automatically initialized to the application ORDERS. To initialize the launch pad explicitly, follow these instructions:

1. Select File | Change Application System. This action displays the Application System dialog box, with which you are familiar now.
2. Select the desired application from the list box.
3. Click OK.

The same steps can be performed inside other Designer/2000 tools to switch the context of the tool from one application system to another.

When the Entity Relationship Diagrammer is displayed on the screen, you notice that this is an MDI application as well. The MDI sheets of this diagrammer are called entity relationship diagrams (ERDs). Objects that you create and maintain from within the Entity Relationship Diagrammer need to reside in ERD diagrams. You can create a new diagram by issuing one of these commands:

❑ Click the iconic button New 🔲 in the toolbar.
❑ Select File | New....
❑ Press CTRL+N from the keyboard.

Save the newly created diagram with the following commands:

1. Select File | Save As... from the menu. Because this is a new application system, the dialog box Save Diagram As appears.
2. Type 'ORDERS ERD' in the Diagram Name text box of the dialog box Save Diagram As.
3. Click OK.

Now you see the name of the new diagram displayed in the title bar of the diagram window.

1.2.4 CREATING ENTITIES AND RELATIONSHIPS

Now that you have a diagram in place, you are ready to create the entities described in Section 1.2.1 and the relationship between them. To create the entity ORDER, follow these steps:

1. Click the iconic button Entity ⬛ from the diagrammer toolbar.
2. Click anywhere inside the diagram. This action brings up the dialog box Create Entity.
3. Enter 'ORDER' in the Name text box of the dialog box. Do not worry about Short Name and Plural, as they will be derived automatically by Designer/2000.
4. Click OK.

Follow similar steps to create the entity LINE ITEM. After the entities are created, you may want to change their position and dimensions in the diagram. To move an entity, click it to select it and, while holding the mouse button down, drag the entity to the desired position. To resize an entity, select it, and then move the mouse over one of the selection handles. When the mouse cursor changes to a horizontal, vertical, or diagonal arrow (depending on which handle you moved it to), click and drag the edge of the entity to the desired size.

Now that the entities are in place, you need to create the relationship between them. Reading the descriptions of the entities ORDER and LINE ITEM provided earlier in the chapter, you can extract the following information:

❑ An ORDER may be composed of zero or more LINE ITEMS.
❑ A LINE ITEM must be part of one and only one ORDER.

The iconic button that allows you to create this type of relationship is the one labeled M:1 (M to O) Relationship, with the following icon: ⬛. The steps listed above allow you to create the relationships:

1. Click the M:1 (M to O) Relationship button ⬛. Notice that the mouse cursor changes to cross-hair symbol.
2. Click the entity where the 'Many' end of the relationship will be attached. This is the entity LINE ITEM, since an ORDER may contain zero or more LINE ITEMS.
3. Click the entity where the other end of the relationship will be attached. Obviously, this is ORDER. At this point the dialog box Create Relationship appears.
4. In the From Name text box, enter the words 'part of.' This is how the relationship sounds when you read it from the entity you clicked first (LINE ITEM) to the second entity (ORDER). In other words, a LINE ITEM must be part of one and only one ORDER.

5. In the To Name box, enter the words *'composed of.'* This is how the same relationship between the entities sounds when you read it in the opposite direction, from ORDER to LINE ITEM. (An ORDER may be composed of zero or more LINE ITEMS)

6. Click OK to complete the process.

Figure 1.9 shows your first entity relationship diagram.

1.2.5 CREATING ATTRIBUTES

After creating the entities and relationships in your system, you can edit each entity to provide additional information, including its attributes. You view and maintain the properties of an entity in the dialog box Edit Entity that is displayed if you double-click the entity. This dialog box is composed of multiple property tabs. The attributes of an entity are created in the Attributes tab.

To create an attribute, for example, ITEM COST for entity LINE ITEM, follow these steps:

1. Click in the first empty record in the record list or click the button Insert Row.

2. Enter *'ITEM COST'* in the text field Name.

3. Enter a number in the text field Seq that reflects the sequence of this attribute among other attributes. The sequence numbers should contain some

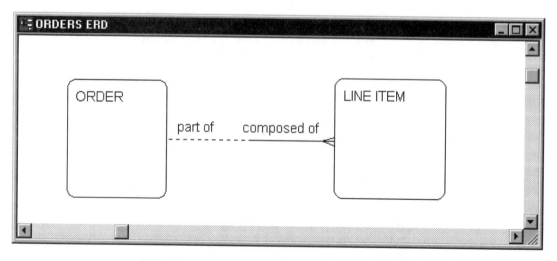

FIGURE 1.9 Your first entity relationship diagram.

gaps to facilitate the process of inserting new attributes or modifying the sequence of existing ones.

4. Click to place a check mark in the check box Opt to indicate that the attribute is optional. For mandatory attributes, this check box should remain unchecked.

5. Select 'NUMBER' from the Format drop-down list. For alphanumeric or date attributes, you should select the corresponding format type (VARCHAR2 or DATE).

6. Scroll right to display the other properties of the attribute and enter '8' in the MaxLen field to indicate the maximum length of this attribute.

7. Enter '2' in the Dec field to express the fact that ITEM COST will be stored with a precision of two digits after the decimal point.

8. Scroll right again and enter 'The cost for this line item.' in the Comment field.

Follow similar steps to create the attributes for entities ORDER and LINE ITEM. The information provided in Figure 1.7 and Figure 1.8 should be used to populate the properties of these attributes.

1.2.6 DEFINING UNIQUE IDENTIFIERS FOR ENTITIES

According to the information provided for the entity ORDER, each order is uniquely identified by an order number. The following is how you enter this information in the Repository:

1. Display the Edit Entity dialog box by double-clicking the entity ORDER in the diagram.

2. Click the tab Attributes and scroll right until you see the check box Primary.

3. Click to place a check mark in the check box Primary for attribute ORDER NUMBER to indicate the fact that this is a unique identifier and also the primary unique identifier for the entity.

For the entity LINE ITEM, the information presented in Section 1.2.1 says that each line item is uniquely identified by the order number and a unique item number within the order. However, you would notice that this entity does not have an attribute to represent the ORDER NUMBER. In fact, this attribute is present implicitly in the entity LINE ITEM through the mandatory end of the relationship that exists between the two entities. Therefore, the relationship end will be part of the unique identifier definition together with the attribute ITEM NUMBER. In order to create the unique identifier for the entity LINE ITEM, follow these steps:

1. Display the Edit Entity dialog box by double-clicking the entity LINE ITEM.
2. Click the tab UIDs.
3. From the Candidate Relationships list box, select 'part of ORDER' and click the iconic button Include ⊞ to add this relationship to the definition of the unique identifier.
4. From the Candidate Attributes list box, select 'ITEM NUMBER' and click the iconic button Include ⊞ to add the attribute to the definition of the unique identifier.
5. Place a check mark in the check box Primary in the Unique Identifiers area of the tab to indicate that this unique identifier will also be the primary unique identifier for the entity.
6. Click OK to save the changes to the database.

Figure 1.10 shows the UIDs property tab for the case discussed above.

1.2.7 DEFINING TEXT INFORMATION FOR ENTITIES

The only thing left now to complete the logical data model is to add some textual information to the entities in order to document their meaning and purpose. The property tab Text allows you to associate textual information with an entity. If you look at this tab, you notice that two text properties can be populated for an entity:

❑ *Description*. This property is used primarily to enter the business meaning of the entity. The language used here is free of technical terms and is such that future users of the system associate with and understand. The narrative paragraphs used in Section 1.2.1 to introduce both entities are good candidates to be stored in the Description property of their respective entities.

❑ *Notes*. The content of this property, when specified, is usually addressed to other designers and developers of the system who will encounter the entity or the table derived from it at some point in time. An example of text stored in this property are the business rules identified for each entity in Section 1.2.1. When the Database Design Wizard creates tables based on the proper-

Designer/2000 derives the name of the primary unique identifier from the *Short Name* property of the entity.

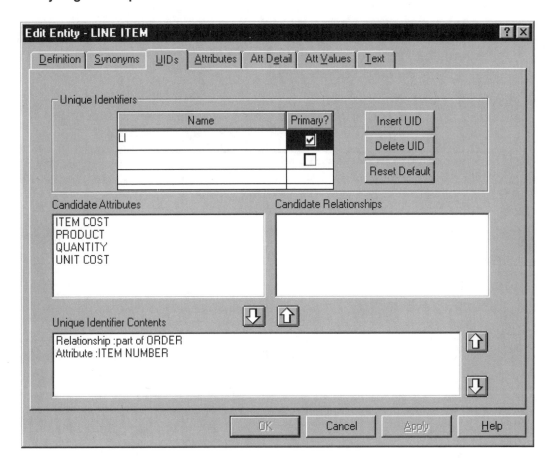

FIGURE 1.10 UIDs property tab.

ties of these entities, it transfers the definitions of these business rules to the tables. The database designer reads these rules and implements them in the physical data model.

Figure 1.11 shows the setting for *Description* property for the entity ORDER.

At this point, the logical data model for the ORDERS application system is complete. The view of your diagram should be similar to Figure 1.12. Notice in this diagram the following conventions:

❑ The character # in front of an attribute indicates that the attribute is part of the primary unique identifier for the entity.

❑ The character * in front of an attribute indicates that the attribute is required.

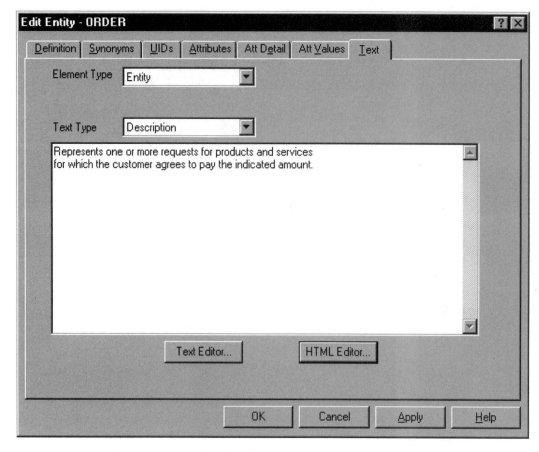

FIGURE 1.11   Contents of the Description property of the entity ORDER.

❑   The character ° in front of an attribute indicates that the attribute is optional.
❑   A dash across the relationship line indicates that the relationship is part of
     the primary unique identifier for the entity.

Save the diagram and exit the Entity Relationship Diagrammer.

1.3   FUNCTION MODELING

Identifying and documenting the data requirements of a system is one important
aspect of the requirements analysis. The other aspect as important as this one is
defining the functional requirements that the system should meet. The Function

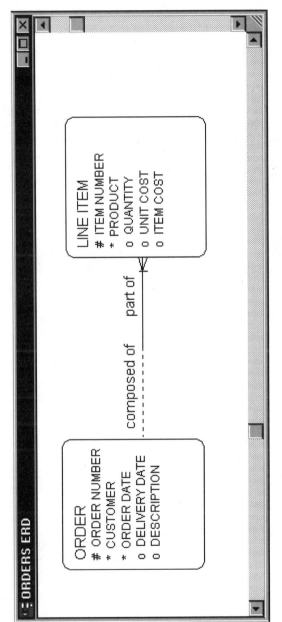

FIGURE 1.12 The final version of the ORDERS application system entity relationship diagram.

Hierarchy Diagrammer is the Designer/2000 tool used to create and maintain the properties of functions in your application systems. The following sections explain how to use this tool to create the functions for the ORDERS system.

1.3.1   FUNCTIONAL REQUIREMENTS OF THE ORDERS APPLICATION

The phrase "functional requirements" is probably as old as computer systems themselves. Throughout the years, it has meant different things to different people. Each methodology and computer science fad has given the phrase its own meaning and has prescribed ways to identify them. This book takes a "best practices" approach and considers functional requirements of a system to be the collection of screens and reports that the system needs to present to its users, joined with the set of business rules that the system needs to enforce and implement.

A critical success factor of software systems today has become their ability to partition and distribute components across multiple physical locations. Experience has shown that when the user interface is defined and implemented separately from the business logic, achieving flexible partitioning of the application code is much easier. In light of this discussion, the user interface requirements of the ORDERS application system are defined as shown in Figure 1.13.

The question of identifying and documenting business rules is a little trickier. You can easily get lost in too many details or succumb to the temptation to capture every little detail in textual format as in the examples shown in Figure 1.13. Always keep in mind that functional analysis and data modeling are activities that happen in concert and complement one another. A good number of business rules of a system are identified during the data modeling. In Section 1.2, all the properties of entities, attributes, and relationships, defined and recorded using the Entity Relationship Diagrammer, are business rules that the system needs to implement. Recording these rules as properties of elements of your data model allows you to implement them declaratively both on the back-end database server and on the front-end user interface applications.

NAME	PURPOSE	DESCRIPTION
Create and manage ordering information.	Enables users to create, view, and maintain ORDER and LINE ITEM data.	This function will initially display a screen with all the attributes of an order. Users may use it to create and maintain orders. In addition, the screen will also view and maintain all the line items of a selected order.
Retrieve and report ordering information.	Enables users to view on the screen and print ordering information.	This function will retrieve ORDER and LINE ITEM data in a master/detail format. Each ORDER record will be followed by all its LINE ITEM records.

FIGURE 1.13   User interface requirements for the ORDERS application system.

Business rules that should be captured and recorded explicitly are those that cannot be implemented declaratively by the Designer/2000 generators or that require some intricate procedural and programming logic to be implemented. As you will see, these generators are very powerful, and a careful setting of objects' properties may reduce significantly the amount of programming you need to do. In Chapter 3, for example, you will create items that will display in the user interface modules, calculated data such as the number of line items included in an order and the total of each order. The code to calculate these items will be generated automatically without requiring that you develop special program units to compute these data elements. This feature allows you to focus your attention on designing and implementing more complex functionality in your applications. As an example, a business rule in the ORDERS application system that falls in this category is presented in Figure 1.14.

1.3.2 CREATING THE FUNCTION HIERARCHY OF THE SYSTEM

In this section, you will create Designer/2000 functions to represent the user interface requirements and business rules presented in Section 1.3.1. The Function Hierarchy Diagrammer is the preferred tool to create and maintain functions. You can access this tool by clicking the icon Function Hierarchy 📊 in the Designer/2000 launch pad. Like other tools discussed in this chapter, this diagrammer is an MDI application in which you can create and maintain different diagrams in their own window. Unlike the diagrams created in the Entity Relationship Diagrammer, the diagrams in this tool are hierarchical in nature. Each diagram is associated with at least one function that serves as the root of the hierarchy. Descendants of the root function are listed under the root in the form of a tree. To create the new functional diagram for ORDERS, issue one of these commands:

- ❑ Click the iconic button New Diagram ▢ from the toolbar.
- ❑ Select File | New.
- ❑ Press CTRL+N from the keyboard.

NAME	PURPOSE	DESCRIPTION
Compute average order total	Compute the average total cost for all orders placed in a given date.	The average total cost for all orders placed in a given date is the sum of the total cost of each order placed in the given date divided by the number of these orders.

FIGURE 1.14 A business rule for the ORDERS application system.

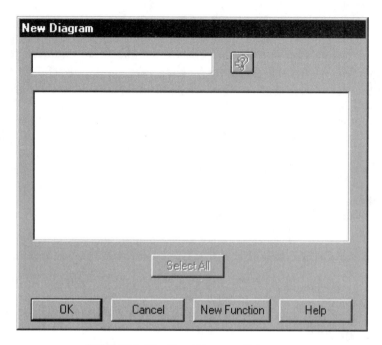

FIGURE 1.15 New Diagram dialog box.

As a result of these commands, the dialog box New Diagram is displayed (see Figure 1.15).

The purpose of this dialog box is to allow you to pick a function as the root of your diagram. The text list control in the center of the dialog box displays all the functions defined in the current application system. You may either select one of the functions in the list box as the root of the new diagram or create a new function and make it the root function by clicking the button New Function. Since no functions are defined in the ORDERS system, click this button to create the root function for the system. This action brings up the dialog box Create Function. Enter 'ORDERS' in the Label field and 'Create and maintain orders' in the Short Definition field as shown in Figure 1.16. To complete the process of creating the root function and the new diagram, click OK.

As you may have already guessed, the function you just created will represent the entire ORDERS system. The next step after defining it is to create two children for this function under which you will group the user interface and the business logic functions. To create a new function that is the child of a function present in the diagram, follow these steps:

1. Click the iconic button Function ⊟ from the toolbar.
2. Click inside the parent function in the diagram. The Create Function dialog box discussed earlier appears.

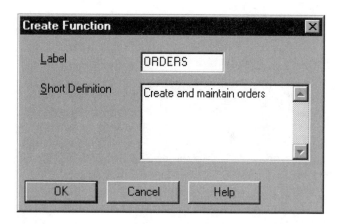

FIGURE 1.16 Create Function
dialog box.

3. Set the properties *Label* and *Short Definition* for the new function. These properties should indicate which category of requirements (user interface or business logic) each function will represent. For example, you could use *'ORDUI'* and *'ORDBL'* to set the property *Label*. The strings *'User interface functions'* and *'Business logic functions'* may be used to set the property *Description*.
4. Click OK.

Now you are ready to create the actual user interface and business rule functions identified in Section 1.3.1. Follow steps similar to the ones described above to create each function. Use unique strings as labels and the text provided in the Name column of Figure 1.13 and Figure 1.14 as the short definition for each function. Although no restrictions exist on the labels you use to identify functions, setting them so that they indicate the position of the function in the hierarchy tree is good. Examples of labels you may use are 'ORDUI001' and 'ORDUI002' for the two user interface functions, and 'ORDBL001' for the business rule.

In a large application system with many functions from each category, the user interface functions are usually kept in their own diagrams separately from the business rule functions. Given the limited size of ORDERS, one functional diagram is sufficient. However, you may still want to distinguish the functions of one type from the other. To do so, you may use different fill colors for each branch of the hierarchy by following these steps:

1. Control-click the functions ORDUI, ORDUI001, and ORDUI002. Controlclicking allows you to select multiple objects in the Function Hierarchy Diagrammer.
2. Click the iconic button Fill Color 🎨 in the toolbar. The Color palette shown in Figure 1.17 appears.
3. Select the desired color and click OK. All the selected functions will be displayed in the selected color.

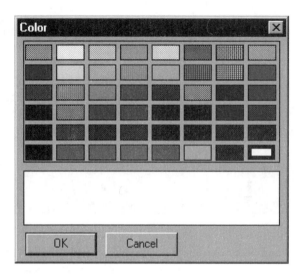

FIGURE 1.17 The Color palette.

Using similar steps, you can set the business logic branch of the hierarchy tree to a different color. Ultimately, your function hierarchy should look like the one shown in Figure 1.18. To complete this leg of the trip, save the diagram under the name ORDERS FHD.

1.3.3 MAINTAINING PROPERTIES OF FUNCTIONS

After creating the functional hierarchy of a system, you need to edit some of the properties of the new functions. Although the hierarchy may contain many functions, not all of them need editing. Usually you focus on those functions that represent a user interface requirement or a business rule. In the ORDERS application system, you should edit the properties of ORDUI001, ORDUI002, and ORDBL001, and not be concerned with the other functions in the higher levels in the hierarchy. You can view and maintain the properties of a function in the Edit Function dialog box, invoked by double-clicking the given function in the diagram. This dialog box is made up of several property tabs. The most frequently used among them are Definition, Entity Usages, Attribute Usages, and Text.

Figure 1.19 shows the Definition tab for the function ORDUI001. Notice in this tab the Label and Short Definition properties for the function and its parent. Notice also the check box Atomic in the upper right-hand corner of the tab, which indicates that this function is a leaf node in the function hierarchy tree. The only property you normally change in this tab is Response. For user interface functions that will correspond to forms, this should be set to *'IMMEDIATE'* to indicate that users interact directly with the function. For user interface functions that will be implemented as reports and for business rules, the property is set to

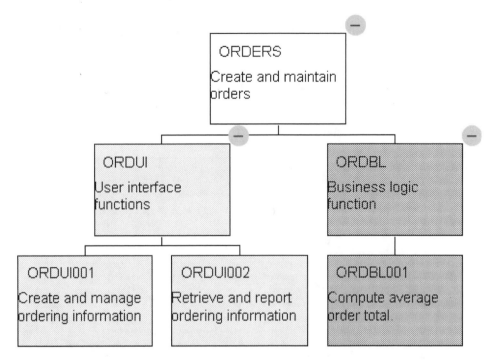

FIGURE 1.18 The function hierarchy for the ORDERS application system.

'OVERNIGHT' to indicate that users will access this function indirectly, through a screen user interface function—hence the 'delay.'

The Text property tab allows you to associate different textual information with the function. As in the case of entities, *Description* is normally used to document the business meaning of the function; *Notes* is used for remarks and information that members of the design and development team want to share with one another. Figure 1.20 shows the *Description* property for function ORDUI001 populated with content from Section 1.3.1.

Besides setting the properties discussed above, for user interface functions you should also specify the ways these functions use data. In other words, associate each function with the entities and attributes it will use and register the kinds of operations that the function will perform with these data elements. These properties are also called the entity and attribute usages of the function and are maintained in the property tabs Entity Usages and Attribute Usages. From the description of the function ORDUI001, you can understand that this function will create, retrieve, update, and delete data from entities ORDER and LINE

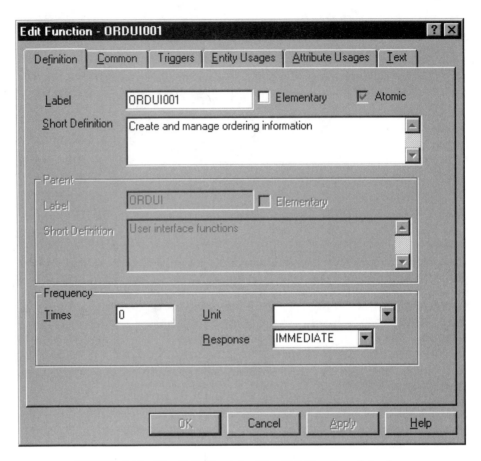

FIGURE 1.19   The Definition tab of the Edit Function dialog box.

ITEM. To enter this information in the form of entity usages for this function, follow these steps:

1. Open the Edit Function dialog box by double-clicking the function ORDUI001.
2. Click the Entity Usages property tab.
3. Select the entity ORDER from the drop-down list box Entity in the first row.
4. Select the entity LINE ITEM from the drop-down list box Entity in the second row.
5. Click to place check marks in the check boxes Create, Retrieve, Update and Delete for both entities. The Entity Usages property tab now should look like the one shown in Figure 1.21.

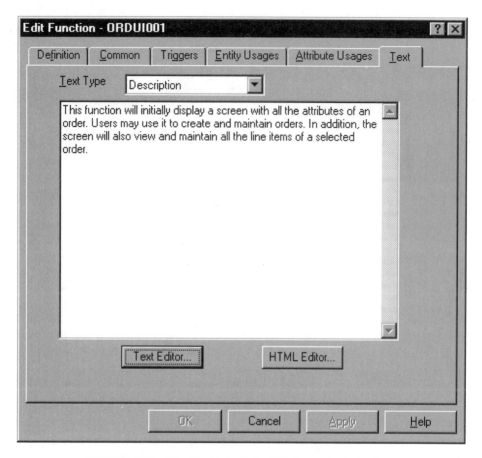

FIGURE 1.20 The Text tab of the Edit Function dialog box.

6. Click Apply to commit the changes without closing the Edit Function dialog box.

Attribute usages are set in a similar manner, except that the kinds of actions a function may perform on an attribute are slightly different. The function, for example, may create or delete instances of an entity, but it can insert or nullify values of an attribute. Assuming that the Edit Function dialog box for function ORDUI001 is still displayed, the following steps populate the attribute usages of this function:

1. Click the Attribute Usages property tab.
2. From the drop-down list box Entity, select the entity ORDER.
3. Click the button Select All to create usages for all the attributes in the entity.

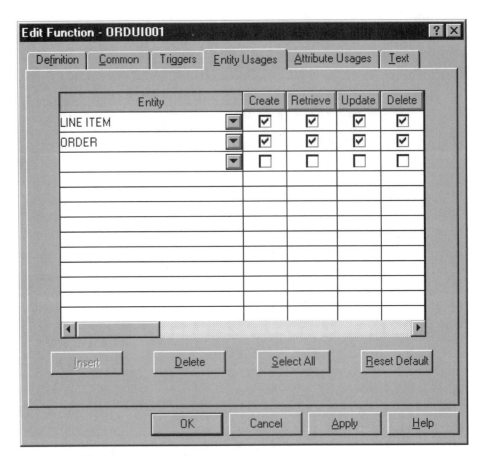

FIGURE 1.21   The Entity Usages tab of the Edit Function dialog box.

Alternatively, you may pick each individual attribute from the list box Attributes. You will notice that when an attribute usage is created, the check boxes Insert, Retrieve, Update, and Nullify are set automatically. Designer/2000 sets these flags based on the usages you have defined for the parent entity of the attribute.

4. Repeat steps 2 and 3 for the entity LINE ITEM.

5. Click OK to commit the changes and close the dialog box.

Note that some of the attribute usages that are set automatically based on the entity usages may not make full sense. For example, the *Update* usage of ORDER NUMBER is set, although a well-known standard dictates that the primary unique identifiers of an entity should not be updatable whenever possible.

Furthermore, the Nullify usage is set for attributes like CUSTOMER and ORDER DATE, which are mandatory attributes in the entity ORDER. Nevertheless, ensuring that the usages of each attribute are set properly is not worth the time for the following two reasons:

❑ The real value of setting attribute usages is to identify which attributes from a particular entity the function will modify.

❑ Properties such as *Updatable* or *Required* for items in generated modules are set by the front-end generators based on the properties of the database schema, which override the settings of attribute usages.

The definition of the data usages for the functions ORDUI001 and ORDUI002 also marks the end of the requirements analysis work you have to do for the ORDERS application system. In Chapters 2 and 3 you will use the information entered in the Repository to design and generate the database schema and front-end modules for the system.

1.4 SUMMARY

This chapter describes all the steps you need to take in order to create your first Designer/2000 application system. It also shows how you can enter the requirements for a simple system you are developing. The main topics of this chapter are listed below:

❑ **Creating a New Application System**
  ❑ Introducing Designer/2000 Launch Pad
  ❑ Introducing the ORDERS Application
  ❑ Repository Object Navigator
❑ **Data Modeling**
  ❑ Data Requirements of the ORDERS Application
  ❑ OLPT and OLAP Applications
  ❑ Introducing the Entity Relationship Diagrammer
  ❑ Creating Entities and Relationships
  ❑ Creating Attributes
  ❑ Defining Unique Identifiers for Entities
  ❑ Defining Text Information for Entities
❑ **Function Modeling**
  ❑ Functional Requirements of the ORDERS Application
  ❑ Creating the Function Hierarchy of the System
  ❑ Maintaining Properties of Functions

Chapter 2

DESIGNING AND GENERATING DATABASE OBJECTS

- ♦ Database Design Transformer
- ♦ Designing the Physical Database
- ♦ Enhancing the Data Design
- ♦ Generating Database Objects
- ♦ Summary

After the requirements of a system are defined, the design and development efforts continue along two tracks. The first one translates the logical data model into a physical database schema. This chapter will walk you through the steps required to create and implement the database schema of the ORDERS system. In the second track, you will design and develop software modules to implement the user interface and the business rules of the system. Activities along this track are covered in Chapter 3.

The transformation of the logical data model of a system into a working physical database schema using Designer/2000 goes through the following stages:

1. Create a first-cut physical design based on the logical data model using the Database Design Transformer.
2. Refine the physical data model using the Design Editor.
3. Implement data-related business rules.
4. Generate DDL statements and create the physical objects in a database using the Server Generator.

The remainder of this chapter will guide you through these steps for the ORDERS application system.

2.1 DATABASE DESIGN TRANSFORMER

Designer/2000 provides a tool that enables you to convert the logical data model of a system, consisting of entities, attributes, and relationships, into a physical data model. This tool, called the Database Design Transformer, can be accessed directly from the Designer/2000 launch pad by clicking the Database Design Transformer icon 🖳. It is also accessible from a number of other tools, such as the Entity Relationship Diagrammer and the Repository Object Navigator.

2.1.1 PURPOSE AND USE

The Database Design Transformer translates the logical data model into a physical data model by reading properties of objects in the Repository and, based on these properties, creating new objects. In particular, the Transformer performs the following tasks:

❑ Creating tables based on properties of entities.
❑ For each table, creating columns based on properties of attributes of the corresponding entity.
❑ Implementing relationships between entities as foreign key constraints associated with the corresponding tables.

2.1.2 POPULATING THE RUN SET

When you initially launch the Database Design Transformer, you see a dialog box similar to the one shown in Figure 2.1. The property tab labeled Mode allows you to run the Transformer in default mode or to customize it. The default mode is the simplest way to use the Transformer. In this mode, the run set includes all the entities in your application system. Database design objects will be created based on the properties of these entities.

The lower right-hand side of the Mode tab contains a summary of the objects included in the run set. In the case shown in Figure 2.1, there are two entities in the set that are not mapped to any tables. Although the entities help define the Transformer's run set, they are not the only members of the set. For each entity, the Transformer automatically includes in the set the attributes of the entity as

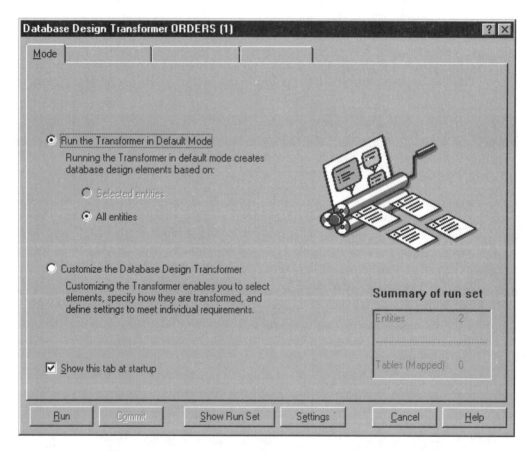

FIGURE 2.1   The Mode tab of the Database Design Transformer.

well as any unique identifiers or relationships defined for the entity. If the entity has already been mapped to a table, the working set may include columns, primary key, foreign key, and unique key constraints, as well as index objects that correspond to foreign keys. In order to view all the components of the Transformer's working set, click Show Run Set. The dialog box Elements in the Run Set appears similar to the one shown in Figure 2.2. Click Close to dismiss it and return to the Database Design Transformer.

If you run the Database Design Transformer with these default settings, the Transformer will create all the tables, columns, keys, and indexes it considers necessary to implement the logical data model. In general, however, the tool is used iteratively multiple times during the design and development efforts of a system. In these cases, the Transformer is used in customized mode. This mode allows you to include in the run set specific objects and provides you with a lot of

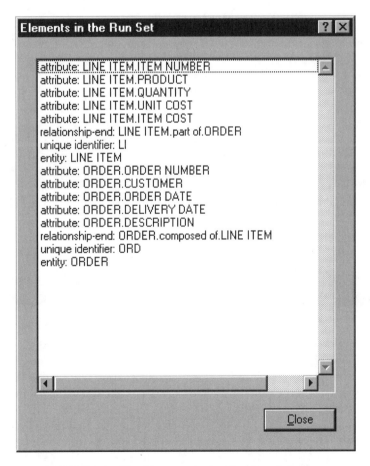

FIGURE 2.2   The Elements in the Run Set dialog box.

flexibility in deciding what actions to perform on which objects of the working set. In particular, you can control the following options:

❑ **Type of action.** You may instruct the Transformer to create new objects or modify properties of existing ones, or to cover both cases.

❑ **Granularity of action.** You may instruct the Transformer to act upon tables, columns, keys, and indexes, or any combination of these objects.

❑ **Scope of properties.** You may select one or more categories of properties that the Transformer will update for the objects in the working set.

Chapter 17 discusses in detail running the Database Design Transformer in customized mode.

2.1.3 RUNNING THE TRANSFORMER

After populating the working set and inspecting the objects included in it, you can kick off the process by clicking the button Run in the Transformer's dialog box. As the Transformer proceeds to create the objects, each action it performs along the way is displayed in the dialog box Database Design Transformer Output Window. After the process is complete, you can click Copy to place this information in the Windows clipboard or simply close the dialog and discard the log records. At the end of the process, the Summary of run set will show that there are two mapped tables in the set. Click Show Run Set to display the dialog box Elements in the Run Set updated with the new objects just created by the Transformer. These objects include the tables ORDERS and LINE_ITEMS with columns, primary keys, and foreign keys, as well as an index on the foreign key of table LINE_ITEMS. To dismiss the Database Design Transformer, click the button Close in the Transformer's dialog box.

2.2 DESIGNING THE PHYSICAL DATABASE

In general, for a full-blown system, a separate thread of activities aims at designing the database that will contain the data model objects. During these activities you identify the architecture of the database and properties of objects related to this architecture. Such objects include databases, tablespaces, data files, rollback segments, storage definition clauses, sequences, database users, and others. They are stored in the Designer/2000 Repository together with objects like tables, views, snapshots, and indexes, which express the data model requirements of the system. The database design objects listed above are created and maintained in the Design Editor. In the following sections, you will create these objects for the ORDERS application system.

2.2.1 STARTING THE DESIGN EDITOR

As a preliminary step, start the Design Editor by clicking the icon with the same name 🖼 in the Designer/2000 launch pad. In the dialog box Welcome To The Design Editor that appears, select the radio button Database Administration as shown in Figure 2.3 and click OK. At this point, the Design Editor is started. Like other Designer/2000 components you have seen so far, this application has a multiple document interface (MDI). There are two windows displayed inside the MDI frame. The first one is similar to the Object Navigator window in the Repository Object Navigator. It is known as the Design Navigator window and contains a list of Repository objects used in application design activities, organized hierarchically by their type. A noticeable difference between the Navigator windows in the Design Editor and the Repository Object Navigator is that the Design Navigator contains four tabs used to organize and group together database objects, modules, database administration objects, and distribution objects. The tab DB Admin is selected automatically when you selected to work with database administration objects in the Welcome To The Design Editor dialog box.

The second window opened automatically when the Design Editor starts is the Database Administration Guide dialog box shown in Figure 2.4. This is one in a series of wizards implemented in Designer/2000 to help you accomplish com-

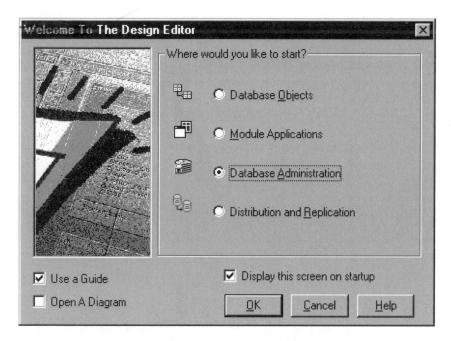

FIGURE 2.3 The Welcome To The Design Editor dialog box.

To hide the dialog box Database Administrator Guide when no longer needed, simply click Close. To display it again select Tools I Database Administrator Guide... from the menu.

plex tasks. In particular, the Database Administration Guide walks you through each step required to define databases, schemas, and related properties in the Repository. It also assists you in the process of recovering the designs of existing databases and storing them in the Repository.

2.2.2   CREATING THE ORDERS DATABASE

Since every object in the ORDERS system will be stored in a database, beginning the process by defining a database object in the Designer/2000 Repository is understandable. I assume here that you have launched the Design Editor and opened the dialog box Database Administrator Guide as explained in the previous section. To create the database objects, follow these steps:

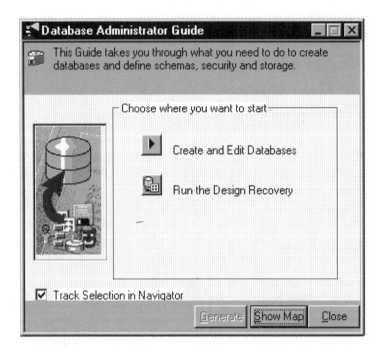

FIGURE 2.4   The Database Administrator Guide dialog box.

You can create a far more complex database than this by following all the steps contained in the dialog box Create Database. Chapter 18 provides details on how you create Oracle and non-Oracle database objects in the Repository.

1. Click the icon ▣ in the dialog box Database Administrator Guide. The layout of the dialog box is transformed to inform you that there are no databases in the application system.
2. Click Create. The Create Database dialog box shown in Figure 2.5 appears.
3. Type 'ORDERS' in the text box Unique name. As you type, the text box Local name is set to the same value.
4. Set the list box Version of Oracle Server to the value that best describes the database where you will create the objects of the ORDERS application.
5. Click the button Finish to complete the transaction and close the Create Database dialog box.

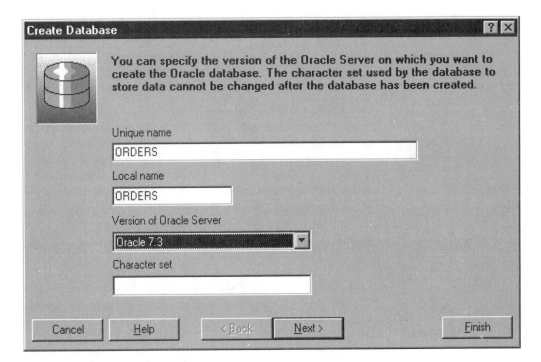

FIGURE 2.5 The Create Database dialog box.

At this point the database ORDERS is created in the Repository. As a visual indicator of this fact, the list box in the Database Administrator Guide dialog contains an entry with the characteristic icon of the database followed by the database name. Click the icon ◼ to return to the entry screen of the Database Administrator Guide, shown in Figure 2.4.

2.2.3   CREATING A DATABASE USER

For every database application you need a database user, also known as schema or database account that will own all the objects required by the application. The following steps describe the process of creating a database user in the Design Editor.

1. In the Design Navigator window, expand the nodes Databases (Oracle) and ORDERS.
2. Select the node Users.
3. Click the icon Create ◼ on the window's toolbar. The dialog box Create Database User appears.
4. Set the properties User name and Initial password. Figure 2.6 shows an example of such settings.
5. Click Finish to complete the process of creating the database user.

The Design Navigator window will be updated to display the newly created user.

2.2.4   RECOVERING THE DESIGN OF EXISTING DATABASE OBJECTS

Having a database object and at least a schema defined in the Repository are minimal requirements for proceeding with the rest of the physical database design activities. However, in order to have a useful design in your hands, you need to add to the Repository additional database structures, like tablespaces, rollback segments, and sequences. One way to populate the applica-

The process of creating a database user was shown in Section 2.2.3 in its most simple form. Full details on the process are discussed in Chapter 19.

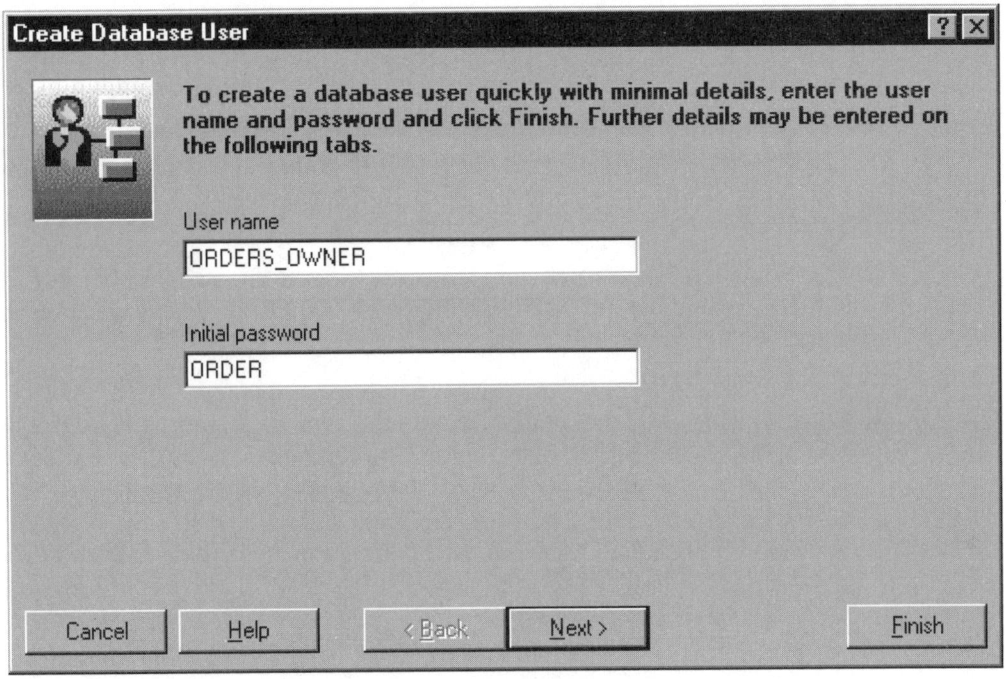

FIGURE 2.6 The Create Database User dialog box.

tion system Repository with such objects is to create them in the Design Navigator window of the Design Editor. This course of action is desired when designing a system that will be implemented in its own database, separate from other systems. However, not every application system you design and develop is large enough to warrant a separate database. The case in point is the ORDERS system, which will require only two tables and a few indexes to be implemented. In cases like this, I recommend that you implement the database objects of the new system in an existing database schema, in which you have the privileges required to create all the necessary objects. For example, you can implement the objects of the ORDERS application system in the SCOTT/TIGER schema that is created by default in any Oracle database, or in your personal account.

Even when database objects will be implemented in an existing Oracle schema, the desirable approach is to bring into the Designer/2000 Repository some of the objects of the existing database that will be associated with the new objects of your system. In the case of the ORDERS system, for example, you may want to create objects that represent the tablespaces of the target database, so that you can distribute the tables and indexes to the appropriate tablespaces.

The Design Recovery utility allows you to read the data dictionary of an existing database and create objects in the Designer/2000 Repository based on the properties of the real objects. In the Design Editor, this utility can be accessed using one of the following two methods:

❑ Select Utilities | Recover Design of | Database... from the menu.
❑ Click the icon Run the Design Recovery 🖳 from the Database Administrator Guide.

The following is a list of steps you need to perform in this utility in order to read the properties of tablespaces from an Oracle database into the Designer/2000 Repository:

1. Open the Design Recover Database dialog box by issuing one of the two commands listed earlier. This dialog box contains two tabs labeled Source and Objects. The tab Source is selected and displayed by default.
2. Select the radio button Oracle in the Source of Design Recovery group of controls. Note that you can recover the design of non-Oracle databases from data definition language (DDL) statements stored in files or by connecting to these databases via ODBC.
3. Set the text boxes Username, Password, and Connect to allow the utility to connect to the database and extract the information you want to recover. In order to recover the tablespace properties of the Oracle database, a schema with database administration privileges, like SYSTEM, is required. At this point, the Source tab should look like the one shown in Figure 2.7.
4. Remove the check mark from the check box Show Results on new Data Diagram. This option is not useful in your case since tablespaces cannot be displayed on data diagrams.
5. Switch to the properties tab Objects.
6. Expand the node Tablespace in the object tree on the left side of the tab labeled Don't Recover. This control contains all the objects of the remove database.
7. Select the tablespace object you want to recover and click the icon 🔳 to transfer it to the list to the right. This list contains all the objects whose design will be recovered. At this point, the tab Objects should resemble the one shown in Figure 2.8.
8. Click Start. The Database Design Recovery utility starts creating the tablespace objects in the Repository. A message window appears at the bottom and displays any errors or warnings that may be encountered in the process. At the end, a message box is displayed to inform you that the design recovery is complete. However, the new objects are not yet saved in the Repository. As a visual indicator of this fact, the background color of the Design Navigator window becomes gray.
9. Click Save to commit the changes to the Repository.

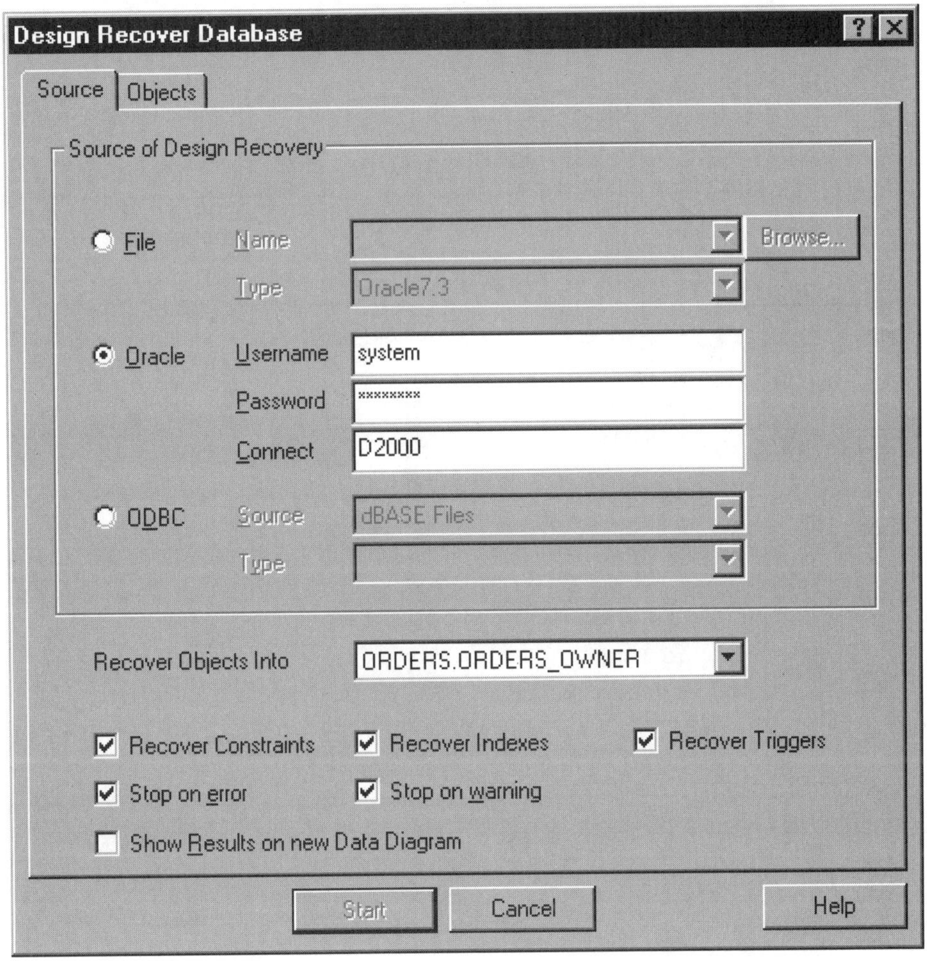

FIGURE 2.7 The Source tab of the Design Recover Database utility.

The following steps allow you to view the newly created objects in the Repository Object Navigator:

1. In the Design Navigator window, expand the nodes Databases (Oracle) and ORDERS.

2. Select the node Tablespaces.

3. Select Edit | Requery Selection from the menu. Notice that the iconic representation of the node Tablespaces changes to indicate that the Repository contains objects of this type.

4. Expand the node Tablespaces. You now see all the tablespaces that you reverse engineered from the Oracle database.

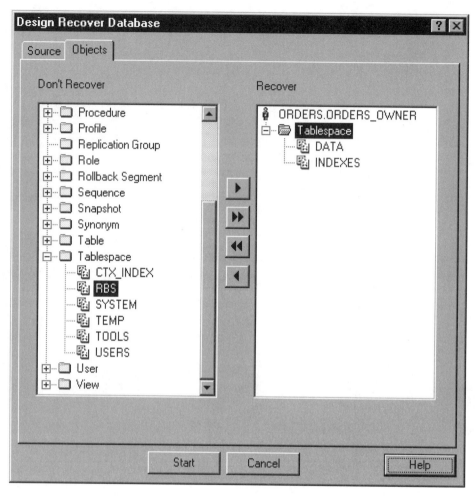

FIGURE 2.8 The Objects tab of the Design Recover Database utility.

At this point, you are ready to proceed into the next section, which will discuss how to present the data model of the new system in data diagrams and enhance the properties of database design objects in the Data Schema Diagrammer.

2.3 ENHANCING THE DATA DESIGN

As mentioned in Section 2.1 of this chapter, the Database Design Transformer utility is used to generate the initial database design based on the properties of your system's data model. This initial design needs to be enhanced and expanded in order to achieve a better implementation of the data requirements and business rules that your system will implement. The Design Editor is the main Designer/2000 tool used to enhance the database design. In the following sections, you will use this tool to modify the properties of database objects in the ORDERS application.

2.3.1 CREATING AND MAINTAINING DATA DIAGRAMS

The Design Navigator window of the Design Editor allows you to create and maintain all the database objects of your application. However, in order to present the concepts and critical points of your design, you need to create data diagrams. The Design Editor allows you to create two types of diagrams: data and module diagrams. To create the first data diagram in the ORDERS application, Select File | New | Data Diagram from the menu. Now follow these commands to populate the diagram with objects:

1. Select Edit | Include. This command brings up the dialog box Include Tables/Views/Snapshots/Foreign Keys.
2. Expand the nodes All Schema Objects and Table Definitions in the navigator control in the center of the dialog box.
3. SHIFT+CLICK the tables ORDERS and LINE_ITEMS to select both of them as shown in shown in Figure 2.9.
4. Click OK to include the selected objects in the diagram.

At this point, the data diagram created should look like the one shown in Figure 2.10. Notice that the contents of this diagram are similar to those of the entity relationship diagram you created in Chapter 1. The only striking difference is the column ORD_ORDER_NUM in the table LINE_ITEMS. While every other column corresponds to an attribute, this one does not have an attribute counterpart in the entity LINE ITEM. The Database Design Transformer creates this column as a component of the foreign key constraint on table LINE_ITEMS. This constraint maps the logical relationship between entities ORDER and LINE ITEM to a physical database object. For each line item, ORD_ORDER_NUM will contain a reference to its parent in table ORDERS. Because the relationship was part of the primary unique identifier of LINE ITEM, the column ORD_ORDER_NUM is also part of the primary key for table LINE_ITEMS.

However, the data diagram also differs in several important ways from the corresponding entity relationship diagram. The following is a list of these differences together with instructions you can follow on the diagram to experience these differences yourself.

❑ Ability to hide or display all the objects owned by a table, including its columns, constraints, synonyms, indexes, and triggers. Icons in the title bar of each table allow you to toggle the display of these objects on or off.

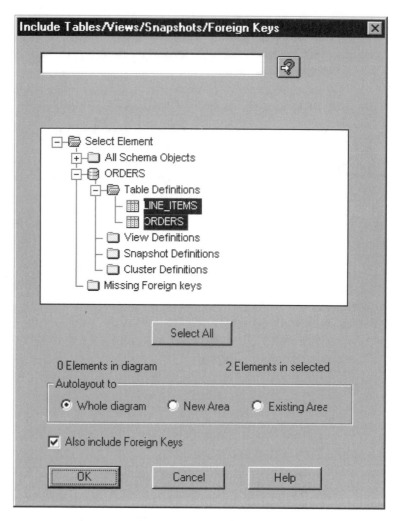

FIGURE 2.9   The Include Tables/Views/Snapshots/Foreign Keys dialog box.

❑ 'Bubble' help for every object displayed in the diagram. By moving the mouse cursor over objects like tables, columns, or foreign keys, you will see context-sensitive text pop up and display the type of object and its name.

In order to complete the process of creating the data diagram for the application, save the diagram by following these instructions:

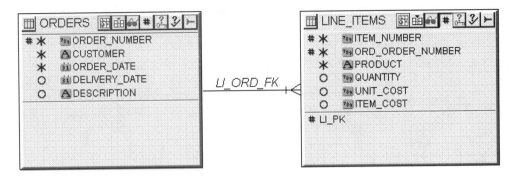

FIGURE 2.10 The ORDERS data schema diagram.

1. Select File | Save Diagram As…. The dialog box Save Diagram As appears.
2. Type *'ORDERS DSD'* in the Diagram Name text box.
3. Click OK.

2.3.2 CREATING TABLE IMPLEMENTATIONS

The table object is a very powerful concept in your application, full of rich features and functionality. However, this richness does not come from properties of the object itself as much as it comes from other objects owned by the table, such as columns, primary, unique, and foreign keys, check constraints, and indexes. Therefore, maintaining the properties of a table means primarily maintaining the properties of these objects. There are, however, a few steps needed to associate the table with a database user who will be the owner of the table and to set properties such as the tablespace and storage parameters of

The Data Schema Diagrammer is similar to the Entity Relationship Diagrammer, since it displays objects related to one another. Many commands and actions, such as selecting, resizing, moving, and modifying color properties of objects in the diagrams, are similar as well. A functionality that you may find very helpful is the in-place editing of names of every object displayed in the diagram. To activate the editing mode, click the name of the object you want to edit twice (but do not double-click). Simply type the new name and click elsewhere in the diagram to save the changes.

It is important to understand the difference between a table and its implementation for a given database user. The first object is used in the logical design of the database; the second object is used in its physical design. While there is only one table object to represent a given table, for example ORDERS, there may be multiple table implementation objects derived from it. Each of them represents the table in a different physical database or database schema.

the table. These steps are performed in the Design Navigator window of the Design Editor and are described here for the tables ORDERS and LINE_ITEMS.

1. Switch to the tab DB Admin of the Navigator.
2. Select the node Databases (Oracle) and click the icon Expand All ⊞. You will see in the hierarchy tree the database ORDERS and the user ORDERS_OWNER you created in Section 2.2.2 and Section 2.2.3.

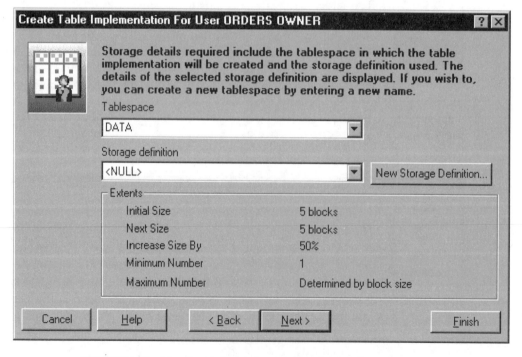

FIGURE 2.11   The Create Table Implementation for User dialog box.

3. Select the node Table Implementation and click Create 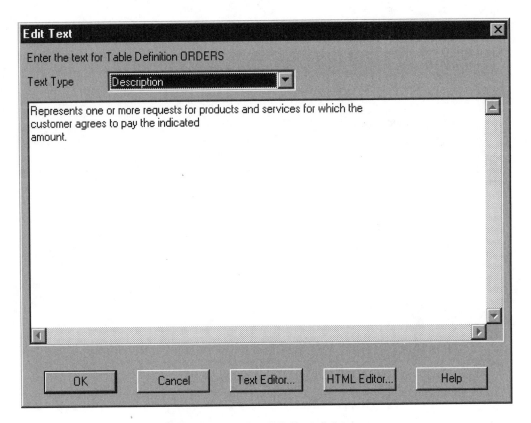. The dialog box Create Table Implementation for User is displayed.

4. Select the first table in the list and click Next.

5. Set the list box Tablespace to the tablespace where this table should reside as shown in Figure 2.11. The tablespaces in this list were created during the design recovery process discussed in Section 2.2.4.

6. Click Finish.

The implementation of the table for the database user is created and displayed in the Navigator. Repeat steps 3–6 for the second table.

Another set of table-related properties is textual properties associated with the table. These properties are maintained in the dialog box Edit Text (see Figure 2.12). To display this dialog box for a given table, select the table in the Design Navigator and then select Edit | Text... from the menu. The list box Text Type in the dialog box allows you to select the text property that you want to view or

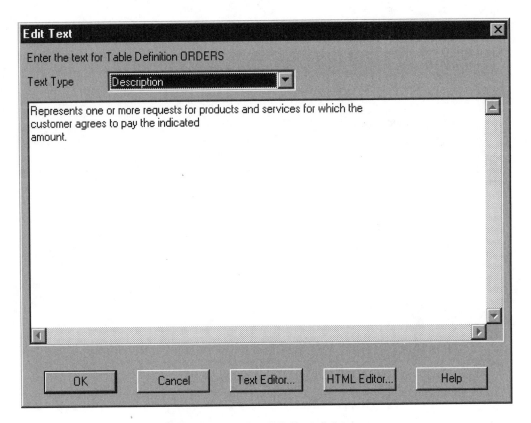

FIGURE 2.12 The Edit Text dialog box.

edit. The contents of the selected property are displayed in the multi-line text object in the center of the dialog box. Note that the Database Design Transformer uses the information you specified in the *Description* property of the entity to populate the properties *Description* and *User Help Text* of the corresponding table. The content of the property *Notes* is transferred from the entity to the table object as well.

2.3.3   MAINTAINING COLUMN PROPERTIES

The properties of columns are viewed and edited in the Edit Table dialog box invoked by double-clicking the desired table object on the diagram or on the Design Navigator window. This dialog is composed of several property tabs, which group together a few properties of the table itself and those of its columns. The tab Name allows you to maintain among others the properties Name and Alias of the table object. This tab is not used as often as the other tabs. The tab Columns contains the most important database properties of each column in the table. These properties influence all the Designer/2000 generators. Figure 2.13 shows an example of this property tab.

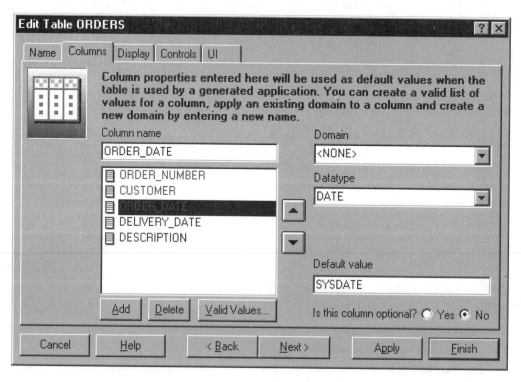

FIGURE 2.13   The Columns property tab of Edit Table dialog box.

The Database Design Transformer transfers the settings for a good number of these properties from the properties of their attribute counterparts, particularly the sequence in which columns are defined, the data type, length, and whether the column is optional or mandatory. Mandatory columns are displayed in red characters to set them apart from the optional columns. The only action you need to perform in the property tab Columns is to set the text box Default value to 'SYSDATE' for the column ORDERS.ORDER_DATE as shown in Figure 2.13. This setting will create software modules that set the date of an order to the current system's date whenever the user does not specify the date explicitly.

The property tab Display allows you to define whether columns from a table will be displayed or hidden in generated applications and the display order of these columns. The property tab Controls is used to set layout properties of items in the generated applications. These properties include *Display Type, Prompt, Width,* and *Height*. The properties you need to set in this tab are as follows:

1. Set the property *Width* to '30' for columns ORDERS.CUSTOMER and LINE_ITEMS.PRODUCT; set property *Width* to '40' for columns ORDERS.DESCRIPTION. The main purpose for reducing the default setting of these VARCHAR2 items is to conserve screen real estate in modules that will contain them.

2. Set the property *Width* to '12' for columns UNIT_COST and ITEM_COST in the table LINE_ITEMS.

3. Set the property *Width* to '4' for column ORDER_NUMBER in the table ORDERS, and for columns ORD_ORDER_NUMBER, ITEM_NUMBER, and QUANTITY in the table LINE_ITEMS.

Figure 2.14 shows this tab for the case of the table ORDERS.

Finally, the tab UI contains properties which control the way data is displayed in the items of the generated application. An example of this tab is shown in Figure 2.15. The following are the steps you need to take in order to set the UI properties of columns in ORDERS and LINE_ITEMS tables:

1. Put a check mark in the check box *Uppercase* for the columns CUSTOMER, ORDER_DATE, and DELIVERY_DATE in the table ORDERS, and for the column PRODUCT in table LINE_ITEMS. Based on this setting, the front-end generators will create items corresponding to these columns that allow users to enter data only in uppercase characters.

2. Set the property *Format* to 'DD-MON-YYYY' for columns ORDER_DATE and DELIVERY_DATE in the table ORDERS.

3. Set the property *Format* to '$999,999.99' for columns UNIT_COST and ITEM_COST in the table LINE_ITEMS.

4. Set the property *Alignment* to 'Right' for columns QUANTITY, UNIT_COST and ITEM_COST in the table LINE_ITEMS.

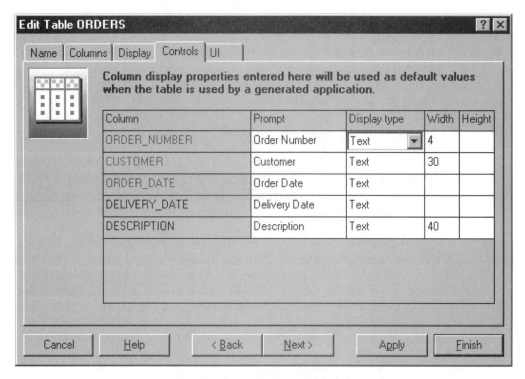

FIGURE 2.14   The Controls tab of the Edit Table dialog box.

2.3.4   MAINTAINING CONSTRAINT PROPERTIES

When the Database Design Transformer converts entities, attributes, and relationships into database design objects, it automatically creates the following table constraints:

❏ **Primary key constraints.** These constraints are defined based on the primary unique identifier of the entity. In the ORDERS system, ORD_PK is the primary key constraint defined for the table ORDERS, and LI_PK is defined for the table LINE_ITEMS.

 The property *Hint* is used by the generators to display a hint message in the message line of generated modules when the application focus is placed inside the items. Its setting is inherited from the *Comment* property of the corresponding attribute.

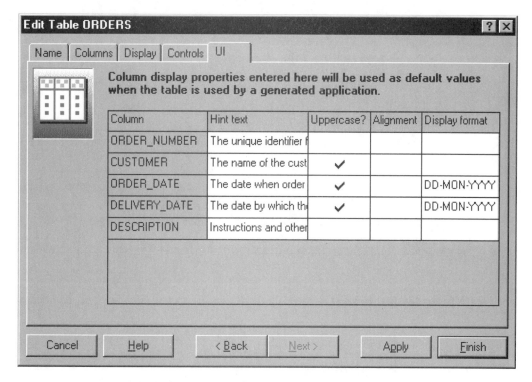

FIGURE 2.15   The UI tab of the Edit Table dialog box.

❑ **Foreign key constraints.** These constraints are defined in tables whose corresponding entity contains the many end of a one-to-many relationship. In
the ORDERS system, the table LINE_ITEMS contains the foreign key constraint LI_ORD_FK, which joins the columns LINE_ITEMS.ORD_ORDER_
NUMBER and ORDER.ORDER_NUMBER.

❑ **Unique constraints.** These constraints are defined based on unique identifiers of the entity other than the primary unique identifier. Since entities
ORDER and LINE ITEM do not have any such unique identifier associated
with them, the corresponding tables do not have unique constraints.

You can view and edit the properties of a primary key in the dialog box Edit Primary Key displayed when you double-click the
object. This dialog box is composed of two tabs: Primary Key
Mandatory and Validation. The following are the actions required to set the properties of the primary key ORD_PK:

1. Display the dialog box Edit Primary Key and switch to the tab Validation.
2. Set the text box Error message to *'An order with this number already exists.'*

The generated applications will return this message when the constraint is violated.

3. Select the radio button Both from the group Validation level. With this setting, the constraint will be implemented as a table constraint by the Server Generator and the front-end generators will create code to implement it in the client modules as well.

4. Click Finish.

Figure 2.16 shows the settings of the Validation tab of the Edit Primary Key dialog box for the case of ORD_PK.

The steps to set the properties for the primary key LI_PK are very similar. The only difference is in the setting of the error message, which now should be *'A line item with this number already exists within the current order.'* The following steps describe the process of setting the properties of the foreign key constraint LI_ORD_FK:

1. Display the dialog box Edit Foreign Key and switch to the tab Validation.

2. Set the text box Error message to *'The order specified for this line item does not exist.'*

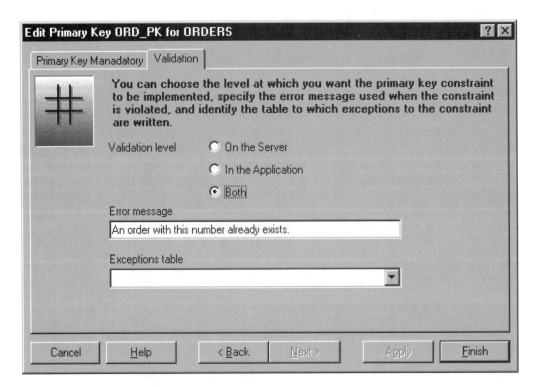

FIGURE 2.16 The Validation tab of the Edit Primary Key dialog box.

3. Select the option Both from the list box Validation level.

4. Switch to the tab Cascade Rules.

5. Select the option Cascades from the list box Cascade delete rule. This list represents the property *Delete Rule* of the foreign key. By default, this property is set to '*Restricted*,' in which case users cannot delete orders if they contain at least one line item. By setting *Delete Rule* to '*Cascades*' you will enable the user to delete an order and, automatically, all the line items that reference this order.

6. Select the radio button No in the group Can the foreign key be updated? This radio group represents the property *Update Rule* of the foreign key. Setting the radio button No is equivalent to setting this property to '*Restricted*,' which means that a line item cannot be transferred from one order to another after its creation.

7. Click Finish.

Figure 2.17 shows the Cascade Rules tab of the Edit Foreign Key dialog box for the foreign key LI_ORD_FK.

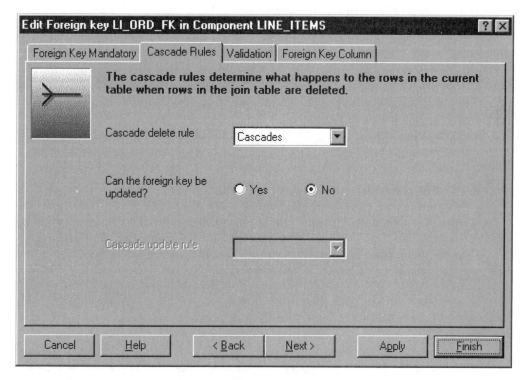

FIGURE 2.17   The Cascade Rules tab of the Edit Foreign Key dialog box.

2.3.5 IMPLEMENTING BUSINESS RULES WITH CHECK CONSTRAINTS

By reading the description of the ORDERS application system presented in Section 1.2.1, you can identify the following business rules that the system needs to implement:

☐ The order date must be on or after the current system's date.
☐ The order delivery date must be on or after the order date if it is not null.
☐ The item cost is the product of quantity by unit cost.

In this section, you will implement the first two rules as check constraints defined on table ORDERS, and the last rule as a check constraint defined on table LINE_ITEMS. I assume here that the Design Editor is running. Follow this list of steps to create a check constraint that enforces the first rule:

1. Switch to the DB Objects tab of the Design Navigator window, expand the nodes Table Definitions and ORDERS.
2. Select the node Check Constraints and click Create ⬚. The dialog box Create Check Constraint in Component appears.
3. Type 'ORD_CK1' in the text box Check constraint name. This will be the name of the check constraint.
4. Enter the following line in the text box Check constraint condition:

```
ORDER_DATE >= SYSDATE
```

5. Click Next and set the text box Error message to a string that describes the business rule you are implementing, for example, *'The order date must be on or after the current date.'*
6. Set the radio button In the application in the group Validation level.
7. Click Finish to complete the process.

The reason for the settings of the Validation Level property in Step 6 is that this constraint cannot be implemented as an in-line check constraint associated with the table ORDERS (the Oracle Server does not allow the use of pseudo-columns like SYSDATE in check constraints). The following steps allow you to create another check constraint to implement the second business rule.

1. Click the button Create ⬚ on the toolbar. The dialog box Create Check Constraint in Component appears again.
2. Type 'ORD_CK2' in the Check constraint name text box.
3. Enter the following line in the text box Check constraint condition:

```
( (DELIVERY_DATE >= ORDER_DATE) OR
(DELIVERY_DATE IS NULL) )
```

In order to insert a new line in the multiline text box Check constraint condition you should press CTRL+ENTER from the keyboard
rather than just ENTER.

Figure 2.18 shows how the dialog box Create Check Constraint in Component should look at this point.

4. Click Next and set the Error message text box to a string that describes the
business rule you are implementing, for example, *'The delivery date must be
on or after the order date, if it is not null.'*

5. Set the radio group Validation level to the option Both.

6. Click Finish to complete the process.

The difference between the two check constraints defined above is that the
first one can be implemented only by the front-end generators, whereas the sec-

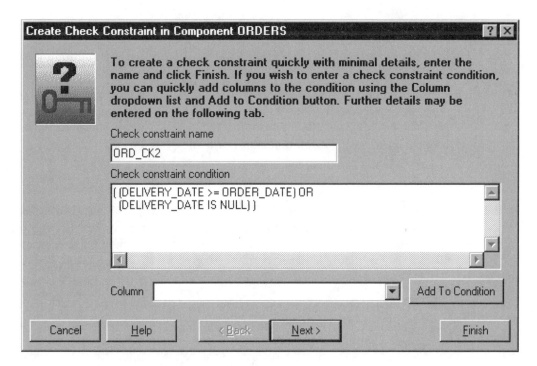

FIGURE 2.18 The Create Check Constraint in Component dialog box.

The first tab of the dialog box Create Check Constraint in Component allows you to select the columns from a list box at the bottom of the tab and click the button Add to Condition to include the column to the Check constraint condition text box. This feature can save you typing efforts in cases when the condition of constraint uses a number of columns. The conditional statement itself can reference only columns from the same table as check constraint table.

ond one can be implemented by the Server Generator at the database level as well. The following steps create a check constraint in the table LINE_ITEMS to ensure that the item cost is the product of the unit cost of merchandise by the quantity of merchandise ordered.

1. Expand the node LINE_ITEMS in the Design Navigator window.
2. Select the node Check Constraints and click Create ▣. The dialog box Create Check Constraint in Component appears.
3. Type 'LI_CK1' in the text box Check constraint name. This will be the name of the check constraint.
4. Enter the following line in the text box Check constraint condition:

```
ITEM_COST = QUANTITY * UNIT_COST
```

5. Click Next and set the text box Error message to a string that describes the business rule you are implementing, for example, 'The item cost must equal product unit cost multiplied by quantity.'
6. Set the radio group Validation level to the option Both.
7. Click Finish to complete the process.

2.3.6   PERFORMING DATA DERIVATION

Chapter 1 identified the following business rule, which describes how to compute the cost of an item: The cost of a line item is the product of the unit cost of merchandise times the quantity of merchandise ordered under the line item.

Naturally, you would want to create front-end modules that compute the values displayed by these items automatically, without user intervention. Designer/2000 provides a property for each column, named *Derivation Expression*, in which you can specify how to derive the content of the column. Unlike the properties of tables and related objects you have set so far, this property is not accessible from any GUI dialog boxes in the Design Editor. You can access this property in the Property Palette of the Editor by following these steps:

1. Click the icon Use Dialogs to toggle it from the pushed state 🖾 to the raised state 🖾.
2. Double-click the column ITEM_COST of table LINE_ITEMS. The Property Palette for this column appears.

By default, the icon Use Dialogs is in pushed state. In this case, double-clicking an object in the Design Navigator window brings up a dialog box with the properties of the object. When the icon is raised, double-clicking the object displays the Property Palette with all the properties of that object. After the Property Palette is displayed, each time you select a different object in the Navigator, the Palette will be refreshed with its properties. You can toggle the icon Use Dialog to its pushed state and continue to view and maintain the properties of the objects using both interfaces.

Now that the Property Palette of the column ITEM_COST is displayed, take these actions:

1. Click the property *Derivation Expression* in the Palette. A TextPad window appears.
2. Enter the following line in the TextPad document:

```
QUANTITY * UNIT_COST
```

3. Click the Save icon 🖾. This action closes the TextPad window. The new setting of the property *Derivation Expression* is shown in the Property Palette.
4. Click the value field of the property *Derivation Expression Type*. Notice how this field turns into a list box.
5. Select the option '*SQL Expression*' from this list box as a setting for the property *Derivation Expression Type.*
6. Click the Save icon 🖾 on the Design Editor's toolbar.

2.3.7 MAINTAINING INDEX PROPERTIES

Recall from the discussion about the Database Design Transformer that for each foreign key created, the Transformer creates an index to facilitate joins between the master and detail tables. In the case of the ORDERS application, the Transformer has created the index LI_ORD_FK_I associated with the foreign key LI_ORD_FK. Furthermore, each primary or unique key constraint defined in your Oracle database is implicitly associated with an index. This means that when the ORDERS tables will be created in the database, two indexes will be created based on the columns that are part of the primary keys ORD_PK and LI_PK.

Like tables and other objects created by the Transformer, these indexes are components of the logical design of the database. In order to add them to the physical design of the system, you need to create implementations of these indexes for a given database schema. As in the case of table implementations, index implementations primarily consist of assigning the index to a tablespace and setting its storage properties. The following steps describe the process of creating an implementation of the index LI_ORD_FK_I for the database user ORDERS_OWNER created in Section 2.2.3.

1. Switch to the tab DB Admin of the Navigator.
2. Select the node Databases (Oracle) and click the icon Expand All ⊞. You will see in the hierarchy tree the database ORDERS, the user ORDERS_OWNER, and the table implementations LINE_ITEMS and ORDERS you created in Section 2.3.2.
3. Select the node Index Storage and click Create ⊡. The dialog box Create Index Storage for User is displayed. Notice that the list Index in this dialog box contains two entries: LI_ORD_FK_I and LI_PK, which represents the index implicitly associated with the primary key of LINE_ITEMS.
4. Select the index LI_ORD_FK_I and click Next.
5. Set the list box Tablespace to the tablespace where this index should reside. In general, to reduce the I/O contention, the indexes and tables should be stored in different tablespaces.
6. Click Finish.

Repeat similar steps to set the storage properties of indexes associated with the primary keys ORD_PK and LI_PK. These actions conclude the work you have to do to enhance the initial logical data design generated by the Database Design Transformer and transform it into a physical database schema. In the next section, you will use the Server Generator to create DDL commands that implement the design in an Oracle database.

2.4 GENERATING DATABASE OBJECTS

After the database design of your system is complete, you use the Server Generator to create SQL DDL statements that implement your design in the database server. The Server Generator can be accessed from the Design Editor. Its interface is simple, and the process of generating and implementing database objects is not complicated at all. In general, it requires that you follow these three steps:

1. Set the target for generation and populate the working set of the Generator with the objects you wish to implement in the database server.
2. Generate DDL statements for the objects in the working set.
3. Execute the generated DDL statements in the database server where the objects will reside.

In the case of the ORDERS application system, the following steps will invoke the Generator and set the target for generation of DDL statements:

1. Switch to the tab DB Admin of the Design Navigator.
2. Select the node Databases (Oracle) and click the icon Expand All 🗔.
3. Select the tables ORDERS and LINE_ITEMS in the Navigator. Standard Windows techniques such as Shift- and Ctrl-clicking can be used to select these objects.
4. Click the icon Generate 🖾 to invoke the Server Generator.
5. In the Target tab, select the radio button File to instruct the generator to produce the DDL statements as text files.
6. Type 'ORDERS' in the list box File Prefix.
7. Type the directory name where the generated files will be written in the list box Directory. Alternatively, click Browse... to select the generation target directory.
8. Select the target database from the list box Type.

At this point, the tab Target should look like the one shown in Figure 2.19.

In order to view the objects included in the working set of the generator, switch to the tab Objects, which is shown in Figure 2.20. Notice that the tables LINE_ITEMS and ORDERS are already included in the working set displayed in the list box Generate in the right half of the tab. The Server Generator has the ability to include in the working set every object selected in the Design Navigator when the tool is launched. Besides the tables ORDERS and LINE_ITEMS, the Generator will create DDL statements for a number of other objects, including indexes and integrity constraints associated with these tables. To see why, click Options... and, in the dialog box Database Generation Options that appears, notice the check marks placed in the check boxes that represent these options. Click OK to close this dialog and return to the Generate Database Objects dialog box.

After populating the working set, click the button Start to initiate the generation process. The progress of this process and any messages raised are displayed in the Messages pane of the Design Editor window. When the generation is completed, a number of Notepad windows are displayed. Each of them contains one of the generated files. The following is a brief description of the generated files:

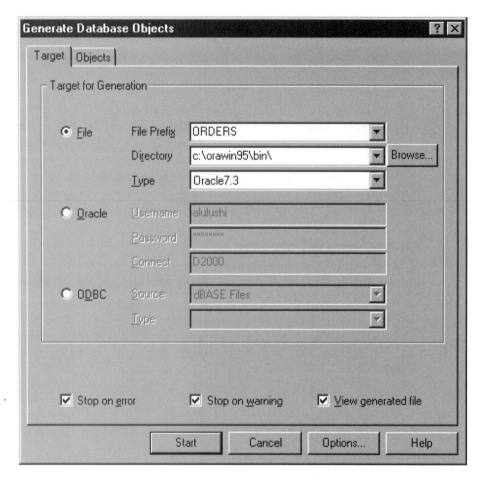

FIGURE 2.19   The Target tab of the Generate Database Objects dialog box.

❑   **ORDERS.sql.** This is the 'master' file that you will execute and that will call all the other files.
❑   **ORDERS.tab.** This file contains the DDL statements that create the tables in the Generator's working set.
❑   **ORDERS.con.** This file contains the DDL statements that create the primary key, foreign key, unique key, and check constraints defined for the tables in the working set.
❑   **ORDERS.ind.** This file contains the DDL statements that create the indexes associated with the tables included in the working set.

The easiest way to run the generated DDL scripts to create the objects in a database account is to start a SQL*Plus session, connect to the database using that

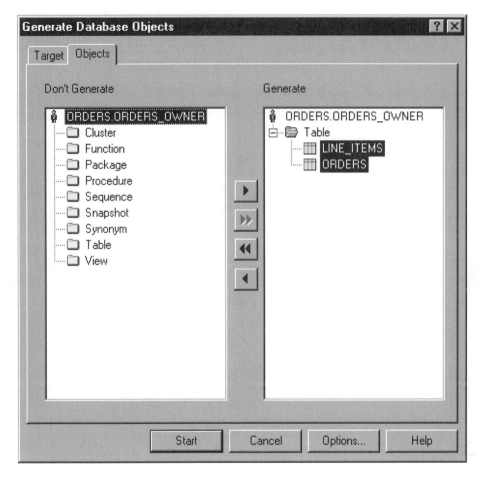

FIGURE 2.20 The Objects tab of the Generate Database Objects dialog box.

account and run the script file ORDERS.sql. This file contains calls to all the other command files in the appropriate order. You can also execute the DDL statements as they are created by the Server Generator by taking these steps:

1. Select the tables ORDERS and LINE_ITEMS in the Design Navigator.
2. Invoke the Generate Database Objects dialog box.
3. Select the radio button Database as the generation target.
4. Provide the database user name, password, and connect string to allow the Generator to connect to the database account where the objects should be created.
5. Click Start.

This procedure, although appealing for its simplicity, is rarely followed in practice. Normally, the generated DDL scripts are reviewed and inspected to ensure their quality before running them against a database account.

2.5 SUMMARY

This chapter guides you through the process of designing and generating the database objects that will be used for the ORDERS application system. The main topics of this chapter include:

❑ **Database Design Transformer**
   ❑ Purpose and Use
   ❑ Populating the Run Set
   ❑ Running the Transformer
❑ **Designing the Physical Database**
   ❑ Starting the Design Editor
   ❑ Creating the ORDERS Database
   ❑ Creating a Database User
   ❑ Recovering the Design of Existing Database Objects
❑ **Enhancing the Data Design**
   ❑ Creating and Maintaining Data Diagrams
   ❑ Creating Table Implementations
   ❑ Maintaining Column Properties
   ❑ Maintaining Constraint Properties
   ❑ Implementing Business Rules with Check Constraints
   ❑ Performing Data Derivation
   ❑ Maintaining Index Properties
❑ **Generating Database Objects**

DESIGNING AND GENERATING SOFTWARE MODULES

♦ Generating the Initial Module Design

♦ Enhancing the Design of User Interface Modules

♦ Expanding Modules with Unbound and Action Items

♦ Designing and Programming PL/SQL Modules

♦ Generating the Application Modules

♦ What Next?

♦ Summary

In the previous chapter, you transformed the data model of the ORDERS application system into a database schema that will support the software modules and implement a number of business rules of the application. This chapter will guide you through the process of designing and generating the user interface modules and the PL/SQL program units that will satisfy the application requirements identified in Chapter 1. The steps to follow in this process are:

1. Generate the first-cut module design using the Application Design Transformer.
2. Refine the design of each screen or report module in the Design Editor.
3. Implement PL/SQL modules in the Design Editor.
4. Generate user interface modules using the Designer/2000 generators.

Each of these steps will be discussed in the rest of this chapter.

3.1   GENERATING THE INITIAL MODULE DESIGN

Designer/2000 allows you to create the first-cut design of the modules in your system based on properties of the functions identified in the Function Hierarchy Diagrammer. The Application Design Transformer is the tool that creates candidate software modules based on the properties of these functions, their entity and attribute usages, and the properties of tables and columns that correspond to these objects. The process of generating the initial modules design for an application system goes through the following two stages:

1. Create the candidate modules using the Application Design Transformer.
2. Select from the generated modules those that will become part of the application.

In the following two sections, you will go through these stages using the ORDERS application system as an example.

3.1.1   APPLICATION DESIGN TRANSFORMER

 The Application Design Transformer is the tool that generates software modules out of the function objects defined in the Repository of an application. Because it translates the logical representation of the system's requirements into physical design objects, this is the counterpart and complementary tool of the Database Design Transformer. The Application Design Transformer can be accessed from the Designer/2000 launch pad by clicking the iconic button Application Transformer 🖳. In order to generate the software modules for the ORDERS application system, follow these steps:

1. Invoke the Application Design Transformer by clicking the iconic button Application Transformer 🐾 in the Designer/2000 launch pad.

2. Select 'ORDUI' from the list box Start Function. The Transformer will process each function in the hierarchy tree that is dependent on the selected function. From the way you defined the function hierarchy in Chapter 1, you can see that only the functions that describe user interface requirements will be processed by the Transformer.

3. Enter 'ORDD2K' in the text box Module Prefix. This setting will instruct the Transformer to prefix the name of each module it creates with the specified characters. (ORDD2K is intended to indicate Developer/2000 software modules for the ORDERS application.)

4. Select the radio button Identical Entities and Usages from the group Merge Granularity. At this point, the Application Design Transformer dialog box should look like the one shown in Figure 3.1.

   This setting will instruct the Transformer to merge into one module those functions that are associated with the same entities and have the same create, retrieve, update, and delete (CRUD) usages for these entities. The default option represented by the radio button Identical Entities will merge the modules if they are associated with the same entities. In the case of the ORDERS application system, the default setting will result in one module created out of functions ORDUI001 and ORDUI002. Setting the second option instead allows you to create a separate module for each function.

5. Click Generate to initiate the module creation process. Since you did not change the options in the Language group of list boxes, the Transformer will generate screens as Developer/2000 Forms modules, and reports as Developer/2000 Reports modules.

As the Transformer works to convert the functions into modules, the progress is displayed in a second dialog box also titled Application Design Transformer. A text box in the center of the dialog displays detailed instructions about each step completed. Click the Close button to remove this dialog box after the processing is completed. If you want to view a report of the work performed by the Transformer, click the button Show Results. This action displays a text file where the Transformer has recorded the modules it generated, their names, and the reason for creating the module, as well as the text you have entered in the Description property of the respective function. Figure 3.2 shows excerpts from this report in the case of the ORDERS application. To dismiss the Application design Transformer, click Cancel.

3.1.2 ACCEPTING CANDIDATE MODULES

The Application Design Transformer generates software modules suggested for further design and development, also known as candidate modules. After the Transformer completes its run, go over

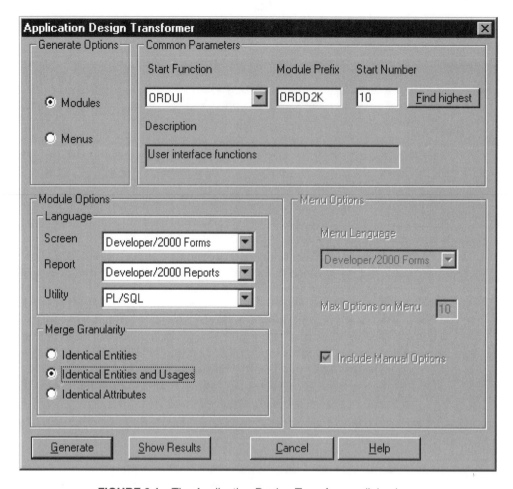

FIGURE 3.1   The Application Design Transformer dialog box.

the list of the candidate modules and identify those with which you want to continue to work in other Design Editors. You do so by setting the *Candidate?* property
of those modules from *'Yes'* to *'No'* in the Design Navigator. To accept the candidate modules for the ORDERS application system, take the following actions:

1. Start the Design Editor from the Designer/2000 launch pad.
2. Click Cancel to dismiss the dialog box Welcome to the Design Editor.
3. Switch to the tab Modules of the Design Navigator.
4. Click the Expand icon ⊞─▢ of the node Modules to expand it. You see two
   modules labeled ORDD2K0010 and ORDD2K0020, which were created by
   the Application Design Transformer.

```
ShortName:ORDD2K0010
Name       :CREATE AND MANAGE ORDERING INFORMATION    Type : SCREEN
Notes      :Developed by Application Design Transformer from
Function ORDUI001 candidate module because it is a leaf
Function
Identified as a screen because response required is immediate

Desc       :PURPOSE:
            Enable users to create, view, and maintain ORDER and
            LINE ITEM data.
            DESCRIPTION:
            This function will initially display a multi-record
            screen with the information about all the orders in
            the database. For each order, users may display
            detailed information together with its line items in
            a separate window by clicking a push button.
```

FIGURE 3.2   Excerpts from the report produced by the Application Design Transformer.

5. Select Options | Use Property Palette from the menu, then double-click the icon of one of the modules to display the Property Palette. Selecting from the menu is equivalent to clicking the icon Use Dialog so that it returns in the raised state ▪, as discussed in Chapter 2.
6. Click the module ORDD2K0010 and CTRL+CLICK the module ORDD2K0020 to select the modules.
7. In the Property Palette click the setting of the property *Candidate?*. As you do so, this setting is replaced by a list box.
8. Select the option 'No' from the list box to indicate that the modules are no longer candidate modules.
9. Click the icon Save ▦ to save the changes.

At this point, these two modules can not only be maintained in the Design Editor, but also generated by the Designer/2000 generators.

3.2   ENHANCING THE DESIGN OF USER INTERFACE MODULES

In this section, you will enhance the design of the user interface modules that will be responsible for the creation and the maintenance of orders and line items. These modules were initially created by the Application Design Transformer and will be maintained in the Design Editor. The following sections will cover some of the main activities you perform in this diagrammer. In particular, they will discuss these topics:

❑ Module diagrams
❑ Detail Table Usages of a module
❑ Detail Column Usages of a module

3.2.1 MODULE DIAGRAMS

 The Design Editor is the Designer/2000 tool that allows you to design the layout properties and data usages of a module. In this Editor you can view and maintain the module properties in Property Palettes as discussed in Section 3.1.2 or in dialog boxes. In addition, you can create and maintain diagrams for each module. Each diagram corresponds to one screen or report module in the application system Repository. To create the module diagram for ORDD2K0010, follow these steps:

1. Switch to the property tab Modules in the Design Navigator.
2. Expand the node Modules and select the module ORDD2K0010.
3. Select File | New | Module Diagram.... Alternatively, right-click the module ORDD2K0010 and from the popup menu that appears select the item Show On Diagram.

This action displays a new diagram for the module in a separate window. Initially the diagram will be displayed in minuscule dimensions on your screen. In order to enlarge it to a comfortable level, click the iconic button Zoom In ⊞ several times. Finally, save the diagram under the name ORDER ENTRY FORM. Repeat the same steps to create a data diagram for the Oracle Report module ORDD2K0020. Save this diagram under the name ORDER REPORT.

3.2.2 VIEWS AND ELEMENTS OF THE MODULE DIAGRAM

Each module diagram has two views. The data view shows only the module data components; the display view shows the layout of these components in windows for the case of screen module, and pages for the case of report modules. In order to switch from the data view to the display view of the module, you can issue one of these commands:

❑ Select View | Display View.
❑ Click the icon Switch to Display View ▦ on the vertical toolbar of the module diagram window.

The following command can be used to switch from the display view to the data view:

❑ Select View | Data View.
❑ Click the icon Switch to Data View 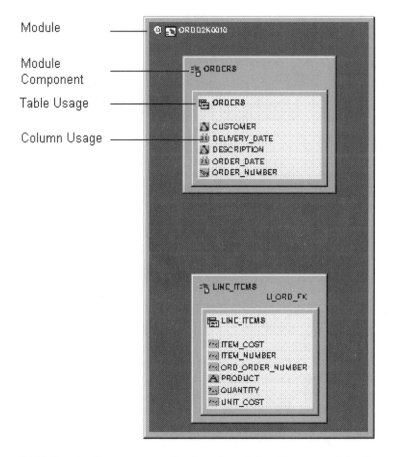.

Figure 3.3 and Figure 3.4 show the module diagram for ORDER ENTRY FORM in data and display view, respectively. There you can notice several important elements of a module diagram:

❑ **Module component.** A module component is a grouping of items that together implement part or all of the functionality of the module. The items in

FIGURE 3.3 Components of a Developer/2000 Forms module diagram in data view.

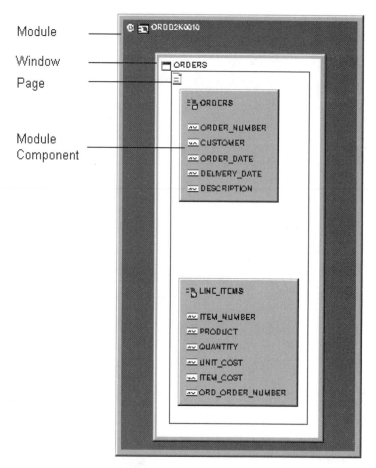

Module

Window

Page

Module
Component

FIGURE 3.4 Components of a Developer/2000 Forms module diagram in display view.

the module component reside in the same placement item (window or page). Although the components ORDERS and LINE_ITEMS shown in Figure 3.3 are based upon a single table, in general, a module component may contain items from different tables. In your modules you may also use components whose items do not map to database resources. Such components are known as control components or control blocks. The biggest advantage that module components offer is the ability to reuse them in multiple modules.

❑ **Module component table usage.** A table usage is a grouping of module items directly related to columns from a database table. Two widely used types of table usages are base and lookup usages. The table usages shown in

Figure 3.3 are both base usages. For Developer/2000 Forms modules, table usages are the blocks of the module; for Developer/2000 Reports modules, they are the groups of the module.

❑ **Item.** The type of an item can be bound, unbound, or action. A bound item maps directly to a database column. All the items shown in Figure 3.3 are bound items. An unbound item does not correspond to one database column, although its values may be derived from one or more such columns. An action item is a special unbound item which offers users a choice of actions, for example navigating to a different module or module component. Bound items exist in the context of a module component table usage, whereas unbound and action items exist in the context of a module component.

❑ **Page and Window layout element.** In the case of Developer/2000 Forms modules, such as the one shown in Figure 3.4, pages represent canvases of the form, and windows represent window objects to which one or more canvases may be attached. Window layout elements are found only in screen modules defined in Designer/2000. Page layout elements are found only in report modules defined in Designer/2000. Developer/2000 Forms modules are the only ones where both these components coexist. Layout elements contain one or more module components.

3.2.3 ARRANGING THE LAYOUT OF MODULE DIAGRAMS

The order in which components appear in the diagram of a module influences the order in which the front-end generators place the corresponding items in the generated modules. If, for example, LINE_ITEMS is placed higher than ORDERS in the module ORDER ENTRY FORM, the generated form will have LINE_ITEMS as the first block and ORDERS as the second one. The simplest way to change the order of a module component is to select a component and drag it above or below another component in the diagram. Similarly, the order of items within the module component is the sequence in which they will be displayed in the generated modules. One way to modify this order is to select the particular item, drag it, and drop it in the desired sequence.

3.2.4 ADDING LINKS TO MODULE DIAGRAMS

Two module components are related if at least one foreign key constraint exists between their corresponding base tables. Obviously, ORDERS and LINE_ITEMS are related components. The relations between module components based on primary and foreign keys are called key based links. Graphically, they are represented using a similar convention as the foreign key constraints in a data schema diagram. Key based links can be created and maintained only in the data view of the module diagram.

When creating links in a module data diagram, I recommend that you follow the convention expressed metaphorically as "Crows always fly south or west." (The crow represents the many end of the link, often referred to as a crow foot.) When the link points south, the module components are in a master/detail relationship. The link points west when the module component contains a base and a lookup table usage. The table usage to the right is a lookup for the table usage to the left.

In order to include the key based links between module components in the form and report module you are designing, issue the following commands:

1. Make sure that the module component ORDERS is sequenced before LINE_ITEMS and the data view of module diagram is displayed.
2. Click the icon Create Link ▦ on the toolbar.
3. Click the table usage ORDERS in the diagram.
4. Click the table usage LINE_ITEMS in the diagram.

The key based link between the table usages is displayed in the diagram. Figure 3.5 shows the data view of the module diagram for ORDD2K0010. You can use similar steps to create a key based link between the components of the module ORDER REPORT.

3.2.5 MAINTAINING PROPERTIES OF MODULE ELEMENTS

The Design Editor provides an easy interface to the properties of elements in the module diagram. As with other objects in the Editor, you can display the properties of a module element in its characteristic dialog box or in a Property Palette window. The following list describes at a high level the functionality provided by the dialog boxes you can invoke for module objects:

❑ **Edit Module.** This dialog is used primarily to maintain context-sensitive help associated with the module.
❑ **Edit Module Component.** This dialog allows you to maintain the name of the components, to specify which data operations are allowed, to choose the number of rows and the overflow style of the component.
❑ **Edit Base Table Usage.** This dialog is used to maintain the properties of the base table usages of module components and, most importantly, of all their bound items. Among properties you can set here are whether an item is dis-

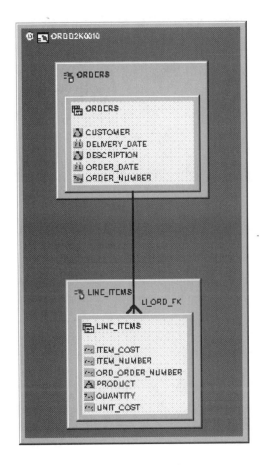

FIGURE 3.5 The module diagram for ORDD2K0010 in data view.

played or not, the display order of items, data operations allowed for each item, and display characteristics of items.

❑ **Edit Item.** There is a different dialog for each type of item (bound, unbound, action item). They allow you to view and maintain properties that control the display and the functionality of the items in the generated application.

The rest of this section will provide instructions on how to set properties of several objects for both the form and the report module. The goals of the activities you will perform here are as follows:

❑ Define the layout of the form.
❑ Define the layout of the report.
❑ Specify default ordering criteria for the data in the form and report modules.
❑ Enhance the display of data items in the form and report modules.

Defining the layout of the form essentially means specifying for each component how the data items will be laid out and how many records the component will display. In addition, you can also define properties of the window in which the data will be displayed. Here is what you have to do to define the properties of the only window in the module ORDER ENTRY FORM:

1. Set the data diagram in display view by selecting View | Display View.
2. Double-click the window layout item to display the Edit Window dialog box.
3. Type 'ORDERS' in the Window name text box. This will be the internal name for the window object in the generated application.
4. Type 'Order Maintenance Form' in the text box Window title. This will be the title of the window in which the module components will appear.
5. Select the radio button Yes from the group Use scroll bars? to provide this window with scrollbars.
6. Click Finish.

In the Size tab, you could specify also the dimensions of the Developer/2000 Forms window object and its position relative to the underlying canvas. However, since estimating the appropriate dimensions is difficult at this point, leaving these properties unset is better. The Form Generator will derive the appropriate settings for these properties and, depending on the options you set for the Generator, it may save these settings in the Repository.

The following actions allow you to define the layout of the component ORDERS:

1. Double-click the ORDERS module component to display the Edit Module Components dialog box, and switch to the Display tab.
2. Select the option Wrap line from the drop-down list Overflow style. With this option, the block ORDERS will have a form layout.
3. Click the radio button Rows and type '1' in the text box associated with it. The block ORDERS will display only one record at a time. Now your tab should look like the one shown in Figure 3.6.
4. Click Finish.

Set the layout properties of the component LINE_ITEMS as follows:

1. Select the option Spread table from the drop-down list Overflow style.
2. Click the radio button Rows and type '8' in the text box associated with it.

With these settings, LINE_ITEMS will be a multi-record block that displays up to eight records in tabular format. The following actions will allow you to define the layout of the ORDERS component for the report module ORDD2K0020:

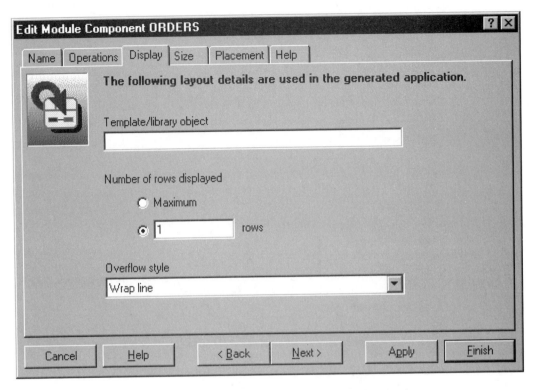

FIGURE 3.6   The Display tab of the Edit Module dialog box.

1. Double-click the module component ORDERS and switch to the tab Display.
2. Select the option Form from the list box Layout style.
3. Type '1' in the text box Number of rows displayed per page. With such a setting, the report will start each new order on a separate page.
4. Click Finish.

For the component LINE_ITEMS select the option Tabular from the list box Layout style. Do not set the maximum number of rows displayed per page so that the Developer/2000 Report engine decides at runtime how many records to include in each page.

As the next enhancement of the modules, set properties in such a way that ORDERS records are always sorted by the order date, starting from the most recent order. In addition, the line items of each order should be sorted by the line item number. This requirement will apply to both the form and the report module.

Since the implementation is identical in both cases, only the steps required to add this functionality in the Developer/2000 Form module are listed below:

1. Click the icon Use Dialogs to set it in raised state ⊡. To set the properties in the following steps you will use the Property Palette of the Design Editor.
2. Double-click the bound item ORDER_DATE on the module diagram. The Property Palette is displayed with all the properties for this item.
3. Scroll down the Palette until you see the group of properties titled Ordering.
4. Set the property *Order By Sequence* to '1' to indicate that this column is the first one in the ORDER BY clause of the SELECT statement that queries data for this table usage.
5. Set the property *Sort Order* to 'Descending.'
6. Save the changes.

You can follow similar steps to set the ordering properties of LINE_ITEMS.ITEM_NUMBER. The only difference is that the *Sort Order* property here must be set to 'Ascending.'

I conclude this section by drawing your attention to the fact that a number of item properties in the modules ORDD2K0010 and ORDD2K0020 are populated although you did not set any of them explicitly. These properties include *Prompt, Alignment, Format Mask, Width, Default Value,* and *Hint,* just to name a few. However, recall that in Chapter 2 you provided setting for the corresponding properties of the database columns that are mapped to these items. During the transformation of the business functions to modules, the Application Design Transformer read these properties from the data model and transferred them to the module. In the case of the ORDERS application, you set the properties once and the Transformer reused these setting in two modules. In a full-blown application system many modules may use the same table or column. Therefore, setting these properties at the data model level may be very advantageous and reduce the amount of work to enhance each individual module. You perform the work once, and the Application Design Transformer will make sure to reuse it for each module it creates.

3.3 EXPANDING MODULES WITH UNBOUND AND ACTION ITEMS

The items in a database application can be grouped in two categories: base table items and control items. A base table corresponds to a unique column in the database. In the Designer/2000 terminology, these items are called bound items. A control item does not have a direct relationship with any database column. The purpose of control items is to display data that are calculated or otherwise derived from base table items, or to allow users to issue a command, as in the case of push button items. The items in this category are known as unbound and action items. In the following sections you will add the following unbound or action items to your Developer/2000 Forms and Reports modules:

❏ An unbound item to display the total cost for each order
❏ An unbound item to display the number of line items for each order
❏ An unbound item to display the average cost of orders for the current date
❏ An action item in the ORDER ENTRY FORM module, which will invoke the ORDERS REPORT module.

3.3.1 FORMULA UNBOUND ITEMS

A formula item is an unbound item, whose value is derived by applying a summary function, such as Sum or Count, to a bound item. Two examples of useful formula items in the modules you are designing in this chapter are the following:

❏ An item that automatically computes and displays the total cost of an order as the sum of item cost for all its items
❏ An item that automatically computes and displays the number of line items in an order

As you will see from the rest of this section, the Design Editor provides for ways to create such items declaratively, by setting selected properties and without requiring any programming. You will start by adding an item that will compute and display the total cost of an order. You know already that this value is given by the sum of ITEM_COST for all the line items of the given order. Follow the steps listed below to create the item in question:

1. Select View | Data View to set the module diagram in data view, if it is not in this mode already.
2. Click the icon Create Item 🔛 on the vertical toolbar of the module diagram.
3. Click the module component ORDERS. The Create Unbound Items dialog box is displayed. (Make sure to click the component ORDERS and not its table usage, also called ORDERS, if you want to create an unbound item.)
4. Type 'ORDER_TOTAL' in the text box Item name; select the option Computed from the list box Item type; click Next.
5. Select SUM from the list box Function; type LINE_ITEMS. ITEM_COST in the combo box Item used; click Next.

6. Click Next to skip the tab where you set the operations allowed for this item.
7. Select NUMBER from the list box Datatype; click Next.
8. Click Next to skip the tab where you specify a list of allowable values for the item.
9. Set the display properties for the item as shown in Figure 3.7; click Next.
10. Type *'The total cost for the order.'* in the Hint text item.
11. Click Finish to complete the process.

At this point, the unbound item is created and is displayed in the module component outside the boundaries of the table usage. You can follow the instructions presented above to create a similar field in the ORDER REPORT module. An important difference you should notice is the need to specify the reset level for the unbound item. Select the radio button Parent group to instruct the Report Generator to compute the formula SUM(LINE_ITEMS.ITEM_COST) for each order.

I will not discuss here the process of adding the unbound item which will display the number of detail records in the component LINE_ITEMS associated with the master record. This process is almost identical to the one described

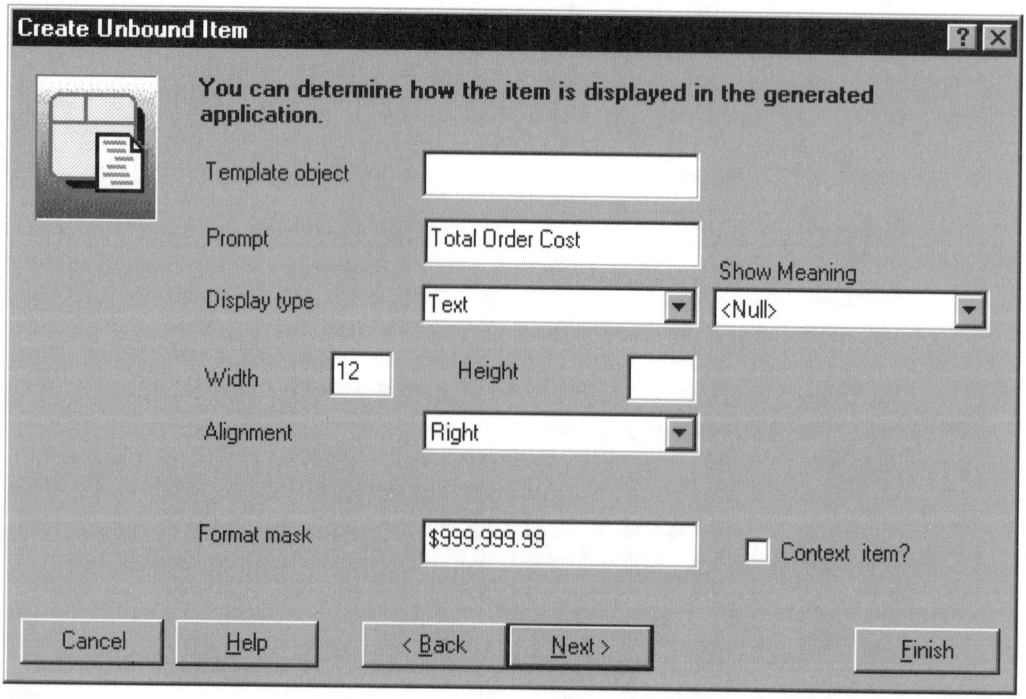

FIGURE 3.7 The Display tab of the Edit Unbound Item dialog box.

above, except for the fact that the function selected to compute the value of the second unbound item is the function COUNT.

3.3.2 DERIVATION UNBOUND ITEMS

Recall from Chapter 1 that the business rule that expresses the requirement to calculate the average cost of all orders for a given date was captured as a separate function in the functional hierarchy of the system (ORDBL001). The reason why the other business rules discussed in Chapter 1 were not entered as separate functions is that they can be implemented fairly simply in a declarative way, either in the form of check constraints that will be enforced at the database server or at the front-end application, or in the form of formula unbound items. The rule ORDBL001, however, requires some programmatic power to be implemented. As you will see in Section 3.4, this rule will be implemented as a PL/SQL function stored in the database server. The definition of this function is as follows:

```
Comp_Avg_Ord_Total(CurrentDate DATE)
RETURN NUMBER;
```

In this section, you will create an unbound item that will become part of the ORDERS module component in the generated Developer/2000 Form module and will display side-by-side the total cost of an order and the average cost of orders placed in the same date as the current order. The value of this item will be computed automatically, without user intervention, using the stored function Comp_Avg_Ord_Total. Here is what you have to do to add such an item to the ORDER ENTRY FORM module:

1. Select View | Data View to set the module diagram in data view, if it is not in this mode already.
2. Click the icon Create Item 🔳 on the vertical toolbar of the module diagram.
3. Click the module component ORDERS. The Create Unbound Items dialog box is displayed.
4. Type 'AVG_ORD_TOTAL' in the text box Item name; select the option Server Side Function from the list box Item type; click Next.
5. Enter the following line in the Derivation Expression text field:

```
Comp_Avg_Ord_Total(ORDER_DATE);
```

6. Click Next twice and select NUMBER from the list box Datatype. Click Next to skip the property tabs until you see the tab where you can set the display properties of the item.

7. Type 'Average Order Cost' in the Prompt field; set the list box Alignment to Right; set Display type to Text; type '$999,999.99' in the text box Format mask, and set Width to '12.' Except for the text box Prompt, this tab should look like the one shown in Figure 3.7.

8. Click Next and set Hint text to 'The average cost of orders on this date.'

9. Click Finish.

3.3.3 ACTION ITEMS

In this section, you will add a push button item to the module component ORDERS in the ORDER ENTRY FORM module. The purpose of this push button is to invoke the ORDER REPORT module. Follow these steps:

1. Select View | Data View to set the module diagram in data view, if it is not in this mode already.

2. Click the icon Create *Action* Item ▦ on the vertical toolbar of the module diagram.

3. Click the module component ORDERS. The Create Navigation Action Item dialog box is displayed.

4. Select the radio group Navigation to a different module; click Next.

5. Type 'INVOKE_REPORT' in the text box Item name; type 'Orders Report...' in the text box Prompt; click Next.

6. Place a check mark in the check box Show modules of all languages?

7. Select the report module ORDD2K0020, identified by its name RETRIEVE AND REPORT ORDERING INFORMATION, as the module where users will navigate when they click the action item you are creating.

8. Click Next and type 'Invoke the orders report module.' in the text box Hint text.

9. Click Finish.

At this point, a push button item is added to the module component. The prompt of this item indicates that it is an action item to navigate to the module ORDD2K0020. If you switch the module diagram into display view, you will see something similar to Figure 3.8. The arrow originating at the action item and terminating at the module ORDD2K0020 is called a module network link.

The actions listed above conclude your design efforts with the form and report modules. Save and close the module diagrams before continuing with the remaining two sections of this chapter.

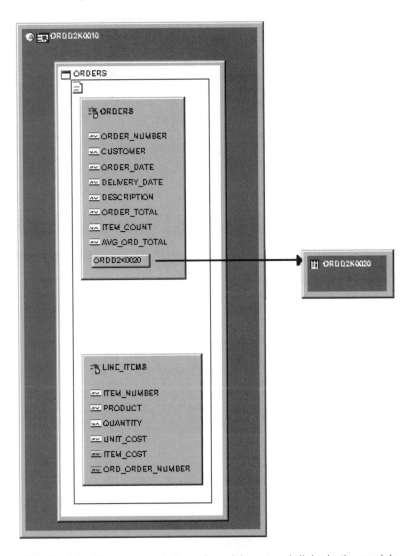

FIGURE 3.8 The representation of module network links in the module diagram.

3.4 DESIGNING AND PROGRAMMING PL/SQL MODULES

From the functions identified in Chapter 1, you have completed the design of the two functions that will implement the user interface of the ORDERS application system, ORDUI001 and ORDUI002. In this section, you will implement the business rule described by the last function, ORDBL001, as a PL/SQL function that will be stored in the application system's database server. Developer/2000 applications share the same programming language, PL/SQL, with the Oracle Server. Therefore, techniques you master when creating stored program units can be used to add to the application logic as well. In this section, you will add application logic code to the module ORDD2K0010, as well.

Program units are created and maintained in the Design Editor. Those that will be deployed in the database server are considered as database objects; those that will be implemented in the front-end modules are associated with modules, module components, table usages, and items. Despite the differences, when creating PL/SQL objects for any of these environments, you perform the following steps:

1. Specify the definition, arguments, return data type, and local variables of the function using the dialog boxes provided by the Design Editor.
2. Enter the PL/SQL statements that make up the body of the function in the Logic Editor.
3. Validate the syntax of the program unit.

The following sections describe each of these steps.

3.4.1   CREATING A PL/SQL FUNCTION

When creating a PL/SQL program unit you will need to provide the following information:

❑   **Specification.** The specification of a program unit includes its name, the type of program unit, the names and datatypes of any arguments, and, if the program unit is a function, the return data type.

❑   **Body.** In the general case, the body of a program unit consists of a declaration part where local variables are declared, the execution part, and the exception handling part.

 In the Design Editor, you can define and maintain declaratively all the components of a program unit, except for the execution section of the body. This piece is edited and maintained in the Logic Editor. The following are the actions you need to take to create the PL/SQL function that will implement ORDBL001.

1. Click the tab DB Objects in the Design Navigator window of the Design Editor.
2. Expand the node PL/SQL Definitions and select the node Function Definitions.
3. Click the icon Create ⬚. The Create PL/SQL Function dialog box appears.

4. Set the Short name, Name, and Purpose text boxes as shown in Figure 3.9 and click Next.

5. Select NUMBER from the list box Return datatype and click Next.

6. Type 'Current_Date' in the text box Parameters; select DATE from the list box Parameter datatype; type 'SYSDATE' in the Default value text box. With these settings, the function will always return a value, even if no data is passed through the argument Current_Date. At this point, the property tab Parameters should look like Figure 3.10.

7. Click Next to skip the exception definition tab.

In order to create a local variable to store the computed total cost of the order, click the Program Data tab and do the following:

1. Type 'Avg_Ord_Total' in the text box Declaration name

2. Select NUMBER from the list box Datatype.

3. Set the radio button Variable in the group Type.

4. Type '0' in the Default value text field.

5. Click Next.

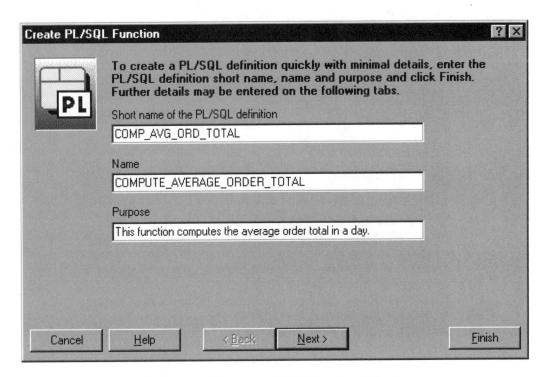

FIGURE 3.9 The Create PL/SQL Function dialog box.

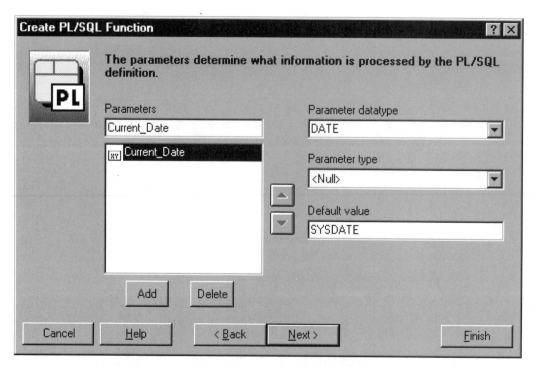

FIGURE 3.10   The Parameters property tab of the Edit Module dialog box.

At this point you are presented with the final tab of the Create PL/SQL Function dialog shown in Figure 3.11. Depending on which radio button you select before clicking Finish, one of the following may occur:

❑ **Set the first radio button.** The PL/SQL program unit is created in the Navigator. At a later point you can invoke the Logic Editor to add and maintain the body of the program unit.

❑ **Set the second radio button.** You are taken to a different dialog box where you can create PL/SQL record and table data structures.

❑ **Set the third radio button.** The program unit is created and the Logic Editor is invoked so that you can start working with the body right away.

In case you selected the first radio button, you can invoke the Logic Editor explicitly by selecting the module in the Design Navigator and performing one of the following actions:

❑ Select Edit | Logic... from the menu
❑ Right-click the function to display the popup menu, then select Edit PL/SQL...

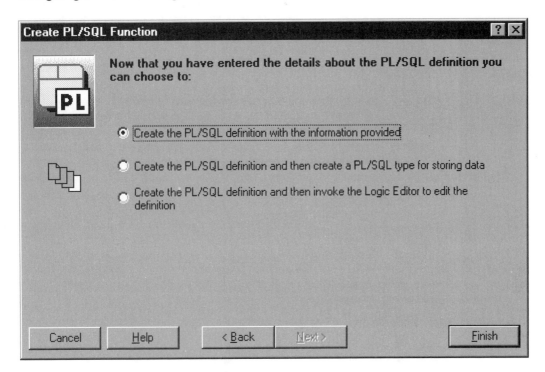

FIGURE 3.11   The final tab of the Create PL/SQL Module dialog box.

3.4.2   THE LOGIC EDITOR

The Logic Editor is the Designer/2000 tool used to edit the content of program units. It is displayed in its own MDI sheet within the Design Editor and this window is made up of two panes. The pane to the right is where you type the PL/SQL statements to implement the program unit. The left pane is where the Editor presents the code you enter in the right pane, in a structured fashion that helps understanding and debugging of the module.

Figure 3.12 shows another window, titled Plsql, which usually remains open in the Logic Editor. This window can be considered the PL/SQL programmer's reference guide, because it contains a lot of information you may need to know when writing PL/SQL programs. In particular, by expanding nodes in the window, you can view the following elements:

❑   The syntactic constructs of PL/SQL, such as looping statements, conditional statements, subprograms, and so on

❑   The statements that can be included in a PL/SQL program, such as INSERT, UPDATE, or SELECT

❑   Static PL/SQL language elements, such as data types, built-in functions, pre-defined exceptions, and so on

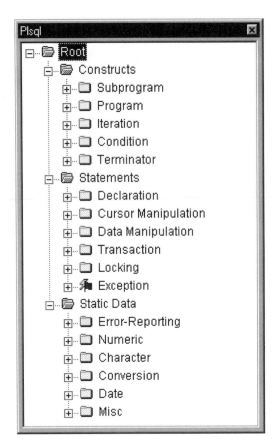

FIGURE 3.12 The PL/SQL programmer's workbench of the Logic Editor.

The beauty of this window is not only that it allows you to expand its nodes and look up any PL/SQL element or the structure of a Repository object, but most importantly, that it enables you to drag any node from the tree and drop it in the editing pane of the module in the form of pseudocode. For this reason, this window is also known as the Selection Tree. As you will see later in the chapter, this capability makes programming PL/SQL modules not only rapid but also fun. Thus, the Selection Tree may also be considered the PL/SQL programmer's workbench.

3.4.3 PROGRAMMING THE BODY OF PL/SQL PROGRAM UNITS

The properties you set in Section 3.4.1 will enable the Server Generator to create the header and the declaration section of the function `Comp_Avg_Ord_Total`. In order to complete the development of this function, you need to enter its body in the editing pane of the module window. The following steps show how you can quickly outline the structure of the code by dragging PL/SQL constructs from the Selection Tree and dropping them in the editor pane.

1. Expand the node Construct, and then the node Program in the Selection Tree.
2. Drag the node Block and drop it in the editor pane. The editor pane now contains the following lines of code:

```
BEGIN
    /*_statements_*/
END;
```

3. Highlight and delete the line '/*_statements_*/' in the editor.
4. Expand the node Statement and then expand the node Data Manipulation.
5. Drag the node Conditional Select and drop it in the editor pane between the keywords BEGIN and END. The content of the editor will now be as follows:

```
BEGIN
    SELECT /*_items_*/
    INTO
        /*_vars_*/
    FROM
        /*_tables_*/
    WHERE
        /*_conditions_*/;
END;
```

At the end, either by dragging and dropping, or by typing the statements in the editor, the body of the function Comp_Avg_Ord_Total should be as shown in Figure 3.13. To store the contents of the editor in the Repository, click the icon Save 🖫 on the toolbar. To ensure that the statements you typed are correct, select Utilities | Check Syntax.... Close the Logic Editor window with any of the standard Windows commands.

3.4.4 CREATING AN APPLICATION LOGIC PROGRAM UNIT

The function Comp_Avg_Ord_Total you created in the previous sections implements the business rule ORDBL001 in the Oracle Server database. However, not every program unit in an application is stored in the database server. In this section you will create a program unit that is invoked when the Developer/2000 Form event WHEN-NEW-FORM-INSTANCE occurs. This program

```
BEGIN
   SELECT avg(sum(line_items.item_cost))
   INTO
      avg_ord_total
   FROM
      line_items, orders
   WHERE
      orders.order_date = current_date
      AND orders.order_number =
line_items.ord_order_number
   GROUP BY line_items.ord_order_number,
orders.order_date;
   RETURN(avg_ord_total);
END;
```

FIGURE 3.13   The body of the PL/SQL property tab of the Edit Module dialog box.

unit will set the title of the MDI frame window to *'Orders Maintenance System'* and will set the window in maximized state. Here is a list of steps you need to follow to accomplish this task:

1. Display the tab Modules in the Design Navigator window.
2. Expand the following nodes: Modules, ORDD2K0010, and Application Logic.
3. Select the node Event and click the icon Create ⬚. The dialog box Create Application Logic is displayed.
4. Select WHEN-NEW-FORM-INSTANCE from the list box Events and click Next.
5. Set the text boxes Name and Comment as shown in Figure 3.14 and click Next.
6. Select the second radio button on the tab and click Finish. The application logic program unit is created and the Logic Editor is displayed.
7. Enter the following statements in the Editor:

```
BEGIN
   SET_WINDOW_PROPERTY(FORMS_MDI_WINDOW, TITLE, 'Order
Maintenance System');
   SET_WINDOW_PROPERTY(FORMS_MDI_WINDOW, WINDOW_SIZE,
MAXIMIZE);
END;
```

8. Click Save.

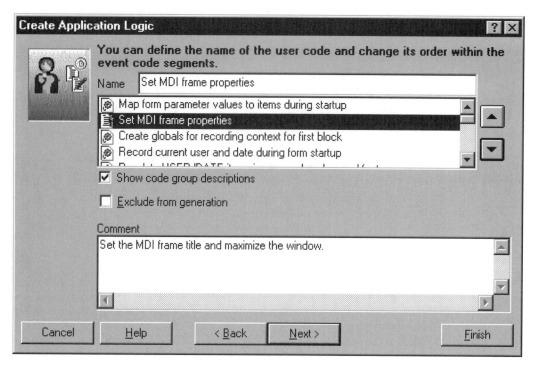

FIGURE 3.14 The Create Application Logic dialog box.

This completes the work to design and develop the modules of the OR-DERS application. Before moving to the generation stage, expand the nodes Events and WHEN-NEW-FORM-INSTANCE. You will be presented with a list of program units that will be executed when this event is triggered (see Figure 3.15). In the Form Generator terminology, these program units are called code groups. You can see from the figure that the Generator combines its internal code groups with the one you specified earlier, but still preserves the distinction between them.

3.5 GENERATING THE APPLICATION MODULES

After the design work with all the modules is complete, you are ready to generate and use them. In this section, you will use Designer/2000 generators to implement the PL/SQL function, the Developer/2000 Form module, and the Developer/2000 Report module you designed earlier in the chapter.

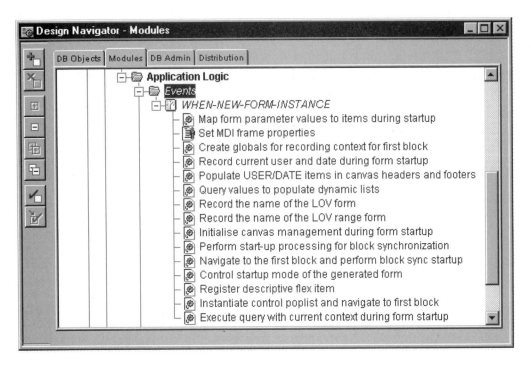

FIGURE 3.15   A combination of Form Generator and user-defined code groups activated during an event.

3.5.1   GENERATING AND INSTALLING PL/SQL MODULES

The process of generating PL/SQL program units and storing them to a database is identical to that of generating other database objects, such as tables and indexes. Since this process was covered in detail in Chapter 2, this section only briefly describes the steps you need to take in order to implement the function Comp_Avg_Ord_Total.

1. Switch to the tab DB Objects of the Design Navigator and expand the nodes PL/SQL Definitions and Function Definitions.

2. Select the function COMP_AVG_ORD_TOTAL and click the icon Generate 🖹.

3. In the Target tab, select the radio button File to instruct the generator to produce the DDL statements as text files.

4. Type 'ORDERS' in the list box File Prefix.

5. Type the directory name where the generated files will be written in the list

You may discover that the Steps 2–6 may not be required if you did not set the settings of the controls in the Target tab since the time you used the Server Generator to create the database objects at the end of Chapter 2. The tool has the ability to remember the settings you specify and will display them the next time you invoke it.

> box Directory. Alternatively, click Browse... to select the generation target directory.

6. Select the target database from the list box Type.
7. Click Start.

After the Generator finishes processing, install the newly-created function in the same database account you used in Chapter 2 to install the other database objects.

3.5.2   OVERVIEW OF DESIGNER/2000 FRONT-END GENERATORS

Before presenting the steps you need to take in order to generate the user interface modules of the ORDERS application system, I will briefly describe how the Designer/2000 front-end generators work. Despite differences between each generator, their architecture is the same. In order to create the module, a generator relies on the following information:

❑ Properties of the module defined in the Module Data Diagrammer, including the layout of module components, table usages, items and other properties associated with the data usages of the module.

❑ Properties of database objects, such as tables and columns, upon which the bound data usages of a module are defined. These include all the data-related business rules captured in the data model in the form of constraints and other properties of these database design objects.

❑ Object libraries, which are containers for objects that help you reuse your design and development efforts and enforce standards across your applications. If, for example, you want to add an iconic toolbar or a visual attribute in your Developer/2000 Form module, you can create these objects in an object library, and point the Designer/2000 Form Generator to this library. When the Generator runs, it will read the definition of the object library and copy or subclass (depending on your preference) these objects in the generated module. Designer/2000 provides an object library used by the Form Generator, which allows you to add an iconic toolbar to your modules with the most commonly used Developer/2000 Form functions in it. You will use this library to generate the ORDER ENTRY FORM module.

❑ Template modules, which are modules of the same kind as the module you want to generate, where you can define objects that you want to include in a number of generated modules. In versions of Designer/2000 prior to Release 2, Developer/2000 Form template modules played the role of object libraries. As with object libraries, Designer/2000 provides a number of template modules that you can use to generate your application.

❑ Preferences, which are a set of data-driven options that you can set to influence how each generator converts the information it collects from the sources listed above into items in the generated forms and reports. Preferences add a lot of flexibility to the generation process and allow you to create software modules with a sophisticated interface with minimal manual intervention. However, you do not need to set a single preference in order to be able to generate software modules successfully. For each generator, Designer/2000 provides an extended set of preferences with predefined settings, called factory settings. These settings are such that you can often achieve the results you want without having to modify any of them. In the ORDERS application system, for example, you will not change any of the factory settings.

3.5.3   GENERATING DEVELOPER/2000 FORMS MODULES

Before starting the generation activities, create the database objects of your application under the schema of the repository user that will perform the generation. These objects allow the Developer/2000 Forms Generator to validate a number of objects during the generation process. After the generation of the modules ORDD2K001 and ORDD2K002 you may remove these objects, as they are no longer needed. The steps you need to take to generate the ORDER ENTRY FORM module are outlined below:

1. Switch to the tab Modules of the Design Navigator and expand the node Modules.

2. Select the module ORDD2K0010 and click the icon Generate ⬛. The dialog box Generate Form appears.

3. Clear the setting of the text box Template Name as shown in Figure 3.16. You will not need a template to generate your form.

4. Click Options... to display the Forms Generator Options dialog box. Skip the tabs Form Option and Menu Option, which contain properties that are rarely changed.

5. Switch to the tab Compile and select the radio button Add to Action List in the group Compile Form/Menu. With this setting, the Generator will display a message when it completes the generation. Double-clicking this message starts the compilation process of the generated module.

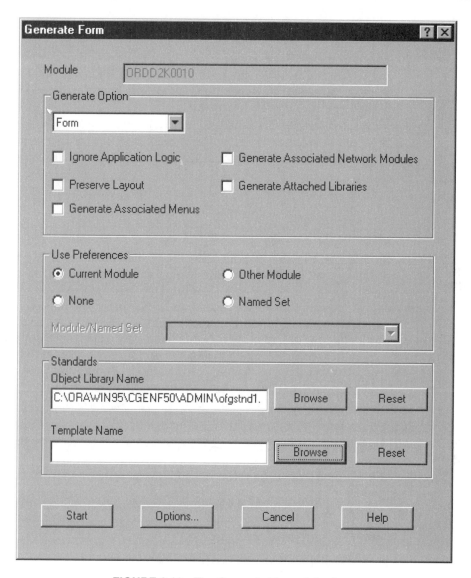

FIGURE 3.16 The Generate Form dialog box.

6. Set the Connect String text box with the string *<user_name>/<password> @<db_connect_string>*. The connection information you provide in this field should allow the Forms Generator to connect to the database account under which you have created the ORDERS database objects and generate the executable version of the module. If you created these objects under the same

account as the one to which you are currently connected, you do not need to set the Connect String property.

7. Switch to the tab Run and select the radio button Add to Action List in the group Run Form. With this setting, the Generator will display a message when it completes the generation. Double-clicking this message starts the execution of the generated module.

8. Set the Connect String text box with the string *<user_name>/<password> @<db_connect_string>*, to allow the Forms Runtime engine to connect to the database account under which you have created the ORDERS database objects.

9. Click OK to close the Forms Generator Options dialog box.

10. Click Start to begin the generation.

As the generator runs, the Message Window of the Design Editor displays warning or error messages produced by the generator. Examples of these messages are shown in Figure 3.17. A few messages are to be expected whenever you generate a module for the first time. The first two messages shown in Figure 3.17, for example, indicate that the Generator has turned off the Update flag of the primary key columns in the blocks ORDERS and LINE_ITEMS. It is normal to let the Generator set some of the properties of Repository objects. At the end of the process, you are presented with a dialog box that prompts you to save, revert, or browse and edit the changes made by the generator. Recall from Chapter 2 that a similar dialog box is displayed when you recover the design of database objects in the Repository. In general, whenever a tool or utility modifies the Repository

---

The messages listed in the Message window are of three types:

❏ **Information messages.** They inform you of the stages and processes completed by the Generator. These messages are displayed in normal font.

❏ **Warnings.** They draw your attention to conflicts encountered during the generation. These messages are displayed in blue.

❏ **Errors.** They report situations that cause the failure of the generation process. These messages are displayed in red.

Right-clicking the warning and error messages displays a popup menu. One of the items in the menu allows you to display help on correcting the error. When the context is appropriate, a second item allows you to navigate to the Property Palette of the Repository objects that caused the violation.

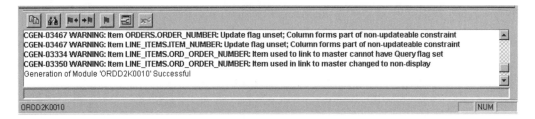

CGEN-03467 WARNING: Item ORDERS.ORDER_NUMBER: Update flag unset; Column forms part of non-updateable constraint
CGEN-03467 WARNING: Item LINE_ITEMS.ITEM_NUMBER: Update flag unset; Column forms part of non-updateable constraint
CGEN-03334 WARNING: Item LINE_ITEMS.ORD_ORDER_NUMBER: Item used to link to master cannot have Query flag set
CGEN-03350 WARNING: Item LINE_ITEMS.ORD_ORDER_NUMBER: Item used in link to master changed to non-display
Generation of Module 'ORDD2K0010' Successful

ORDD2K0010   NUM

FIGURE 3.17   The Message window of the Developer/2000 Form Generator.

implicitly, Designer/2000 offers you the choice to accept, reject, or view the changes.

The Designer/2000 Form Generator stops when the binary version of the module is created successfully. You can compile and run this module independently using the Developer/2000 Form tools, or you can perform these tasks from the Design Editor by following these steps:

1. Select Messages | List Actions… from the menu or click the icon 🔲 on the Message Window toolbar. The dialog box Build Action appears as shown in Figure 3.18.

2. Select the action Generate Form:ORDD2K0010 and click Run. The Developer/2000 Form Compiler builds the executable version of the module.

3. Select the action Run Form:ORDD2K0010 and click Run. The Developer/2000 Form Runtime executes the module.

When you run the generated application, enter a few records in each block to discover some of the features of the created form. Notice, for example, how the created form:

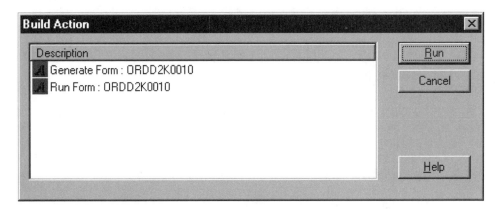

FIGURE 3.18   The Build Action dialog box.

❑ Supplies the order date automatically and enforces the business rules you identified for this and the order delivery date.

❑ Enforces uppercase characters for items, such as PRODUCT and CUSTOMER.

❑ Compares the cost of an item automatically.

❑ Refreshes the line item count and the order total for each new line item added to the order.

❑ Ranks the orders by order date and line items by line item number upon query.

❑ Calculates the average cost of all orders for a given date and displays it with each order.

All this functionality was built into the application system during the work you did before the generation. One of the strengths of the Developer/2000 Form Generator is its ability to convert properties of Repository objects defined declaratively into working software modules like the one you just created. Figure 3.19 shows how your generated form should look at this point.

3.5.4   GENERATING DEVELOPER/2000 REPORTS MODULES

The Designer/2000 Reports Generator is similar to the Designer/2000 Forms Generator, and its interface is even simpler. You can start it by selecting the report module in the Design Navigator and clicking the icon Generate ▒. The layout of the dialog box Generate Report that appears is even simpler than that of the dialog Generate Form, shown in Figure 3.16. The following steps allow you to generate the module ORDD2K0020:

1. Select the module in the Design Navigator and invoke the dialog box Generate Report.

2. Click Options... to display the Reports Generate Options dialog box.

3. Provide the information required to connect to the database during the compilation and execution of the report. To avoid any errors, the runtime user should be the database account under which you have created the ORDERS database objects.

4. Click OK to close the Reports Generate Options dialog box.

5. Click Start to begin the generation.

Like the Form Generator, the activities of the Report Generator are displayed in the Message Window of the Design Editor. You can compile and execute the generated report from the dialog box Build Action, as explained in the previous section.

When you run the report, you will notice that the generated module contains a front page and a trailer, and that each order is displayed on its own page.

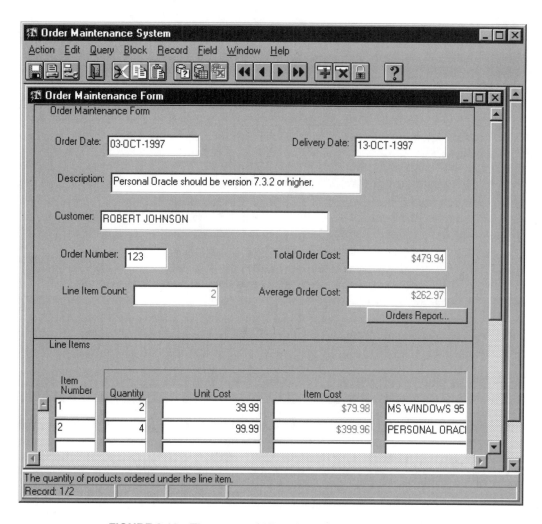

FIGURE 3.19 The generated Developer/2000 Forms module.

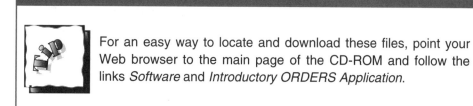

For an easy way to locate and download these files, point your Web browser to the main page of the CD-ROM and follow the links *Software* and *Introductory ORDERS Application*.

The generator has included from the template reports useful data, such as the name of the user who ran the report, the current page indicator, and the total number of pages in the report. As in the case of the Developer/2000 Forms module, you utilized the power of Desginer/2000's Repository-driven generation to convert properties of Repository objects into working software modules.

The companion CD-ROM contains a number of software modules you have developed in these three chapters. They are organized in three folders inside the folder \SOFTWARE\ORDSMALL. The following list is a description of these folders:

❑ **Designer.** This folder contains the application discussed in these chapters exported in the file ORDERS.DMP. Import the file into your Repository to view the settings of all the properties and objects of the ORDERS application system. Chapter 5 provides instructions on how to import an application system in Designer/2000.

❑ **Developer.** This folder contains the Developer/2000 Forms module ORDD2K0010 you generated in this chapter and the Developer/2000 Reports module ORDD2K0020.

❑ **DDL.** This folder contains the files created by the Server Generator to implement the database objects of the ORDERS application system.

3.6 WHAT NEXT?

At this point, stop the work and consider what you have done in these three chapters. Using a concrete situation, you stepped into each phase of a software development effort using Designer/2000. In Chapter 1, you identified and stored in the Repository the logical data model, the user interface requirements, and the business logic rules of the ORDERS application system. In Chapter 2, you converted the logical data model into a physical database schema, implemented several business rules by enhancing the properties of the data schema, and, finally, generated and implemented the DDL statements that create the schema in a physical database. In this current chapter, you converted the user interface requirements into screen and report modules, and complex business logic rules into PL/SQL modules. You designed the layout of the interface modules and expanded their functionality by introducing summary items, push buttons, and formula items. Finally, you generated working software modules full of functionality, which can be used to enter, manipulate, and retrieve data, without requiring any manual modifications.

Although the number of components in the ORDERS application you implemented is limited, the path you followed remains essentially the same for larger systems as well. The rest of this book will help you broaden your set of skills and knowledge about Designer/2000 and will enable you to tackle problems of a larger complexity. The remaining chapters in this part will discuss the purpose and features of the major categories of Designer/2000 tools. They will teach you how to work with navigators, diagrammers, matrices, and other tools in Designer/2000.

Part Two will discuss in detail the role and use of Designer/2000 in strategic planning, business modeling, and business process reengineering activities. Part Three will discuss how to define, analyze, and store in the Repository the requirements of an information system. Part Four will present all the tools used during data modeling, database design, and application design activities. It will also focus on the implementation of data-related business rules that your systems will enforce and on PL/SQL programming. Part Five will be dedicated to the generation and implementation of software modules of your applications. I will discuss the generation of the database schema of the system and the role of preferences and templates in shaping the generated modules. Two chapters in this part will show you different ways to generate Developer/2000 Forms modules from the definitions stored in the Repository.

3.7 SUMMARY

This chapter shows how you can convert the functional definitions of the ORDERS system into software modules. It also focuses on techniques to enhance the design and functionality of these modules, and explains how to use the Developer/2000 Forms and Reports Generators to implement these modules. The following is a list of highlights from this chapter.

- ❏ **Generating the Initial Module Design**
  - ❏ Application Design Transformer
  - ❏ Accepting Candidate Modules
- ❏ **Enhancing the Design of User Interface Modules**
  - ❏ Module Diagrams
  - ❏ Views and Elements of the Module Diagram
  - ❏ Arranging the Layout of Module Diagrams
  - ❏ Adding Links to Module Diagrams
  - ❏ Maintaining Properties of Module Elements
- ❏ **Expanding Modules with Unbound and Action Items**
  - ❏ Formula Unbound Items
  - ❏ Derivation Unbound Items
  - ❏ Action Items
- ❏ **Designing and Programming PL/SQL Modules**
  - ❏ Creating a PL/SQL Function
  - ❏ The Logic Editor

❑   Programming the Body of PL/SQL Program Units
❑   Creating an Application Logic Program Unit
❑   **Generating the Application Modules**
❑   Generating and Installing PL/SQL Modules
❑   Overview of Designer/2000 Front-End Generators
❑   Generating Developer/2000 Forms Modules
❑   Generating Developer/2000 Reports Modules
❑   **What Next?**

Chapter 4

UNDERSTANDING THE DESIGNER/2000 ARCHITECTURE

- ♦ Overview of Designer/2000
- ♦ Designer/2000 Repository Model
- ♦ Repository Administration Utility
- ♦ Extending and Customizing the Repository
- ♦ Summary

Designer/2000 is not a single application, but rather a constellation of tools and utilities used in a variety of tasks and activities in which Information Technology professionals engage today. This chapter will cover the architecture of Designer/2000 and a series of related topics, including:

❑ An overview of Designer/2000
❑ The Designer/2000 Repository model
❑ Creating and maintaining Repositories
❑ Creating and maintaining Repository users
❑ Extending the Designer/2000 Repository
❑ Designer/2000 configuration

4.1 OVERVIEW OF DESIGNER/2000

This section will briefly discuss some characteristics of software engineering as an engineering discipline, and then will introduce Designer/2000 as a modern software engineering tool used to implement database systems.

4.1.1 SOFTWARE ENGINEERING AND TOOLS

Software engineering is a business activity whose ultimate goal is the production and implementation of high-quality software systems and applications on schedule and within allocated budgets. Although relatively new, software engineering shares many characteristics with older and more established engineering disciplines, like mechanical, electrical, or construction engineering. In particular, it produces its outputs by using and converting resources from the following four categories:

❑ **Business Community.** Software engineering is a business activity whose products solve one or more business problems. As such, it is closely related to the business community. This community supplies software engineers with two important resources: problems to solve, and money to reach the solutions.
❑ **Science.** Like any other engineering discipline, software engineering resides upon solid scientific foundations. The science that provides software engineers with methodology, tools, and algorithms to solve business problems is Computer Science.
❑ **People.** Despite the high degree of automation that software engineering employs, people remain a very important factor in every solution designed and implemented by the discipline. As software engineering becomes more and more mature, the level of skills of the people who practice it, the soft-

ware engineers, increases constantly. The most successful projects today are carried out by SWAT (Skilled, With Advanced Tools) teams of software engineers.

❑ **Management.** A software engineering project cannot succeed without a strong and committed management team. Like the coach of a successful sport team, the manager of a software engineering team provides guidelines and direction to the team during its effort to build successful software systems.

Figure 4.1 shows a diagram that represents the relationships between software engineering and these four important factors that influence its results.

As I said earlier, the goal of software engineering is to produce high-quality software systems. Much is said and written about the definition of a high-quality software system. In general, a software system is considered of good quality if it displays the following characteristics:

❑ It meets the business needs of the user community.
❑ It meets or exceeds the requirements of its users for performance, reliability, and availability.
❑ It is easy to learn and use.
❑ It requires little maintenance during its life.

In addition to having good quality, software systems need to be delivered in time and within budget. Like engineers from other disciplines who face similar constraints in their activities, software engineers today have at their reach a variety of tools that they use to build their products. In their origins, these tools were called computer-assisted software engineering (CASE) tools. They were helpful in defining and documenting the requirements of a software system, often in the form of diagrams that were easy to build and understand. They also enforced a system-

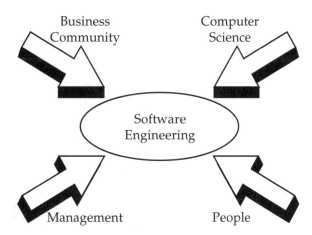

FIGURE 4.1 Relationships between software engineering and influencing factors.

wide dictionary of terms and facilitated the task of cross-checking and discovering inconsistencies in the system's requirements. The next generation of software engineering tools were the integrated CASE (I-CASE) tools. They extended the capabilities of CASE tools and allowed software engineers to convert the requirements of their systems into software modules generated automatically by the tool.

Today, software engineering and its practitioners see themselves in positions of increasing importance and prominence within corporations and businesses. Once sideline players in most companies, today they are actively shaping the business of these companies and the direction in which they are headed. Success stories of companies such as FedEx and Wal-Mart, which have seen themselves clearly ahead of the competition thanks to a carefully planned, designed, and implemented information systems infrastructure, give software engineers the credibility and affirmation they need. The tools that they use have evolved as well. In addition to providing more sophisticated features in support of design, development, and implementation of software systems, they enable software engineers to model and document business processes and activities.

4.1.2 COMPONENTS OF DESIGNER/2000

Designer/2000 is a suite of tools that falls in the category of advanced software engineering products. As mentioned earlier in the book, more than a dozen components make up Designer/2000. In the previous three chapters, you had the opportunity to work with a good number of them. The following list displays the way in which these components are most commonly grouped:

❑ **Business modeling components.** The most important tool in this group is the Process Modeller. Other tools, like Function Hierarchy Diagrammer, Repository Object Navigator, and Matrix Diagrammer, are used to model business processes as well.

❑ **System modeling components.** Function Hierarchy Diagrammer and Entity Relationship Diagrammer are the tools normally used to model software systems. Dataflow Diagrammer is also used, although not as frequently as the other two components. These diagrammers are widely used to create the information model of enterprises and business areas, independently of software systems, as well.

❑ **System design components.** Two important tools in this group are the Database Design Transformer and the Application Design Transformer. They translate the system model into a first-cut system design, composed of database objects and modules. You can refine the system design using the Design Editor.

❑ **Software generator components.** This group is the most crowded of Designer/2000 components, and the most dynamic one as well, since each major release of Designer/2000 adds new components in this group. Tools in this group convert the design of database objects and software modules into software programs that you can install and distribute in your user environment. The most important pieces in this group are the Server Generator, a number of generators for Developer/2000 components, and other Oracle development tools, such as Power Objects and Oracle WebServer. The C++ Object Layer Generator allows you to create a set of C++ classes used to access the database objects of your application from a C++ programming environment.

❏ **All-purpose components.** This group includes tools that are used in all the software engineering activities in which you can use Designer/2000. For this reason, they could be included in all the groups listed previously. Tools in this group are Repository Object Navigator, Matrix Diagrammer, and Repository Reports Navigator. Because of their widespread use, they are often considered utilities.

❏ **Repository administration tools.** As you will see later in the chapter, the Repository is an important part of Designer/2000. The Repository Administration Utility is the most important tool used to create and maintain the Repository. In addition, since the Repository is nothing but a set of database objects stored in an Oracle database, SQL*Plus is often listed as a Repository administration tool of Designer/2000.

Designer/2000 also provides a utility, called the Designer/2000 launch pad, from which you can start each major tool or component. The launch pad was introduced and discussed in the previous three chapters and is shown in Figure 4.2. You can see from this figure that the launch pad organizes the Designer/2000 components according to their membership in one of the functional groups described above. The ability to clearly see how each major component of Designer/2000 fits into the whole picture is also the major benefit that the launch pad provides to you, as a user of Designer/2000.

4.1.3 CHARACTERISTICS OF DESIGNER/2000

Each component of Designer/2000 enjoys the following important properties:

❏ It runs on a client/server environment.
❏ It is Repository-driven.
❏ It has a three-tiered architecture, described by the thin client, fat server metaphor.

The distribution of the code for each component is based on the client/server model. The user interface of each diagrammer or navigator you use in your desktop is the client part of the software. This client interface allows you to create, view, and maintain information related to your business and systems in

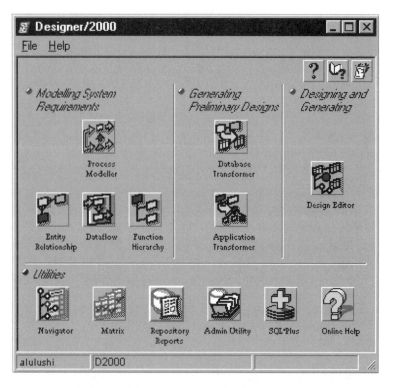

FIGURE 4.2   The Designer/2000 launch pad.

windows drawn and displayed on your client machine. The information itself, as well as a variety of check and enforcement business rules with which data must comply, are stored in the Designer/2000 Repository. The Repository is a group of database objects that reside in an Oracle Server database in the back end. The objects that make up the Designer/2000 Repository can be grouped in the following three categories:

❑ **Repository tables.** These are tables where all the information about a Designer/2000 project or activity is stored. Relatively few such tables exist compared with the number of different objects for which you store information in the Repository. For example, only one table, SDD_ELEMENTS, stores the information for most Designer/2000 objects, like entities, functions, tables, and modules. The structure of these tables tends to be flat and highly denormalized. Few relationships exist among the tables themselves.

❑ **Repository views.** The Repository views are defined upon Repository tables to represent a more normalized picture of the data stored in these tables. The number of views is significant, compared to the number of

Repository tables. For example, dozens of views are defined upon the table SDD_ELEMENTS. Views, like CI_ENTITIES, CI_FUNCTIONS, and CI_TABLE_DEFINITIONS, restrict access to records of this table that correspond to Designer/2000 objects, like entities, functions, tables, and modules. These views are also known as business views of the Designer/2000 Repository. They are documented as part of the entire product in the form of several entity relationship diagrams, which represent the logical relationships that exist between these views.

❑ **Repository API.** In order to implement the rules that Designer/2000 must enforce for each object it supports, the Repository contains a number of PL/SQL program units stored in the Oracle Server schema of the Repository owner. These program units, mostly PL/SQL packages, are also known as the Repository application programmatic interface (API). The Repository API is used by all the tools and utilities of Designer/2000 that you access from the client environment. It is also the recommended method of interacting with the Repository from other applications that you may develop yourself.

From the description of the Designer/2000 Repository, you can easily realize that the architecture of the entire Designer/2000 tool set is fundamentally a three-tiered architecture. The three tiers, or layers, of this architecture are the presentation layer, the business logic layer, and the data management layer. However, given that the business logic and data management layers are implemented almost entirely in the Oracle Server database, this architecture can be described as a thin client, fat server architecture. Figure 4.3 represents the Designer/2000 architecture graphically.

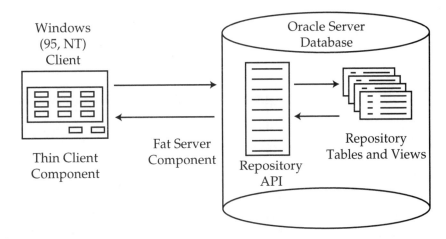

FIGURE 4.3 The three-tiered, thin client, fat server architecture of Designer/2000.

The presentation layer consists of all the tools and components of Designer/2000 that make up its suite of GUI user interface applications. Users create, view, and maintain data through the components of this layer. In Figure 4.3, the dialog box Create Entity from the Entity Relationship Diagrammer is used to represent a presentation layer component. The data management layer resides on the opposite side of the architecture and serves the needs of Designer/2000 users to store persistent data. The table SDD_ELEMENTS, in which data about the new entity will be stored, serves to represent this layer in Figure 4.3. The business logic layer serves the purpose of transferring requests for data services from the presentation layer to the data management layer and for returning responses from this layer to the user interface application. In addition, the business logic layer checks and validates a number of rules that data sent from the presentation layer must satisfy in order to be processed by the data management layer. This layer is implemented in the form of Repository business views and APIs and is represented in Figure 4.3 by the API call CIOENTITY.INS and the business view CI_ENTITIES.

4.1.4   INSTALLING AND CONFIGURING THE DESIGNER/2000 CLIENT SOFTWARE

As I said in the previous section, the Designer/2000 software has a three-tier architecture. However, two of these tiers are implemented in the Oracle Server database. Therefore, the installation process of Designer/2000, in general, goes through the following two steps:

1. Install and configure the client software.
2. Install and configure the Designer/2000 Repository in the Oracle Server database.

The process of installing the Designer/2000 client software is simple and covered in detail in the Oracle Designer/2000 Installation Guide, provided with the software. Depending on the options you select during the installation, differ-

Although the part of the installation process discussed here is called client installation, consider installing the software in a file server rather than on the individual PCs of each member of your design team. Given the considerable size of Designer/2000, installing it locally, in each PC, would result in a waste of disk space. On the other hand, the performance of the tools may suffer if the software is installed on the file server. Like every other decision you make, you have a trade-off to make here between the benefits and cost of each configuration you choose.

ent software components may be stored in your PC. In the most general case, the client installation process stores the presentation layer software for all the Designer/2000 components and the script files required to create and maintain the Designer/2000 Repository in the Oracle Server database. The Repository Administration Utility is the GUI tool that you can use to run these scripts in the proper order. This tool will be further discussed in Section 4.3.

I conclude this section by describing the actions you need to perform in order to create separate shortcuts for the diagrammers of Designer/2000. As a preparation step, you need to open the program folder Oracle Designer/2000 on your desktop. Follow the list of steps below:

1. Right-click the Start button and select Open from the popup menu. This action displays the program folder Start Menu.
2. Double-click the icon Programs in the Start Menu folder to open the program folder Programs.
3. Double-click the icon Oracle Designer/2000 in the Programs folder to open the program folder Oracle Designer/2000.

By default, the Oracle Designer program folder contains shortcuts to the Oracle Designer/2000 launch pad program and the online documentation. In order to add a shortcut for the Entity Relationship Diagrammer in the folder, follow these steps:

1. Select File | New | Shortcut from the Oracle Designer folder menu. This displays the dialog box Create Shortcut.
2. Click Browse in this dialog box to display the standard Browse dialog box of the Windows Explorer.
3. Use the Browse dialog box to select the executable file for this program. These files are located in the BIN directory of the Oracle home directory for your PC, for example, C:\ORAWIN95\BIN. You can easily identify these programs by their characteristic icons, also used in the Designer/2000 launch pad utility.
4. Click Next to move to the tab Select Title for Your Program.
5. Enter the title you want to associate with the program, for example, 'Entity Relationship Diagrammer.'
6. Click Finish to complete the process.

When you access the Designer/2000 components from such shortcuts, you will be prompted with two dialog boxes that allow you to connect to the Repository as a valid user and initialize the component for a valid application system within that Repository. I recommend that you create shortcuts for all the Designer/2000 tools shown in Figure 4.4.

DESIGNER/2000 TOOL	EXECUTABLE
Process Modeller	BPMOD20.EXE
Entity Relationship Diagrammer	AWE30.EXE
Dataflow Diagrammer	AWD30.EXE
Function Hierarchy Diagrammer	AWF30.EXE
Design Editor	DWFDE20.EXE
Repository Object Navigator	CKRON20.EXE
Matrix Diagrammer	AWM30.EXE
Repository Reports	CKRPT20.EXE
Repository Administration Utility	CKRAU20.EXE

FIGURE 4.4 Characteristic icons and executables for the Designer/ 2000 components.

4.2 DESIGNER/2000 REPOSITORY MODEL

The Repository is to Designer/2000 what the brain is to the human body. It stores, controls, and coordinates all the information that you collect, process, and use during the analysis, design, and development of information systems. It also contains the intelligence to process this information and generate the application code in multiple flavors of native programming environments, such as Developer/2000 Forms, Oracle WebServer, Visual Basic, and others. Thus, for the application being modeled, the Repository at the same time serves as a knowledge warehouse and as an expert system. The knowledge warehouse of the Designer/2000 Repository is its set of database tables; the logic and the intelligence of the Repository is implemented by the Repository views, PL/SQL APIs, and database triggers.

The Designer/2000 Repository is organized in application systems that can be accessed by any number of Repository users. Multiple applications can coexist in the same Repository, and multiple users can access these applications. However, with any of the Designer/2000 tools, a user can be connected to only one application system at any given time. The contents of the Repository are accessed using different tools and utilities of Designer/2000. As I mentioned earlier, different tools are used at different stages of the software development life cycle. These tools not only allow you to enter and edit information, but also to maintain multiple versions of applications; exchange information with other software packages; and browse, search, display, and print the information in the form of reports and matrices. The vast information managed by the Repository can be classified in the following categories:

❑   Elements
❑   Associations
❑   Topological information about diagrams
❑   Rules

The following sections provide information about each category.

4.2.1   ELEMENTS

Elements are units of data in which the Repository stores information about the application. The Designer/2000 Repository provides support for over 90 types of elements, and, in addition, it allows you to create your own customized object types. Examples of object types are business units, entities, attributes of an entity, modules, and so on. Instances of element types are the actual objects about which the Repository collects information. Examples of element instances are the business unit SALES DEPARTMENT, the entity ORDER, the attribute ORDER DATE of this entity, the module ORDER ENTRY FORM, and others like these.

As you can see from the examples listed above and from the work you did with these elements in the first three chapters, not all elements are alike. Some elements, like business units and entities, can stand for themselves, whereas others, like attributes, need to be associated with other elements. This fact leads to the following classification of elements in the Designer/2000 Repository:

❑   **Primary Access Controlled (PAC) elements.** These elements are owned and controlled by the application system. They can be created and modified directly, without going through another element of the Repository. Entities, modules, and tables are examples of primary access elements of an application system.
❑   **Secondary Access Controlled (SAC) elements.** These elements are owned and controlled by PAC elements, and, through them, by the application system. They can be created and modified only in the context of the PAC element that owns them. As an example, an attribute can be created only for a defined entity and accessed through the interface of its parent entity. Likewise, a database column exists only in the context of its parent table.

Elements in the Designer/2000 Repository are distinguished by their properties. The number of these properties depends on the type of object, but common properties found in most elements are:

❑   The application system that owns the element
❑   The Repository user who created the element and the date it was created
❑   The Repository user who last updated the element and the date it was last updated

❑ The type of the element
❑ Identification
❑ Name
❑ Different text properties that provide for remarks, notes, and the like

A number of these properties are set automatically by the different Designer/2000 tools you use to create and maintain the Repository elements. This automation reduces the number of properties you have to set yourself. On the other hand, Designer/2000 tools have the ability to read properties of certain elements you have defined in the Repository and create other elements with properties derived from the original elements. The Database Design Transformer, for example, can create table elements from properties of entities. The Application Design Transformer can create modules using property settings of elements like entities, functions, and tables.

4.2.2 ASSOCIATIONS

Associations represent relationships between elements in an application. As in the case of elements, the Repository of Designer/2000 contains types and instances of associations. An association type expresses the relationship that *may* exist between two elements, whereas an association instance denotes a relationship that *already* exists between two elements. In Designer/2000 parlance, associations are often referred to as *usages*. Some usages you will encounter in your modeling and design activities are table entity usages, which map database tables to entities; function entity usages, which describe the types of actions functions perform upon entities; module function usages, which document the business functions implemented by a module; and so on. Often associations between Repository elements have a meaning of their own in the application system. Relationships between entities, for example, or detailed table usages and detailed column usages of a module, are examples of such associations.

As in the case of elements, different Designer/2000 tools you use to create and maintain associations also populate a good number of their properties with the necessary values. Furthermore, tools like the Application Design Transformer and the Database Design Transformer create a good number of the associations you need in your application systems. The Database Design Transformer, for example, creates table–entity associations automatically. The Application Wizard, on the other hand, creates the initial detailed table and column usages of a module based on the function–entity associations and on the properties of table and column elements.

4.2.3 TOPOLOGICAL INFORMATION ABOUT DIAGRAMS

Diagrams allow you to visualize the elements in an application system and the associations among them. Figure 4.5 shows the example of an entity relationship diagram from the application system you developed in the first three chapters. The elements and their associations are annotated in this figure.

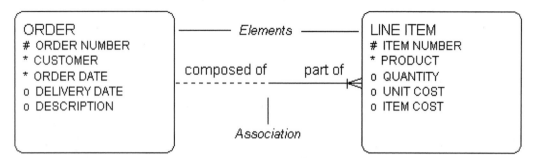

FIGURE 4.5 An entity relationship diagram with Repository elements and associations.

The majority of Designer/2000 tools are sophisticated diagramming packages that allow you to represent the contents of your Repository in a logical, visual, organized, and synchronized fashion. By creating objects in a diagram document, or by moving and rearranging them, you strive for a clear representation of the *meaning* of your design. In order to provide you with the same consistent view of a diagram each time you access it, Designer/2000 stores in its internal structures the *topology* of the diagram. The information in this category includes the coordinates of objects, their relative position with regard to other objects in the diagram, and their size. It also includes visual attributes of objects in the diagram, such as fill color, line color, line thickness, font style, and so on.

4.2.4 RULES

As I said previously, besides serving as a warehouse for storing information about the application, the Repository also functions as an expert system. Hundreds of rules implemented in the Repository guide you through the process of analyzing, designing, and developing the application. Some of these rules check the syntax of your definitions, provide for consistency and completeness, and perform cross-checking of objects and associations you create. Other important rules implemented in the form of transformers allow you to perform complicated tasks, such as transitioning from the logical data model of your application to a database design model, or generating modules from definitions of business functions. Yet another set of rules is implemented in the form of generators, which provide you with ready-to-run software modules created from the definitions and properties of these modules stored in the Repository.

An important category of rules includes those that govern what can be stored in the Repository, in what format, and under what conditions. A common statement is that these rules provide data about the data. Collectively, they are known as *metadata* rules, and their relations form the *metamodel* of the Repository. The Designer/2000 Repository metamodel is documented in the form of five entity relationship diagrams that you should have received together with the software. These diagrams are identified by the following names: Business Planning Model, Business Requirement Model, Module Design Model, Database Design Model, and Database Administrator Model. Coupled with the Designer/2000 Application Programming Interface (API), these metamodels guarantee the openness and accessibility of the Repository from third-party or custom-developed applications.

4.3 REPOSITORY ADMINISTRATION UTILITY

The Repository Administration Utility is the Designer/2000 component that allows you to install, upgrade, and maintain the Repository. You can access it by clicking the Admin Utility icon ▨ in the Designer/2000 launch pad. Only the Repository owner can enter the Repository Administration Utility; all other users, despite their roles or privileges, are not allowed to access the Repository through the Repository Administration Utility. The primary screen of the Repository Administration Utility is shown in Figure 4.6.

The functionality of the Repository Administration Utility is always one mouse click away, and is offered in the form of five iconic buttons in the toolbar and several more in the main area of the screen. As with other iconic buttons in Designer/2000, you can get a brief description of each tool in the form of popup text by positioning the mouse cursor over the button; or you can invoke the on-line help by first clicking the context-sensitive help button ▨ in the toolbar, and then clicking on the desired tool.

You can perform four major tasks in the Repository Administration Utility:

❑ Installing, upgrading, exporting, and importing the Repository
❑ Diagnosing and optimizing the Repository
❑ Creating and maintaining Repository users
❑ Extending and customizing the Repository

The following sections show you how to perform each of these tasks.

4.3.1 UNDERSTANDING THE PHYSICAL LAYOUT OF THE REPOSITORY

The process of creating a new Repository in an Oracle database, or upgrading an existing one, is described in detail in the Oracle Designer/2000 Installation Guide that comes with Designer/2000. Therefore, I discuss it only briefly here. Recall from discussions earlier in this chapter that the Designer/2000 Repository contains the data management layer and the business logic layer of the Designer/2000. The Repository installation process, then, can be seen as a two-stage process. In the first stage, the tables, sequences, and indexes that make up the data management layer are created. Most of the objects created in this stage

FIGURE 4.6 The Designer/2000 Repository Administration Utility.

are empty, since they are not populated with data until you create application systems and populate them with design and analysis objects. Nevertheless, planning ahead for the future growth of your Repository, assign the objects created in this stage into their own tablespaces, separate from data of other applications that may share the same database instance as the Repository. Furthermore, in order to avoid bottlenecks during data access operations, I recommend that tables and indexes be stored in distinct tablespaces. As you will see in Section 4.3.3, the Repository Administration Utility offers a fine level of granularity for distributing the objects of your Repository across different tablespaces.

The second stage of the installation creates the objects that make up the Designer/2000 business logic layer. As I mentioned earlier, these objects are a set of views, stored program units, and database triggers that enforce and implement the Repository rules. As such, they will reside in the data dictionary tables of the Oracle Server database. These tables are stored in the SYSTEM tablespace and are internally maintained by the database kernel. Before starting the Repository installation process, you need to make sure that the SYSTEM tablespace has enough contiguous space to allow for the data dictionary tables to be extended during the installation. The Oracle Designer/2000 Installation Guide provides the amount of free space the SYSTEM tablespace needs to have. A number between 50 MB and 60 MB is usually sufficient.

Recall from what I said earlier that the Designer/2000 Repository is composed of two components. The first one is the business logic layer of Designer/2000. This component is physically located in the SYSTEM tablespace and is fixed in size throughout the life of the Repository. The second component is the data management layer. Its tables and indexes are physically located in tablespaces that you assign during the installation process. The size of this component varies throughout the life of the Repository and typically increases as the number of application systems in the Repository increases. The Repository Administration Utility allows you to configure the size of the Repository based on the following three models:

❑ **Small.** A small Repository is optimized for storing no more than 20,000 elements.
❑ **Medium.** A medium size Repository is optimized for storing between 20,000 and 100,000 elements.
❑ **Large.** A large Repository is optimized to store over 100,000 elements.

The Repository Installation Utility discussed in Section 4.3.3 allows you to select one of the sizing models described above. Based on this model, the storage parameters of Repository tables and indexes will be configured to optimize the storage of your application systems.

4.3.2   PREPARING FOR THE CREATION OF THE REPOSITORY

Each Designer/2000 Repository is closely related to a special Oracle Server user known as the *Repository owner*. This database user is the account that owns all the database objects created during the Repository installation process, including stored program units, tables, views, and database triggers. During the installation procedure, you connect to the database using this account. The installation process then creates all the Repository objects under the schema of the owner account. Clearly, in order for the installation to succeed, the owner schema needs to have all the appropriate privileges and grants. In particular, you need to make sure before the installation begins that the Repository owner has been granted the following privileges:

❑ Appropriate quotas in the tablespaces where the Repository tables and indexes will be created.

❑ The Oracle Server role CONNECT.

❑ The Oracle Server role RESOURCE.

❑ The Oracle Server role DES2000_OWNER. This role is created especially for granting the required privileges to a Designer/2000 Repository owner. To create this role, connect to SQL*Plus from the PC where you have installed the Designer/2000 software and issue the following command:

```
@ <ORACLE_HOME>\REPADM20\UTL\ckrole.sql
```

The argument <ORACLE_HOME> in this command should be substituted with the home directory of your Oracle installation, for example, C:\ORAWIN95 or C:\ORANT.

❑ EXECUTE privilege on the packages DBMS_LOCK and DBMS_PIPE owned by the Oracle user SYS.

Another modification to consider before running the Repository installation utility is to create a large rollback segment that will be used by the installation processes. This segment will ensure that these processes, some of which may run for a considerable amount of time, will complete successfully. In order for the large rollback segment to be utilized by the installation processes, you must take offline the other rollback segments normally used by the database instance. Furthermore, in order to avoid fragmentation of the tablespace dedicated to regular rollback segments, consider creating a tablespace in which the large rollback segment will be created. This tablespace and the associated rollback segment may be brought online when you are about to initiate the installation or upgrade process of the Repository. They may be taken offline as soon as these processes complete successfully.

The Repository Administration Utility allows you to check the privileges of the Repository owner schema before the installation and during the maintenance of the Repository. In particular, you can view the tablespaces in which the Repository owner has quota privileges, the value of these quotas, and the available free space for each tablespace. You can also view the privileges and database roles granted to this schema. Section 4.3.5 later in this chapter will show how you can use this information to diagnose and optimize the Repository.

4.3.3 CREATING THE DESIGNER/2000 REPOSITORY

After ensuring that you have taken all the preliminary steps for a successful installation of the Repository, you can perform the actual installation by following these steps:

1. Click the iconic button Install 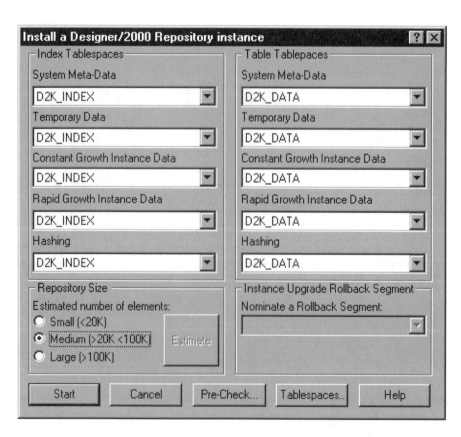 in the Repository Management group of the Repository Administration Utility (see Figure 4.6). Note that this button is enabled only if no Designer/2000 Repository is installed under the current database schema. When the Repository is installed successfully, this button is disabled.

2. In the dialog box Install a Designer/2000 Repository Instance that appears, select the appropriate tablespaces from the groups of list boxes Table Tablespace and Index Tablespace. By default, these list boxes are set to the default tablespace of the Repository owner. Replace these settings with the tablespaces you have created for the Designer/2000 Repository tables and indexes. Figure 4.7 shows an example of this dialog box.

3. Click the Pre-Check... button for a final review of the privileges of the current schema. The database privileges required to complete the installation successfully are listed in the Operation Requirements dialog box (see Figure 4.8). If all the check boxes in this dialog box contain check marks, you may

FIGURE 4.7 The Install a Designer/2000 Repository Instance dialog box.

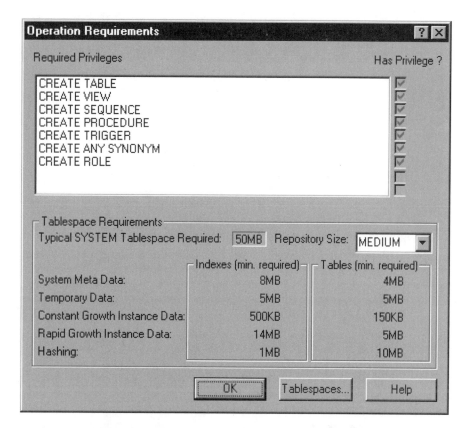

FIGURE 4.8 The Operation Requirements dialog box.

proceed with the installation. Otherwise, you need to grant the missing privilege to the would-be Repository owner as discussed in Section 4.3.2. The lower half of this dialog box displays the tablespace requirements to create the Repository. The SYSTEM tablespace requirement is fixed at 50 MB. The size of the configurable part of the Repository varies with the sizing model you choose. When you select one of the three options (SMALL, MEDIUM, and LARGE) from the list box Repository Size, the dialog box displays the appropriate tablespace requirements for indexes and tables by category of Repository objects.

4. In order to ensure that the tablespaces you selected in Step 2 have the free space recommended by Step 3, click the button Tablespaces… to display the Tablespace Analysis dialog box. This dialog lists all the tablespaces on which you have quota privileges and the amount of available space in these tablespaces. If a tablespace you have targeted to store Repository objects does not have the amount of free space estimated in Step 3, add a new data

file to the tablespace or move the objects to a different tablespace before
moving on to the next step.

5. Click the button Start in the Install a Designer/2000 Repository Instance dialog box to initiate the installation process.

The dialog box Control Status displays information about each step of the
installation process. In an example of this dialog shown in Figure 4.9, the stage of
the installation process is CKTABS Creating the Repository tables. The object
being currently processed is the table CK_CKDBSZ_DBU_TMP. This is the 29th of
93 objects that will be processed in this stage. The icons at the bottom of the Control Status dialog box allow you to pause the installation process, to restart it after
the pause, to skip a stage forward or backward, or to interrupt the process altogether. A powerful feature of the Installation utility is the ability to remember the
stage where you stopped the installation. The next time you invoke the tool, you
are prompted to start from the beginning or to resume from the place you left.

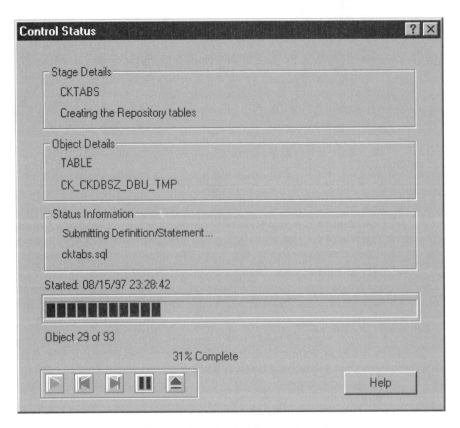

FIGURE 4.9   The Control Status dialog box.

4.3.4 MAINTAINING THE DESIGNER/2000 REPOSITORY

After the installation of the Repository is completed, you need to maintain it. Some maintenance functions, such as export and import, should be part of the larger maintenance scheme designed for your databases and systems. Other functions can and should be performed at the Repository level using the Repository Administration Utility maintenance tools. Here is a list of maintenance tasks you can complete from the Repository Administration Utility.

❑ **Upgrade the Repository**. The upgrade utility is invoked by clicking the Upgrade button ▨. Invoke this utility whenever you decide to upgrade your existing Repository to a more advanced version of Designer/2000. As with the installation process, during the upgrade, carefully follow the instructions provided by the Oracle Corporation.

❑ **Remove the Repository**. To remove all the database objects of the Repository, click the Remove Repository button ▨. This process may be required if the Repository installation fails and you want to restart it from the beginning. This step may also be used if you are about to restore a Repository that was backed up using an export of the Repository tables or of all the tables owned by the Repository owner schema.

❑ **Remove all the objects owned by the Repository owner**. To remove all the database objects owned by the schema under which you are logged on, click the Remove All Objects button ▨. As with the previous step, this process may be required if the installation of the Repository fails. It is required if you want to restore a Repository backed up using a full export of the Repository owner schema.

❑ **Back up the Repository**. The Repository Administration Utility integrates this function with the Oracle Server Export utility. You can perform three types of exports using the Repository Administration Utility. You may perform a full export of all the objects owned by the Repository owner schema, you may export only the tables that make up the Repository instance, or you may export all the tables owned by the Repository owner. The exported data is written to a file, which then can be backed up and archived. The backed up export file may be used to restore the Repository in case it is corrupted or to import it into another Repository in a different Oracle instance. The following steps can be used to perform the export process:

  1. Click the Export icon ▨. The dialog box Export Options appears (see Figure 4.10).
  2. Select the appropriate check box in the dialog box Export Options and click Continue….
  3. Set the name and location of the export file in the Windows File Export dialog box that appears and click Save. The duration of the Export process varies, depending on the export option you select and on the

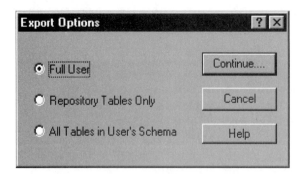

FIGURE 4.10 The Export Options dialog box.

size of the Repository being exported. The list of activities performed during the process is displayed in the dialog box Export Status.

4. Click Close in the Export Status dialog box to return to the Export Options dialog box. Note that this button is enabled only if the export process has completed.

5. Click Cancel to dismiss the Export Options dialog box.

❑   **Restore the Repository**. The Repository Administration Utility uses the Oracle Server Import utility to restore a Repository. A prerequisite to restoring a Repository is that it should be in the schema of the current Repository owner. If you need to restore a version of the Repository over an existing one, clear the existing Repository first by clicking the Remove Repository ⬚ icon or the Remove All Objects ⬚ icon. Which method you choose to clear the existing the Repository depends on the kind of export file you are about to restore. If the file was produced by an export of the Repository tables or all the tables of the owner schema, use the former option. If the file was created by a full export of the owner, use the latter option. The Import iconic button ⬚, which is used to invoke the Import utility, is not active until you clear the Repository objects with one of these methods.

When you click the Import button, a Windows File Import dialog box is displayed. Use this dialog to select the file from which you want to restore the Repository. When the file is selected, the Import process is started. At the end of this process, if you performed a full restore of the Repository owner, you need to reconcile the privileges granted by this schema to other Oracle users. This process is explained in Section 4.3.6.

❑   **Recreate and recompile Repository objects.** Cases may occur when not all the Repository objects are installed successfully, or the compile status of some package may be invalid, or some object is dropped accidentally from the database. Other situations may occur, where the performance of Designer/2000 tools will benefit from the recreation of the Repository indexes and hash tables. In such cases, you may click the Recreate button ⬚ to invoke the dialog box shown in Figure 4.11.

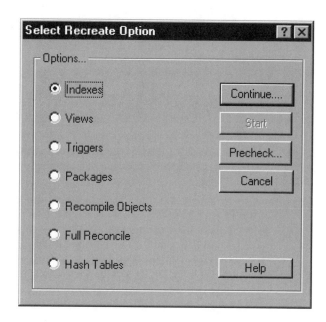

FIGURE 4.11 The Select
Recreate Option dialog box.

In the dialog box Select Recreate Option, you can choose any of the
first four radio buttons to invoke the utility that recreates indexes, views,
triggers, and packages the Repository. You can also select one of the last
three radio buttons if you want to recompile the Repository's PL/SQL objects, perform a full reconciliation of Repository users with objects, or recreate the Repository hash tables. When recreating triggers or hash tables, you
may click the Continue button to display a dialog box in which you can select the tablespace where the new objects will be stored. You may also click
the Precheck button to see whether you have all the privileges required to
perform the desired operation. When you are ready to perform the operation, click Start.

4.3.5 DIAGNOSING AND OPTIMIZING THE REPOSITORY

In addition to the tasks discussed in the previous section, you can
also perform several important diagnostics on the Repository that
allow you to spot and avoid problems before they hinder the activities of other Repository users. The first diagnostic tool you can
use is invoked by clicking the View Objects button 🖳. This brings
up the View Object Options dialog box shown in Figure 4.12.

Choose the radio button Object Status and click Continue to display the
Repository Objects Status dialog box shown in Figure 4.13.

This dialog box allows you to monitor the status of constraints, indexes,
packages, package bodies, sequences, synonyms, tables, triggers, and views, indi-

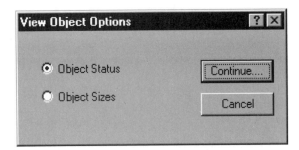

FIGURE 4.12 The View Object Options dialog box.

vidually or all together. You may display objects that are valid, invalid, missing, disabled, or enabled; or you may display the objects in all these states. Figure 4.13 shows all the Repository objects in any of the possible states. The number of elements in the list is shown in the lower right-hand corner of the dialog box. To focus the selection on a particular object type or state, make the appropriate selections from the list boxes Object Type and Status in the upper part of the dialog box. Needless to say, before starting to recreate any of the objects with the recre-

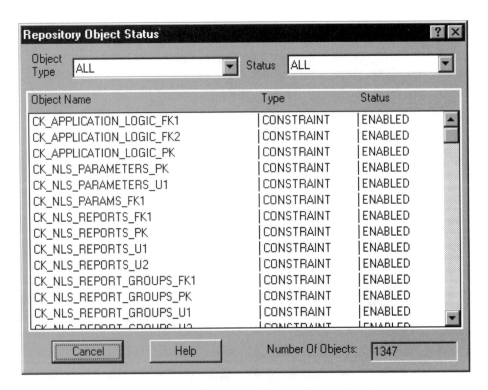

FIGURE 4.13 The Repository Objects Status dialog box.

ate utility discussed above, check their status in the Repository Object Status dialog box.

If you select the Object Sizes radio button in the View Object Options dialog box, you see the Check Object Sizes/Limits dialog box shown in Figure 4.14.

This dialog box displays the storage parameters for the Repository tables and indexes. The key parameter to observe here is the number of extents, which is an indicator of the fragmentation of the object. A large number of extents for an object means higher fragmentation of that object and, therefore, slower access and retrieval of data stored in that object. This ultimately results in decreased performance of Designer/2000 tools that access these objects. Also, if the number of extents is close to the maximum number of extents allowed, the object is near its maximum storage capacity. A proactive approach to Repository management would require you to avoid the fragmentation and increase the storage capacity of the objects before the crisis occurs. The dialog box Check Object Sizes/Limits allows you to easily retrieve the necessary information to avoid the crisis.

Another diagnostic tool you can use is the Tablespace Analysis dialog box shown in Figure 4.15. You can invoke it by clicking the View Tablespaces button

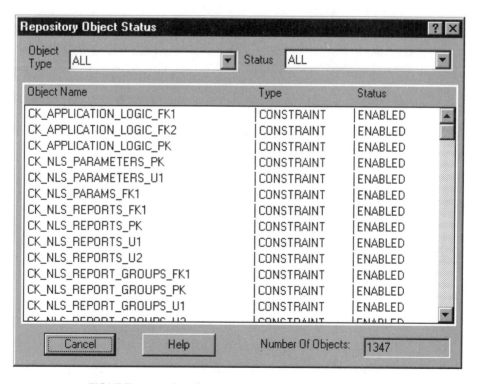

FIGURE 4.14 The Check Object Sizes/Limits dialog box.

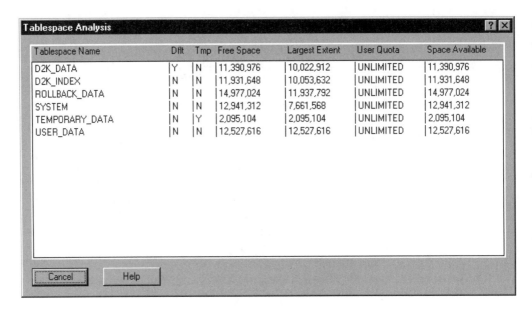

FIGURE 4.15   The Tablespace Analysis dialog box.

in the Repository Administration Utility main screen. Recall from the discussion in Section 4.3.3 that this dialog box can be invoked to check the space availability before initiating the installation process.

This dialog box lists the tablespaces on which the Repository owner has quota privileges. When an Oracle Server schema has quota privileges on a tablespace, that schema can take up free space from the tablespace up to the amount indicated by the quota. In the particular case when the quota of a user on a tablespace is set to 'Unlimited,' that user may occupy as much space as possible from the given tablespace. The key variables to look for in the Tablespace Analysis dialog box are Free Space and Largest Extent for each tablespace, since they control the size of objects that can be created in that tablespace. I recommend that you use the Tablespace Analysis utility not only before installing or upgrading the Repository, but also each time you are about to recreate the Repository objects.

So far, you have seen two steps you can take to enhance the performance of the Repository: recreating the hash tables and identifying fragmented objects. Another step is to "pin" frequently accessed Designer/2000 packages into the system global area (SGA) of the Oracle Server database in which the Repository is installed. Packages are loaded in memory when one of their components is invoked. They remain in the SGA until the aging algorithm employed by the database decides to swap them out. The performance of Designer/2000 can be improved if the packages that its components use the most are kept in the SGA even when the aging algorithm decides to evict them. Pinning marks these packages so

The number of Designer/2000 packages that will remain in the SGA if you pin them in the Repository Administration Utility is quite large. In total, they occupy about 13 MB of the shared memory of the database. Use this option only if you can dedicate this much memory to your Designer/2000 users without affecting the other database users.

that once loaded in the SGA, they are not removed from it as long as the database instance is up and running.

You can pin the Designer/2000 packages in the SGA by clicking the Pin button ▨ in the toolbar. Since this utility invokes the Oracle package DBMS_SHARED_POOL, this package must exist and the Repository owner must have EXECUTE privilege on it. If any of these conditions are not met, an error box instructs you on how to satisfy them. If you no longer want the packages pinned in the SGA, click the Unpin button ▨. From that moment on, these packages will age out of the SGA like any other package.

4.3.6 CREATING AND MAINTAINING REPOSITORY USERS

When the Repository is installed, only one user can access it—the Repository owner. Eventually, you would want to enable more users to access it. The Maintain Users utility of the Repository Administration Utility allows you to manage the access to the Repository by other users. To launch this utility, you click the button Maintain Users ▨ in the Repository Administration Utility main screen. The dialog box User Maintenance shown in Figure 4.16 appears. As you can see from this figure, the central area of this dialog is occupied by a navigator control which allows you to view the users organized by their Repository privileges. Applications owned by a particular user may be shown as well.

In order to create a user for the Designer/2000 Repository, click the icon Add ▨. The dialog box Repository User Properties is displayed (see Figure 4.17). In this dialog you should select the Oracle user from the list box Oracle User Name. The text boxes Full User Name and Description can be used to clarify the definition of the Repository user. By default, they are set when you select from the list box Oracle User Name.

Valid users of the Repository can be created either with the Manager or with the regular User role. An account with Manager privileges is normally used to create applications, maintain different versions of applications, and control the access by other users to the application. It should not be used for regular design activities, for which an account with the User role is more appropriate. To assign the user one of these Repository roles, select MANAGER or USER from the list box Type.

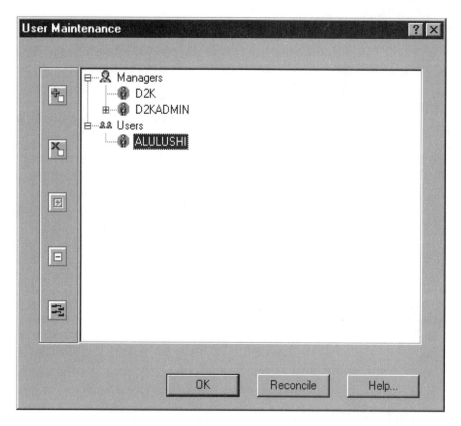

FIGURE 4.16   The User Maintenance dialog box.

Creating or modifying users does not automatically enable them to access the Repository. After you make the desired changes and save them, run the reconcile utility by clicking the Reconcile button in the User Maintenance dialog box. This utility invokes the Control Status dialog box described in Section 4.3.3. This dialog runs a series of scripts, which adjust the privileges of the users on Repository objects according to your changes. Note that the creation of new users or modifications to existing users will not take effect until you run the Reconcile utility.

A more advanced form of reconciling user definitions with Repository objects is offered by the Full Reconcile utility. Rather than reconciling grants of an individual user, this utility performs a global reconciliation of all the Repository users. In order to perform a full reconciliation of the Repository, take the following actions:

1. Click the iconic button Recreate ▨ in the Repository Administration Utility dialog box. This action displays the dialog box Select Recreate Option (see Figure 4.11).

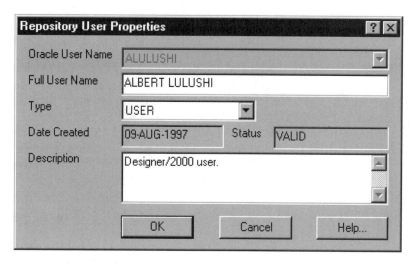

FIGURE 4.17   The Repository User Properties dialog box.

2. Select the radio button Full Reconcile in the dialog box Select Recreate Option.
3. Click Start. This command invokes the Control Status dialog box, which performs the actual reconciliation process. After these scripts are completed, the control returns to the dialog box Select Recreate Option.
4. Click Cancel.

When you initially define the Repository users, the Full Reconcile utility may be a good alternative to reconciling the grants of each user individually. Furthermore, use this utility each time one of the following occurs:

❑ The Repository is restored from a full Repository owner backup. Backing up and restoring the Repository was discussed in Section 4.3.4, earlier in this chapter.

❑ The Repository is extended with user-defined elements and associations. The user extensions of the Repository will be discussed Section 4.4.

❑ An application system is imported from a different Repository. Chapter 5 will discuss the process of creating and maintaining application systems in the Designer/2000 Repository.

In any event, be aware that the full reconciliation process may be a long-running one, especially if the Repository contains multiple users and several application systems.

4.4   EXTENDING AND CUSTOMIZING THE REPOSITORY

The Repository of Designer/2000 contains a large number of element types and associations among the element types, with an extensive range of properties for each object. This allows it to accommodate requirements of methods and methodologies of all kinds. However, what makes the Repository truly flexible and useful for every design and development methodology you choose is the ability of its architecture to extend and accommodate user-defined elements and associations. The following sections will discuss the ways in which you can extend the Designer/2000 Repository with your own objects.

4.4.1   WAYS TO EXTEND THE DESIGNER/2000 REPOSITORY

The architecture of the Repository is extended in the User Extensibility dialog box. You can display this dialog box by clicking the Maintain User Extensions button in the Repository Administration Utility main screen. Figure 4.18 shows an example of this dialog box.

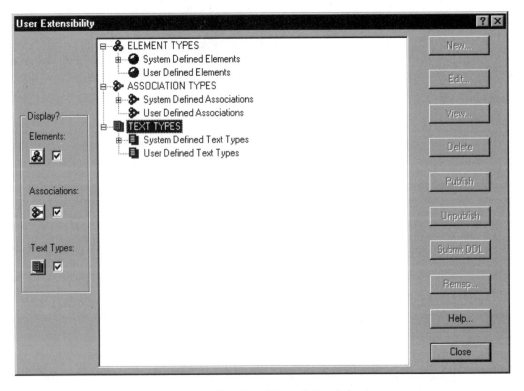

FIGURE 4.18   The User Extensibility dialog box.

You can extend the Designer/2000 Repository in several ways:

❑ **Define new properties for existing element types and associations.** All the predefined objects and associations contain properties set aside to satisfy your needs to expand and customize the Repository. You can see these properties in the right pane of the User Extensibility dialog box under names such as Usrx0, Usrx1, and so on. For certain objects, some of these properties may be already in use; however, for the majority of the objects, they are available for use.

❑ **Create new element types.** In addition to the ninety-some existing element types that exist in the Designer/2000 Repository, you may create brand-new types with up to twelve properties and as many text type properties as needed.

❑ **Create new associations between elements.** If the system you are designing requires associations between element types that do not exist in the Repository, you can define your own associations with up to eleven properties and additional text type properties.

❑ **Create new text types.** In addition to thirty-some text type objects already defined in the Repository, you can create your own text types to support the requirements of your applications.

4.4.2 STEPS TO EXTEND THE DESIGNER/2000 REPOSITORY

Whether you are creating a new object, association, or text type, or simply adding a property to an existing one, follow the steps listed below to extend the Repository:

1. Carefully assess and justify the need for extending the Repository. Make sure that what you want does not already exist or cannot be implemented in one form or another by existing structures. Identifying and justifying this need requires that you know the contents of the Repository from the inside out; extending the Repository is not a task you should tackle in your first week of working with Designer/2000.

2. Create the new object and edit its properties to suit your needs. The following sections will discuss the process of adding new properties to existing objects and that of creating new element types, association types, or text types.

3. Review and confirm the newly-created type or property.

4. Publish the extension to the Repository. Publishing informs the Repository about your extension and creates a programming interface so that other Designer/2000 tools may access the new object or property. Publishing is an important step because it is irreversible: once an extension is published, it cannot be edited or deleted from the Repository. You must review carefully all proposed extensions before publishing them; otherwise you will end up with a cluttered and confusing Repository.

5. Submit the DDL statement that creates the element type or association type in the Repository. This step applies only to these two types of extensions; when creating a new text type or extending a property, you do not need to submit the DDL statement to the database.

4.4.3 EXTENDING PROPERTIES OF EXISTING OBJECTS

The process of extending the properties of existing objects is the same for element types and associations. The following actions allow you to extend the properties of the predefined element type Database (Non-Oracle) to include the name of the vendor of the database package.

1. Invoke the dialog box User Extensibility as described in Section 4.4.1.
2. Extend the node ELEMENT TYPES and then the node System Defined Elements. All the base elements of the Designer/2000 Repository are displayed in the Navigator.
3. Expand the element type ANS Database (Non-Oracle) from the list of element types. This is the first element in the list.
4. Expand the properties of this element. You see that this element type has only two properties defined: *Name* and *Comment*. On the other hand, there are twenty columns identified as Usrx0 through Usrx19 which you can use to extend the properties of this element type.
5. Select the column Usrx0 from the list of properties and click the button Edit…. The dialog box Property Details appears.
6. Set the properties *Displayed Name*, *Datatype*, and *Length* in the Property Details dialog box as shown in Figure 4.19 and click OK. The newly-created property appears in the list of properties. Note that unlike the properties *Database Name* and *Comment* whose characteristic icon is green, the property *Vendor* still has a red icon since you have not published it yet.
7. Click the button Publish in the right panel of the User Extensibility dialog box to publish the new property. Now the characteristic icon of the property becomes green.
8. Collapse the nodes ANS Database (Non-Oracle) and System Defined Elements.

4.4.4 CREATING NEW ELEMENT TYPES

This section describes the process of adding a new element type to the Designer/2000 Repository. This new element type allows you to record information about executives in an enterprise. Such information may be used during enterprise modeling activities with Designer/2000. I assume here that you have invoked the di-

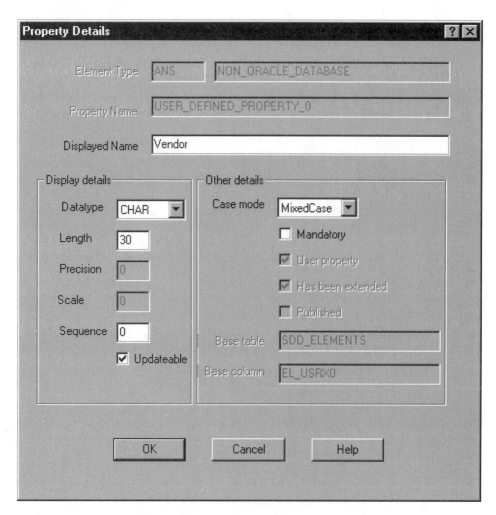

FIGURE 4.19 The Property Details dialog box.

alog box User Extensibility, as described in Section 4.4.1. To create the new element type, follow these steps:

1. Select the node User Defined Elements.
2. Click the button New.... The dialog box Element Type Details appears.
3. Set the properties in the dialog box Element Type Details as shown in Figure 4.20. Note that the *Short Name* property should be set to a label following the pattern 'E1' through 'E99.' By looking at the list of system defined element types, you can notice those that were added to the Repository as

user-defined extensions by the Oracle engineers. They include element types like Objective, Critical Success Factor, and Key Performance Indicator.

4. Click OK. The new element type is created and inserted in the list.

5. You can edit the properties of the new element by clicking the button Edit.... The same dialog box as the one shown in Figure 4.20 appears. However, in this case, the Details group of properties is populated with the name of the view, CI_EXECUTIVES, and the package, CIOEXECUTIVE, through which you will access and maintain the objects of this new element type.

6. Click Publish to publish the newly-created type. As the process runs, you are reminded that you should run the Full Reconcile utility after extending the Repository. Note that after the element type is published, the button Delete is disabled. As I mentioned earlier, be really sure about the extension to the Repository when you publish it, since you cannot un-publish or otherwise delete the user extension after it has been published. Once the publishing process is complete, an alert box prompts you to submit the DDL to generate the views and packages.

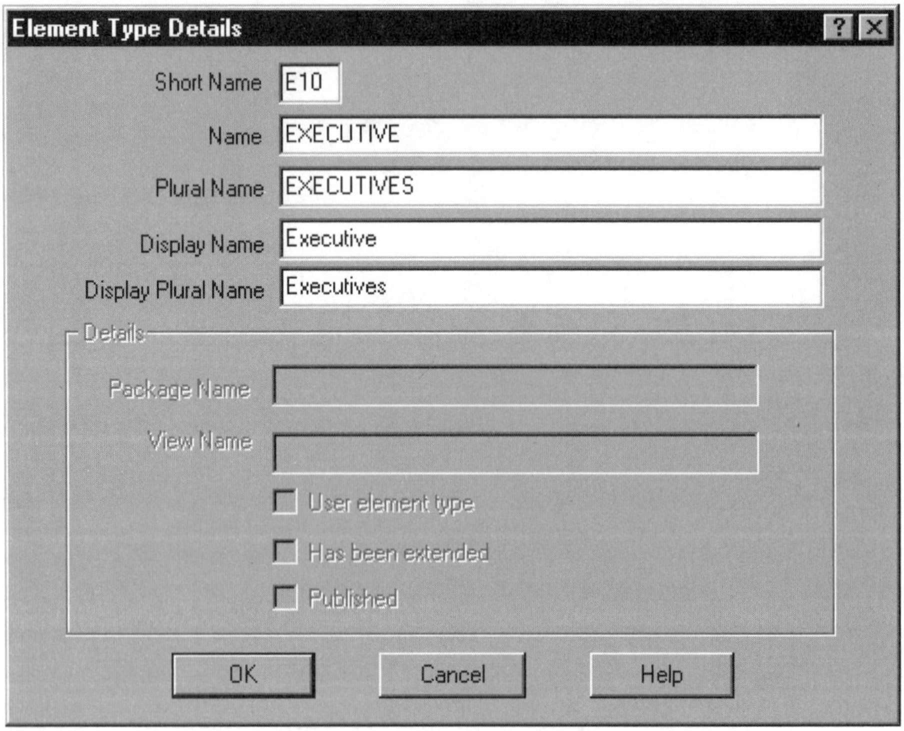

FIGURE 4.20   The Element Type Details dialog box.

7. Click OK in the alert box to add these objects in the Repository. Alternatively, you can simply close the alert by clicking Cancel. When you return to the User Extensibility dialog box, submit the DDL by clicking the button Submit DDL.
8. Collapse the node User Defined Elements.

By default, the new element type has only two properties defined, *Name* and *Comment*. Follow the instructions presented in Section 4.4.3 to add any new properties to this element type.

4.4.5 CREATING NEW ASSOCIATION TYPES

 The process of creating new association types is very similar to that of creating new element types. This section describes the steps you can follow to create an association type that will record the role that executives play in business units of an enterprise. As in the previous sections, I assume that the dialog box User Extensibility is available.

1. Expand the node ASSOCIATION TYPE and select User Defined Associations.
2. Click the button New.... The dialog box Association Type Details appears.
3. Set the properties in the dialog box Association Type Details as shown in Figure 4.21. The property *Short Name* should be set to a label following the pattern 'A1' through 'A99.' You can notice that several associations in the default Designer/2000 Repository are extensions defined by the Oracle engineers.
4. Select the element type 'EXECUTIVE' from the list box *Element type* in the OWNING ELEMENT group of properties. Select the element type 'BUSINESS_UNIT' from the list box *Element type* in the TO group of properties. Leave the *Cardinality* list boxes set to '*Many*.' With these options, you are enabling your association to handle cases where an executive plays a role in several business units, and cases where a business unit may be associated with multiple executives.
5. Click OK to close the Association Type Details dialog box and return to the User Extensibility dialog box. The new association type is created and inserted in the list.
6. Click the button View... to see the names selected by the User Extensibility utility for the view and package that will be created for the new association type.
7. Add a new property to this association. The process is similar to the one described in Section 4.4.3. For the new property, type 'Role' in the Displayed Name text box and select the check box Mandatory.

8. Click Publish to publish the newly-created association type and its property.
9. Click OK in the alert box that prompts you to submit the DDL to generate the views and packages.

4.4.6 CREATING NEW TEXT TYPES

Finally, extend the Repository with a new text type that will hold biographical information about executives in the enterprise. Follow these steps to add the text type from the User Extensibility dialog box:

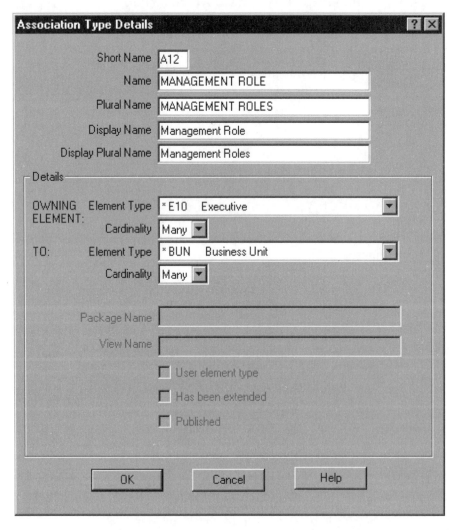

FIGURE 4.21   The Association Type Details dialog box.

1. Expand the node TEXT TYPES and select the node User Defined Text Types.
2. Click the button New…. The dialog box Text Type Details appears.
3. Set the properties in the dialog box Text Type Details as shown in Figure 4.22. The property *Name* must be set to a string with up to six characters, the first two of which must be 'UE.' Furthermore, notice that the *Maximum Length* property indicates only the maximum length of text displayed in one line by the Designer/2000 text editor. You can have as many such lines associated with a text type object as necessary.
4. Click OK to dismiss the Text Type Details dialog box.
5. Click Publish to publish the newly-created text type.

Notice that the button Submit DDL is not active for text type objects. The reason is that, unlike the other two Repository object types, multi-line text properties are not accessed though Repository views or API packages. In order to add the Biographical Notes text type to the Executives element type, follow this list of actions:

1. Expand the node UEBIO Biography and select the node Extended Usages.
2. Click the button New…. The dialog box Text Type Usage Details appears.
3. Set the radio button Element Type and select E10 Executive from the list box Text type, as shown in Figure 4.23.

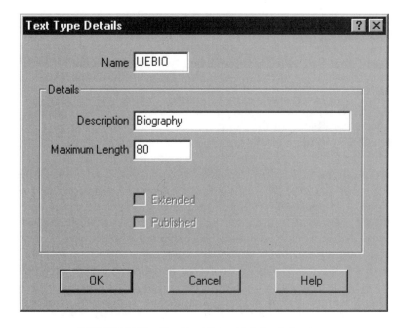

FIGURE 4.22 The Text Type Details dialog box.

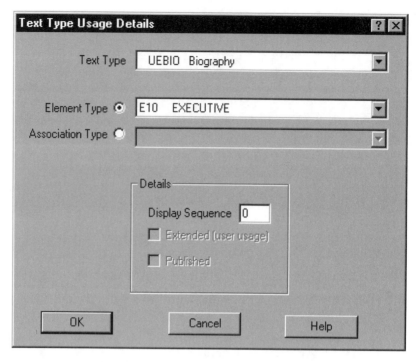

FIGURE 4.23   The Text Type Usage Details dialog box.

4. Click OK to close the dialog box Text Type Usage Details.
5. Click Publish in the right panel to publish the modification.
6. Click Cancel to close the dialog box User Extensibility.

4.4.7   EXTRACTING AND LOADING USER EXTENSIONS

Like other objects of the Repository, you may want to back up or move user extensions to other repositories. To help you in the process, the Repository Administration Utility provides utilities for extracting and loading user extensions. They
are implemented with the Oracle Server Export and Import tools and can be accessed by clicking the buttons Extract User Extensions and Load User Extensions , respectively. When you extract the user extensions of your Repository,
the Repository Administration Utility presents you with a report of all the extensions that will be exported. The report details the properties of each element type,
association type, and text type that you have added. In addition, new properties
and text type usages of element and association types are reported as well. The
report is produced in the form of a text file that you can save for your records.
The same report is produced when you are about to load user extensions from a
dump file.

4.5 SUMMARY

Designer/2000 is a client/server, multi-tiered, and database-driven suite of advanced software engineering tools. This chapter explains the architecture of Designer/2000 and focuses on the Repository model of the tools. Creating, maintaining, and expanding the Repository are major topics of this chapter. Other issues discussed here are:

- ❑ **Overview of Designer/2000**
  - ❑ Software Engineering and Tools
  - ❑ Components of Designer/2000
  - ❑ Characteristics of Designer/2000
  - ❑ Installing and Configuring the Designer/2000 Client Software
- ❑ **Designer/2000 Repository Model**
  - ❑ Elements
  - ❑ Associations
  - ❑ Topological Information about Diagrams
  - ❑ Rules
- ❑ **Repository Administration Utility**
  - ❑ Understanding the Physical Layout of the Repository
  - ❑ Preparing for the Creation of the Repository
  - ❑ Creating the Designer/2000 Repository
  - ❑ Maintaining the Designer/2000 Repository
  - ❑ Diagnosing and Optimizing the Repository
  - ❑ Creating and Maintaining Repository Users
- ❑ **Extending and Customizing the Repository**
  - ❑ Ways to Extend the Designer/2000 Repository
  - ❑ Steps to Extend the Designer/2000 Repository
  - ❑ Extending Properties of Existing Objects
  - ❑ Creating New Element Types
  - ❑ Creating New Association Types
  - ❑ Creating New Text Types
  - ❑ Extracting and Loading User Extensions

Chapter 5

MAINTAINING APPLICATION SYSTEMS

- ♦ Creating and Maintaining Application Systems
- ♦ Creating and Maintaining Application Objects
- ♦ User-Defined Object Sets
- ♦ Summary

The work performed using the Designer/2000 tools and components is organized by application systems. At any point in time, you analyze, model, design, and generate in the context of one application. Every piece of information you enter and all the Repository objects you create fall into a hierarchy tree that has an application system at the root. Part Two of the book will discuss how to divide the information "pie" of your enterprise into "slices," or application systems. This chapter will explain how you can create and maintain application systems and objects within these application systems.

5.1 CREATING AND MAINTAINING APPLICATION SYSTEMS

All the application management functions in Designer/2000 are performed in the Repository Object Navigator. These include creating, opening, closing, renaming, saving, and deleting the application; maintaining multiple versions of an application; and controlling user access. In order to be able to create new applications or maintain existing ones, the Repository user account you use must be assigned a role Manager. Chapter 4 explained how you can assign this role to one or more Repository users. The following sections will detail a series of actions you can perform in the Repository Object Navigator to create and maintain application systems. In order to launch the Repository Object Navigator from the Designer/2000 launch pad click the Navigator button 🔲.

When you first launch the Repository Object Navigator, you are presented with the dialog box Welcome To The Repository Object Navigator shown in Figure 5.1. This dialog helps you get started with tasks like creating a new application system, opening an existing one, searching the Repository, and filtering out groups of objects in the Navigator. The following sections discuss these and many other tasks accomplished in the Repository Object Navigator.

5.1.1 CREATING APPLICATION SYSTEMS

You can create a new application system by selecting the radio button Create a New Application in the Welcome dialog box shown in Figure 5.1. To create an application system explicitly, issue one of the following commands:

❑ Click the icon New Application 🔲 on the Repository Object Navigator toolbar.
❑ Select File | New Application... from the Repository Object Navigator menu.
❑ Press CTRL+N.

In all cases, an application will be created in its own untitled window, and the cursor will be positioned in the application Name node, waiting for your

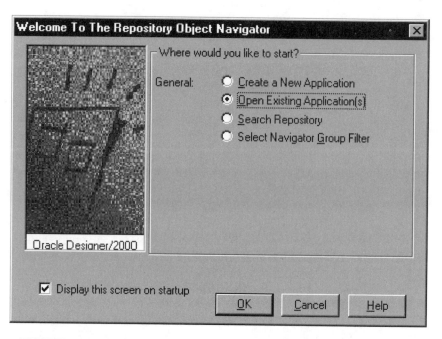

FIGURE 5.1 The Welcome To The Repository Object Navigator dialog box.

input. You can type the application name here or you can click the property *Name* in the application's Property Palette and enter it there. Usually, the abbreviated name of the information system serves as its name in the Designer/2000's Repository. Acronyms of the system are often good candidates to name an application system, provided they are well understood by your audience and are not cryptic.

Name is the only property required for an application to exist. A visual indicator of this is that, when the application is created, this property is displayed in red in the Property Palette. Other properties, such as *Owner* and *Version Date*, are automatically filled in when the new application is saved. They are displayed in

 By default, the dialog box Welcome To The Repository Object Navigator will appear each time you launch the Navigator. Fairly soon, you will become familiar with the Navigator to the point where you will not need the assistance of this dialog to accomplish the tasks discussed here. To stop displaying the Welcome dialog box, select Options | General Settings… and clear the check box Show Welcome Screen.

In order to create an application system, you must be a Repository user with the Manager role.

green in the Property Palette of the application. The other properties, displayed in normal color, may not be filled in when the application is created, but should be populated during the requirements definition and analysis phase of the system. Figure 5.2 shows the property settings of a new application system.

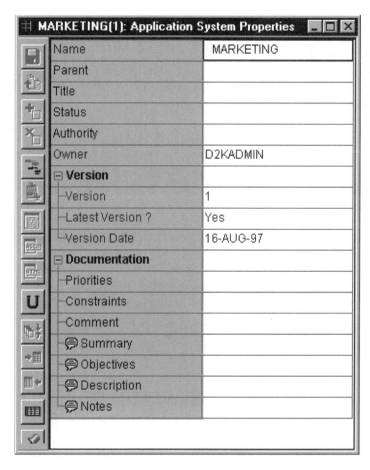

FIGURE 5.2   The Property Palette of a new application system.

5.1.2 SAVING APPLICATION SYSTEMS

A visual indicator that the application system contains uncommitted changes is the appearance of the iconic button Save on the Repository Object Navigator's horizontal toolbar. If the button is enabled, as in ▣, changes to the application properties still need saving; if the button is disabled, as in ▐, the application represents a committed view of the Repository. Another indicator that the application may have changes pending is the enabled Save button in the Property Palette of the application. You may commit changes to properties of an application in any of the following ways:

❑ Click the Save button ▣ on the Repository Object Navigator toolbar or on the Property Palette toolbar.
❑ Select File | Save from the Repository Object Navigator menu.
❑ Press CTRL+S.

5.1.3 OPENING APPLICATION SYSTEMS

You may open an existing application system by selecting the radio button Open Existing Application(s) or by issuing any of the following commands:

❑ Click the Open button ▣ on the toolbar.
❑ Choose File | Open from the Repository Object Navigator menu.
❑ Press CTRL+O.

The dialog box Open Application that appears lists all the applications that you can access (see Figure 5.3). By default, only the latest versions of the application systems is listed, although you can force all the versions of the applications to be displayed by clearing the check box Show Current Versions Only?. The name of the Repository user who owns the application is displayed together with the application. Select the check box Show Privileges? as shown in Figure 5.3, to list the privileges you have on each application. To open one or more applications, select them from the list and click OK. Use the standard Windows SHIFT+CLICK and CTRL+CLICK commands to select multiple applications. To open the application in ReadOnly mode, place a check mark in the check box Open in ReadOnly Mode? at the bottom of the list.

5.1.4 FILTERING GROUPS OF OBJECTS

The Repository Object Navigator organizes objects by groups according to their use in the system analysis, design, and development tasks. Figure 5.4 shows the groups of objects displayed by default in the Navigator. The classification of objects in these groups is based on their purpose, therefore you may find the same

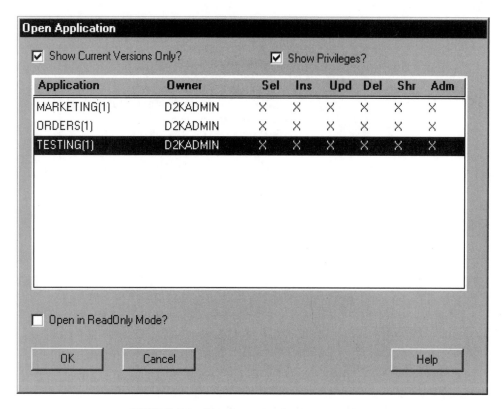

FIGURE 5.3   The Open Application dialog box.

object under more than one group. For example, entities are members of the groups Enterprise Modelling, Entity/Relationship Modelling, and C++ Object Layer Generator.

You can control which of these categories are displayed in the Navigator by selecting View | Include Navigator Groups… from the menu. In the dialog box Include Navigator Groups select those groups that you want to view in the Navigator and clear the ones you do not want to see. Figure 5.5 shows this dialog with the default groups selected.

5.1.5 CLOSING APPLICATION SYSTEMS

You can close an application in either of the following ways:

❑   Choose File | Close from the Repository Object Navigator menu.
❑   Press CTRL+W.

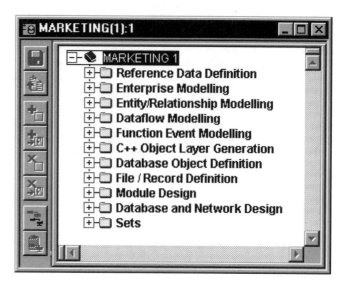

FIGURE 5.4 The object groups displayed by default in the Repository Object Navigator.

If unsaved changes exist, you are prompted to commit them to the database before closing the application.

5.1.6 RENAMING APPLICATION SYSTEMS

One way to rename an application is to open it and then modify the *Name* property in the Property Palette. A second way, which allows you to rename multiple applications without opening them, is to select Application | Rename... from the Repository Object Navigator menu. This action brings up the dialog box shown in Figure 5.6.

In this dialog box, enter the new name of the application to the right of the current name and click Rename to execute the command.

5.1.7 FREEZING AND UNFREEZING APPLICATION SYSTEMS

On some occasions, you need to take a snapshot of the application and preserve it in this state for a period of time. On such occasions, you may "freeze" the application, or prevent users of the Repository from modifying any of the objects in that application. The reverse may also be true. You may want to return a previously frozen application to an updateable state. To perform these tasks, select Application | Freeze/Unfreeze... from the Repository Object Naviga-

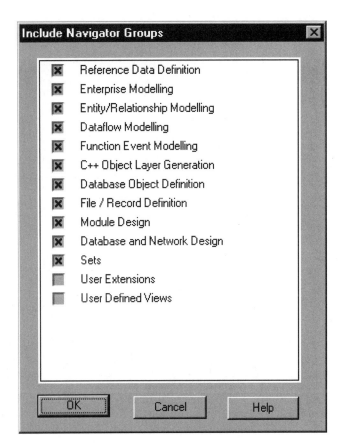

FIGURE 5.5 The Include Navigator Groups dialog box.

tor menu. The dialog box Application Freeze/Unfreeze appears, as shown in Figure 5.7. This dialog box lists all the applications that the current user can modify. To reverse the freeze/unfreeze state of one or more applications, select them in the list and click the Freeze/Unfreeze button.

5.1.8 CREATING MULTIPLE VERSIONS OF APPLICATION SYSTEMS

For long-running or large projects, you often need to maintain multiple versions of the applications. For example, when major milestones are reached, such as the conclusion of the requirements planning phase, the analysis phase, or the design phase, you may want to baseline the application and create a new version for use in the next phase. To create a new version of an application, select Application | New Version from the Repository Object Navigator

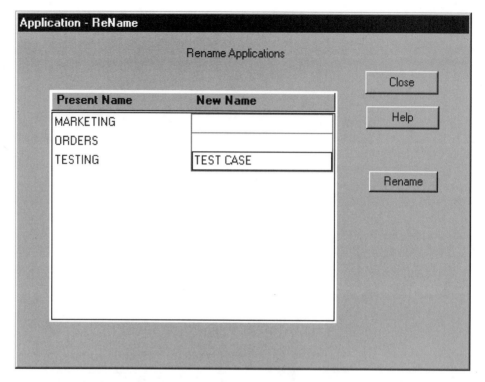

FIGURE 5.6   The Application Rename dialog box.

menu. In the Application New Version dialog box that appears (see Figure 5.8), select the desired application and click the button New Version.

At this point, the current version of the application is frozen and a new version is created. If the application contains a large number of objects, the process of creating a new version of it may require long-running transactions that modify the Repository. These types of transactions would benefit from a dedicated large rollback segment. The drop-down list box at the bottom of the dialog box allows you to assign the transaction of creating a new version to a particular rollback segment.

When the Repository Object Navigator creates a new version of the application system, it simply increments the current version number by one unit. So the version numbers of these systems are 1, 2, 3, and so on. On some occasions, you may want a finer granularity of the version numbers of these applications. For example, you may want to maintain versions 1.1, 1.2, and 1.3 of the ORDERS application system for ongoing minor modifications and switch to version 2.0 when a major upgrade of the system occurs. In order to implement this type of version-

Application - Freeze/UnFreeze

Change Status of Application System Versions

| Close |
| Help |

Application	Status
MARKETING(1)	
ORDERS(1)	
TESTING(1)	

| Freeze/Unfreeze |

| Objects Shared From Other Applications... | Objects Shared by Other Applications... |

FIGURE 5.7 The Application Freeze/Unfreeze dialog box.

ing scheme, click inside the text box Version and type the new version number of the application.

5.1.9 COPYING APPLICATION SYSTEMS

During extensive design and development activities it is often desirable to create a new application as a copy of an existing one. For example, during the analysis of the business areas of the enterprise it is very common to maintain information that applies to the entire business area in one application system. As information systems are developed to address the needs of the business area, the design effort for these systems may start from a copy of the business area application system. To copy applications, select Application | Copy... from the Repository Object Navigator menu. This action displays the dialog box Application Copy, shown in Figure 5.9. Select the application you want to copy, provide the name of the new application in the New Name text box, then click Copy. As

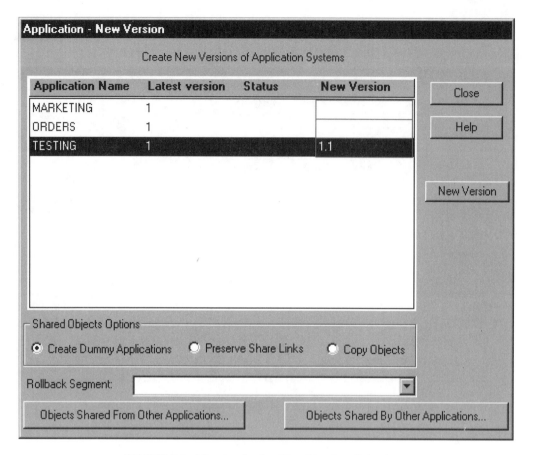

FIGURE 5.8 The Application New Version dialog box.

in other similar situations, assign the transaction to a dedicated large rollback segment by selecting it from the list box Rollback Segment.

5.1.10 DELETING APPLICATION SYSTEMS

In order to delete applications, select Application | Delete... from the Repository Object Navigator menu. This action displays the dialog box Application Delete, shown in Figure 5.10.

In this dialog box you can pick one or more applications from the list and press the Delete button to remove them from the Repository. This operation is another that may benefit from a large dedicated rollback segment. You can associate the delete process with a rollback segment by picking it from the drop-down list box at the bottom of the screen.

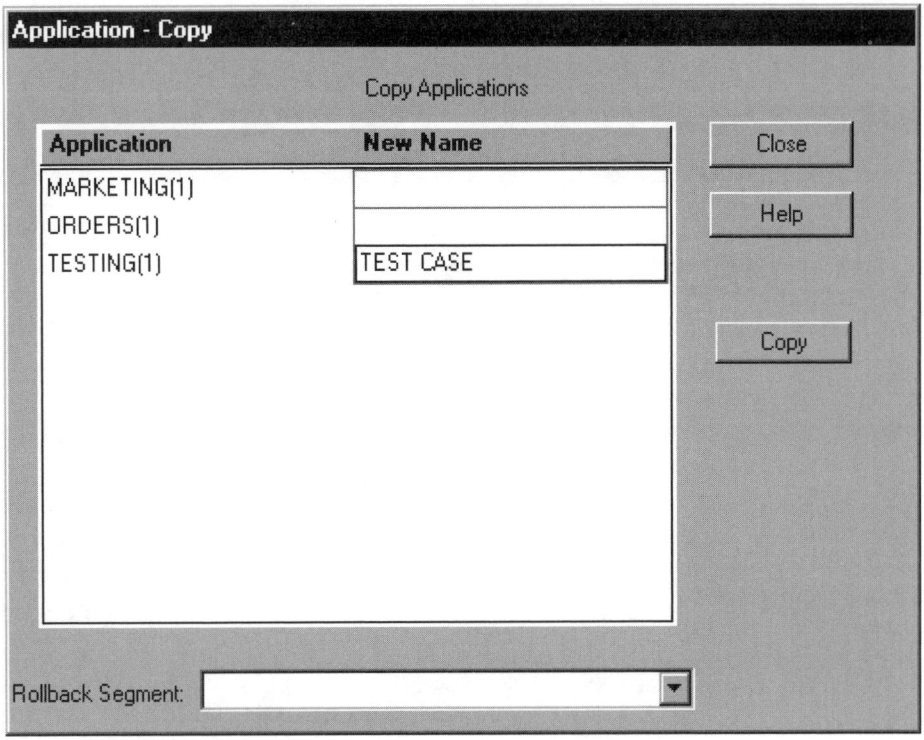

FIGURE 5.9 The Application Copy dialog box.

As you will see later in the chapter, objects of an application may be shared with other applications. When you delete the application that contains the master objects, also decide what to do with the replicas of these objects shared by other applications. You can stop sharing these objects, make another application system their owner, or copy them to each application that references them. Until you resolve these references, though, you will not be able to delete an application. To view the shared objects of the application you are about to delete, click the button Objects Shared by Other Applications... in the dialog box Application Delete. This action invokes the dialog box shown in Figure 5.11.

In this dialog box, you can select one or more shared objects and decide to stop sharing them with the other applications or to transfer their ownership to one of these applications. I assume that you have selected the shared entity ORDER as shown in Figure 5.11. When you click the button UnShare, any references of this entity are removed from the sharing application system MARKET-ING; when you click Transfer, the ownership of the object is moved from the application ORDERS about to be deleted to the application MARKETING that

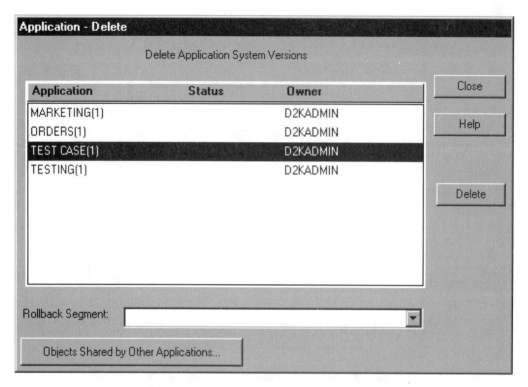

FIGURE 5.10   The Application Delete dialog box.

references the object thus resulting in a copy of the shared entity to the application MARKETING.

5.1.11 MANAGING USER ACCESS

Analyzing the requirements and designing an application system are teamwork that requires the contribution and effort of multiple persons. In order to succeed in the effort, you must manage carefully the access of users to the information in the Repository. As discussed in Chapter 4, the Repository Administration Utility allows you to create three levels of users beside the owner of the Repository: application managers, users with read/write privileges, and users with only read privileges.

A finer set of privileges may be granted to Repository users in the Repository Object Navigator. Here you can grant privileges on a particular application to one or more users, or you can grant one user privileges on one or more applications. The privileges that can be granted to a user are Select, Insert, Update, Delete, Share, and Admin. The first four privileges allow users to select, insert, update, and delete Primary Accessed Control objects of an application; Share al-

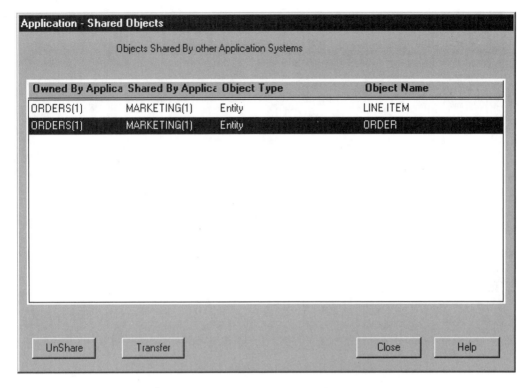

FIGURE 5.11   The Application Shared Objects dialog box.

lows users to share these objects with other applications; and Admin, when granted to users who already have the Repository role of Manager, enables them to manage application access by other users, to rename, to freeze and unfreeze, and to maintain multiple versions of the application.

To grant privileges to one or more users one application at a time, you must select Application | Grant Access by Appl... from the Repository Object Navigator menu. In the dialog box Application – Grant Access by Application that is displayed, pick the desired application from the drop-down list box For Application, as shown in Figure 5.12.

In order to be able to provide other Repository users access to an application, you must either be its owner or be granted Admin privileges on it. At the same time, you must have the Repository role Manager.

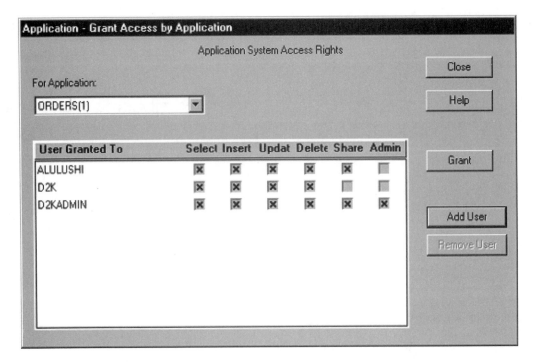

FIGURE 5.12   The Grant Access by Application dialog box.

When you do so, the multi-record area of the dialog box is populated with the Repository users that have privileges on the chosen application. The actual privileges are displayed as well. At this point, you can do one of the following actions:

❑   Check or uncheck the check boxes to grant or revoke privileges to users.
❑   Click the button Add User to display a list of Repository users who do not have privileges on the application; you can pick one or more users from this list and give them the appropriate access rights.
❑   Select a user and click the button Remove User to revoke all privileges on the application from this user.

To grant privileges for one or more applications to a particular user, choose Application | Grant Access by User... from the Repository Object Navigator menu. In the dialog box Grant Access by User (see Figure 5.13), select a user from the drop-down list box For User.

All the applications for which this user has privileges will be displayed in the multi-record area of the dialog box. At this point, you can do one of the following actions:

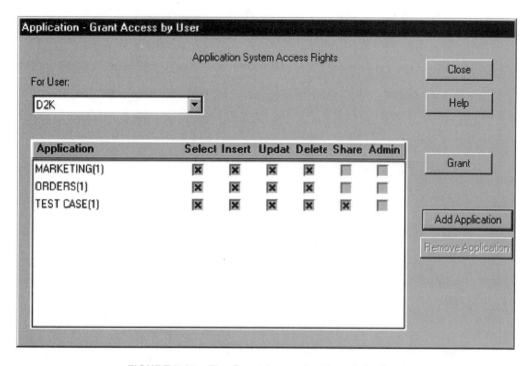

FIGURE 5.13 The Grant Access by User dialog box.

❏ Check or uncheck the check boxes to grant or revoke privileges of the user for applications.

❏ Click the button Add Application to display a list of applications for which the current user does not have access. From this list, you can pick one or more applications to allow the selected user to access them.

❏ Select an application and click the button Remove Application to prevent the user from accessing the application.

5.1.12 TRANSFERRING THE OWNERSHIP OF APPLICATION SYSTEMS

Although no limit exists on the number of applications a user may own, the maintenance and management of the Repository will benefit if some limit exists on the number of applications owned by any given user. Therefore, in cases when one user owns a number of applications, I recommend that she transfer the ownership of some of these applications over to other users. To transfer the ownership of an application, you must be the owner of the application and choose Application | Transfer Ownership... from the Repository Object Navigator menu. This action causes the dialog box shown in Figure 5.14 to be displayed.

The dialog box Application Transfer lists all the applications that you currently own. To transfer the ownership of an application to another user, click the New Owner drop-down list, pick the name of the new user from the list, and click the button Transfer.

5.1.13 ARCHIVING APPLICATION SYSTEMS

Another important group of application management operations that you can perform in the Repository Object Navigator is archiving an application in the Repository archive tables, exporting the archive tables to an operating system file, importing from an export file into the archive tables, and restoring an application in the Repository from the archive tables. The main purpose of archiving and restoring is to port an application from one Repository to another; software configuration management comes a close second.

In order to export an application to a file, all the data that the application contains must be transferred first to a set of tables that serve as a staging area. These tables are known as XT tables because their names begin with 'XT.' To initi-

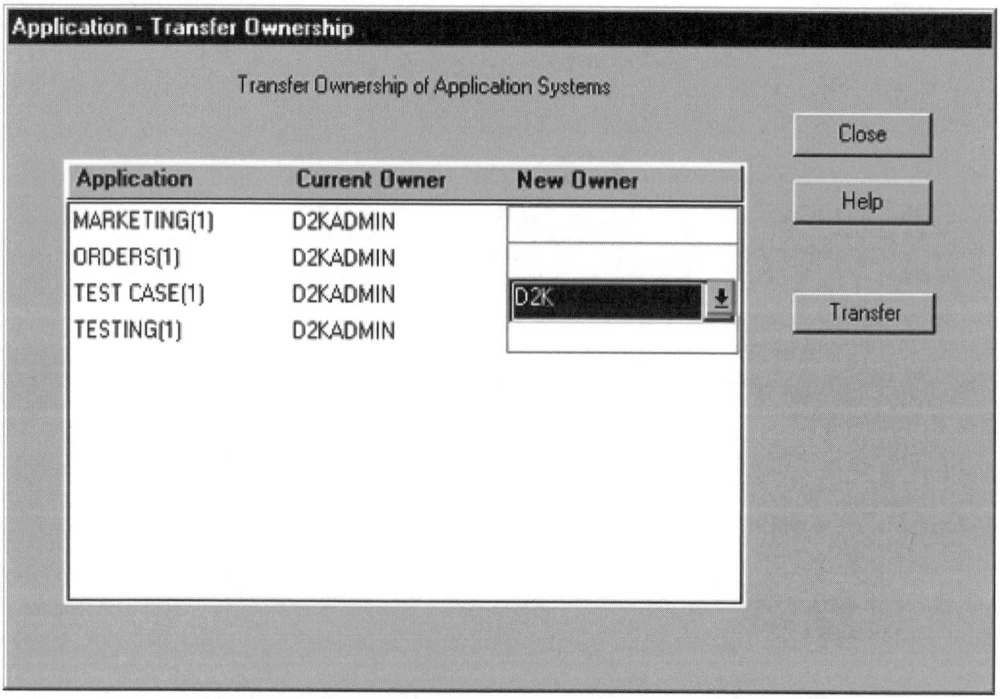

Application - Transfer Ownership

Transfer Ownership of Application Systems

[Close]

[Help]

Application	Current Owner	New Owner
MARKETING(1)	D2KADMIN	
ORDERS(1)	D2KADMIN	
TEST CASE(1)	D2KADMIN	D2K
TESTING(1)	D2KADMIN	

[Transfer]

FIGURE 5.14   The Application Transfer Ownership dialog box.

The drop-down list New Owner contains only Repository users who have been assigned the role Manager.

ate the transfer, select Application | Archive... from the Repository Object Navigator menu. If this is the first time you invoke this utility, the Repository Object Navigator asks you to specify the tablespaces where the XT tables and corresponding indexes will be created. You must create these tables to be able to proceed with the archiving. On the other hand, if you have archived an application system before, and the archive is not empty, the Repository Object Navigator asks you to clear the archive before proceeding. Choosing Application | Archive... from the menu invokes the Application Archive dialog box shown in Figure 5.15.

In this dialog box, you may select one or more applications from the list and click Archive to begin the transfer of data from the Repository tables to the XT tables. For large applications, this operation may initiate long transactions that would benefit from a large dedicated rollback segment. You can pick such a segment from the drop-down list at the bottom of the screen.

After the archiving process completes, the Repository Object Navigator automatically invokes the Application Export dialog box, shown in Figure 5.16. You can invoke this dialog box by selecting Application | Export... from the menu, as well, provided that at least one application has been archived in the archive tables.

In this dialog box, you can specify the name and location of the file where data from the XT tables will be written, and click Export to initiate the export

In Figure 5.15, the application MARKETING is selected for archival, but Figure 5.16 shows that the archive contains an additional application ORDERS of type Skeleton. The reason is that the application MARKETING is sharing some objects from the application ORDERS. In order to maintain the integrity of the application when it is archived, these referenced objects must be archived as well. Since objects can exist only in the context of an application, the Repository Object Navigator artificially creates a 'skeleton' application for the sole purpose of hosting the shared objects in the archive.

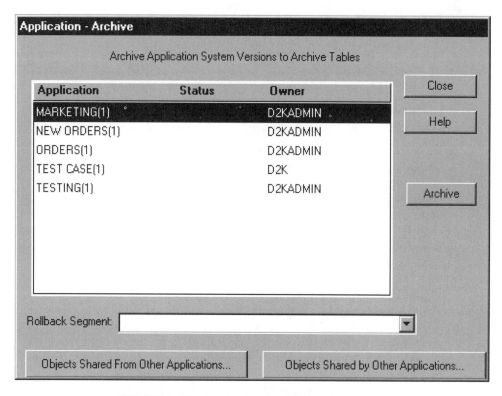

FIGURE 5.15 The Application Archive dialog box.

process. Clicking the List... button displays the standard Windows Open dialog box, which allows you to browse the directory structure of your file system in order to find the location of the export file. After the export is complete, you can back up the file or transfer it to the physical location of the Repository where you intend to migrate the application.

5.1.14 RESTORING APPLICATION SYSTEMS

In order to complete the opposite task, that is, loading an application in the Repository from an archive, you must select Application | Restore... from the Repository Object Navigator menu. In the Application Restore dialog box (see Figure 5.17), specify the file that contains the exported application and click Import to bring the data over to the archive tables. If the XT tables are not empty, you are prompted to clear them before proceeding with the import. You may also clear the archive by clicking the Reset button. After the application is in the archive, you can click Restore to move it to the regular Repository structures.

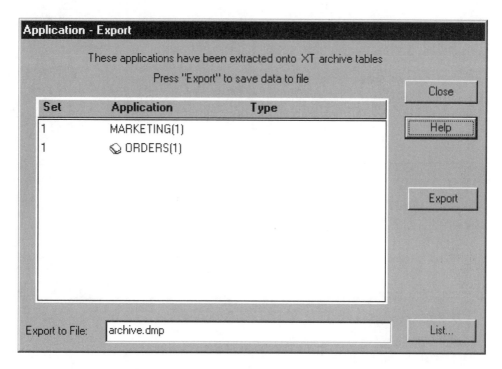

FIGURE 5.16   The Application Export dialog box.

If the Repository contains an application with the same name as one of the applications being restored, you need to provide a new name for the incoming application in the New Name column, as shown in Figure 5.17. After the restore operation completes successfully, the status of the application in the archive becomes "Restored."

If the application being restored contains user extensions that conflict with the Repository, the button UE Report is enabled. By clicking this button, you can see a listing of the conflicting objects and take steps to resolve the conflicts. Specifically, you may want to load the user extensions from the source Repository into the target Repository. Chapter 4 discussed the process of archiving and restoring the user extensions of a Designer/2000 Repository.

After you finish restoring the data, you may want to clear the archive structures. For this, click the Reset button in the Application Restore dialog box, or select Application | Reset from the Repository Object Navigator menu. When you export an application system into a dump file, you export the Repository access privileges that users have on the application. When the exported application is loaded into another Repository, these access privileges are moved into the target Repository together with the rest of the application data. However, the target and

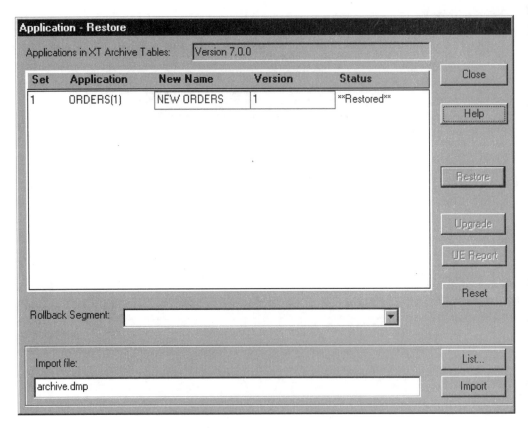

FIGURE 5.17 The Application Restore dialog box.

destination repositories may not have the same set of users with the same set of privileges. In order to synchronize the user access privileges of an application system loaded from a different Repository, you must run the Full Reconcile utility in the destination utility. Chapter 4 discusses how to perform a full reconciliation from the Repository Administration Utility.

5.2 CREATING AND MAINTAINING APPLICATION OBJECTS

As I discussed earlier in the chapter, all objects in the Repository exist in the context of an application. Designer/2000 tools, such as Business Process Modeller, Entity Relationship Diagrammer, and Function Hierarchy Diagrammer, allow you to easily create or update most of the objects in your application system. Each of these tools serves the purpose of grouping the Repository objects based on the phase of the project and on the type of analysis being done. The Repository Object Navigator, on the other hand, because it offers a unified view of the Repository, allows you to access, create, and modify all the object types. Although the chapters to come will discuss extensively how to create and maintain properties of objects, this section will discuss issues related to managing objects in application systems. These issues include:

- ❑ Sharing and unsharing objects
- ❑ Transferring ownership of objects
- ❑ Copying and deleting objects

5.2.1 SHARING AND UNSHARING OBJECTS

 An application system in Designer/2000 normally models one business area of your enterprise. In an enterprise-wide information engineering scheme, the most important, if not all, business areas are modeled, thus resulting in several applications in the Repository. Because the business areas of your enterprise share data and information, your models in the Repository need to share data as well. When an object is shared between two or more applications, the application that owns the object maintains the master copy of the object; the other applications reference this master copy and contain a read-only version of it.

In order to share an object, you must have the privilege Share on the application that owns the object, and follow these steps:

1. Select the object you want to share in the Repository Object Navigator object tree.
2. Choose Utilities | Share.... The Share Objects dialog box appears, as shown in Figure 5.18.
3. Select the application with which you want to share the object from the drop-down list Share with Application, to the right.
4. Refine the granularity of the Share operation. Refer to Section 5.2.4 for more details on this topic.
5. Click Share to complete the task.

When you open the application that shares the object, you see the object in the hierarchy tree preceded by the open hand icon ☜, which indicates that the object is shared. Although you can view the properties of the object in the Property Palette, you cannot edit any of them, since only the owner application can modify the object.

An elegant way to share objects between applications is the following:

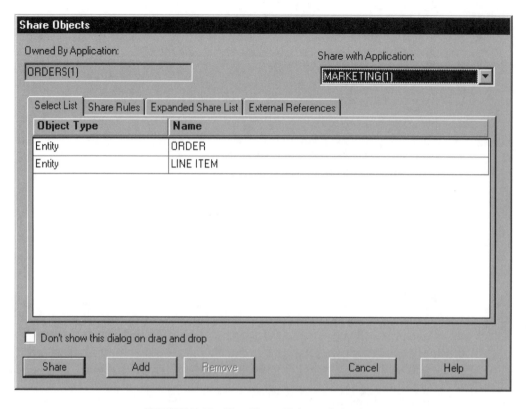

FIGURE 5.18   The Share Objects dialog box.

1. Open the applications in the Repository Object Navigator; size and position the windows so you can see both of them.
2. Select the object to be shared, drag it over, and drop it in the window of the application that will share the object. The Share Objects dialog box appears.
3. Click Share to complete the task.

While sharing is used to offer your objects for use to other applications, unsharing removes the shared references of objects from your application. To unshare an object, follow the steps listed here:

1. Select the shared object in the Repository Object Navigator object tree. Look for the iconic indicator ➥ that distinguishes shared objects.
2. Choose Utilities | UnShare.... Alternatively, you may press DELETE from the keyboard. The UnShare Objects dialog box appears (see Figure 5.19).
3. Click UnShare to complete the task.

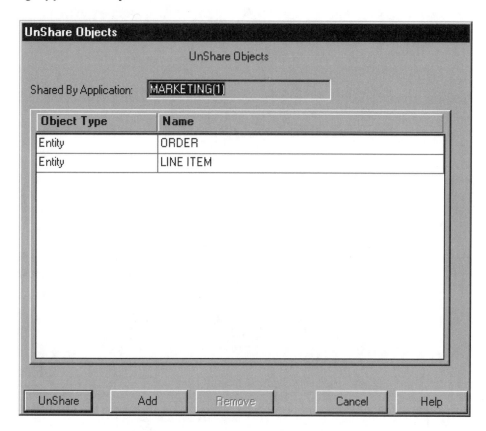

FIGURE 5.19   The UnShare Objects dialog box.

Note that you share an object from the application that owns the object, but unshare it from the application that references the shared object.

5.2.2 TRANSFERRING OWNERSHIP OF OBJECTS

 When sharing objects, the application that owns the object remains its owner, and the target application receives a reference read-only copy of the object. Transferring the ownership of an object is in a sense the opposite of sharing. Transferring an object from the current application to another one makes the other application the owner of the object and leaves a shared copy of the object in the current application. In order to be able to transfer the ownership of an object, you must have the Share privilege in the application that owns the object, and Insert and Update privileges in the target application. Furthermore, only Primary Accessed Component (PAC) objects may be transferred; Secondary Access Component (SAC) objects can be transferred only if the PAC object that owns them is transferred.

To transfer the ownership of an object, perform these steps:

1. Select the object in the Repository Object Navigator object tree.
2. Choose Utilities | Transfer Ownership.... The Transfer Ownership of Objects dialog box appears, as shown in Figure 5.20.
3. Select the application that will become the new owner of the object from the drop-down list Transfer to Application to the right.
4. Click Transfer to complete the task.

5.2.3 COPYING OBJECTS

Sharing, unsharing, and transferring ownership of objects are tasks that can be completed only for PAC objects in the application. Another command in this category is Copy. This command

---

Transfer Ownership of Objects

Owned By Application:	Transfer Ownership to Application:
ORDERS(1)	MARKETING(1) ▼

Object Type	Name
Entity	ORDER
Entity	LINE ITEM

☐ Don't show this dialog on drag and drop

| Transfer | Add | Remove | Cancel | Help |

FIGURE 5.20   The Transfer Ownership of Objects dialog box.

creates a new copy of PAC objects and new instances for all the SAC objects that depend on it. For example, copying an entity creates a new entity that contains the same attributes and associations as the original entity. Follow these steps in order to copy an object:

1. Select the object in the Repository Object Navigator object tree.
2. Choose Utilities | Copy.... The Copy Objects dialog box appears (see Figure 5.21).
3. From the drop-down list to the right, select the application where the new copy of the object will be created. By default, this is the current application.
4. Enter the name and short name for the new object in the fields to the right of the old object, as shown in Figure 5.21. These attributes are required only if the application where the objects will be copied already contains objects with the same name or short name.
5. Click Copy to create the new object.

An easier way to copy an object is to select it in the source application, and, while pressing CTRL, drag and drop it in the hierarchy tree of the destination application. This action invokes the dialog box Copy Objects, from which you can

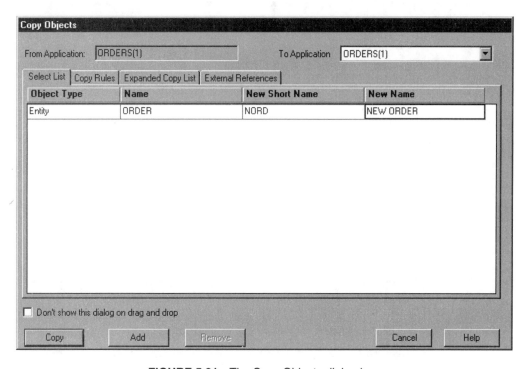

FIGURE 5.21 The Copy Objects dialog box.

copy the object as discussed above. I assume here that both the source and the destination application systems are opened in the Repository Object Navigator.

5.2.4 REFINING THE GRANULARITY OF SHARE AND COPY OPERATIONS

The process of sharing and copying objects is very easy and straightforward. However, you need to be aware of the way the Repository Object Navigator performs these operations in order to take advantage of them. As I mentioned earlier, you can issue the Copy or Share command only against PAC objects; by default, the Navigator will extend the operations to all the appropriate SAC elements of such objects. The Share Objects and Copy Objects dialog boxes allow you to control the granularity of the operations and to select precisely those associated elements that you want to share or copy together with the parent object.

In order to better understand this feature, consider an application system that contains two entities ORDER and LINE ITEM with a one-to-many relationship defined between them. The ends of this relationship are stored in the form of SAC elements dependent on each entity, just like the attributes or the unique identifiers are. When you copy the entity ORDER you can decide whether or not

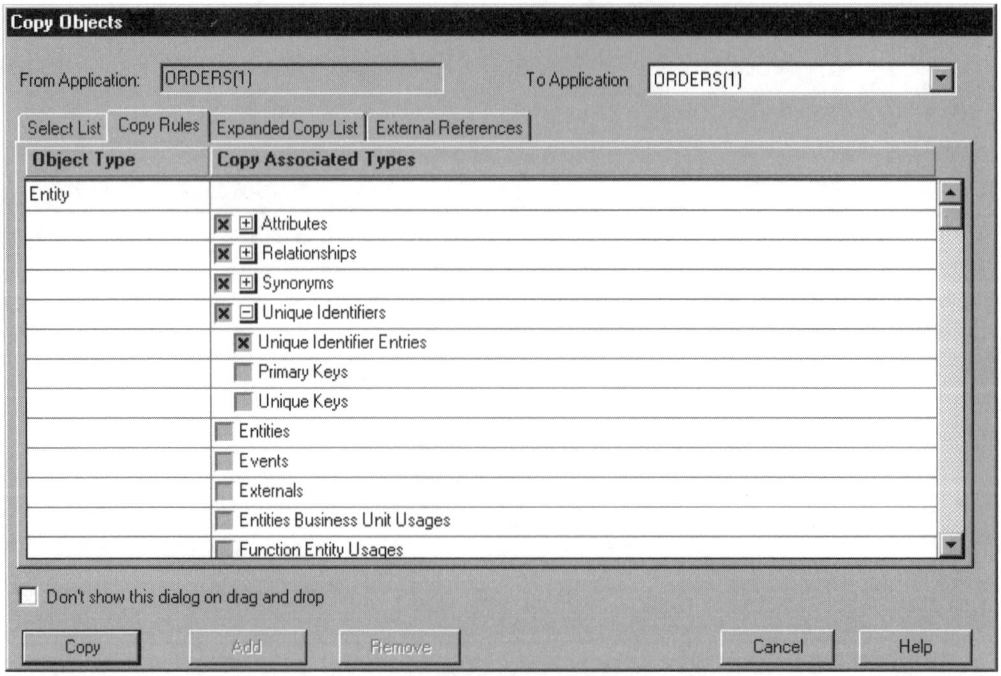

FIGURE 5.22 The Copy Rules tab of the Copy Objects dialog box.

these elements are copied. In the Copy Rules tab of the Copy Objects dialog box, you can select which categories of SAC objects will be affected by the operation. In the tab shown in Figure 5.22, attributes, relationships, synonyms, and unique identifiers will be copied with the entity. Each of these categories may have other categories of elements that depend on it, as in the case of unique identifiers. To remove one of these categories, clear the corresponding check box.

For a finer level of granularity, switch to the tab Expanded Copy List, shown in Figure 5.23. This tab displays the actual elements from the categories selected in the tab Copy Rules. By selecting or clearing the check boxes associated with each element, you instruct the Repository Object Navigator to include or exclude the element from the operation.

In the case shown in Figure 5.23, the relationship 'ORDER composed of LINE ITEM' is included in the working set. This relationship can be copied only if the entity LINE ITEM is included in the set. To resolve this problem, the Navigator creates a shared copy of the entity LINE ITEM in the target application. You also have the option to copy this entity together with the relationship end that requires it. To achieve this, switch to the tab External References and select the check box Copy for the entity. To include all the details of this entity in the copy list, click the button ReExpand. The tab External References is shown in Figure 5.24.

Copy Objects		

From Application: ORDERS(1)   To Application: ORDERS(1)

Select List | Copy Rules | Expanded Copy List | External References

Copy	Object Type	Object Name
☒	Entity	ORDER
☒	Relationship	ORDER composed of LINE ITEM
☒	Unique Identifier	ORDER ORD
☒	Unique Identifier Entry	⊟ ORDER ORDER NUMBER
☒	Attribute	─ORDER ORDER NUMBER
☒	Attribute	─ORDER CUSTOMER
☒	Attribute	─ORDER DESCRIPTION
☒	Attribute	─ORDER DELIVERY DATE
☒	Attribute	└ORDER ORDER DATE

☐ Don't show this dialog on drag and drop

Copy	Add	Remove		Cancel	Help

FIGURE 5.23 The Expanded Copy List tab of the Copy Objects dialog box.

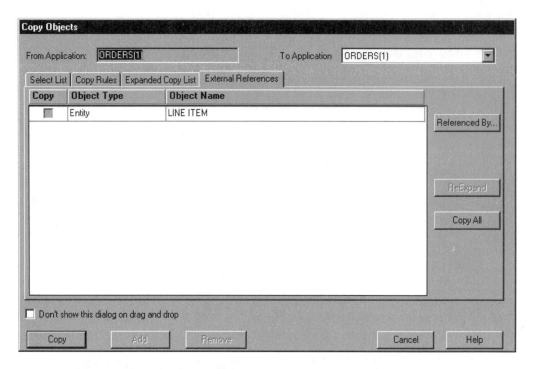

FIGURE 5.24   The External References tab of the Copy Objects dialog box.

Although the example provided in this section applies to the copy operation, similar actions can be taken to control the granularity of share operations. The Share Objects dialog box contains tabs that resemble in layout and functionality the tabs discussed in this section.

5.2.5   DELETING OBJECTS

In order to delete an object in the Repository Object Navigator, you simply select it in the hierarchy tree and choose Edit | Delete Object. If the object contains dependent objects and associations, the delete process is restricted, that is, it does not complete successfully if the object references or is associated with other PAC objects. Force Delete is the command used to remove from the Repository the PAC object being deleted and all its references and associations with other objects. In order to Force Delete a PAC object, do the following:

1. Select the object in the Repository Object Navigator object tree.
2. Choose Utilities | Force Delete.... The Force Delete dialog box appears. The Select List tab of this dialog contains a list of all the objects you selected to delete.

3. If you do not want to delete one or more objects in the list, select them and click the button Remove.

4. Click OK to proceed with the Force Delete of the objects that remain in the list.

Before starting the delete process, I recommend that you consider the scope of the action by inspecting the other three property tabs of the Force Delete dialog box. The Delete Rules tab shows the categories of objects that may be affected by the delete and what will happen to them if you proceed with the operation. The tab shown in Figure 5.25 captures the delete rules for attributes. You can see, for example, that the delete rule for allowable values is 'Delete' and for columns is 'Nullify Reference.' The meaning of these rules is that if an attribute is deleted, all the allowable values associated with it will be deleted; if a column refers to this attribute (because it is mapped by the Database Design Transformer, for example), the reference will be deleted but the column will not be otherwise affected.

For a condensed list of the actual objects that will be deleted when you carry on the operation, switch to the tab Expanded Delete List. To view the objects whose references to the element you are about to delete will be nullified, switch to the Expanded Nullify List tab.

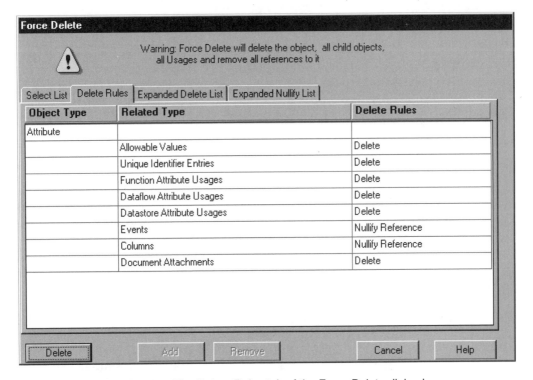

FIGURE 5.25 The Delete Rules tab of the Force Delete dialog box.

Because you cannot undo the Delete or Force Delete command, use it with caution and only after making sure you really want to delete an object.

5.3 USER-DEFINED OBJECT SETS

Section 5.2 discussed how you can share, copy, or transfer objects from one application to another within the same Repository. Although the functionality described there covers a good number of situations, it does not address the need to move objects between applications that reside in different repositories. Section 5.1.13 discussed how to move applications across repositories using the support of Designer/2000 for archiving and restoring application systems, but the functionality described there can be used only at the application level. This section shows how user-defined sets of objects can help you accomplish the same objectives, but at a finer level of granularity. In particular, this section will focus on the following topics:

❑ Creating and populating object sets
❑ Locking and unlocking object sets
❑ Checking objects in and out
❑ Loading and unloading objects

5.3.1 CREATING AND POPULATING OBJECT SETS

Object sets are objects that allow you to group together PAC objects from your application for the purpose of managing locks, backing them up, or transferring them to another Repository globally with one command, rather than individually. Object sets are listed at the bottom of the Repository Object Navigator's tree of PAC object types, under the listing group Sets. There are two types of sets:

❑ **Diagrams.** These are the diagrams you create and maintain using tools like the Entity Relationship Diagrammer, the Process Modeller, or the Design Editor.
❑ **User-Defined Sets.** Theses are groups of objects you create explicitly.

In the Repository Object Navigator you can create only user-defined sets by selecting the node User Defined Sets, and issuing one of the following commands:

❑ Select Edit | Create Object from the Repository Object Navigator menu.
❑ Click the icon Create Object 🔲 on the toolbar.

After the object set is created, enter its name in the object tree of the Navigator or in the Property Palette and save it. In order to add objects to the user-defined set, you must follow these steps:

1. Expand the node that represents the object set and then select the node Set Members.
2. Click the icon Create Association 🔲 on the toolbar.
3. In the dialog box Select Type that appears, select the element type you want to include in the set, for example, Business Functions.
4. Click OK to dismiss the Select Type dialog box. This action displays the dialog box Create Set Member Items that lists all the objects of the chosen type that exist in your application. Figure 5.26 shows this dialog box populated with business functions in the ORDERS application you created in the first three chapters.
5. Select one or more items in the list and click OK to add them to the object set.
6. Click Save.

If you want to remove an object from the set, simply select it and press DELETE.

5.3.2 LOCKING AND UNLOCKING USER-DEFINED SETS

One use of user-defined sets is to prevent modifications of several objects with one command, also known as locking. You can lock an object set by following these steps:

One way to create an object set and populate it at the same time is to select objects and check them out. This approach is discussed in Section 5.3.3.

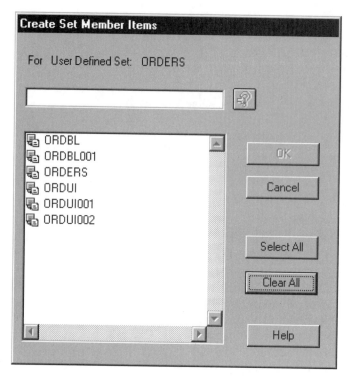

FIGURE 5.26 The Create Set Member Items dialog box.

1. Select the object set in the Repository Object Navigator's hierarchy tree.
2. Choose Utilities I Lock Set....
3. In the Lock dialog box that appears, click OK to lock the selected set.

After the set is locked, all its member objects in the application become read-only, and the lock iconic indicator 🔒 is displayed to the left of their names. In the Property Palette of the object set, the property *Status* is set to *'Locked,'* *Locked By* is set to your user name, and *Date Locked* is set to the date the set was locked.

Unlocking the set is done in the same fashion, except that you choose Utilities I Unlock Set... from the Repository Object Navigator menu.

5.3.3 CHECKING IN AND CHECKING OUT OBJECTS

You can use the Repository Object Navigator's check in/check out utility to back up and restore objects in your application, or move them from one Repository to another. In order to check out objects, they must be bundled in an object set. This set can be created and populated before the checkout procedure, or simultaneously in one action.

To check out objects, you must either select the object set in which they are placed, or, if that set does not exist, select the individual objects in the Navigator. Then choose Utilities | Check Out... to display the dialog box shown in Figure 5.27.

The layout of this dialog box is similar to dialog boxes used to copy or share objects. It contains four tabs whose functionalities are described below:

❏ **Set Objects.** This tab allows you to view, add, or remove the objects that will be checked out.

❏ **Check Out Rules.** This tab lists the element types that may be checked out together with the elements included in the set. You can set or clear the check boxes associated with these entries to include or exclude them from the set.

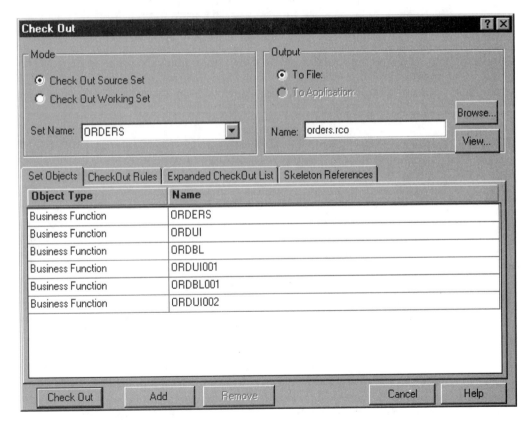

FIGURE 5.27 The Check Out dialog box.

❑ **Expanded Check Out List.** This tab lists the elements that may be checked out. You can include or exclude them according to your needs.

❑ **Skeleton References.** This tab lists all the objects referenced by objects included in the set. If the check box that precedes these elements is not set, only the references will be checked out. If the check box is set, the reference and the referenced object will be checked out.

By selecting a radio button in the Mode group, you can control how the objects will be checked out. When Check Out Source Set is selected, the Navigator will write out all the details needed to create the objects from scratch when the file is checked in; this option, known as source check out, corresponds to a full backup of the selected objects. When Check Out Working Set is selected, the check out file contains only the details required to update the objects that must already exist in the Repository where the file will be checked in; this option, also known as the working check out, corresponds to an incremental backup of the selected objects.

Your selection in the Mode group affects the extension of the file in which the object set will be checked out. Source sets are written to files with extension .RCO, whereas working sets are written to files with extension .RCI. You can click the button Browse... in the Output group of properties to display the Windows dialog box Check Out Object Set to File, which allows you to pick the location and name of the file where the information will be unloaded. After you have specified all the options, click Check Out to initiate the process. The progress of the work is shown in the dialog box Check Out Progress.

Checking files in is the reverse process. You select File | Check In... and specify your parameters in the Check In dialog box shown in Figure 5.28.

The radio button Check In to Source Application should be set if the objects you are about to check in already exist in the application you have selected from the list box Name, and if you want to update their properties. This option requires that you specify a file of extension .RCI in the Input group of properties. This file should have been produced by the Check Out process executed with the Check Out Working Set mode.

The radio button Check In to Working Application should be selected if the objects you check in do not exist in the application system chosen from the list box Name. In the Input group of properties, set the input file to a file with extension .RCO. Such a file must have been produced by a checkout process run with the Check Out Source Set option.

Finally, you may decide to upload the new objects to a new application. To do so, select the radio button Create New Working Application in the Mode group. Notice that the list box name is converted to a text item in which you can type the name of the new application. The input file in this case should be set to a

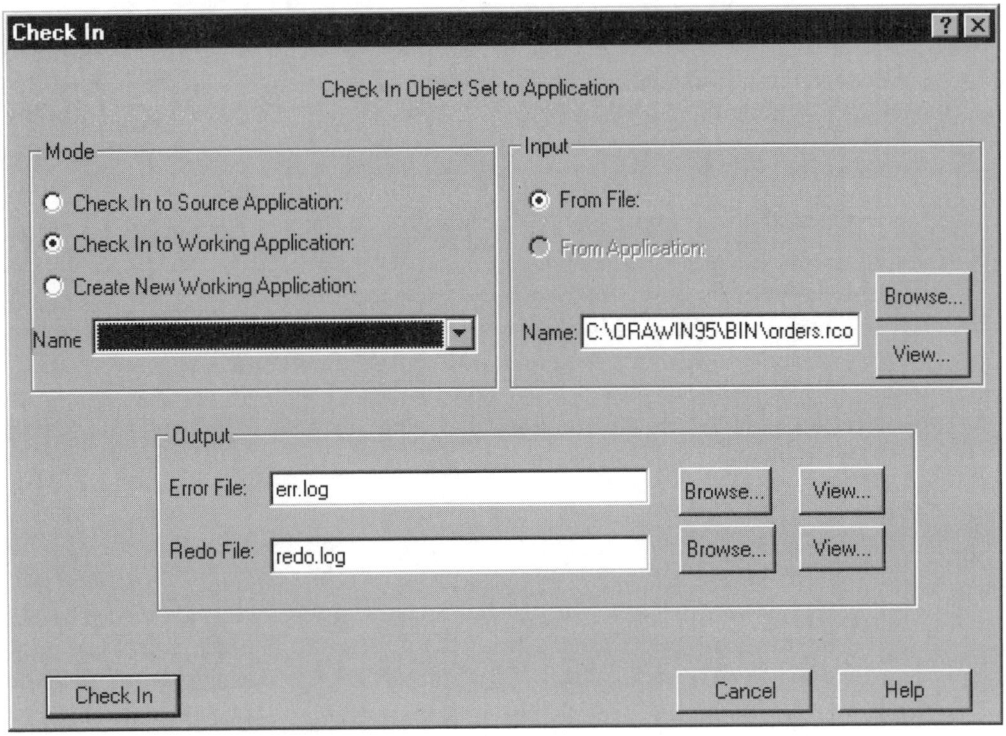

FIGURE 5.28   The Check In dialog box.

.RCO file. The Output group of properties in the Check In dialog box allows you to specify the name and location of an error log and redo file.

After all the settings are defined, click Check In to start the loading process. The status of the process is displayed in the dialog box Check In Progress. If the Check In process uploads objects in the source application, after the process completes, any locks to these objects are removed.

5.3.4   SAMPLE DESIGNER/2000 CONFIGURATION MANAGEMENT SCENARIO

The following scenario shows how you can use user-defined sets, the locking mechanism, and the check in/check out utilities of the Repository Object Navigator to enhance your productivity with Designer/2000. This scenario assumes that you have worked with an application system throughout the week and want to perform some additional tasks during the weekend. The Repository of your application is located in a UNIX database server, but you also have a smaller

Designer/2000 Repository created in the Personal Oracle database in your laptop. Here is how you can use this smaller Repository to work during the weekend and upload the modifications on Monday morning without violating the integrity of the application system.

Friday afternoon:

1. Connect to the Designer/2000 Repository in the UNIX server.
2. Create a user-defined set and include in the set all the objects you will need to access during the weekend.
3. Check out the set using the option Check Out Source Set. You obtain an .RCO file with all the data needed to create these objects in the Personal Oracle Repository. The process also locks the objects you checked out so that other people may not update their properties while you will be working with them.

Saturday morning:

1. Connect to the Designer/2000 Repository in the Personal Oracle database.
2. Check in the .RCO file you created at work on Friday. If this is the first time you are checking in objects from the application system, select the option Create New Working Application in the Check In dialog box and provide a name for the application that will be created. Otherwise, use the option Check In to Working Application.
3. Work with the objects in the application as you normally would.

Saturday afternoon:

1. Complete the work for the weekend.
2. Check out the object set you loaded in the morning. Use the option Check Out Working Set when checking out the objects. This process produces an .RCI file that you will use to upload the changes in the master Repository on Monday morning.

Sunday: Have a Good Time!

Monday morning:

1. Connect to the master Designer/2000 Repository in the UNIX database server.
2. Check in the .RCI file you created at home on Saturday. Select the option Check In to Source Application to perform the upload. This updates the properties of the objects in the object set with the latest changes you did over the weekend and releases the locks on these objects.
3. Continue working normally with the objects in the application.

When you unload a group of objects, Designer/2000 unloads not only the objects you have included in the working set, but also all the objects that are in a relationship or that are being referenced by the components of the working set.

5.3.5 LOADING AND UNLOADING OBJECTS

So far, you have seen two levels at which data may be transferred in and out of the Repository: at the application level, using archive, export, and restore; and at the object set level, using the check in and check out utilities. The load and unload utilities allow you to go one level further in the granularity of the objects. Using these utilities, you may migrate one or more individual PAC objects without having to bundle them in user-defined object sets.

In order to unload one or more objects, you must select them first in the Navigator, and then choose Utilities | Unload.... The dialog box Unload that is displayed is very similar to the dialog box Check Out, discussed in Section 5.3.3, therefore I will not go to any details here. After reviewing the objects you are about to unload, specify the location and the name of the file where data about objects will be written and click Unload to start the process.

When you want to load data in the Repository, select Utilities | Load... from the menu. In the Load dialog box that appears (see Figure 5.29), set the options according to your case and click Load.

Besides providing you with ways to specify the application name, the data file, and the log files, the Load dialog box allows you to specify several other options for the loading process, some of which are discussed here. The options in the Process radio group are used to instruct the Loader to load all the elements from the data file, only primary access elements, or only secondary access elements.

In the Mode group, the Insert option instructs the Loader to record in the error log any objects in the data file that have names conflicting with objects in

A particular case of unloading objects to a file is when you load them in the Repository of a different product, such as ErWin, using Oracle Exchange. In this case, select the objects you wish to unload and choose Application | Unload for Exchange....

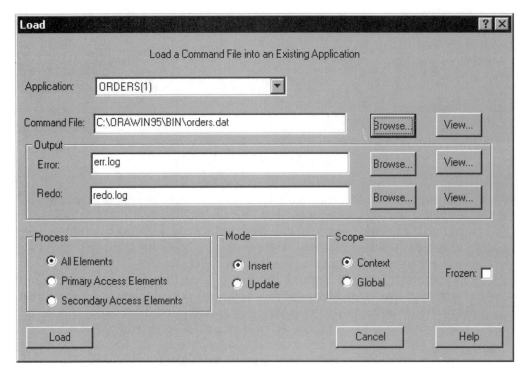

FIGURE 5.29 The Load dialog box.

the application; the Update option is used to update the application objects with specifications from file objects when duplicate objects are encountered.

The Scope group determines the applications where the Loader looks for objects whose names conflict with objects from the file. When the Context button is selected, only the application system specified in the upper right side of the screen is searched; when the Global button is selected, the Loader searches for conflicting names in the current application and in all the applications for which you have the Share privilege.

5.4 SUMMARY

The work you do in Designer/2000 is organized by application systems—a set of objects in the Repository that apply to a common business situation that you are modeling or analyzing. Application systems and the tasks you perform to create and maintain them are the subject of this chapter. A list of topics discussed here follows:

❏ **Creating and Maintaining Application Systems**
  ❏ Creating Application Systems
  ❏ Saving Application Systems
  ❏ Opening Application Systems
  ❏ Filtering Groups of Objects
  ❏ Closing Application Systems
  ❏ Renaming Application Systems
  ❏ Freezing and Unfreezing Application Systems
  ❏ Creating Multiple Versions of Application Systems
  ❏ Copying Application Systems
  ❏ Deleting Application Systems
  ❏ Managing User Access
  ❏ Transferring the Ownership of Application Systems
  ❏ Archiving Application Systems
  ❏ Restoring Application Systems

❏ **Creating and Maintaining Application Objects**
  ❏ Sharing and Unsharing Objects
  ❏ Transferring Ownership of Objects
  ❏ Copying Objects
  ❏ Refining the Granularity of Share and Copy Operations
  ❏ Deleting Objects

❏ **User-Defined Object Sets**
  ❏ Creating and Populating Object Sets
  ❏ Locking and Unlocking User-Defined Object Sets
  ❏ Checking In and Checking Out Objects
  ❏ Sample Designer/2000 Configuration Management Scenario
  ❏ Loading and Unloading Objects

Chapter 6

OBJECT NAVIGATORS IN DESIGNER/2000

- Components of Object Navigators
- Working with Navigator Windows
- Working with Property Palettes
- Summary

Object navigators provide an easy interface for browsing and searching a large number of objects organized and grouped in several levels of hierarchy. They also allow you to quickly add or remove objects, and to view or modify their properties. Object navigators rely on a metaphor that was introduced and popularized first by Graphical User Interface (GUI) file access utilities, such as File Manager and Windows Explorer in MS Windows, and then became a common commodity thanks to the explosion of Internet and Web browsing utilities. Designer/2000 has three components that are implemented as object navigators: Repository Object Navigator, Design Editor, and Repository Reports. Although each of these tools is used for a specific purpose and has its own distinct functionality, they all rely on common concepts shared by all object navigators. This chapter discusses these concepts and explains how to work with object navigators in general, and the specific functionality of each tool will be discussed in the appropriate context in the chapters to come.

6.1 COMPONENTS OF OBJECT NAVIGATORS

The object navigators in Designer/2000 are all Multiple Document Interface (MDI) applications that contain at least two windows. One of them, known as the Navigator window, contains the hierarchy tree of the objects that the navigator services. The other window, usually referred to as the Property Palette, contains the properties of the objects selected in the Navigator window. Figure 6.1 shows the components of a typical object navigator application.

The navigator's MDI frame contains the menu and the toolbar of the application on top of the window, and a status bar at the bottom. The Navigator window and the Property Palette are always displayed inside the MDI frame. By default, each navigator displays the toolbar and the status bar. If you do not want them displayed, uncheck the menu items View | Toolbar and View | Status Bar. The Design Editor uses a horizontal pane attached to the MDI frame to display messages issued during the process of generating application components. This pane is known as the Message Window and its display is controlled from the menu item View | Message Window.

6.1.1 NAVIGATOR WINDOW

Each entry listed in the Navigator window is also called a node. Two kinds of nodes exist: object types and object instances. Object types are names of categories of objects that the particular navigator displays. Each object type node has the following format:

```
[Expand/Collapse Status Indicator] [Object Type Name]
```

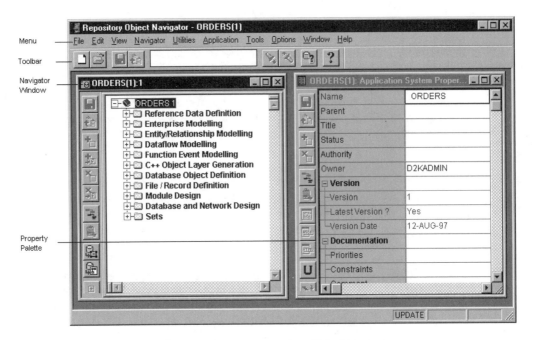

FIGURE 6.1 Components of an Object Navigator.

The Expand/Collapse Status Indicator can be one of the following icons:

⊢☐ Indicates that no objects of this category are in the application yet. In the Repository Object Navigator, double-clicking the icon creates a new object of the associated type. In the other navigators, you do not create any new objects; therefore this icon is not used.

⊞☐ Indicates that this category of objects is already populated. At least one object of that type is in the application. Clicking this icon expands the object type node and displays all the objects of that type. For clarity, the objects are indented below the corresponding object type node.

⊟☞ Indicates that the object category is already expanded. All the objects of that category are listed below the node, indented according to the hierarchy level. Clicking this icon collapses the object category and hides its instances from sight.

The object instances represent actual objects created and used in the application. Each object instance node has the following format:

```
[Expand/Collapse Status Indicator] [Object Type Icon]
[Object Name]
```

The Expand/Collapse Status Indicator can have one of the following states:

⊞🗐 Indicates that this object may own other objects. Clicking this icon expands the object and displays the types of objects it may own. These types may be populated or not, depending on the particular situation.

⊟🗐 Indicates that the object is already expanded. Clicking this icon collapses the object and hides its children.

The Object Type Icon serves as a visual indicator of an object's type. Because of the large number of objects that are displayed and manipulated in the navigators, you see a large variety of object type icons. The Object Name uniquely identifies the instance of an object in the navigator. When you create new objects in the Repository Object Navigator, you are asked to enter the name of the object before being able to move on to another object.

The number of objects displayed in the Navigator window is quite large. To help you to find your way easily through these objects, Designer/2000 navigators organize them in functional groups. The Design Editor uses a tabbed interface to present its groups. By default, these tabs are displayed horizontally and identified by the following text labels: DB Objects, Modules, DB Admin, and Distribution. You can modify this layout by right-clicking an area of the window—but not an object in the window. The following is a list of modifications you can achieve by selecting items from the popup menu that appears:

❑ Display the tabs vertically by selecting Vertical Tabs.
❑ Replace the text labels with icons by selecting Show Icons On Tabs.
❑ Hide tabs by selecting Hide Tabs.

The Repository Object Navigator organizes its objects in groups. Although the default display mode of this Navigator is the regular hierarchy control tree, you can display each group in its own tab by right-clicking the node that represents the group and selecting Split View from the popup menu. To hide the tab, right-click the group node again and select Remove Split View from the popup menu.

During the work with the Navigator tools, you may easily open several windows. While you can always activate the Navigator window by selecting it from the Window menu, a quick way to accomplish this task is to press F3.

6.1.2 PROPERTY PALETTE

The Property Palettes are identical in the Repository Object Navigator and De-sign Editor. They list the properties of objects and allow you to view and modify them. In the Repository Reports, the Property Palette allows you to specify para-meters before running a report and, for this reason, it is called the Parameters Palette.

By default, the Property Palette is displayed as a two-column property sheet. The column to the left contains the names of properties. The properties are orga-nized in groups which can be collapsed or expanded as needed. The length of the property list depends on the object or group of objects selected and on whether the property groups are collapsed or expanded. The column on the right of the Prop-erty Palette shows the setting for each property in the window. To modify the set-ting for a property click the setting area. Depending on the type of the property, the control where the property is set can be one of the following types:

❑ **Text field**. If the property setting can be specified by a text string or a digit, the bar displays a text field, where you can enter the desired value. If the property is already set, the text in the text field is highlighted, so that it can be typed over more easily.

❑ **Drop-down list**. If the property setting must be chosen from a list of pre-de-fined values, the properties setting bar displays a drop-down list. This list contains the valid settings for the property, from which you must choose one. When appropriate, this list allows you to set the property to NULL.

❑ **Multi-line text**. If the text for the property setting can be particularly long, the text iconic ⬛ precedes the name of the property. Clicking the property's name, brings up TextPad, a text editor embedded in Designer/2000, which you can use to type and edit the text more easily. Long text can be edited in an ASCII editor by clicking the property setting area and then the icon Ascii Edi-tor ⬛ in the Palette's toolbar. The text can also be viewed in a Web browser by clicking the property setting area and then the icon HTML Editor ⬛.

Recall from the discussion of the Designer/2000 Repository that each object in your application system is stored in Repository tables and accessed through Repository views and Repository APIs. The properties of objects that you view in

By default, the ASCII editor is Notepad and the HTML editor is Netscape's browser. You can change these settings by selecting Options | Text Editor Options… from the menu. In the dialog box Text Editors that appears select the command to run your fa-vorite ASCII editor and HTML browser.

the Property Palette of the Repository Object Navigator are stored as columns of these tables and views. To view the physical implementation details of a property, select its value in the Property Palette and press F5 from the keyboard. The dialog box Property Details that appears provides you with details not just of the selected property, but also of the object that owns it. Figure 6.2 shows the Property Details dialog box for the *Name* property of table LINE_ITEMS that you created in Chapter 2. In the Object Details group, you can see that this object is an element of type TABLE_DEFINITION, which is stored in the Repository table SDD_ELE-MENTS and uniquely identified by the number 965. The Property Details group shows that this property is stored in the column EL_NAME of table SDD_ELE-MENTS but exposed as NAME by the Repository view. You can also see that this is a mandatory property of data type VARCHAR2, and of length 30. Understanding the value stored internally in the Repository tables, which may be different

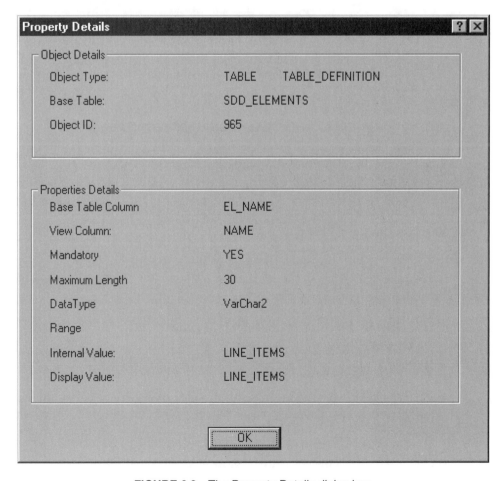

FIGURE 6.2 The Property Details dialog box.

A quick way to activate the Property Palette is to press F4 from the keyboard.

from that displayed in the Property Palette, allows you to add flexible query criteria to the query that populates the Repository Object Navigator hierarchy tree.

6.2 WORKING WITH NAVIGATOR WINDOWS

Section 6.1.1 earlier in this chapter introduced the Navigator windows in the Designer/2000 navigators. The following sections will discuss functions you can perform in these windows, such as navigating, selecting, expanding, collapsing, and marking objects.

6.2.1 EXPANDING AND COLLAPSING OBJECT TREES

In order to better manage and organize the information about objects, each navigator provides expanding and collapsing services. These services include expand/collapse status indicators that show the state of a node, and commands to actually expand or collapse nodes in the navigator. The different status indicators were explained in Section 6.1.1. The rest of this section deals only with the commands to perform these operations.

Four commands expand or collapse nodes in the navigators.

The Expand command displays all the dependent nodes at the hierarchical level immediately below the object currently selected. It can be accessed in one of the following three equivalent methods:

❑ Click the ⊞▭ icon on the left of the node.
❑ Click the Expand icon ⊞ on the toolbar.
❑ Select Navigator | Expand.

The Collapse command hides the nodes immediately below the currently selected object. To collapse a node in the Navigator, do one of the following:

❑ Click the ⊟🗀 icon on the left of the node.
❑ Click the Collapse icon ⊟ on the toolbar.
❑ Select Navigator | Collapse.

The commands Expand and Collapse act upon nodes that are in the hierarchy level immediately below that of the current node. Some instances require displaying or hiding the whole hierarchical tree of objects under a certain object. The commands Expand All and Collapse All are used in these situations.

The Expand All command displays all the dependent nodes at every hierarchical level below the currently selected object. It expands each node under the current node all the way down to the atomic level. This command can be accessed in one of the following equivalent methods:

❑ Click the Expand All icon ▣ on the toolbar.
❑ Select Navigator | Expand All.

The Collapse All command hides all the subnodes below the currently selected object. It collapses all the hierarchies under the current node. To perform this action in the Navigator, do one of the following:

❑ Click the Collapse All icon ▣ on the toolbar.
❑ Select Navigator | Collapse All.

In the conclusion of this section, I want to mention that the Navigator memorizes the expand/collapse state of the object tree. If you collapse one branch of the tree, the next time you expand it, the tree displays the same configuration as before being collapsed.

6.2.2 NAVIGATING, SEARCHING, AND SELECTING OBJECTS

The easiest way to navigate to an object is to click it with the mouse in the hierarchy tree. In order to do so, the target object must be visible in the Navigator window. If it is not, scrolling up and down the node list may be necessary. If the desired object is in a level of the hierarchy tree that is currently collapsed, expand the parent objects as necessary and then select the object (expanding and collapsing were explained in the preceding section). To navigate up and down the list, you may also use the up-arrow and down-arrow keys from the keyboard.

Left- and right-arrow keys provide navigational and expand/collapse functionality from the keyboard. The right-arrow key expands the current node and moves the focus to the first node immediately below it. If the node cannot be expanded, the right-arrow key simply moves the focus of the navigator one object down. The left-arrow key moves the focus one object up the tree, and if this object is the parent of the original object, it collapses it.

The Find utility of the navigators is very useful in locating target objects in the hierarchy tree. It is made up of a text field where search criteria are entered and two iconic buttons specify the direction of search. The Search Forward icon searches forward, whereas the Search Backward icon searches backwards. By default, lists are searched from top down, or forward. When the bottom of the list is reached, the search resumes from the top. To search backwards, enter the search string and click the Search Backwards button. The search stops at the first entry in the lists that satisfies the search criteria. This entry is highlighted by the navigator. When a match occurs, all parent nodes of the newly-found object are expanded as necessary. The find utility searches forward as you type, therefore you may find the object you are searching by typing only the first few characters of its name.

Once you navigate to an object, you have also selected it, because the focus of the navigator is placed on the object. When you need to select multiple objects, you may use standard Windows techniques, such as SHIFT and CTRL selecting. SHIFT selecting allows you to select a range of objects by clicking the first object in the range, pressing the SHIFT key and clicking the last object. CTRL selecting allows you to add individual objects to the set of selected objects by pressing the CTRL key while clicking the desired object. This action is used to deselect an already selected object as well. Once the objects are selected, you can perform group operations on them, such as moving them to different locations, setting common properties, unloading, and so on. As a matter of fact, performing these types of operations is the main purpose for selecting multiple objects.

6.2.3   SEARCHING REPOSITORY OBJECTS

The Find utility described in the previous section is a simple tool that allows you to quickly find objects in the hierarchy tree of the Navigator window. For a powerful way to query the Repository, you can use the advanced features of the Repository Object Navigator's search engine. You can invoke this engine with one of the following commands:

❑   Click the Search Repository icon on the Navigator's MDI toolbar.
❑   Select Navigator I Search Repository… from the menu.

The dialog box Repository Search that appears as a result of these actions allows you to search the Repository of objects of a given type using criteria defined on the properties of the object type. You can select the desired element or association type by selecting from the list For Object Type. By default, the search will span all the most recent versions of the application systems that exist in the Repository. To search all the application systems, clear the Search Latest Versions of Application Only? check box. The central part of the dialog box Repository Search is occupied by a tabbed control. The three properties tabs of this control are described in the following paragraphs:

❑ **Search Conditions.** This tab allows you to specify the criteria used by the Navigator to search the Repository. In order to add a condition, simply select it in the list and type the parameter in the Condition field. Standard SQL wildcards can be used in the condition. If a list of values exists for the selected property, the icon ▤ appears in the Condition field. Click this icon to select a value from the list of available values.

The properties in the Search Conditions tab are initially listed in the order in which they are defined in the Repository. This may not necessarily match the order in which these properties are used to populate the search condition set. To move a list element up or down, select it and click the icons ▲ and ▼. When multiple conditions are defined, the Boolean operator that joins them is AND, by default. You can explicitly assign the Boolean operator to a condition by clicking the icons ▧ and ▧. You can also group conditions with parentheses by selecting them in the list and then clicking the icon ▣. Removing a set of parentheses can be achieved by selecting the conditions inside the parentheses and then clicking the icon ▣. There may be situations in which you may want to apply more than one condition on the same property. Clicking the icon ▣ inserts a duplicate element that can be used to specify an additional condition for the query. Finally, if you want to clear the condition defined for a property, select the property and click the icon ▣. Figure 6.3 shows an example of conditions you can specify in the Search Condition tab.

❑ **Sort Sequence.** This tab allows you to specify how the result list will be sorted. The Navigator sorts the objects found by the search in ascending order, based on one or more default properties. To add a property to the sorting conditions, select the check box Order By for that entity. To sort the result list in descending order, place a check mark in the check box Descending.

❑ **Show Properties.** This tab allows you to choose what properties of a given object will be displayed in the result list. (The application that owns the object and the type of object are always displayed.) As in the other tabs, set or clear the check box associated with the property to include or exclude it from the list.

The criteria you specify in the Search Conditions tab are positional. This means that when you select a different item from the list For Object Type, any parentheses, Boolean operators, or conditions you may have entered for the previous object will be applied to the properties of the new object. You have to consider these conditions carefully, since, in general, they may not apply to the properties of the new object type.

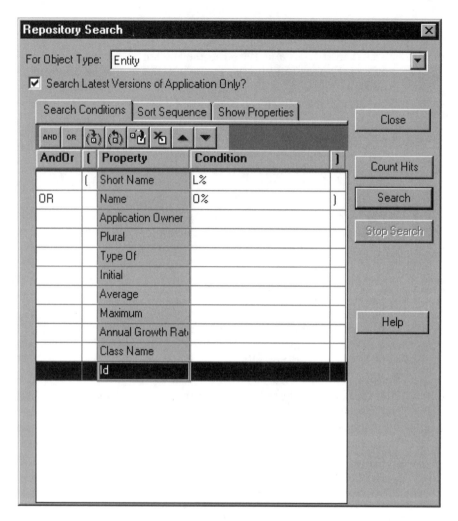

FIGURE 6.3 The Search Conditions tab of the Repository Search dialog box.

 When you select an element in the tabs Search Conditions, Sort Sequence, and Show Properties, the list controls move it from its original position in the list to the last position in the group of other selected elements. If the selection check box is cleared, the element returns to its original position. As in the Search Conditions tab, you can modify the sequence of the elements in the list using the icons ▲ and ▼.

When the specifications of the query are set, you can click Count Hits to see the number of objects that will be found by the search. I recommend that you do this before actually running the query. If you see that the number of hits is large, you can refine the search conditions to reduce the result set to a manageable size. To perform the search, click the button Search. The results are displayed in the dialog box Repository Search Matches, an example of which is shown in Figure 6.4. In this dialog, you can click New Query to return to the dialog box Repository Search to refine your query or enter a new one. You can also select an element from the result list and see where it is being used by clicking the button Show Where Used. To navigate to that element on the Navigator window, click Locate in Navigator.

6.2.4 MANAGING FILTERS OF REPOSITORY OBJECTS

Now that you have seen how the search engine of the Repository Object Navigator works, you can easily set and maintain filtering criteria for objects in the hierarchy tree of the Navigator window. To enter conditions that restrict which objects are displayed in the tree, select Navigator | Filter... from the menu. The Navigator Filter Query dialog box is displayed and the tab Filter Conditions is active (see Figure 6.5). To specify the order in which the objects should be listed, select Navigator | Sort...; the same dialog box is displayed, but now the tab Sort Sequence is active. To control what properties are displayed in the Navigator window for a category of objects, select Navigator | Show Properties...; Show Properties is now the active tab of the dialog box Navigator Filter Query.

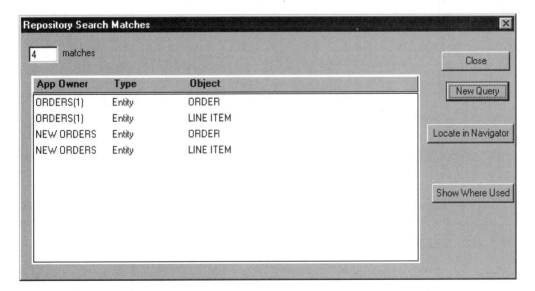

FIGURE 6.4 The Repository Search Matches dialog box.

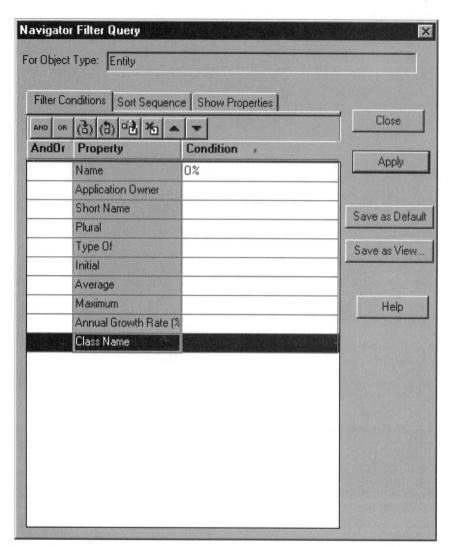

FIGURE 6.5 The Filter Conditions tab of the Navigator Filter Query dialog box.

By comparing Figure 6.3 and Figure 6.5, you can tell that the layout and usage of the tabs in this dialog box closely resembles the dialog box Repository Search discussed in Section 6.2.3. Some of the differences are outlined below:

❑ **Scope.** The Repository Search dialog allows you to search the entire Repository, whereas the Navigator Filter Query dialog is limited in scope to a particular object type in a given application system.

❑ **Outcome.** The outcome of a Repository search is a list of objects in the Repository Search Matches dialog box. The outcome of a filter query is a different listing of objects in the Navigator window.

The filtering conditions you set remain in effect as long as the application system remains open in the Repository Object Navigator. To remove them for a category of objects, select Navigator | Clear Selected Filter; to remove all the filters in the Navigator window, select Navigator | Clear All Filters. You can use the filters across multiple sessions by defining them as default filters in the dialog box Navigator Filter Query. However, be conservative with the modifications you make to the default interface of the Navigator which has been carefully tuned and optimized by the Oracle engineers.

The option I recommend is to create a user view of the filtered objects by clicking the button Save As View... in the Navigator Filter Query dialog box and providing a name for the view when prompted by the Navigator. In order to display this and other views in the Navigator window, select View | Include Navigator Views.... In the dialog box Include Navigator Views that appears, place a check mark for each user-defined view you want to include in the Navigator and click OK.

The Design Editor offers a filtering interface although not as sophisticated as the one implemented by the Repository Object Navigator. In principle, they both work the same, therefore I will simply show in Figure 6.6 the Options dialog box that you use to set filters. You can access this dialog box by selecting Options | Customize....

6.2.5 MARKING OBJECTS

Setting marks and navigating to them is another facility provided by the navigator to help you quickly access objects in your application. Every node in the Navigator window can be marked. To mark an object, you simply select that object and issue one of the following commands:

❑ Click the Mark icon ▣ on the toolbar.
❑ Select Navigator | Set Mark.

Once a node is marked, the navigator can navigate to that node from any position in the Navigator window. To navigate to a marked object, follow one of these steps:

❑ Click the Goto Mark icon ▣ on the toolbar.
❑ Select Navigator | Goto Mark.

If the target node is collapsed, the Object Navigator expands the object tree as necessary. Only one mark can be set in each Navigator window. A mark remains effective until one of the following events occurs:

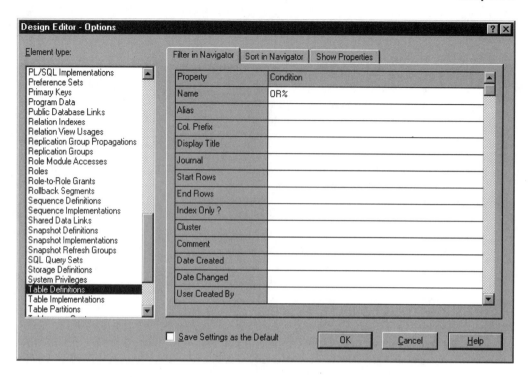

FIGURE 6.6   The Options dialog box of the Design Editor.

❑   A new object is marked, thus overriding the current mark.
❑   The marked object is deleted.
❑   The application or module that contains the marked object is closed.
❑   The navigator application terminates.

6.2.6   CREATING OBJECTS IN THE REPOSITORY OBJECT NAVIGATOR

The Repository Object Navigator and the Design Editor not only allow you to navigate, search, and select objects, but also give you the ability to act upon these objects. Actions such as create or delete for a number of Repository objects can be accessed from other specialized Designer/2000 tools, as well. For example, entities, attributes, and relationships can be created and modified in the Entity Relationship Diagrammer, business functions in the Function Hierarchy Diagrammer, and tables and columns in the Data Diagrammer. But with their unified view of the application objects, the Navigators give uniformity and coherence to these actions. The Repository Object Navigator also allows you to modify objects for which no specialized diagrammer or dialog box exists in Designer/2000, such as objectives, critical success factors, and problems.

Before creating an object, you must decide the location of that object in the hierarchy tree. This location depends on the type of the object. Primary access objects such as entities, modules, objectives, and others go right under the respective object type nodes. If the object is a secondary access object, than the parent object must be selected first. For example, before adding an attribute, you must decide in which entity that attribute will go; before creating a column you must decide in which table it will be attached.

If no objects of the same type exist as the object you want to create, the expand/collapse status indicator will be the icon ⊢▢. As I explained earlier, double-clicking this icon creates a new object. If other objects for a given element or association type already exist, to create the new one, simply select the object type node or one of the existing objects to indicate the location where the new object will be placed. The new object will be created immediately below the current selection. To create an object, issue one of the following commands:

- ❑ Click the Create icon ▯ on the toolbar.
- ❑ In the Repository Object Navigator, select Edit | Create Object or Edit | Create Association, depending on the context. In the Design Editor, select Edit | Create.

The Repository Object Navigator and the Design Editor offer a Fast Create technique that may be useful when creating a large number of objects in the Navigator window. When you create an object in this window, type its name and press RETURN. The Navigator will save the newly-created object and create a new one below. You can repeat this as often as needed.

Such a technique interacts with the database every time a new object is created. To avoid the overhead in network traffic, the Design Editor implements a more sophisticated Fast Create technique. To use it, select the object type in the Navigator and choose Edit | Fast Create from the menu. In the dialog box that comes up, you can enter a minimal set of properties, usually only the name, for each object you want to create. When you click OK, these objects are added to the Repository.

Combined with the spreadtable view of the Property Palette, the Fast Search techniques discussed here allow you to create a number of objects and their properties quickly and efficiently.

6.2.7   DELETING OBJECTS IN THE REPOSITORY OBJECT NAVIGATOR

Objects in the Repository Object Navigator can be deleted one at a time, or in groups. The only difference in the process is during the selection of the candidates for deletion. You have different ways to delete an object, after it is selected:

❑ Press DELETE.
❑ Click the Delete icon ⌷ on the toolbar.
❑ In the Repository Object Navigator, select Edit | Delete Object or Edit | Delete Association, depending on the context. In the Design Editor, select Edit | Delete.

In all cases, the Repository Object Navigator prompts you with a dialog box to confirm that you want to delete the object. The delete will be successful only if the object is not referenced by other objects in the Repository. For example, you cannot delete a table that is referenced by the foreign key constraint of another table. Before deleting the object, you need to remove all the references in which this object is the destination or the 'To' end of the association. In the Repository Object Navigator you can also use the Force Delete mechanism discussed in Chapter 5. This mechanism allows you to understand the impact that deleting an object may have on other objects. The restrictions placed on the ability to delete an object are to ensure the data consistency of your application system and to protect you from unwanted actions that are easy to perform but from which recovery is difficult.

6.2.8   REQUERYING OBJECTS IN THE NAVIGATOR WINDOW

After the Navigator is initially populated and displayed, the properties of objects in the hierarchy tree may change as a result of the work that you or other Repository users may perform. In order to refresh the properties of an object with the latest changes, you select the object in the Navigator, then issue one of the following commands:

❑ Click the icon Requery Selection ⌷.
❑ Select Edit | Requery Selection.

No matter which type of delete command you issue, you must be very cautious with it, since the command is applied immediately to the Repository database and is not reversible.

The previous commands requery only selected objects. You may also requery the entire hierarchy tree by clicking the icon Requery All 🖺 or by selecting Edit | Requery All. Understandably, the second requery option may be expensive, especially for large application systems. To help you easily identify the objects you need to requery, Designer/2000 provides a utility that broadcasts messages to other Repository users when properties of an object change. This utility is also responsible for receiving notification messages from other Designer/2000 users participating in the broadcasting scheme. You can view the notification options of your workstation by selecting Options | Broadcast Options… from the menu. The dialog box Broadcast Options shown in Figure 6.7 appears.

The notification options you can choose are explained in the following paragraphs:

❑ **Disabled.** You will not send or receive any notification when this option is selected.

❑ **Desktop.** With this option, when you modify an object in one tool, for example, the Repository Object Navigator, a message will be broadcast to all the other Designer/2000 tools running in your desktop that are active and contain the object in question.

❑ **Network.** This option extends the scope of the messages sent when modifications occur. Now, all the Repository users who have set their broadcast notification option will receive a message when you modify the properties of an object.

When a Designer/2000 tool receives the notification that one of the objects has been modified, it marks the object with a characteristic icon. Figure 6.8 shows this icon for the Navigator window in the Design Editor.

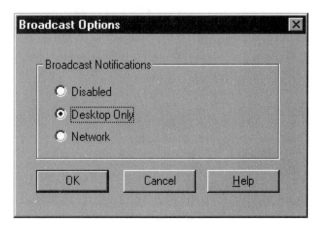

FIGURE 6.7 The Broadcast Options dialog box.

FIGURE 6.8 Iconic identification of changed objects.

6.3 WORKING WITH PROPERTY PALETTES

The behavior and functionality of objects in an application are determined by their properties. Upon creation, each object is assigned a set of default properties, which can be changed and reset based on the needs of the application. The Property Palettes are one of the interfaces that the navigators provide to access and modify properties of objects. In the case of the Design Editor, diagrams and tabbed dialog boxes are two other important interfaces. In these windows, you can display and edit the properties of one or more objects, and copy properties of one object to another. The following sections explain how to perform these actions.

The broadcast notification option may be set from a number of Designer/2000 tools. The setting applies to the entire workstation; all the tools will share the same option set in any of them.

By default, the Design Editor displays the properties of objects in dialog boxes. To display them in Property Palettes, click the icon Use Dialogs ▆ to set it in raised state or select Options | Use Property Palette from the menu.

6.3.1 SETTING PROPERTIES OF OBJECTS

You can set the properties for one or more objects in the properties setting bar of the Property Palette. If the property you want to set is a text item, you simply type the new setting; if the setting must be chosen from a predefined list of values, you can select it from the list or double-click the property in the properties list to go through the list sequentially until you find the desired setting; if the setting is in the form of a long, multi-line text, you can click the property name in the list to bring up the Designer/2000 text editor. If more than one object is selected, setting a property propagates the setting in all the objects that contain that property. The action overwrites any existing settings of that property in all the objects.

6.3.2 REVERTING CHANGES OF PROPERTIES

The changes you make can be reverted as long as you have not navigated to another object in the Navigator window or saved the changes. To revert changes, you can issue one of these commands:

❑ Click the Revert icon 🔄 on the navigator toolbar.
❑ Select Edit | Undo.
❑ Press CTRL+Z.

6.3.3 COPYING AND PASTING PROPERTIES OF OBJECTS

Designer/2000 navigators extend the concept of copying and pasting objects to that of copying and pasting their properties. You can copy and paste properties at the object level, where all the properties for an object are copied and pasted onto other objects; you can also copy and paste them at the property level, where you can copy the values for an individual property and paste them to the same property of another object.

To copy properties of objects, follow these steps:

1. On the Navigator window, select the object or group of objects whose properties you want to copy.
2. Click the Copy Properties icon 🔄 from the navigator toolbar or choose Edit | Copy Properties.

To copy settings of individual properties, follow these steps:

1. Select one or more properties in the Property Palette.
2. Click the Copy Properties icon ⬛ on the Property Palette toolbar or choose Edit I Copy Properties.

In both cases, the navigator places the properties settings in the clipboard, ready to be pasted onto another object. You can also view the properties copied to the clipboard by choosing Edit I View Copied Properties.... The View Copied Properties dialog box that appears (see Figure 6.9) allows you to delete any of the unwanted properties from the list.

To paste properties at the object level, issue the following commands:

1. Select the object or group of objects on which you want to paste the properties.
2. Click the Paste Properties icon ⬛ on the navigator toolbar or choose Edit I Paste Properties.

Be cautious when copying and pasting properties at the object level, because these commands act upon all the properties of the selected objects. If, for example, you copy the properties of an entity and paste them onto another entity, all their properties, except name, become identical. Uniqueness constraints on the entity objects do not allow the modified object to be saved to the Repository.

To paste properties at the property level, issue the following commands:

1. Select the object or group of objects on which you want to paste the properties.
2. Click the Paste Properties icon ⬛ on the Property Palette toolbar or choose Edit I Paste Properties.

View Copied Properties	
Alias	LI
Col. Prefix	
Display Title	
Journal	None
Start Rows	1

[Delete] [OK] [Cancel]

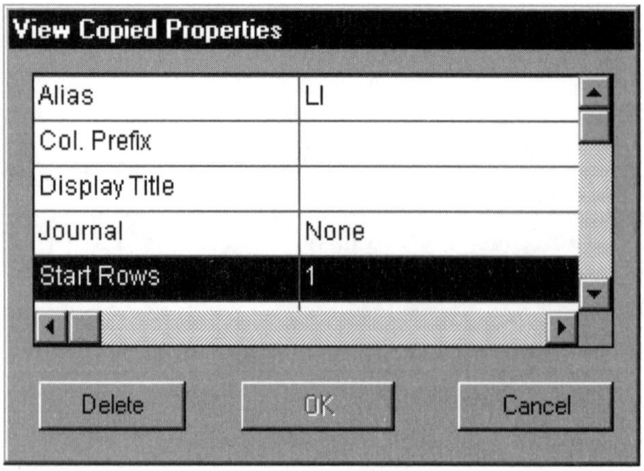

FIGURE 6.9 The View Copied Properties dialog box.

6.3.4 PINNING PROPERTY PALETTES

The default behavior of the Repository Object Navigator and the Preferences Navigator is to synchronize the contents of the Property Palette with the object selected in the Navigator window. In synchronized mode, when you select a new object in the hierarchy tree, the Property Palette is refreshed with the properties for that object. The visual indicator of the synchronized mode is the Pin button ⊠ on the Property Palette toolbar.

If you want the properties of an object to remain in a Property Palette even after that object is no longer selected, "pin" them to the Property Palette. Click the Pin button ⊠ on the Property Palette toolbar to pin the properties of the object to that window. When you do, the mode of the window changes to pinned, and the iconic button you clicked is replaced by the Synchronize button ⊡. To set the window back to synchronized mode, click the Synchronize button.

If a Property Palette is in pinned mode, you cannot see the properties of another object unless you open an additional Property Palette. Double-clicking an object in the Navigator window is the easiest way to open a new Property Palette for the object.

6.3.5 MANAGING PROPERTIES OF MULTIPLE OBJECTS

As I mentioned earlier, you can select multiple objects in the Navigator window. In the Repository Object Navigator, the properties displayed depend on whether the Property Palette is in intersect mode or in union mode. The Property Palette is in intersect mode if the iconic button ⊞ is displayed on its toolbar. In this mode, the window displays only the common properties of the selected objects. Clicking the button toggles the window's mode to union. The Property Palette is in union mode if the iconic button ⊞ is displayed on its toolbar. In union mode, the window displays all the properties of selected objects. Clicking the icon toggles the window's mode back to intersect.

When multiple objects are selected, the Property Palette displays values only for the properties that share the same setting. Properties with different settings are displayed using a series of '#' characters, as shown in Figure 6.10. You can view and edit the properties of individual objects while still maintaining the

The spreadtable view of the Property Palette can be combined with Fast Create techniques to quickly create and set the properties of a number of objects.

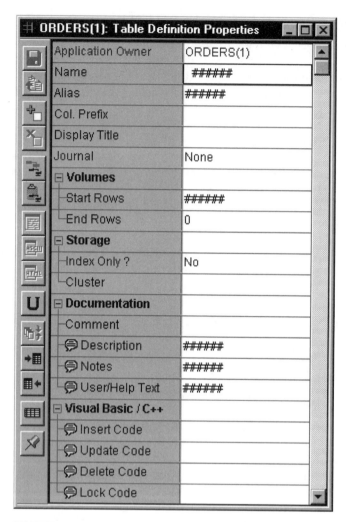

FIGURE 6.10   Default view of the Property Palette when multiple objects are selected.

selection of multiple objects by clicking the icons Next Object ◨ or Previous Object ◨. To return to the default view of the properties, click the icon Set ◨, which is enabled only if the Property Palette displays the properties of one out of several objects selected in the Navigator.

An elegant way to display the properties of multiple objects is to display the Property Palette as in a matrix format, rather than in the usual two-column tabular format. Click the icon SpreadTable View ◾ to view the Palette in this mode. Figure 6.11 shows the example of a property palette in spreadtable view.

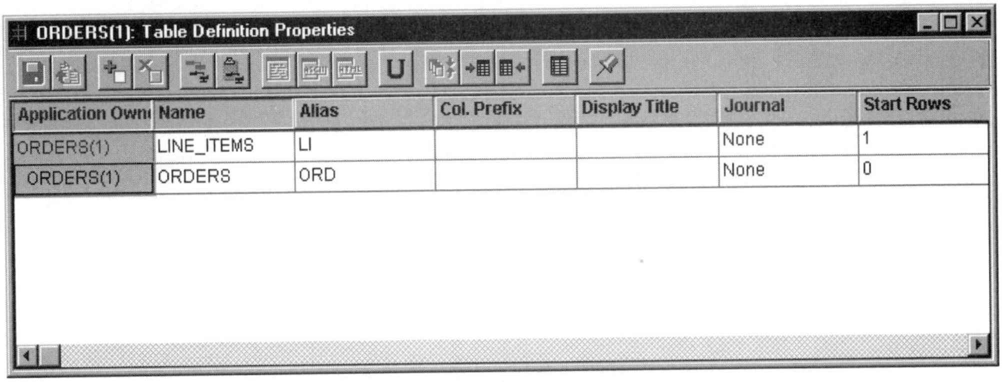

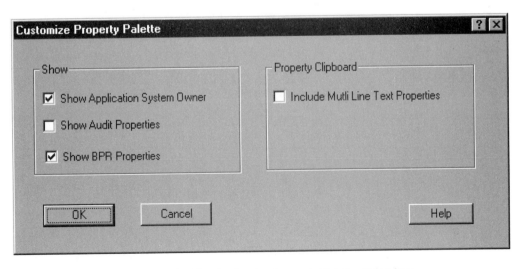

FIGURE 6.11   Spreadtable view of the Property Palette when multiple objects are selected.

6.3.6   CUSTOMIZING THE PROPERTY PALETTE OPTIONS

The Repository Object Navigator allows you to customize the properties displayed in the Property Palette by selecting Options | Customize Property Palette... from the menu. The dialog box that is displayed as a result of this action is shown in Figure 6.12. By setting or clearing the check boxes in the Show group, you can instruct the Navigator to show or hide the application system owner, audit properties, such as date when the object was created or updated, and properties used during business analysis and business process reengineering. The check box Include Multi Line Text Properties is not checked by default. This means that when you copy properties of objects, the multi-line text properties are not copied.

FIGURE 6.12   The Customize Property Palette dialog box.

6.4 SUMMARY

Designer/2000 has several tools that are built around the Windows Explorer metaphor. These tools are commonly referred to as Object Navigators. This chapter highlights the common functionality of the navigators in Designer/2000. It focuses, among others, on the following topics.

❑ **Components of Object Navigators**
  ❑ Navigator Window
  ❑ Property Palette
❑ **Working with Navigator Windows**
  ❑ Expanding and Collapsing Object Trees
  ❑ Navigating, Searching, and Selecting Objects
  ❑ Searching Repository Objects
  ❑ Managing Filters of Repository Objects
  ❑ Marking Objects
  ❑ Creating Objects in the Repository Object Navigator
  ❑ Deleting Objects in the Repository Object Navigator
  ❑ Requerying Objects in the Navigator Window
❑ **Working with Property Palettes**
  ❑ Setting Properties of Objects
  ❑ Reverting Changes of Properties
  ❑ Copying and Pasting Properties of Objects
  ❑ Pinning Property Palettes
  ❑ Managing Properties of Multiple Objects
  ❑ Customizing the Property Palette Options

Chapter 7

DIAGRAMMERS IN DESIGNER/2000

- Diagrams and Diagrammers
- Components of Diagrammers
- Working with Diagrams
- Working with Objects in Diagrams
- Customizing Diagrammer Preferences
- Enhancing Diagrams with OLE Technology
- The Matrix Diagrammer
- Summary

In order to build any system successfully, you need a plan of action, skilled people to carry out the plan, a design of the system, and appropriate tools to build it. This statement is true whether you are building a bridge, a computer chip, the engine of a car, or an information system. In long-established professions, such as architecture, mechanical engineering, and electrical engineering, people use diagrams and diagramming techniques to represent and convey their design ideas clearly and unequivocally. When software engineering grew from its infantile stage to a full-fledged profession and began to attack and solve problems of significant size, diagramming techniques were developed to help professionals design their systems. Alongside these techniques, diagramming tools were developed to assist the systems engineers draw their diagrams. In the early 1980s, these led to the invention, production, and marketing by several companies of computer-assisted software engineering (CASE) tools, which stored information about the meaning of diagrams in a format that could be read, checked, and retrieved by the computers. With CASE tools, software engineers were able to design large systems of high complexity that they could not approach when diagrams and design documents were created, maintained, and synchronized manually.

Integrated CASE (I-CASE) tools were a natural evolution of the original CASE tools. They added the ability to automatically convert one type of diagram into another, enhanced the process of checking the integrity and validity of the design, and allowed analysts to generate application code straight from design specifications stored in a centralized Repository.

As the responsibilities of software engineers have grown, they are contributing in areas such as strategic planning, enterprise modeling, business area analysis, and business process reengineering. To succeed in the new role as mediators between business and technology, they need not only strong analytical skills and technical knowledge, but also tools to clearly present the findings of their analysis. These tools should provide all the functionality of the early I-CASE tools. In addition, they should allow analysts to represent visually in an understandable model enterprise, components such as complex organizational hierarchies, intricate business processes, complicated flows of resources and materials, and the relations and dependencies among them.

Designer/2000 is a set of business modeling and systems design tools that provides you with all this functionality through its diagrammers and other components. This chapter will discuss the importance of diagrams and the common functionality of diagramming tools in Designer/2000.

7.1 DIAGRAMS AND DIAGRAMMERS

The following sections discuss the properties of diagrams in software engineering and the diagramming tools of Designer/2000, also known as diagrammers.

7.1.1 DIAGRAMS

Diagrams can be considered languages that software engineers use to materialize and communicate their ideas about information systems. Although you can express the design of an information system using a natural language, such as English or French, the fuzziness of these languages may lead to misinterpretations and slow down the communication between designers, developers, management, and users. System design documents written in the form of paragraph after paragraph of descriptions often produce situations like the one depicted in Figure 7.1.

Because they express the concepts and ideas of design in visual form, diagrams convey more information more quickly than natural languages. An entity relationship diagram, for example, is often sufficient to express the ideas of a team about the data model; these ideas, presented in a natural language format, would require entire pages of narrative text. The issue is even more important when applications are designed in multi-lingual, multi-national environments. In these situations, a diagram prepared by a team of American software engineers will be understood much faster by their oversees colleagues than any written document.

Finally, for the diagrams to be useful, they must always represent the most up-to-date knowledge gathered about the system. Although drawing an initial diagram in a drawing package or even by hand is not difficult, trying to maintain it and all the relationships it involves as the design process evolves becomes a challenge. For this you need a computerized diagramming tool.

FIGURE 7.1 Fuzziness of natural languages may lead to misunderstandings of requirements and undermine the design of systems.

As a summary, for the purposes of the discussion in this book, diagrams are means of communications that are:

❑ Precise and non-ambiguous
❑ Universal
❑ Computerized

7.1.2 DESIGNER/2000 DIAGRAMMERS

The following is a brief description of the diagrammers in Designer/2000:

❑ **Process Modeller.** It is used to create diagrams about business processes performed by one or more organizations within the enterprise. It is used primarily during strategic planning and business process reengineering tasks.
❑ **Entity Relationship Diagrammer.** It is used to create and maintain the data model of the application, the entities that are part of this model, and the relationships among them. It is used in strategic planning, business process reengineering, and business area analysis, as well as during the requirements analysis and definition of information systems.
❑ **Function Hierarchy Diagrammer.** It is used to model the business functions, their decomposition, and dependencies. It is also used to create associations between the business functions and the data structures of the enterprise. It is used in strategic planning, business process reengineering, and business area analysis. During requirements definition and analysis, this diagrammer is used to record user interface requirements and business rules that the information system will implement.
❑ **Dataflow Diagrammer.** It is used to model the business functions from the perspective of flows of data and resources. It is used mostly in business area analysis but also in strategic planning and business process reengineering.
❑ **Data Diagrammer.** This diagrammer is part of the Design Editor and is used to maintain the logical and physical database design of the application in the system design phase of the development project. You use this diagrammer to maintain the definitions for tables, columns, constraints, indexes, and other database objects.
❑ **Module Diagrammer.** This diagrammer is also a component of the Design Editor used to create and maintain the layout of user interface modules during the system design phase of the project. It allows you to organize the components of your application's modules according to the user's needs.

Obviously, each of these diagrammers has its own unique features and functionality. However, the interface they offer is comparable, and a core of fundamental functions is performed similarly, if not identically, in all of them. The interface of diagrammers and common functions performed with them, such as creating and maintaining diagram documents, creating and maintaining objects in diagrams, enhancing diagrams with OLE technology, and so on are the subject of the rest of this chapter.

7.2 COMPONENTS OF DIAGRAMMERS

When you start a diagrammer, you see something similar to Figure 7.2. Despite the differences, all the Designer/2000 diagrammers are Multiple Document Interface (MDI) applications. The main components of these diagrammers are the MDI sheets, or diagrams, the menu, and the toolbar. The following sections provide details about these components.

7.2.1 MULTIPLE DOCUMENT INTERFACE APPLICATIONS

Each of the Designer/2000 diagrammers is a Multiple Document Interface (MDI) application. The MDI frame, which is also referred to as the application window or the diagrammer window, serves as a container for the diagrammer's menu,

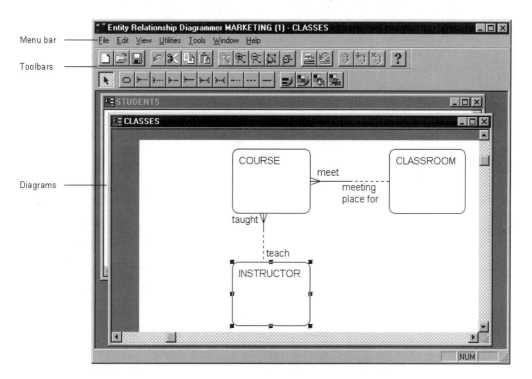

FIGURE 7.2 Components of a typical Designer/2000 diagrammer.

toolbar, and the MDI sheets. In a particular diagrammer, you create and maintain diagram documents of a certain type defined by the diagrammer. You can work simultaneously with as many diagrams as you need. These diagrams can be resized, maximized, minimized, tiled, cascaded, moved around, and scrolled vertically and horizontally, while always staying within the boundaries of the diagrammer's window.

The title bar of each diagrammer window contains the name of the diagrammer, the name and version of the application to which you are logged on, and, if you have open diagrams, the name of the current diagram. Figure 7.2, for example, shows the Entity Relationship Diagrammer for the application MARKETING (1). Two diagrams are open; CLASSES is currently selected, and STUDENTS is inactive in the background.

7.2.2 MENU

The MDI frame of each diagrammer contains the menu bar on top. Each of these menus has at least the following submenus as part of it:

❏ **File menu.** It provides access to functionality that applies to the diagram as a whole, such as creating, opening, saving, closing, and printing diagrams. The commands that can be issued from this menu will be discussed in Section 7.3.

❏ **Edit menu.** The items of this menu invoke functionality required to edit and maintain the objects in a diagram, such as Cut, Copy, Paste, and Delete. They also include different commands used to select objects present in a diagram, or to include objects from the Repository in the diagram. Most of these functions will be discussed in the chapters to come.

❏ **View menu.** It contains several menu items that control the layout of the diagram and the zoom level of the window. In addition, it allows you to display or hide the diagrammer's toolbars and status bar.

❏ **Utilities menu.** This menu provides access to utilities that are particular to each diagrammer. Most of these utilities will be discussed in the context of each diagrammer, in the coming chapters.

❏ **Tools menu.** Items in this menu launch other Designer/2000 components to which the diagrammer is related. From each diagrammer, you can start at least the Repository Object Navigator, Repository Reports, and the Matrix Diagrammer. Other tools that can be launched depend on the diagrammer. For example, from the Entity Relationship Diagrammer, you can start the Function Hierarchy Diagrammer, the Data Flow Diagrammer, and the Design Editor.

❏ **Window menu.** This menu allows you to access standard Windows commands for MDI applications: Cascade, Tile Horizontally, Tile Vertically, and Arrange Icons. It also contains the menu item New Window, which opens a new window for the current diagram. If multiple windows are open in the diagrammer, their titles are listed in the Window menu; you can navigate to any of these windows by selecting its title in the menu.

❑ **Help menu.** This menu gives you access to online help for the particular diagrammer. When you begin working with Designer/2000, you will find especially helpful the Cue Cards item, which contains concise, step-by-step instructions for performing different tasks in the diagrammer. Figure 7.3 shows one cue card for the Entity Relationship Diagrammer.

FIGURE 7.3 An example of a diagrammer cue card.

The items in each of the submenus described above can be grouped in two categories:

❑ **Conventional menu items.** These are the standard menu items that you find in any GUI application. Usually they execute a command, such as opening a diagram or copying an object; they also launch a different Designer/2000 tool. If the command is rather complicated and requires additional parameters, a dialog box follows the selection of the menu item. In this dialog box, you can specify the necessary data and execute the command. The labels of all the menu items that invoke dialog boxes end with an ellipsis, as in File │ Save As....

❑ **Check menu items.** These menu items are used to toggle the setting of a property. In unchecked mode, they look like ordinary menu items; in checked mode, their name is preceded by a check mark. This type of item is encountered mostly in the View submenu.

7.2.3 TOOLBAR

Each diagrammer comes with two toolbars: the standard toolbar and the drawing palette. Both these toolbars contain iconic buttons that allow you to access often-used functionalities of each diagrammer with one click of the mouse. The standard toolbar for all the diagrammers contains buttons to create new diagrams, as well as to open and save existing ones; buttons to control the zooming levels of the window; buttons to organize the layout of the diagram; and finally, a button for context-sensitive help ▤.

The drawing palette contains buttons to create objects that are maintained by the particular diagrammer. In the Entity Relationship Diagrammer, for example, this palette includes icons to create entities and different kinds of relationships between entities. In addition, the drawing palette for each diagrammer contains four iconic buttons that allow you to change the line width and color, fill color, and font attributes of objects in your diagrams. You will learn more details about these icons in Section 7.4.7.

7.3 WORKING WITH DIAGRAMS

While the Repository Object Navigator and the Navigator component of the Design Editor serve as a centralized interface for creating and maintaining the objects of your application, the diagrammers allow you to organize the objects and their relationships visually in diagram documents. Each diagrammer accesses a limited number of object types used in a particular context. Despite the different purposes and uses of the diagrammers, many tasks are completed similarly in all of them. These tasks are the subject of the following sections.

7.3.1 CREATING DIAGRAMS

You can create a new diagram by issuing any of the following commands:

❑ Click the New Diagram button 🔳 on the toolbar.
❑ Select File | New.
❑ Press CTRL+N.

In all cases, a new diagram document is created. The title of the document is set to an acronym of the diagrammer followed by a sequence number, for example, ERD1 for the Entity Relationship Diagrammer or MSD3 for the Module Structure Diagrammer.

In the case of the Process Modeller, Function Hierarchy Diagrammer, and Data Flow Diagrammer, a new diagram must be associated with at least one function; in the case of the Data Schema Diagrammer, the diagram applies to a particular module. In these diagrammers, the action of creating a new diagram initially displays a dialog box in which you pick the required object from a list of existing objects of the same type, or create the new object as you create the diagram.

7.3.2 OPENING DIAGRAMS

In order to open a diagram that already exists in the Repository, take one of these steps:

❑ Click the Open button 🔳 on the toolbar.
❑ Select File | Open....
❑ Press CTRL+O.

The Design Editor integrates its Design Navigator with the Data Diagrammer and Module Diagrammer. In this tool, you create a new diagram by selecting File | New | Data Diagram or File | New | Module Diagram. The icon New here opens a new Design Navigator window. An elegant way to create a new module or data diagram in the Design Editor is to right-click the module or database object you want to include in the diagram. Then, select the option Show on Diagram from the popup menu that appears.

The command to open a diagram in the Design Editor is File | Open | Data Diagram... or File | Open | Module Diagram.... You can launch a diagrammer and open a diagram with one single action by double-clicking the diagram object in the Navigator window of the Design Editor or the Repository Object Navigator.

If no diagrams of the given type exist in the Repository, the diagrammer displays a message box to inform you of the fact; otherwise, the Open Diagram dialog box shown in Figure 7.4 is displayed.

In this dialog box, you can pick the diagram you want to open from the list of available diagrams and click OK. Like most MDI applications, all the diagrammers maintain a list of diagrams accessed most recently. They are found under the File menu, right before the Exit item. By selecting one of the items in the list, you can open the corresponding diagram with just one click of the mouse.

7.3.3 CLOSING DIAGRAMS

To close a diagram, you can either select File | Close, or issue one of the standard Windows commands to close the diagram window. If the diagram contains unsaved changes, you are prompted to save them before closing it.

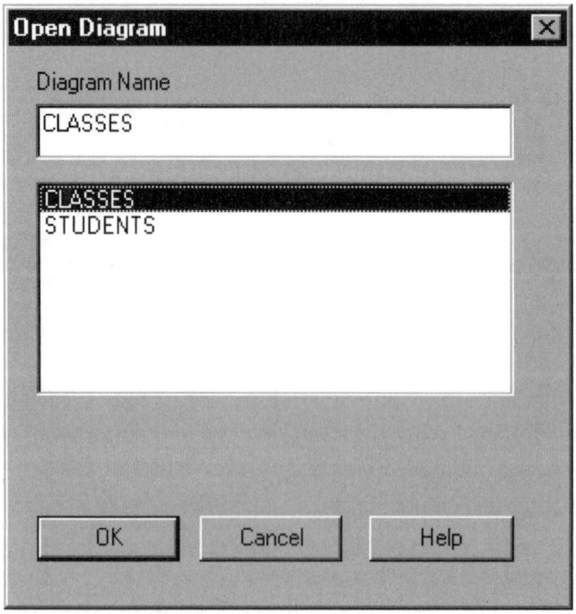

Open Diagram   ☒

Diagram Name

CLASSES

CLASSES
STUDENTS

OK   Cancel   Help

FIGURE 7.4 The Open Diagram dialog box.

In the Design Editor, the command to save a diagram is File | Save Diagram or File | Save Diagram As....

7.3.4 SAVING DIAGRAMS

You can save a diagram by issuing any one of the following commands:

❑ Click the Save button 🖫 on the toolbar.
❑ Select File | Save....
❑ Press CTRL+S.

Any of these actions saves topological information of the diagram, such as the position, dimensions, visual attributes of the objects, and the layout of the diagram. Properties of objects in the diagram are saved to the Repository after the objects are created or edited.

If you want to save the current open diagram under a different name, choose File | Save As.... A dialog similar to the one shown in Figure 7.5 appears.

FIGURE 7.5 The Save Diagram As dialog box.

In the Design Editor, you invoke the Delete Diagram dialog box by selecting File | Delete Diagram from the menu.

In this dialog box, you can see the names of existing diagrams and you can specify the new name of the diagram.

7.3.5 DELETING DIAGRAMS

You can delete diagrams by selecting File | Delete... from the diagrammer's menu. In the dialog box Delete Diagram that appears (see Figure 7.6), you can select the name of the diagram you want to delete from the list of available diagrams. After you click OK, the diagrammer displays a warning box and requests that you confirm your intention to delete the diagram.

When deleting a diagram, you are discarding only the topological information of that diagram. All the objects inside the diagram remain untouched in the Repository. If they are included in other diagrams, their position in these diagrams does not change.

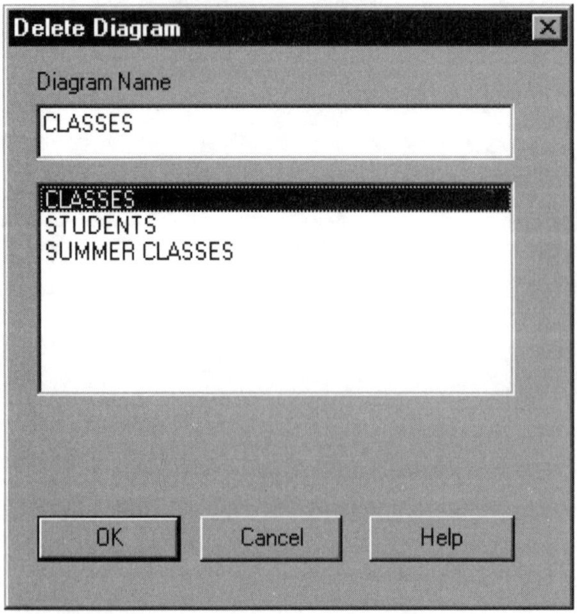

Delete Diagram　　　　　　　　　　　　　　　　⊠

Diagram Name

CLASSES

CLASSES
STUDENTS
SUMMER CLASSES

OK　　　　Cancel　　　　Help

FIGURE 7.6 The Delete Diagram dialog box.

7.3.6 MAINTAINING SUMMARY INFORMATION OF DIAGRAMS

Each diagrammer allows you to maintain and control the display of a series of information items associated with diagrams, such as name, title, author, change history, and notes. Some of this information is maintained and updated automatically by the Repository as you work with the diagram. The rest you can enter and maintain.

In order to access this information for each diagram, choose File | Summary Information... from the diagrammer's menu. The Summary Information dialog box appears. Figure 7.7 shows a typical Summary Information dialog box.

The Summary Information dialog box lists all the items that you can display on the diagram. The items that are grayed out are maintained internally by the Repository; you can enter and edit only the enabled items. To the left of each item is a check box. You need to check it if you want the item to be displayed on the diagram. This dialog box also allows you to enter longer information about the

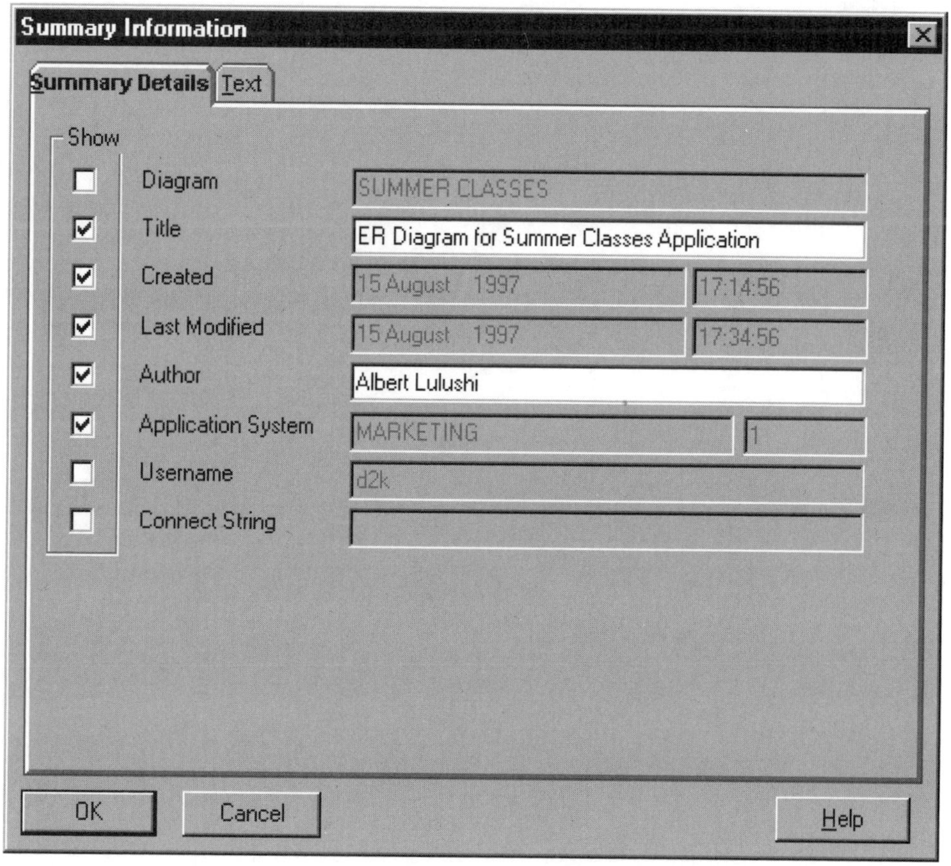

FIGURE 7.7 The Summary Information dialog box.

diagram in the free-text format fields Change History, Description, and Notes. If the dialog box is implemented as a tabbed dialog box, as shown in Figure 7.7, you can access these fields by clicking the tab Text, and then picking the desired type from the list box Text Type. In some diagrammers, such as the Data Diagrammer, the text tab of the dialog box is displayed if you click the button Text in the dialog box Summary Information.

7.3.7 PRINTING DIAGRAMS

In your activities as systems analyst and designer, creating and maintaining diagrams is as important as presenting and showing them to others. As you prepare deliverables for different tasks of your project, you will need to include different diagrams as attachments to these deliverables. In order to assist you with producing hard-copy versions of your diagrams, each diagrammer comes with wide printing options that you can use.

In order to print a diagram, issue one of these commands:

❑   Select File | Print....
❑   Click the icon Print 🖺 where available.
❑   Press CTRL+P.

In the dialog box that comes up (see Figure 7.8), you can specify the pages to print, the number of copies, and the print quality. If you want all the diagram to

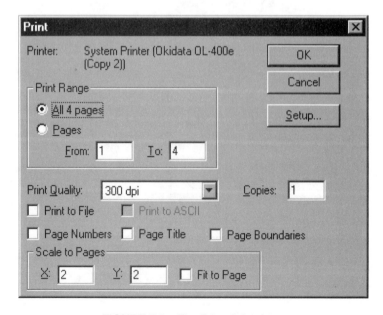

FIGURE 7.8   The Print dialog box.

be printed in one page, check the Fit to Page check box. If you want the diagram to be saved in a file in Postscript format, check the Print to File check box. In addition, by setting the options in this dialog box, you can print numbers and titles on the pages of your diagrams or scale the diagram across a number of pages.

In order to set properties and options of your printer, click the button Setup in this dialog box. This action displays the standard Windows Print Setup dialog box, which can also be accessed directly by choosing File | Print Setup....

In order to preview your diagram before sending it to the printer, select File | Print Preview. This action replaces the diagrammer window with the Print Preview window, where you can view your diagram as it will appear when printed. You can display one or two pages on the screen, zoom in and out, and send the diagram to the printer from this window.

7.3.8 CHANGING CONNECTION AND APPLICATION SYSTEM

While working in a particular diagrammer, you may need to log on as a different Repository user, or connect to a different application system. To log on as a different user, choose File | Change Connection.... If diagrams are open, they are first closed; you are prompted to save any pending changes, if they exist. When all the diagrams are closed, the Connect dialog box appears. Here you can specify the new user name, password, and database connect string.

To change the application system, select File | Change Application System... from the designer's menu. This action displays the dialog box Application Systems, which lists all the applications you can access. From this list, choose the new application to which you want to connect.

7.3.9 CHANGING ZOOMING LEVELS OF DIAGRAMS

As your diagrams grow in size, displaying their components entirely in the diagrammer's window becomes difficult. Although occasionally you would still want to view the entire diagram on the screen, most of the time you would prefer to focus on particular areas of the diagram where objects that interest you lay. Each diagrammer in Designer/2000 offers a lot of flexibility in setting the zooming level of your diagrams to different levels.

In order to zoom in on a diagram, follow one of these steps:

❑ Click the Zoom In button 🔍 on the toolbar.
❑ Select View | Zoom In.

You can zoom out a diagram by issuing one of these commands:

❑ Click the Zoom Out button 🔍 on the toolbar.
❑ Select View | Zoom Out.

You can repeat these commands as many times as is necessary to reach a comfortable viewing level for your diagram.

If you want to focus on a particular object in the diagram, select the object and click the button Fit Selection 🖬 on the toolbar. If you want to focus on a particular area of the diagram, select View | Fit to Area from the menu and click the area where you want to focus.

You can also ask the diagrammer to display the full diagram according to its own algorithm, by issuing one of the following commands:

❑   Click the Fit to Diagram button 🖬 on the toolbar.
❑   Select View | Best Fit Diagram.

Finally, each time you want to cancel the last zoom action you performed, take one of the following actions:

❑   Click the Zoom Reset button 🖬 on the toolbar.
❑   Select View | Zoom Reset.

7.3.10   MAINTAINING THE LAYOUT OF DIAGRAMS

As you work with diagrammers, you want to arrange the objects in positions that express more clearly the contents of your diagram. As you will see in Section 7.4.3, positioning the objects on a diagram is as easy as dragging and dropping them to the desired location. If you want the diagrammer to draw the diagram for you, you can invoke one of the layout utilities provided with it.

To invoke the diagrammer's layout utility, follow one of these steps:

❑   Click the Autolayout button 🖬 on the toolbar.
❑   Select Utilities | AutoLayout.

By default, the autolayout utility redraws the objects of the new diagram in the same area of the diagram occupied by the existing objects. You can ask the diagrammer explicitly to draw the new diagram in the same area as the old diagram by selecting Utilities | AutoLayout to Same Area. If on the other hand you want to redraw the diagram to a new area, select Utilities | AutoLayout to New Area and click the new diagram location where you want the objects to be placed.

You can always revert the diagram to its previous layout state by issuing one of these commands:

❑   Click the Previous Layout button 🖬 on the toolbar.
❑   Select Layout | Previous Layout.

The functionality discussed in this section is offered by all the diagrammer tools of Designer/2000 except for the Module Diagrammer component of the Design Editor, where the layout of diagrams is not complex enough to warrant it.

The algorithm used to lay out diagrams automatically has different flavors, as shown by the options discussed above. Often, when the autolayout mechanism is used, the diagrams span multiple pages. If this layout is not acceptable, you can choose Layout | Minimize Number of Pages to draw objects so that they take the least amount of space in the diagram. If even this option does not produce the desired outcome, select Layout | Rescale Diagram.... In the Rescale Diagram dialog box that appears (see Figure 7.9), you can specify the precise number of horizontal or vertical pages that you want your diagram to occupy.

In the Rescale Diagram dialog box, if the check box Scale Fonts is checked, the text labels of the diagram objects are resized proportionally with their parent objects. If the check box Maintain Aspect Ratio is checked, the ratio between horizontal and vertical pages in the new layout is the same as in the previous one. In other words, if the current diagram takes two horizontal pages and one vertical one, and you want the new diagram to span two vertical pages, the diagrammer automatically sets the number of horizontal pages to four to maintain the ratio setting as shown in Figure 7.9.

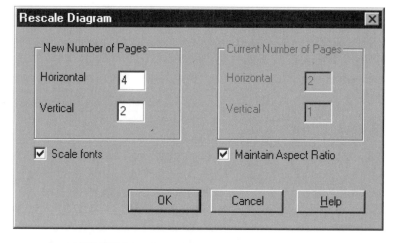

FIGURE 7.9   The Rescale Diagram dialog box.

7.3.11   MAINTAINING THE LAYOUT OF FUNCTION HIERARCHY DIAGRAMS

Function hierarchy diagrams express relationships of dependency among the objects in the diagrams. They usually contain a root object on which one or more children depend. Each of these children may in turn have one or more dependents, and so on. You can use two major types of layout in the Function Hierarchy Diagrammer: horizontal and vertical. A diagram is in horizontal layout when the root object is on top, all its children are aligned horizontally in the next level down, and so on. Each "generation" of objects is one level below the parent object. Figure 7.10 shows a function hierarchy diagram with horizontal layout.

A diagram is laid out vertically when the dependents of the root object are aligned vertically and indented to the right, their dependents are indented another level further to the right, and so on. Figure 7.11 shows the same function hierarchy diagram shown in Figure 7.10, but this time in a vertical layout.

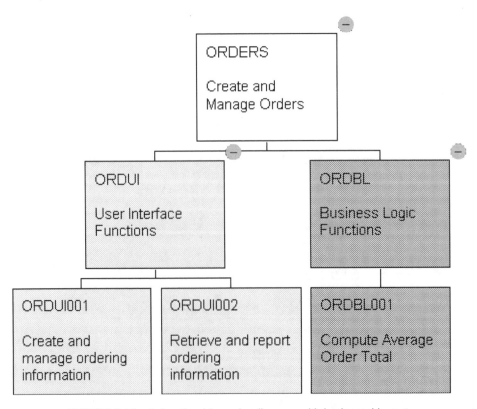

FIGURE 7.10   A function hierarchy diagram with horizontal layout.

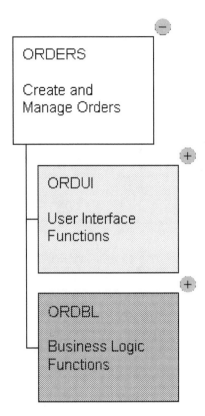

FIGURE 7.11 A function hierarchy
diagram with vertical layout.

Either of the following two commands can be used to make the diagram appear in horizontal layout:

❑ Click the Horizontal Layout button ▦ on the toolbar.
❑ Select Utilities | Horizontal Layout.

To set the diagram to a vertical layout, use one of these commands:

❑ Click the Vertical Layout button ▦ on the toolbar.
❑ Select Utilities | Vertical Layout.

In order to make your diagrams more readable and easier to follow, the Function Hierarchy Diagrammer also allows you to mix the two layout styles in the same diagram. One way to combine horizontal and vertical layout in a diagram is to issue one of the following commands:

❑ Click the Hybrid Layout button ▦ on the toolbar.
❑ Select Utilities | Hybrid Layout.

In each case, the diagrammer displays the first generation of objects horizontally and the second generation vertically, and it continues to alternate the style for each following generation. If you want to have more control on the layout of a specific branch in the hierarchy tree of objects in your diagram, select the object where this branch starts and do one of the following:

❑ Click the button Vertical Selection Layout ▣ to display all the direct dependents of that object vertically.

❑ Click the button Horizontal Selection Layout ▣ to display all the direct dependents of that object horizontally.

These commands can also be issued by selecting Utilities │ Vertical Layout Selection or Utilities │ Horizontal Layout Selection.

7.3.12 EXPANDING AND COLLAPSING
FUNCTION HIERARCHY DIAGRAMS

The Function Hierarchy Diagrammer, like other Designer/2000 tools that manage hierarchies of objects, allows you to expand and collapse objects in the diagrams. The techniques discussed in this section can be very useful, especially in diagrams that include a large number of objects, because they allow you to focus, or expand, only on the part of the diagram with which you are currently working, while hiding, or collapsing, details or other unnecessary objects. In these diagrams, objects with dependents have an icon by their side that serves as a visual indicator of their status. The plus-shaped icon ➕ indicates that the object is currently collapsed; the minus-shaped icon ➖ indicates that the object is expanded. Objects that do not have either icon by their side are leaf objects in the hierarchy tree of the diagram.

In order to expand an object in the diagram, use one of these commands:

❑ Click the Expand button ⊞ on the toolbar.
❑ Select Navigator │ Expand.
❑ Double-click the Expand icon ➕ displayed with the object on the diagram.

You can collapse an object in one of the following ways:

❑ Click the Collapse button ⊟ on the toolbar.
❑ Select Navigator │ Collapse.
❑ Double-click the Collapse icon ➖ displayed on the side of the expanded object.

Like the navigators discussed in the previous chapter, these diagrammers allow you to expand or collapse all the objects starting from a point in the hierarchy tree. To expand all the objects that depend on a given object, select that object and do one of the following:

- ❑ Click the Expand All button ⊞ on the toolbar.
- ❑ Select Navigator | Expand All.

To collapse all the hierarchies under an object you have already selected, issue one of these commands:

- ❑ Click the Collapse All button ⊟ on the toolbar.
- ❑ Select Navigator | Collapse All.

7.4 WORKING WITH OBJECTS IN DIAGRAMS

The previous section discussed a variety of tasks that you can complete in order to work with and maintain diagrams. This section offers an overview of generic actions you can take to create and maintain objects in these diagrams. Detailed information about specific objects in particular diagrammers will be discussed in the chapters to come.

7.4.1 CREATING OBJECTS

In Section 7.2.3, you learned that each diagrammer in Designer/2000 comes with two toolbars: the standard toolbar and the drawing palette. Buttons in the standard toolbar provide functionality that applies to the diagram as a whole; buttons on the drawing palette offer access to functions that apply only to objects characteristic for the diagram. Among others, each drawing palette contains icons to create these diagrammer-specific objects. For example, the Entity Relationship Diagrammer contains one icon to create entities and several others to create relationships of different kinds; the Function Hierarchy Diagrammer contains an icon to create new functions; and the Data Diagrammer has icons to create tables, views, snapshots, and different referential integrity keys.

In order to create a new object on the diagram, follow these steps:

1. Click the corresponding iconic button on the drawing palette. The mouse pointer usually changes shape to indicate that you are in "drawing" mode.
2. Click the diagram where you want the new object to appear.

At this point, a dialog box that depends on the type of object you are creating is displayed. The purpose of this dialog box is to gather the minimal information about the object required to create it in the Repository. If the information you enter in this dialog box is sufficient and does not conflict with existing Repository objects, the new object is created and displayed on the diagram.

The diagrammer assigns default dimensions to newly-created objects. But it also allows you to specify their dimensions when you create them. To size an object when you create it, follow the additional step 3:

3. While holding the mouse button down, draw the object to the desired size.

7.4.2 SELECTING OBJECTS

Before moving, resizing, cutting, pasting, or doing anything with an object, you must first select it. Selecting is therefore the most frequent action in any diagrammer. For this reason, the Select button ▮ is, by default, always active on the drawing palette of each diagrammer. To select an object, just move the mouse on the object and click. When the object is selected, handles appear around it. Handles are dark gray boxes on the corners and middle points of the object. They are used to change the size of the selected object.

Often, you need to select more than one object. Diagrammers provide two ways to select multiple objects. The first one selects one object at a time:

1. Select the first object.
2. Hold down CTRL and select each additional object.

This method allows you to select only those objects you need, anywhere on the diagram. But it can be tedious if the number of objects to be selected is large. The second method is used in this case.

1. Place the mouse pointer further to the left and higher up than any object.
2. Holding the left mouse button down, draw a virtual selection rectangle large enough to enclose entirely all the objects to be selected.

After you release the left mouse button, all the objects completely inside the selection rectangle are selected. Selecting objects this way is particularly helpful if the objects are adjacent or near one another. However, other objects may be selected together with the desired objects. If this is the case, deselect any unwanted objects. To deselect an object, follow these steps:

1. Hold down the CTRL key.
2. Click the unwanted object.

Sometimes, you may need to select all the objects on the current diagram. A quick way to select all the objects in a diagram is to choose Edit | Select All. In some diagrammers, you can also press CTRL+A.

7.4.3 MOVING AND RESIZING OBJECTS

As discussed in Section 7.4.1, diagrammers allow you to place newly created objects where you want on the diagram. They also allow you to size the object as you create it. Nevertheless, after an object is created, you may need to move and resize it. You can perform these actions on individual objects or multiple objects simultaneously. The only difference is when you select them. Multiple objects are moved as a group and, when resized, their dimensions change proportionally.

To move an object after it is selected, follow these steps:

1. Click anywhere in the object and hold the left mouse button down. Make sure not to click one of the handles.
2. While holding the left button down, drag the object to the position you want on the canvas.
3. Release the button when you are satisfied with the new position.

You can also use the arrow keys to move an object. Each time the arrow key is pressed, the object moves one grid unit in the direction of the arrow.

To resize an object after it is selected, click and drag its handles. If only the width of the object needs to be changed, use the handles on the vertical edges of the selecting rectangle. Handles on horizontal edges are used to adjust the object's height. The handles on all four vertices of the selecting rectangle are used to resize an object horizontally and vertically at the same time.

To resize an object, proceed as follows:

1. Click the appropriate handle of the object.
2. While holding the left mouse button down, drag the handle until the object reaches the desired size.
3. Release the left mouse button when you are satisfied with the new size of the object.

In the Function Hierarchy Diagrammer, all the objects on the diagram have the same dimensions. In these diagrammers, resizing one object resizes all the objects on the diagram.

 In the Function Hierarchy Diagrammer, the position of the object on the diagram has important meaning for the object and reflects its relationships with other objects. This diagrammer does not allow you to move the objects freely around the diagram.

7.4.4 REVERTING CHANGES TO DIAGRAMS

The last move or resizing action performed in the diagrammer can be reversed by the command Undo. This is a helpful command that protects your diagrams from accidental and unwanted actions. Understand that diagrammers implement only a one-level Undo command. This means that if you want to undo something, do so immediately after the action or command is executed, without performing anything else in between.

You have three ways to invoke the Undo utility:

❑ Click the Undo button ⊡ on the toolbar.
❑ Select Edit | Undo.
❑ Press CTRL+Z. This is also the standard Microsoft Windows Undo command.

In all three cases, your last action is reversed. When you issue the Undo command, the Undo menu item in the Edit menu changes to Redo.

Like any other command, you can undo the Undo command as well. In other words, the action you wanted to undo can be redone. You can perform the Redo command only if nothing else has happened since your last Undo. To redo an undone command, take any of the following steps:

❑ Click the Undo button ⊡ on the toolbar.
❑ Select Edit | Redo.
❑ Press CTRL+Z.

7.4.5 DELETING OBJECTS

To delete objects in a diagram, you must first select them. Then do one of the following:

❑ Press DELETE.
❑ Select Edit | Delete.

In both cases, the objects are removed not only from the diagram, but also from the Repository. Once an object is deleted from the Repository, it cannot be recovered easily. Use backups and exports of the application system to restore it. Since the process is not straightforward, use this command very carefully and only when you intend to remove the object entirely from your application. To protect you from unintentional deletes, the diagrammer prompts you with a confirmation message box each time you request to delete an object.

7.4.6 CUTTING, COPYING, AND PASTING OBJECTS

If you want to remove objects from the diagram without deleting them from the Repository, use the Cut command. This command places the information about the object in the diagrammer's "clipboard." To cut an object or group of objects from the diagram, do one of the following things:

❑ Click the Cut button 🔲 on the toolbar.
❑ Select Edit | Cut.
❑ Press CTRL+X.

Selected objects are removed from the diagram and placed in the clipboard. However, they are not removed from the application system Repository, as is the case when you issue a delete command. So whenever you want to remove objects from a diagram, cut them rather than deleting them from the diagram. If you want to place just a copy of the objects in the clipboard without removing them from the diagram, use the Copy command. To copy an already selected object or group of objects, take one of these actions:

❑ Click the Copy button 🔲 on the toolbar.
❑ Select Edit | Copy.
❑ Press CTRL+C.

Once the clipboard is populated with the cut or copied objects, you can paste its contents onto another diagram. To do so, first switch to that diagram, and then issue one of the following commands:

❑ Click the Paste button 🔲 on the toolbar.
❑ Select Edit | Paste.
❑ Press CTRL+V.

From what I said above, you can easily conclude that the combination copy and paste is used to place the same objects on multiple diagrams; cut and paste is used to move objects from one diagram to another. Understand that when copying in Designer/2000 diagrammers, you are merely copying the presence of the same object in another diagram. You are not creating copies of the objects in the Repository; this task is completed in the Repository Object Navigator, as explained in Chapter 5.

7.4.7 MAINTAINING VISUAL PROPERTIES OF OBJECTS

Each object in the Designer/2000 diagrammers is created with a set of predefined visual attributes, which include the font of text labels, the color and thickness of the borderline, and the fill color. These predefined settings allow you to create diagrams with uniform look and feel. At the same time, each diagrammer allows you to change these visual attributes for any individual object. Before changing the visual properties of one or more objects in your diagrams, you must first select them, and then click one of the iconic buttons on the drawing palette of the diagrammer used to maintain the visual attributes of objects.

To change the font properties of objects, click the Font button 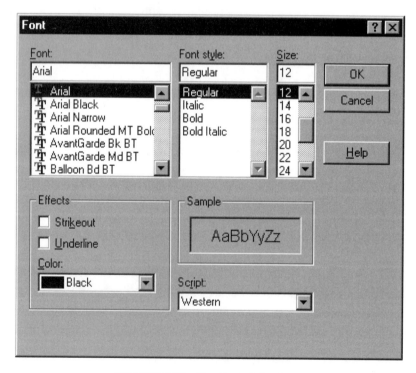 on the toolbar. This action displays the Font dialog box shown in Figure 7.12.

The main components of the Font dialog box are the lists of options from which attributes settings can be selected. The list Font on the left displays all the fonts available to the diagrammer. Windows TrueType fonts are preceded by the indicator ⱦ. By default, diagrammers use the font Arial, but you can select any font installed on your environment. The list Font style in the middle allows you to select the font style. It can be regular, **bold**, *italic* or ***bold italic***. The list Size to the right allows you to specify the size of the chosen font. Usually, only TrueType fonts support different sizes of their characters. For example, Arial font shown in Figure 7.12 supports a whole range of font sizes, but System font, which is not TrueType, supports only characters of size 10. In the lower left corner of the Font dialog box, you can specify two additional font attributes: Underline and Strikeout. If the check boxes are marked, then the text will have <u>underline</u> and ~~strikeout~~ effects, respectively. Furthermore, you can pick a color for the font from the dropdown list Color in the Effects group. The Font dialog box offers you a chance to see the outcome of your selections in the Sample field. In this field, you can see

FIGURE 7.12   The Font dialog box.

how the text objects you are modifying will look, before actually making the changes.

In order to change the line width of the objects, you need to click the Line Width button 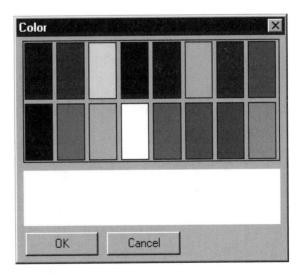 on the toolbar. This action displays a list of ten possible settings for this property, from which you can pick the one that best suits your needs. To change the color of the borderline, click the Line Color button ⬛ on the toolbar. This action displays a color palette in a dialog box similar to the one shown in Figure 7.13. In this dialog box, you can click one of the 16 basic colors and then click OK to set the color of lines for the selected objects.

Finally, to change the fill color of an object, you click the Fill Color button ⬛ on the drawing palette. A Color dialog box similar to the one shown in Figure 7.13 appears. The Color palette for this tool has more options than the one shown in Figure 7.13. Functionally though, they are the same: you pick a color from the palette and click OK to set the fill color of the selected objects.

7.4.8 EDITING OBJECTS

Besides maintaining objects in diagrams with the actions described above, you also need to edit the properties of these objects. The properties that you most likely set in diagrammers are generally presented to you in the form of tabbed dialog boxes. You may display this dialog box in one of the following two ways:

❑ Double-click the object whose properties you want to view and edit.
❑ Select Edit | Properties....

Figure 7.14 shows a typical dialog box of this kind.

FIGURE 7.13 The Color dialog box.

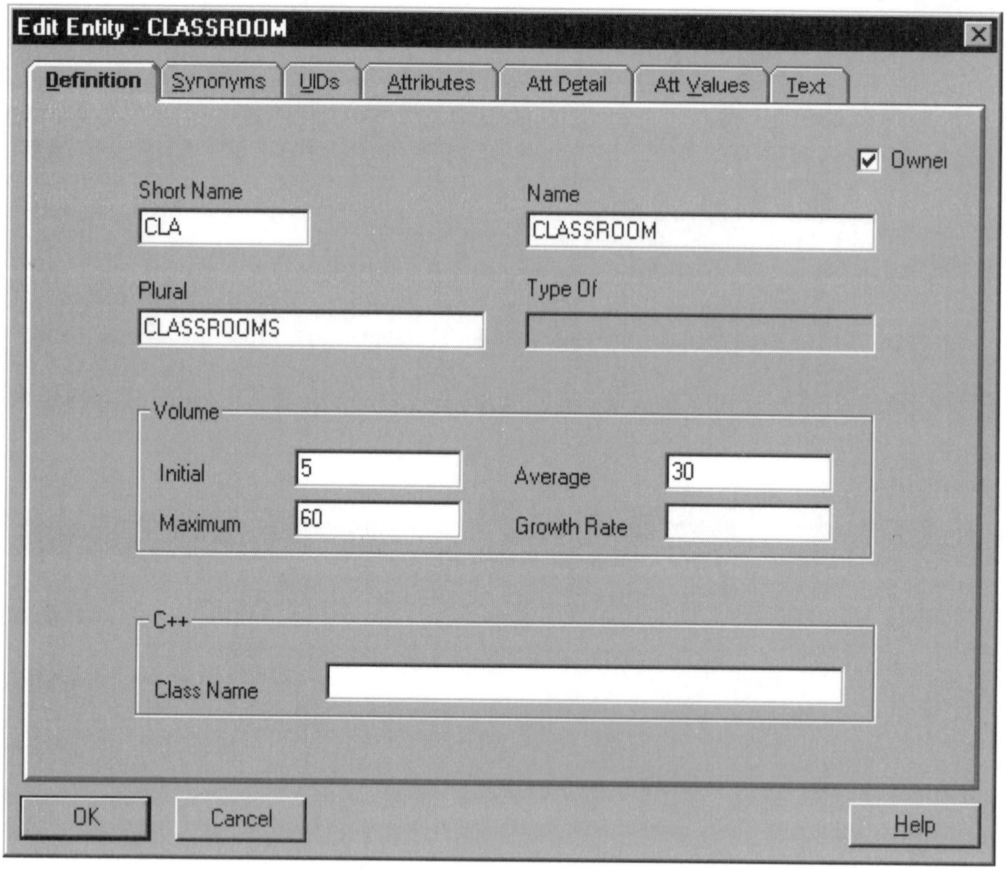

FIGURE 7.14 A typical tabbed dialog box.

The title bar of tabbed dialog boxes contains the type and name of the object being edited. The properties of the object are grouped usually by functionality and placed in separate property sheets according to the metaphor of folders in a file cabinet. Each property sheet is a folder, and the tabbed index on top of the dialog box contains the names of the folders. To access the properties under a functional group, you need to click the corresponding tab in the index.

Each tabbed dialog box comes with at least four buttons aligned horizontally at the bottom. In order to save the changes made in all the property tabs, and close the dialog you must click OK. (In general, dialog boxes in the Design Editor have replaced OK with Finish.) To save the changes without closing the dialog box, click Apply. If you do not want any of these changes to take effect, click Cancel. The button Help always brings up context-sensitive help for the current tab of the dialog box. When the dialog box for an object is initially opened, the button Apply is disabled. This button is enabled as soon as you change a property's setting.

7.5 CUSTOMIZING DIAGRAMMER PREFERENCES

Each diagrammer has a set of preferences that control the color and dimensions of objects created on the diagram, which objects are displayed on the diagram, the grid of the diagram, and so on. You can view and maintain these preferences by selecting Option | Customize... from the diagrammer's menu. Figure 7.15 shows the Customize dialog box for the Entity Relationship Diagrammer, which is also a typical Customize dialog box.

The Customize dialog box in different diagrammers contains a set of options grouped under the group Elements that control the visual attributes of objects in the diagram. The Type list box allows you to set the visual attributes for a particular type of object on the diagram. Below this list, one or more text items show the current font setting of text labels for the objects in the diagram. The

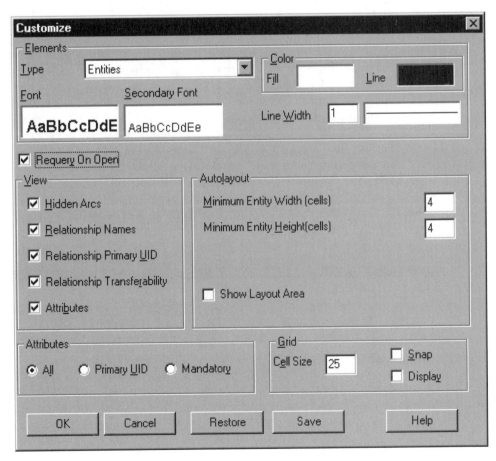

FIGURE 7.15 A typical Customize dialog box.

Customize dialog box shown in Figure 7.15 has two such items, labeled Font and Secondary Font. The first one displays the font of entity names in the diagram; the second one displays the font of attribute names. The items in the group Color show the current settings of the Fill Color and Line Color properties. The items in the Line Width group display the settings of this property. In order to modify the visual preferences of a diagram, click in the appropriate text item, and in the dialog box that appears, set the properties as discussed in Section 7.4.7. For example, to change the font of entity names, click the text item Font and set the desired properties in the Font dialog box shown in Figure 7.12.

The Customize dialog box also contains fields that allow you to set the minimum size of objects that the Autolayout utility uses, the cell size for the diagrammer's grid, whether the grid should be displayed or not, and whether objects should snap to grid or not. All these properties are grouped together in the Autolayout group of properties.

An important preference that I recommend setting is Requery On Open. If this preference is set, each time a diagram is opened, the diagrammer retrieves the most up-to-date settings of objects from the Repository; if the preference is not set, the diagrammer retrieves only the visual image of the diagram. In cases when objects are modified or deleted in the Repository Object Navigator, or in another diagram, the current diagram continues to display the image of these objects as they were the last time the diagram was saved. If you do not requery the diagram when it is opened, you need to requery it manually. Like the Navigators discussed in the previous chapter, diagrammers allow you to requery properties of selected objects by selecting Edit | Requery Selection or clicking the icon Requery Selection ⬚. All the objects in the diagram may be requeried by selecting Edit | Requery All or clicking the icon Requery All ⬚.

Finally, the Customize dialog box contains options that are specific to the particular diagrammer that owns the dialog box. Figure 7.15, for example, which shows the Customize dialog box for the Entity Relationship Diagrammer, con-

The Design Editor does not have a unified Customize dialog box like the other diagrammers. The command Options | Customize... in this editor displays the filter dialog box that was discussed in Chapter 6. When the context of the Design Editor is a diagram, three items under the menu Options allow you to maintain and administer the colors, font, style, what elements to hide and what to show, as well as the layout of the diagrams. These items, Color/Font/Style..., Show/Hide..., and Layout..., essentially are used for the same purpose as the dialog box Customize discussed earlier.

tains options under the View and Attributes groups that allow you to control the type of objects that the diagram displays.

7.6 ENHANCING DIAGRAMS WITH OLE TECHNOLOGY

OLE is a technology developed by Microsoft Corporation that is based on the integration and reusability of different software components in one application. Formerly known as Object Linking and Embedding, hence its name, today OLE includes a much wider range of features and functionality. Due to the growth in popularity of ActiveX controls, which are the latest development in the OLE technology, people often identify OLE with ActiveX. One aspect of OLE, OLE Documents, allows the creation of compound documents through the linking or embedding of objects from OLE servers in the body of OLE client applications. Examples of OLE servers are applications such as Microsoft Word, Excel, and components of Designer/2000 such as the Entity Relationship Diagrammer, Business Process Modeller, and so on. These applications are also OLE clients. Some applications, such as Developer/2000 Forms, are only OLE clients. In the context of Designer/2000 diagrammers, OLE Documents enables you to enrich your analysis and design diagrams with functionality from other applications. For example, when engaged in Business Process Reengineering (BPR) activities, you can help your audience grasp the conclusions of your analysis or the advantages of the new processes you propose, by inserting in the process model diagram video or sound clips that show how the process is conducted in real life. Chapter 11 will discuss to a greater extent the use of multimedia applications in process modeling. The following sections discuss how to implement linking and embedding of OLE components in the Designer/2000 diagrammers.

7.6.1 INSERTING OLE OBJECTS IN DIAGRAMS

To insert a new object from an OLE server in an open diagram, select Edit | Insert New Object.... This action displays the Insert Object dialog box, shown in Figure 7.16.

In this dialog box, you specify the type of object to be created, whether to create this object from scratch or from an existing file, and whether to display the new object in its full size or as an icon on the diagram. The list box Object Type contains all the applications that the Windows Registry has recorded as OLE servers. You specify the type of application you want to insert by picking the entry for the application from this list. The options shown in Figure 7.16 will create a new entity relationship diagram that will be displayed as an icon on the client diagram. Clicking OK in this case will launch the Entity Relationship Diagrammer and open a new diagram.

If the object you want to insert in the diagram exists as a file, for example, a Microsoft Word document or Excel chart, you may insert the object from the file

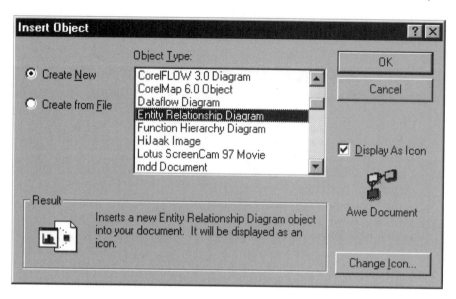

FIGURE 7.16 Creating a new object in the Insert Object dialog box.

by selecting the radio button Create from File in the Insert Object dialog box. When you pick this option, the dialog box changes to the one shown in Figure 7.17.

In this dialog box, you can click Browse to display a standard Windows dialog box that allows you to search the directories tree and select the file to insert.

If the OLE server application can save objects as files (for example, Microsoft Word or Excel), you may be better off creating a link to this file rather than embedding its contents in the body of the diagram. The reason is that when you embed an object, the diagram saves all the binary information required to start the embedded application and open the object, when you decide to edit it. This may increase significantly the size of the diagram and the time the diagrammer takes to transfer it back and forth between the Repository and your workstation. When linking is used instead of embedding, the diagram saves only a "pointer" to the Registry entry for the linked application and to the location of the file in the file system. In order to insert an object in linked form, simply check the option Link in the Insert Object dialog box shown in Figure 7.17.

7.6.2 EDITING OLE OBJECTS IN DIAGRAMS

Once you have inserted an object from an OLE server application in your diagram, you can use that object from within your diagram without having to open it from the application that created it. The information stored with the embedded or linked object is all the diagrammer needs to launch the server application and allow you to manipulate the object.

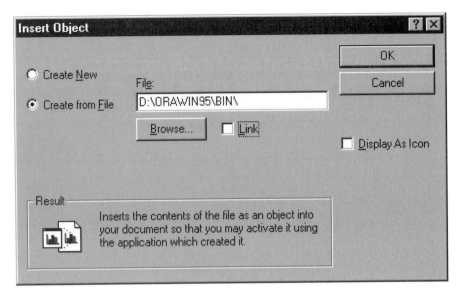

FIGURE 7.17   Creating an object from a file in the Insert Object dialog box.

You can perform a limited number of actions on an embedded or linked document. These actions are also known as verbs of the OLE objects. Typically, document servers, such as a Microsoft Word document or an Entity Relationship Diagram, expose two verbs: Edit and Open. Multimedia servers, such as Microsoft Video or Microsoft Sound, expose the verbs Play and Edit.

All the verbs of an OLE object are displayed under Edit | Object. This is the last item in the Edit menu and is enabled only if you select an OLE object on the diagram. From the verbs that each OLE server exposes to the surrounding environment, one has priority over the others. For document servers, this is the verb Edit; for multimedia applications, this is the verb Play. You can activate the default verb of an OLE object by double-clicking that object.

7.6.3   MAINTAINING LINKS TO OLE OBJECTS

If a diagram contains links to files, you can maintain them by selecting Edit | Links... (this menu option is disabled if the diagram has no linked documents in it). This command invokes the Links dialog box, shown in Figure 7.18.

This dialog box lists all the linked objects that the diagram contains. The central area of this dialog repeats concisely the information displayed at the bottom. The Source is the name and location of the file linked to the OLE object. The Type corresponds to the OLE class that produced the object. The update mode by default is Automatic. This means that whenever the contents of the file change, the modifications are seen immediately and auto-

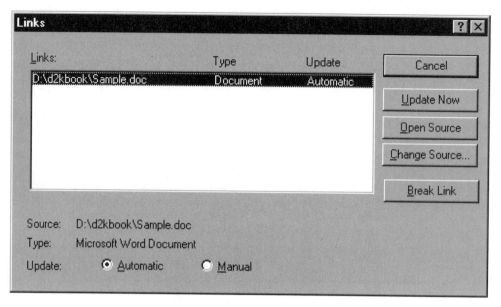

FIGURE 7.18   The Links dialog box.

matically by the diagrammer. If the radio button Manual is checked instead, the only way to update the OLE object in the diagrammer is to click the button Update Now in the Links dialog box.

In this dialog box, you can also change the file linked with the OLE container by clicking the Change Source... button. A standard Browse dialog box is displayed, which you can use to search for the new file. If you want to launch the server application, click the button Open Source.

Finally, if you click the button Break Link, the link between the OLE container and the file is disrupted. You are left with just a static picture of the object, and any editing functionality is lost. In this case, only the bitmap remains after you break the link. If, for example, the object is an Excel graph, what remains after you break the link with the source file is just a pictorial representation of the chart, with no data or editing capabilities behind it.

7.7 THE MATRIX DIAGRAMMER

A special type of diagrammer in the family of Designer/2000 tools is the Matrix Diagrammer. This is used to create and maintain a variety of matrices that document the relationships between objects of two different types. Typical matrices are the ones that map business functions to business units, business functions to entities, and so on. You will see several examples of matrices throughout this book. In this section, you will learn how to work with the Matrix Diagrammer.

A large number of similarities exist between the Matrix Diagrammer and the diagrammers discussed in general in previous sections of this chapter. Like the other diagrammers, the Matrix Diagrammer is an MDI application that allows you to open and edit several matrix diagrams at the same time. Many diagram-level actions, such as open, save, print, change application system, change connection, and so on, are performed identically in the Matrix Diagrammer as in the other diagrammers. Given this similarity, the following sections will discuss only functionality that is unique to the Matrix Diagrammer.

7.7.1 CREATING AND MAINTAINING DOCUMENTS

As in other diagrammers, to create a new matrix document in the Matrix Diagrammer, issue one of the following commands:

- ❑ Click the New Matrix button ▣ on the toolbar.
- ❑ Select File | New.
- ❑ Press CTRL+N.

Any of these commands displays the New Matrix dialog box, shown in Figure 7.19.

This dialog box is made up of two list boxes. The list Row on the left helps you define which object will populate the rows of the matrix; the one to the right, labeled Column, is used to define the column of the matrix. When the dialog box appears initially, both lists contain all the object types defined in the Repository. Selecting one object in one list defines the first coordinate of the matrix and automatically restricts the options on the other lists to only those objects that can be associated with the first object. Picking an object from this list defines the second dimension of the matrix.

After selecting the dimensions of the matrix, click OK. This action displays the Settings dialog box (see Figure 7.20).

The Settings dialog box is a tabbed dialog box like the ones discussed in Section 7.4.8. It always has three tabbed properties sheets whose contents depend on the objects you selected earlier to populate the rows and columns of the matrix. The first tab displays all the properties of the object that will occupy the rows of the matrix; the second tab lists all the properties of the object that will serve as the column of the matrix.

Check the check box View for each property you want to include in the matrix. In the case shown in Figure 7.20, properties *Name* and *Annual Growth Rate* will be displayed for each entity. In order to sort the rows or the columns of the matrix by the values of a property, you can pick A for ascending and D for descending from the Order list box. Furthermore, you can restrict the contents of

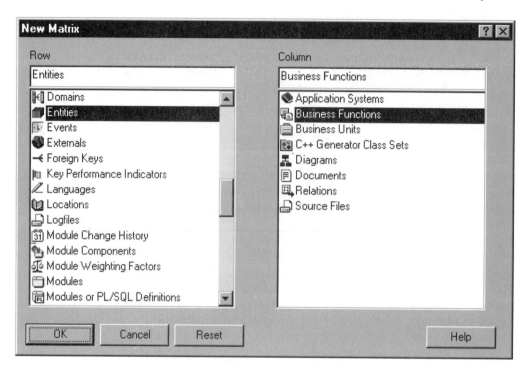

FIGURE 7.19 New Matrix dialog box.

the matrix by applying restriction criteria in the Filter text items. For example, the matrix shown in Figure 7.20 will be populated with only those entities whose *Annual Growth Rate* is greater than 20 percent.

In the first two tabs, you can also control some visual attributes of the elements of the matrix. You can specify, for example, the width in number of characters for the columns of the matrix, the way the contents of each cell will be aligned, or the number of lines in which the setting of a property can be broken if it cannot fit on one line. If you want to modify the default font settings for the whole matrix, click the Font button at the bottom of the dialog box. This action displays the same Font dialog box discussed earlier and shown in Figure 7.12.

The third tab of the Settings dialog box is used to specify what will go in the intersection cells of the matrix. Figure 7.21 shows an example of this tab.

The properties displayed in this tab are defined by the association between the two object types that form the matrix. Again here, mark those properties that you want to be displayed in the matrix cells by checking the check box View. If you plan to include more than one property in each cell, separate them with a literal specified in the field Separator in the bottom, right-hand corner of the tab. You may also want to recast missing values to some conventional string, such as 'N/A,' as shown in Figure 7.21. The group Displayed as, to the right of the prop-

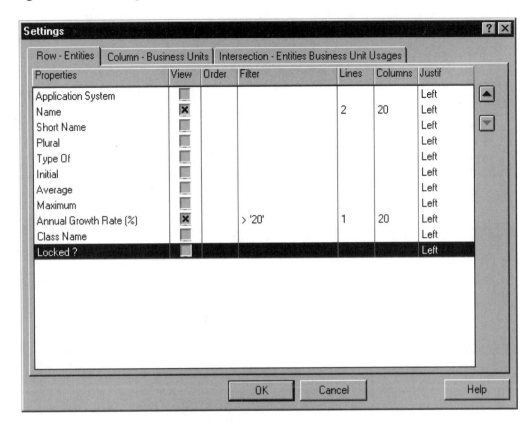

FIGURE 7.20   The Settings dialog box.

erty tab, will be populated with different items according to the contents of the matrix. For example, in a matrix like the one discussed here that shows the usage of entities by business functions, the text items Create, Retrieve, Update, and Delete are enabled. To have the cells populated with the letters C, R, U, and D, you do not need to change the settings of any of these items. If you want to specify different values, simply enter your own string in the appropriate fields.

The properties displayed in the tabs of the Settings dialog box are displayed based on their internal order in the Repository. However, the Matrix Diagrammer allows you to change this order by using one of the icons to the right of the list control. In order to move a property one step up or down the list of properties, click the icons ▲ or ▼, respectively.

After the matrix is created, you can modify the contents of its rows, columns, and cells by invoking Edit | Settings... from the diagrammer's menu. This action again displays the Settings dialog box, in which you can make your modifications as discussed above. Another modification you can make to the matrix is to change its view mode. By default, the Matrix Diagrammer displays ma-

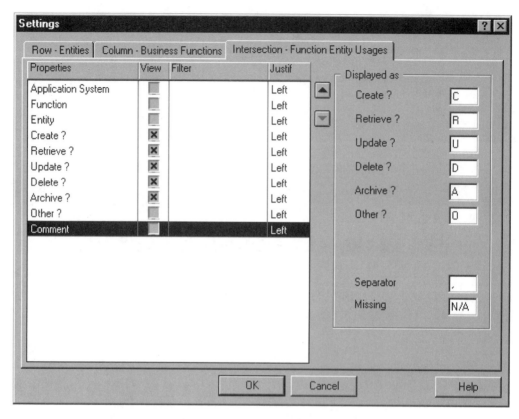

FIGURE 7.21   The Intersection tab of the Settings dialog box.

trices as rows and columns of properties with values in the intersection cells displayed as text strings. Figure 7.22 shows the example of a matrix displayed in default mode.

You can have check marks placed in the cells that contain data by putting the matrix in iconic mode. You can view the matrix in iconic mode by issuing one of these commands:

Business Functions / Entities	Create and Manage Orders	User Interface Functions	Business Logic Functions	Create and manage ordering information	Retrieve and report ordering information	Compute Average Order Total
LINE ITEM				CRUD	R	
ORDER				CRUD	R	

FIGURE 7.22   A matrix diagram in default mode.

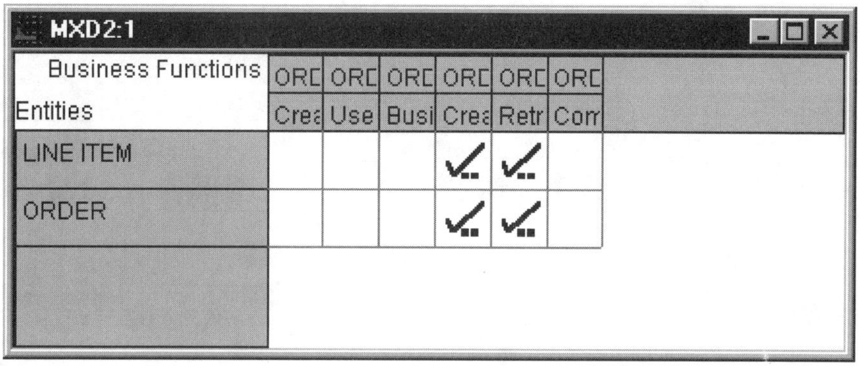

FIGURE 7.23 A matrix diagram in iconic mode.

❑ Click the Iconic View button 🔳 on the toolbar.
❑ Select View | Iconic.

Figure 7.23 shows the same matrix in iconic mode.

If the matrix contains a large number of elements in the horizontal or vertical axes, you can use micro view mode to quickly locate the part of the matrix with which you want to work, and then switch to standard mode. Micro view mode is also known as micromap mode. In order to change the matrix to micro view, do one of the following:

❑ Click the Micro View button 🔳 on the toolbar.
❑ Select View | Micro.

Figure 7.24 shows the matrix used here as an example displayed in micromap mode.

Finally, in order to set the matrix back to standard view mode, issue one of these commands:

❑ Click the Standard View button 🔳 on the toolbar.
❑ Select View | Standard.

7.7.2 CREATING AND MAINTAINING OBJECTS

A matrix document does not serve only as a convenient tool to display the associations between objects, but also provides you with ways to view and edit the properties of each object, whether it is displayed in the rows, columns, or intersection cells of the matrix. Furthermore, you can create new objects and add them to the rows or columns of the matrix, or delete existing objects from the matrix and the Repository.

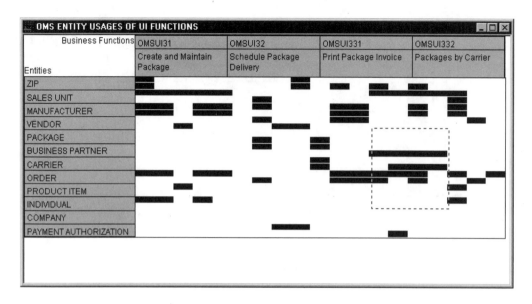

FIGURE 7.24   A matrix diagram in micromap mode.

The properties of objects are displayed and maintained in Properties windows similar to the ones you use in the Repository Object Navigator, discussed in Chapter 6. Double-click an object or select Edit | Properties... to display the first Properties window in the matrix diagram (see Figure 7.25).

You can edit the properties of one or more objects at the same time; the only difference is when you select them. In order to select multiple cells in the matrix, you can use the standard Windows SHIFT+CLICK method for a range of objects and CTRL+CLICK method for individual objects.

In order to create new objects in the matrix, issue one of the following commands:

❑   Click the Create button ⬛ on the toolbar.
❑   Select Edit | Create.

In the Properties window for the new object, fill out the properties according to the definition of the new object. As in other Properties windows, the mandatory properties here are displayed in red until you supply a value for them.

In order to delete an object, issue one of these two commands:

❑   Click the Delete button ⬛ on the toolbar.
❑   Select Edit | Delete.

FIGURE 7.25 A typical Properties window in the matrix diagram.

As in other diagrammers, deleting an object from a matrix document removes the object from the matrix and from the Repository; therefore the command must be used with care.

7.8 SUMMARY

The majority of Designer/2000 tools fall in the category of diagrammers—MDI applications—which allow you to create and maintain several types of diagrams. These diagrams are used to represent the objects of your analysis and design in a clear and concise manner. This chapter covers all the generic functionality that is common across Designer/2000 diagrammers. In particular, it focuses on the following topics:

- ❑ **Diagrams and Diagrammers**
  - ❑ Diagrams
  - ❑ Designer/2000 Diagrammers
- ❑ **Components of Diagrammers**
  - ❑ Multiple Document Interface Applications
  - ❑ Menu
  - ❑ Toolbar

❏ **Working with Diagrams**
   ❏ Creating Diagrams
   ❏ Opening Diagrams
   ❏ Closing Diagrams
   ❏ Saving Diagrams
   ❏ Deleting Diagrams
   ❏ Maintaining Summary Information of Diagrams
   ❏ Printing Diagrams
   ❏ Changing Connection and Application System
   ❏ Changing Zooming Levels of Diagrams
   ❏ Maintaining the Layout of Diagrams
   ❏ Maintaining the Layout of Function Hierarchy Diagrams
   ❏ Expanding and Collapsing Function Hierarchy Diagrams

❏ **Working with Objects in Diagrams**
   ❏ Creating Objects
   ❏ Selecting Objects
   ❏ Moving and Resizing Objects
   ❏ Reverting Changes to Diagrams
   ❏ Deleting Objects
   ❏ Cutting, Copying, and Pasting Objects
   ❏ Maintaining Visual Properties of Objects
   ❏ Editing Objects

❏ **Customizing Diagrammer Preferences**

❏ **Enhancing Diagrams with OLE Technology**
   ❏ Inserting OLE Objects in Diagrams
   ❏ Editing OLE Objects in Diagrams
   ❏ Maintaining Links to OLE Objects

❏ **The Matrix Diagrammer**
   ❏ Creating and Maintaining Documents
   ❏ Creating and Maintaining Objects

Part II

STRATEGIC PLANNING AND BUSINESS AREA ANALYSIS

Chapter 8. Modeling the Business Direction of the Enterprise

Chapter 9. The Enterprise Functional and Information Models

Chapter 10. Modeling Business Processes

Chatper 11. Business Area Analysis

Chapter 12. Business Process Reengineering

MODELING THE BUSINESS DIRECTION OF THE ENTERPRISE

- Setting the Scene
- The Enterprise Model
- Business Units
- Goals and Objectives
- Problems
- Critical Success Factors
- Key Performance Indicators
- Assumptions
- Summary

Part One offered an overview of Designer/2000 tools and introduced the major skills and techniques you need in order to work with these tools. The remaining chapters of the book will enable you to turn Designer/2000 into a major asset for your success in activities such as enterprise and business process modeling, systems analysis and design, and application design and development.

8.1   SETTING THE SCENE

So that you can better relate the concepts discussed here with situations you are likely to encounter in real life, these chapters extensively use a fictional company, The American Software Club (TASC). Although fictional, you will see that TASC represents a typical enterprise where analysts equipped with the right knowledge and tools can make a difference. Information about this company will be introduced in appropriate form when the context requires it. Section 8.1.1 offers an initial overview of this company.

The other important character in this book is the person who will set up the information infrastructure to support and stimulate the growth of the enterprise; who will identify problems and offer solutions; who will analyze business needs and propose information systems to meet these needs; and finally, who will design, develop, and deploy these information systems. This person is you, and Section 8.1.2 describes the roles you will play and the qualities you will develop while reading this book.

8.1.1   THE AMERICAN SOFTWARE CLUB

The American Software Club is a mail-order company that specializes in software products for home and office. TASC purchases the products directly from the software companies at discounted wholesale prices, which are negotiated semi-annually. TASC is responsible for picking up products from the vendors' warehouses and transporting them to its own warehouses and distribution centers spread across the United States. TASC markets the products through catalogs, published and distributed monthly to its current and potential customers. Customers interested in a product contact their regional sales representative through an 800 number. Besides responding to product inquiries, sales representatives also take orders and proactively contact customers with various promotional offers.

The customer base of TASC can be divided into two major segments. The first one includes corporations that are interested primarily in business software and office suites. The business generated by this segment accounts for 35 percent of the total sales of TASC. The second segment is made up of individual customers who purchase primarily educational software, games, and tax packages. The sales to this segment are highly seasonal, unlike the sales to the first segment, which tend to be constant throughout the year. The Holiday Season at the end of the year is the busiest period for the company. Other peak periods are the last six weeks before April 15, when almost 80 percent of the tax software is ordered and delivered, and the period from mid-August to mid-September, when about 50 percent of educational software products is sold.

For the last five years, the annual sales of TASC have grown by 20 percent, to $60 million posted this year. Currently, the company employs 200 people full-time. According to data published in business magazines and newspapers, the management of TASC believes it has a 10 percent share in software sales nation-wide. Fifty percent of this market is owned by large software manufacturers which distribute their products through their own channels. However, TASC considers these companies its allies rather than competitors and its strategy has been to negotiate with them large-quantity purchases at wholesale prices for products that it can then offer to customers at a modest markup. The remaining 40 percent of the market is shared by three nation-wide retail chains, which offer hardware and software products to individual customers in about 1000 locations across the country. TASC is disadvantaged in competing with these companies because they can obtain products from vendors at larger quantities and deeper discounts. However, being a mail-order business, TASC does not have to incur the cost of maintaining and operating retail stores. The reduced overhead costs allow TASC to offer three out of four products at lower prices than its competi-tors. In addition, TASC is a major source of distribution for products developed by small companies, often individual entrepreneurs, which are not considered important enough by the large retail chains. TASC intends to maintain this niche market by working closely with the small vendors. As part of the efforts to main-tain warm relations with them, TASC publishes a quarterly newsletter and main-tains a forum on the Internet dedicated to small and start-up software businesses.

On a final note, TASC is managed by an aggressive team of executives who continuously seek ways to raise the level of customer satisfaction, improve the overall performance of the company, expand its share on the market, and reward achievements of its employees.

8.1.2 YOUR ASSIGNMENT

The Chief Information Officer (CIO) of TASC has brought you in as an outside expert to help the company in strategic planning, to identify and analyze its busi-ness areas, to evaluate existing information systems, and to assess the need for additional ones. During the second phase of your assignment, you will design and develop applications identified in the earlier term. As a top-notch software engineer, you will need to wear several hats to meet the expectations of the CIO. In particular, you will be required to serve as:

❑ **Strategic Planning Facilitator.** You will determine an overall enterprise model for TASC, which will include, among others, the organizational chart, the functional areas, and the data subjects of the company. Furthermore, you will help identify, analyze, and document the company's mission, objectives, goals, problems, critical success factors, and key performance indicators.

❑ **Modeler of Business Processes.** You will help identify, understand, analyze, and document the company's major processes, and the steps, triggers, outcomes, and flows associated with them.

❑ **Reengineering Champion.** You will identify processes that, if redesigned and reengineered, will improve the measurable productivity parameters radically. You will make the case for reengineering these processes, and will promote information systems as important factors that will make the new processes succeed.

❑ **Business Area Analyst.** You will identify and analyze the business areas of the company. In particular, you will create and maintain the data model, the functional hierarchy, and the data flows of each business area.

❑ **Database Designer.** From the data model for a particular business area, you will derive the physical database schema. You will enhance and customize this schema to support the applications that will use the data items included in it.

❑ **Application Designer and Developer.** You will design and develop applications that meet needs and requirements identified in earlier stages of your analysis.

As an outsider, you will bring to the table your impartial and objective perspective to the business problems. On the other hand, you will have to adapt to the new environment, become familiar with the company's culture, traditions, and policies, and begin contributing to the project more quickly than in other situations. Figure 8.1 contains a list of the top ten qualities you need to have or develop in order to fulfill your assignment successfully.

❑ Problem Solver
❑ Good Listener
❑ Excellent Communicator
❑ Quick Learner
❑ Big-Picture Thinker
❑ Skilled and Knowledgeable
❑ Agent of Change
❑ Leader
❑ Team Player
❑ Self-Disciplined and Self-Motivated

FIGURE 8.1 The top ten qualities of a successful software engineer.

In this job, you need to be able to identify problems and propose solutions. In order to identify important problems in a timely manner, you need to learn quickly how the company conducts its business, and the best way to learn is to listen carefully to internal resources that have been around the block a few times. The solutions you propose should be presented clearly and communicated efficiently. The quality of these solutions will depend on your vision and ability to "think big." Your skills, mastery of tools, and experience also play an important role. Your presence and knowledge should serve as a catalyst for change because as an outsider, you will feel more comfortable taking risks than insiders who may be directly affected by any change in the way the company conducts its business.

Your job does not end with the presentation and articulation of your solutions. In order for these solutions to become something more than nicely bound reports shelved in the company's library, they need to come to life, be accepted, and implemented. Your solutions will be accepted if you enthuse people and rally their support behind them, and you can achieve this by being a leader, not as much by position as by character. Your solutions will be implemented if you are a strong contributor on the implementation team. This result will often require that you work hard in pursuit of your goals with discipline and determination, until you fulfill them.

8.2 THE ENTERPRISE MODEL

In the rest of this chapter and in the following chapters, you will create a high-level executive model for The American Software Club. This model will serve as the framework around which all the subsequent design and development work will be conducted. The components of the TASC enterprise model are:

❑ Business units and organizational chart
❑ Functional areas
❑ Data subjects and entity types
❑ Goals and objectives
❑ Problems
❑ Critical success factors
❑ Key performance indicators

After identifying and entering these components in the Designer/2000 Repository, you will be able to identify the scope of the information needs of TASC, divide it into business areas, and prioritize these business areas for the purpose of further analysis and design. Another benefit that you will gain by creating the TASC enterprise model in the Designer/2000 Repository is that you can continuously maintain it to reflect changes and modifications in the way the company conducts its business.

In order to create the overall enterprise model, you will use the Function Hierarchy Diagrammer, the Entity Relationship Diagrammer, and the Repository Object Navigator. As a preliminary step, start Designer/2000 and create a new application in the Repository Object Navigator. Name this application 'STRATEGIC PLAN' and enter any additional information in the other properties, such as *Comment, Description,* or *Notes.* The Repository Object Navigator groups together all the objects needed to store information collected during enterprise modeling activities. The Navigator group for these objects is called Enterprise Modelling.

8.3 BUSINESS UNITS

When you begin creating the enterprise model in Designer/2000, one of the first things to do is to enter information about the business units of the corporation in the Repository. Very often, you get the business units and their dependencies in the form of an organizational chart such as the one shown in Figure 8.2. Transfer the information from such a chart into the appropriate structures of the Repository.

The organization chart of an enterprise may come in different flavors and shapes. However, from this chart and from other sources in the company, collect and store in the Repository the following information:

- ❑ Name, abbreviation, and short description of each business unit in the company
- ❑ Geographic location for each business unit
- ❑ Executive or manager who oversees the business unit
- ❑ Number of full-time employees who work in each business unit

Based on the information shown in Figure 8.2, you can now enter data about TASC's business units in an application system called STRATEGIC PLAN. Follow instructions provided in Part One to create such an application system in the Repository Object Navigator.

8.3.1 CREATING AND MAINTAINING BUSINESS UNITS

In this section, you will learn how to create and maintain business units in the Repository Object Navigator. As you will see in coming chapters, you can perform these functions in the Process Modeller as well. Start by creating a business unit object that represents the entire TASC corporation:

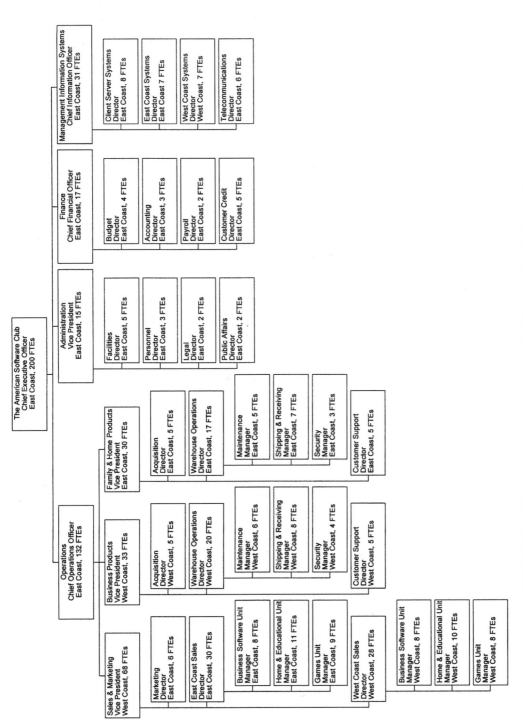

FIGURE 8.2 A high-level organizational chart for The American Software Club.

1. Switch to the Repository Object Navigator and select the object type node Business Units. You can find this node in the Enterprise Modeling category of the Navigator.
2. Click the button Create Object ⚁ on the Navigator's toolbar.
3. In the Property Palette for the new object, set *Short Name* to 'TASC,' and *Name* to 'The American Software Club.'
4. Scroll down in the Property Palette until you see the properties that belong to the BPR (Business Process Reengineering) group. Set the property *Headcount* to '200,' based on the number shown in Figure 8.2 for this organizational unit. This is to indicate that TASC has 200 employees.

Now you can create the four divisions into which TASC is divided.

1. Expand the node Sub Divisions.
2. Click the button Create Object ⚁ and enter the data for the Operations division of TASC.
3. Repeat Step 2 for the other divisions: Finance, Administration, and Management Information Systems.

It is clear that now you should enter the business units that make up each of these divisions, until you get to the bottom of the hierarchy list. Refer to Figure 8.2 for the names and other properties of these business units. Notice that when you enter subdivisions of a business unit, the Navigator places these subdivisions in two places: under the hierarchy branch of their parent organization, but also in the list of all the business units in the Repository. Figure 8.3, for example, shows the Operations division as a child of TASC, but at the same time, as a business unit equal to TASC; likewise, Sales and Marketing is a second generation dependent of TASC, but it is found as an independent business unit in the Navigator as well.

Other properties you can set for a business unit are *Primary Contact*, where you can store information about the point of contacts for that business unit, or any of the text-type properties, such as *Comment*, *Description*, or *Notes*. If you want the business units to appear in the Process Modeller in a particular order within their parent, such as the order of objects in Figure 8.2, set the property *Sequence in Parent* to the desired order number. You can also specify information about the business unit location by setting the property *Primary Location*. However, this information will be stored in text format for that particular business unit. In situations where multiple business units share the same location, maintain the location as a separate object in the Repository and create associations between the location and the business units.

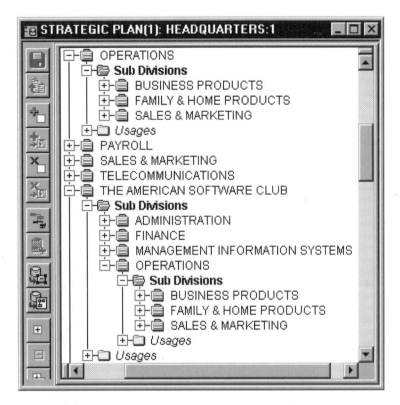

FIGURE 8.3   Business units for The American Software Club.

8.3.2   CREATING AND MAINTAINING LOCATIONS

From the organizational chart shown in Figure 8.2, you can see that TASC classifies the geographic location of its offices in two regions: East Coast and West Coast. However, after talking to a few people and reading some information about the business of

In order to quickly navigate to the highest level occurrence of a business unit in the hierarchy tree, click the characteristic icon that precedes the name of the business unit. This feature is not specific to business units. Whenever you are in a situation where an object is part of the decomposition of a higher level object, but has meaning independently, the Navigator will allow you to perform this type of navigation.

the corporation, you realize that this company has regional offices and warehouses in five cities across the United States. Some additional research allows you to come up with the information about these offices shown in Figure 8.4.

Enter this information in the Repository following these steps:

1. Switch to the Repository Object Navigator and select the object type node Locations.
2. Click the button Create Object 🔳 on the toolbar.

REGION	SITE	OFFICE	ADDRESS
East Coast	New York	Headquarters	1212 Norman Avenue New York, NY 11111 Contact: Allen Brown Phone: 212.909.3223
	Baltimore	Baltimore Office	121 Roman Way Baltimore, MD 21111 Contact: Heather Jones Phone: 410.909.3223
		Baltimore Warehouse	121 Roman Way Baltimore, MD 21111 Contact: James Green Phone: 410.909.3224
	Atlanta	Atlanta Office	3243 Prosperity Boulevard Atlanta, GA 41111 Contact: Mary Young Phone: 813.909.3223
		Atlanta Warehouse	3243 Prosperity Boulevard Atlanta, GA 41111 Contact: Chris Donaldson Phone: 813.909.6578
West Coast	San Diego	San Diego Office	1829 20th Street San Diego, CA 90023 Contact: Sam Johnson Phone: 415.779.8223
		San Diego Warehouse	1829 20th Street San Diego, CA 90023 Contact: Harold Jones Phone: 415.779.1236

FIGURE 8.4 Geographic locations of TASC offices.

3. In the Property Palette for the new object, set *Name* to *'EAST COAST,'* and *Type* to *'REGION.'*
4. Follow steps 1–3 to create a location for the West Coast region.

The technique you used to enter the divisions and subdivisions of TASC in the previous section can be applied very successfully in the case of locations as well. You can enter New York, Baltimore, and Atlanta as sub-locations of East Coast, the Atlanta office and warehouse as sub-locations of Atlanta, and so on. Figure 8.4 provides you with the data you need to enter for each location. Figure 8.5 shows all the sub-locations of East Coast, as well as the Property Palette for the location of TASC headquarters. Following this example, set the properties of the Atlanta, Baltimore, and San Diego offices and warehouses.

8.3.3 CREATING AND MAINTAINING PLANNING ITEMS

Thus far, you have entered in the Repository the business units and locations of the TASC corporation. The information you stored either applies to a particular object or allows you to associate objects of the same type in a hierarchical parent-child relationship. However, you need to create associations between the business units and the geographic locations of an enterprise. This need is primarily driven by the fact that in general an organizational unit may have representatives

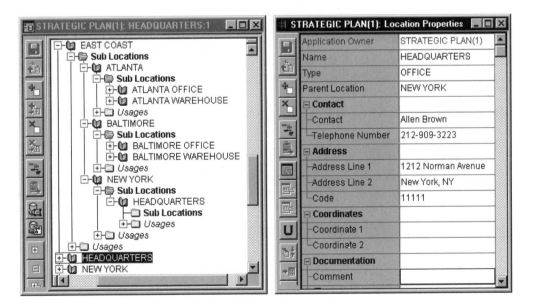

FIGURE 8.5 Sample properties for a TASC business location.

in several locations, and, vice versa—each location may house offices and employees from several business units.

Designer/2000 allows you to create associations between business units and locations in the form of planning items. Among other things, a planning item allows you to set, view, or modify the number of employees from an organizational unit that work at a particular location, or the amount of money allocated to the part of a business unit in a particular location. Proper definition and maintenance of planning items will allow the TASC managers to respond to questions such as:

❑ How many employees from the Sales and Marketing division work at each office in the East Coast Region?
❑ How many employees from each business unit work in the Atlanta office?
❑ How is the budget allocated to the Baltimore warehouse distributed among business units found there?
❑ From the total amount of budget set aside for the Marketing division, how much goes to the East Coast region, and how much goes to the West Coast region?

You have two ways to create and maintain planning items in Designer/2000. The first one is to create associations between a location and the business units that are present at that location in the Repository Object Navigator. Suppose, for example, that from your conversations with the Director of Personnel, you obtained some information regarding employees who work in the company's headquarters in New York. Among other things you learn that the New York office hosts five employees from the CEO office, eleven from the Finance division, five from the MIS division, nine from Administration, and twenty-five from Operations. In order to enter this information, follow these steps:

1. Select and expand location HEADQUARTERS, and expand the node Usages.
2. Click the icon Create Association 🔖 or double-click the node Business Unit Planning Items. The dialog box Create Planning Items appears .
3. Select the following business units from the multi-selection list of this dialog box: ADMINISTRATION, THE AMERICAN SOFTWARE CLUB, FINANCE, MANAGEMENT INFORMATION SYSTEMS, and OPERATIONS.
4. Click OK. The dialog box is closed and five planning items are inserted in the hierarchy tree.
5. Select all the planning items, switch to the Property Palette and click the icon Spread Table View ▪ to display the properties of these planning items in matrix format.
6. Click the header columns Application Owner, Location, Business Unit. No-

tice that they are in pushed state now. This is a visual indicator that these three columns are context columns for the spread table. You can scroll right to view and set other properties, but these properties will always be visible.

7. Set the properties of the planning items as shown in Figure 8.6. The setting 'FTE' of the property *Headcount Unit* stands for Full-Time Employee.

The Repository Object Navigator is very flexible because it allows you to create and edit planning items as objects dependent on business units and locations. You just created planning items starting from the location HEADQUARTERS. You could create planning items starting from the business units equally fast. There are occasions where looking at the planning items from the business unit perspective is more advantageous. For example, if you consider the list of questions presented earlier in this section, the first and the last ones are better responded to by looking at planning items that exist for a particular business unit.

However, this method is not very flexible when you need to maintain for an extended period of time mappings between multiple business units and locations. The most flexible way to create and maintain planning items in such situations is to edit one or more matrix documents in the Matrix Diagrammer. Typically, you would need two matrices to represent the relationships between business units and locations, one to represent the distributions of employees and the other one the allocation of budget for each part of a business unit at a particular location. Suppose now that, after interviewing the Director of Budget, you obtained the financial data shown in Figure 8.7 regarding the budget of the MIS division at TASC.

STRATEGIC PLAN(1): Planning Item Properties

Application Owner	Location	Business Unit	Headcount	Headcount Unit
STRATEGIC PLAN(1)	HEADQUARTERS	ADMINISTRATION	9	FTE
STRATEGIC PLAN(1)	HEADQUARTERS	CLIENT SERVER SYSTEMS	9	FTE
STRATEGIC PLAN(1)	HEADQUARTERS	FINANCE	11	FTE
STRATEGIC PLAN(1)	HEADQUARTERS	MANAGEMENT INFORMATION SYSTEMS	5	FTE
STRATEGIC PLAN(1)	HEADQUARTERS	OPERATIONS	25	FTE
STRATEGIC PLAN(1)	HEADQUARTERS	THE AMERICAN SOFTWARE CLUB	5	FTE

FIGURE 8.6   Setting properties for planning items.

MIS Division FY98 Budget

Client Server Systems

        Headquarters $5,000,000.00

        San Diego Office $4,500,000.00

East Coast Systems

        Headquarters $3,000,000.00

        Atlanta Office $2,000,000.00

        Baltimore Office $2,500,000.00

West Coast Systems

        San Diego Office $4,000,000.00

Telecommunications

        East Coast Region $1,000,000.00

        West Coast Region $ 900,000.00

FIGURE 8.7   Sample budget data for a division of the TASC corporation.

In order to enter these numbers in the Repository, follow the steps below:

1. Launch the Matrix Diagrammer and create a new diagram.
2. In the New Matrix dialog box, select Business Units as the row and Locations as the column of the matrix.
3. In the Settings dialog box, display the names of business units and locations by placing a check mark in the corresponding check box items in the tabs Row-Business Units and Column-Locations.
4. In the Intersection tab of the Settings dialog box, check Budget and Budget Unit.
5. Click OK to display the diagram.

Now you are ready to enter the data listed in Figure 8.7. To enter the first budget figure, for example, do the following:

1. Click at the intersection cell of business unit Client Server Systems and location Headquarters. This cell represents a planning item.
2. Display the Property Palette of the cell by selecting its title from the Window menu. The properties listed in this window are the same properties displayed in the Repository Object Navigator for a planning item.
3. Set *Budget* to '5000000' and *Budget Unit* to 'USD' and the new item to the Repository.

After entering all the data shown in Figure 8.7, save this matrix in the Repository. In the future, as you accumulate more data or need to update existing ones, you can edit this document to reflect the most current budget situation in the corporation.

8.3.4 CREATING AND MAINTAINING EXECUTIVES

From the organization chart of TASC shown in Figure 8.2, you can see that each business unit in the company is under the direct responsibility of an executive. A desirable approach is to store the information about these executives together with the other information in the STRATEGIC PLANNING application system. A quick look at the Repository Object Navigator tells you that no element type is intended to store information about executives. Recall, however, from Chapter 4 that you can extend the Designer/2000 Repository structures to accommodate the needs for element and association types that are not provided by the default Repository. In fact, that chapter provides detailed instructions on how you can extend the Repository with the element type Executive and the association type Executive Role between the element types Executive and Business Unit. The discussion in the rest of this section assumes that you have extended the Repository with these additional types. I also assume that you have modified the settings of the Repository Object Navigator group to show the user extensions. The following steps help you make this modification:

1. Select Options | Customize Navigator Groups... from the menu. The dialog box Customize Navigator Groups appears.
2. Set the check boxes Show/Enable and Show on Open for the group User Extensions as shown in Figure 8.8.
3. Click OK and restart the Repository Object Navigator so that changes may take effect.

Follow these steps to enter an executive in the Repository Object Navigator:

1. Expand the node User Extensions and select the node Executives in the hierarchy tree.
2. Click the button Create Object 🔳.
3. Type *'JOHN MILLER'* in the new node created in the Navigator window or in the property *Name* in the Property Palette.
4. Save the changes to the Repository.

In order to store the fact that John Miller is the CEO of TASC, issue the following commands:

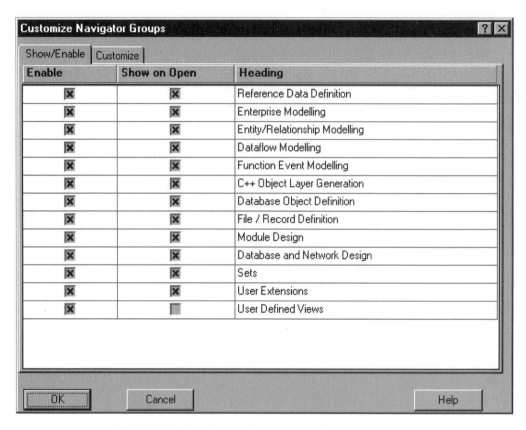

FIGURE 8.8   The Customize Navigator Groups dialog box.

1. Expand the nodes Business Units and THE AMERICAN SOFTWARE CLUB.
2. Extend the nodes User Extended Associations and Executives.
3. Click the button Create Association 📥. The dialog box Create Management Roles appears (see Figure 8.9).
4. Select JOHN MILLER and click OK to close the dialog box.
5. Switch to the Property Palette and set the *Role* property to *'Chief Executive Officer.'*
6. Save the changes to the Repository.

Similar actions can be used to enter the information about the other executives at TASC and their roles in the business units of the corporation.

FIGURE 8.9   The Create Management Roles dialog box.

8.4   GOALS AND OBJECTIVES

The TASC corporation, like any other business or human endeavor, has certain goals and objectives that guide its activities. One of the most important tasks you need to accomplish when creating the high-level model for an enterprise is to identify and document its goals and objectives. At the least, these will create a set of quantifiable criteria that the management can use to measure the progress of the company. In the best case, by going through the formal procedure of defining goals and setting objectives, you will ignite a process of reflection and evaluation, the end result of which could be a radical improvement in the way the company does business.

8.4.1   CHARACTERISTICS OF GOALS

Goals are targets, results, or achievements toward which an effort is directed. For example, here are two goals identified by executives of TASC:

❑ The East Coast Sales department will increase 20 percent the ratio of sales calls that result in an order of $50 or more in the third quarter of the fiscal year by improving the skills of employees and the selection of products. (Source: Director of East Coast Sales department)

❑ The Marketing division will improve the visibility of TASC in the marketplace by sponsoring *Sesame Street* on PBS next year and setting up an Internet site by the end of this quarter. (Source: Director of Marketing)

By looking at these goals, you can identify the characteristics of the goals as follows:

❑ **Goals should clearly specify who will be responsible for accomplishing them.** Tracking the fulfillment of goals is more difficult if they are unassigned, or stated in general terms such as "The company will ...."

❑ **Goals should be defined in such a way that you can measure their accomplishment.** They should explain the *results* that will be achieved. The first goal, for example, is set against a very clear parameter, the ratio of sales calls that result in an order of $50 or more over all the sales calls. At the end of the third quarter of FY97, you can measure this parameter and tell unambiguously whether the East Coast Sales department met its goal or not. Stating this goal as "Improve sales significantly ..." is not acceptable because it does not provide a reliable mechanism to check the organization's success in meeting it.

Note, however, that some goals, such as the second goal above, may not state explicitly the measurement mechanism that will be used. Nevertheless, this mechanism should be set for the goal to be valid and helpful. For example, although no direct way exists to measure the visibility of the company, the Marketing division may conduct several surveys in the market that could provide clues about the fulfillment of the goal.

❑ **Goals should indicate a series of actions to follow for their achievement.** In both examples shown above, you can easily deduce the game plan that management plans to follow in order to meet the goals. The course stated in the definition of a goal becomes the starting point for planning and implementing the actions that will make the business unit meet the goal.

❑ **Goals should be set for a very specific time frame.** Defining a time window in which the goal is effective has three advantages. First, it allows you to measure your progress towards fulfillment of the goal. Second, it provides you with a timeline for all actions required to accomplish the goal. Third, it allows you to evaluate your business periodically, reevaluate the needs, and adjust your goals as the business changes.

Thus, to summarize, when setting goals, provide answers to the first four of the famous five questions a good journalist asks: *Who?*, *What?*, *When?*, *How?*, and *Where?*

8.4.2 OBJECTIVES

While goals define targets to be reached by an organizational unit in a given time frame and following specific actions, objectives generally set the direction in which the organization intends to move. Objectives set the business course for the whole corporation and its business units, whereas goals define the steps to take at a given point in time in that direction. The following are two objectives defined by the Sales and Marketing division of TASC:

❑ Develop strategies that improve the outcome of sales calls.
❑ Make TASC a household name as a provider of software games and products for families across America.

The goals discussed in Section 8.4.1 are steps that specific business units within the Sales and Marketing division will take to progress toward these objectives.

8.4.3 MISSION STATEMENT

The highest-level objective for a corporation is expressed in the mission statement. The mission statement expresses the fundamental reasons for the existence of the enterprise, what it aims to achieve, and why it is different from everybody else. The mission of a company directly reflects the vision of the founders and upper management about the purpose and role of the company. It contains qualitative and quantitative information that allows everyone to measure the advancement of the corporation. It can be a single sentence, such as Microsoft's famous "A computer on every desk and in every home," or it can span several paragraphs. However, in general, a mission statement is brief and to the point. Here is the mission statement defined by the upper management of TASC:

> The mission of The American Software Club is to provide customers with software products of superior quality for office, home, and entertainment, in a timely manner and at prices they can afford.

8.4.4 PLANNING HORIZON, HIERARCHIES, AND PRIORITIES

One of the preeminent characteristics of successful businesses today is their ability to change and adapt to new conditions in the marketplace. As a reflection of this, corporations should plan their activities both in tactical and strategic terms. Simply defining goals and objectives is not enough. Companies should also decide whether they contribute to the short-term growth of the business, thus being tactical, or whether they will remain valid for longer terms (over five years), thus being strategic ones. Thus, a planning horizon is assigned to each goal and objective.

In addition, corporations must create a hierarchy of goals and objectives. At the top of this hierarchy resides the mission statement of the enterprise. Directly dependent on the mission statement may be long-term strategic objectives, which are broken down in tactical objectives, and so on. The same applies to the goals. Another way to organize objectives and goals in hierarchies is to break them up based on the organizational chart of the company. In other words, the mission statement helps define a set of objectives and goals for each division; these are further divided into objectives and goals for departments within a division, and so on. High-level goals and objectives are customarily set in terms of broad financial indicators, for example, a sales quota that a division must achieve. As they are filtered down the organizational chart, they are converted into actions to be taken in order to meet these indicators.

Accomplishing a goal or objective, or failing to do so, directly impacts its parent in the hierarchy tree. Not every goal or objective, though, has the same impact on its parent. Therefore, goals and objectives are ranked based on the impact they have on the parent.

8.4.5 GOALS AND OBJECTIVES IN DESIGNER/2000

 The Designer/2000 Repository has one object type that can be used to create and maintain the enterprise mission statement, its objectives, and goals. In this section, you will enter in the Repository the mission, objectives, and goals for TASC that were discussed earlier. These are summarized in Figure 8.10.

Enter this information in the Repository following these steps:

1. Switch to the Repository Object Navigator and select the object type node Objectives.
2. Click the button Create on the toolbar.
3. In the Property Palette for the new object, set *Name* to *'MISSION OF TASC,'* *Type* to *'MISSION STATEMENT,'* *Set By* to *'CEO,'* and *Planning Horizon* to *'PERMANENT.'*
4. Double-click the property *Description* to bring up the TextPad window and enter the mission statement shown in Figure 8.10.
5. Close the TextPad window saving the changes and click the Save button on the properties window toolbar to commit the new object to the Repository.

The process of entering the objectives is similar. The only difference is in the properties you set for the new object. Figure 8.11 shows the properties set for the first objective. Note here that the property *Parent Objective* is set to *'MISSION OF TASC.'*

Likewise, entering the goals in the Repository is only a matter of setting the appropriate properties of the newly created object with values from the definition

Mission	The mission of The American Software Club is to provide customers with software products of superior quality for office, home, and entertainment in a timely manner, and at prices they can afford.
	Source: Chief Executive Officer
Objectives	❑ Develop strategies that improve the outcome of sales calls.
	❑ Make TASC a household name as provider of software games and products for families across America.
	Source: Vice President of Sales and Marketing
Goals	❑ The East Coast Sales department will increase 20 percent the ratio of sales calls that result in an order of $50 or more over all the sales calls in the third quarter of FY97 by improving the skills of employees and the selection of products.
	Source: Director of East Coast Sales department
	❑ The Marketing division will improve the visibility of TASC in the marketplace by sponsoring *Sesame Street* on PBS next year and setting up an Internet site by the end of this quarter.
	Source: Director of Marketing

FIGURE 8.10   Mission statement, objectives, and goals for TASC.

and analysis of goals. Figure 8.12 contains a way you could set the properties for the first goal.

8.4.6 ASSOCIATING BUSINESS UNITS WITH GOALS

When a business unit sets a goal, usually all its subordinate units work towards meeting that goal. A common practice is to quantify the contribution that each of these units can make towards the goal in the form of a mini-goal. Most of the time, setting mini-goals does not require you to create new goals for each subordinate organization of the business unit. Often, creating associations between business units and goals is sufficient. Like other associations in Designer/2000, you can create and maintain associations between business units and goals in the Repository Object Navigator or in the Matrix Diagrammer. As an example, consider the following scenario:

> The management of the East Coast Sales department reviews the goal to increase 20 percent the ratio of sales calls that result in an order of $50 or more over all the sales calls in the third quarter of FY97 by improving the skills of employees and the selection of products. The Business Software Unit agrees that it can increase the ratio 25 percent, the Home and Educational Unit agrees to 22 percent, and the Games Unit 13 percent. These targets should become the goals for the respective units in this department.

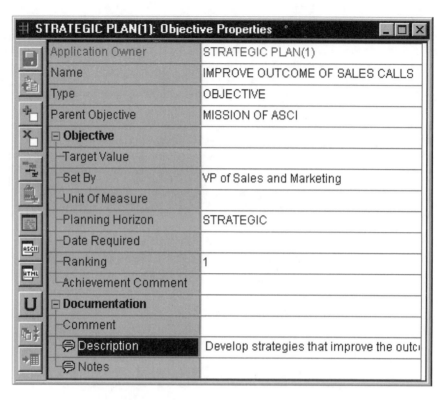

FIGURE 8.11   Setting properties for objectives.

In order to enter this information in the Repository Object Navigator, follow these steps:

1. Select and expand the node BUSINESS PRODUCTS under Business Units.
2. Expand the node Usages and double-click the node Objectives to create a new association. The dialog box Create Business Units to Objectives appears.
3. In this dialog box, pick the objective IMPROVE OUTCOME OF SALES CALLS: EC SALES and click OK. A new association is created.
4. Switch to the Property Palette for the new object and set the property *Value* to '25.'
5. Follow Steps 1–3 to create associations for the other two units.

Alternatively, you can use the Matrix Diagrammer to enter the same information:

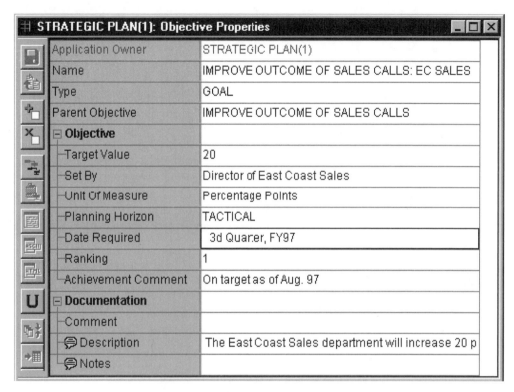

FIGURE 8.12 Setting properties for goals.

1. Create a matrix document that has Objectives in the rows and Business Units in the columns.
2. Select the property *Value* to go in the intersection cells of the matrix.
3. Select the cell at the intersection of objective IMPROVE OUTCOME OF SALES CALLS: EC SALES and business unit BUSINESS PRODUCTS.
4. Switch to the properties window of this object and set the property *Value* to '25.'
5. Repeat Steps 1–4 to create associations for the other units.
6. Save the matrix document for further use.

8.5 PROBLEMS

As you work to identify and document the goals and objectives of the enterprise, you will inevitably run into problems that inhibit the achievement of these goals. Even if these problems do not appear at first sight, your interviewing strategies and research should be such that when executives and management state a goal, they think and tell you about existing or potential problems that may arise when trying to meet this goal.

When you discover a problem, collect as much information as possible about it, starting from the person who identified it and the date it was identified. Often, grouping problems in several categories is helpful. For example, you can group together problems that are related to information systems currently in place at the corporation; in another group, you can place problems related to information systems that will be developed in the future; in a third one, you can place problems that are not related to any current or future information system; and so on. Another way to group problems is by their cause, which could be lack of raw materials, market instability, Congressional regulations, employee turnover, and so on. Yet another way to group the problems is to associate a severity level with each of them. The severity level influences directly the priority level assigned to the problem, since the higher the severity of a problem, the higher it must be in the list of things to resolve. Other factors that influence the priority level of a problem are the opportunities created by the solution of the problem and the benefits that the company will draw by resolving the problem.

8.5.1   ENTERING PROBLEMS IN THE REPOSITORY

In order to create a problem in the Repository Object Navigator, do the following:

1. Select the node Problems in the Navigator.
2. Click the Create Object icon on the toolbar.
3. Switch to the Property Palette for the new problem and set its properties according to your case.

 As an example, consider the following problem identified by the Telecommunications unit when the Marketing department requested that it set up an Internet site for TASC (in accordance with one of their goals described earlier).

In order to protect the investment and property of the company from intruders, the Telecommunications group must set up a firewall that will separate the Internet server that the world will access from all the other servers and routers inside the firewall. The hardware, software, and training cost to accomplish this task amounts to $40,000. This amount is not included in the budget for the current quarter.

Figure 8.13 shows an example of how you could enter this problem in the Repository. Note that the problem described above was broken into two problems: one that addresses the budget shortage of the Telecommunications group,

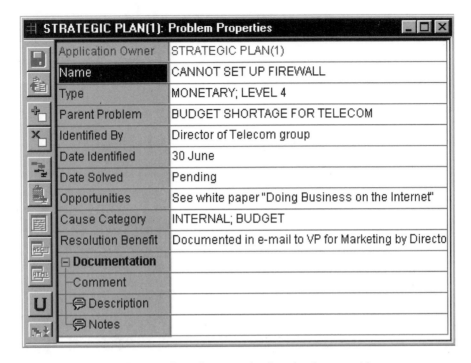

FIGURE 8.13 Sample properties for a business problem.

and another, shown in Figure 8.13, that addresses the inability to set up the firewall for the Internet server.

8.5.2 ASSOCIATING PROBLEMS WITH BUSINESS UNITS

As discussed in Section 8.4, each business unit in the organization must have its own set of goals and objectives. Since problems often are identified when people think how to achieve their goals, you naturally want to associate these problems with the business units that they affect. In the example discussed in the previous section, for example, you would associate the problem BUDGET SHORTAGE FOR TELECOM with the following business units: Telecommunications unit, Budget office, and Marketing department. Like other associations, you can create business units to problems associations in the Repository Object Navigator or in the Matrix Diagrammer. To associate the Budget office with the problem discussed here, follow these steps:

1. Select and expand the node BUDGET under Business Units.
2. Double-click the node Business Units to Problems to create a new association. The dialog box Create Business Units to Problems appears.

3. In this dialog box, pick BUDGET SHORTAGE FOR TELECOM and click OK. A new association is created.

Now you can set the properties of this association so that they describe, for example, what the Budget office intends to do to solve this problem, or a contact person in that office who will respond to inquiries about the status of the problem. Following the same steps, you could associate the problem with the other two program offices. If you decide to use the Matrix Diagrammer instead, do the following:

1. Create a matrix with Problems in the rows and Business Units in the columns.

2. Select one or more association properties that will populate the intersection cells of the matrix.

3. Select the cell that corresponds to the problem BUDGET SHORTAGE FOR TELECOM and any of the three offices mentioned above, and enter the desired information.

8.6 CRITICAL SUCCESS FACTORS

For each organizational unit, starting from the enterprise itself and going down the hierarchy, several elements contribute to the favorable or prosperous outcome of its business activities. These elements are commonly referred to as success factors. Often managers are aware of the success factors that apply to their business units, but sometimes they lie deep in their subconscience. Strategic planning of the enterprise is responsible for identifying the success factors for each unit.

Among all the success factors, a few have an impact on the success of the business unit that is much stronger than the others. These are called the Critical Success Factors (CSF) of the business unit. When they occur, the business unit will most likely succeed; otherwise failure is almost guaranteed.

CSFs should be identified for each hierarchy level in the organization. At the highest level, CSFs are those crucial elements that contribute to the fulfillment of corporate's mission. For each division and business unit underneath, CSFs are the important factors that allow the unit to meet its objectives and goals.

Often CSFs have a relatively short life span. They tend to express what must happen *at present* in certain areas of the business activity in order to guarantee success. For example, a critical success factor for the Family and Home Products department at TASC is the following:

Stock enough tax preparation packages (100,000 units) in warehouses to meet all demands.

Clearly, this CSF is really critical only in the first few months of the year; after April 15, it will not play an important role in the success or failure of this business unit. If the CSF can be quantified, associating a target value for it is important, as in the example above, so that you can easily verify whether it occurred or not. Also record any external factors on which this CSF may depend. In the CSF listed above, an external dependency would be the software vendors, because if they do not produce and deliver enough units of tax packages, the CSF will not be met.

 Designer/2000 allows you to enter all the success factors of your business units (critical or non-critical) through the Repository Object Navigator. As an example, follow these steps to enter the CSF listed above in your application:

1. Select the node Critical Success Factors in the navigator.
2. Click the Create button on the toolbar.
3. Switch to the Property Palette and set the properties as shown in Figure 8.14.

Critical success factors have a dual relationship with goals and objectives of organizational units. First, when a CSF is identified, it can be converted almost automatically into one or more goals or objectives that the business unit must meet in order to guarantee its success. For example, the CSF just discussed may generate the following two goals for the Acquisition and Warehouse groups within the Home and Family Products department:

❑ By September, the Acquisition group will secure contracts with tax software vendors for 100,000 units of tax packages for the current year.
❑ By December, the Warehouse group will set up storage space (100 cubical feet) for 100,000 units of tax packages.

On the other hand, for each objective or goal, management may define critical success factors that, if met, will help the unit meet the goal. They may even quantify the effect of each of these CSFs on the objective or goal. In order to document this in the Repository, you need to create associations between objectives and critical success factors. As other types of associations, these can be created in the Repository Object Navigator or in the Matrix Diagrammer. To associate an objective with a critical success factor, do the following:

1. Select and expand the desired objective.
2. Double-click the node Objectives to CSFs to create a new association. The dialog box Create Objectives to CSFs appears.

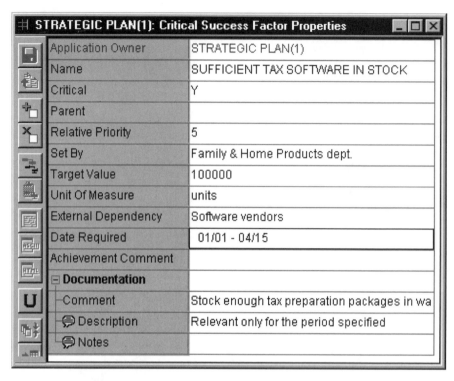

FIGURE 8.14 Setting properties for a critical success factor.

3. Pick the success factor that will contribute to the objective from the list of available CSFs and click OK. The new association is created.

4. In the Property Palette for the new association, describe the reason why this factor contributes to the fulfillment of the objective, how it will contribute to the fulfillment of the objective, and enter the value of this contribution, if you can quantify it.

The process of mapping objectives to success factors that influence their fulfillment in a matrix document is very similar to other mappings discussed in this chapter. You need to follow these three steps:

1. Create a matrix that maps Objectives to Critical Success Factors.
2. Fill the intersection cells with the properties you want to display.
3. For each intersection cell in the matrix, enter the contribution of the CSF to the objective as described above.

8.7 KEY PERFORMANCE INDICATORS

The performance of any activity or process depends on a number of factors determined by their complexity and size. A few parameters exist, though, whose values you monitor constantly in order to have a good idea about how well the activity or process is going. For example, as you drive your car every day, you always keep an eye on a few things, such as the oil pressure, engine temperature, gas level in the tank, and air pressure in the tires. As long as they remain at normal levels, you have no reason to worry; you can go about minding other things in your life. However, if one of them falls into the "red" zone, you have good reason to get alarmed and pull over at the next gas station to see what's wrong. Periodically, you will go to the mechanic, who will diagnose and fix all the nuts and bolts of the car, but routinely the parameters above are all you need to monitor to be sure that the car is performing as it should.

Similarly, in any business activity, a small number of items indicate right away the state of that activity. These are pieces of information that are indispensable for management, the kind of things they would choose to have on a deserted island in order to judge the health of the business. They are all referred to as Key Performance Indicators (KPI).

You encounter key performance indicators every way you turn in your day-to-day activities. Consider, for example, the leading economic indicators published periodically by the federal government. They are a reliable source of information about the current and future health of the economy and, because of their significance, often cause the stock market to rally up or to take a nosedive. Or think about the report card that concerned parents check frequently. It gives them a fairly good idea about their child's academic progress in school.

 Given the importance that tracking and measuring KPIs has, always include them in the overall model of the enterprise and its business. When capturing a KPI, be sure to not only describe the parameter itself, but also collect as much information as possible about how to measure it, who maintains and sets it, and so on.

Also specify a value that serves as the checkpoint for the KPI. Depending on the meaning of the KPI, a warning flag should be raised if the value of the indicator falls below or jumps over the target value. In order to enter a KPI in the Designer/2000 Repository, follow these steps:

1. Select the node Key Performance Indicators in the Repository Object Navigator.
2. Click the Create button on the toolbar.
3. In the Property Palette for the new object, set the properties with data collected during your interviews and analysis (see Figure 8.15).

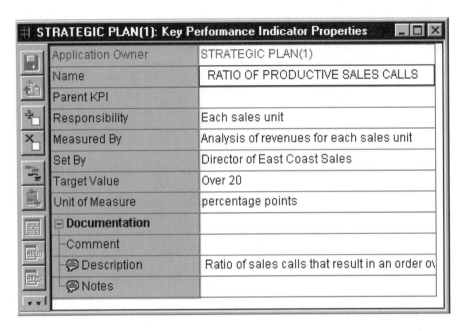

FIGURE 8.15 Sample properties for a key performance indicator.

As an example, consider the following KPIs defined by the management of East Coast Sales department:

❑ Ratio of sales calls that result in an order
❑ Quarterly average of hours staff members spend in training
❑ Employee turnover rate

Figure 8.15 shows the properties of the first KPI populated with data from the analysis of the indicator.

From the importance that KPIs have in the success of the business, each organizational unit must set at least one goal or objective that aims at maintaining the indicator within healthy bounds. On the other hand, some important goals and objectives may identify the need for a key performance indicator to measure their achievement. Designer/2000 allows you to create this last kind of association between objectives and KPIs. For example, in order to associate the objective IMPROVE THE OUTCOME OF SALES CALLS discussed in Section 8.4 with the KPI described above, do the following:

1. Select and expand the objective IMPROVE THE OUTCOME OF SALES CALLS in the Repository Object Navigator.

2. Double-click the object type Objectives to KPIs to display the dialog box Create Objectives to KPIs.
3. From the list of the available KPIs, select RATIO OF PRODUCTIVE CALLS and click OK.
4. In the Property Palette of the newly-created association, enter the reason why this KPI would serve as a monitoring flag for the fulfillment of the objective.

Like other associations, you can also use a Key Performance Indicators to Objectives matrix to create and maintain the association between these objects in your application. This process will not be discussed here, since it is entirely similar to others discussed in this chapter.

8.8 ASSUMPTIONS

When you analyze, model, and document the mission of any business unit, you will always discover that what people tell you contains, embedded in it, beliefs that these people hold about the business of their organization. For example, look carefully at the following goal identified in Section 8.4:

> The East Coast Sales department will increase 20 percent the ratio of sales calls that result in an order of $50 or more in the third quarter of the fiscal year by improving the skills of employees and the selection of products.

You can easily understand that the Director of the East Coast Sales department who identified this goal believes the following:

❏ Stronger employee skills improve the chances that each phone call will conclude with a sale.
❏ A rich selection of products makes it easier to conclude a sales call successfully.
❏ The most significant part of business for the department comes from orders totaling $50 or more.

 These beliefs are assumptions that the manager makes about the way to conduct the business activity of her department. You must identify and document in the Repository each assumption. You can create an assumption in the Repository Object Navigator by following these steps:

1. Navigate to the object type node Assumptions.
2. Click Create on the toolbar.
3. Switch to the Property Palette and enter the data collected about the assumption.

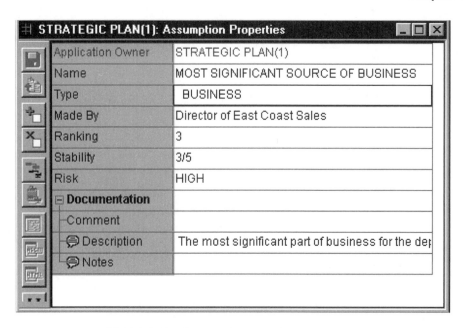

FIGURE 8.16   Sample properties for assumptions.

Figure 8.16 shows settings you can use to enter the third of the above assumptions in the Repository.

Notice that in addition to standard properties such as *Name, Made By*, and *Description*, you can also specify a type for the assumption, rank it among all the other assumptions, express the level of confidence you have in the stability of the assumption, and evaluate the risk level to your business if the assumption turns out to be false.

Capturing business assumptions provides you with the opportunity to question and challenge each of them. As you will see in coming chapters, identifying and destroying existing assumptions is one of the most important techniques used in Business Process Reengineering to envision new business processes, radically different from existing ones, that offer breakthrough improvements of key performance indicators.

8.9   SUMMARY

Designer/2000 provides you with the ways and means to store information you collect during strategic planning activities for your enterprise. This information is very useful in understanding the business mission of a company, its major challenges, goals, and objectives. This chapter shows how you can enter strategic planning data in the Repository for the case of a fictional corporation, The American Software Club. The major topics of this chapter are listed below:

- ❑ **Setting the Scene**
  - ❑ The American Software Club
  - ❑ Your Assignment
- ❑ **The Enterprise Model**
- ❑ **Business Units**
  - ❑ Creating and Maintaining Business Units
  - ❑ Creating and Maintaining Locations
  - ❑ Creating and Maintaining Planning Items
  - ❑ Creating and Maintaining Executives
- ❑ **Goals and Objectives**
  - ❑ Characteristics of Goals
  - ❑ Objectives
  - ❑ Mission Statement
  - ❑ Planning Horizon, Hierarchies, and Priorities
  - ❑ Goals and Objectives in Designer/2000
  - ❑ Associating Business Units with Goals
- ❑ **Problems**
  - ❑ Entering Problems in the Repository
  - ❑ Associating Problems with Business Units
- ❑ **Critical Success Factors**
- ❑ **Key Performance Indicators**
- ❑ **Assumptions**

THE ENTERPRISE FUNCTIONAL AND INFORMATION MODELS

- Defining the Functional Model of the Enterprise
- Defining the Information Model of the Enterprise
- Modeling Mutual Exclusivity of Data and Relationships
- Associating Entities with Other Repository Objects
- Summary

As explained in the previous chapter, the first step to model the enterprise is to create its organizational chart, identify its mission, objectives, and goals, recognize its critical success factors, and quantify its key performance indicators. This gives you a good idea about the key players in each organization and what they are trying to achieve.

The next step becomes understanding the business of the enterprise, what functionality each of its units fulfills, and what activities occur during its lifetime. Recognizing and modeling the information and data required to complete the business functions is a task that goes hand-in-hand with this step. This chapter explains how you can use the Function Hierarchy Diagrammer and the Entity Relationship Diagrammer in combination with other Designer/2000 tools to create a high-level functional and information model of the enterprise or any of its business units.

9.1 DEFINING THE FUNCTIONAL MODEL OF THE ENTERPRISE

The purpose of each business unit, starting from the enterprise as a whole and all the way down to each individual employee, is to contribute to the fulfillment of the enterprise's business objectives. The reason for a business unit to exist is to *do* something in accordance with the strategy and mission of the enterprise. Business functions are collections of activities performed in order to achieve business goals and objectives; business function modeling is a modeling technique that aims at identifying and classifying the business functions of a corporation and its organizations.

9.1.1 FUNCTIONAL AREAS OF THE ENTERPRISE

The mission statement of an enterprise is also its first function. All the other business functions and activities are designed to help the company fulfill this mission. Often business functions are grouped into major areas of activity. These are called functional areas of the enterprise. Figure 9.1 shows the functional areas of the TASC corporation and the major business functions for each area.

Although companies have their own unique character that distinguishes them from the others, finding functional areas that are the same or similar in a number of them is not unusual, especially if they are from the same branch of the industry. For example, each company defines functional areas such as Accounting, Sales and Marketing, or Human Resources; manufacturing corporations have areas such as Plant Operations, or Planning and Production; educational institutions have functional areas such as Student Affairs, or Research and Development; and so on.

ACQUISITION

❏ Identify products in the marketplace
❏ Select vendors
❏ Plan and schedule product acquisitions
❏ Control product inventory
❏ Price products

DISTRIBUTION

❏ Plan supply and demand for products
❏ Negotiate rates and schedules with distributors
❏ Process customer orders
❏ Operate and maintain warehouses
❏ Control product inventory

FINANCE

❏ Plan and analyze financial situation
❏ Prepare budgets
❏ Provide credit to customers
❏ Bill customers
❏ Negotiate financial terms with vendors
❏ Maintain accounts payable and accounts receivable
❏ Maintain payroll

SALES AND MARKETING

❏ Research marketplace
❏ Present customers with introductory offers
❏ Enter customer orders for products
❏ Provide customer service
❏ Advertise and promote products

ADMINISTRATION

❏ Maintain offices and work areas
❏ Manage legal affairs
❏ Manage public relations

HUMAN RESOURCES

❏ Administer employee benefits
❏ Recruit, hire, and terminate employees
❏ Maintain job classifications and compensations

MANAGEMENT INFORMATION SYSTEMS

❏ Develop and maintain client/server systems
❏ Maintain legacy systems
❏ Configure and maintain local area networks
❏ Configure and maintain database systems
❏ Configure and maintain telecommunication services

FIGURE 9.1 Functional areas and major functions of TASC.

9.1.2 FUNCTIONS AND FUNCTIONAL HIERARCHIES

Business functions are presented and maintained hierarchically. For the enterprise-wide functional model, the mission of the enterprise serves as the root of the functional hierarchy. All the business functions required to fulfill this mission are listed underneath. Usually, functional areas occupy the level immediately below the enterprise mission. They are broken down into a series of major functions within each area. Each of these functions may need a number of other functions to be carried out; they belong to the next hierarchy level, and so on. The process of identifying business functions required to fully complete a given function is known as *decomposition* of that function. When the functional hierarchy is presented graphically, it is called a function hierarchy diagram or function decomposition diagram. Figure 9.2 shows part of the high-level function decomposition diagram for TASC. Note that the functions displayed in this diagram are the same as those shown in Figure 9.1.

9.1.3 CREATING FUNCTIONS IN THE FUNCTION HIERARCHY DIAGRAMMER

In Designer/2000, functional hierarchy diagrams are created and maintained in the Functional Hierarchy Diagrammer. Chapter 7 discussed generic properties and functionality of this diagrammer. Here you will use it to create the high-level functional diagram of TASC.

Start by launching the Function Hierarchy Diagrammer and click the New Diagram button ⬜ on the toolbar to create the new diagram document. The New Diagram dialog box that appears (see Figure 9.3) displays a list of all the functions that exist in the current application. You can either pick a function from the list or create a new function that will serve as the root of the new hierarchy.

Since you have not created any functions in the application system STRATEGIC PLAN, the list box is empty, as shown in Figure 9.3. Click the New

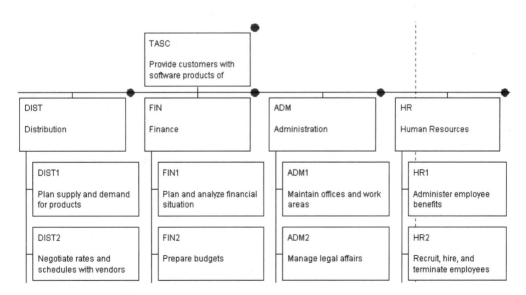

FIGURE 9.2 Part of a function hierarchy diagram.

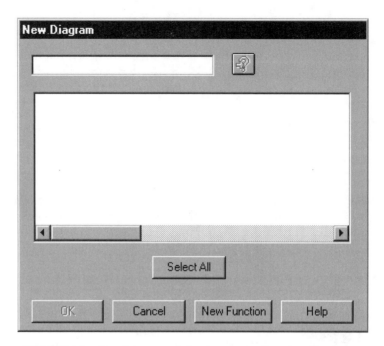

FIGURE 9.3   New Diagram dialog box in the Function Hierarchy Diagrammer.

Function button to create the new function. In the dialog box Create Function that appears, enter the specifications for the root function of the hierarchy as shown in Figure 9.4. Click OK in this dialog box to create the new function in the new diagram.

You must specify two properties in order to be able to create a new function. First you must provide a label for the function. This can be considered a tag that is attached to the function for easier identification. In your case, the label for the mission statement will be TASC, since this function identifies what the company does. Then the labels for the functional areas shown in Figure 9.1 could be ACQ, DIST, FIN, S&M, ADM, HR, and MIS. Often labels are defined in such a way that they imply the position of the function in the hierarchy. For example, the functional area Finance (FIN) could be decomposed into functions with labels FIN1, FIN2, and so on. Each of these functions, for example FIN1, could be decomposed into functions with labels such as FIN11, FIN12, or FIN13. This convention exists so that, when you encounter a function labeled FIN1223, you can tell exactly the position of the function in the functional hierarchy. In fact, this label tells you that to get to that function, you need to expand functional area FIN, function FIN1 within FIN, FIN12 within FIN1, and finally, FIN122 within FIN12. The fact that function labels are padded with numbers does not imply any

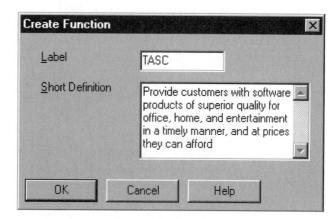

FIGURE 9.4 The Create Function
dialog box.

sequence or priority in which functions are executed. In other words, if the functional area HR is decomposed into functions HR1, HR2, and HR3, HR1 is not necessarily the first function to be executed within that area, and HR2 doesn't necessarily come after HR1.

The second property that you provide in order to create a new function is a description of what the function does. This description should be brief but clear. It should avoid lengthy discussions, and, in particular, it should not describe how something is done or who does it. When defining the meaning of a function stick to the *what*; wandering into the *how* and *who* may be like casting in stone the way business is done now and may limit the ability of the corporation to change and renew itself. The description of the function should also be precise and to the point. Usually you do not need more than one strong, active, and direct sentence to describe what the function should accomplish.

Now that you created the root function of TASC, you can proceed on your own to enter the functional areas and functions of TASC. Follow labeling conventions like the ones discussed above, and use the definitions shown in Figure 9.1 as

If the function object represents a functional area in the enterprise, you may set its *Definition* property to one or two nouns or gerunds, rather than to a complete active sentence. By looking at Figure 9.2, for example, you can see that the functional areas of TASC are defined with nouns like Distribution, Finance, and Administration. The functions into which they are decomposed, however, are defined with full sentences.

descriptions for the functions. The following paragraphs discuss some techniques that you may find helpful when creating the functional hierarchy diagram.

In order to create a function as a child of a function that already exists on the diagram, do the following:

1. Click the Function button 🔲 on the drawing toolbar of the diagrammer. The cursor changes shape to a soft box.
2. Click the function that will serve as the parent of the new function.
3. Enter the label and short description for the new function as discussed above.

If in step 2 above you click the diagram instead of another function, you create a new root function. Although technically this is allowed, your functional model should contain only one root: the enterprise mission. Everything else should fit in the appropriate level of the hierarchy. In order to assign these "loose" functions to a parent, or to change the current parent of a function, simply drag the function over the new parent and drop it inside the rectangle that represents the parent.

As I said above, the sequence in which functions are displayed in the hierarchy should not imply any precedence or order in which they are completed. However, on some occasions, you would like to change this sequence. In order to resequence a function within its parent, drag the function to the target location being careful not to drop it inside another function, which will reparent the function.

Finally, remember that you can enhance the way your diagram looks by switching between horizontal layout and vertical layout, or by combining them for different levels of the hierarchy. Refer to Chapter 7 for instructions on how you can perform these actions in hierarchy diagrammers such as the Function Hierarchy Diagrammer.

9.1.4 TYPES OF FUNCTIONS

The top-level function in the diagram is called the *root* of the diagram. In Figure 9.2, the mission of TASC is the root function. The functions immediately below it are the functional areas, which are decomposed in other functions. Eventually,

When you reparent or resequence a function, the diagrammer gives you visual clues about allowed positions in the diagram where the function can go. As you drag the object, the mouse cursor changes to indicate whether you can or cannot drop the function in the location where the mouse pointer is.

functions will exist in each hierarchy diagram that are not decomposed any further. They are called *atomic* business functions for the diagram. A function can be atomic in one diagram but decomposed in another diagram. But if an atomic function represents a business activity that does not require further activities to complete, then this function cannot be decomposed into further levels in any diagram in which it is included. This type of function is called an *elementary* business function.

As you decompose the business functions into more and more details, you may find out that you need to create functions that are already shown in other areas of the diagram, under another hierarchy. For example, one of the functions under the functional area Acquisition is Control Product Inventory. By looking at the high-level functions shown in Figure 9.1, you can see that the same function appears under the functional area Distribution. Obviously, if the functions are the same, you do not want to maintain them in two or more separate places. In this case, identify one of them as the *master* function and make the others *copy* functions of this master. After that, you need to maintain the properties and decomposition of the master function only; the copy functions automatically inherit any changes that you make to the master. Business functions that appear in more than one place in the hierarchy diagram, whether they are master or copy functions, are referred to as *common* functions.

 As an example, you can turn the TASC functions Control Product Inventory mentioned above into common functions. Since they are identical, identify one of them, for example ACQ4–Control Product Inventory, to be the master function. You do not need to take any further actions to turn a function into a master function. Instead, you turn the other functions into copies of this function. In order to turn DIST5–Control Product Inventory into a copy of the master, follow these steps:

1. Double-click the function DIST5 in the diagram. The Edit Function tabbed dialog box appears.
2. Click the tab Common to display its properties.
3. Pick the application that owns the master function in the Application System list box (see Figure 9.5). In your case, it is STRATEGIC PLAN.
4. Pick the master function ACQ4 in the Master Function list box (see Figure 9.5). This list shows the labels of all the functions in the application ordered alphabetically.
5. Click OK to complete the process.

After the dialog box is closed, the diagrammer displays double bars along the vertical lines of the box that represents the function. These distinguish copy functions from other functions in the diagram. However, they do not allow you to tell

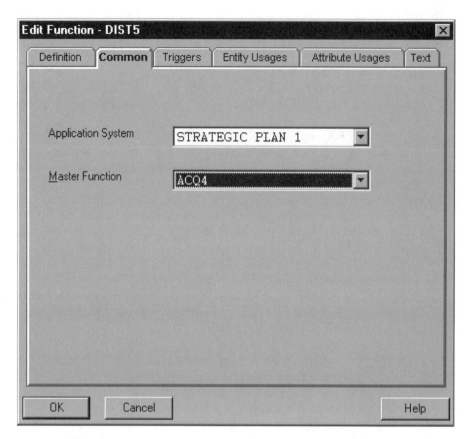

FIGURE 9.5 Creating common functions in the Function Hierarchy Diagrammer.

which is the master of a copy function. Often, when reviewing and discussing a diagram, having that type of information associated with the function comes in handy. You can do this by adding a reference to the master function in the short description of the copy function. The following section explains how you can edit the properties of functions in the Function Hierarchy Diagrammer.

9.1.5 MAINTAINING FUNCTIONS IN THE FUNCTION HIERARCHY DIAGRAMMER

When you create a function in the Function Hierarchy Diagrammer, you can specify only its label and short description. In order to add more information about the function and maintain it over time, you need to edit the function. You can maintain the properties of a function in the Edit Function dialog box. The easiest way to display this dialog box is to double-click the function you want to edit. The previous section discussed how you can use the Common properties tab to turn function DIST5 into a copy of function ACQ4. Figure 9.6 shows the Definition properties tab for another function.

On this properties tab, you usually maintain the label and the short definition of the function. You can also flag a function as elementary by checking the check box Elementary to the right of its label. You can view information about the parent of the function but you are not allowed to change it. In order to enter a longer description for the function, or additional notes, switch to the Text tab in the dialog box and pick the desired text type.

The information described above is more or less all you enter and maintain about functions at this point of the analysis. The reason is that, when creating the high-level model of the enterprise, you do not want to obscure the picture with too many details. They should be gathered and analyzed when you narrow the

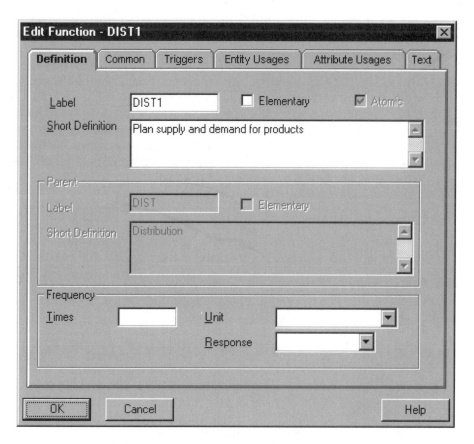

FIGURE 9.6 Definition properties in the Edit Function dialog box.

In the application system you developed in the first three chapters of the book, the settings *'Immediate'* and *'Overnight'* of the property *Response* had another meaning. This difference is to be expected since the element type Business Function in Designer/2000 represents different things in different contexts. In the context of defining the functional hierarchy of the enterprise, a function represents a business activity. When defining the requirements of an information system, a function represents a user interface requirement or a business rule that will be implemented by the system. As the discussion in this book progresses, you will return to some of these properties tabs and fill in additional information appropriate for the topic.

scope and focus in a particular business area or further down in an information system.

Suppose for example that you are analyzing the Human Resources business area of the TASC corporation and decide to decompose the function HR2–Recruit, Hire, and Terminate Employees in the following three sub-functions: HR21–Recruit Employee, HR22–Hire Employee, and HR23–Terminate Employee. During conversations with the Director of Human Resources, you learn that recruiting is an ongoing process at TASC; they are always on the lookout for the brightest and the best. This activity results in about 20 new hires every quarter, which compensate for an average of 5 resignations or terminations and satisfy the growing staffing needs of the company.

You can enter the frequency information identified above on the Definition tab of the Edit Function dialog box. For example, for the function HR22, you would enter '20' in the field *Times* and pick *'Quarter'* from the *Unit* list box. Likewise, you could set the *Response* to one of the two allowed values: *'Overnight'* or *'Immediate.'* Hiring or firing an employee is usually a lengthy process; therefore the *Response* would be set to *'Overnight,'* but for a function such as Enter Employee Hours in Payroll System, the *Response* should be set to *'Immediate.'*

9.1.6 ASSOCIATING FUNCTIONS WITH OTHER REPOSITORY OBJECTS

In the example presented at the end of the previous section, I assumed that the functions HR21, HR22, and HR23 are performed by one business unit, the Human Resources department. Some functions in a company are performed by more than one business unit. You saw earlier that the function ACQ4–Control Product Inventory is the same as function DIST5 with the same description.

However, they are performed by different business units in different contexts. Function ACQ4 is executed by the Acquisition group in the Business Products or Home and Family Products departments; function DIST5 is performed by the Warehouse group within the same departments. In order to express the fact that the same function is performed by four business units, but also to enter data about the frequency with which each business unit performs the functions, you create associations between them. Other information that your business functions analysis should reveal is how they contribute to the achievement of business objectives, and whether they monitor, report, or set a target value for any key performance indicators. This information is stored in the Repository in the form of associations as well. The following paragraphs describe how you can use the Repository Object Navigator to create and maintain these associations.

To create associations between a function and the business units that perform this function, follow these steps:

1. Select and expand the node that corresponds to the desired business function.
2. Expand the node Usages and then select the node Performing Functions.
3. Click the icon Create Association 🔛 to create a new association. The dialog box Create Function Business Unit Usages appears.
4. In this dialog box, pick the business units that execute the selected function and click OK. A new association is created between the function and each business unit.
5. Switch to the Property Palette for each new association and set the properties *Frequency, Frequency Unit,* and *Response Required* so that they describe accurately the frequency with which the business unit performs the function.

You can document which business functions contribute to the fulfillment of a particular objective by doing the following actions:

1. Select and expand the node that represents the objective in the Repository Object Navigator.
2. Expand the node Usages and select the node Of Business Functions.
3. Click the icon Create Association 🔛. The dialog box Create Objectives of Business Functions appears.
4. In this dialog box, select one or more business functions that help to achieve the objective and click OK. A new association is created between the objective and each business function you selected.
5. Switch to the Property Palette and set the properties of the new objects so that they describe or measure the contribution of the function to the objective.

Finally, for each key performance indicator, identify business functions that establish targets for them, or that monitor and report their performance against the targets. To enter the accumulated information in the Repository, do the following:

1. Select and expand the desired KPI in the Repository Object Navigator.
2. Expand the node Usages and select the node Controlled by Business Functions.
3. Click the icon Create Association 🔁. The dialog box Create Key Performance Controls appears, listing all the business functions available in the Repository.
4. Select one or more business functions that set, monitor, or report on the chosen KPI and click OK. An association is created between the KPI and the selected business functions.
5. For each new association, switch to the Property Palette and set the properties according to data from your analysis.

Like any other association between objects in Designer/2000, the associations discussed above can be created and maintained in the Matrix Diagrammer as well. In the new matrix, business functions occupy one dimension of the matrix; business units, objectives, or key performance indicators occupy the second dimension. The intersection cells represent the association objects.

9.2   DEFINING THE INFORMATION MODEL OF THE ENTERPRISE

Information strategic planning follows two parallel tracks: one that builds the enterprise functional model, and the other one that builds the enterprise data model. Section 9.1 discussed how you can create the functional model. In this section, you will see how you can use Designer/2000 tools, primarily the Entity Relationship Diagrammer, to create the data model.

Whereas the functional model of an enterprise is highly hierarchical, the data model is usually much flatter. Nevertheless, a top-down approach to presenting the model usually adds clarity and helps its understanding. Therefore, this section will introduce first the high-level data subjects, then the entities, and finally relationships among entities.

9.2.1   DATA SUBJECTS, ENTITIES, AND ATTRIBUTES

The starting point of building the information model is to identify broad categories or subjects of data that the enterprise needs to maintain in order to fulfill its business mission. For example, the TASC corporation needs to collect, process, and administer data on the following subjects:

❑ Employees
❑ Customers
❑ Vendors
❑ Products
❑ Orders
❑ Equipment and Facilities

Each data subject can be further analyzed and broken down into entities. An entity is something of real existence that is relevant for the business and has significance in the way a business unit fulfills its objectives. Figure 9.7 shows some entities identified for each of the data subjects listed above.

Besides the relevancy and significance to the business, data subjects must possess other properties in order to be considered and modeled as entities. In particular, the following three points should be true:

❑ **Entities must represent information that is stored and maintained by the organization.** Not every piece of important information needs to be maintained by the enterprise or its business units. This fact becomes particularly true in this age of exploding information sharing and distribution. For example, employees in the Finance department must know the latest developments in the stock and bond markets. However, instead of storing and maintaining all the financial indicators themselves, they rely on financial and business publications or public information services.

EMPLOYEES	PRODUCTS
❑ Employee	❑ Product
❑ Business Unit	❑ Location
❑ Job	❑ Manufacturer
CUSTOMERS	**ORDERS**
❑ Customer	❑ Order
❑ Location	❑ Order Item
❑ Profile	❑ Delivery
VENDORS	**EQUIPMENT AND FACILITIES**
❑ Vendor	❑ Site
❑ Location	❑ Warehouse
❑ Industry	❑ Office Equipment
❑ Contract	❑ Computer Equipment

FIGURE 9.7   High-level data entities for the TASC corporation.

❑ **Entities must have occurrences in the business.** Clearly, you do not need to analyze, model, or plan to store some information that will never materialize in concrete form. On the other hand, for entities that have or will have multiple instances, determining some volumetric parameters is good, such as the initial, average, or maximum number of instances, and the growth rate of that entity.

❑ **Entities must be uniquely identified.** While representing multiple instances of information, entities should also provide you with ways to uniquely identify one instance from another. Information items that cannot be uniquely identified are not eligible to be considered entities and could be part of a larger entity

Whereas entities represent relevant information that business units need to collect and store, the attributes are details that describe the entity. Figure 9.8 contains some attributes of the entity EMPLOYEE.

This figure shows clearly that attributes identify (Employee Number), qualify (Name, Hire Date), group (Department Number), quantify (Salary, Bonus), or describe the status (Status) of a particular instance of the entity. The attributes that uniquely identify each instance of an entity are called unique identifiers. In Figure 9.8, the attribute Employee Number is the unique identifier of the entity Employee.

9.2.2 CREATING ENTITIES IN THE ENTITY RELATIONSHIP DIAGRAMMER

Like business functions, entities are identified in close interaction and with the participation of the people who perform the work in the organization. While listening carefully to the way they describe their work, pay attention to the nouns in their language, because they represent the entities. On the other hand, familiarity with the business is probably the greatest advantage one can have in defining the entities of a business. Given the ease with which data modeling techniques can be picked up by many people, training business persons in data modeling and making them part of the modeling team is often easier than relying on a data analyst, often an outside consultant, to grasp all the details and intricacies of the business.

❑	Employee Number	❑	Salary
❑	Last Name	❑	Bonus
❑	First Name	❑	Hire Date
❑	Department Number	❑	Status

FIGURE 9.8   Sample attributes of the entity EMPLOYEE.

For a detailed data model, you need to capture detailed information about the entity and about each of its attributes. Also identify and document business rules that affect the state of an entity or of its attributes. This last activity becomes especially important when data modeling occurs as part of the efforts to define and design an information system.

However, if you are working on a high-level data model that is part of information strategic planning efforts, focus only on the major entities and their descriptions. Because the strategic plan should allow the management to look at the "large picture," it should not contain many details, such as attributes or detailed business rules that affect the data. After the strategic plan is complete and the business areas are defined and prioritized, you can begin to gather all these details. In this section, you will create some of the entities shown in Figure 9.7. Here are excerpts from a conversation with the Director of Human Resources at TASC that allows you to get the information you need:

...

You: How many employees work for TASC right now?

Director: First of all, I want to emphasize that employees are the most important asset of our corporation, because through their hard work and dedication we can meet our business objectives. Currently TASC has 200 employees, and each year the staff grows by about 60 employees. According to our measurements, we hire 20 new employees each quarter to compensate for about 5 employees who resign or are terminated, and to provide for the growth of the company.

You: Are they all full-time employees?

Director: Yes. Those 200 I mentioned are all full-time employees, or FTEs as we often abbreviate. However, we have other people who work for us and contribute to the growth of the company, such as some contractors and 30 intern students we bring on board each summer. Although we do not offer them any benefits or guarantee them employment for any period of time, for the purposes of my department, they are considered to be like any other TASC employee.

You: Why? Why don't you distinguish FTEs from contractors or interns?

Director: Because we have to make sure that they are interviewed properly and are briefed about TASC's rules and policies when hired. We follow their progress and development throughout the time they work for us, just like for our regular employees. In fact, when their assignment or contract expires, we offer full employment with the company to about half of them.

...

Enter now the information you can gather from this conversation in the Designer/2000 Repository. As a preliminary step, launch the Entity Relationship Diagrammer and create a new diagram that contains TASC's high-level information model. To define the entity EMPLOYEE, do the following:

1. Click the button Entity ◩ on the diagrammer's drawing toolbar. Notice that the mouse cursor changes shape to a soft box.
2. Click in the diagram. The dialog box Create Entity appears (see Figure 9.9).
3. Type 'EMPLOYEE' in the Name field and click OK to create the new entity.

This dialog box contains the three properties of an entity that must be set in order to create it. Normally, you supply only the name, and let the diagrammer fill in the short name and the plural name for the entity. The settings of these two properties are used by the other Designer/2000 components such as the Database Design Transformer, the Server Generator, and several front-end generators.

9.2.3 MAINTAINING ENTITIES IN THE ENTITY RELATIONSHIP DIAGRAMMER

After creating an entity, you need to provide additional information related to the entity and maintain it. In order to edit the properties of an entity in the Entity Relationship Diagrammer, double-click the diagram object that represents the entity. This action displays the dialog box Edit Entity, where you can access and modify the properties of the entity. Figure 9.10 shows this dialog box for the entity EMPLOYEE.

The Edit Entity dialog box contains several properties tabs. The one shown in Figure 9.10 allows you to maintain the general definition of the entity, such as names or volumetric information. Note in this figure that properties like *Initial* and *Growth Rate* in the Volume group are set based on the interview with the Director of Human Resources presented above. That interview shows that the initial

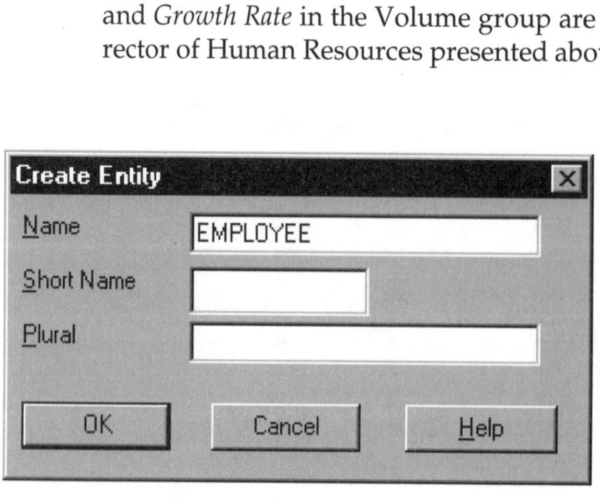

Create Entity   ☒

Name | EMPLOYEE

Short Name |

Plural |

[OK]   [Cancel]   [Help]

FIGURE 9.9 The Create Entity dialog box.

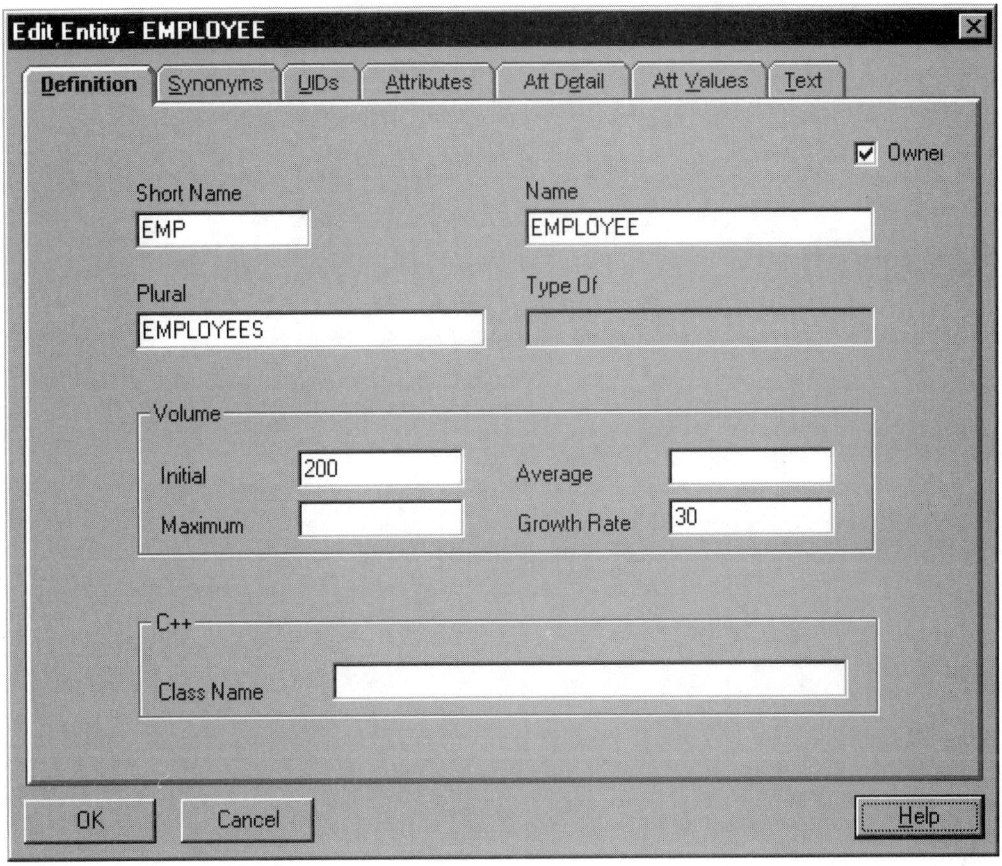

FIGURE 9.10   The Definition tab of the Edit Entity dialog box.

number of instances for the entity EMPLOYEE is estimated to be 200, and the average annual growth rate is estimated to be 30 percent.

Other things you can deduce from this interview are that from the HR perspective, an employee is also known as a full-time employee or FTE; and contractors and intern students are considered employees as well. This information should be included when you model the entity EMPLOYEE. In the Edit Entity dialog box, you need to click the Synonyms tab and enter the synonyms in the multiple record window, as shown in Figure 9.11.

The other information provided in the interview presented earlier should allow you to come up with a good description of the entity. You can enter it in the Repository by clicking the Text tab in the Edit Entity dialog box and selecting *Description* from the *Text Type* list box. The description should be concise and clear.

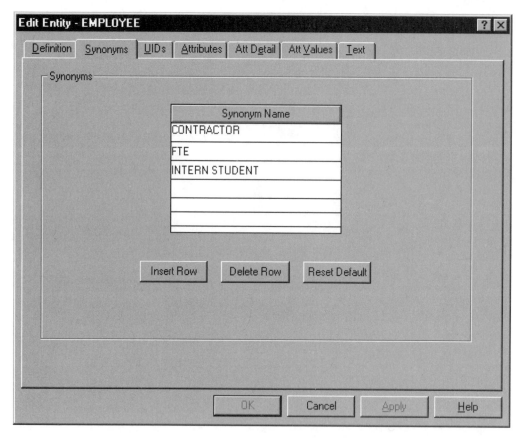

FIGURE 9.11 The Synonyms tab of the Edit Entity dialog box.

For lengthier discussions or further clarifications, you can use the *Notes* associated with the entity.

The description of an entity should fit the following formula:

An instance of <ENTITY NAME> has significance as <Entity Description>.

According to this formula then, the description for entity EMPLOYEE could be:

A salaried worker who contributes to the growth of The American Software Club. For the Department of Human Resources, EMPLOYEE is considered any full-time worker, contractor, or intern student.

This convention allows you to standardize the description of all the entities in the Repository. One more reason is that some predefined Repository reports that you

You will encounter the interface offered on the Synonyms tab on several other properties tabs in the Entity Relationship Diagrammer and other Designer/2000 tools. The multiple-record block in the center allows you to append records at the bottom of the list by clicking the first empty row in the list and entering the appropriate data. If you select an existing record and click the Insert Row button, a new record is created before the one you selected. This method allows you to insert a new record anywhere in the list. In order to delete a record, simply select it and click the Delete Row button. If the record contains multiple fields, you can navigate to them by pressing the TAB key. You can also move up and down the list of records by pressing UP ARROW and DOWN ARROW from the keyboard.

may want to include with your analysis reports expect the entity descriptions to follow this formula.

9.2.4 RELATIONSHIPS

When a significant business association exists between two entities, this association must be analyzed and documented in your data model. This association is called a relationship between the entities. The process of analyzing entities is so interwoven with that of defining the relationships into which these entities enter, that they are often considered one common data modeling process, called entity relationship modeling. Relationships between entities are always expressed in dual form. For example, the relationship between CUSTOMER and ORDER may be presented as follows:

Each CUSTOMER may be originator of one or more ORDERs.
Each ORDER must be originated by one and only one CUSTOMER.

The first sentence expresses the CUSTOMER aspect of the relationship; the second one the ORDER aspect of it. The combination of both sentences qualifies the relationship between the entities in its entirety.

The clauses in the example above are intentionally indented to indicate the different components in the definition of a relationship. First comes the name of the entity that serves as the initial point of the specific aspect of the relationship. This is followed by the Optionality variable, whose values can be either *may be* or *must be*. If the optionality of the relationship is *may be*, then the left-side entity can exist without necessarily entering into a relationship with the right-side entity. In the case above, a customer can call TASC with an inquiry, can be sent promotional materials, and so on. In all these cases, TASC would like to gather data about the customer, even if she is not calling in to order a product. In particular cases, numerous ones hopefully, the customer will place an order. In these cases, the relationship "Each CUSTOMER may be originator of one or more ORDERs" will be materialized.

If the optionality of the relationship is *must be*, then an instance of the left-side entity cannot exist if it is not associated with at least one instance of the right-side entity. In the example above, an order cannot exist without a customer to whom the order, and of course the bill, will be sent.

The Optionality variable is followed by the description of the relationship. No restrictions exist here, except that the description should reflect the business reality and the sentence should read well. After that comes the Cardinality variable, which can be either *one or more* or *one and only one*. When the cardinality of the relationship is *one or more*, each instance of the left-hand entity may be associated with more than one instance of the right-hand entity. In the example above, each customer may place more than one order. When the cardinality is *one and only one*, an instance of the entity to the left may be associated with one instance of the other entity at most. According to the business rules of TASC, an order cannot be originated by more than one customer. As a way of summarizing the discussion above, Figure 9.12 represents a matrix that you could fill out for each relationship that you identify or analyze.

When it comes to representing relationships in data diagrams, no consistent way is used universally. Each methodology represents them with its own conventions and nuances. This book will use the Oracle Method convention, which is supported by Designer/2000. In the Oracle Method, the relationship is presented as a line that connects the entities. The description of the relationship from one entity to the other one is placed closer to the first entity. The optionality of the relationship is represented by the line that originates at the first entity. If it is a solid line, the optionality is *must be*; if it is a dashed line, the optionality is *may be*. The cardinality of the relationship is represented by the line that terminates at the second relationship. If it is a straight line, the cardinality is *one and only one*; if it is a crow-foot symbol ✦, the cardinality is *one or more*. Figure 9.13 illustrates the

Each	Entity Name	Optionality	Relationship Description	Cardinality	Entity Name
Each	CUSTOMER	may be	originator of	one or more	ORDERs
Each	ORDER	must be	originated by	one and only one	CUSTOMER

FIGURE 9.12   A matrix for representing a relationship between two entities.

Each CUSTOMER may be originator of one or more ORDERs

Each ORDER must be originated by one and only one CUSTOMER

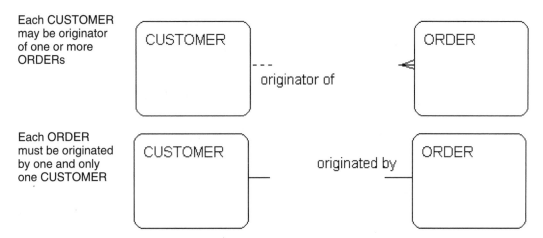

FIGURE 9.13 The Oracle Method diagramming conventions for representing relationships.

Oracle Method diagramming conventions for entity relationships for the same relationship between CUSTOMER and ORDER that I discussed earlier.

When expressing the relationship discussed here with words, you need a set of two sentences to fully describe the relationship. The power of diagramming is that it allows you to unify the two-directional representation of the entities. The Entity Relationship Diagrammer merges the relationship displayed in Figure 9.13 in one consolidated line as shown in Figure 9.14.

9.2.5 TYPES OF RELATIONSHIPS

The relationship shown in Figure 9.14 is also the one that you encounter the most in your data modeling practice. It is described as mandatory many to optional one, and is often abbreviated as M:1 (M:O). In addition to this relationship, especially at the high-level modeling stage, you will define a good number of optional many to optional many relationships, represented as M:M(O:O).

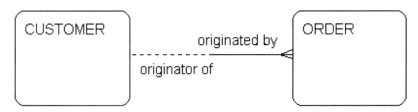

FIGURE 9.14 A representation of entity relationships in the Entity Relationship Diagrammer.

The syntax of the abbreviated notation of relationships shown above is described by the following rules:

1. Describe the cardinality of each relationship end by using "M" for "many" and "1" for "one."

2. Describe in parentheses the optionality of each relationship end by using "M" for "mandatory" and "O" for "Optional."

Figure 9.15 shows an example of the relationship that exists between products and warehouses at TASC.

The relationship shown in Figure 9.15 expresses the fact that a product may be stored in more than one warehouse, in addition to the trivial fact that each warehouse serves as a storage place for one or more products. M:M relationships are acceptable, sometimes encouraged, when used in the strategic planning phase, because they often hide unnecessary details. But when you move to the systems analysis and design stage, the data model should be fully normalized, requiring, among other things, that you remove from the model any M:M relationships. A M:M relationship is removed or, as it is often said, resolved by introducing an intersection or associative entity and splitting the original relationship into two M:1 relationships. You will see in coming chapters that the Database Design Transformer can resolve M:M relationships automatically when creating a first-cut database design from the data model.

Another type of relationship that is encountered frequently is the recursive M:1 relationship. In the majority of cases, this relationship expresses a recursive association of instances from an entity with instances from the same entity. A classical example of a recursive M:1 relationship is the one shown in Figure 9.16.

The diagram shown in this figure expresses the fact that an employee may be manager of many employees, and that each employee may be managed by another employee. Both ends of the recursive M:1 relationship need to be optional.

FIGURE 9.15   A typical M:M (O:O) relationship.

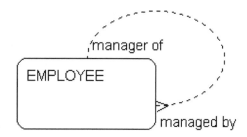

FIGURE 9.16 A recursive M:1 relationship.

Since not every employee is a manager, the optionality of the 1 end is generally understood. Where some confusion may arise is on the optionality of the M end. Look at Figure 9.16 and imagine that the M end of the relationship is mandatory. Then the relationship from that end would read as follows:

Each EMPLOYEE must be managed by one and only one EMPLOYEE.

This means that no matter how high you go in the TASC organizational chart, each employee you pick, even the CEO, must be managed by another employee. Clearly, such a relationship models an infinite recursive association that cannot occur in real-life situations.

Here is a list of all the iconic buttons on the diagrammer's drawing toolbar and the corresponding relationships you can create with them:

❑ **M:1(M to O) Relationship icon** ⬛. This is the most frequently used button. It allows you to create a mandatory many to optional one relationship.

❑ **M:1(O to O) Relationship icon** ⬛. This button allows you to create an optional many to optional one relationship. In this case, the entity on the many end of the relationship may be associated with zero or one instance of the other entity.

❑ **M:1(O to M) Relationship icon** ⬛. This button allows you to create an optional many to mandatory one relationship. In this case, the entity on the

The relationships covered here are the types of relationships that would meet your needs in almost every case. Question seriously other types of relationships and use them only if you are convinced and can convince others that they reflect the real world.

one end of the relationship must be associated with at least one instance of the other entity. Because such a relationship cannot be enforced by regular database referential integrity constraints, you need to implement it programmatically, if it is to be included in a database application.

❑ **M:1(M to M) Relationship icon** ▣. This button allows you to create a mandatory many to mandatory one relationship. In this case, the instance of each entity must be associated with at least one instance of the other entity. This relationship is impossible to implement using regular referential integrity constraints, since the first record to be inserted in the tables that represent these entities violates the constraint and no way exists to insert records simultaneously in both tables.

❑ **M:M(M to O) Relationship icon** ▣. This button allows you to create a mandatory many to optional many relationship. Such a relationship is resolved in two relationships of type M:1(M to M) and M:1(M to O). From what I said in the previous paragraph, this relationship cannot be implemented using the database referential integrity mechanisms.

❑ **M:M(O to O) Relationship icon** ▣. This button allows you to create an optional many to optional many relationship. Such a relationship is resolved in two relationships of type M:1(M to O) and M:1(M to O). It is often encountered in high-level data modeling efforts.

❑ **1:1(M to O) Relationship icon** ▣. This button allows you to create a mandatory one to optional one relationship. Instances of each entity cannot be associated with more than one instance from the other entity.

❑ **1:1(O to O) Relationship icon** ▣. This button allows you to create an optional one to optional one relationship. Instances of each entity may be associated with zero or, at most, one instance from the other entity.

❑ **1:1(M to M) Relationship icon** ▣. This button allows you to create a mandatory one to mandatory one relationship. Like other relationships that are mandatory on both sides, this relationship cannot be implemented in the database using referential integrity constraints. Often entities associated with such a relationship are split artificially when, in fact, they represent one entity. Therefore, I recommend that you model them as one entity.

9.2.6 CREATING RELATIONSHIPS IN THE ENTITY RELATIONSHIP DIAGRAMMER

In order to create a relationship between two entities in the Entity Relationship Diagrammer, both entities should be present in the diagram. Your job will be much easier if you have filled out the matrix shown in Figure 9.12 and have an idea in your mind about how the relationship will be drawn in the diagram. A pencil-drawn sketch on a piece of paper is often sufficient to give you this idea. Here is a list of steps to follow when you want to create the relationship:

1. Choose the relationship tool that matches the type of relationship you want to create on the diagrammer's drawing toolbar. Each button on the toolbar contains an iconic representation of the relationship.
2. Click the entity that will appear on the left side of the iconic representation of the relationship. For example, if the selected icon is 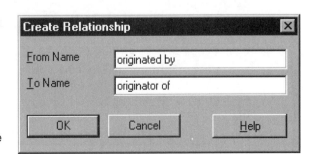, the first entity to click is the one that will have the *many* side of the relationship.
3. Click the second entity. This action displays the Create Relationship dialog box (see Figure 9.17).
4. Enter the two-directional description of the relationship in the properties *From Name* and *To Name*. The *From Name* contains the text that will be on the side of the entity you clicked first; the *To Name* contains the text that will be associated with the second entity.
5. Click OK to complete the creation of the relationship.

By following the steps above, the relationship will be created as a straight line that connects the two entities. When the diagram contains many entities and relationships, they may cause some of the lines to intersect. A diagram with intersecting relationships is often unclear, complicated to read, and difficult to comprehend. To avoid straight line relationships, create them as multiple-edged lines. Each of the relationship drawing tools can be used as a multi-line drawing tool. After selecting the first entity and before selecting the second one, you can click at any number of intermediate points in the diagram to obtain a multi-line relationship.

Another way to avoid crossing relationship lines is to use the Autolayout utility of the diagrammer. In this case, the algorithm that the utility executes guarantees that relationships will not intersect. However, use the tool with caution, since it may change radically the layout of your diagram. After the diagram has been shown, discussed, and reviewed by your audience, minimize dramatic changes to its layout.

FIGURE 9.17 The Create Relationship dialog box.

9.2.7 MAINTAINING RELATIONSHIPS IN THE ENTITY RELATIONSHIP DIAGRAMMER

After you create a relationship, you may need to maintain its appearance on the diagram and its contents in the Repository. In the diagram, the relationship appears as a combination of the line connecting the entities, and two text labels that contain the relationship description. You can select these objects and drag their selection handles to resize and reposition them. You can also move the text labels to a better position on the diagram and you can drag the edge of a relationship and drop it on different areas of the entity to change their connection point. If you drop the edge onto another entity, you effectively delete the current relationship and create a new one between the entity on the other side of the relationship and the entity where you drop the edge of the relationship.

In order to change properties of a relationship such as optionality, cardinality, or description, double-click the object to display the Edit Relationship dialog box, shown in Figure 9.18.

This dialog box shows both ends of the relationship, and allows you to change the description, optionality, or cardinality of each end. You can read each direction of the relationship displayed on the left and right sides of the dialog box by filling in the placeholders in the following templates with data from the dialog box:

Each <Left Entity> <Optionality> <From Name > <Degree> <Right Entity>
Each <Right Entity> <Optionality> <To Name > <Degree> <Left Entity>

In Figure 9.18, the left half of the dialog box reads: Each ORDER must be originated by one and only one CUSTOMER. The right half reads: Each CUSTOMER may be originator of one or more ORDERs.

9.3 MODELING MUTUAL EXCLUSIVITY OF DATA AND RELATIONSHIPS

Often instances of an entity can be grouped together so that they create partitions of an entity into mutually exclusive sub-entities. These entities are modeled using supertypes and subtypes. Associations between entities can have an exclusive character as well. Mutually exclusive relationships are modeled with arcs. The following sections will show you how to create supertypes, subtypes, and arcs to model entities and relationships that are mutually exclusive.

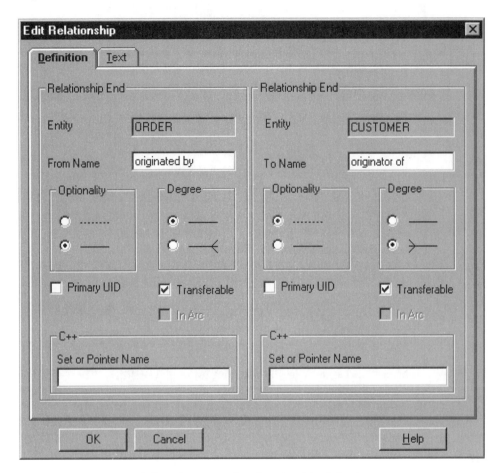

FIGURE 9.18   The Edit Relationship dialog box.

9.3.1 SUPERTYPE AND SUBTYPE ENTITIES

Recall from Chapter 8 that TASC markets and sells three types of software products: business products, family products, and games. Here is an excerpt from a memo by the company's Chief Operating Officer that sheds some more light on these products.

> For each product type, the company needs to track several information items, such as title, price, hardware requirements, installation and troubleshooting procedures, and so on. The procedures for acquiring and storing products in warehouses are similar as well. Where things change is in the way TASC sells these products to its customers. Business products are

purchased by corporations, which usually send us purchase orders. When TASC ships the order, a bill is attached to a copy of the purchase order. Customers pay the bill when they receive it together with the product. Family products and software games, on the other hand, are mostly purchased by individuals ordering by phone. For these orders, TASC requests a credit card authorization or asks the customer to send a money order. If the sales price can be charged to a credit card, the product is shipped right away together with an invoice. Otherwise, the order is booked, but not shipped until the money order is received and cashed. In any event, TASC delivers the products to individual customers only after they have paid.

Clearly, TASC's products have many attributes and relationships in common, but at the same time, they also need to be treated as separate entities. Similarly, TASC's customers share many things, but they are also treated differently when it comes to ordering and shipping products.

One way to model these situations is to create a separate entity for each type of product and customer. The disadvantage to this approach is that you will repeat the common attributes and relationships for each entity. This repetition requires unwanted replication of efforts and complicates the maintenance of common attributes and relationships in the future.

The best way to model these situations is to create a super-entity, such as PRODUCT or CUSTOMER, that contains all the shared attributes of the individual entities and enters in all the common relationships. Then you can create "smaller" sub-entities, which describe the different types of the super-entity. Conventionally, the "large" entity is called a *supertype* entity, and the "small" ones are called *subtypes* of this supertype. In the example above, then, subtypes of supertype PRODUCT could be BUSINESS PRODUCT, ENTERTAINMENT PRODUCT, and GAME PRODUCT. Subtypes of supertype CUSTOMER could be CORPORATION and INDIVIDUAL.

The easiest way to create supertype and subtype entities is to create them as regular entities and then drag the subtype and drop it inside the supertype. This action automatically sets the property *Type Of* of the subtype entity to the name of the supertype entity. Conversely, by dragging a subtype outside the boundaries of its supertype, you break the subtype/supertype relationship between them. In each case, the Entity Relationship Diagrammer displays a message box that informs you of the outcome of the action. Figure 9.19 shows how the Entity Relationship Diagrammer would display the subtype entities discussed above.

When modeling supertypes and subtypes, carefully avoid some common pitfalls.

❑ **The subtype entities must form a disjoint partition of the supertype.** In other words, each instance of the supertype entity must relate to one instance in one and only one subtype entity. Conversely, each instance in any

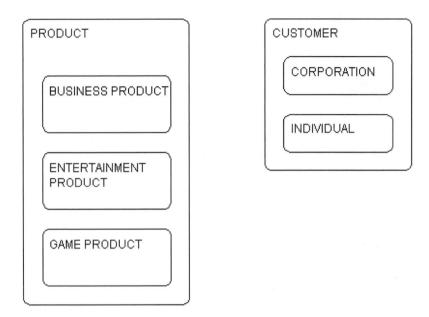

FIGURE 9.19 Supertype and subtype entities in the Entity Relationship Diagrammer.

of the subtype entities must have one and only one instance in the supertype entity. In the example above, you can proceed with the subtypes of PRODUCT, only after making sure that each product must be a business product, an entertainment product, or a game product, and nothing in between. If you cannot guarantee such a partition, then introduce an additional subtype that will store all the exceptions. For example, if the TASC executives plan to introduce new lines of products in the near future, you can create a fourth subtype for supertype PRODUCT and call it OTHER PRODUCT. This way, you make your model flexible enough to handle any changes in the business of TASC.

❏ **Do not overdo it.** If you have the time and the nerve, you can convert every entity, even the simplest one, into a supertype by defining subtypes that partition its instances according to some arbitrary criterion. However, the quality test for the subtypes and supertypes must be their usefulness to the business you are modeling. For example, from previous discussions, you may decide to split the entity EMPLOYEE into the subtypes FTE, CONTRACTOR, and INTERN STUDENT. However, they will not provide any benefits to the Human Resources department, which considers all three categories of workers for all purposes identical.

9.3.2 ARCS

Subtype entities model entities that are mutually exclusive. Sometimes relations in which an entity takes part are mutually exclusive. For example, from the executive memo quoted in Section 9.3.1, you can conclude that an order can be paid for by credit card, money order, or if the customer is a corporation, by issuing a purchase order and subsequent billing by TASC. In order to represent the mutually exclusive nature of the relationships in which an entity takes part, the Entity Relationship Diagrammer allows you to create *arcs* that join these relationships. Figure 9.20 shows how the situation described above can be modeled using arcs.

The way to read the relationships shown in Figure 9.20, starting from the entity ORDER is:

> Each ORDER must be paid for by one and only one CREDIT CARD, or
>
> must be paid for by one and only one MONEY ORDER, or
>
> must be paid for by one and only one PURCHASE ORDER.

Notice that the intersection of the arc line with the relationship line is a small empty circle to indicate that the relationship is part of the arc. If a relationship intersects the arc but is not a member of the arc, the intersection point is not a circle.

In order to create an arc in the Entity Relationship Diagrammer, create at least two relationships that will be part of the arc, and CTRL+CLICK each of them to select them as a group. Then do one of the following:

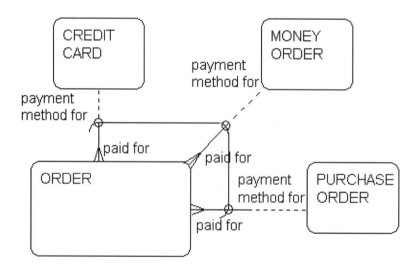

FIGURE 9.20   An arc representation of exclusive relationships.

❑ Click the icon Create Arc 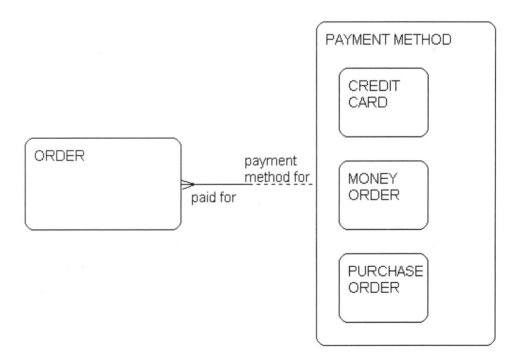 on the toolbar.
❑ Select Utilities | Create Arc.

The arc should be seen as a string that bundles together similar relationships that originate from an entity. The relationships must be either all optional or all mandatory. Often they have the same description as in the example shown in Figure 9.20. Furthermore, a relationship can be part of only one arc, although an entity can have its relationships grouped in more than one arc.

After you create an arc, you can add or remove relationships from the arc. To add a relationship to an existing arc, CTRL+CLICK the arc and the new relationship to select them and issue one of these commands:

❑ Click the button Add to Arc ▣ on the toolbar.
❑ Select Utilities | Add to Arc.

To remove a relationship from an existing arc, CTRL+CLICK to select the arc and the relationship, and then do one of following actions:

FIGURE 9.21 Replacing arc relationships with subtype and supertype entities.

❑   Click the button Remove from Arc ▓ on the toolbar.

❑   Select Utilities | Remove from Arc.

Normally, arcs make a diagram more difficult to read; hence, try to avoid them as much as possible. A good strategy that you can often follow is to shift the mutual exclusivity from the relationships that end in the entity that owns the arc to the entities that are on the other side of these relationships. In the case of Figure 9.20, you can create a subtype called PAYMENT METHOD that has the current entities CREDIT CARD, MONEY ORDER, and PURCHASE ORDER as its subtypes. The three existing relationships are replaced by only one relationship between ORDER and PAYMENT METHOD that has exactly the same optionality, cardinality, and definitions as any of the previous ones. As Figure 9.21 shows, the readability and clarity of the diagram is enhanced significantly when arc relationships are replaced with subtype and supertype entities.

9.4   ASSOCIATING ENTITIES WITH OTHER REPOSITORY OBJECTS

In order to integrate the information model with data collected during the analysis of the enterprise mission and of the functional model, you need to create associations between entities and other objects in the Repository. For strategic planning purposes, you need to create and maintain two types of associations. The following section will discuss how you can associate entities with business functions. Section 9.4.2 explains how to associate entities with business units.

9.4.1   ASSOCIATING ENTITIES WITH BUSINESS FUNCTIONS

For the sake of clarity, this chapter introduced the creation of the functional model first and the creation of the information model next. However, in practice, both activities occur in parallel. You will find out and learn more about the data by discussing business models of the enterprise; you will discover new functionality by modeling the entities and the relationships of the enterprise. Of particular interest are the following questions:

❑   What entities does a business function require in order to be completed successfully?

❑   Which of the following actions does a business function perform on these entities: Create, Retrieve, Update, Delete, Archive?

Ask these questions of yourself and the people you are working with over and over again, to ensure that your model presents an accurate and clear picture of the enterprise. You have several ways to enter the answers to the above questions in the Designer/2000 Repository. You can use the Edit Function dialog box in the Function Hierarchy Diagrammer, create a matrix that maps entities to functions in the Matrix Diagrammer, or rely on the tried and true Repository Object Navigator.

In order to create associations between a function and the entities it uses, you can edit the function in the Function Hierarchy Diagrammer and switch to the Entity Usages properties tab of the Edit Function dialog box. Figure 9.22 shows this properties tab for the business function HR22: Hire Employee.

In this spreadsheet-like properties tab, each row represents an association between the function and an entity. You can select the entity by choosing its name from the drop-down list. Then you can specify how this function acts on the entity by checking one of the following check boxes: Create, Retrieve, Update,

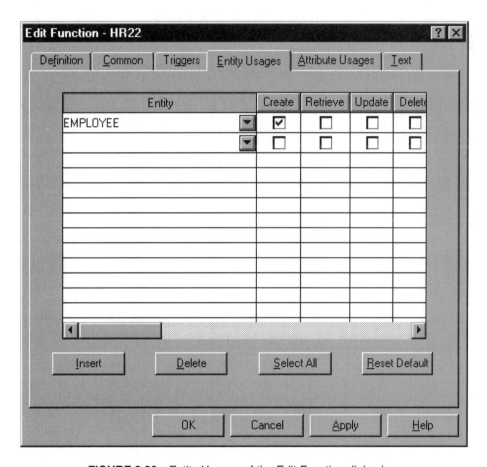

FIGURE 9.22   Entity Usages of the Edit Function dialog box.

Delete, Archive, or Other. You can also add notes in the Comments field about the way the entity is used by the function. In order to view the items mentioned here but not shown in Figure 9.22, scroll the spreadsheet to the right by using the horizontal scrollbar. When you have specified all the desired function entities usages, click Apply to save the changes without closing the dialog box, or click OK to save the changes and exit the dialog.

You can enter the same information in the Repository Object Navigator by following these steps:

1. Select and expand the node that corresponds to the desired business function.
2. Double-click the node Function Entity Usages to create a new association. The dialog box Create Function Entity Usages appears.
3. In this dialog box, pick one or more entities used by the function and click OK. A new association is created between the function and the entities.
4. Switch to the Property Palette for each new association and set the properties *Create?*, *Retrieve?*, *Update?*, *Delete?*, *Archive?*, or *Other?* to reflect the use of the entity by the function.

If you want to view and set the entity usage for several or all the functions at the same time, create a matrix that maps business functions to entities. This matrix is often called the CRUD matrix because it usually displays C, R, U, or D in the intersection cells if the properties *Create?*, *Retrieve?*, *Update?*, or *Delete?* are set. You can change the default characters of this matrix by switching to the Intersection properties tab of the Settings dialog box for the matrix, and by modifying the settings of the respective fields in the Displayed As group. Figure 9.23, for example, shows how the Archive property is represented by the letter B for Backup; the Other property is represented by the letter E for External source of data.

The CRUD matrix is especially useful when used to examine and validate the functional and information models. Because it offers a global view of the associations between business functions and entities, it allows you to pinpoint holes and discrepancies in your analysis, such as entities that are not created by any function, or business functions that do not use any entity. Chapter 16 will provide more details about the quality checking of your models at the end of the information strategy planning.

9.4.2 ASSOCIATING ENTITIES WITH BUSINESS UNITS

Another association that you should create and maintain in the strategy planning phase is that among entities and business units. The main purpose of this association is to clarify how much a business unit contributes to the volume and average growth rate of the instances of an entity.

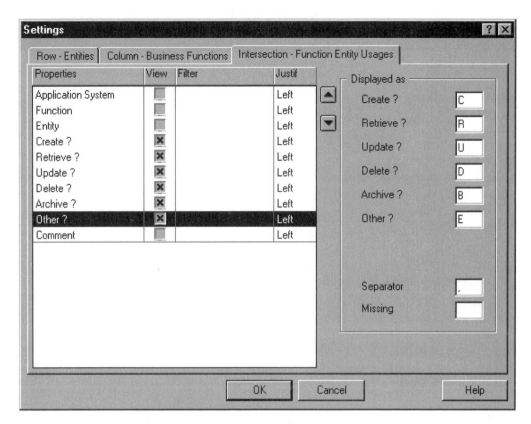

FIGURE 9.23   Changing labels of a CRUD matrix.

To create associations between an entity and the business units that use it,
follow these steps:

1. Select and expand the node that represents the entity in the Repository Object Navigator.
2. Double-click the node Entities Business Unit Usages to create a new association. The dialog box Create Entities Business Unit Usages appears.
3. In this dialog box, pick the business units that change the volume of data in the entity and click OK. A new association is created between the entity and each business unit. Note that you do not need to create associations between the entity and business units that simply read the data, since they do not affect the volume of data.
4. Switch to the Property Palette for each new association and set the properties *Initial, Maximum,* and *Average* so that they describe accurately the impact of the business unit on the entity.

9.5   SUMMARY

One of the most important activities that occurs when collecting data for the strategic planning of an enterprise is defining its functional model and the information model. The functional model describes the functional areas into which the corporation is divided and the major business functions that each of them performs. The data model focuses on the data subjects, entities, and their relationships. This chapter shows how you can use Designer/2000 to capture and maintain the functional and data model of the enterprise. Highlights of this chapter are:

❑ **Defining the Functional Model of the Enterprise**
   ❑ Functional Areas of the Enterprise
   ❑ Functions and Functional Hierarchies
   ❑ Creating Functions in the Function Hierarchy Diagrammer
   ❑ Types of Functions
   ❑ Maintaining Functions in the Function Hierarchy Diagrammer
   ❑ Associating Functions with Other Repository Objects

❑ **Defining the Information Model of the Enterprise**
   ❑ Data Subjects, Entities, and Attributes
   ❑ Creating Entities in the Entity Relationship Diagrammer
   ❑ Maintaining Entities in the Entity Relationship Diagrammer
   ❑ Relationships
   ❑ Types of Relationships
   ❑ Creating Relationships in the Entity Relationship Diagrammer
   ❑ Maintaining Relationships in the Entity Relationship Diagrammer

❑ **Modeling Mutual Exclusivity of Data and Relationships**
   ❑ Supertype and Subtype Entities
   ❑ Arcs

❑ **Associating Entities with Other Repository Objects**
   ❑ Associating Entities with Business Functions
   ❑ Associating Entities with Business Units

Chapter 10

MODELING BUSINESS PROCESSES

♦ What Are Business Processes?

♦ Why Model Business Processes?

♦ Creating the Process Model of the Enterprise

♦ Creating Processes in the Process Modeller

♦ Modeling the Customer

♦ Analyzing the Business Areas of the Enterprise

♦ Summary

In the previous two chapters, you learned how to capture and model in the Designer/2000 important data for the information strategy planning phase, such as organizational structure, business objectives, critical success factors, key performance indicators, high-level functional model, and high-level data model of the enterprise. As I mentioned there, this data gives you an idea about what the company is trying to do, about its business challenges and opportunities, and about the players who will turn these opportunities into reality.

An important piece missing from the puzzle is how all the TASC activities fit together. Although you created the functional hierarchy diagram for the company, that diagram is very much organized along organizational lines. It has the advantage that it allows you to see how a large function is divided into smaller ones. But it has the disadvantage that it does not show you how the job gets done. At this point, can you tell how TASC fulfills its goals and objectives? Who does what? How long it takes? How much it costs?

In order to provide answers to these and other similar questions, you need to analyze the *business processes* of the corporation. This chapter will discuss the importance of business process analysis and modeling and how to create the high-level process model of the enterprise. At the end of this chapter, the information required to plan the information strategy of the TASC corporation will be in your hands and in the Designer/2000 Repository. This will allow you to transition to the analysis of the business areas within the company.

10.1   WHAT ARE BUSINESS PROCESSES?

Probably the first question to ask is "What is a business?" In the traditional meaning, a business is the purchase and sale of goods with the intent to make a profit. This definition has well described many corporations for a long time. However, the problem with it is that it highlights the effect while hiding the cause. Making a profit, although being a reasonable goal for each corporation, does not define its business. It is the effect of its activity, but not the cause or the reason for it. The existence of a business is defined by the needs of a particular group of people, its customers, and needs that the business fulfills with its products or services. Thus, the business is an endeavor that intends to provide customers with some products or services of value that satisfy their needs.

Business processes are collections of activities through which a corporation creates value for its customers. They can be seen as mechanisms that convert business inputs into outputs of value for the customers. Figure 10.1 graphically represents business processes.

When you model a business process, you will need to understand, analyze, and document in the Repository the following components:

FIGURE 10.1 Processes are mechanisms that convert business inputs into outputs of value to customers.

❑ Business events that activate a process
❑ Business inputs in the process
❑ Business outputs that the process will produce
❑ Business activities required to convert the input into the desired output
❑ Organization units that carry out each activity within the process
❑ Flow of work from one activity to another within the process

In the following sections, you will learn how to capture this information and model it in the Process Modeller.

10.2 WHY MODEL BUSINESS PROCESSES?

Traditionally, corporations have organized their existence around the functions they perform. Starting from the high-level enterprise functions, they are broken down into simpler functions, which themselves are broken into smaller functions, and so on, until the level of elementary business functions is reached. The functional hierarchy of the corporation often defined its organizational hierarchy, since it was considered appropriate to group employees that performed similar functions in the same organization unit, for example, all the accountants in the Accounting department, all the salespersons in the Sales department, and all the engineers in the Engineering department.

The reasons for such an organization were clearly laid out by the Scottish philosopher and political economist Adam Smith in his masterwork *An Inquiry into the Nature and Causes of the Wealth of Nations* (1776). This work, universally known as *The Wealth of Nations*, is the first great work in political economy. Its fundamental thesis is that the annual production of goods and services, also known as the wealth of a nation, tends to grow. The ultimate driver of the society's ability to increase its productivity is the division of labor. In fact, *The Wealth of Nations* opens with the now famous description of a pin factory in which ten workers specializing in a few simple tasks produce 48,000 pins a day, compared to just a few, perhaps only one, that each of them could have produced alone.

Smith's principle of division of labor was raised to near perfection by Henry Ford and the assembly lines he implemented in his factories. Ford's idea was to break a complex task such as building an automobile into simple, elementary tasks that could be performed by workers with basic skills. The natural result of such radical division of labor was the creation of a myriad of business units within the corporation. Managing and coordinating their activities was a nightmare until the administrative genius of Alfred Sloan, president and CEO of General Motors for a quarter century, appeared. Sloan divided the administrative and management tasks into smaller and simpler ones. While he decentralized General Motor's production into the five divisions that exist even today, he centralized administration, creating a large hierarchy of financial and management advisers headed by a powerful central office, whose purpose was to coordinate and oversee the company's business. The division of production by Ford complemented by the division of management by Sloan were the principles after which the successful corporations of the twentieth century were modeled.

In the 1980s and early 1990s, many of these corporations began experiencing serious problems. Some of them, which had reached the status of American symbols around the world, such as PanAm, ceased to exist; some others, such as IBM, failed to notice radical changes in the marketplace; some others, like Sears or the three big automakers, were posting huge losses quarter after quarter. To the surprise of their managers and directors, these companies were rapidly losing ground even though they were following the same proven principles and practices that had helped them become so successful in the first place.

In 1993, Michael Hammer and James Champy wrote *Reengineering the Corporation* (1993, HarperCollins), in which they explain that many corporations today face similar problems not because they do not follow or implement traditional business and management practices well, but exactly because they *do*. The fundamental concept of the book is that, given the new character of forces driving business today, the time has come to replace the principles and lessons learned during the past two centuries. These forces, which Hammer and Champy call the three Cs, are Customer, Competition, and Change.

Until the 1980s, the market had constantly been a seller's market, which allowed businesses and corporations to produce without much consideration for the real needs of individual customers. By the 1980s, the roles began reversing, and since the early 1990s the buyers, the customers, decide to buy one product versus another based on the quality, price, and on how well this product meets their individual needs. The competition has taken on a new character as well. The large Goliaths often lose sight of the athletic Davids until they find themselves outdone and outsold. The case in point is the phenomenal rise of Microsoft from one of the many IBM suppliers, chosen almost by accident in 1981 to provide the operating system of IBM's PC, to one of the giants of the software industry. The motto of traditional businesses is "You can have it good, cheap, and fast. Pick two!" Their hungry, startup competitors can do it better, cheaper, *and* faster. Finally, businesses today face a world that changes constantly. To rephrase a political slogan often heard today, the era of stable and static businesses is over. Companies that cannot adapt to rapidly changing market situations are doomed to fail. Companies that can shift their priorities and change their profiles have a great chance at succeeding. In the late 1980s and early 1990s, the big three American automakers were rapidly losing ground in favor of their Japanese competitors partly because they took much longer to design, produce, and market new car models in a time when the customer demands were changing rapidly.

In face of these three factors—customers, competition, and change—only those companies that understand well how they conduct their business will be able to adjust to the changing nature of the marketplace. Paradoxical as this may sound, the problem that many corporations face in the 1990s is that they do not have a clear understanding of how they do what they do. Functional division of labor into simpler and smaller tasks, according to Adam Smith's principles, tells you what is done. Understanding and analysis of business processes tells you how it is done. Put in the words of Hammer and Champy, "It is no longer necessary or desirable for companies to organize their work around Adam Smith's division of labor. Task oriented jobs in today's world of customers, competition, and change are obsolete. Instead, companies must organize work around *processes.*" Starting from the early 1990s, many corporations have begun looking at their business processes. Only those that can improve and change these processes to the benefit of their customers position themselves for a good start of the new century.

The first step towards converting a corporation from task-oriented into process-oriented is to understand its current processes. You can say that you understand a process if you can identify its beginning and end, the steps required to complete it, the resources it needs, and how it relates with other processes. After understanding the processes, you will be able to measure their performance, compare it with the performance of similar processes in other businesses, and decide which processes need improvement. Experience has shown that, at this point, many executives realize how ineffective their business processes are and how radically they must be transformed in order for the company to remain competitive and achieve its goals. The radical transformation of business processes in order to achieve dramatic improvements in key performance indicators is the substance of Business Process Reengineering (BPR). Processes that are not so hopelessly broken as to need BPR or processes between BPR stages can be enhanced using continuous improvement approaches, such as the Total Quality Management (TQM).

An effective tool you can use to model the business processes of your corporation is the Designer/2000 Process Modeller. The rest of this chapter and the following chapter will show you how to use the Process Modeller in this context.

10.3 CREATING THE PROCESS MODEL OF THE ENTERPRISE

As for the case of functions and data subjects, during the strategy planning, analyze and model the high-level processes of the enterprise. This activity allows you to understand what the major business activities are that the corporation performs. As is the case with the enterprise functional model or data model, you need to understand that in this stage, you are trying to model only the major processes. Although each of them can be decomposed into subprocesses and activities, do not obscure the high-level picture with details.

10.3.1 CRITERIA FOR DEFINING HIGH-LEVEL PROCESSES

Here are some criteria to follow when modeling the major processes of a corporation:

❑ In order to recognize and model the enterprise processes, you need to change the way in which you see the business. Vertical partitioning and decomposition of functionality is no longer in question. Instead, look across to understand how one activity is followed by another and how the work flows from one process to the other.

❑ You cannot invent processes. They are there, in the way the company performs its business, probably hidden in the labyrinth of departments, functional units, and organization units, but decidedly present in the reality.

❑ Despite the complexity of the corporation, your high-level process model should contain only its six to eight most important business processes. The details should be identified and modeled during the business area analysis.

❑ The process model should reflect the purpose of the company for being in the business. Remember from Section 10.1 that the ultimate reason that any company is in business is to fulfill some needs of its customers.

❑ As a continuation of the previous point, your process model should reflect the customers and their interaction with the corporation.

❑ The high-level process model should also represent the interaction of the corporation with other external entities, such as its vendors, suppliers, business partners, competitors, and so on.

❑ Processes should be named and described with active sentences that clearly express the purpose of the process.

❑ Processes should be clearly defined in terms of the business unit or agent that performs them. They should turn some input into output that ultimately has value for the customer.

10.3.2 TASC'S HIGH-LEVEL PROCESSES

So what are the high-level processes at The American Software Club? Here is an excerpt from an interview with the company's Chief Executive Officer, which may help you answer this question:

You: How would you define the purpose of TASC?

CEO: I think I have mentioned earlier that our mission is to provide customers with software products of superior quality for office, home, and entertainment, in a timely manner and at prices they can afford. You can tell from this statement that we are in the business to fulfill the needs of our customers for software products.

You: How do you assess these needs?

CEO: In a variety of ways. We always keep open the channels of communications with our customers. We use market surveys and carefully interview selected samples of our customer population. We consider very important the fact that customers themselves should express their needs and wants. We create ways for them to tell us what they want and we do our best to listen to them. Understanding the customers' needs and wants is part of the ongoing activities that we conduct in order to understand and define the market requirements.

You: How do you define your business requirements?

CEO: Well, based on the market and customers' requirements, we develop and periodically enhance the strategy and vision of our company. A byproduct of the strategic plans are the requirements that our business must meet. These requirements are used to identify key products in the software market that we can acquire and market to our customers.

You: What happens after these key products are identified?

CEO: We contact vendors with requests for information about each product. Often we receive evaluation copies that we use here to become familiar with the features and functionality of each application. If we decide to purchase the product, we send an order to the vendor, which ships the requested copies to our warehouses. Meanwhile, the Marketing and Sales department sends selected customers brochures and facts about the new product; they also contact customers via telephone with special sales and promotional offers. These efforts are aimed at producing as many orders from customers as we can handle.

You: How long do customers wait between the time they place an order and the time they receive the product?

CEO: This depends on a variety of factors, such as the location of customer, the warehouse location of the product, the type of customers, and so on. What we try to do is to minimize the time we take to fulfill a customer's order. This is important to us, because the sooner customers receive their product, the happier they are, and the faster they will pay us for the purchase. A happy customer allows us to collect what we are due, pays our salaries, and creates the profit for the shareholders of our corporation. In the end, everybody wins.

Carefully review the information that the CEO offers in this interview. All the major business processes appear in one way or another in between the lines. Figure 10.2 contains a list of these processes. For each process, this table lists the agent responsible for the completion of the process, its business inputs and outputs, and a brief description of the process.

10.4 CREATING PROCESSES IN THE PROCESS MODELLER

In this section, you will use the Process Modeller to create the high-level processes of the TASC corporation. Before starting, note that Designer/2000 uses the same repository element types—business functions—to store processes and

AGENT	INPUT	PROCESS DEFINITION	OUTPUT
Customer	Software Needs	Express Requirements for Software Products	Customer Needs and Wants
TASC	Customer Needs and Wants	Understand Markets and Customers	Market Requirements
TASC	Market Requirements	Develop and Enhance TASC's Strategy and Vision	Business Requirements
TASC	Business Requirements	Identify and Acquire Products from Vendors	Inquiries and Orders
Vendor	Inquiries and Orders	Supply Products to TASC	Products
TASC	Products	Market and Sell Products to Customers	Marketing Materials, Sales Calls
Customer	Marketing Materials, Sales Calls	Place Orders with TASC	Orders
TASC Products	Orders	Fulfill Customer Orders	Delivered
Customer	Delivered Products	Pay Bill to TASC	$$$
TASC	$$$	Distribute Revenue to Employees and	Profit, Value

FIGURE 10.2 Major business functions of TASC.

process steps as well as functions and subfunctions. The reason is that fundamentally, each step of a business process will appear as a business function somewhere in the functional decomposition of the enterprise or the business area. Conversely, each business function should represent an activity that is performed in at least one of the business processes of the enterprise. Figure 10.3 shows graphically the relationship between business processes and business functions.

This figure clearly shows one more time the importance of business process modeling. Focusing only on business functions causes you to view the enterprise as many narrow stove pipes that hardly communicate with each other. You can think "out of the box" and look across organizational and functional boundaries only if you focus on the processes of the enterprise that naturally traverse these boundaries.

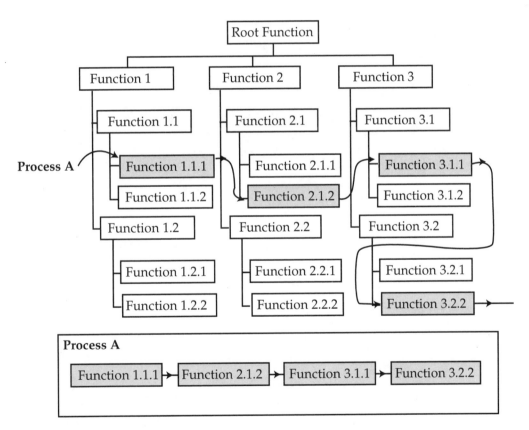

FIGURE 10.3 The relationship between business processes and business functions.

In order to create the process model based on the contents of Figure 10.2, you need to go through the following steps:

1. Create a new diagram and a new "root" process that will represent the mission of TASC.
2. Create the agents or organization units that appear in Figure 10.2.
3. Create each process in the order it appears in Figure 10.2.
4. For each process, create its business inputs and outputs, as described in Figure 10.2.

The following sections will discuss each of these steps in detail.

10.4.1 CREATING A NEW ROOT PROCESS

 Begin by launching the Process Modeller from the Designer/2000 tools window. Create a new diagram by clicking the button New on the diagrammer's toolbar. The dialog box New Diagram is displayed (see Figure 10.4).

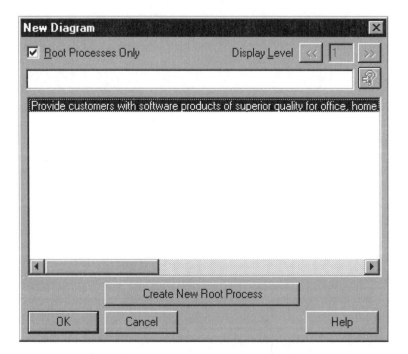

FIGURE 10.4 The New Diagram dialog box.

Before continuing further, I want to discuss for a minute the functionality contained in this dialog box. In the center, the dialog box lists processes or functions that are defined in the Repository. By default, only the root processes or functions are displayed. But if you remove the check mark from the check box Root Processes Only in the upper left-hand corner, you see all the functions listed. The controls in the upper right-hand corner of the dialog box are used to determine how many levels of the hierarchy tree will be displayed. These controls are enabled only if you are viewing all the functions or processes and not just the root ones. If Display Level is set to '1,' all the functions that depend directly on the root are listed indented one level to the right; if Display Level is set to '2,' the second "generation" of functions is displayed indented one more level to the right; and so on.

The long text item across the dialog box serves as a search engine if the list of available functions is very long. It has automatic find capabilities that allow you to navigate to the desired element in the list by typing only the few first characters of its name. After selecting the process you want to model, you can click OK.

You can also create a new root process directly from this dialog box by clicking the button Create New Root Process. In the situation discussed here, you want to create a new root process for TASC's mission. In the dialog box Create Process Step that appears after clicking the button, enter the short definition and the label of the process, as shown in Figure 10.5.

10.4.2 CREATING ORGANIZATION UNITS

Together with the new root process to represent the mission of TASC, a new diagram is created, as shown in Figure 10.6. This diagram represents the entire process. A visual indicator of this is the name of this diagram, displayed in the title bar of the Process Modeller window, which is the same as the short description of the new process.

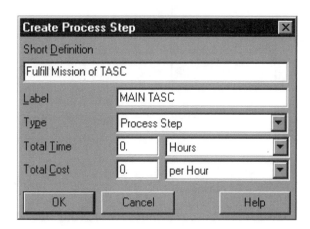

FIGURE 10.5   The Create Process Step dialog box.

The Create Process Step dialog box contains fields where you can specify quantitative information about the time and cost required to perform the process. Other similar dialog boxes you will see in the coming sections, used to create other components of a business process diagram, contain the same or similar items. They are rarely used, though, especially when preparing the high-level process model of the enterprise. As you will see in Chapter 11, the quantitative data and detailed information for business processes is widely used during business area analysis.

The window of a process diagram is divided into two vertical panels. The right panel is where you create and display all the steps that make up the process. The left panel contains the organization units that are responsible for performing the process steps. In business process modeling, they are also known as agents. Each process diagram contains a generic agent called Unspecified. You can use this agent to indicate that a certain step or activity in a process is performed by a unit outside your scope of consideration. The new diagram contains a horizontal lane defined by the width of the organization unit Unspecified. Each agent that

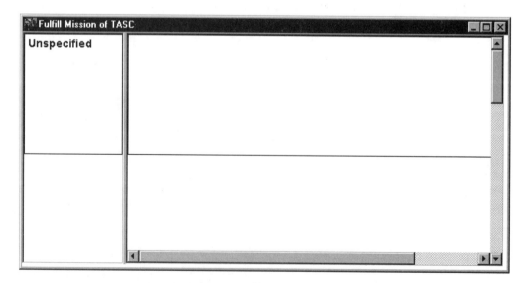

FIGURE 10.6   A newly-created process model diagram.

will be added to the diagram has its own lane where all the process steps that this agent performs reside. These lanes are often called swim lanes.

The list of high-level processes in Figure 10.2 contains three distinct process agents: TASC, Customer, and Vendor. From these, the first one already exists in the Repository. You created it when you created the organizational chart of the company in Chapter 8. In order to include it in the diagram, follow these actions:

1. Select Edit | Include | Organization unit.... This action displays the dialog box Include Organization Unit.
2. Select the unit that corresponds to TASC from the list.
3. Click OK to include the selected organization unit in the diagram.

You see that a new swim lane corresponding to this unit appears across the diagram. Now create a new agent that will correspond to Customer.

1. Select the button Create Organization Unit ▣ on the diagrammer's drawing toolbar.
2. Click in the left panel of the diagram on or below the organization unit Unspecified. The dialog box Create Organization Unit appears (see Figure 10.7).
3. Enter the specification of the new agent as shown in Figure 10.7 and click OK.

Following these steps, you can easily create the agent VENDOR. In step 2 above, do not click in the box that corresponds to TASC. If you do, the new organization unit that you create becomes a dependent of TASC. The new diagram now should be as shown in Figure 10.8.

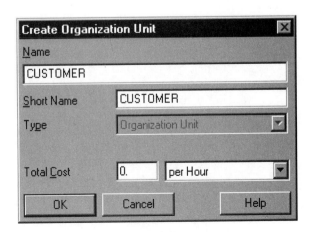

FIGURE 10.7 The Create Organization Unit dialog box.

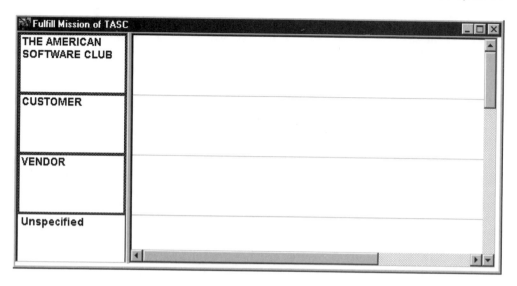

FIGURE 10.8 The process diagram with three agents defined in it.

Chapter 8 showed you how to create and maintain the organization units in the Repository Object Navigator. As you can see here, the Process Modeller offers you another way, probably more elegant, to create them. In order to edit the properties of an organization unit, display the dialog box Organization with one of these two commands:

❑ Double click the organization unit in the diagram.
❑ Select the organization unit, choose Edit | Object | Organization Unit..., and select the desired object from the Edit Organization Unit dialog box that appears.

The properties appear in the Organization Unit dialog box. Figure 10.9 shows this dialog box for the newly created agent CUSTOMER.

By default, the swim lanes that correspond to organization units in a process diagram have a transparent background. Often you may want to highlight or separate the activities performed by each agent more than by just placing them in separate lanes. You have two ways to emphasize the distinction between swim lanes using colors. In the first one, you change the fill color of an organization unit and make the whole swim lane that corresponds to that unit adopt the same color. The steps required to change the fill colors of the organization units are listed below:

1. Select the desired organization unit in the left pane of the process diagram.
2. Click the Fill Color button 🎨 on the diagrammer's drawing toolbar.
3. Pick the desired color in the Color palette that appears.

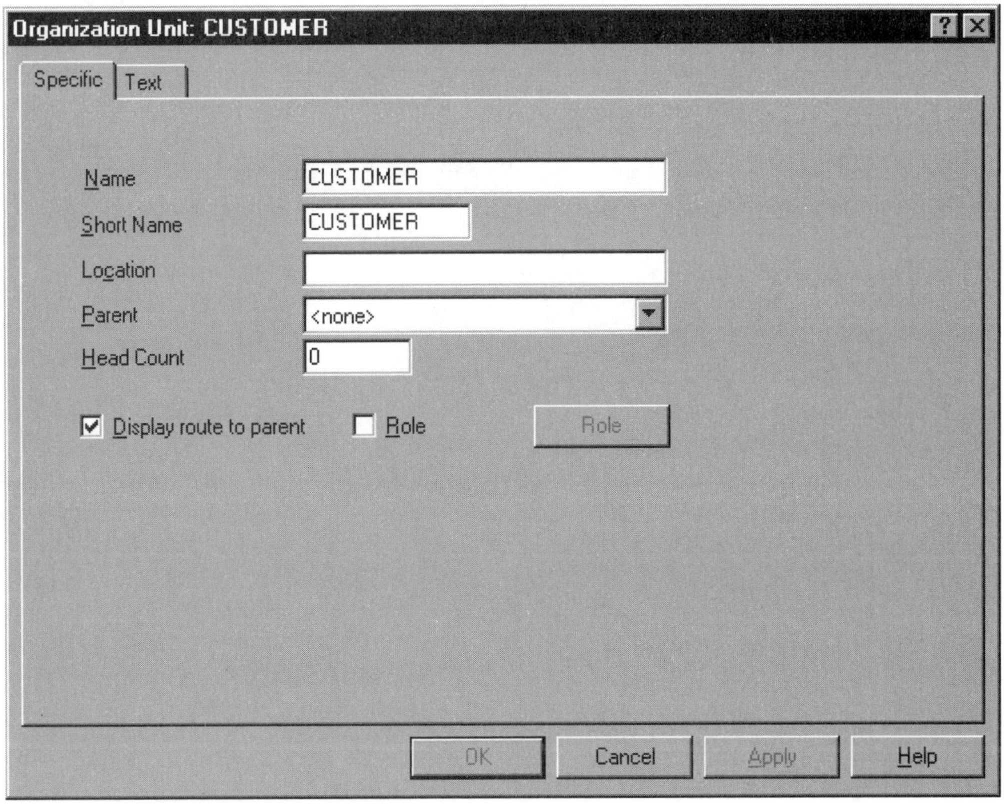

FIGURE 10.9 The Organization Unit dialog box used to edit properties of organization units in the Process Modeller.

In order to make the swim lanes have the same fill color as the organization units associated with them, modify the preferences of the Process Modeller in the dialog box Customize-Graphics. You can access this dialog box by selecting Options I Customize I Graphics... from the diagrammer's menu.

In the dialog box Customize - Graphics, place a check mark in the check box Use Organization Fill Color in the Swim Lanes group of properties, as shown in Figure 10.10. This way, each swim lane will have the same fill color as its corresponding agent.

The second way in which you can distinguish the swim lanes is to assign a color to each of the boxes in the Swim Lane group of the dialog box Customize-Graphics shown in Figure 10.10 and to uncheck the check box Use Organization Fill Color. In such a case, the colors of the swim lanes will alternate according to your settings. The fill colors of the organization units, if you have defined them, will exist and be maintained independently from those of the swim lanes.

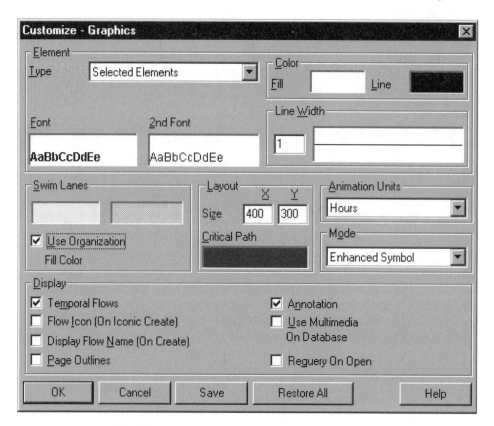

FIGURE 10.10 The Customize-Graphics dialog box.

When you create organization units, the Process Modeller places them in the left pane in the order in which they are created, leaving the Unspecified unit always at the bottom. You can change this order by selecting the organization unit and pressing the UP ARROW and DOWN ARROW keys until it reaches the desired position. Also, the width of the swim lanes is determined by the width of the objects you can create in the diagrammer. On some occasions, you would want to expand the width of the swim lane in order to fit more objects or to organize the existing ones better. In order to expand the swim lane, select its corresponding organization unit and, while holding the SHIFT key down, press DOWN ARROW. To reduce the size of the swim lane, hold SHIFT down and press UP ARROW. If the diagrammer cannot reduce the size of the swim lane, it informs you with an alert box.

10.4.3 CREATING PROCESS STEPS

Creating the high-level processes of TASC is very easy and, to a certain point, similar to the way you created the root process in Section 10.4.1. For example, to create the first process listed in Figure 10.2, do the following:

1. Select the Create Process Step iconic button ⬛ on the diagrammer's toolbar.
2. Click in the right panel of the process diagram, inside the CUSTOMER swim lane, to create the new process. The dialog box Create Process Step appears. This is the same dialog box discussed in Section 10.4.1 and shown in Figure 10.5.
3. Fill the fields in the dialog box Create Process Step with the definition of the process from Figure 10.2 and a label of ten characters or less.
4. Click OK to close this dialog box and create the new process.

After creating the process, select it and drag it along the CUSTOMER swim lane. As long as you move the object along the same swim lane, its association with the business unit remains unchanged. In order to associate a process with another organization unit that is present in the diagram, simply drag and drop it in the swim lane that corresponds to the new unit.

Following the steps above, create all the processes listed in Figure 10.2. You have to scroll the diagram window right, in order to enter all the processes performed by TASC. If you want to modify the default settings of the font properties or if you want to change the default dimensions of the grid unit in the diagrammer, invoke the Customize-Graphics dialog box shown in Figure 10.10 and change these properties according to your needs. The state of the process diagram now is shown in Figure 10.11.

10.4.4 CREATING PROCESS INPUTS AND OUTPUTS

Now that you have created the major processes of the TASC corporation, you can easily add to the diagram the business inputs and outputs that are listed for each process in Figure 10.2. To start, note that every process must have at least one event that triggers it and at least some business output that it produces. In the case of the root process you created, the event that triggers it is a need that customers experience for software products. This starts the chain of business activities that TASC performs, the ultimate outcome of which is profit for the company and value for the customers.

In order to create the event that triggers the TASC's root process, follow these steps:

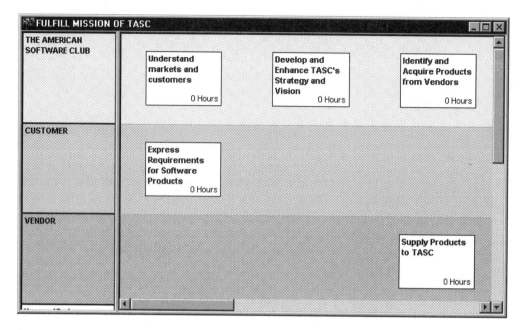

FIGURE 10.11   The state of the new process diagram.

1. Select the button Create Trigger ⬛ on the diagrammer's drawing toolbar.
2. Click the first function in the CUSTOMER swim lane with the description "Express Requirements for Software Products." The dialog box Create Trigger appears (see Figure 10.12).
3. Enter the definition of the trigger as shown in Figure 10.12.

In order to create the outcome of the process, do the following steps:

1. Select the button Create Outcome ⬛ on the diagrammer's drawing toolbar.
2. Click the last function in the TASC swim lane with the description "Distribute Revenue to Employees and Shareholders." The dialog box Create Outcome appears (see Figure 10.13).
3. Enter the definition of the outcome as shown in Figure 10.13.

10.4.5   CREATING PROCESS FLOWS

In Figure 10.2, you may notice that the way the major business processes are defined, the outcome of one process becomes input for the next process. So, for example, the needs and wants of the customers, which are the outcome of the process "Express Requirements for Software Products," become the input for the

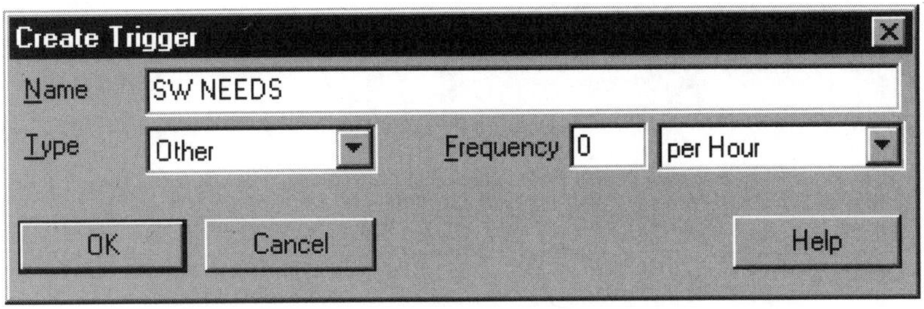

FIGURE 10.12   The Create Trigger dialog box.

process "Understand Market and Customers." The output of this process, "Market Requirements," becomes input for the process "Develop and Enhance TASC's Strategy and Vision," and so on until the last process. In situations like this, where the output of one process becomes input of another process, a *flow* exists from the first process to the second one. You can create a flow between two processes in the diagram by following these steps:

1. Select the button Create Flow ⇥ on the diagrammer's drawing toolbar.
2. Click the process that will serve as the origin of the flow.
3. Click the process that will serve as the extremity of the flow. The dialog box Create Flow appears (see Figure 10.14).
4. Enter the name of the flow according to your specific case.

Follow these steps to create the flows in the high-level process model of TASC. By default, the Process Modeller does not display the name of the flow when you create it. However, in your case, the model will gain in clarity if you show the descriptions of flows from one process to the other. In order to display the name of

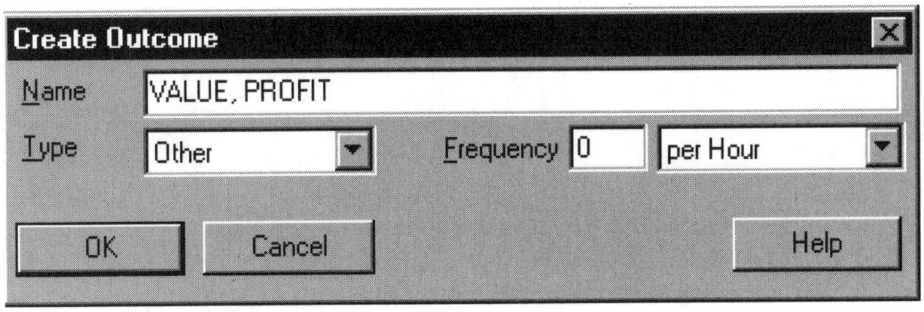

FIGURE 10.13   The Create Outcome dialog box.

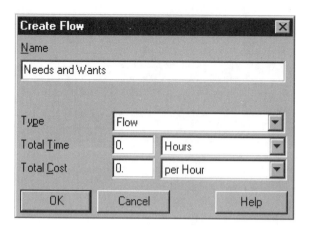

FIGURE 10.14 The Create Flow dialog box.

the flow on the diagram, invoke the Customize-Graphics dialog box and check the check box Display Flow Name in the Display group as shown in Figure 10.10.

Note also that when the name of the flow appears on the diagram, it can be moved freely, independently of the flow. This capability allows you to drag and drop the description of the flow at the most appropriate place in your diagram. Figure 10.15 shows part of TASC's high-level process diagram.

In this figure, you can notice the characteristic symbols used by the Process Modeller to represent process triggers, steps, and flows.

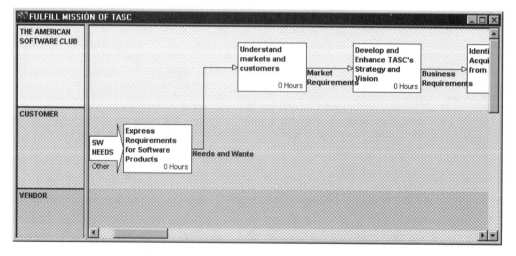

FIGURE 10.15 Part of TASC's high-level process model.

10.5 MODELING THE CUSTOMER

Up to this point, the analysis and modeling of TASC has been done primarily from the company's perspective. You can easily notice, though, a powerful player that insists upon entering the scene: the customer. Indeed, recall from Chapter 8 that the mission of TASC was defined as:

> Provide customers with software products of superior quality for office, home, and entertainment, in a timely manner and at prices they can afford.

Recall also that the purpose of TASC for being in business, like that of any other company, is to create and provide services and products of value to the customers. Furthermore, the high-level process model discussed in Section 10.3 identified the customer as one of the three principal agents that influence the business process in which TASC participates.

The importance that customers have in the fortunes of any modern business makes their modeling a very crucial component of the strategic planning. Modeling the customers requires that you switch the angle of observations and analysis. Now you should look at the corporation with their eyes. Focus only on those aspects of business that the customers see and feel. Internal processes and activities that may be necessary for the existence of the company, but that do not have any importance for the customers or do not add any value to the products and services they receive, are filtered out of the model. For example, the way in which TASC hires and manages employees or the methods it uses to acquire products from software vendors are completely irrelevant to the way customers look at the company. Customers couldn't care less whether TASC uses full-time employees for its warehouse operations or contracts out these activities; whether it distributes bonuses to the sales force at the end of the year or at the end of each quarter; or whether TASC arranges for the transportation of products from vendors' warehouses to its own warehouses or vice versa. All these issues have their importance and impact on the overall situation and health of the company, but they are not experienced or felt directly by the customers. Therefore, they are not included in the customer model of the corporation.

10.5.1 GATHERING INFORMATION FOR THE CUSTOMER MODEL

You can use several methods to gather the information you need in order to create the customer model of a company. First, the company itself may have accumulated data about its customers. Recall, for example, that one of the major processes within TASC is "Understand Markets and Customers." This implies that several people at TASC may interview customers periodically and create profiles for them, based on several social, geographic, or economic parameters.

Use all this information for your analysis. Furthermore, you can go out and talk to customers yourself or, better yet, interact with the company from the standpoint of a typical customer. Other techniques often used are polling and surveying the customers and inviting customer representatives to participate in key analysis and strategy sessions.

The following passages are excerpts from a typical interview that you may conduct with a customer of TASC. This particular customer has been purchasing software products from TASC for over three years. As you will notice from the interview, she keeps coming back to TASC because its salespeople consistently perform better than competitors when it comes to providing her with enough information to decide what is the right product for her. However, you can also notice a couple of problems that TASC needs to fix in order not to lose its longtime customers.

...

You:	How did you learn that a company exists out there called TASC?
Customer:	About three years ago, I needed to do a comparative analysis of word processing packages that our division could buy. For each package, I had to list its features, options, functionality, cost, ease of use, and how well it integrated with other applications we were using. The deadline was tight and I felt I didn't have enough time to call and ask for this kind of information from the four or five companies that were making word processors at that time. I raised the concern at the weekly meeting of our group. A colleague of mine suggested that I give TASC a try. He regularly buys software games for his daughters from them and he mentioned this database of products they maintain that allows them to provide their customers with comparative reports for products in different categories.
	As soon as the meeting was over, I called the sales rep for our region, told him about my problem, and, *voilà*, in two hours I had all the data I needed for my analysis. I was so impressed with the response that I did not hesitate to place with TASC the order for 80 copies of the word processor we selected at the end of the month.
You:	And you have continued to use them ever since?
Customer:	Yeah, we keep in touch. I receive marketing materials from our sales rep on a regular basis. He even drops by once in a while just to see how things are going and whether we need anything. I have ordered several products from him, although I wish he could help me with other product lines they have as well as with the office products.

You: What do you mean?

Customer: Well, from what I understand, each of these salespersons specializes in some products. That may be good for them, but it bothers me that I talk all year long to one guy about spreadsheets and word processors, and in January and February, when I need some tax software, I have to call somebody else who deals with family products. This setup may suit TASC, but I'd rather have what they call "one stop shopping."

You: Why do you think that splitting work like this suits TASC?

Customer: I don't think it is to their benefit, but I see they do it all the time. For example, after I place the order, I get a phone number I can call and an order ID that I can use to track the order status through their telephone system. However, I have no way to make a modification to the order, even if it is a minor one. The way it works is that I have to place a new order, and when the first one is delivered, I just send it back.

                The salesperson with whom I communicate right until I order the product is no longer in the loop after the order is placed. Somebody somewhere is responsible for assembling and shipping the product, but I have never been able to speak with this person. It seems like the order goes inside a black box and nobody knows what happens to it until it gets out of it anywhere between two to three weeks later. I understand the delay if I order two thousand copies of an exotic application that TASC has to custom order from the manufacturer, but this happens consistently, even with the most generic products.

You: So is two weeks the quickest turnaround time you have had with TASC?

Customer: Well, if they want to do it quickly, they can do it, I think. Let me tell you what happened last year. I placed a sizable order four days before the end of TASC's last financial quarter. The way our company deals with TASC is that we don't pay the bill until we receive the product we ordered and we are happy with it. Normally, between the time to place an order, receive the product, and send the check to TASC for the billed amount, four to six weeks have passed. However, in that case, we got the delivery in two days and the sales guy was insisting that I write the check before the end of the quarter so that he could meet some quota for the quarter and get his bonus. I don't know how big the bonus must have been, but I know the guy was really eager to get it. He walked the order through the system himself and even rented a truck to deliver the products because their carrier wouldn't guarantee overnight delivery.

You: Yeah, something seems wrong here. Besides the difficulties you have had after placing orders, where do you think TASC should improve its work?

Customer: One suggestion I might have is related to their database of products I mentioned earlier.

You: The one where they store detailed information about each product and use for product comparisons?

Customer: Exactly. They do a really good job trying to maintain it. But their delivery mechanism has started to wear out a little bit. They have to put that database on the Internet and allow users to query and print reports online. They can still count on existing customers to request and receive information in the traditional way, but it would be very hard to attract new customers this way. Sooner or later, if TASC does not put its system on the Web, some of its competitors will, and then even some of the old-timers like me will have to convert.

...

You can get a lot of information out of this conversation, which you will see referenced in the sections and chapters to come. The most important thing to notice is that, from the customer's perspective, two clearly distinct processes go on within TASC. The first one encompasses all the activities from the moment when the customer experiences a need for a software product until either an order is placed or the customer is not convinced that TASC can provide her with the best value for the money and decides to go to a competitor. This process will be called TASC's pre-sales process. The second process, which will be called TASC's after-sales process, begins when the customer places an order with TASC, continues with the business activities required to process this order and ends either with a happy customer who pays her bill or an unsatisfied one who returns the product. The following two sections will discuss these processes in more detail and will show you how to enter them in the Process Modeller.

10.5.2 TASC'S PRE-SALES PROCESS MODEL

This process is triggered by software needs of customers that push them to inquire about the TASC products. TASC takes these product inquiries and matches them with data from the product information database it maintains. All this activity is done so that when a sales representative responds to a customer inquiry, he or she has the necessary information to expand the knowledge of the customer about the product. Obviously, the company does not wait for customers to come to it with product information requests. As Michael Hammer puts it in his book *Beyond Reengineering* (HarperCollins, 1996), "customers are people whose behavior the company wishes to influence by providing them with value." Therefore, TASC tries to expand the customers' knowledge about products through marketing materials and sales calls. Recall that the process that produces this outcome was identified as one of the major business processes at TASC.

The ultimate goal of providing customers with data about TASC's products and services is to enable them to decide whether TASC's offerings meet their needs. If yes, then the customers will place an order with TASC; if customers need additional information, they can inquire further and communicate their needs to the sales representatives; and if no, then they will go to a competitor. This third outcome obviously results in lost sales, and the company would like to reduce it as much as possible.

Figure 10.16 shows how this process could be represented in the Process Modeller. In the following paragraphs you will create this model in your Repository.

Begin by creating a new diagram and a new root process. Enter "Pre-Sales Customer Model" as the short description and "CUST PRESL" as the label of the root process. Now include organization units THE AMERICAN SOFTWARE CLUB and CUSTOMER from the Repository. Choose different fill colors for each

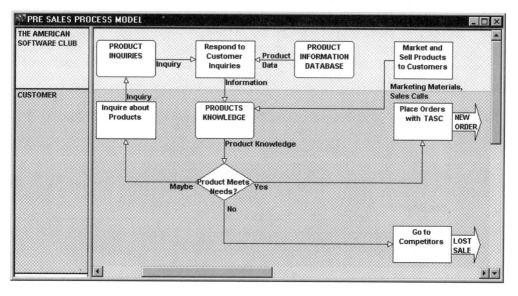

FIGURE 10.16 TASC's pre-sales customer process model.

of them and make sure that the graphical preferences of the diagrammer are such that the swim lanes use the fill color of the organization units. As a final preparatory step, choose View | Enhanced Symbol from the menu so that the Process Modeller will use enhanced symbols in the new diagram rather than regular symbols.

Of the process steps shown in Figure 10.16, two of them already exist in the Repository as part of the high-level process model of the corporation. Include them in the diagram by following these steps:

1. Select Edit | Include | Global Process Step…. The dialog box Include Global Process Step appears (see Figure 10.17).
2. Choose the processes "Market and Sell Products to Customers" and "Place Orders with TASC" from the list box and click OK.
3. Move the inserted processes further to the right in order to make room for the new objects you will create.

One of the items of the submenu Edit | Include is Process Step. The difference between choosing this option and the option Global Process Step is that the first one shows only those process steps that are under the hierarchy of the root process. In this case, since you just created the root process, choosing Edit | Include | Process Step does not show any processes. But had you created some process steps for the root process in another diagram, you could include them in the current diagram with this command.

Now create the three process steps that are new for this process. Their *Short Description* properties should be set to *'Inquire about Products,' 'Respond to Customers Inquiries,'* and *'Go to Competitors.'* In order to set the *Label* properties, use some sort of abbreviation no longer than 10 characters that indicates the root

You can distinguish the differences between symbol and enhanced symbol view of a process diagram by comparing Figure 10.15 with Figure 10.16. As you can see, in enhanced mode, the diagrammer does not display the time required to complete a process step. Another difference is that a decision point is shown as a regular process step in the symbol mode, whereas the enhanced symbol mode displays it in the more conventional form of a diamond. A third mode of displaying the process diagram is the iconic mode, which will be discussed in the following chapter.

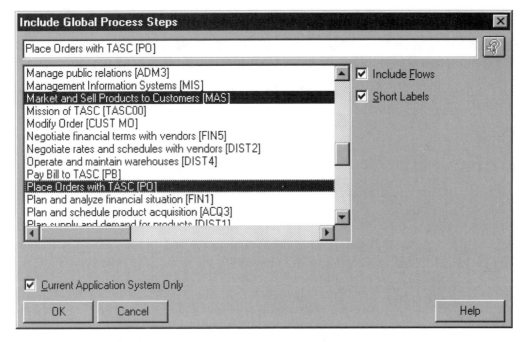

FIGURE 10.17 The Include Global Process Step dialog box.

process as well as the individual process steps. For example, you could use the following labels to identify these steps: *'PRESL IP,' 'PRESL RCI,'* and *'PRESL GC.'* After creating the process steps, place them on the diagram in positions similar to those shown in Figure 10.16.

Following steps similar to the ones described in Section 10.4.4, create the trigger SW NEED for the process step "Inquire about Products," the outcome NEW ORDER for the step "Place Order with TASC," and the outcome LOST SALE for the process step "Go to Competitors."

From the way the pre-sales process is described, you can easily identify the need to store some information or materials. For example, TASC stores information about the products it sells in a database that sales representatives can use to respond to customers inquiries. Not all the information needs to be stored in databases, files, or electronic format. It can reside on notebooks and planners as in the case of product inquiries to which sales people will respond; or it can reside in the customers' heads in the form of knowledge about products that makes them decide to order or not.

Create the first store in the diagram by following these steps:

1. Select the iconic button Create Store ⊒ on the toolbar.
2. Click the diagram region where you want the new store to appear. The dialog box Create Store appears (see Figure 10.18).
3. Set the properties *Name* and *ID* for the store as shown in Figure 10.18 and click OK.

As you can notice in your diagram, the Process Modeller symbol for stores is a soft rectangle. With similar steps, create a store that represents the product information database and a store that represents the customers' knowledge about products. Place these stores in relative positions in the diagram, as shown in Figure 10.16.

Another new object that is needed in the pre-sales customer model of TASC is a decision point. As the name would indicate, a decision point is an activity where branching of process steps occurs based on whether a condition is met or not. In the case of this process, a decision point is created in each customer's head after they receive product information from TASC's sales representative. They have to decide whether to go ahead and order the product, request more information, or go to another vendor of software products.

In order to create this decision point in your diagram, do the following:

1. Select the iconic button Create Process Step ⊒ on the diagrammer's drawing toolbar.
2. Click the diagram where you want to place the new object. The dialog box Create Process Step appears.

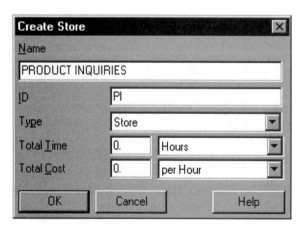

FIGURE 10.18 The Create Store dialog box.

3. Fill in the *Short Definition* and *Label* properties as shown in Figure 10.19.
4. Change the property *Type* of the process step to *'Decision Point'* by selecting the appropriate option from the list box.
5. Click OK.

You can notice that one difference between a regular process step and a decision point resides in the wording of their descriptions. Whereas for the first type of object, the description is a direct active sentence, the description of the decision point should be such that it expresses the ambiguity of the activity and the need to make a decision one way or another at the end of it. As mentioned earlier, in enhanced symbol mode, you can distinguish visually between decision points represented as diamonds and process steps represented as regular rectangles.

Finally, in order to wrap up the pre-sales customer process model, you need to create the flows between process steps and stores you have included in the diagram. Conceptually, you know how to do everything about this activity. Follow the model shown in Figure 10.16 to create the flows in the diagram.

10.5.3 TASC'S AFTER-SALES PROCESS MODEL

The after-sales customer process is triggered by the event NEW ORDER, which is one of the outcomes of the pre-sales process described in the previous section. After the order is placed, from the customer's perspective, somebody receives it and queues it up for processing. The process that fulfills the customer order takes the order from this queue, matches it up with the ordered products from the inventory, and delivers it to the customer. When the customer receives the product, he can decide to keep it and pay the bill to TASC if he is satisfied with the prod-

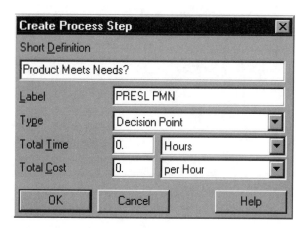

FIGURE 10.19 Creating a decision point in the Process Modeller.

uct. Or he may decide to return the product if he is not satisfied with it. Figure 10.20 shows how you could represent this process in the Process Modeller.

The overall process of creating this diagram in the Process Modeller is very similar to the one described in Section 10.5.2. Therefore, only a brief list of steps to follow is presented here:

1. Create a new diagram and a new root process called "After-Sales Customer Model."
2. Include the global process steps "Fulfill Customer Orders" and "Pay Bill to TASC" created in the high-level process model of the company.
3. Create the new process steps "Receive Customer Orders," "Modify Order," and "Return Product."
4. Create the decision point "Satisfied with Product?"
5. Create the stores INVENTORY and ACCOUNTS RECEIVABLE.
6. Create the outcome SATISFIED for the process step "Pay Bill to TASC" and the outcome UNSATISFIED for the process step "Return Product."
7. Position the objects on the diagram as shown in Figure 10.20.
8. Create flows between objects in the diagram following the layout of Figure 10.20.

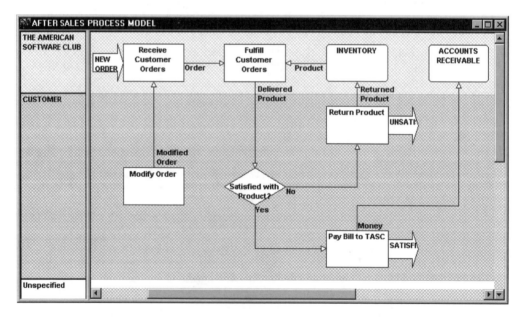

FIGURE 10.20   TASC's after-sales customer process model.

You may have noticed that no mention appears in the steps above of the event NEW ORDER that triggers the whole after-sales process. In the Process Modeller, you can create a trigger or an outcome and, at the same time, associate them with a process step. So far you have created a trigger and two outcomes for the pre-sales process as well as two outcomes for the after-sales process. Now you want to make the outcome NEW ORDER of the first process the trigger for the second one, and in particular, the process step "Receive Customer Order." Here is what you have to do:

1. Launch the Repository Object Navigator and open the application STRATE-GIC PLAN.
2. Expand the node Events in the Navigator group Enterprise Modelling.
3. Expand the node that corresponds to the event NEW ORDER in the navigator.
4. Double-click the node Triggering Functions to create a new trigger association between this event and the process (here it is called a function) in question. The dialog box Create Event Triggers appears (see Figure 10.21).
5. Select the function Receive Customer Order from the list of functions and click OK to create the new association.
6. Click Commit on the toolbar to save the changes in the Repository.

Now that the association between the event and the function is created, you can include it in the diagram where the process appears by following these steps:

1. Switch to the Process Modeller and select the process Receive Customer Order.
2. Choose Edit | Include | Trigger... from the diagrammer's menu. The dialog box Include Trigger appears, listing all the events that trigger the selected function.
3. Select the trigger NEW ORDER from the list and click OK. The trigger is included and shown in the diagram.

 For a simple way to locate and download these files, point your Web browser to the main page of the CD-ROM and follow the links *Software* and *Enterprise Strategic Analysis*.

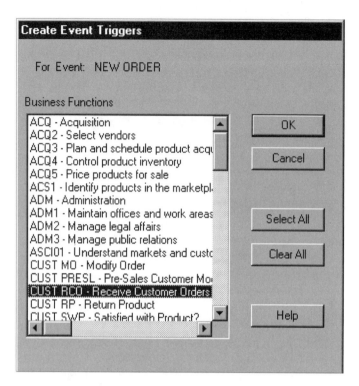

FIGURE 10.21   The Create Event Triggers dialog box.

After completing these steps, your diagram should look similar to the one shown in Figure 10.20. The companion CD-ROM contains the application system STRATEGIC ANALYSIS with all the objects and diagrams discussed in the last three chapters. This application is exported in the Oracle Export dump file STRG-PLAN.DMP, which is located in the folder \SOFTWARE\STRGPLAN. Import the file and restore the application system in your Repository to see the information provided in it.

10.6   ANALYZING THE BUSINESS AREAS OF THE ENTERPRISE

The final stage of information strategy planning is dividing the enterprise into business areas and deciding which business area to analyze first. The following two sections define business areas and discuss some ideas for ranking and prioritizing them.

10.6.1 DEFINING BUSINESS AREAS

As James Martin defines it in his trilogy *Information Engineering* (Prentice Hall, 1990), "a business area is a naturally cohesive grouping of business functions and data." Naturally, cohesive means that the functions and data are related and communicate with each other in the way that the company conducts its business. From the meaning and definition of processes, you will have no difficulties realizing that a business area is nothing more than a grouping of one or more business processes of a corporation. Often, the high-level process model of the corporation, combined with the customer model, offers a good starting point for the definition of business areas. The processes identified in these models can form a business area themselves, or be combined with one or more other processes from the model. For example, the process "Market and Sell Products to Customers," defined in the high-level process model of TASC, could be considered a business area in itself; the processes "Receive Customer Order" and "Fulfill Customer Order" can be grouped and analyzed together in the business area Process Customer Orders.

10.6.2 PRIORITIZING BUSINESS AREAS

After the business areas of a corporation are defined, you need to rank them in order to determine what areas to analyze first. Several factors can make you decide in favor of one business area over another. For each business area, you need to score these factors and then sum up all the scores. The business area that scores the highest is the one that will be analyzed first. The following is a list of factors you can consider when prioritizing business areas:

❏ **State of processes within the business area.** If you suspect that several processes within the business area are not performing reasonably well, you need to gather additional information in order to judge for remedial actions or even replacement of these processes. The analysis of the business area gives you the information required to understand and fix the problems.

❏ **Impact of processes on customers.** This is another factor that is very impor-

More formal methods exist for identifying the business areas of a corporation. For example, in the second book of the trilogy mentioned earlier, Martin describes two ways in which the CRUD matrix of entities usage by functions can be clustered into groups of functions and data subjects that fit naturally together.

tant when prioritizing business areas. As with processes, each business area within the enterprise has its own importance. However, in process- and customer-oriented corporations, where the mentality is that the customer pays everybody's salary, processes and business areas that have an impact on customers should be understood really well and made as flawless as possible. For this reason, business areas that have an impact on the customers should be among the first to be analyzed.

❑ **Possibility for success.** Analyzing a business area should not be considered an intellectual exercise, but a business activity that, like every other activity, should be carefully planned and executed only when you have a good indication that it will be beneficial for the corporation.

From the interview with the customer shown in Section 10.5.1, you can sense that the processes grouped in the business area Process Customer Orders are suffering in performance, directly affect the satisfaction of the customers, and, if fixed, will have a great potential for success. Therefore, this business area should be on top of the list of business areas to be analyzed. In Chapter 11, you will analyze this business area in full details.

10.7 SUMMARY

Many corporations today find themselves in dire need to understand their business processes. Therefore, strategic planning of the enterprise cannot be considered complete without identifying its high-level processes. This chapter explains how you can use the Process Modeller to capture the processes of the enterprise in the Designer/2000 Repository. The most important concepts discussed in this chapter are listed below:

❑ **What Are Business Processes?**
❑ **Why Model Business Processes?**
❑ **Creating the Process Model of the Enterprise**
    ❑ Criteria for Defining High-Level Processes
    ❑ TASC's High-Level Processes
❑ **Creating Processes in the Process Modeller**
    ❑ Creating a New Root Process
    ❑ Creating Organization Units
    ❑ Creating Process Steps
    ❑ Creating Process Inputs and Outputs
    ❑ Creating Process Flows

- ❑ **Modeling the Customer**
    - ❑ Gathering Information for the Customer Model
    - ❑ TASC's Pre-Sales Process Model
    - ❑ TASC's After-Sales Process Model
- ❑ **Analyzing the Business Areas of the Enterprise**
    - ❑ Defining Business Areas
    - ❑ Prioritizing Business Areas

Chapter 11

BUSINESS AREA ANALYSIS

- Defining Business Area Processes
- Analyzing Processes in Detail
- Animation and Multimedia
- Synthesizing the Business Area
- Summary

In the previous chapter, you were introduced to business process modeling and completed the high-level process model of The American Software Club. You also singled out the business area Process Customer Order for further analysis. This chapter is dedicated to this analysis. Here you will identify the major processes in this business area, their activities, triggers, and outcomes. You will also learn how to store and manipulate in the Process Modeller analytical data about processes and activities, such as time and resources required to complete them.

11.1 DEFINING BUSINESS AREA PROCESSES

The first step to define the processes of a business area is to understand in general terms what happens in this business area and who the major players are. Here again you do not want to lose sight of the big picture by digging too deeply into details. Your objective in this phase is to define the processes and understand their relationships. After doing that, you will explore and analyze each process more closely.

You can use several techniques to gather the information required at this stage. Some of them, such as reviewing existing documentation, reading reports from previous analysis activities, and interviewing, have been discussed in earlier chapters, since they can be used successfully for other activities during the strategic planning phase. An important technique is to walk through the business area following the flow of activities. Recall that a business area is a process in the sense that it normally includes all the activities that transform one or more inputs into an output. By following the input through all the stages until it is transformed to the desired output, you have a good opportunity to observe and understand the processes performed by the business area.

11.1.1 INPUT AND OUTPUT OF THE BUSINESS AREA

The primary input in the business area Process Customer Order is nothing more than an order from a customer. TASC has designed a standard purchase order that each customer must complete and submit to a sales representative. In its journey through this business area, the order is transformed until it comes out at the end as a product delivered to the customer. Figure 11.1 shows a sample purchase order filled out by one of TASC's customers.

The following paragraphs are a summary of how the business area discussed here transforms an order into a product delivered to the customer, in the words of TASC's Chief Operations Officer:

> The best way to describe how we handle orders here is to compare it with an assembly line. Orders are fed in at one end of the line. As they travel

The American Software Club

Serving America's software needs, one customer at a time®
1434 North Main Avenue
Farifax, Virginia, 21102-9087
800.432.2343 Fax 703.546.4343

P.O. NUMBER: 1237545-445

Bill To:	Ship To:
North American Database Experts, Inc. P.O. Box 12334 Arlington, VA 28201-2334	Julie H. Adams 2526 North Wayne Street Baltimore, MD 32201

P.O. DATE	CREDIT CARD NO	MONEY ORDER NO	DELIVERY DATE	DELIVERY TERMS
04/23/97			On or before 05/12	FedEx Early Morning

ITEM NO	QTY	DESCRIPTION	UNIT PRICE	TOTAL
1	1	MS Windows '95	$ 98.00	$ 98.00
2	2	Oracle Designer/2000	$ 1,999.00	$3,998.00
3	3	Oracle Developer/2000	$ 1,999.00	$5,997.00

SUBTOTAL	$10,093.00
SALES TAX	$ 454.19
SHIPPING & HANDLING	$ 48.99
OTHER	
TOTAL	$10,596.18

ADDITIONAL INSTRUCTIONS:
Please notify us immediately if you are unable to ship as specified. Send all correspondence to:
Julie H. Adams
North American Database Experts, Inc.
2526 North Wayne Street
Baltimore, MD 32201
410.211.2334, ext. 320; Fax 410.211.2300

FOR OFFICE USE ONLY: Please do not write below this line

Department or Office	Received By	Receive Date	Reviewed By	Review Date	Approved By	Approve Date
Sales						
Customer Credit						
Customer Service						
Warehouse						

FIGURE 11.1 Sample purchase order filled out by one of TASC's customers.

through the line, different departments and organizational units add something to them until they are transformed into products delivered at the customer's door.

Customers place orders after discussing their needs with one of our sales representatives. The sales offices we have are in general responsible for the accuracy and completeness of the orders. They must ensure, for example, that necessary customer information is captured, or that the prices of products are correct and up-to-date. After reviewing and approving the orders they receive, the sales offices forward them to our Customer Credit office in New York.

The Customer Credit office is a central point through which all orders must pass before being booked. The reason is that we need to be sure of the credit worthiness of customers, especially those who are new or request to be billed after receiving the product. This office reviews the purchase order, goes over the numbers there, and looks at the credit history or payment history of the customers. After the orders are approved, they are divided into two groups based on the type of products they contain. Orders for business products are sent to the Business Products division in San Diego; those for games and family products are sent to the Family and Home Products division in New York for further processing.

Each of these divisions has a Customer Support office that receives the orders. The persons that work here verify that each order has the appropriate approvals from the Sales and Customer Credit units and then books the order in our Inventory System. They are partly responsible for monitoring the supply levels for products in the system. If they fall below a certain threshold, they alert the Acquisition office, which then purchases additional copies of the software.

On the other end of our Inventory System, we have the warehouses. People that work there take booked orders out of the queue on a first-come, first-served basis. They are responsible for retrieving all the products listed on the purchase order and assembling them in one package. They also attach an invoice to the package, move the package to the shipping dock, and schedule one of our carriers to pick up and deliver the package. Since both carrier companies we use guarantee delivery within two business days, we consider the process on our end pretty much complete once the packages are picked up by them.

11.1.2 STATES OF ORDERS

From the description of the business area presented in the previous section, you can easily recognize that before being transformed into a finished product ready to be delivered to the customer, an order has to go through a series of states. Figure 11.2 lists the name and a brief description of each of these states.

ORDER STATE	STATE DESCRIPTION
New	Order has been submitted to the Sales office. No action has occurred on it yet.
Approved	Order has been reviewed and approved by the appropriate Sales office. It has been handed over to the Customer Credit office.
Credit Approved	Credit history of customer has been reviewed and approved by the Customer Credit office. Order has been forwarded to the appropriate Customer Service office.
Booked	Order has been booked by the Customer Service office and queued in the Inventory System.
Assembled	Products for each order line have been assembled in one package by the warehouse staff. Package has been transferred to the shipping area.
Picked	Package has been picked by carrier.

FIGURE 11.2   States of an order in the Process Customer Orders business area.

The way an order moves from one state to the other is best presented by a state transition diagram, which is shown in Figure 11.3. In this diagram, you can see not only the stages through which a purchase order is transformed into a product, but also the processes in the business area that are responsible for these transformations. The order state transition diagram serves as a starting point for creating the model of the business area in the Designer/2000 Repository.

11.1.3   ENTERING BUSINESS AREA PROCESSES IN THE REPOSITORY

Your ultimate goal is obviously to maintain the processes and other information related to the business area in the Designer/2000 Repository. As you saw in the previous chapter, you can take full advantage of the Process Modeller capabilities in this direction by expressing your knowledge about the business area in terms of processes, agents, stores, flows, and so on.

The information provided in Section 11.1.1 and Section 11.1.2 allows you to identify five major processes within the business area Process Customer Orders. Figure 11.4 contains a list of the label, short definition, and description for each of these processes.

From the way these processes are performed in the business area, you can distinguish five agents that are responsible for each of the processes. These agents are Sales, Customer Credit, Customer Service, Warehouse, and Carrier. Note that the term *agent* is more appropriate in this case than *organization unit*, since several of these may perform similarly in the role of an agent. For example, the agent Sales represents three sales offices that are responsible for one product type, in

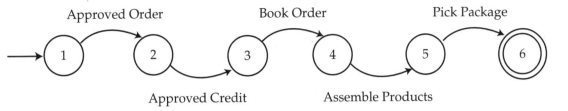

LEGEND:
1 – New
2 – Approved
3 – Credit Approved
4 – Booked
5 – Assembled
6 – Picked

FIGURE 11.3 A state transition diagram for orders in Process Customer Orders.

PROCESS LABEL	SHORT DEFINITION	DESCRIPTION
PCO1	Approve Order	Review purchase order, verify prices, approve it, and hand it over to the Customer Credit office.
PCO2	Approve Credit	Review credit or payment history of customer, approve order, and forward it to the Customer Service office.
PCO3	Book Order	Book the order and place it in the Inventory System queue.
PCO4	Assemble Products	Take order from Inventory System queue, assemble products, transfer package to shipping area, and schedule pickup.
PCO5	Pick Package	Pick up product from shipping area and send it to delivery hub.

FIGURE 11.4 Major processes in business area Process Customer Orders (PCO).

each region, for a total of six organization units. However, for the purposes of analysis of a business area, each of these units plays the same role in the process of reviewing and approving orders; therefore, they can be considered from a unified perspective.

The process model of the business area can gain clarity if you introduce stores into the picture. These stores represent staging areas from which processes take their input and where they place their outputs. Figure 11.5 contains a list of the stores you will need at this point. Note that some of these stores represent real objects, such as the Inventory System. Others represent abstractions, such as the New Orders containers, which could be considered a consolidated look at all the IN mailboxes of the sales representatives.

At this point, you are ready to enter the business area processes in the Process Modeller. As a preliminary step, create a new application PROCESS ORDERS that will contain the information about the business area in question. The idea is that while the application system STRATEGIC PLAN was used for tasks related to strategic planning and identification of business areas of the enterprise, each business area, when analyzed in detail, should have its own separate application system in the Repository.

After creating the new application system, launch the Process Modeller and create a new diagram. When prompted, create a new root process with label PCO and description "Process Customer Order." Figure 11.6 shows how the process diagram could look after you have entered the information discussed here. You can create this diagram by following these steps:

1. Create the agents for this business area in this order: Sales, Customer Credit, Customer Service, Warehouse, and Carrier.

STORE ID	STORE NAME	DESCRIPTION
NO	New Orders	Container for all the new orders arriving by mail or fax; located in Sales offices.
AO	Approved Orders	Container for all orders arriving from Sales; located in Customer Credit office.
CAO	Credit Approved Orders	Container for all orders arriving from Customer Credit; located in Customer Support offices.
INVSYS	Inventory System	Database system that records data about each warehouse inventory.
SA	Shipping Area	Collective name for the shipping rooms of each warehouse where packages reside until picked up by carriers.

FIGURE 11.5   Stores in the Process Customer Orders business area.

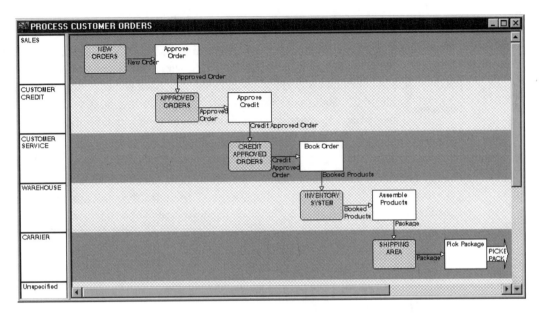

FIGURE 11.6　A process diagram for business area Process Customer Orders.

2. Create processes using data from Figure 11.4.
3. Create stores using data from Figure 11.5.
4. Create flows between processes and stores, as shown in Figure 11.6.

In the following sections, you will analyze in detail these processes and enter in the Repository the quantitative data that will be provided for them.

11.2　ANALYZING PROCESSES IN DETAIL

The next step after defining the major processes in a business area is to take each of them apart, and understand the activities that occur, events, and flows. At this time, important measurements are taken, such as the time, cost, and resources required to complete each activity. In the following sections, you will analyze in detail the first process, Approve Orders, which is performed by the agent Sales.

11.2.1　HOW APPROVE ORDERS WORKS

Here is a description of the process Approve Orders in the words of the manager of the Business Software Unit in the East Coast Sales division.

The visual attributes of the diagram shown in Figure 11.6 are adjusted in order to improve its readability. For example, the view size is reduced and the swim lanes are filled with two colors that alternate. Because the number of agents in this diagram is relatively big, choosing a particular color for the swim lane that corresponds to them would burden the picture.

Our salespeople spend about 30 percent of their time reviewing purchase orders they receive from the customers. These orders arrive usually by mail or by fax. There is a lot of interaction between the salesperson and the customer to come up with the right order, and this is done mostly through personal exchanges or phone conversations. We consider this part of the sales job. However, we cannot start processing an order until the customer sends a hard copy with appropriate signatures to us.

When a salesperson receives an order, he or she first determines its type. If it is a new order, the information contained in it must be carefully revised mostly to make sure that customers are using correct and updated prices for products. If the order looks correct, the salesperson places a copy of it in the customer file, marks his or her name in the Reviewed By box at the bottom of the order, and places it in the pile of orders that I must approve. If the order contains irregularities, the customer is contacted and the problem is usually resolved within the day. Typically, a salesperson processes two to three orders each day. Our group that has six full-time salespersons reviews about 15 orders a day; the sales divisions in two regions combined process around 100 orders a day.

Every day at 2:00 p.m., I begin approving the orders that salespersons have placed in my FOR APPROVAL box. I normally skim the order and make sure that the salesperson has not overlooked some important fact or forgotten to sign his or her name in the review box. About 90 percent of the orders have no problems. For them, I sign my name and the date in the appropriate boxes at the bottom of the order and place them in the APPROVED box. Occasionally, I find some error with the order. In this case, I write my comments and place the order in the DISAPPROVED box.

My administrative assistant is responsible for managing these boxes. Every morning at 11:00 a.m. she empties them from the orders I have reviewed and approved the previous day. She places approved orders in envelopes and sends them to the Customer Credit office for credit approval. Disapproved orders are sent back to the salesperson responsible for them for additional review. Mail goes out at 2:30 p.m. every day. Therefore, reviewed orders must be ready for pickup by this time.

In these paragraphs, the process "Approve Orders" is described in narrative language, as you will most likely encounter it in normal circumstances. In order to model it in the Process Modeller, you need to formalize the definitions of its components a bit. At the same time, since you are describing the process at a lower level than previous processes you have analyzed, gather and enter in the Repository detailed information for its components. The following sections will describe these activities. As a preliminary step, create a new diagram for this process. In the dialog box New Diagram, uncheck the check box Root Processes Only, and select the process Approve Order (PCO1) from the list of available processes.

11.2.2 ROLES

From the description of the process offered in Section 11.2.1, you can easily identify three groups of people who perform its activities. These are salespersons, sales managers, and sales assistants. In the Processes Modeller, they are equivalent to organization units or agents that you have seen before. In order to create these agents in your new diagram, follow these two steps:

1. Include in the group the agent SALES, defined earlier during the analysis of the business area.
2. Create the organization units SALES PERSON, SALES MANAGER, and SALES ASSISTANT as dependents of SALES.

You may collect additional information about each of these agents, which you want to store in the Repository. As I mentioned earlier, you can enter this information in the Repository Object Navigator. But in the Process Modeller, you can double-click the desired organization unit to bring up a dialog box that allows you to edit its properties. This dialog box is composed of two property tabs: Specific and Text. Figure 11.7 shows the tab Specific for the agent SALES PERSON. This tab contains several items that you can fill with results from your analysis and research, such as Location and Head Count. The tab text contains the text items Description and Notes.

An important difference exists between the agents you created here and those created during the strategic planning phase or when the processes in the business area were defined. Now, you have drilled down to a level where agents no longer represent organization units. At this point, they are better described as categories of workers or roles. To indicate the fact that the agents SALES PERSON, SALES MANAGER, and SALES ASSISTANT are roles, check the check box with the same name in the dialog box Organization, as shown in Figure 11.7.

When dealing with roles, you can collect additional data items and store them in the Repository. You can maintain these items in the Organization–Role

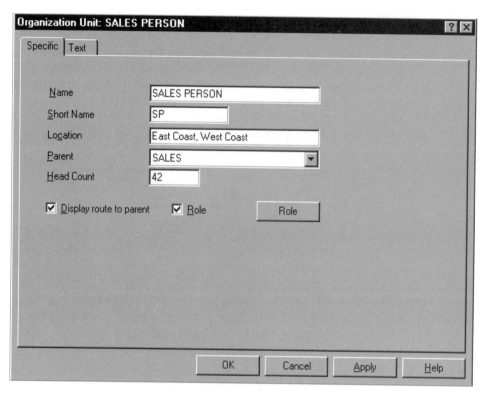

FIGURE 11.7 The Specific tab of the Organization dialog box.

dialog box, which is displayed if you click the button Role in the dialog box Organization. This button is active only if the check box Role is checked, as shown in Figure 11.7.

Figure 11.8 shows the Organization–Role dialog box with information about the role SALES PERSON. As you can see from this figure, you can list here the responsibilities and skills required to complete the process in question successfully. You must understand that the responsibilities and skills listed here should apply only to the process in which the role participates. For example, salespeople may have many skills and may be assigned several responsibilities; however, in order to process purchase orders, they need only those shown in Figure 11.8. In addition, you can also enter information about the cost that the company incurs for using the role in the process. According to Figure 11.8, for example, it costs TASC $40.00 an hour to have salespeople process orders. This is an average cost that includes not only their salaries and commissions, but also other costs, such as office expenses, stationary, and telephone and fax usage.

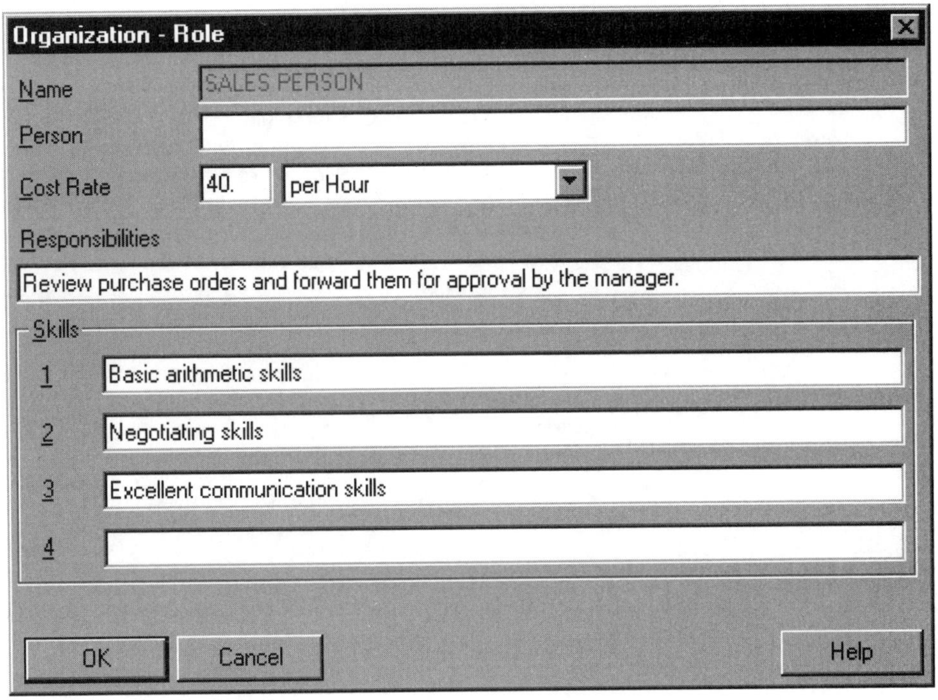

| Organization - Role | ☒ |

Name `SALES PERSON`

Person ` `

Cost Rate `40.` `per Hour` ▼

Responsibilities

`Review purchase orders and forward them for approval by the manager.`

Skills

1 `Basic arithmetic skills`

2 `Negotiating skills`

3 `Excellent communication skills`

4 ` `

[OK]   [Cancel]   [Help]

FIGURE 11.8   The Organization–Role dialog box.

11.2.3 PROCESS STEPS

From the description of the process Approve Order in Section 11.2.1, you can easily identify the steps that need to be performed in order to complete this process. Figure 11.9 contains a listing of these steps, which you can easily create in your diagram. Keep in mind that process steps PCO11, PCO12, and PCO13 are performed by role SALES PERSON; PCO14 is performed by SALES MANAGER; and PCO15 is performed by SALES ASSISTANT.

After creating the process steps, double-click each of them to display the Edit Process Step dialog box. In this dialog box, you can enter and maintain all the important information about the activity. For example, the Specific tab contains the *Short Definition*, *Type*, and *Label* properties. On the Text tab, you can enter information such as the description or notes related to the process step. However, the property tab Main is probably the most important one for a process step. This property tab allows you to enter and maintain two important groups of quantitative data about the activity: time and cost. Additionally, you can enter the frequency with which this step is performed and the percentage of time that the organization unit or role spends on it.

PROCESS LABEL	SHORT DEFINITION	DESCRIPTION
PCO11	Receive Order	Receive purchase order and determine its origin.
PCO12	Process Order	Verify order information and file a copy for the record. Contact customer for additional information if necessary.
PCO13	Submit Order for Approval	Group reviewed orders and place them in manager's FOR APPROVAL box.
PCO14	Review Sales Orders	Review each order. Approve valid ones and place them in the APPROVED box. Annotate orders with problems and place them in the DISAPPROVED box.
PCO15	Forward Reviewed Orders	Take orders from APPROVED box and send them to the Customer Credit office.

FIGURE 11.9 The steps of the process Approve Order.

Figure 11.10 shows the Main property tab for the activity Process Order. Measuring the time it takes to complete a process step is a useful technique that allows you to judge the efficiency of the process. Note however that not every process needs to be timed. In the case of the business area Process Customer Orders, the time from when an order is placed until a product is delivered is a key performance indicator. Therefore, understanding the time requirements of each process and, in particular, of Process Order, is very important. But if the cost were a key measure, then dedicating resources to timing activities is not very helpful. Also note that the time measurements need not, and probably cannot, be exact. In cases where abstractions are made, such as in the case where the role SALES PERSON represents 42 salespersons at TASC, you need to come up with averaged or estimated figures. The Measured Time group of properties on the Main property tab allows you to enter up to two of the times you observed.

You can divide the time required to complete a process step into three components:

❏ **Prior Delay.** This is the time from the moment the flow of work enters the boundaries of the process step until the actual work on it begins. According to the measurements for the activity Process Order, each purchase order spends on the average one hour on the sales representative's desk before any work begins.

❏ **Activity Time.** This is the time required to do the work for the task. This time is split into *Work* and *Quality Check*. As the names indicate, the first parameter measures the time it takes to finish the work, for example, review the order. The second parameter represents the time to check that the work

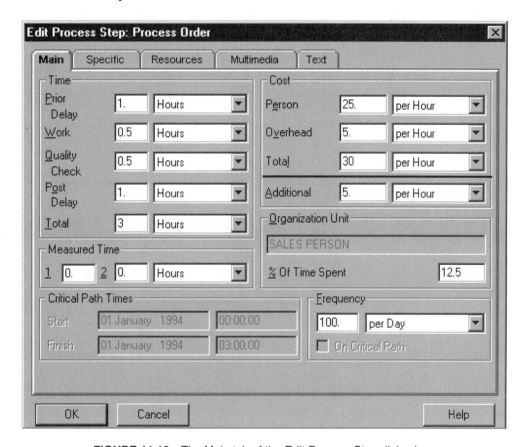

FIGURE 11.10 The Main tab of the Edit Process Step dialog box.

is done properly. In the case of Figure 11.10, it takes half an hour to process an order and another half an hour to check the accuracy of the work.

❑ **Post Delay.** This is the time from the moment when the activity stops until the output of the process is picked up by the next process step. In the step in question, a one hour wait occurs from the moment the processing of the order is complete until the sales manager moves it to the manager's FOR APPROVAL box.

An important parameter derived from the ones described above is the total time required to complete the process step, displayed in the text field *Total*. Normally, this is a sum of the other four time parameters. The Process Modeller automatically computes this total each time you modify one of the above measurements. Each of these parameters can be expressed in a series of units, which range from seconds to years.

Other important items on the Main property tab are those under the group Critical Path Times. You cannot directly edit these items. The diagrammer maintains them when it calculates the activities that are in the critical path of the process. Section 11.4.4 later in the chapter explains how to use the Process Modeller for critical path analysis.

As interesting as these parameters are, even more significant are ratios you can form with them. For example, the ratio *Work / Total* for the process shown in Figure 11.10 is 0.167, which means that in this activity, actual work is being performed only 16.7 percent of the time. On the other hand, *(Prior Delay + Post Delay) / Total* is around 0.667, which means that 66.7 percent of the time, this process step remains idle with the flow waiting in queues.

The other group of parameters that you can maintain in the dialog box Edit Process Step is Cost. As you can see from Figure 11.10, you can estimate the average cost per person and an overhead cost per unit of time. The Process Modeller automatically maintains a total of these two costs each time you update one of them. A third parameter is also provided to enter any additional cost that you do not wish to include in the above categories.

For some activities, you want to record the cost not only in time and human resources but also in other resources. For example, in the process step Forward Reviewed Orders, the assistant to the sales manager stuffs approved orders in envelopes, types the addresses in labels with the electric typewriter, places the stamps on the envelopes, and sends them to the Customer Credit office by mail. You can associate these material resources consumed by the activity by clicking the tab Resources in the Edit Process Step dialog box and entering them in the list of resources, as shown in Figure 11.11.

On this property tab, you can also register the efficiency of the activity in the *Yield (Quality Percentage)* field. Figure 11.11 shows that, according to the estimates, reviewed orders are forwarded correctly 99 percent of the time.

11.2.4 EVENTS

Closely related to the identification of steps for a process is the analysis of events that trigger or are triggered by some or all of these steps. In a sense, a process is nothing more than a planned reaction of the business to an event. In the case of the process step Forward Reviewed Orders, you can easily identify three events that cause some activity to happen. The first event occurs whenever a new order arrives. This event triggers the step Receive Order. The other two events occur in specific moments in time. One happens every day at 2:00 p.m. and causes the

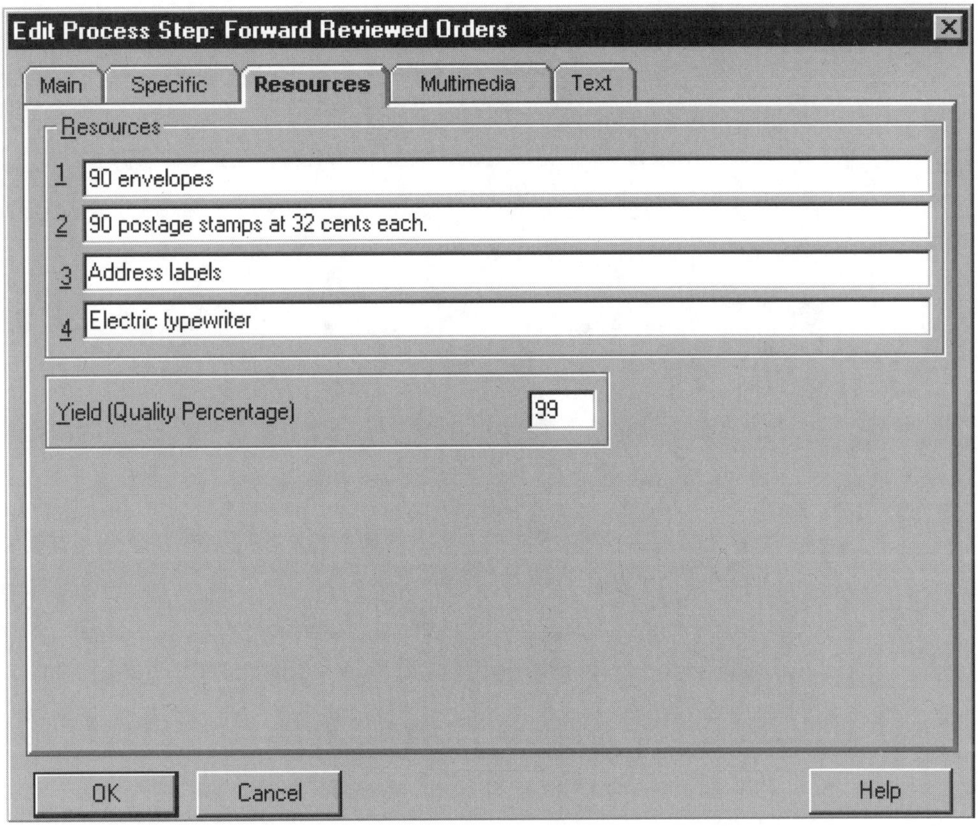

FIGURE 11.11 The Resources tab of Edit Process Step dialog box.

manager to begin approving orders. The other happens daily as well, at 11:00 a.m., at which time the assistant to the manager forwards the reviewed orders to the appropriate destination.

Another type of event is the outcome of a process. Although a process may have more than one outcome, the process step Forward Reviewed Orders has only one outcome. This is reviewed orders that go in the mail every day at 2:30 p.m. From activities performed earlier in the book, you already know how to create triggers and outcomes. Therefore, here I will simply show the edit dialog box for the first event of the process. This dialog box is composed of the tabs Specific and Text. Figure 11.12 shows the Specific tab of the dialog box for the event that triggers the step Receive Order. As you can see, this event occurs on the average 100 times a day, every time a new order comes in. The other events, including the outcome of the process occur only once a day. Since all these events occur at a specific moment, their type should be Time.

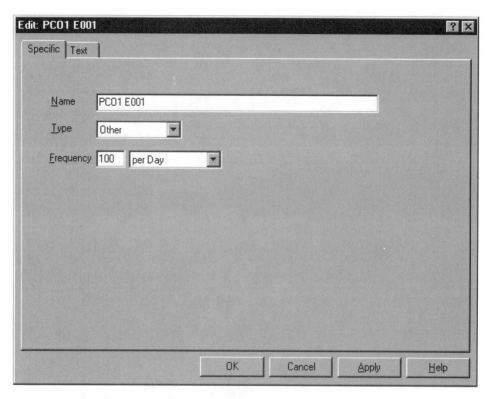

FIGURE 11.12 The Specific tab of the Edit dialog box for events.

11.2.5 STORES

The information about the time and different costs associated with a process step can be collected and entered in the Repository in a similar way for other components of a process model, such as stores and flows. For example, if orders lie in the manager's FOR APPROVAL box for four hours every day, you can capture this information in the Repository as a prior delay for the store that represents this box. If the store represents a database, you can estimate the cost to maintain this database and enter it in the appropriate fields on the Main property tab of the edit dialog box.

Of particular interest for stores are estimates about the quantity of data or objects they contain. They are entered on the Specific property tab of the store. Figure 11.13 shows this property tab for the store FOR APPROVAL BOX. As you can see from this figure, since the store holds objects, its *Type* is *'Material Store.'* A database, spreadsheet, or computer file would be a data store. This property tab also contains volumetric information, such as the estimated minimum, maximum, and average number of orders that reside in this store. You can enter simi-

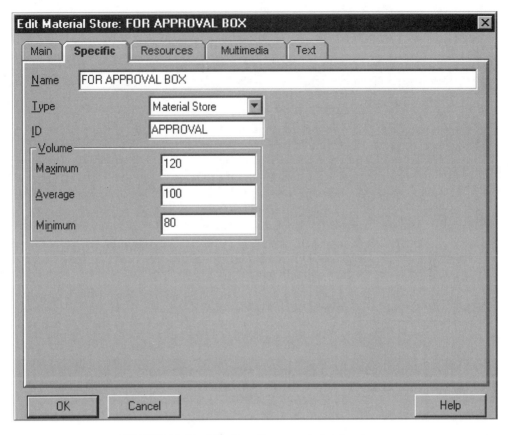

FIGURE 11.13 The Specific property tab for stores.

lar information for the other two stores involved in this process: APPROVED BOX and DISAPPROVED BOX.

11.2.6 FLOWS

As in other cases, in the diagram of the process Approve Order, you need to create flows between its components to represent how orders transition from one stage to another. However, differently from the other high-level models you have created previously, here you do not need to display the names of the flows in the diagram. The reason is that when focusing inside a single process, you should not normally observe shifts in the state of inputs so radical as to require explanations in the diagram. In the process being discussed here, for example, you are dealing with a hard copy version of the order that moves from one activity to the next one without turning, say, into an assembled package.

At this point, you have enough experience with creating flows to add them on your own to the diagram. Figure 11.14 shows the completed version of the diagram for the process Approve Order, shown in the enhanced symbolic mode.

The time or the resources that are needed when the order actually transitions from one step to the other are negligible in this process. For example, when the salespeople need to submit their orders in the FOR APPROVAL box of their manager, they simply walk across the hall and drop them. In some processes, however, flows are associated with costs. For example, if the flow represents a physical move of materials from one location to the other, you would be interested to record how long it takes and how much it costs to transport the materials. In such cases, you can use the Main property tab in the Edit dialog box of the flow to enter and maintain these data items. Three major types of flows exist:

❑ **Material flows.** These represent movement of objects or materials from one point of the process to another. For example, when orders move from the process step Submit Order for Approval into the FOR APPROVAL box, real pieces of paper exchange hands.

❑ **Data flows.** These are similar to material flows, except that they represent an exchange of data. For example, a sub-activity of the step Process Order is

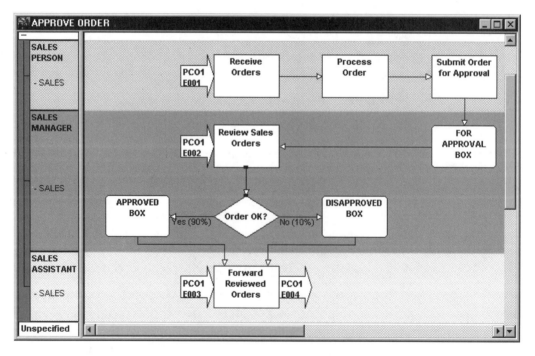

FIGURE 11.14   The finished diagram of the process Approve Order.

to look up the prices in a catalog of TASC products to ensure that they are correct. The flow in that case would be a data flow, since it represents the information that the salesperson retrieves from the catalog and matches against the order.

❑ **Temporal flows.** These flows should be defined between two process steps when a time dependency exists between them. In other words, if the activity at the source of the flow must be completed before the activity at the destination begins, the flow between them should be defined as temporal flow.

You can set the type of the flow upon creation, but you can also modify it at a later time in the Specific tab of the Edit Flow dialog box. Figure 11.15 shows this tab for the flow that connects the decision point "Order OK?" with the store AP-PROVED BOX (see Figure 11.14).

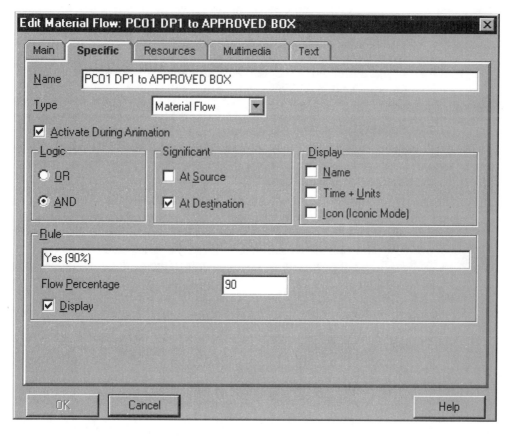

FIGURE 11.15   The Specific property tab for flows.

This property tab contains other data items specific to the flows that you can use. If the flow has some particular importance at the source, at the destination, or at both extremities, you can check the appropriate checkbox in the Significant group. In the example shown in Figure 11.15, the flow has particular significance at the destination APPROVED BOX, since this flow is followed 90 percent of the time. The Display group of check boxes controls the information that you can display with the flow on the diagram. By checking the options *Name* and *Time + Units*, you can visually associate the corresponding information with the flow on the diagram. In addition, if the option *Icon (Iconic Mode)* is set, the flow will be represented as an icon when the diagram is displayed in iconic mode.

The fields in the group Rule are particularly important for conditional flows like the one displayed in Figure 11.15. Here you have the possibility to describe the value of the condition for which the flow is activated. You can decide to display this information as in the case above by checking the check box *Display*. Furthermore, if you know the percentage of times the process follows the flow, you can enter it in the *Flow Percentage* field. In the example shown in Figure 11.15, you know in advance that 90 percent of the orders are approved, hence the value entered in this field.

Other important options that you can set on this property tab are the radio buttons in the group Logic, and the check box *Activate During Animation*. Using animation and multimedia to document and demonstrate processes is the subject of the following section, which will also discuss the meaning of these options.

11.2.7 NAMING CONVENTIONS

I conclude this section with some words about conventions to follow for names and labels of the components of a process. First and foremost, conventions should exist and be followed consistently throughout the analysis and documentation of business processes. Which conventions you follow and how you establish them have little importance, as long as you are committed to using them. The label of the process discussed here was PCO1. Choosing the labels of all its sub-processes so that they indicate their parent is natural. So PCO11, PCO12, PCO13, and PCO14 would be appropriate labels for them. If any of these activities is further expanded into additional steps, the pattern should continue. The components of PCO11 would be PCO111, PCO112, and so on. Decision points, although a type of process step, are not normally considered as such. Nevertheless, for the sake of clarity, enumerate them as in PCO1 PD1 for the first and only decision point in the diagram of Approve Orders.

The events inside the process should be enumerated as well. Referring to Figure 11.14, the events for process PCO1 are *PCO1 E001, PCO1 E002, PCO1 E003,* and *PCO1 E004*. Names and IDs of stores should describe their purpose as clearly as possible. Finally, flows at this level of detail should be named to indicate the source and destination. Examples of flow names used in the diagram of

Approve Order are *PCO1 DP1 to APPROVED BOX* shown in Figure 11.15, *PCO11 to PCO12*, and so on.

11.3 ANIMATION AND MULTIMEDIA

The Process Modeller as a business process diagramming tool has several advantages over other tools on the market today. The most important one is that it is a GUI interface to the centralized Repository of knowledge about your business. Each time the contents of the Repository are modified, even if through other interfaces, the Process Modeller can display the changes automatically, as soon as the diagrams are synchronized.

Another crucial advantage of using the Process Modeller to represent your business processes is the versatility and flexibility you have to display the diagrams in ways that are easier to follow and understand. So far, you have displayed the diagrams in Symbol and Enhanced Symbol modes. What differentiates diagrams you create in the Process Modeller from diagrams created with other tools is that you are able to represent the components of a process as icons and images or associate them with multimedia files and other applications. The following sections will explain how you can accomplish these two tasks.

11.3.1 MULTIMEDIA PROPERTIES

You can turn the process diagram into a very effective demonstration and presentation tool. Using the Process Modeller's support for multimedia features, you can clearly communicate your understanding of the process to the audience. In particular, you can associate each component of your diagram with an image file, a video clip, and a text or graphic annotation. Furthermore, you can link the component to a program installed on your machine that can be launched to show some additional characteristics of the component. You can specify all this information on the Multimedia tab of the Edit dialog box for process steps, store, or flow. Figure 11.16 shows this property tab for the activity Process Order.

If an image would help in the understanding of the object, you can capture it in the form of a GIF file and place it in the directory where the Process Modeller looks for images. Then you can associate it with the object by selecting it from the elements of the drop-down list *Image* on the Multimedia property tab. Similarly, to associate the process component with a video file, place the file in the directory where the Process Modeller looks for video clips, and select it from the list *Video*.

If you would like to launch an application associated with the component, enter the command in the field *Execution string* of the Multimedia tab. In the ex-

The Process Modeller looks in four directories for multimedia files. They are called ICONS, IMAGES, SOUNDS, and VIDEOS. By default, they are under the home directory of the Process Modeller—\ORAWIN95\BPMOD20 or \ORANT\BPMOD20. You can change the settings of these directories as described in Section 11.3.3.

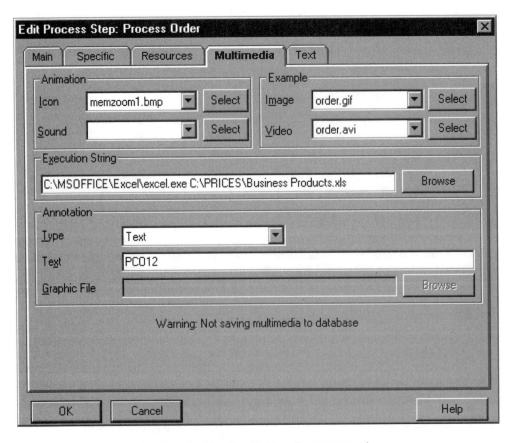

FIGURE 11.16   The Multimedia property tab.

ample shown in Figure 11.16, the activity Process Order is associated with an Excel spreadsheet that contains the prices of products sold by TASC. During the discussions of this activity, you can bring up this spreadsheet with a click of the mouse to show the documents that salespersons consult to check the prices of products in a purchase order.

The Process Modeller simplifies the process of selecting the multimedia file that meets your needs by allowing you to view the contents of this file without leaving the diagram. Notice in Figure 11.16 that each multimedia file type has a button to its right labeled Select. Clicking this button displays the dialog box Multimedia Select shown in Figure 11.17.

In this dialog box, you can view the contents of the directory where the files of the chosen multimedia type are stored. These directories are set in the configurations of the Process Modeller as explained in Section 11.3.3. If you have configured an application that will be used to view or edit the files, the button

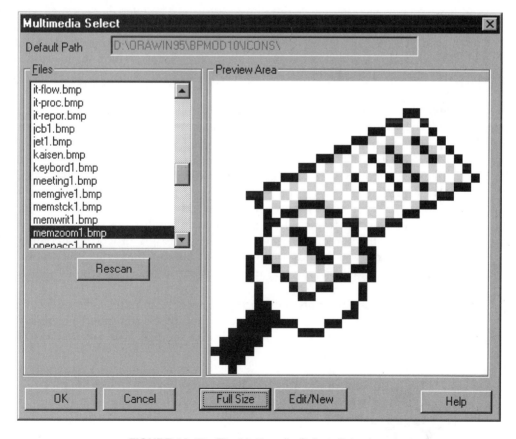

FIGURE 11.17 The Multimedia Select dialog box.

Edit/New at the bottom of the dialog box is enabled. By clicking it, you can launch the application and edit the file. Section 11.3.3 will discuss how you can configure these applications as well.

In the case of icons, you can view the icons in their normal size or have them displayed in the whole preview area by clicking the button Full Size at the bottom of dialog box Multimedia Select. In the example shown in Figure 11.17, the icon MEMZOOM1.BMP is displayed in its full size.

You can also enter some annotations in the form of text or graphics. I recommend, for example, that you display the labels for all the process steps in your diagram. You can achieve this display by setting the *Annotation Type* to '*Text*' and entering the label in the field Text, as shown in Figure 11.16. If you want to annotate the object with a graphic, then set the property *Annotation Type* to '*Graphic*' and provide the name of the graphic file that will be used.

11.3.2 ANIMATING THE PROCESS DIAGRAMS

Each process step, store, or flow in the Process Modeller is associated with an icon that can be used to represent the object on the diagram. You can display a diagram in iconic mode by selecting View | Icon from the diagrammer's menu. When you initially switch the diagram to iconic mode, its components use the default icons associated with them. These icons are listed below:

❑   The "Shoveling Man" icon 🏃 is the default for process steps.
❑   The "Cylinder" icon ➖ is the default for stores.
❑   The "Conveyer Belt" icon 🏃 is the default for flows.

Normally, flows are not shown in iconic mode, unless you set the check box Icon on the Specific tab of the Edit dialog box for that flow (see Figure 11.15). Designer/2000 comes with a number of icons other than the default ones that you can use in your diagrams. They are located in the ICONS subdirectory of the Process Modeller's home directory. In order to assign an icon to a component, you should bring up the Edit dialog box for that object and click the Multimedia tab. Then select the appropriate icon from the drop-down list Icon in the Animation group.

You can also associate the process steps with an audio file by selecting the file from the list *Sound* in the Animation group of the Multimedia property tab. This list contains all the sound files located in the SOUNDS subdirectory of the Process Modeller directory.

In order to animate the process diagram, select the process steps where the animation will start. Then issue one of these commands:

❑ Click the Animate button 🔁 on the diagrammer's toolbar.
❑ Select Utilities | Animation | Start.
❑ Press ALT+S.

Animation occurs when the diagram is in Iconic mode. If not, the Process Modeller automatically switches the mode of the diagram to Iconic. During the animation of the diagram, the Process Modeller highlights the component where work is being currently performed. If a sound file is associated with the object, it plays when the process execution reaches it. However, you can turn this default behavior off by unchecking the menu item Utilities | Animation | Sound.

When the animation process reaches a component in the diagram, the icon that represents it is replaced with a series of frames that replace each other and create the impression of animation. The Process Modeller uses a simple and very flexible animation algorithm that allows you to expand its capabilities. In the example shown in Figure 11.16, the icon that represents the process step is the file MEMZOOM1.BMP. During the animation, the Process Modeller uses this as the first frame, and then it replaces it with MEMZOOM2.BMP, if it exists. This icon in turn is replaced by MEMZOOM3.BMP, if it exists, and so on. When the sequence of these files is interrupted and the animation needs to continue, the Process Modeller starts from the beginning.

The flexibility of this algorithm lies in the fact that you can change both the starting point and the number of frames that implement the animation. Here is a list of steps to follow in order to create your own animation icons:

1. Create a new icon and save it with a name that terminates with a numerical digit, as in NEWICON1.BMP. A generic program such as Windows Paint can be used to create the bitmap image file.
2. Create additional icons similar to the first one, which, if viewed sequentially will give the impression of movement. Save them with the same name as the first icon, but the digit at the end should indicate the sequence of the icon in the series of icons you have created. So you can have NEWICON2.BMP, NEWICON3.BMP, and NEWICON4.BMP.
3. Place the new icons in the ICONS directory.
4. Set the property Icon on the Multimedia tab of the desired component to the first icon, NEWICON1.BMP.

By default, each frame during the animation corresponds to one hour in the life of the process. Hence, an activity that lasts three hours uses three frames, a store where materials stay for six hours uses six frames, and so on. This feature is very useful because it allows you to flavor a realistic simulation of the process. Each "tick" of the Process Modeller's clock is visually displayed by a change in the iconic frames and represents a certain amount of time in the life of the real process (one hour, by default). You can change the length of this unit and other animation properties by selecting Utilities | Animation | Options... from the diagrammer's menu. This action displays the dialog box Animation Options, which is shown in Figure 11.18.

Besides adjusting the granularity of time, you can use this dialog box to change the values of different units of work time. In addition, you can turn on and off the ability of the Modeller to track the flow of the animation and always display in the window the currently active component. By default, the check box Automatic Animation Tracking is not set. In this case, the diagram view on the window does not change during the animation. If the diagram is too big to fit in the window, you cannot see the animation when it flows to components outside the current view. However, if you place a check mark in this check box, the Process Modeller follows the animation and scrolls the window, if necessary to maintain the current component in the center of the view.

11.3.3 CONFIGURING THE PROCESS MODELLER FOR MULTIMEDIA FILES

Before you can start using the multimedia files associated with a process step, flow, or store, you need to tell the Process Modeller which software applications to use in order to run these files. The Process Modeller has several configuration parameters that you set in order to identify these applications. You can access and maintain these parameters in the dialog box Customize–Basic, which is accessed by selecting Options | Customize | Basic.... Figure 11.19 shows an example of configuration settings in this dialog box.

The basic configuration settings of the Process Modeller are grouped in Multimedia Commands, User Defined Commands, and File Locations, listed here

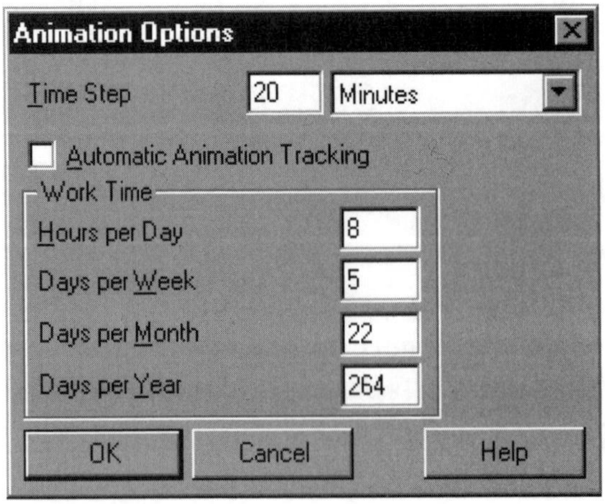

FIGURE 11.18 The Animation Options dialog box.

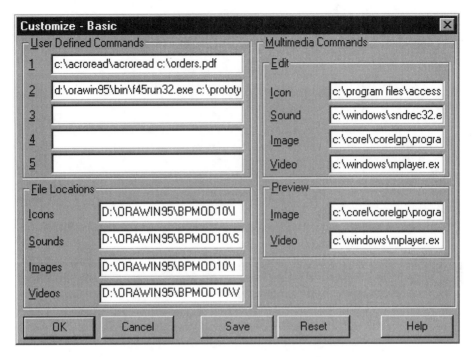

FIGURE 11.19 The Customize–Basic dialog box.

by the frequency with which you are likely to use them. In the Multimedia Commands group, you can enter the path to the applications that will be used to edit iconic, sound, image, and video files. According to the settings shown in Figure 11.19, these programs will be the standard Microsoft Paint, Player, and Sound Recorder for icons, videos, and sounds, respectively. Images will be edited using Corel's Photo-Paint application.

Also specify the applications you will use to view images and videos in your diagrams. Normally, these programs are the same as the ones you use to edit them, except in cases when you are not licensed to run editing programs for images or videos, but own applications that allow you to view them, which are generally distributed for free by their vendors. In such cases, you can enter the names of these applications in the Preview group and leave the names blank in the Edit group.

From the Process Modeller, you can invoke up to five user-defined commands directly from the menu. First, you must enter these commands in the Customize–Basic dialog box, as shown in Figure 11.19. Once you save these configurations, these commands become part of the diagrammer's menu and you can access them by selecting Tools | User Defined Command. This feature can be used very effectively during live presentations or demonstrations. For example, the first command in Figure 11.19 would display an actual order filled out by a customer, which you may capture in the popular Portable Document Format (PDF) and view using Adobe's Acrobat Reader. The second command could invoke a Developer/2000 Forms application that prototypes some enhancement that you propose to do in the current process.

The third group of items in this dialog box, File Locations, allows you to set the locations of the multimedia files. When you activate the lists Icon, Sound, Image, and Video on the Multimedia property tab (see Figure 11.16), the Process Modeller displays the contents of the directories listed in the File Locations group of configurations. By default, these properties are set to point to the directories ICON, SOUND, IMAGE, and VIDEO of the Process Modeller's home directory.

11.3.4 USING MULTIMEDIA FILES

After having associated the components of your diagram with multimedia files and set the configuration parameters of the Process Modeller according to the environment in your workstation, you are ready to use the enhanced diagram.

You can display the image associated with a component in the diagram by issuing one of the following two commands:

❑ Click the iconic button Show Image ▣ on the diagrammer's toolbar.
❑ Select Utilities | Multimedia | Show Image.

To listen to the audio file associated with a component in the diagram, use one of the following two commands:

❑ Click the iconic button Play Sound ▣ on the diagrammer's toolbar.
❑ Select Utilities | Multimedia | Play Sound.

You can view the video file associated with a component in the diagram with one of these commands:

❑ Click the iconic button Play Video ▣ on the diagrammer's toolbar.
❑ Select Utilities | Multimedia | Play Video.

Finally, if you have associated a command with a component in the diagram, you can execute it in one of these ways:

❑ Click the iconic button Execute Program ▣ on the diagrammer's toolbar.
❑ Select Utilities | Multimedia | Execute Process.

The iconic buttons or menu items mentioned above are enabled only if you have selected a process step, store, or flow, and an association exists between the object and a multimedia file of the appropriate type.

PROCESS STEP OR DATA STORE	NEW ICON
PCO11–Receive Orders	⬛ ENVELOP1.BMP
PCO12–Process Order	⬛ MEMWRIT1.BMP
PCO13–Submit Order for Approval	⬛ MEMGIVE1.BMP
PCO14–Review Sales Order	⬛ MEMZOOM1.BMP
PCO15–Forward Reviewed Orders	⬛ TRUCK1.BMP
PCO1 DP1–Order OK?	⬛ BUBBLE1.BMP
FOR APPROVAL BOX	⬛ MEMSTCK1.BMP
APPROVED BOX	⬛ MEMSTCK1.BMP
DISAPPROVED BOX	⬛ MEMSTCK1.BMP

FIGURE 11.20   Icons for steps of the process Approve Orders.

11.3.5 SETTING ICONS FOR PROCESS STEP APPROVE ORDER

I conclude this section by enhancing the look of the diagram for the process Approve Order. In this diagram, you could replace the default icons that represent the process steps with icons that describe the contents of these activities better. Figure 11.20 lists a set of icons that come with Designer/2000 that you can use.

You can also use your own icons as long as you place them in the ICONS subdirectory of the Process Modeller multimedia directories. Recall from previous discussions on animation that in order to take advantage of this functionality, the name of the new icons you create must include at the end the index of the icon in the set of frames that form the animation.

Figure 11.21 shows a final look at the diagram for the process Approve Order in Iconic mode.

11.4 SYNTHESIZING THE BUSINESS AREA

The analysis of the business area should begin with identification of its business processes and a detailed understanding of each of them. You performed these tasks in the previous sections of this chapter. Although only one of the processes was discussed in its entirety, the approach is the same for the remaining components of the business area.

After each process is analyzed, collect all the detailed information and summarize it in order to create a better picture of the business area as a whole. The Process Modeller itself performs some summarization and synthesis of the information you enter in its diagrams. You can view this if, after entering the details for the process Approve Orders as described in the previous section, you open

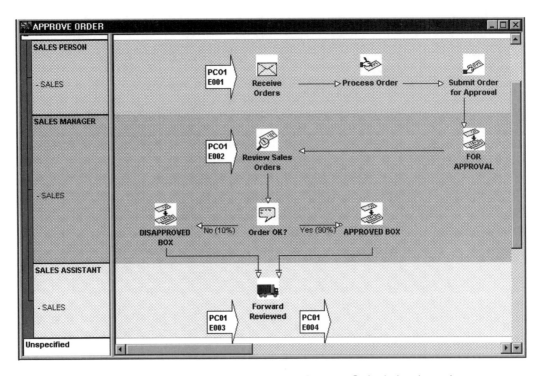

FIGURE 11.21   A diagram of the process Approve Order in Iconic mode.

the main diagram of the business area Process Customer Orders in the standard Symbol mode (see Figure 11.22). You see that the rectangle that represents the process Approve Orders contains in the lower right-hand corner the duration of this process in hours. This value is calculated automatically based on the duration of each activity that you specified in the detailed diagram.

Note also that the rectangle contains an ellipsis in the lower left-hand corner, which indicates that the subprocess Approve Orders is decomposed into smaller steps in another diagram. To open the diagram Approve Orders from the main business area diagram, select the process and then choose File | Open Down. Conversely, you also have the ability to quickly open the diagram that contains the parent of the process presented in the current diagram. To do so, choose File | Open Up.

If you want to go beyond this basic functionality, follow the discussion presented in the next sections, which concentrate on identifying the value-added activities in the business area, calculating several cost factors for each activity, and analyzing the critical path of each process.

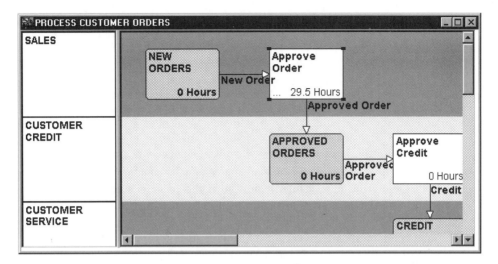

FIGURE 11.22 The Process Modeller sums up the duration time of the activities of a parent process.

11.4.1 IDENTIFYING VALUE-ADDING PROCESSES

The purpose of this task is to quantify or estimate the value that each process step in the business area adds to the outcome of the business area. Before you engage in the activity, clearly define what are the parameters or the performance indicators to which the process steps add value. If your analysis is performed with the customers in mind, these indicators are factors that affect the level and quality of goods and services that these customers are receiving. For example, the outcome of the business area Fulfill Customer Orders is a package of software products delivered to the customer according to his or her request. Some of the indicators that would have an impact on the satisfaction of the customer are the time to process the order, the quality of products, the completeness and correctness of order, and so on. Naturally, you consider value-adding activities to be those process steps that contribute positively to the above factors.

In general, each business organization performs activities that either add value themselves to the output or control the performance of other value-adding activities. The value that the activities in the second group add to the overall product or service is small, often negligible. Nevertheless, in task-oriented organizations, where the work is broken down into many small, relatively simple tasks, you often find that the time and resources spent on control activities often surpass those spent in value-adding activities. The purpose of identifying value-adding activities in a business area then is to question each of its processes and subprocesses, and to quantify the contribution that each of them makes in the fulfillment of key performance indicators for the business area.

After deciding whether and how an activity adds value to the business output, you can enter this information in the Process Modeller by following these steps:

1. Double-click the process step to display its Edit properties dialog box.
2. Click the Text property tab.
3. Pick the category *Value Chain Notes* from one of the drop-down lists of the text types that can be associated with a process step.
4. Describe how the process step adds or does not add value to the business output in the multiline text field below the list box.
5. Select the level of contribution of the process step from the list box *Value Added* to the left.

Figure 11.23 shows an example of notes of this type for the process step Process Order. Although the value-adding analysis is performed usually for activities within a process, Designer/2000 allows you to enter results of these analyses for

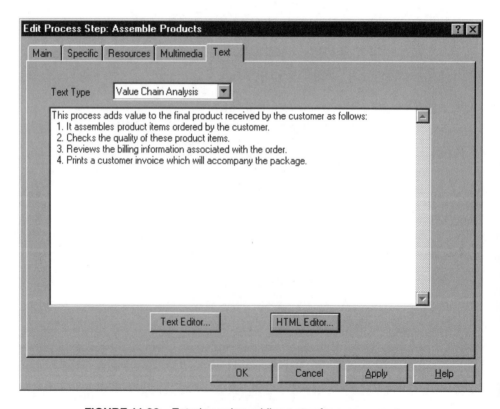

FIGURE 11.23   Entering value-adding notes for a process step.

other components of a process model, such as stores and flows. The procedure is entirely similar to the one described above; therefore it will not be discussed here.

11.4.2 BENCHMARKING

Benchmarking is a business activity during which you compare the performance of your processes with that of similar processes performed by leading organizations around you. This comparison is done with a two-fold goal in mind. First, you want to know how much better or worse than other players in the business arena you perform certain processes. Second, you want to learn from the experience of others and implement your processes in a more effective way.

Several business processes and many more subprocesses and activities may be ongoing in a business area. Trying to benchmark all of them is at best a waste of time and often proves to be unfeasible, since no two companies organize their business alike, even if they belong to the same industry. Benchmarking must be conducted after the value-adding analysis of the business area for the following reasons:

❑ Benchmarking is an activity that requires comparing measurable and measured business elements. Losing sight of the most important factors of a business area is easy, those that determine how the customer evaluates the efficiency of this business area. Recall that determining these factors is among the first steps to identify the value-adding activities in a process.

❑ As mentioned earlier, activities in a business area can be divided into value-adding and control activities. Focus your attention mainly on the value-adding ones, although sometimes you may need to benchmark control activities as well. The distinction between value-adding and control activities is drawn clearly only during the value-adding analysis of activities in a process.

Benchmarking is not an intellectual exercise conducted to satisfy the curiosity of business managers but a tool that provides ideas on how to perform better and run the business more efficiently. Therefore, you need to engage in this activity with a clear set of processes and performance indicators about which you want to collect data. Once you have collected the information, you can enter it in the Designer/2000 Repository by following these steps:

1. Double-click the process step to display its Edit properties dialog box.
2. Click the property tab Text.
3. Pick the category *Competitive Index Notes* in one of the multiline text boxes.
4. Enter in the text field a description about the index, what it expresses, methods of measurements you used, and so on.
5. Enter the value of the index in the field *Index Value Added* to the right.

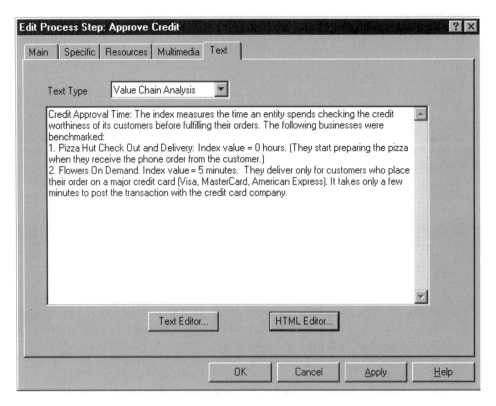

FIGURE 11.24 Entering competitive index notes for a process step.

Figure 11.24 contains an example of competitive index notes for a process step. Note that the value that you specify for the chosen competitive index is usually a ratio between the value of your performance indicator and that of the entity against which you are benchmarking. A value between 0 and 1 means that you are being outperformed; the closer the index is to zero, the worse your performance is, compared to the other entity. A value greater than one means that you are performing better than the benchmark entity.

11.4.3 ACTIVITY-BASED COSTING

Performing activity-based costing for a business area allows you to create an idea about how much the processes are costing in time and money. The first step that enables you to perform activity-based costing is to collect detailed data about each process step in the business area and to enter this data in the Repository.

Section 11.2.3 discussed how to use the Process Modeller in order to enter quantitative data about the time and human cost involved with running a process step.

After collecting the detailed data, the information needs to be aggregated and summarized. As I mentioned earlier, the Process Modeller offers some default functionality along these lines. Additional information can be obtained by running the Repository reports titled Activity-Based Costing, under the group of reports Enterprise Modelling. For a given process within an application, this report lists all the process steps, stores, and flows defined for that process. For each entry in the list, you can see the total time spent on it, the cost per unit of time, and the total cost to run the component. In addition, the report shows the percentage of time and cost of each component versus the time and cost of the entire process. Thus, you can see not only the actual values of time and cost for a component but also its weight in the whole process. Furthermore, the report shows the time during which work is performed and calculates the ratio of this time over the total time required by the component. Finally, it shows the value-adding factor of the component and the agent responsible for it, as defined in the Process Modeller. Figure 11.25 shows part of the Activity-Based Costing report for the process Approve Order.

To perform a finer analysis and reporting of the data stored in the Designer/2000 Repository, you can transfer the information into a spreadsheet application, such as Microsoft Excel, and use the large variety of tools that it provides. Transferring the information is a two-step process that requires you to first export the data to a text file on your hard disk, and then open the exported file and convert it to a spreadsheet file.

28-JUL-97   **Activity Based Costing Report**

Diagram: APPROVE ORDER
Parent Process: PCO1

Activity	Total Time	Cost per Unit	Total Cost	Time %	Cost %	Work Time
Receive Orders	2.50 Hour	25.00 Hour	62.50	10.20	16.03	0.50 Hour
Process Order	3.00 Hour	30.00 Hour	90.00	12.24	23.08	0.50 Hour
Submit Order for Approval	0.50 Hour	25.00 Hour	12.50	2.04	3.21	0.25 Hour
Review Sales Orders	3.00 Hour	45.00 Hour	135.00	12.24	34.62	2.00 Hour
Order OK?	0.00 Hour	0.00 Hour	0.00	0.00	0.00	0.00 Hour
Forward Reviewed Orders	4.50 Hour	20.00 Hour	90.00	18.37	23.08	2.00 Hour
FOR APPROVAL BOX	5.00 Hour	0.00 Hour	0.00	20.41	0.00	0.00 Hour
APPROVED BOX	2.00 Hour	0.00 Hour	0.00	8.16	0.00	0.00 Hour
DISAPPROVED BOX	4.00 Hour	0.00 Hour	0.00	16.33	0.00	0.00 Hour

FIGURE 11.25   Part of the Activity-Based Costing report from predefined Designer/2000 reports.

Depending on the configurations of the Repository Reports tool, you may not see the report Activity Based Report under the group Enterprise Modelling. To add the report to this group select the node Enterprise Modelling in the Navigator window, then choose Edit | Add Report to Group.... In the dialog box that appears select the report Activity Based Costing and click OK. The report is added to the group.

The Process Modeller allows you to export the data of one or more components of a process that you have selected in the diagram, or to export the data of all the elements in the process diagram. The following steps are required to export the information about the process to a file:

1. Select Utilities | Export Data... from the diagrammer's menu. The Export Data dialog box appears (see Figure 11.26).
2. Specify the name of the file where the Process Modeller will write the data.
3. Select the file type from the drop-down list with the same name.
4. Click OK.

By default, the file is written in the BIN subdirectory of your Oracle home directory. Enter the full path in the field File Name if you want it written to a different location. The export utility can write the information in different formats, which are explained here:

❑ **Oracle CASE 5.1.** This is included for backward compatibility to allow you to transfer the data to an earlier version of Designer/2000.

❑ **Organization (spreadsheet).** Files in this format contain one record for each organization unit being exported. The fields of each record are comma delimited, and a header is provided. This file is a dump of useful data collected during the business area analysis, such as the name of the organization unit, a reference to the parent organization unit, cost rate and unit, responsibilities, and skills required by this organization. The records can very easily be transferred into a database table, thus making the data gathered during the analysis available to any other application.

❑ **Process (spreadsheet).** Files in this format contain one record for each process step, store, and flow that is being exported. Categories of objects are separated by labels, and the fields of each record are separated by commas. This export format is the default. This file contains all the data you have col-

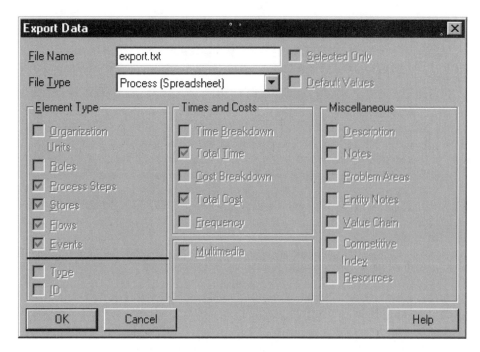

FIGURE 11.26   The Export Data dialog box.

lected about the process components that are maintained on the Main property tab, including all the time and cost information, the critical path times, frequency, and organization unit information related to the component. As with the data exported by the previous section, you can very easily load this information into database tables ready for use by other applications.

❑ **Proprietary.** This is a format proprietary to the Process Modeller that does not have any practical value in activity-based costing analysis. However, since data exported with this format contains internal information that you normally do not see in other places, like IDs for the objects, this type of export may come in handy in cases when you are trying to debug or trace information in the Repository.

❑ **Text.** The files in this format are not suitable for loading to spreadsheets, since each data item is written in its own line for the exported objects. However, this type of export is easy to read and can be easily incorporated into reports and deliverables that you may want to produce. Figure 11.27 shows a sample from an export file produced with this format.

The most useful export format for activity-based costing is Process (spreadsheet). After you have exported the process diagram in such a format, you can

```
Process Data
Name: Receive Orders ( Process Step ) ID: 3959 (PCO11)
Organization Unit: SALES PERSON
Work Time: 0.5 Hours
Post Delay Time: 2 Hours
Total Time: 2.5 Hours
Person Cost: 20 per Hour
Overhead Cost: 5 per Hour
Total Cost: 25 per Hour
Frequency: 100 per Day
% Time Spent: 5
Quality %: 0
```

FIGURE 11.27   Sample export data produced with the Text format.

launch your favorite spreadsheet application and open the text file that contains the data. Each spreadsheet program has its own tools to convert text files. In Excel, for example, you can use the Text Import Wizard, which in three simple steps opens the text file and converts it to the spreadsheet format.

Once the file is in the spreadsheet document, you can cut and paste the data, apply different formats, and present them visually in enhanced mode using different graphs. Figure 11.28 shows data similar to the ones produced by the Activity-Based Costing report, extracted from the contents of the export file. Quantities, such as the percentage of time each step takes in the whole process, or the distribution of time in an activity between productive work and wait time, can be presented much more clearly in the form of graphs and charts, as shown in Figure 11.29 and Figure 11.30.

11.4.4   CRITICAL PATH ANALYSIS

The critical path is another important factor you should determine for the processes that make up the business area. The critical path is the set of those process steps that determine the total time required by the process to complete. In other words, a task is in the critical path if and only if, by lengthening or shortening its completion time, you lengthen or shorten the completion time for the process as a whole. Determining which activities are in the critical path of a process is very important when you want to decide which activities to improve or replace with better performing ones. Obviously, you want to concentrate on

Sub-Component	"PrDlyTm"	"WrkTm"	"QChkTm"	"PoDlyTm"	"TotTm"	"PerCst"	"AddCst"	"TotCst"	"OHdCst"	"Freq"
Process Data										
Approve Order	12	12	23	2	28.5	0	0	0	0	0
Approve Credit	23	23	23	23	34	0	0	0	0	0
Book Order	23	32	23	3	23	0	0	0	0	0
Assemble Products	23	3	3	2	11	0	0	0	0	0
Pick Package	3	2	2	2	25	0	0	0	0	0
Total Cost	84	72	74	32	121.5					

FIGURE 11.28 Data exported from the Process Modeller and formatted in Excel.

those that are in the critical path, since improving an activity outside the path does not affect the completion time of the parent process.

The critical path calculation, like the activity-based costing, is based on and should be performed after detailed time information is collected and entered in the Repository. After analyzing each process step in detail, you can calculate the critical path in the Process Modeller by following these steps:

1. Select Utilities | Calculate Critical Path. This menu item is enabled only if the critical path needs to be recalculated. The Process Modeller keeps track of its status.
2. In the Critical Path Analysis dialog box that appears, enter the date and time when the calculation of the critical path should begin (see Figure 11.31).
3. Click OK.

At this point, the Process Modeller asks you whether you want to write the base process total time to the database. If you click Yes, the total time of the parent process of the diagram is updated with the total length of the path. After the criti-

Time Distribution for Process Steps

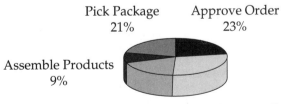

Pick Package 21%
Approve Order 23%
Assemble Products 9%
Approve Credit 28%
Book Order 19%

FIGURE 11.29 Graphical presentation of the weight of each activity in the parent process.

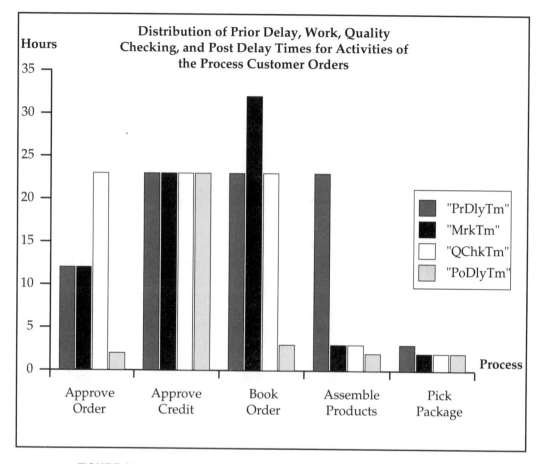

FIGURE 11.30   Graphical representation of the cost distribution for each process step.

 The companion CD-ROM contains the application system PROCESS ORDERS with all the objects and diagrams discussed in this chapter. This application is exported in the Oracle Export dump file PRCSORD.DMP, which you can download from the Web page of the CD-ROM browsing utility by following the links *Software* and *Process Orders Model*. Import the file and restore the application system in your Repository to see the information provided in it.

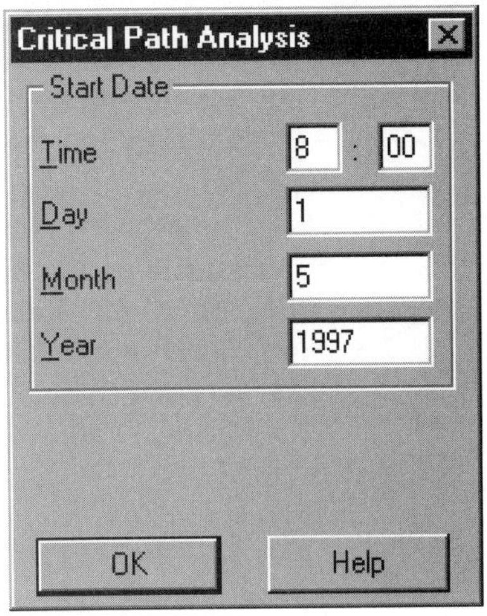

FIGURE 11.31 The Critical Path Analysis dialog box.

cal path is calculated, the contours of process steps, stores, and flows that are in the path are redrawn in red lines. These allow you to distinguish clearly the members of the critical path and focus your attention on them.

11.5 SUMMARY

When business areas of an enterprise are analyzed, their business processes should be identified and detailed in order to understand the activities, events, stores, and flows that they contain. The Process Modeller provides excellent support for creating and maintaining detailed process diagrams of your business areas. This chapter shows how you can complete these tasks for the case of the Approve Orders business area of TASC. Major points in this chapter are:

❑ **Defining Business Area Processes**
    ❑ Input and Output of the Business Area
    ❑ States of Orders
    ❑ Entering Business Area Processes in the Repository
❑ **Analyzing Processes in Detail**
    ❑ How Approve Orders Works
    ❑ Roles
    ❑ Process Steps
    ❑ Events
    ❑ Stores
    ❑ Flows
    ❑ Naming Conventions

- ❑ **Animation and Multimedia**
  - ❑ Multimedia Properties
  - ❑ Animating the Process Diagrams
  - ❑ Configuring the Process Modeller for Multimedia Files
  - ❑ Using Multimedia Files
  - ❑ Setting Icons for Process Step Approve Order
- ❑ **Synthesizing the Business Area**
  - ❑ Identifying Value-Adding Processes
  - ❑ Benchmarking
  - ❑ Activity-Based Costing
  - ❑ Critical Path Analysis

Chapter 12

BUSINESS PROCESS REENGINEERING

- ◆ Symptoms of Aching Processes
- ◆ Prescriptions for Aching Processes
- ◆ Preparing for Reengineering Business Processes
- ◆ Reengineering
- ◆ Reengineering TASC
- ◆ Summary

The first step to shifting from a traditional Industrial Age task-oriented company to a process-centered one is the analysis of its business areas. As explained in the previous chapter, during the business area analysis, you identify the processes and collect detailed information on their performance, cost, consumption of resources, and other important indicators. These indicators should give you an idea about the health of the processes and the organization as a whole, much the same as results from clinical tests give a physician a way to understand the health of the patient. In this chapter, you will learn how to interpret the results of the business area analysis, how to recognize the symptoms of poorly performing business processes, and how to achieve a dramatic healing and recovery through drastic change of these processes.

12.1 SYMPTOMS OF ACHING PROCESSES

I begin by listing some typical symptoms reflected by business processes that are in dire need of fixing. As an example, this section will use the TASC's process of fulfilling customer orders, which was discussed in previous chapters. The following paragraph is a summary of the description of this process.

Fulfill Customer Orders

A salesperson receives the purchase order from the customer by mail or fax and files it in the Sales office archives. Then the order is reviewed for accuracy and is passed on to the office manager for approval. The manager verifies that the order is reviewed correctly and approves it. From here, the order travels to the Customer Credit office. Here, someone makes sure that the order has the right approval from the Sales office and sends it back if it does not. For those that are correctly approved, the payment method is established. If the customer will be billed, the credit worthiness of the customer must first be established and approved. If the customer is new for TASC, a credit report is requested; for existing customers, the payment history is compiled and analyzed to look for any glitches. The manager of the Customer Credit office is responsible for reviewing the collected materials, assessing the risk of the customer, and approving or rejecting the order, based on that risk. For those orders that are not approved, an explanation letter is sent to the customer.

The approved orders are sorted by the type of products ordered (business or family product) and are forwarded to the Customer Service office in the division that covers those products. The Customer Service representative (CSR) in this office reviews incoming orders and ensures that they contain appropriate approvals from the Sales and Customer Credit offices. If everything is correct, the products that make up the order line items are booked in the Inventory System, and the order is sent to the warehouse that will package the order. At the same time that an order is booked, the CSR monitors the number of products in the inventory and notifies the Acquisition office if this number falls beyond a certain threshold. The staff in this warehouse assembles in one package the products based on the order line items, generates a customer invoice, and attaches the invoice to the package. Next, a carrier is selected to pick up the package, and the whole order is transferred to the shipping and receiving area. At the scheduled time, the carrier picks up the package and delivers it to the customer.

The way this process is performed at TASC conforms with Adam Smith's principle of division of labor. The process is divided into many small, repetitive, and relatively simple tasks that do not require advanced skills from the employees that perform them. However, in today's world, the customer defines the purpose and existence of a business. From the customer's perspective, this process is hopelessly broken. Recall from the interview with a representative customer reported in Chapter 10 that after she places an order, it seems to fall into a black hole, and no one can tell her accurately where the order is in the system. This effect is typical of task-oriented work. By breaking up a process into many small tasks, the responsibility for the process as a whole and its ultimate outcome, a satisfied customer, is lost. Although each organization unit may work hard to complete its piece of work quickly and efficiently, nobody is in charge to oversee that all the pieces of the puzzle are put together on time and accurately.

Even from TASC's narrow interest and perspective, this process is far from perfect. You can easily notice that within TASC, a purchase order must go through four organization units: Sales, Customer Credit, Customer Service, and Warehouse. Recall from the previous chapter that just to approve the order in the Sales office three persons had to be involved. This state of affairs, although dictated by the need to split the process into small steps, inevitably creates the possibility for errors. Each time the process is handed over to a different organization unit, the possibility of introducing an error is increased. Thus, the overall process becomes more vulnerable and riddled with problems.

To fence off problems that may arise from such situations, many checks and controls are introduced into the process. Sales managers check the work of salespersons, credit officers check the approvals from the sales department, credit managers check the credit and financial data gathered by the credit officers, and so on. Basically, for each handoff that occurs, a check exists on both the sending side and the receiving side to ensure the correctness of the procedure. The down side to this, often a very significant one, is that each handoff is also accompanied with queues, delays, and time spent waiting rather than doing work valuable to the customer. The ratio of work time over the total activity time often drops to single digit percentage points, as you saw for some activities in the process Approve Order. The activity-based costing analysis of the business area, discussed in the previous chapter, is the best tool to shed light on such activities.

Another characteristic of the process Fulfill Customer Order at TASC is that many tasks cannot be considered value-adding activities from the customer's perspective. The whole credit checking process, for example, exists totally for the benefit and protection of TASC, but does not contribute in any way to orders being completed more quickly or accurately. On the contrary, it may slow the whole process down, not because the Customer Credit office does not do its job well, but exactly because it does. The priority of the other organization units involved in the process is to move the order as quickly as they can through the system. Customer credit representatives on the other hand are evaluated based on whether or not customers live up to their commitments and pay the bills. Therefore, they want to do a full review of the credit or payment history of a customer, even if this may take several days of their time. The identification of value-adding activities and the activity-based costing analysis of the business area are great tools to understand process steps like this and quantify the impact they have on the business as a whole.

If TASC is like many companies that you may encounter today, the information contained on the single-page purchase order may be stored in several systems and rekeyed several times by the time the process order changes into a packaged product ready to be delivered to the customer. A typical scenario could be the following:

> The sales representatives keep the customer data in a contact management package that they share within their office. Their managers record every sale in a spreadsheet in order to determine the bonuses for their department. The Customer Credit office maintains a database of current customers, which is shared with the Accounting office. The Customer Service office has its own database implemented in a client/server environment, which, besides the customer information, records also the products that each customer orders, for the purpose of profiling them. In addition, this office has access to the mainframe Inventory System used to book orders. When orders are booked, the customer service representatives must update the local database by entering the products ordered through the client/server application.

You can easily see that many data items must be entered in separate applications by several people as the process order goes through the system. The picture looks so dark that one would think the worst enemies of TASC came up with a scheme to bog its employees down in typing and retyping over and over the same information, or almost the same, since errors and discrepancies are unavoidable. In fact, many businesses that grow from small start-up companies end up organizing their work this way, as the load and responsibilities increase incrementally. Analyzing the business processes gives you an opportunity to identify such duplications of effort and data redundancy. Many companies today attempt to reduce the duplication of effort by creating complicated interfaces between systems and rekeying the data electronically rather than manually, in the form of massive batch jobs that transfer information back and forth over the corporation's networks. Nevertheless, automation does not solve but hides the problem of rekeying information and data redundancy. The same data items being entered multiple times within the business area are a good indicator that some processes are broken.

In summary, some symptoms of processes that are broken and disrupt the business of a corporation are the following:

❑ People know what their individual tasks are but cannot identify what the processes of the business area are and who has responsibility over them.
❑ The process winds through a large number of organization units. Work is handed over several times until the process is completed.
❑ The ratio of time spent on actual work over the total time it takes the process to complete is low.
❑ The ratio of value-adding activities over control activities is low.
❑ A considerable amount of data rekeying and redundancy occurs across organization units.

In the following section, you will see some prescriptions for healing these broken processes.

12.2 PRESCRIPTIONS FOR ACHING PROCESSES

Clearly, a company whose processes are displaying the symptoms described in the previous section sooner or later must change the way it works. These symptoms have manifested themselves in corporations around the world for quite some time, since, as I explained earlier, they are rooted in the way these companies organize their business around tasks and functions. Obviously, different remedies have been tried; the three most popular ones are listed below:

❑ **Automation.** This approach became widespread as the computing power that companies could afford increased rapidly in the 1970s. Many tasks previously performed laboriously by hand now were given to computers, which could complete them much more quickly and accurately than entire teams of office workers. Automation is an effective tool for improving the efficiency of many tasks that is used nowadays and will be used successfully in the future. However, automation alone cannot cure all the symptoms described above. Automating work without changing the way work is done provides only tools, systems, to perform tasks more quickly. But if the whole task-oriented approach to business is flawed, automating individual tasks in the long run is like digging deeper the hole in which businesses find themselves.

❑ **Restructuring.** This approach consists of reshuffling and reorganizing the human resources in the company with the hope of improving the way tasks are performed. Besides adding to the confusion within the company, the restructuring achieves little improvement and leaves the task-oriented approach to business fundamentally unchallenged.

❑ **Rightsizing.** This is a technique that aims at changing the staffing quotas and job responsibilities in response to changing business circumstances. Rightsizing is really nothing more than a knee-jerk reaction to the market demands for the products and services offered by the company. When the demand drops, the company lays off its workers and divests some of its assets; when the demand increases, these workers or their replacements, are called back. Significant, for example, is the fact that on the same day, September 17, 1996, *The Wall Street Journal* reported that IBM planned to lay off 5,000 of its nonsales-related personnel, while United Airlines announced that it had recalled the last of the airline pilots laid off during the downsizing wave of the 1980s.

The common characteristic of the three approaches listed above is that they strive for incremental improvements of tasks that the company performs. *Total Quality Management (TQM)* is a business improvement method that distances itself from all of them by focusing on understanding and improving the business *processes*. TQM programs were introduced in the United States by managers who were trying to understand the key to the 1980s success of their Japanese competitors. These programs aim at the continuous improvement (*kaizen* in Japanese) of existing business processes. The improvement is sought in the quality with which these processes perform as measured by key performance indicators of the process, such as speed, accuracy, and customer satisfaction.

Successful implementation of TQM programs, given the nature of these programs, results in gradual improvements of the processes. But in the early 1990s, the business literature began reflecting success stories of companies that were im-

The whole essence of reorganization is captured by Scott Adams in his book *The Dilbert Principle* (HarperCollins, 1996):

Managers are like cats in a litter box. They instinctively shuffle things around to conceal what they have done. In the business world this process is called "reorganizing." A normal manager will reorganize often, as long as he's fed.

proving the quality and the performance of their processes by orders of magnitude rather than by 10 to 20 percent offered by TQM methods. These companies were implementing drastic overhauls of their processes, their mentality, and the way of doing business. In 1993, Hammer and Champy defined this activity as *business process reengineering* (BPR). In their book *Reengineering the Corporation*, quoted earlier, they define reengineering as "the fundamental rethinking and radical redesign of business processes to achieve dramatic improvements in critical, contemporary measures of performance such as cost, quality, service, and speed." Important characteristics of reengineering that distinguish it from other approaches to fixing business problems are:

❑ **Reengineering acts upon processes.** Processes or business activities that take some input and transform it into output of value to the customers are the domain of reengineering. You do not reengineer companies, organizational units, or functions, but processes. In this quality, reengineering falls into the same group as TQM and differs from automation, restructuring, and rightsizing.

❑ **Reengineering dramatically improves performance indicators.** Unlike TQM, which is for continuous, incremental improvement of these indicators, reengineering aims to achieve giant leaps forward. Reengineering is not done to improve the performance of processes by 10 or 20 percent. Instead, a company reengineers its processes if it must, needs, or wants to improve its performance by orders of magnitude.

❑ **Reengineering requires you to fundamentally rethink business processes.** In order to reengineer, you must go to the core of the business process and question everything you encounter on the way. Everything must be on the table, every belief or assumption must be challenged, especially if it has been around and taken for granted for a long time.

❑ **Reengineering radically changes the business processes.** Reengineering business processes transforms the company from the traditional Industrial Age corporation based on Adam Smith's principle of division of labor, to the 21st-century Information Age corporation. It is not a gradual or incremental transformation of the same type of company that has existed and flourished for the last two centuries, but the radical change of it, the rebirth of a new type of corporation, centered and organized around processes. Reengineering deeply changes not only the way the company performs its processes, but also its culture, philosophy, beliefs, organization structure, management techniques, and everything else that defines the company.

The purpose of this book is not to discuss all the details, aspects, and requirements of reengineering. Many books have been written on the subject, among which stand out the classics *Reengineering the Corporation* and *Beyond Reengineering* by Michael Hammer (HarperCollins, 1996). *The Reengineering Handbook*

(AMACOM, 1996) by Raymond Manganelli and Mark Klein offers a 5-phase, 54-step methodology to follow when engaging in reengineering efforts. Business magazines and newspapers publish articles about reengineering on a regular basis, as well. Use all these and other resources to fully understand what reengineering is and how it works. The remainder of this chapter will simply outline some of the concepts encountered most often during the reengineering of business processes.

12.3 PREPARING FOR REENGINEERING BUSINESS PROCESSES

In the following sections, you will see which companies launch reengineering efforts, who are the players in this undertaking, how reengineering happens, and how the companies look after their processes have been reengineered. As usual, the TASC example will be used to explain and provide examples for the concepts encountered here.

12.3.1 WHY REENGINEER?

As I mentioned earlier, reengineering promises big payoffs in terms of dramatic improvement in the quality and performance of business processes, customer satisfaction, and other important factors. On the other hand, these payoffs are realized only through radical changes to existing processes, which unavoidably disrupt and wreak havoc in the current work and life of the company. The failure of many companies in the efforts to overhaul their processes, especially in the early 1990s, indicates that reengineering is an undertaking with a great deal of risk. Despite this risk, more and more corporations are embracing the principles and ideas of reengineering. What pushes these companies to put on the line the structures, philosophy, principles, and values that made them successful over the years? The answer to this question is three-fold: need, fear, and ambition.

❑ **Need.** This factor drives the reengineering of those processes that are hopelessly broken. The performance factors of these processes lag far behind those for comparable processes performed by the competition. Incremental improvements achieved through conventional management methods may narrow the gap, but do not allow the company to catch up with its competitors. A well-designed and well-conducted reengineering effort is the only hope these corporations have to reenter the competition game.

❑ **Fear.** On some occasions, something is in the air that creates unease in managers. The business operates well, the numbers look healthy, the products sell; however, nobody knows how long this tranquillity is going to last. The environment is charged with tension and everybody fears that any day a competitor may sprint forward with a brand new product or idea. In such situations, people who want to push the business beyond this zone of uncertainty turn to reengineering as the only method that will catapult them forward a healthy distance from the competition.

❑ **Ambition.** This force pushes those companies that outperform the competition towards reengineering, and those that are leaders in the industry and see themselves in a brilliant position. Nevertheless, visionaries within these companies do not stop thinking about improving the business. They use reengineering to place themselves even further ahead and set new standards of performance. Their competitors, they hope, will break their necks trying to meet these higher standards.

Each of these factors, working independently or in conjunction, drives a corporation towards reengineering. But in order for the effort to succeed, several things must happen. The following section is dedicated to what it takes to succeed at reengineering.

12.3.2 PREREQUISITES TO REENGINEERING

As I mentioned earlier, corporations enter the reengineering way because they need or want to change their business processes. However, not every corporation is ready to undertake the reengineering effort. Several conditions must exist in order to guarantee a successful beginning and continuation of the effort. The following list is a summary of such conditions:

❑ **Executive-level support.** When reengineering business processes, you are reshaping not only the existing processes, but also the functional division of work, organizational boundaries, job descriptions, rules, and assumptions that seemed cast in stone for a long period of time. The only way you will succeed is if you have the full and unequivocal commitment of the highest officers of the corporation. Reengineering efforts step on so many toes and touch so many nerves that they are destined to be killed unless they have the heavy weight of top executives behind them. They are the only ones who can rise above the narrow interests of provincial-minded managers who want to defend their corporate fiefdoms. Executives are the only ones who can set aside resources to support the effort until it succeeds. Reengineering is far from a smooth and clean effort. You can be assured that any reengineering effort sooner or later will find itself in muddy waters with too many people around calling for its dismissal. (If not, you are not going deep enough into your designs and revamping of new processes.) Only the support from executives within the company will not allow opponents and critics to pull the plug too soon on the effort.

❑ **People with appropriate skills and commitment to reengineering.** While executives protect the reengineering train from those who want to derail it,

you need skilled and committed people to man it and do all that it is required to push it forward. These people should be grouped together in
reengineering teams and should be given the mandate to change the existing processes as much and in any way they like. No limitations or constraints should be placed on the reengineering team; otherwise the creativ-
ity and spontaneity of their work will be severed. The members of the
reengineering team should be familiar enough with the way current
processes work to understand what the business goals and priorities are.
But remember that the longer they have performed the processes they are
tasked to change, the heavier their baggage will be and the harder it will be
for them to part with ways processes were performed in the past. These
people should be encouraged to think "outside the box," over and beyond
the boundaries of their former organization units. They should all work together as a group and discontinue their old reporting relationships in order
to avoid the protection of narrow interests from becoming issues during
the reengineering sessions. The reengineering team should stay together
throughout the length of the effort, until the reengineering process is complete.

❑ **Well defined methodology principles.** In the early 1990s, when reengineering was being defined and the first corporations were experimenting with
it, a widespread belief existed that a methodology was not necessary, but
that, on the contrary, it was harmful to the goal of reengineering. The "clean
sheet of paper" approach, professed by the fathers of reengineering as a
technique to stimulate the creative thinking and design of the reengineering
team, was often misinterpreted as a call to abandon all methodology principles. However, as more experience was gathered, the need for a methodical
approach to reengineering was not only recognized, but also fulfilled to
some extent. The collective experience of corporations that have gone
through the ups and downs of reengineering has begun to crystallize in a
system of methods, principles, and rules that should be followed by reengineering teams. Hammer and Champy laid out several of them in *Reengineering the Corporation*. Manganelli and Klein, in their book *The Reengineering
Handbook*, document the Rapid Re™ methodology, an integration of existing
management techniques such as process modeling, activity-based costing,
value-adding analysis, and benchmarking for use in business process
reengineering.

❑ **Advanced technology.** No success story exists in business process reengineering today where the technology in general, and information technology
in particular, has not played a crucial role. Often, the breakthrough performance and visionary structure of the processes can become reality and be
implemented thanks only to advanced technological features. For example,
The Wall Street Journal reported on 13 September 1996 how Rowe Furniture
Corp. reengineered its process of fulfilling custom orders for upholstered

furniture. Traditionally, customers would go to a showroom, where they could see only a limited selection of furniture items with an even more limited selection of fabrics. The company offered a wide variety of fabrics, but the customers had to place a special order and wait for several months to get furniture with the fabrics of their choice. The company reengineered the process of special orders in such a way that dramatically cut the delivery time and the cost to the customers. An important enabler of the new reengineered process is a computer network that allows customers to match the fabrics and styles online and create their own customized furniture items interactively.

On the other hand, the role of technology in reengineering must not be confused with that of technology as a means to automate work. As explained earlier, automation aims at completing existing tasks faster. Reengineering is all about modifying the way work is currently performed. The technology in reengineering serves as a tool that allows you to accomplish things that you cannot do now, but that will be performed by the new processes you envision.

Reengineering transforms the face of the company not only radically but also irreversibly. Once its processes are reengineered, the company cannot go back to the pre-reengineering way of doing business. The only option is to move forward on the reengineering path. The only way to keep this movement uninterrupted is to ensure that the conditions listed above are always met.

12.4 REENGINEERING

The first time a company undertakes a reengineering effort, it goes through the following steps:

1. Prepare for reengineering.
2. Analyze the enterprise business areas.
3. Choose and understand the process to reengineer.
4. Envision the new process.
5. Implement the vision of the new process.
6. Constantly improve the reengineered process through gradual improvement techniques such as TQM.

Afterwards, when subsequent reengineering projects are performed, the need for the first two steps is minimal. Normally, the experience and lessons learned from the previous efforts feed back into the overall corporate experience, and the modifications to the initial business areas are reflected in the business knowledge repository. The effort then proceeds directly to step 3 and the ones that follow it.

The scenario above assumes that the corporation reengineers one process at a time. This is the path that is chosen more often, since it reduces the impact on the company and minimizes risk associated with reengineering. However, cases exist in which companies have overhauled several and even all of their processes. In fact, most of the successful reengineering initiatives have tackled multiple processes at the same time. A very concise list of steps to reengineer business processes follows. More details are provided in references quoted earlier in the chapter and other materials that appear regularly in the bookstores and in articles of business newspapers and magazines.

12.4.1 PREPARE FOR REENGINEERING

This step identifies the strategic goals and problems that the company is facing. It makes the case for reengineering and builds the commitment of executives for the effort. Only after an executive agreement and consensus for the project occur, proceed to build the reengineering team. Choose people in such a way that the common pool of skills that everyone contributes is large enough to support the team in its effort. Compare the skills needed to the skills that the team already has acquired and plan for developing missing or inadequate skills. Training sessions, self-paced study of literature, and attending professional conferences and seminars are just a few ways you can add or update skills and knowledge of your team members.

Carefully balance the "insiders" on the team with the "outsiders." Insiders are those who know all or parts of the process you are trying to reengineer. However, as said earlier, they should not be so much attached to it as to present resistance to new ideas and changes. Outsiders, on the other hand, are people who do not know the current process. They may come from other different business areas of the company, or they may be hired consultants or facilitators. Be sure to include outsiders in every reengineering team, because they will bring with them none of the beliefs, facts, or knowledge about the current process that insiders inevitably bring.

Also insist on having the team work as a group at the same location. Long distance reengineering usually does not work. Face-to-face discussions are the best way to ignite discussions and generate new ideas. If the team members belong to different organization units, they should be transferred formally and permanently to a common unified business unit and break old reporting ties with their former managers. Executive support is essential here to make sure that disgruntled managers will not drag their feet or tie the process up in the web of bureaucracy.

12.4.2 CHOOSE THE PROCESS TO REENGINEER

Before any reengineering effort is undertaken, the company must complete its strategic planning and business area analysis, as discussed in Chapters 9, 10, and

11, which dealt with these topics. Strategic planning allows you to understand the mission, objectives and goals of the enterprise, the problems it faces, the success factors that are critical to the achievement of these goals, and the key performance indicators that measure the achievements. Business area analysis determines the principal business processes of the enterprise, and dissects these processes into subprocesses and activities that need to be performed. Methods like activity-based costing, value-adding analysis, and benchmarking are used to identify the processes that are riddled with problems.

Only if reengineering is done in the framework of strategic planning and business area analysis will you be able to decide objectively which processes to tackle first. Based on the facts you have gathered and documented in the knowledge repository, you can create a good idea about the levels of important performance factors such as cost, time, customer satisfaction, and quality. You can then combine these measures with strategic objectives and goals of the enterprise and create a prioritized list of processes to be reengineered.

Reengineering after strategic planning and business area analysis also enables you to assess the success based on reliable tangible facts. If you have done all the preliminary work, you will have a good idea about the performance of current processes. After the reengineered processes are instituted, you can measure the same parameters and document them in the enterprise repository. By comparing the performance indicators of processes before and after reengineering, you can objectively evaluate the improvement that the new processes bring to the business.

12.4.3 ENVISION THE NEW PROCESS

This step is where the character of reengineering as an art and as a science is fully displayed. Envisioning the new processes that will replace the existing, broken ones is an art because it requires inspiration, fantasy, and creative spirit. Remember that reengineering is about dramatic improvement. Measures that improve the situation incrementally are easy to identify and suggest, but they will not yield the improvement rates that reengineering delivers. Quick and small fixes are attractive, but should not be allowed to lure the reengineering team away from the promised land upon which it has set its eyes. The breakthrough idea or innovation that will double productivity or result in a five-fold reduction of order processing time is what reengineering needs and what will take the team to the end of its journey. Coming up with such an idea, like writing, composing, or painting, is not easy. The reengineering team will go through the agonies, pains, and difficulties that every artist experiences.

The fact that envisioning new processes is an art does not mean that it is an eerie activity out of touch with reality. On the contrary, it is an activity that, like every other business activity, must be conducted under constraints and limitations. Many traditional constraints and barriers should be lifted in order to enable the reengineering team to envision the new process. However, fundamental business constraints remain in place and should be respected even by the wildest visionary. Designing an efficient process that will send the company to bankruptcy does not benefit anyone. These business constraints often have opposite effects that the new process must balance. The envisioning of new processes is a science because it finds the process that offers an optimal solution to a business problem under well defined business constraints.

Once you have a vision, you need to communicate it to the rest of the company. You need to convey with clarity the crisis the company faces if it continues with the existing processes and how the vision you have for the new process will avoid this crisis. A great communicator must present the vision so that everyone is not only convinced but also enthused and excited about the new way of doing business. Lee Iacocca, former CEO of the Chrysler Corporation, was able to present his vision for reinventing a company on the verge of collapse in such a way that rallied the support of politicians, press, and ordinary citizens for the biggest corporate bailout in American history.

12.4.4 DESIGN THE NEW PROCESS

When you present your vision, also show the path to follow in order to reach this vision. The first step on this path is to redesign the processes. During the redesign, you define the way the new process will work, the new business rules that will apply, what information systems will be implemented, how they will interact with existing systems, what equipment and tools will be purchased, how they will be deployed, and so on.

The next step is to explain the social effect of the new processes. These include changes in the organization structure, job descriptions, career directions of employees, recruitment and hiring strategies, employee training and certification programs, and so on. Here you must explain how management and measurement policies and procedures will change under the new process, what will define the compensation, how performance will be evaluated and rewarded, how promotions will be handled, and so on. Reengineering can happen only if new processes are established in a new corporate environment. Therefore, reengineering impacts all the factors that determine the culture and environment, such as the ones mentioned above. Your responsibility is to plan for the changes and explain them to everyone who will be affected.

12.4.5 IMPLEMENT THE DESIGN

The hardest part in a reengineering effort is implementing the design of the new process. The potential for failure increases dramatically at this stage, and things missed during the design could prove to be fatal for the success of the whole effort. Implementation lasts longer than any of the other reengineering stages, anywhere from six to eighteen months. Many things may change during this time. A new law passed by Congress, new technological achievements or discoveries, the retirement of the reengineering champion, and many other factors like this may have a considerable impact on the project.

On the other hand, up to this point, the impact of the reengineering effort on the company has been limited. When you start implementing the new process, the changes you introduce will start having a real effect on real people. Reengineering fundamentally changes the way people work. It replaces many simple, repetitive tasks with broader, multi-dimensional tasks that require more responsibilities and decision-making skills. It collapses several hierarchy levels into flatter and wider organizations. It replaces jobs that reward showing up and working eight-hour days with jobs that reward value created or services offered to the customer. All these changes and disruptions will thrill many, but will certainly meet the resistance of those that feel uncomfortable with the new life. You must always have executive support to go ahead, help those who want to be helped, and let go those who cannot adapt to the new environment.

When implementing a reengineered process, you are often wise to start out with a pilot project. Out of the whole business area affected by the process, you can carve a piece where business will be done following the requirements of the new process. The rest will continue to perform the traditional process. After the pilot project is implemented successfully, you can extract the lessons learned and apply them to transform the entire business area. Pilot projects are important especially when reengineering large business areas, because they remove the size dimension from the universe of problems facing the reengineering team. They also reduce and isolate the impact that the change will bring to the business area, thus minimizing the number of those who will oppose the project. Furthermore, a successful implementation of the pilot project creates a dynamic working process in which the participants are excited to work, the productivity soars, and the customers feel great about the service they are getting. The glaring contrast between this and the old, inefficient process is the best argument in support of a full-scale deployment of the new reengineered process.

12.4.6 CONSTANTLY IMPROVE THE REENGINEERED PROCESS

After the new process is implemented, you need to constantly monitor the results and evaluate the performance. Constant changes in customer needs and aggressive competition that every business faces will force you to revise and improve the process. A reengineered process that is left intact for a period of time may end up with the same amount of problems as the process it replaced. The freshness and elasticity of the reengineered process can be maintained only through uninterrupted maintenance and care for the process.

In the process-centered organization, change and improvement of processes becomes a way of life. Gradual process improvement techniques such as TQM can be used successfully for small-scale, incremental improvements. If the gap between the actual performance measures of the process and those required by the customers or dictated by the competition is too wide to be filled by TQM, the process must be reengineered again. Michael Hammer, in his book *Beyond Reengineering*, discusses in detail problems and issues related to the process-centered organization and to the maintenance and improvement of business processes after reengineering.

12.5 REENGINEERING TASC

The previous sections offered a rather theoretical overview of the steps to reengineer the business processes of an enterprise. This section explains the initiatives taken at TASC to reengineer the process of fulfilling the customers' orders. The new reengineered process will be entered in the Designer/2000 Repository using the Process Modeller. The reengineering team at TASC will focus its attention on the following four areas:

- ❏ Breaking old assumptions in the order fulfillment process
- ❏ Reorganizing the existing business units into order management teams with increased responsibilities
- ❏ Reorganizing the relationships with customers and business partners in order to optimize the order fulfillment process
- ❏ Identifying new information systems that will assist the order management team in performing the new reengineered process

12.5.1 BREAKING OLD ASSUMPTIONS

As I explained earlier, one of the major delays in TASC's existing order fulfillment process occurs when the Customer Credit office checks the credit of customers that place orders. The credit checking activity is based on the assumption that a customer ordering a product may default on the payment of the required price to the company. This assumption is as old as TASC and reflects more the mentality of "us against the customers," rather than the newly defined mission of TASC, to provide customers with software products at prices they can afford. In addition, a simple and informal benchmark of the current ordering process with similar processes performed by other companies reveals that almost all these companies require that customers provide the payment at the same time they place an order, thus bypassing the need to check the credit of the customers. Therefore, the reengineering team at TASC proposes the following change:

> TASC is in the business of satisfying the needs of customers for software products on time and with high professionalism. We believe that, as long as we fulfill this goal, our relationship with the customers will be a friendly and cooperative one, rather than an adversarial one. Therefore, the new

order fulfillment process will not require checking the credit history of a customer before processing the order. Instead, the customers will provide the payment together with their purchase order. The payment will be in the form of a credit card charge, money order, or personal check.

When the first two methods of payment are used, the verification process is almost instantaneous. If the credit card transaction is posted or the money order is valid, the order can be processed right away. In the opposite case, the request will be returned to the customer with the appropriate explanation. When customers pay with personal checks, TASC will assume that the check is valid and will begin processing the order as soon as it receives the request. Within two business days, our bank can inform us if there is a problem with the check. In such an event, we will cancel the order and return the request to the customer with the appropriate explanation. In any case, we will almost eliminate the time between receiving the purchase order and starting its processing.

12.5.2 REORGANIZING THE BUSINESS UNITS

One of the major problems with the existing order fulfillment process at TASC is that it involves too many organization units. As mentioned earlier, each time a handoff occurs between different business units, checks are performed to avoid any mistakes. These checks bring unavoidable delays and do not add any value to the ultimate product that the customer receives. Furthermore, recall from Chapter 10 the following two concerns expressed by the customers about the way TASC currently processes orders:

❑ The process is divided into two sub-processes—pre-sales and after-sales—which are very distinct in the eyes of the customer. In addition, the attention that customers receive differs widely, depending on whether the order is in the first or the second sub-process.

❑ Each salesperson specializes in a selected number of products. So customers interested in a wide range of products have to interact with different representatives from the company, when they would prefer to establish and maintain contact with only one person.

In order to address these problems, the reengineering team proposes the following modifications to the organizational structure of TASC:

❑ Organize the operations of the company by geographic regions. The current organization in three divisions (Sales and Marketing, Business Products, Family and Home Products) separates artificially the sales and marketing efforts from efforts to fulfill customer orders. In addition, it groups the products that TASC offers into categories that are not meaningful to customers, thus requiring them to deal with different business units within TASC.

❑ Create a new organization unit called Order Management Team. The Baltimore, Atlanta, and San Diego offices will each have their own order management team. Members of this team will work together to help customers order products from TASC and fulfill these orders. Each team will be organized into a Sales unit and a Warehouse unit.

❑ Close the Customer Credit office within the Finance division and reassign its members to the regional order management teams.

Figure 12.1 shows the new organizational chart of TASC proposed by the reengineering team. You can see from this figure that the structure of the company represents the customer-centric approach that the reengineering team has followed. For the purpose of comparison, Figure 12.2 shows the current organizational chart of TASC, which was discussed in Chapter 8. You can see from this figure that a customer in New York, who wants to order Personal Oracle (a business product) and Microsoft Encarta (a family and home product) has to deal with two sales representatives from the East Coast Sales department. In order to fulfill her request, two different warehouses (on the West Coast and East Coast) have to get involved. Throughout the process, duplication of effort, time, and resources occurs, which leads to delays in fulfilling the order and cuts the profits of the company. With the proposed organization structure, on the other hand, all the customer has to do is contact her regional TASC office in Baltimore and place the order with the sales representative. This sales representative will be responsible for satisfying her needs for software products in the future as well. After the order is placed, it is fulfilled within the same unit by people who work closely with the sales representative to complete the order in the shortest time possible.

By comparing the existing organizational chart with the proposed one, you may note that changes triggered by the reengineering of the order fulfillment process have a wide effect on the corporation. Some business units, like Customer Credit Office or Customer Support Office, may be dissolved; others, like the Acquisition offices, may be merged into a single unit; others, like the groups in the Management Information Systems department, may be reorganized. As emphasized earlier, only an empowered reengineering team that enjoys the support of upper management in the corporation may be able to recommend overhauls of this scale without risking self-destruction.

12.5.3 REORGANIZING THE RELATIONSHIPS WITH CUSTOMERS AND BUSINESS PARTNERS

The new reengineered order fulfillment process can succeed only if customers and business partners of TASC are engaged and participate in its activities just as easily as members of the order management teams. Following is how the reengineering team describes the role that customers will play in the new process:

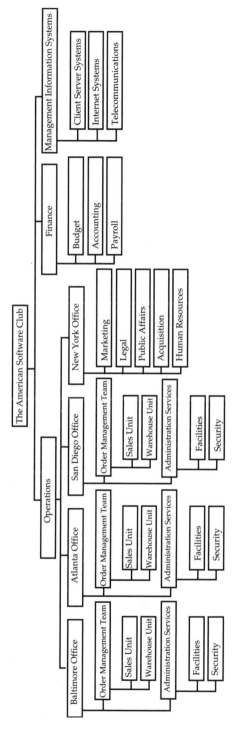

FIGURE 12.1   The organizational structure of TASC proposed by the reengineering team.

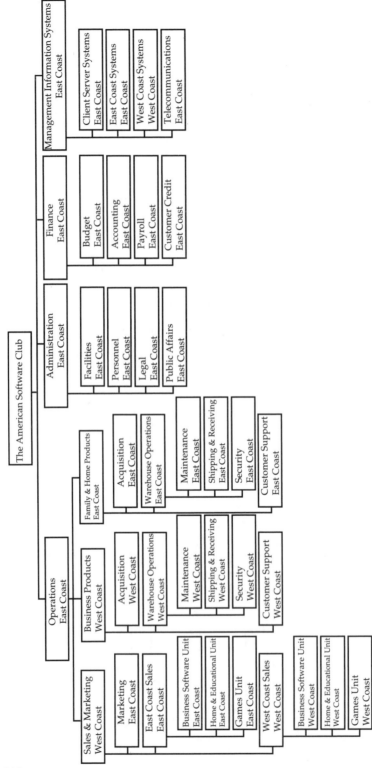

FIGURE 12.2 The organizational structure of TASC before reengineering.

We urge our customers to play an active part in placing orders with us. We will provide them with information about the products we offer in electronic format, on our Web site, and in more traditional formats, through printed catalogs and literature. These will enable them to select the products they need more easily and submit a purchase order electronically or in hard copy. Together with the purchase order, they will submit the appropriate payment information that will enable us to process the order immediately. We will extend the current telephone status tracking system to include updated information about the order as it is being processed by us. We will implement a Web-enabled version of this system that our customers will access from our Web site.

The business partners that the reengineering team identified as agents in the new order fulfillment process are manufacturers and vendors of software products, as well as carriers of packaged products. These agents are involved in the existing process; however, the role that they will assume in the new process is much more active, and the relationship between them and TASC becomes a close partnership. Here is how the reengineering team describes the changes in relationships with its business partners:

❑ **Manufacturers.** The product information we currently obtain from manufacturers is not refreshed often enough. On the other hand, the diminishing length of life cycles of such products renders the information we have obsolete fairly quickly. To avoid this problem, we want to link our product information Web pages with the home sites of each manufacturer. This link will allow our customers to always get the most up-to-date information about a product.

❑ **Vendors.** Today our Warehouse Operations group is responsible for monitoring the supply of product items in each warehouse. When the supply falls beyond established levels, we order additional items from contracted vendors. We want to completely revamp this process by allowing our vendors to directly access our inventory system and monitor the supply levels of those product items that they are responsible for delivering. This setup will eliminate the need for us to place an order with our vendors each time the supplies run low.

❑ **Carriers.** The relationship with the carriers today is similar to that with our vendors. When we pack products, we have to call them and schedule the pickup and delivery of the packages. In order to avoid delays, we will install in our warehouses scheduling and tracking systems provided by each of these vendors. These systems will allow us to electronically log pickup and delivery requests for each package. Bar-coded labels will be automatically printed, and we will stick them on the packages to facilitate the work of the carriers. Carriers on the other hand will be able to monitor online the number of packages we have scheduled for pickup and delivery each day.

12.5.4 THE REENGINEERED ORDER FULFILLMENT PROCESS

In order to better present the vision of the new order fulfillment process, the reengineering team organized the steps and activities of this process according to the agents that are responsible for completing them. Here are the activities that customers will perform in the reengineered process:

❑ **Place Orders.** In this activity, customers will submit requests for software products to TASC. The input to the activity will be the needs of customers for software products, information about product offerings that TASC provides, and the method of payment for the order. The output of the activity is a purchase order submitted to the sales representative from the regional order management team of TASC.

❑ **Modify Orders.** This activity allows customers to change the information they have provided in previous orders.

❑ **Check Orders Status.** The purpose of this activity is to allow customers to track the fulfillment of their orders.

Each regional order management team will perform the following process steps:

❑ **Create, Maintain, and Book Orders.** The sales unit will perform this activity in order to electronically store the purchase orders submitted by customers and to associate available product items from the warehouse with products requested in their orders. The output of this step is a booked order that will be processed by the warehouse unit. This activity also modifies orders at customers' request and updates the status of orders.

❑ **Process Orders.** This activity will be performed by the warehouse unit and will assemble all the product items booked by the sales unit for a given order into one package. The status of the order will be updated accordingly.

❑ **Schedule Pickup.** This activity schedules a package for delivery by one of the carriers contracted by TASC. It will be performed by the warehouse unit, normally right after the ordered products are packed. The status of the orders will be updated with the tracking number generated by the carrier's scheduling and pickup system.

The business partners of TASC will perform the following steps in the reengineered order fulfillment process:

❑ **Check for Scheduled Packages.** Carriers will use their scheduling systems installed in each warehouse to check twice a day for packages that may have been scheduled for pickup and delivery by the order management team.

❑ **Pick up and Deliver Packages.** If the order management team has scheduled packages for pickup and delivery, the carrier will receive these packages from the warehouse and will deliver them to the customers.

❑ **Check Product Item Levels.** Vendors of TASC will be responsible for checking the levels of available product items in the warehouses of TASC.

❑ **Deliver New Product Items.** Software vendors perform this activity if their check reveals that the number of product items in a warehouse has fallen below established levels. Vendors will supply the warehouse with the necessary product items within the time frames established in their contractual agreements with TASC.

❑ **Provide Product Information.** This activity will be performed by software manufacturers and will allow TASC to offer its customers up-to-date information about the products it offers.

Chapters 10 and 11 discussed how you can use the Process Modeller to represent existing business processes in the enterprise. This Designer/2000 tool can also be used to design new processes and convey to the audience the way they will perform. The representation by the Process Modeller of business units, process steps, stores, and flows makes it easier to explain the purpose of each component and its relationships with other components. Furthermore, the animation features of the Process Modeller allow you to show live simulations of the new process. Figure 12.3 shows part of the diagram of the reengineered order fulfillment process in enhanced symbol mode. The companion CD-ROM contains the reengineered order fulfillment process in an application system archived and exported in the Oracle Export dump file RPRCSORD.DMP, which you can download from the Web page of the CD-ROM browsing utility by following the links *Software* and *Reengineered Process Orders Model*. Import the file and restore the application system in your Repository to see the information provided in it.

12.5.5 DEFINING INFORMATION SYSTEMS TO IMPLEMENT THE NEW PROCESS

Conceiving and presenting the vision of the new reengineered process is only the beginning of the effort. The hardest job lies ahead, in the implementation of the vision. Because business process reengineering changes radically the way a company conducts its business processes, its impact is significant and multi-faceted. The solutions that the reengineering team must provide should minimize this impact, help the corporation implement the new process, and address the problems that may arise in the process. These solutions are usually grouped in the following two categories:

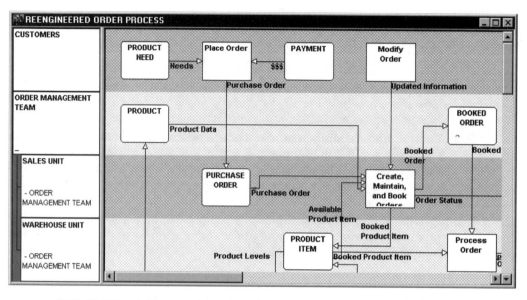

FIGURE 12.3 A diagram of the reengineered order fulfillment process at TASC.

❑ **Social solutions.** Social solutions address the human and social problems that reengineering business processes causes. Such solutions may include addressing the uncertainty about the future of employees affected by reengineering, training the personnel that will perform the new process with the appropriate skills, building relations with business partners that will enable the new process, explaining the new changes to the customers, and many others.

❑ **Technical solutions.** These solutions provide the information infrastructure that is required to implement the reengineered process. They may include new telecommunication services, databases, and software systems that make up this infrastructure.

The reengineering team at TASC identified the need for the following two systems to enable the new order fulfillment process:

❑ **Order Management System.** This system will allow members of the order management team to create, maintain, and book orders received from the customers. A Web-enabled module of this system will allow customers to submit the purchase orders electronically. Furthermore, the system will be used to record the assembly of product items into packages and the scheduling of the pickup and delivery of these packages. The system will also provide for the interface between TASC and its business partners required by the reengineered order fulfillment process. The Order Management System will be a department-level system that will be deployed at each of the order management team locations, in Baltimore, Atlanta, and San Diego. The data for each system will be stored in operational databases located at each of these offices.

❑ **Sales Analysis System.** This system will be implemented at the New York Office and will allow the executives at TASC to analyze sales data of each team, aggregate them at a corporate level, discover patterns, and forecast trends. The regional databases from the Baltimore, Atlanta, and San Diego offices will regularly feed data to the data warehouse of the Sales Analysis System.

The remaining chapters in this book will discuss the design and implementation of these systems using Designer/2000.

12.6 SUMMARY

Business Process Reengineering is the radical redesign and implementation of business processes in an enterprise with the goal of achieving dramatic improvements in the performance of these business processes. If you are involved in any way in strategic planning and business area modeling activities, you will very likely run into processes that, for one reason or another, need to be overhauled using the methods and practices of reengineering. This chapter provides you with the essential knowledge about business process reengineering requirements and steps. Important topics of this chapter include:

❑ **Symptoms of Aching Processes**
❑ **Prescriptions for Aching Processes**
❑ **Preparing for Reengineering Business Processes**
   ❑ Why Reengineer?
   ❑ Prerequisites to Reengineering
❑ **Reengineering**
   ❑ Prepare for Reengineering
   ❑ Choose the Process to Reengineer
   ❑ Envision the New Process
   ❑ Design the New Process
   ❑ Implement the Design
   ❑ Constantly Improve the Reengineered Process

❏ **Reengineering TASC**
    ❏ Breaking Old Assumptions
    ❏ Reorganizing the Business Units
    ❏ Reorganizing the Relationships with Customers and Business Partners
    ❏ The Reengineered Order Fulfillment Process
    ❏ Defining Information Systems to Implement the New Process

Part III

SYSTEMS REQUIREMENTS DEFINITION AND ANALYSIS

Chapter 13. Requirements Analysis

Chapter 14. Data Modeling

Chapter 15. Business Rules Modeling

Chapter 16. Quality Assurance of the System Requirements

REQUIREMENTS ANALYSIS

♦ Business Requirements and System Requirements

♦ Using Designer/2000 in Requirements Analysis

♦ Building the High-Level System Model

♦ Documenting the High-Level System Design

♦ Defining the User Interface Requirements

♦ Summary

The requirements gathering, modeling, and documentation are the first step and a very important one in the life cycle of the software system. Before you design or develop the system, you need to know what the customers expect from it. Knowing the requirements means that you not only understand what is expected from the system, but also are able to convey clearly your understanding and agree with your customers on what they should expect and what you will deliver. Thus, analyzing the system requirements lays the foundation of your work for the next few months and clarifies the terms of the services you are offering to the customers. A well defined set of requirements is the starting point for a successful design and implementation of the system. At the same time, it serves as an effective checklist that you can use at the end of the effort to assess the outcome of the effort. In this chapter, you will learn how to use Designer/2000 in the requirements definition phase of the system's development life cycle.

13.1   BUSINESS REQUIREMENTS AND SYSTEM REQUIREMENTS

A requirement is a thing that is demanded or obligatory. For example, in order to fly abroad, the airline agent will demand and you are obliged to produce a valid ticket and a passport. Stated otherwise, the ticket and the passport are requirements to travel. Only if you meet these requirements are you allowed to fly overseas. Similarly, business requirements are those "things" that must happen so that a business activity is successful. Strategic planning and business area analysis are aimed ultimately at identifying and understanding the business requirements that face an organization.

The universe of business requirements varies with the type and size of the business itself. However, since the first busess started, when *Homo Sapiens* began hunting mammoths and digging roots, business requirements have been divided into two categories. The first includes those requirements that are met by mere human physical and mental labor. The second category includes requirements for which tools are used.

When a business runs for some time, certain tools tend to condense into relatively distinct groups that are used together as a unit. The Greeks defined these combinations of things as *systema*, which means a whole compounded of several parts. Over the years, as the knowledge and technology evolved, people have been using mechanical, hydraulic, electric, and other types of systems to meet the requirements of their businesses. A relatively recent development in the field are computer systems, an organized set of programs, applications, and utilities designed to achieve specific business objectives through the use of computers. Those business requirements that are met by a computer system are known as application requirements, program requirements, or, under the more generic term, system requirements.

System requirements analysis is the activity that determines which business requirements may and will be implemented by a system. In this context, you can clearly see why system requirements are best determined in the framework of strategy planning and business area analysis. If you understand the business objectives, goals, and problems, if you understand the business events and processes and activities that they trigger, if you understand the overall business functions and data entities of the business area, you will be in a better position to decide which of the business requirements should be implemented as computer systems. This last activity is often referred to as defining the scope of the system.

The system requirements can be divided into several groups:

- User interface (UI) requirements
- Data requirements
- Functional requirements
- Security requirements
- Intersystem interface requirements
- Documentation requirements
- Physical, environment, and resources requirements
- Reliability, availability, and serviceability (RAS) requirements

A complete and detailed system requirements analysis should address all the categories of requirements listed above. The following sections provide some explanations and examples for each category of requirements.

13.1.1 USER INTERFACE REQUIREMENTS

User interface (UI) requirements include primarily the layout of screens and reports that will be part of the system. They spell out issues like the ones listed below:

- Number and ranking of screens and reports
- Items that will be displayed in a screen or report, including their properties and layout
- Procedures for invoking each screen or report

Ways to define UI requirements range from textual descriptions of the screens and reports, to pictorial drawings, to prototype applications that demonstrate mainly the layout and ordering of items. UI requirements also include profiles for the users of the system, the skills they must possess, and the training they need. They also include requirements like the flexibility of the system, its ease of use, and potentials for abuse.

13.1.2 DATA REQUIREMENTS

Data requirements describe the content and the format of data items manipulated by the system, their volume when the system is initially implemented and the expected growth rate, the rules under which they can be transformed, which data items are used by which functions, and how.

Most of the data requirements are identified during data modeling and database design activities. They are presented graphically in the form of entity relationship diagrams, but can also be listed in textual mode in a report format. Some data requirements, especially those that describe transformation and dependency rules, are documented like the functional requirements of the system. Other data requirements, such as the data items used by functions, are best presented in the form of matrices. Figure 13.1 contains a sample of data requirements presented in report format.

13.1.3 FUNCTIONAL REQUIREMENTS

Functional requirements describe what the system will do and how often, which business events cause a reaction on the system, what the constraints are on the execution time, response time, and throughput, under what conditions the system can be changed, and so on.

Functional requirements are usually defined in hierarchical format. The root of the hierarchy represents the entire system; its immediate children may be its subsystems; and their children represent the major functions that each subsystem will perform. The hierarchical tree that results from the functional requirements definition is also known as a functional decomposition diagram. The components of a function hierarchy diagram do not necessarily imply the order in which sys-

```
CUSTOMER, also known as COMPANY or INDIVIDUAL.
Has significance as:   An individual or corporation to
which TASC provides software goods and services in
return for payments of prices agreed upon by both sides.
Information includes   customer number,
                            city,
                            phone, etc.
Each CUSTOMER may be initiator of one or more ORDERS
and may be issuer of one or more PAYMENT AUTHORIZATIONS.
Initial number of CUSTOMERS:1000
Average number of CUSTOMERS:2000
```

FIGURE 13.1 An example of data requirements.

OMS12:   Create order. This function will allow users
            to store information in the database for
            each new order they receive. The function is
            expected to be performed 200 times a day.

OMS121:   Create order line items. This function will
            enable users to associate the line items
            with each order in the database. Since each
            order contains on the average five line
            items, this function will be performed 1000
            times each day.

OMS123:   Compute total charge for order. This
            function will compute the total amount of
            money that the customer owes the company for
            a given order. The system will compute the
            total charge automatically based on the
            price of each item, the quantity of items
            ordered, discounts applied, shipping and
            handling charges, and sales taxes where
            applicable. Users will not be allowed to
            enter the total manually.

FIGURE 13.2   Sample functional requirements.

tem functions are conducted. System process diagrams may be used to represent the order in which different functions are performed in the system, events that trigger each function, and the flow of data from one component to the other. Figure 13.2 shows a few examples of functional requirements.

13.1.4 SECURITY REQUIREMENTS

Security requirements define the control mechanisms over different parts of the system, which users can access them, and with what privileges. They include archival, backup and recovery procedures, protection schemes from catastrophic events, protection measures against intruders and viruses, and so on. The security requirements also identify the database privileges that will be granted to each application user, as well as a strategy for managing these privileges in the most effective way. In the simplest case, these requirements are listed in textual format. Requirements, such as user access and privileges, may be presented concisely in matrices. Other requirements, like archival, backup, recovery, and virus protection, are documented in the form of operational procedures that should be fol-

```
1. The users of the system will belong to one of the
   following groups:
   SALES UNIT. Users in this group will be able to
     execute all the functions of the system required
     to create, maintain, and book orders.
   WAREHOUSE UNIT. Users in this group will have
     access to all the functions used to view booked
     orders, assemble them in packages, and schedule
     packages for pickup and delivery by the carriers.
   VENDOR. Members of this group will be able to view
     the number of available product items in each
     warehouse as well as the number of product items
     ordered but not booked, so that they can schedule
     new deliveries according to the quotas.
   CUSTOMER. Customers will be allowed access to the
     functions used to enter a purchase order and to
     view the status of the order.
2. The system administration personnel will perform a
   full backup of the database server every week.
   Incremental backups of the archived log files will be
   performed every three hours.
```

FIGURE 13.3   Sample system security requirements.

lowed when the system becomes a production system. Figure 13.3 contains examples of some system security requirements.

13.1.5   INTERSYSTEM INTERFACE REQUIREMENTS

These requirements define issues such as the protocol of communication between systems, the topology of the network and its components, what information will be exchanged, under what format, and in what ways. They can be formulated in a variety of ways, such as network diagrams, documents that describe standards for interfacing between systems, and descriptions of protocols for exchanging information. Figure 13.4 shows an example of an intersystem interface requirement.

13.1.6   DOCUMENTATION REQUIREMENTS

Documentation requirements define the amount of documentation that is required, the format and media of delivery, the target audience, and so on. A sample documentation requirement is shown in Figure 13.5.

```
TASC will receive updated product information from its
   vendors on a monthly basis. The data will be
   delivered on CD-ROMs or will be sent electronically
   in the form of an e-mail message attachment. The
   information will be stored in ASCII text files with
   one record per line. Each record will contain five
   fields that will be separated by the sequence of
   characters '^^.' The layout of each record is as
   follows:

ID^^NAME^^VERSION^^PRODUCT DATE^^DESCRIPTION
```

FIGURE 13.4 An example of intersystem interface requirements.

13.1.7 PHYSICAL ENVIRONMENT AND RESOURCES REQUIREMENTS

These requirements define the physical locations of different components of the system, environmental and climatic conditions for these locations, the amount of material, human, and financial resources needed to develop, use, and maintain the system, and so on. The table shown in Figure 13.6 is an example of requirements in this category. This table lists the hardware resources needed to run the application.

```
OMS User's Guide will contain a description of the
functionality that will be available to the users of the
OMS system. It will contain three parts and fifteen
chapters. The first part is a tutorial that shows order
processing employees how to accomplish the five
essential tasks of their job using the OMS system. The
second part contains a description of each screen and
report provided by the OMS system in the order they are
organized in the OMS application menu. The last part is
built in the form of a reference manual and lists
alphabetically all the functions that users can perform
using the OMS system.
```

FIGURE 13.5 A sample documentation requirement.

HARDWARE TYPE	QUANTITY	MANUFACTURER	OPERATING SYSTEM	RAM	DISK SPACE
Database Server	1	Sun Microsystems	Sun Solaris, 2.5	512 MB	80 GB
Application Server	2	DELL	Windows NT, 4.0	128 MB	8 GB
Client PC	40	DELL	Windows 95	32 MB	2 GB

FIGURE 13.6   Hardware requirements for an application system.

13.1.8   RELIABILITY, AVAILABILITY, AND SERVICEABILITY REQUIREMENTS

These requirements, commonly knows as RAS, determine the conditions in which the system is considered available or non-available, the meaning of system failures, the mean time between failures, the mean time to repair failed components, system up-time, minimal allowed down-time, and so on. Figure 13.7 contains examples of a few typical RAS requirements for an application system.

13.2   USING DESIGNER/2000 IN REQUIREMENTS ANALYSIS

The information gathered during the analysis of requirements for a database system can be stored in a variety of formats. Multiple tools can be used to create and maintain this information, ranging from simple text editors, to word processing, spreadsheet, and drawing packages, to CASE and I-CASE tools. Designer/2000, with its Repository-centric approach, provides a unified environment for storing

```
The OMS system will be considered non-available if
more than 50 percent of its users cannot access any
one of its components due to software, operating
system, hardware, or network failure.
The OMS system is a 6x20 system. It should be
available Monday through Saturday, from 4:00 A.M
until 11:59 P.M.
In case of catastrophic failure, the system should be
restored to operational state and become available
within 8 hours from the time of failure.
```

FIGURE 13.7   An example of RAS requirements for an application system.

and editing the requirements of a system. Technically, you can store any requirement in the Designer/2000 Repository in one form or another. However, its tools are better suited for certain categories of requirements. In particular, Designer/2000 tools like the Entity Relationship Diagrammer, Functional Hierarchy Diagrammer, and Matrix Diagrammer provide excellent support for storing data, functional, user interface, and security requirements in the Repository. These tools, together with the Process Modeller and the Repository Object Navigator, can be used very effectively to identify the system's requirements. The following paragraphs briefly describe the role of these components of Designer/2000 in the requirements analysis process.

- ❑ **Function Hierarchy Diagrammer.** This diagrammer can be used in general to define all those requirements that are decomposable and hierarchical in nature. Since most of the business functions implemented by the system fit this description, they are modeled using the Function Hierarchy Diagrammer. When documenting the high-level model of the system, this diagrammer may be used to represent the subsystems into which the system is decomposed. In addition, user interface requirements are also defined in the Function Hierarchy Diagrammer.
- ❑ **Entity Relationship Diagrammer.** This is the primary tool for building the data model of your system. It allows you to create and maintain all the data requirements of your system. The data diagrams created with the Entity Relationship Diagrammer allow you to graphically present important data requirements, such as entities and their attributes, or relationships between entities.
- ❑ **Process Modeller.** This tool is used primarily to model transitions from one activity to another and to represent flows of data between components of the system. The Process Modeller can be used in different contexts during requirements analysis activities. One context, for example, is to show how different parts of the system will exchange data. Another use of the Process Modeller is to show the flow between different components of the user interface. Yet another way to use the Process Modeller is to represent the communication of the system with other systems.
- ❑ **Data Flow Diagrammer.** Essentially this diagrammer can be used in the same manner as the Process Modeller. However, since the functionality provided by the Data Flow Diagrammer is only a subset of what the Process Modeller offers, this tool is rarely used in requirements analysis activities.
- ❑ **Matrix Diagrammer.** This tool is used primarily to create, edit, and display requirements that are expressed in the form of associations between objects stored in the Repository. For example, although the entities and attributes used by a user interface component can be specified for each function in the Function Hierarchy Diagrammer, the Matrix Diagrammer allows you to complete this task for all the components defined in your system from a common diagram.

❑ **Repository Object Navigator.** On one hand, the Repository Object Navigator can be used as an alternate tool to complete any task that can be performed in the other tools discussed above. On the other hand, the Navigator provides the only method to access the properties of certain object types for which you want to store information in the Designer/2000 Repository. In particular, if you have extended the Repository in order to better capture some requirements for your system, the data for these requirements can be maintained only through the Repository Object Navigator.

13.3 BUILDING THE HIGH-LEVEL SYSTEM MODEL

Conceptually, building the high-level system model is similar to building the high-level process model for the business area. You want to paint the picture with thick brush strokes, giving the gist of what the system will do, but saving the details for the next iteration. The following sections use the Order Management System as a case study. Recall that this is one of the systems that the reengineering teams at TASC identified as enabler of the new, reengineered order fulfillment process. The following steps may be followed to define the high-level model for this system:

1. Define the categories of requirements that will be maintained hierarchically in the Designer/2000 Repository.
2. Define the user roles of the system.
3. Define the major components of the system, also known as subsystems.
4. Define the major data entities and data flows of the system.

These steps are discussed in detail in the following sections.

13.3.1 DEFINING THE FIRST DECOMPOSITION OF THE SYSTEM

As I mentioned above, the Function Hierarchy Diagrammer may be used to document a large number of requirements that are hierarchical in nature. Each of these hierarchies will originate in a root object, stored as a business function with no parent in the Designer/2000 Repository. Technically, multiple root functions may be defined in an application system. However, the better situation is if the only root function corresponds to the system that you are analyzing and designing. In that case, the first level of function objects into which the root is decomposed may represent the categories of requirements that you want to record in the Repository. Figure 13.8 shows how you would decompose the Order Management System in the Function Hierarchy Diagrammer. As shown in the figure, the categories of requirements that will be documented in the form of functional hierarchies for this system include its subsystems, the user interface requirements, and the business rules.

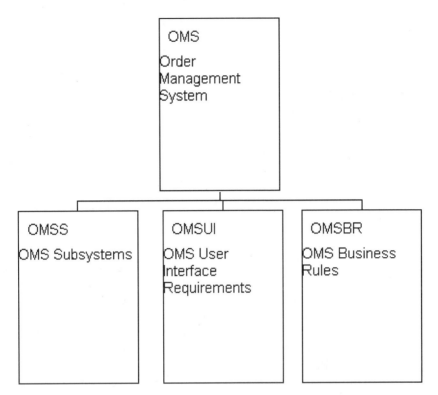

FIGURE 13.8 Categories of Order Management System requirements that will be maintained in the Function Hierarchy Diagrammer.

13.3.2 DEFINING THE USER ROLES

An important step in documenting the high-level model of a system is to identify the groups of users that will interact with the system. This information is stored in the Designer/2000 Repository in the form of business unit objects, for which the property *Role* is set to 'True.' As the requirements of the system are refined, associations between these user roles and other objects, such as functions, entities, and stores, are created. You create the same type of associations during enterprise modeling and business area analysis activities. However, the meaning of these associations in those stages is different from their meaning during the analysis of an information system. In the first case, these associations express responsibility, the business units that are responsible for a function, process, or data entity. In the second case, they represent access privileges.

Three major groups of users will need to access the OMS application. They correspond to the business units ORDER MANAGEMENT TEAM, VENDOR, and CUSTOMER used in Chapter 12 to describe the reengineered process. In addition, ORDER MANAGEMENT TEAM will be divided into two groups of users, SALES UNIT and WAREHOUSE UNIT, which need different access privileges for different components of the system.

13.3.3 DEFINING THE SUBSYSTEMS

Subsystems in an information system are clusters of software modules accessed usually by a distinct number of users. Identifying these subsystems is part of the activities that occur during the high-level design of the system. The Order Management System (OMS) will assist TASC's Order Management Team (OMT) and its business partners in the process of fulfilling customer orders. The system will provide its users with a functionality that can be grouped into the following subsystems:

❑ **Create and Maintain Orders.** This subsystem will allow users to extract data from hard copy purchase orders and store them electronically. These data include information about the customer, the order itself, its line items, payment, delivery method, and so on. In addition to entering ordering information, the subsystem will be used to retrieve an existing order and modify it, based on new information provided by customers.

❑ **Book Order.** This subsystem will assist members of the sales unit to associate line items from orders with product items in the warehouse. In order to avoid multiple bookings of the same product item, the subsystem will remove booked product items from the pool of available items.

❑ **Pack Order and Schedule Delivery.** This subsystem will show members of the warehouse unit the product items booked for a given order as well as their warehouse locations, to assist these users in the process of fulfilling an order. The subsystem will allow the users to create an electronic representation of the packages and print a delivery invoice that will be associated with the package.

❑ **Interface with Business Partners.** This subsystem will contain modules that handle the exchange of data between TASC and its business partners. In particular, the subsystem will allow customers to place orders and check their status from the Internet, it will allow vendors to check the levels of product items in a warehouse, and it will allow TASC to transfer shipping information to the scheduling systems provided by its carriers and receive tracking numbers for its packages.

13.3.4 DEFINING THE MAJOR SYSTEM DATA ENTITIES AND FLOWS

An important part of the high-level design of the system is identifying the major data entities used by each user group and subsystem, as well as the data flows between the components of the system. The high-level data entities identified in this step become the starting point for the data analysis of the system; however, for the purpose of the high-level system design, not too many details are required. The following list contains the major data entities of the Order Management System:

- ❑ Customer
- ❑ Order
- ❑ Payment
- ❑ Product
- ❑ Product item
- ❑ Package
- ❑ Carrier

At the high-level system design, the data entities are often represented as data stores. The use of these data entities by different subsystems is presented in the form of data flows.

13.4 DOCUMENTING THE HIGH-LEVEL SYSTEM DESIGN

 Several Designer/2000 tools may be used to enter the high-level system design in the Repository. However, only the Process Modeller allows you to present in a single diagram all the components of the high-level design, including the user groups, subsystems, data stores, and data flows. Therefore, this is the favorite tool used at this stage of the system's requirements definition efforts. Figure 13.9 shows the high-level design diagram of the Order Management System maintained in the Process Modeller.

An alternative to using the Process Modeller for representing the inputs, outputs, and components of a system is to create data flow diagrams in the Data Flow Diagrammer. Data flow diagrams became very popular years ago when pioneers like Edward Yourdon and Tom DeMarco founded the structured software engineering methodology. Until then, natural languages like English were used to describe the system requirements. The structured methodology removed the inevitable fuzziness and confusion by defining standards for a graphical representation of the requirements. What was revolutionary about the new way of defining the requirements was that only four symbols were needed to express the flow of data through the system. These symbols—process, data store, external data store, and data flow—finally allowed systems analysts to clearly present their understanding of the system to the users' community and opened the way for the active participation of users in the requirements definition process.

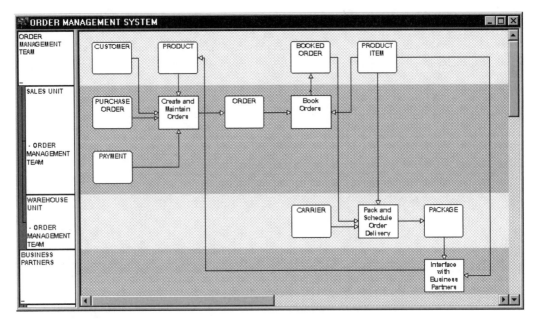

FIGURE 13.9   A high-level design diagram of the Order Management System created in the Process Modeller.

In Designer/2000, though, data flow diagrams are only a subset of process diagrams that you can create in the Process Modeller. Processes and subprocesses of a data flow diagram are process steps in a process diagram, data flows are a particular case of flows, and data stores and externals are a special case of stores. Thus, everything that can be diagrammed in the Data Flow Dia-

The companion CD-ROM contains the application system TASC OMS (REQ) with all the objects and diagrams related to the requirements analysis of the Order Management System as discussed in this chapter. This application is provided in the Oracle Export dump file OMSREQ.DMP, which you can download from the Web page of the CD-ROM browsing utility by following the links *Software* and *Order Management System Requirements*. Import the file and restore the application system in your Repository to see the information provided in it.

grammer can be presented in the Process Modeller as well and often much better. Besides the fact that a process diagram can contain flows and stores of types other than those related to data, the Process Modeller allows you to present the events that trigger an activity and the organization units that carry out the activity or that are responsible for the store. These reasons, coupled with several ways to view a process diagram and the animation features of the Process Diagrammer, make process diagrams a far superior tool for communicating the understanding of requirements to the users' community. Therefore, data flow diagrams will not be discussed to any extent in the rest of this book. Just as a working exercise, you can start the Data Flow Diagrammer and create the high-level data flow diagram for the Order Management System. Follow these steps to create the diagram:

1. Click the iconic button New Diagram ⬜ on the diagrammer's toolbar. The New Diagram dialog box appears.
2. Select 'OMSSUBS–OMS Subsystems' from the list of functions available in the Repository in this dialog box. The diagram is created with a soft rectangle that represents the chosen function.
3. Choose Edit | Include | Function… and select all the subsystems of OMS in the dialog box Include Function. Make sure to check the option *With Dataflows* to include the data flows between the subsystems in the diagram.
4. Choose Edit | Include | Datastore… and select all the stores listed in the dialog box Include Datastore. Here again, check the option *With Dataflows* to include the data flows between the subsystems and data stores in the diagram.

At this point, you need to rearrange the components of the new diagram in order to improve its readability. Figure 13.10 shows one example of such a rearrangement.

13.5 DEFINING THE USER INTERFACE REQUIREMENTS

When you take the first cut at defining the system requirements, you identify the major functions that the system will support. If the system you are working on will ultimately be a set of windows, dialog boxes, and reports that the users will interact with, you need to identify the requirements of users for these interface objects. At the same time, you want to enter them in the Designer/2000 Repository in a way that will facilitate your work during the system design and development phases, which will follow the requirements analysis. Techniques to help you entering user interface requirements in the Designer/2000 Repository are the subject of the following sections.

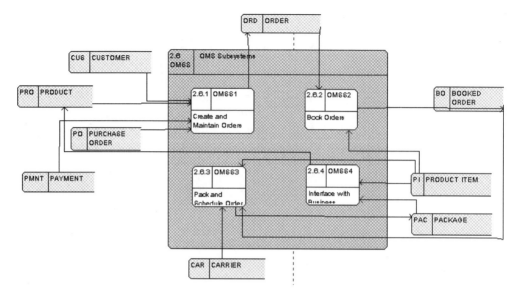

FIGURE 13.10   A high-level data flow diagram for the Order Management System.

13.5.1   DEFINING THE HIERARCHY

Defining interface requirements ultimately means identifying ways in which users want to access the data on their computers in order to accomplish the business functions that the system performs. For example, one of the functions of the OMS system is to create and maintain orders, identified in the high-level model as the subsystem OMSSUBS1. To define the user interface for this function, you may ask questions such as, "What screens are necessary to accomplish this function?" or "How would you prefer to navigate from one screen to the other?" or "Do you need any reporting tools to verify quality of the process?" and so on. If the system will replace existing interfaces, they are a good starting point, as long as you keep in mind that they are being replaced for a good reason. Maybe they are obsolete and inefficient, maybe the existing process is being replaced with a new reengineered one, and so on. Make sure that you critique and discuss these interfaces carefully so that you benefit from them, without carrying any of the old baggage associated with them.

The user interface requirements are modeled using the Function Hierarchy Diagrammer. I discussed earlier that a separate branch should be created in this diagrammer to represent these requirements. In the case of the application system TASC OMS (REQ) I recommended that you load earlier, the root of the user interface requirements is the function OMSUI–OMS User Interface Requirements.

The number of user interface functions may be large, especially for complex systems. In order to better understand and document these functions, they need to be grouped into hierarchical groups. The user interface functions can be grouped hierarchically in many ways. The simplest one is to group together user interface functions that are part of each subsystem. For example, the first level of grouping of the OMS user interface functions is the functions OMSUI1–Create and Maintain Orders, OMSUI2–Book Orders, OMSUI3–Pack Order and Schedule Delivery, and OMSUI4–Interface with Business Partners.

Suppose now that after appropriate research and discussions with users, you identified the interface required to implement the function OMSUI1–Create and Maintain Orders as follows:

❑ **Create Order.** Using this function, users will create a new order and the line items associated with it. Besides entering information directly related to the order, they will be able to associate it with other data, such as customer, payment, and delivery information.

❑ **Maintain Existing Order.** Through this interface, users will be able to retrieve an order that already exists in the database and update its data elements. It includes the ability to retrieve and edit the line items and other information associated with the order.

❑ **Report Ordering Information.** Under this option, users will be able to run three reports that will return useful data about the ordering process. The first report will produce information about orders by ordering customer. The second report will retrieve data for orders placed between two given dates. The third report will return information about orders placed for each product.

❑ **Enter and Maintain Customer Information.** This interface will be used to create new customer records or maintain data about current customers in the system.

The following steps allow you to enter these functions in the application system used as an example in this chapter:

1. Start the Function Hierarchy Diagrammer and open the diagram ORDER MANAGEMENT SYSTEM FHD.
2. Expand the functions OMS, OMSUI, and OMSUI1.
3. Create four functions dependent on OMSUI1. Set the *Label* property of these functions to '*OMSUI11*,' '*OMSUI12*,' '*OMSUI13*,' and '*OMSUI14*.' Use the text in italics from the above list to populate the property *Short Description* of the new functions.
4. For all the functions, except for OMSUI13, display the Edit Function dialog

box, click the Text property tab, and enter in the *Description* property the longer text provided with each function in the list.

13.5.2   IDENTIFYING ELEMENTARY FUNCTIONS

The reason you should not enter the description for the function OMSUI13 is that this function is slightly different from the other three functions. Indeed, by looking carefully at the definitions of these functions, you can conclude that a requirement on OMSUI11, OMSUI12, and OMSUI14 is that they leave the system in a consistent state. For example, OMSUI11 either completes the creation of a new order, with its line items and other associations attached, or rolls it back. Likewise, OMSUI14 updates the information about a customer and commits the data to the database, or cancels the operation and leaves that customer as it was. Furthermore, they cannot be decomposed into smaller subfunctions that enjoy the same property. OMSUI11 may require that several steps be performed so that an order is created, but these should all be performed together. If one of those fails, for example, the order cannot be associated with the customer, and the entire OMSUI11 function cannot complete.

OMSUI13 on the other hand, can be decomposed into subfunctions that can be carried out independently. These subfunctions can be OMSUI131–Orders by Customer, OMSUI132–Orders per Time Window, and OMSUI133–Orders by Product.

Functions like OMSUI11, OMSUI12, OMSUI131, OMSUI132, OMSUI133, and OMSUI14 are called elementary functions. To indicate that a function is elementary, you need to display the Edit Function dialog box and check the checkbox *Elementary* on the Definition property tab. Note that although elementary functions are also atomic functions, the inverse is not true all the time. Until the requirements analysis is complete, some functions may not be decomposed, simply because you have not had a chance to study them yet. However, by the end of the requirements analysis phase, the user interface functional hierarchy tree must be such that all its "leaves," or atomic functions, are also elementary functions.

Identifying the elementary functions carefully is very important, since the

 Another common property of all the functions in the user interface model is *Response*, which must be set to *'Immediate.'* This property is located on the Definition property tab of the Edit Function dialog box. The other properties that are part of the group Frequency on this tab, *Times* and *Unit*, are used mostly during business area analysis, but do not have a major impact on the requirements definition or other stages in the system development life cycle.

Application Design Wizard converts them into screen and reports modules, through which users will access the system. The functionality of these functions must cover completely the objectives and functionality of the system. Gaps in the definition of elementary functions will result in functionality that the system will not deliver. On the other hand, discrepancies and lack of standards will result in an inconsistent user interface. The application system TASC OMS (REQ) provided in the archive file OMSREQS.DMP on the companion CD-ROM contains, together with the other requirements, all the user interface functions defined for this system. You can download this file from the HTML page of the CD-ROM browsing utility by following the links *Software* and *Order Management System Requirements*. Import the file and restore the application system in your Repository to see the information provided in it.

13.6 SUMMARY

The activities to design and develop an information system begin with the analysis of business requirements that the system will satisfy. These requirements are in general related but not identical to all the requirements that must be met by a business process. This chapter explains how you use Designer/2000 to analyze and document the functional requirements and the user interface requirements of the system. Important topics discussed in this chapter include:

- ❑ **Business Requirements and System Requirements**
  - ❑ User Interface Requirements
  - ❑ Data Requirements
  - ❑ Functional Requirements
  - ❑ Security Requirements
  - ❑ Intersystem Interface Requirements
  - ❑ Documentation Requirements
  - ❑ Physical Environment and Resources Requirements
  - ❑ Reliability, Availability, and Serviceability Requirements
- ❑ **Using Designer/2000 in Requirements Analysis**
- ❑ **Building the High-Level System Model**
  - ❑ Defining the First Decomposition of the System
  - ❑ Defining the User Roles
  - ❑ Defining the Subsystems
  - ❑ Defining the Major System Data Entities and Flows
- ❑ **Documenting the High-Level System Design**
- ❑ **Defining the User Interface Requirements**
  - ❑ Defining the Hierarchy
  - ❑ Identifying Elementary Functions

Chapter 14

DATA MODELING

- Techniques and Approaches to Data Modeling
- Entity Modeling
- Domains in Designer/2000
- Relationship Modeling
- Normalization and Denormalization of Data
- Data Modeling for Data Warehouses
- Maintaining Multiple Data Models
- Summary

The data model is a cornerstone for every computer system, because it describes the entities that the system will create and maintain during its lifetime. Building the data model is probably the most important activity during requirements definition, because in the process of understanding how the data is organized and identifying the relationships that exist between entities, you can discover most of the functionality that the system will satisfy. The data model of a business area tends to be relatively stable, compared, for example, to the set of operational procedures or organizational structure, which changes frequently. Therefore, basing the implementation of the future system upon a well-defined data model is a good first step towards developing a system that meets the real requirements of the users.

14.1 TECHNIQUES AND APPROACHES TO DATA MODELING

Two techniques are used interchangeably to model the data of a system: entity relationship modeling and data normalization. The first one aims at identifying the entities that are part of the system, the attributes that make up these entities, and the dependencies between entities. The second one, normalization, makes the data model created using the first technique more robust and extends the life of systems based on the model. Both these techniques go hand in hand and should be applied conscientiously during data modeling activities.

You can take one of two approaches to data modeling: top-down or bottom-up. When you follow the first one, the entities are identified first, then the relationships among them are discovered, and the attributes that should be stored for each entity are defined. In the bottom-up approach, user views of data are collected and analyzed. These may be paper forms that the system will replace, computer screens, reports, and so on. Each data item in these views is analyzed and understood. Then all the little pieces are synthesized together as attributes of entities. Relationships between the entities are discovered in the process. Often both approaches are followed simultaneously, and data normalization principles are applied consistently until a satisfactory data model is created.

In the previous chapters, you were exposed to entity relationship diagramming in a top-down approach. The following sections will combine it with the bottom-up approach to analyze the data items in TASC's new purchase order. In the process, important concepts related to data normalization will be discussed.

14.2 ENTITY MODELING

Chapter 9 introduced entity relationship (ER) modeling in the context of strategic planning as the activity through which you identify and document the information model of the enterprise. ER modeling is also one of the major activities during the analysis and definition of requirements of an information system. In this context, ER modeling allows you to map data from the business world into structures that can be created and maintained by the system. In the particular case when the system uses a relational database to store the data, ER modeling aims to identify and define the following information:

❑ Data about data
❑ Entities
❑ Attributes for each entity
❑ Relationships between entities

The following sections discuss each of these topics.

14.2.1 COLLECTING DATA ABOUT DATA

Any information system you develop manipulates data that correspond to objects or people in real life, such as orders, warehouses, students, and customers. These data are stored in the form of records in database tables. In order to build these tables so that they form a well-performing system, you need to collect and analyze information about the data you will store in them. The information about data used to define database tables is also known as metadata. The amount and complexity of metadata you collect and analyze depends obviously on the complexity of the system, but also on the amount of resources that you can dedicate to the effort. Examples of metadata items include the following:

❑ Name of a data record type. This generally serves as the basis for the name of the entity or table that implements that record type.
❑ Number of initial records, average number of records, maximum number of records, and expected yearly growth rate of records for a given type.
❑ Name, data type, and length of each attribute within a record type.
❑ Constraints for data elements, such as whether they can contain NULL values or whether they uniquely identify a record.
❑ Relationship between record types.

Metadata information can be collected and stored in a variety of ways and forms, starting from pencil-drawn notes scribbled on pieces of paper, to tables created and maintained with word processing packages, to full-blown data modeling and database design tools. However, for information systems with a relevant level of complexity, a Repository-driven data modeling tool like the Entity Relationship Diagrammer is the most efficient way to create and maintain the metadata. The following sections will discuss how you can use the Entity Relationship Diagrammer to create entities, their attributes, and relationships among entities, based on metadata information collected during the system requirements and analysis phase.

14.2.2 CREATING AND MAINTAINING ENTITIES

For the purpose of requirements analysis of a system, entities are business objects or events for which the system will store and manage data. In the OMS, for example, Customer, Order, and Product are entities. Assuming that the system will not process payroll information for the employees of TASC, Salary and Health Benefit are not modeled as entities of the system. Previous chapters showed how you can use the Entity Relationship Diagrammer to create entities. This section will briefly summarize the process of setting the properties and specifying the metadata of entities.

The properties of an entity are organized in the Edit Entity dialog box in the form of several property tabs. In the Definition tab of this dialog, you can enter and maintain the following properties:

❑ *Name.* This is the primary business name by which the object or event represented by the entity is known. It is normally a singular noun like VENDOR, CUSTOMER, or ORDER.

❑ *Short Name.* This is an abbreviation of an entity's name used primarily by Designer/2000 tools, such as the Database Design Transformer or different front-end generators, to name objects that reference the entity. Assuming, for example, that the value of this property for entity EMPLOYEE is EMP, the Database Design Transformer will name the primary key of the corresponding table EMP_PK; the Oracle Forms generator will use EMP as the basis for the name of any blocks based on this table.

❑ *Plural.* This property is used to name the database table that will be created by the Database Design Transformer based on the properties of an entity.

❑ *Volume.* This is a group of four properties (*Initial, Average, Maximum,* and *Growth Rate*) that you can use to record the initial number of records for the entity when the system becomes operational, the average and maximum number of records during the life of the system, and the yearly growth rate in percentage points. This information is used when planning the storage needs and the capacity of the system.

❑ *C++ Class Name.* This property is used by the C++ Class Generator to name the class that will represent persistent objects corresponding to the entity in C++ applications. As you will see in Chapter 30, this generator provides a utility that sets this property to the name of the entity for all the entities in the C++ class set. Therefore, you will have to set this property only when you want it to be different from its default value.

The Definition tab contains most of the properties that you will set for entities during requirements definition. Other tabs of the Edit Entity dialog box used for defining metadata of entities are Synonyms and Text. The Synonyms tab is used to document other names by which the users' community recognizes the entity, in addition to its primary name. The Text tab allows you to enter and maintain a description of the entity from the business perspective in the *Description* property. This is used primarily in reports presented to users in order to ensure that the analysis has captured the correct information about the entity. *Notes* is the other text property accessible from the Text tab. This property is used to record information about the entity addressed primarily to the designers and developers of the system. As you will see in Chapter 15, this property is used to record business rules that will be implemented programmatically rather than declaratively by one of the Designer/2000 generators.

14.2.3 CREATING AND MAINTAINING ATTRIBUTES

In general, attributes are characteristics about the entity that the system will populate with values and maintain during its life. For examples, First Name, Last Name, Phone, Fax, and Email may be some attributes (characteristics) of the entity Customer. For each persistent instance of the entity stored in the database, its attributes may contain data values. These values may be numeric, alphanumeric, date, and other types of values. They may have a defined length, they may be required or optional for each record, they may uniquely identify the record, and so on. During requirements analysis activities, you need to identify and document all this information, or metadata, for each attribute. The Edit Entity dialog box of the Entity Relationship Diagrammer is an important interface through which you enter the attributes' metadata in the Repository. The property tabs Attributes, Att Detail, and Att Values of this dialog box used in the process are discussed in the rest of this section.

The Attributes tab is used primarily to create attributes of an entity. Its spreadsheet layout allows you to view up to nine attributes at a time and is designed to optimize the process of initial creation of attributes and subsequent sequencing of them within the entity. Figure 14.1 shows an example of the Attributes property tab.

In order to create a new attribute on this tab, either click the first empty record in the list, or click the button Insert Row. To remove an attribute from the entity, select it from the list and click the button Delete Row. The following paragraphs describe the properties that you can access and set on the Attributes tab:

❑ *Name.* This is the name of the attribute. It can be entered in natural language format, as in 'LAST NAME' or 'ORDER DATE.' The Database Design Transformer, which maps attributes to database columns, will convert these names into computer language format, as in 'LAST_NAME' or 'ORDER_ DATE.'

❑ *Seq.* This property determines the order in which attributes exist within the entity. If not defined, the attributes will be stored and displayed in alphabetical order. I recommend that you use numbers with gaps between them

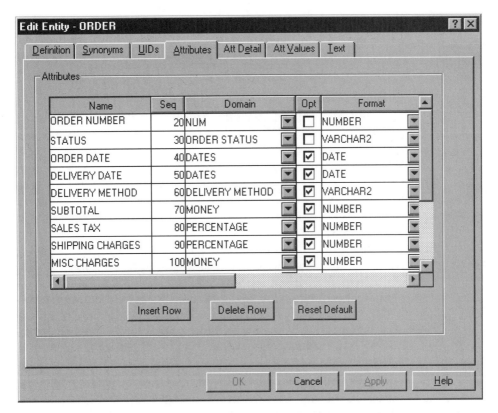

FIGURE 14.1 The Attributes property tab of the Edit Entity dialog box.

to set the property *Seq* of attributes, since they will minimize your work when modifying the sequence order of attributes. Indeed, imagine an entity with four attributes whose *Seq* property is set to '1,' '2,' '3,' and '4.' To insert a fifth attribute in the second position, you will have to modify the sequence order of the last three attributes. If, on the other hand, you set the *Seq* property to '10,' '20,' '30,' and '40,' you can easily insert the new attribute in the second position by setting its *Seq* property to '15.'

❑ *Domain*. This drop-down list allows you to assign the attribute to an existing domain defined in the Repository. Assigning attributes to a domain is a way to standardize properties of data elements in your system. The process of creating and maintaining domains in the Repository will be discussed in more detail in Section 14.3.

❑ *Opt*. When this check box is checked, the attribute is optional, meaning that it can have NULL values for an instance of the entity. When the property is not checked, the attribute is mandatory.

❑ *Format.* This, in a way, indicates the type of data represented by the attribute. Despite the number of options you can select from this list box, only some of them are widely used. VARCHAR2 attributes contain alphanumeric data of variable length; CHAR attributes are for alphanumeric data of fixed length; NUMBER attributes are used for numeric data; and DATE attributes are used for date items. Other formats of attributes less often used are TIME, MONEY, IMAGE, PHOTOGRAPH, SOUND, TEXT, and VIDEO.

❑ *MaxLen.* This property contains the maximum length of data that the attribute can contain. This property is required for some format types, like CHAR and VARCHAR2. For other format types, like NUMBER or DATE, a default setting exists for the property, which you can override by setting *MaxLen* explicitly. Other format types, like IMAGE, PHOTOGRAPH, SOUND, TEXT, and VIDEO, cannot be constrained by a setting of the *MaxLen* property. For attributes of this type, the property *MaxLen* cannot be set explicitly.

❑ *Dec.* The setting of this property is meaningful only for attributes of format type NUMBER and MONEY (for attributes of this last format, the property *Dec* is required). It allows you to specify the precision after the decimal point, that is, the number of digits after the decimal point that the attribute will accept. If, for example, the maximum length of an attribute is 6 digits and the precision is 2, the attribute will accept values such as 89.99 or 1323.55, but it will not allow values such as 32.998 or 34543.99.

❑ *Primary.* This property, in the form of a check-box item, allows you to indicate that an attribute is part of the primary unique identifier of the entity.

❑ *Comment.* You can use this property to describe the meaning, purpose, or other special characteristics of the attribute. The Database Design Transformer and Application Design Transformer use this property to set the Hint property—an explanation about the meaning of the attribute—for user interface items that implement this attribute. Careful setting of this property during the requirements analysis may save you a lot of time during the system design and development.

Ultimately, the attributes of an entity will be implemented as columns in database tables. The setting of the *Format* property and the type of database in which the table is implemented will define the data type of the corresponding column. Figure 14.2 shows the correspondence between settings of the *Format* property for attributes and the *Datatype* property for columns in an Oracle database. Figure 14.3 maps the *Format* property to the *Datatype* property for ANSI databases.

14.2.4 MAINTAINING DETAILED PROPERTIES FOR ATTRIBUTES

As I mentioned earlier, the Attributes tab is intended to quickly create the attributes of an entity and define their most important properties. Its multi-record, spreadsheet-like layout displays by default only the first four properties dis-

FORMAT PROPERTY SETTINGS	COLUMN DATA TYPES FOR ORACLE DATABASES
NUMBER, MONEY	NUMBER
INTEGER	INTEGER
CHAR, VARCHAR2	VARCHAR2
TEXT	LONG
DATE, TIME, TIMESTAMP	DATE
IMAGE, PHOTOGRAPH, SOUND, VIDEO	LONG RAW

FIGURE 14.2 The mapping between settings of the Format property of attributes and the Datatype property of Oracle database columns.

cussed in the previous section. You need to scroll the tabs in order to view the remaining properties. The property tab Att Detail, on the other hand, presents all the properties of an attribute in a form layout. Figure 14.4 shows an example of settings in this tab.

The Att Detail property tab allows you to view and modify the properties of a single attribute. The name of the attribute is selected from the list box Name at the top of the tab. The check box Primary UID, when set, indicates that the attribute is part of the primary unique identifier of the entity. The check box Optional? indicates whether the attribute is mandatory or not. These properties are equivalent to the check boxes Primary and Opt in the Attributes tab.

The items Initial and Average in the group Percentage Used indicate the percentage of record instances of the entity, for which the attribute will contain a non-NULL value. Understandably, these properties are both set to 100 for mandatory attributes, to indicate that every record will contain values in such attributes. For optional attributes, these properties are set by default to 50. One of the goals during the analysis of system requirements is to adjust this setting to a

FORMAT PROPERTY SETTINGS	COLUMN DATA TYPES FOR ANSI DATABASES
NUMBER, MONEY	NUMERIC
INTEGER	INTEGER
CHAR, VARCHAR2	VARCHAR
TEXT	LONG
DATE, TIME, TIMESTAMP	DATE
IMAGE, PHOTOGRAPH, SOUND, VIDEO	BLOB

FIGURE 14.3 The mapping between settings of the Format property of attributes and the Datatype property of ANSI database columns.

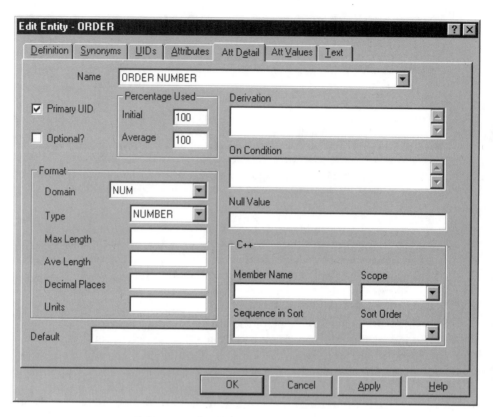

FIGURE 14.4   The Att Detail property tab.

value closer to reality. If, for example, you expect 95 percent of the orders to have a value in the ORDER DATE attribute and only 20 percent of these orders to contain special instructions in the attribute DESCR, then the *Average Percentage Used* property for these attributes should be set to '95' and '20,' respectively. These properties, together with entity-level properties in the Volume group of the Entity tab, are transferred by the Database Design Transformer to the table that corresponds to the entity and are used to estimate the size of tables and indexes in the physical implementation of the database.

Most of the properties in the group Format on the left side of Att Detail tab are present in the Attributes tab, including *Domain, Format Type, Max Length*, and *Decimal Places*. In addition, this group contains the property labeled *Ave Length* to store the average length of data for the attribute, and the property *Units* to better qualify the contents of the attribute.

If you can identify a value for an attribute that is used by a good number of instances of an entity, you can enter this value in the property *Default*. The setting is transferred to the column of the corresponding database table by the Database Design Transformer and the Server Generator. The front-end generators create user interface modules that populate this attribute in new records with the default value. Because the setting of the *Default* property will be applied to database records whenever the value of the corresponding attribute is not set explicitly, be careful when setting this property. Attributes with this property set always contain values, either explicitly set or implicitly derived from the *Default* property. Therefore, this property is usually set only for required attributes.

Null Value is another property that is rarely set for attributes. It is intended for cases when, by convention, a special character or series of characters will be used to indicate the absence of data for the attribute. In Oracle-based systems, this situation is normally handled by setting the attribute to NULL.

The Att Detail property tab contains two properties intended to document business rules that affect the attribute. You may use the property *Derivation* to describe how the value of the attribute is derived. The *On Condition* property is used to describe the conditions under which values of an optional attribute are generated. Although descriptions entered in these properties are closely related to the attribute, in general, the business rules that affect the attribute are documented in the *Notes* text field of the entity. This property is chosen for two principal reasons. First, all the business rules that affect the entity and all its attributes are documented in one location. Second, several business rules may affect more than one attribute; therefore, they should not be attached to any particular attribute. Chapter 15 will discuss in more detail the documentation of business rules related to entities and attributes.

Finally, the Att Detail tab contains four properties that affect the code created by the C++ Object Layer Generator. These properties, located in the lower right-hand corner of the tab, under group C++, are called *Member Name, Scope, Sequence in Sort,* and *Sort Order*. The property *Member Name* is normally set to the name of the attribute; the C++ Object Layer Generator comes with a utility that automatically sets this property to the attribute name for you. By default, the class member that corresponds to the attribute is a public member. To override this setting, set the property *Scope* to 'Private' or 'Protected.' If you want the C++ Query method for the class to return the records sorted by the values of one or more of its attributes, set the property *Sequence in Sort* for each of these attributes. By selecting 'Ascending' or 'Descending' from the list *Sort Order*, you may specify the order in which these records will be returned.

14.2.5 SPECIFYING ALLOWABLE VALUES FOR ATTRIBUTES

As explained earlier, the property *Default* is used to specify an attribute value used by a considerable number of entity instances. If the values of an attribute can be enumerated or fall in a well defined range, you can enter these allowable values on the Att Values property tab. This tab has a spreadtable format to facilitate the process of entering, viewing, and maintaining these values. Figure 14.5

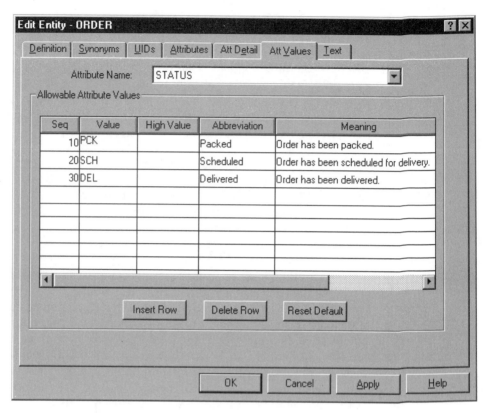

FIGURE 14.5 The Att Values property tab of the Edit Entity dialog box.

shows how you would enter some of the allowable values for the attribute STATUS of the entity PRODUCT ITEM.

The following is a description of the properties in this tab:

❑ *Seq.* This property is used to order the individual values or ranges of allowable values of the attribute.

❑ *Value.* For attributes with enumerated values, this property contains the value of the attribute that will be stored in the database. For attributes with value ranges, the setting of this property corresponds to the lower bound of the range.

❑ *High Value.* When this property is NULL, the allowable value is an enumerated one; otherwise, the setting of the property indicates the upper bound of the range of allowed values.

❑ *Abbreviation.* This property allows you to enter a 20-character description of the value or range.

❑ *Meaning.* This property is used to enter a longer description (up to 60 characters) for the allowed value or range.

The allowed values of an attribute are just another business rule that you need to identify and document during the requirements analysis. Like other business rules, they can be implemented in the database server or in the front-end application, or a combination thereof. In database engines like the Oracle Server, enumerated values are implemented as check constraints. Only the *Sequence, Low Value,* and *High Value* properties are used in this case. In client applications, these values are implemented as elements of list items by front-end code generators. The properties *Abbreviation* and *Meaning* are normally used to populate the values with which users will interact in these applications. For this reason, you must carefully choose the words you use to set these properties.

14.3 DOMAINS IN DESIGNER/2000

Often, more than one attribute shares common format properties and allowable values. For example, several numeric attributes in your system may express currency values. Setting the format properties for each individual attribute not only will be a waste of effort but may also lead to inconsistencies. On the other hand, several entities may contain attributes to hold their name and description. Although you can define the data type and length of these attributes individually, your database and user interface applications will gain consistency if you set these properties to common values for similar attributes. Designer/2000 provides a separate type of object, called domain, which allows you to specify properties such as *Datatype* and *Length* only once at the domain level, and inherit them for each attribute or column included in the domain. The following sections will discuss the process of creating and using domains in Designer/2000.

14.3.1 CREATING DOMAINS

Domains are Repository objects that can be created and maintained from the Repository Object Navigator, the Entity Relationship Diagrammer, and the Design Editor. To access the domains and their properties in the Entity Relationship Diagrammer, select Edit | Domains.... This action displays the dialog box Domains, which has four property tabs. The Definition tab has a tabular layout optimized for creating, listing, renaming, or deleting the domains of an application system. An example of this tab is shown in Figure 14.6. The major actions performed on this tab are described below.

❑ **Create a new domain object.** To create a domain, either click at the first empty record in the list of existing domains or place the cursor in an exist-

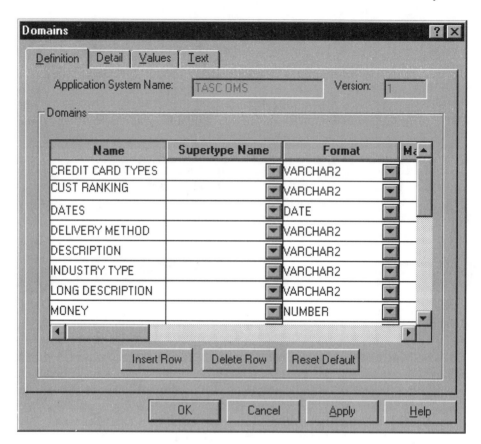

FIGURE 14.6   The Definition tab of the Domains dialog box.

ing row and click the button Insert Row. In the new record, specify the
name and other properties of the domain.

❑   **Subtype a domain.** The main purpose of domains is to allow one or more at-
     tributes and columns to inherit properties from the same source. Domains
     themselves may inherit their properties from other domains by becoming
     subtypes of these supertype domains. You subtype a domain by selecting the
     name of an existing domain from the list Supertype Name of that domain.

❑   **Rename a domain.** In order to rename a domain, simply click in the text box
     Name and enter the new name.

❑   **Delete a domain.** To delete a domain, select it from the list of available do-
     mains and click Delete Row. Note that the delete will succeed only if the do-
     main is not referenced by other objects in the Repository. As in other cases
     when an object cannot be deleted because it is referenced by other objects,
     your alternatives are either to remove these references and delete the do-

main, or to apply a cascade delete, that is, delete the domain and all the objects that reference it. The latter option can be implemented only in the Repository Objects Navigator, by selecting the domain and choosing Utilities | Force Delete....

14.3.2 MAINTAINING PROPERTIES OF DOMAINS

The Definition tab allows you to specify some format properties of the domain as well, but viewing and maintaining these properties is easier on the Detail tab. Figure 14.7 contains an example of this tab.

This tab displays detailed properties of a single domain object. You can select the name of the domain from the list box *Name* at the top of the property tab. The left-hand side of the tab allows you to set properties such as *Null Value, Default, Units,* and *Derivation*. These properties are identical in meaning and pur-

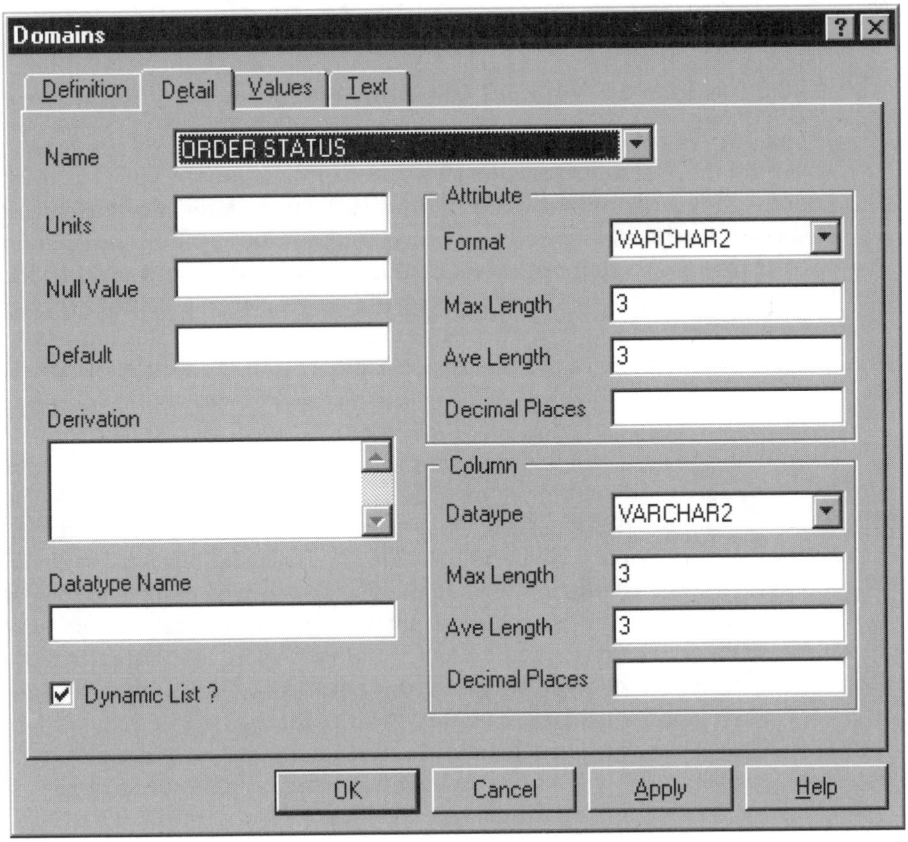

FIGURE 14.7   The Detail property tab of the Domains dialog box.

pose to the attribute properties with the same name discussed in Section 14.2.4. In addition, this side of the tab contains two properties used by code generators to implement items assigned to the given domain. The first one, *Datatype Name*, is essential for creating C++ classes to access your data using the C++ Object Layer Generator. This generator requires each attribute to be in a domain and the property *Datatype Name* of this domain to be set to a C++ data type recognized by the generator. The second property, *Dynamic List?*, is significant when the domain contains allowable values. Windows applications usually represent these values in the form of drop-down lists or text lists. By setting the property *Dynamic List?*, you enable the front-end generators to populate these items dynamically rather than hard-coding the values in the application.

The right-hand side of the Detail tab contains format properties for the domain. Since domains are used to drive properties of attributes and columns, the format properties of domains are organized into the Attribute Format group and Column Format group. When defining the system's requirements, you need to collect and enter format information about attributes. In the system design and development stages, you use the column definitions.

14.3.3 ALLOWED VALUES OF A DOMAIN

A major reason for using domains is to associate allowed values or ranges of values with an attribute. As you saw earlier in the chapter, you can associate such values with each individual attribute. However, if several attributes share the same set of values, you end up reentering them for each attribute. A better solution is to create a domain object that contains these values and include each attribute in the domain. The process of entering allowable values or ranges for domains is very similar to that of entering values for attributes and is done on the Values property tab of the dialog box Domains. In the example shown in Figure 14.8, the domain ORDER STATUS contains several allowable values to represent different states of an order, such as Entered, Booked, and Packed.

The question whether you should associate allowable values or ranges with an attribute or with a domain must be carefully evaluated when entering the data model in the Repository. As a rule of thumb, whenever you can identify a set of values for an attribute, defining them in a domain and placing the attribute in the domain is better. If, during further analysis and enhancements to the data model, you discover that another attribute shares the same values, all you have to do is include this attribute in the domain. If the values are associated with the first attribute instead, when you encounter the second attribute, you have to repeat the task, often laborious, of entering these values for the new attribute.

One of the ways in which you can leverage the advantage of domains is to create domains in which you can include a large number of attributes. For example, a domain called NAME of type VARCHAR2, maximum length 80 and average length 30, could well describe a large number of attributes, from an address line to the name of a software product. A domain called DESCRIPTION of type

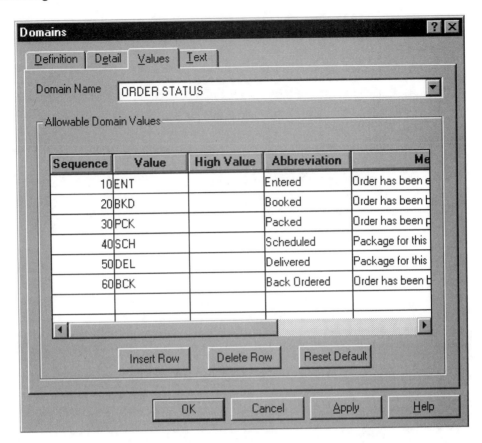

FIGURE 14.8 The Values property tab of the Domains dialog box.

VARCHAR2 and maximum length 240 could drive the properties of all the descriptive attributes in the system. Domains like SHORT NAME, LONG DESCRIPTION, and others like these could also be very useful. Establishing and using them consistently from the earliest stages of requirements definition can save you a lot of effort and help you design and develop consistent applications with a consistent interface.

14.3.4 MAINTAINING DOMAINS IN THE DESIGN EDITOR

Domains are important objects not only for data modeling activities but also for database design tasks. Therefore, the Design Editor allows you to create new domains and maintain existing ones from its components. The following steps will allow you to create a new domain in the Design Navigator:

1. Select the tab DB Objects and expand the node Domains.
2. Click the icon Use Dialogs in the Design Editor's toolbar to ensure that it is in pushed state .
3. Click the icon Create . The dialog box Create Domain appears.
4. Enter the name of the domain and click Next.
5. Set the data type, length, and any default value you want to associate with the domain. Click Next.
6. Enter any allowed values to be associated with the domain. Also specify whether you want the front-end generators to create modules that query these values from database structures at runtime, or that have these values hard coded in their body.
7. Click Finish to complete the process.

To edit the properties of an existing domain, double-click its characteristic icon on the Design Navigator. The dialog box Edit Domain that appears has the

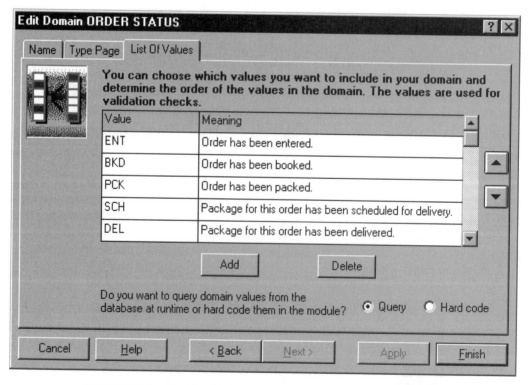

FIGURE 14.9   The List Of Values tab of the Edit Domain dialog box.

same three property tabs that you go through when you define the domain. Figure 14.9 shows the tab List Of Values of this dialog box. As you can easily notice, the Edit Domain dialog box implemented by the Design Editor has a simpler and friendlier interface than the dialog box with the same name implemented invoked from the Repository Object Navigator.

14.3.5 UPDATING PROPERTIES INHERITED FROM DOMAINS

When an attribute or column is initially included in a domain, the values for properties such as *Datatype*, *Maximum Length*, or the list of allowable values are copied from the domain. If, during the data modeling and database design activities, you need to modify the properties of a domain, the new settings of properties will not cascade automatically to the attributes and columns in the domain. In order to update the properties of these objects, you need to follow these steps:

1. Launch the Repository Object Navigator.
2. Expand the node Domains in the hierarchy tree.
3. Select one or more domains that have been modified.
4. Select Utilities | Update Attributes in Domain.
5. Select Utilities | Update Columns in Domain.

In the Design Editor you can update only columns in a domain by selecting the domain in the Design Navigator and choosing Utilities | Update Columns in Domain.

14.4 RELATIONSHIP MODELING

In system requirements analysis, relationships represent associations between data entities that will be stored and managed by the system. As explained in Chapter 9, each relationship has two relationship ends, one for each entity it connects. Each relationship end is characterized by properties such as *Name*, *Cardinality*, and *Optionality*. Based on the cardinality of each relationship end, relationships are grouped in one-to-one, one-to-many, and many-to-many relationships. The process of creating relationships and maintaining their properties in the context of defining the enterprise data model was presented in Chapter 9. The same tasks are performed when the data model is defined as part of the requirements of an information system. Therefore, the following two sections will discuss only the following activities that occur more frequently in the second context:

❑ Resolving many-to-many relationships in the data diagrams
❑ Including relationship ends in the primary unique identifier of an entity

14.4.1 RESOLVING MANY-TO-MANY RELATIONSHIPS

The data model of an information system is not considered complete if it contains many-to-many relationships between its entities. This type of relationship is more common in high-level data models, although finding them even after the data model is detailed and normalized is not unusual. Figure 14.10 shows two examples of many-to-many relationships in the OMS data model. The first one exists between the entities ORDER and CUSTOMER. It expresses the fact that a customer may place multiple orders and that many customers may be involved during the life of an order. The second many-to-many relationship is between entities ORDER and PRODUCT and indicates the fact that an order may be for one or more products and a product may be requested in one or more orders.

The process of eliminating many-to-many relationships is called resolving these relationships. Many-to-many relationships between two entities are resolved by following these steps:

1. Introduce a third entity, called the intersection entity.
2. Delete the many-to-many relationship between the two original entities.
3. Create two one-to-many relationships between the original entities and the newly added entity. The many side of both these relationships must end at the intersection entity and must be mandatory. The one side of the relationships ends at the original entities and may be optional or mandatory.

The intersection entities that resolve many-to-many relationships often represent legitimate entities that are encountered in the real world. For example, in the data model shown in Figure 14.11, the entity LINE ITEM is an intersection entity that resolves a many-to-many relationship between ORDER and PRODUCT. At the same time, it is an entity with which any user of the system is familiar. In other cases, the intersection entity is less real. For example, the entity that re-

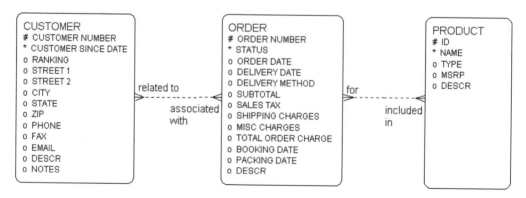

FIGURE 14.10 Examples of many-to-many relationships between entities.

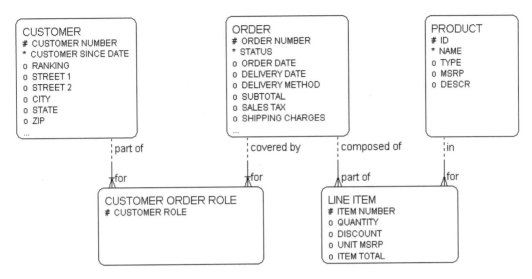

FIGURE 14.11 Resolving many-to-many relationships by introducing an intersection entity.

solves the many-to-many relationship between CUSTOMER and ORDER can be called CUSTOMER ORDER ROLE. One attribute that could be defined in this entity is CUSTOMER ROLE, which tells whether the customer associated with the record is the person placing the order, paying for it, or receiving the product. Figure 14.11 shows how the data model looks after the many-to-many relationship is resolved.

From the description of the relationship between entities CUSTOMER and ORDER, you can see that an order can be associated with up to three customers at any one time. No limit exists, on the other hand, on the number of orders that a customer can place, pay for, and receive. Technically, the relationship between these two entities is many-to-many, although the cardinality of the ORDER end of the relationship end is a finite, low number (three in this case.) Such many-to-many relationships are often resolved by introducing several one-to-many relationships instead of a third intersection entity. Figure 14.12 shows the three relationships that may be created between entities CUSTOMER and ORDER instead of the entity CUSTOMER ORDER ROLE.

Each of the approaches described above has its own benefits and drawbacks. The first one is the most generic solution and will always work, no matter how large the cardinality of each relationship end is. However, an extra entity is required, which results in added complexity in the applications and in slower performance of the queries that join data from the entities CUSTOMER and ORDER. The second approach simplifies the complexity of the applications and queries, since a direct relationship exists between the ORDER and the CUS-

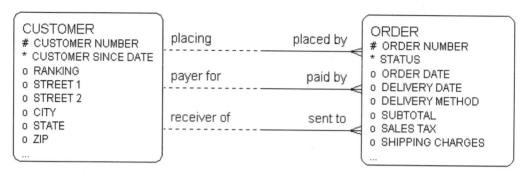

FIGURE 14.12 Resolving many-to-many relationships by introducing multiple one-to-many relationships.

TOMER that places it, pays for it, or receives the ordered products. On the other hand, this approach is beneficial only if the cardinality of the relationship end is small and is not expected to change during the life of the system. A system built on the data model shown in Figure 14.12 will not be able to support a new type of relationship between orders and customers that may evolve over time, without structural changes. A system built on the data model presented in Figure 14.11 can easily accommodate the new relationship by adding a new role type in the entity CUSTOMER ORDER ROLE. Deciding on the approach to take requires that the advantages and disadvantages of each alternative be considered carefully. The solution should be seen as part of the larger issue of normalizing and denormalizing the data model of a system, which will be discussed in Section 14.5.

14.4.2 INCLUDING RELATIONSHIPS IN UNIQUE IDENTIFIERS

In Figure 14.11, notice that the intersection entity CUSTOMER ORDER ROLE contains only one attribute. Nevertheless, each instance of this entity must uniquely identify one customer and one order. You have two ways to express this fact in the Entity Relationship Diagrammer. The first one is to create the attributes that make up the primary unique identifiers for CUSTOMER and ORDER in the intersection entity and make them part of the primary unique identifier of this entity. The second one is to make the relationships of the intersection entity with the other two entities part of the primary unique identifier. When relationships are part of the primary unique identifier, the Entity Relationship Diagrammer draws a vertical bar across the relationship line as a visual indicator of this fact on the diagram, as seen in Figure 14.11.

Including relationships in the definition of the primary unique identifier is preferable to creating duplicate attributes. Indeed, if the definition of the primary unique identifier for the entity on the other end of the relationship changes, no changes should occur in the intersection entity, if the relationship is part of its primary unique identifier.

When relationship ends are part of unique identifiers for an entity, they are often used in combination with attributes of that entity. In the case of the entity CUSTOMER ORDER ROLE, for example, since an association between a customer and an order may exist in three contexts, depending on the roles of the customer in the order, just the relationships are not enough to uniquely identify an instance of the entity. But if the attribute CUSTOMER ROLE is added to this combination, then you have a unique identifier.

The unique identifiers of an entity are maintained on the UIDs property tab of the Edit Entity dialog box, shown in Figure 14.13. To create a new unique identifier, click an empty row in the two-column spreadsheet Unique Identifiers or click the Insert UID button. To make a unique identifier a primary unique identifier, select the check box Primary? as in Figure 14.13.

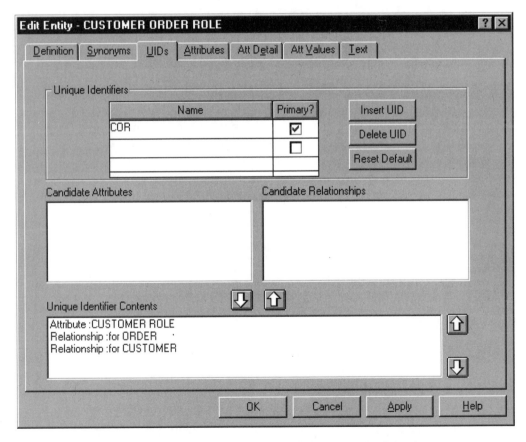

FIGURE 14.13 The UIDs property tab of the Edit Entity dialog box.

The lower half of the property tab is used to specify the elements of the unique identifier. The selection boxes Candidate Attributes and Candidate Relationships list all the attributes and the relationships whose many end terminates at the entity. To add one of these attributes or relationships to the definition of the unique identifier, simply select it and click the Include iconic button ⊞. The element is removed from the list of candidates and added to the list Unique Identifier Contents. To remove a component of the unique identifier, select it from this list and click the Exclude button ⊟. The diagrammer places the element in the appropriate list box, depending on its type.

14.5 NORMALIZATION AND DENORMALIZATION OF DATA

The picture that the users of your systems have about the data is formed from forms, reports, graphs, charts, and other business-related representations. It is often referred to as the business view of data, to distinguish it from the system view, which is the way the items and records of data are physically stored in the system. Although the business views are more closely related to the business functionality of the system, they usually have a moderate to high level of complexity. Furthermore, they are not stable and are characterized by redundant storage and replication of data elements. System data, on the other hand, are stored in smaller and simpler structures that are maintained more easily. The process of transforming complex business views into simpler and more stable data structures is called data normalization. It is performed following these steps:

1. Start with unnormalized data contained in business views.
2. Transform entities in the First Normal Form by moving repeating groups of attributes into separate entities.
3. Transform entities in the Second Normal Form by moving attributes that are partially dependent on the primary unique identifier into separate entities.
4. Transform entities in the Third Normal Form by moving attributes that depend on other nonkey attributes into separate entities.

The following sections will discuss the process of data normalization with an example from the OMS system.

14.5.1 UNNORMALIZED DATA

Figure 14.14 shows the new order that TASC's reengineering team designed. Starting with a top-down approach, you can easily identify at least two entities in this purchase order: CUSTOMER and ORDER. Attributes of CUSTOMER are

American Software Club, Inc.

Serving America's software needs, one customer at a time®
1434 North Main Avenue
Farifax, Virginia, 21102-9087
800.432.2343 Fax 703.546.4343

P.O. NUMBER: 1237545

Bill To:	Ship To:
North American Database Experts, Inc. *P.O. Box 12334* *Arlington, VA 28201-2334* *Customer Number: 10282*	*Julie H. Adams* *2526 North Wayne Street* *Baltimore, MD 32201*

P.O. DATE	CREDIT CARD NO	MONEY ORDER NO	DELIVERY DATE	DELIVERY TERMS
04/23/97			On or before 05/12	FedEx Early Morning

ITEM NO	QTY	DESCRIPTION	UNIT PRICE	TOTAL
1	1	MS Windows 95	$ 98.00	$ 98.00
2	2	Oracle Designer/2000	$2,999.00	$5,998.00
3	3	Oracle Developer/2000	$2,999.00	$8,997.00

SUBTOTAL	$15,093.00
SALES TAX	$ 758.60
SHIPPING & HANDLING	$ 48.99
OTHER	
TOTAL	$15,900.59

ADDITIONAL INSTRUCTIONS:
Please notify us immediately if you are unable to ship as specified. Send all correspondence to:
  Julie H. Adams
  North American Database Experts, Inc.
  2526 North Wayne Street
  Baltimore, MD 32201
  410.211.2334, ext. 320; Fax 410.211.2300

FIGURE 14.14   TASC's new purchase order.

data items such as CUSTOMER NUMBER, NAME, STREET, CITY, STATE, ZIP, PHONE, and FAX. For the TASC environment, CUSTOMER NUMBER uniquely identifies a customer. A combination of NAME and PHONE serves as a unique identifier as well; however, CUSTOMER NUMBER is chosen to be the primary unique identifier of this entity.

Some attributes of the entity ORDER are ORDER NUMBER, ORDER DATE, and DELIVERY DATE. The unique identifier for this entity is ORDER NUMBER. This is also the primary unique identifier, being the only one unique identifier of the entity. Clearly, a many-to-many relationship exists between these two entities. Customers may be related to one or more orders. They may place orders, pay for them, and receive shipments. Thus, each order in the system may be associated with up to three different customers. Sections 14.4.1 and 14.4.2 showed that one way to resolve the many-to-many relationship between CUSTOMER and ORDER is to introduce the intersection entity CUSTOMER ORDER ROLE. Figure 14.15 shows the relationship diagram among these three entities.

14.5.2 FIRST NORMAL FORM

By closely examining the attributes of the entity ORDER in Figure 14.15, you can see that ITEM NUMBER, QUANTITY, PRODUCT, UNIT PRICE, and ITEM TOTAL are repeated for each line item in the purchase order. Clear disadvantages exist to using the entity ORDER in this form. First, you have to set the number of line items to a certain limit for orders. If this limit is set too low, you have orders whose line items you cannot maintain. If, on the other hand, the limit is set

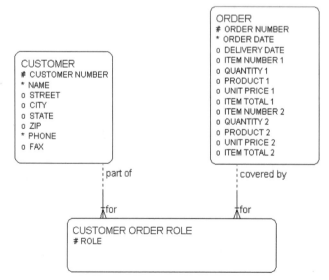

FIGURE 14.15 An example of unnormalized entities.

The diagram shown in Figure 14.15 illustrates the following conventions used by the Entity Relationship Diagrammer to represent attributes of an entity:

❑ Attributes that are part of the primary unique identifier of an entity are preceded by the character '#.' Examples of such attributes are CUSTOMER NUMBER and ORDER NUMBER.

❑ Attributes that are mandatory for the entity are preceded by the character '*.' Examples of mandatory attributes are NAME and ORDER DATE.

❑ Attributes that are optional are preceded by the character '°.' Examples of optional attributes in Figure 14.15 are FAX and DELIVERY DATE.

too high, you have unused data items. Furthermore, if you need to find out whether or not an order contains a software product such as TurboTax in a line item, you have to first retrieve the record for the particular customer, and then scan all the PRODUCT attributes in that record for the desired value.

The anomalies listed above are eliminated by removing repeating attributes or groups of attributes and placing them in a separate entity that has a one-to-many relationship with the original entity. An entity that does not contain repeating attributes or groups of attributes is said to be in the First Normal Form, often abbreviated as 1NF. In the case of the entity ORDER, you would separate the attributes listed above and put them in the entity LINE ITEM. Each order must be composed of one or more line items, and each line item must be part of one and only one order.

Another example of repeating attributes is the address-related data items in the order form shown in Figure 14.14. As you can see from this figure, the same address may correspond to multiple customers. So moving the attributes STREET, CITY, STATE, and ZIP to a separate entity called ADDRESS is better. The unique identifier of the new entity may be the combination of STREET 1 and ZIP. Each customer must be addressed at one and only one address; each address may be for zero or more customers. Figure 14.16 shows the entities discussed here in the First Normal Form.

14.5.3 SECOND NORMAL FORM

An attribute B of an entity E is functionally dependent on attribute A if for every value of A only one value of B exists in the same record. ORDER DATE, for example, is functionally dependent on ORDER NUMBER because for each ORDER

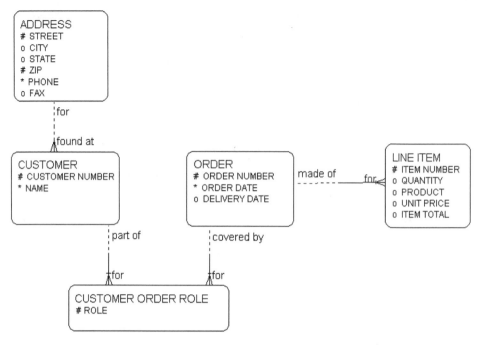

FIGURE 14.16   Entities in the First Normal Form.

NUMBER only one ORDER DATE exists. Since knowing the value of A, ORDER NUMBER in this example, allows you to find the value of B, ORDER DATE, the definition of functional dependency is equivalently stated as "A identifies B." An attribute may be functionally dependent on more than one attribute. For example, the QUANTITY of products ordered in a line item depends on the unique identifier of LINE ITEM, made up by the attribute ITEM NUMBER and the relationship end 'part of' between this entity and ORDER.

   Recall from earlier discussions that an attribute or set of attributes that identifies all the other attributes of an entity is called a unique identifier for the entity. An entity may have more than one unique identifier. One of them is usually given priority over the others and qualified as *primary* unique identifier of the entity. By definition, an entity is in the Second Normal Form (2NF) if it is in the First Normal Form and, in addition, all its attributes depend fully on the primary unique identifier. An entity that contains attributes that depend only on part of the primary unique identifier is not in the Second Normal Form.

   Clearly, every 1NF entity that has only one attribute as primary unique identifier is a 2NF entity as well. Therefore, you must look for entities that are not in the 2NF among those that have more than one attribute in the primary unique identifier. As an example, consider the entity ADDRESS in the example being discussed in these sections. An address is uniquely identified by the street and the ZIP code of the address. Thus, the combination STREET and ZIP is a unique identifier. The attributes STATE and CITY are functionally dependent on the primary unique identifier, but not on the whole identifier. They depend only on ZIP. Indeed, as long as you have a value for ZIP, you can identify the city and state where this ZIP is located.

Entities that are not in the 2NF have their own problems associated with them. First, for all the addresses located in a ZIP code area, you enter the same values for CITY and STATE, thus wasting storage space. In addition, suppose that you need to edit the city or state associated with a particular ZIP code. In the existing situation, you have to edit each address record for that ZIP code.

These problems are avoided by moving the attributes that depend partially on the primary unique identifier to a separate entity that now serves as the parent of the original entity in a one-to-many relationship. What is left of the original entity is in the Second Normal Form. In the example discussed here, you would create the new entity called ZIP CODE with attributes ZIP, CITY, and STATE, and with the primary unique identifier ZIP. A one-to-many relationship is created between entities ZIP CODE and ADDRESS to describe the fact that a ZIP code may be for zero or more addresses, and that each address must be in one and only one ZIP code. Figure 14.17 shows the entity relationship diagram with entities discussed here in the Second Normal Form.

14.5.4 THIRD NORMAL FORM

Some attributes in an entity may depend indirectly on the primary unique identifier of the entity. For example, in the entity LINE ITEM, the attribute UNIT PRICE—the retail price for one unit of a product—depends directly on the attribute PRODUCT. Since PRODUCT itself depends on the unique identifier of LINE ITEM, UNIT PRICE depends indirectly on the primary unique identifier. Dependencies like this, where A depends on C because A depends on B and B depends on C, are called transitive dependencies.

Entities with transitive dependencies represent problems and anomalies. The waste of storage space and update difficulties described in the previous section apply to these entities as well. Furthermore, suppose that a new product just arrived. Under the current model, you have no way to enter its information unless a customer places an order for it. Similarly, if all the orders placed for a product were deleted, the information about the product itself would be lost, thus requiring you to reenter it the next time that product is ordered.

Clearly, by removing the attributes that do not depend directly on the primary unique identifier and placing them in a separate entity called PRODUCT, the product information will be maintained independently of the fact that this product is being ordered or not. The new entity is related to the entity LINE ITEM by a one-to-many relationship, expressing the fact that a product may be ordered under zero or more line items and that a line item must be for a product.

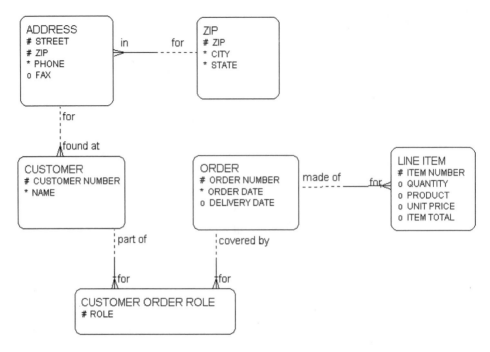

FIGURE 14.17   Entities in the Second Normal Form.

Entities in 2NF that do not contain transitive dependencies are said to be in the Third Normal Form (3NF). An entity in 3NF is such that all its attributes depend on the primary unique identifier, only the primary unique identifier, and nothing but the primary unique identifier. Figure 14.18 shows the entities being discussed here in the Third Normal Form.

Two advantages exist to transforming the data model from an unnormalized form to the Third Normal Form, which are implied in the way the process is conducted. First, as can be seen from the examples provided here, normalizing entities forces you to think about the meaning of the data. In the process, you generate new entities, question and therefore understand each attribute, and identify additional attributes and data rules that may not be visible at first sight. Second, practice has shown over and over again that a data model in the Third Normal Form, by being crisp and clear, is much easier to explain to people who are not familiar with the intricacies of the system.

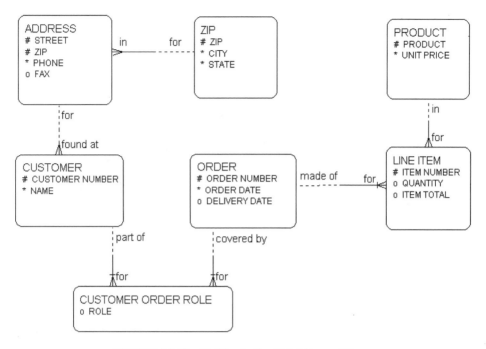

FIGURE 14.18 Entities in the Third Normal Form.

Theoretically, there are at least three other normal forms that are stricter than the Third Normal Form. These are the Boyce-Codd Normal Form (BCNF), the Fourth Normal Form (4NF), and the Fifth Normal Form (5NF). They are discussed usually in works on the theory of databases, such as *Fundamentals of Database Systems* (1994, The Benjamin/Cummings Publishing Company, Inc.) by Elmasri and Navathe. However, from a practical perspective, the data model is considered fully normalized if all the entities in it are in the Third Normal Form.

14.5.5 DENORMALIZATION

If you go back to the previous three sections and read carefully the description of anomalies that each normal form addresses, you will notice that they are related to the lack of flexibility of the data model as new data elements are introduced, the ineffectiveness of data storage, and the inefficiency of data manipulation operations, such as inserts, deletes, and updates. In fact, these were the principal motives behind two seminal papers by Edward F. Codd—*A Relational Model or Data for Large Shared Data Banks* (June 1970, CACM 13-6) and *Further Normalization of the Data Base Relational Model* (in *Data Base Systems*, ed. Randall Rustin,

Prentice Hall, 1972)—which pioneered the relational database theory and technology.

However, as Codd hinted in the conclusion of the second paper mentioned above, a data model in the Third Normal Form, although addressing the important problems mentioned earlier, may require that queries join terms from different entities more often than in a less normalized data model. Relational database management systems, such as Oracle RDBMS, have several tools to improve the performance of queries, such as indexes and different flavors of query optimizers. However, often the database designers are required to deviate consciously from a Third Normal Form model for the sake of data retrieval efficiency. This process is known as denormalization of the data model.

Distinguishing between an unnormalized data model and a denormalized one is important. The first one is where little or no analysis is performed, whereas the second one is arrived at only from a model in the Third Normal Form, after the reasons and impact of denormalizing some entities are identified and weighed. When parts of the data model are denormalized, the rules for maintaining the redundant data must be defined clearly and implemented programmatically, in order to avoid the anomalies discussed in the previous sections. For example, in a denormalized version of the BUSINESS PARTNER entity, ZIP, CITY, and STATE may be defined as attributes of the entity whose value is derived from entity ZIP and stored redundantly with the other address properties of each BUSINESS PARTNER. In order to maintain the data consistency, you may define and later implement the following business rules:

❑ The values of attributes CITY and STATE will be updated only in the entity ZIP. In all the other entities where these attributes are denormalized, applications may insert and select but not modify these attributes.

❑ When the attributes CITY and STATE of entity ZIP are modified, the changes will be propagated in all the denormalized CITY and STATE attributes of other entities.

 E. F. Codd founded the theory of relational databases based on the algebraic theory of relations. Asked several years later why he chose the term "normalization," he answered that at the time (1972), President Nixon had just returned from his acclaimed visit to China, which normalized the relations between China and the United States. So, he said, if relations between countries can be normalized, so can relations between data items and entities.

A denormalized data model should be seen as a form in which the normalized data model is reshaped in order to meet the needs of a particular application system. Only one fully normalized data model of a business exists, which represents the data entities, attributes and relationships in an objective manner, independently of their usage in any information system. However, multiple denormalized versions of this normalized model may exist, each of them tailored to the needs and requirements of a specific system. In each of these versions, specific normalized entities and relationships precipitate into simpler, flatter, and denormalized structures, as dictated by the application system.

14.6 DATA MODELING FOR DATA WAREHOUSES

Issues of balance and tradeoffs between normalizing and denormalizing the data model have become especially important since the explosion in the marketplace of On-Line Analytical Processing (OLAP) systems and data warehouses. These systems differ from traditional On-Line Transaction Processing (OLTP) systems, in that they often gain more from a denormalized data model than they lose. OLAP and data warehousing systems perform usually, but not always, data retrieval and analysis tasks. The majority of data is often read-only, loaded to the database by batch processes, and derived from operational data by summarizing, tabulating, or otherwise transforming or computing these data. In such a case, much of the insert and update overhead that normalization eliminates does not exist, or at least does not affect the users visibly. The redundancy of denormalized data still exists, but its negative effects are less considerable in these days, characterized by the constant drop in costs of storage devices and increase in performance of hardware components. The speed of data retrieval, on the other hand, is such an important critical success factor of these systems that the denormalization of data models becomes an imperative task. Success stories in these applications happen when a normalized data model has been carefully defined, and from it a denormalized model is created artfully and diligently.

The process of creating the data model of a data warehouse can be decomposed into the following steps:

1. Define the questions that the system will help answer. These questions directly affect the extent and complexity of the data model for the data warehouse and of the OLAP system in general.
2. Identify the entities and attributes that the system will analyze. In the terminology of OLAP applications and data warehouses, these entities are called facts and their attributes are called measures.
3. Identify the entities and attributes by which facts and measures will be analyzed. Each of these entities is a dimension in the analysis of a measure.

4. Organize the dimensions in a hierarchy of entities. These hierarchies are also the major paths through which the data warehouse records will be mined and analyzed.

After the data model is prepared and the data warehouse is designed, the OLAP application is designed and implemented. The following sections explain how you can perform the steps above to model the data requirements for TASC's Sales Analysis System.

14.6.1   DEFINING THE QUESTIONS

In general, any information system provides its users with answers to their questions or satisfies their needs for information. These questions and needs affect the structure and design of the system, including its data model and the user interface. In the case of OLTP applications, the data model is closer to the Third Normal Form, which represents an objective view of data and their relationships in the business of the enterprise. The specific needs of the application users are usually met by the user interface modules. The data model of the system is not influenced or affected significantly by these needs. In fact, the same (almost fully normalized) data model can often satisfy the needs of multiple application systems.

The data models of OLAP applications, on the other hand, are considerably affected by the needs of their users. I mentioned earlier that in order to achieve the requirements that these applications have to retrieve and query data, the fully normalized business data model is heavily denormalized. But denormalization is not an activity that can be performed across the board, with the entire data model. It is targeted to key entities and relationships that are determined by the needs of the users and the application system. Thus, understanding the ultimate needs of these users and the purpose of the system has a significant impact on the data model of OLAP applications. In order to understand these needs, you need to identify all the questions for which the users of an application want to get answers from the data. The process is as elaborate as defining other requirements of the system. Assume that after talking to managers of TASC at the Headquarters office in New York, you identify the following information they would like to extract from the ordering data that are recorded and manipulated every day by each order management team:

❑ How many orders do we process every week by geographic region, area, state, and zip code?

❑ What is the average price of each product we sell and how does it compare with the manufacturer's suggested retail price?

❑ What is the average monthly order amount by customer, customer type, and industry?

❑ What is the average monthly order amount for individual customers, by state, zip, year, and product type?

❑ Which is the best performing order management team (the one with the highest total sales) for the last twelve months for all the product types and categories that we carry?

❑ What is the trend of orders (measured by number of orders) from the states of Virginia and Maryland for the last two quarters, for products manufactured by Oracle and Microsoft?

❑ What is the average order amount by payment method, state, zip, and product category?

14.6.2 DEFINING THE MEASURES AND FACTS

The questions for which the users of your application need answers are the cornerstone of the OLAP application and its data model. They must be carefully reviewed and understood in order to identify the attributes that the users will analyze to find answers to their questions. These attributes are also known as measures. The entities that group the measures together are called fact entities. When the data model is implemented in a physical database, the tables that correspond to these entities are called fact tables. Figure 14.19 shows the fact entity ORDER FACT used by the Sales Analysis System. The measures of these tables are the attributes QUANTITY, UNIT PRICE, and TOTAL, because by analyzing these attributes, users may find answers to questions like those listed in the previous section. The meaning of the other attributes in the entity ORDER FACT will be discussed in the next section.

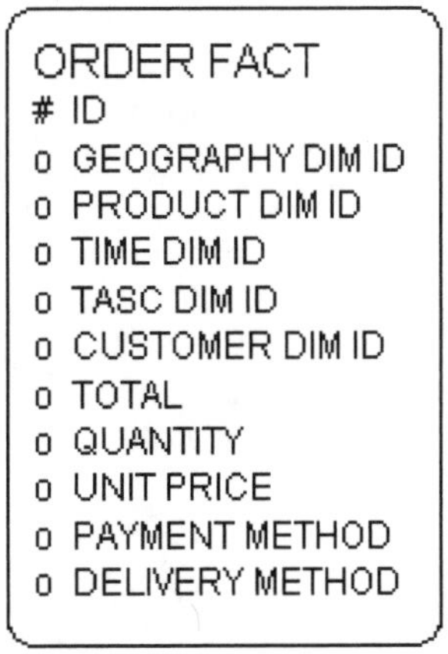

```
ORDER FACT
# ID
o GEOGRAPHY DIM ID
o PRODUCT DIM ID
o TIME DIM ID
o TASC DIM ID
o CUSTOMER DIM ID
o TOTAL
o QUANTITY
o UNIT PRICE
o PAYMENT METHOD
o DELIVERY METHOD
```

FIGURE 14.19 The ORDER FACT entity and its measures in the TASC Sales Analysis System.

14.6.3 DEFINING THE DIMENSIONS

By examining the questions listed in Section 14.6.1, you can easily notice that users often request to analyze measure attributes by another entity or attribute. For example, they want to know the number of orders by geographic region, area, state, and zip; or the average monthly order amount by customer, customer type, and industry. Attributes like state, region, and customer type, by which measure attributes are examined and analyzed, are called dimensions. Like other attributes, dimension attributes are grouped together in dimension entities, which when the data model is physically implemented, become dimension tables. Figure 14.20 shows the dimension entities for the TASC Sales Analysis System. ─────────────────────────────────────

As you can see from Figure 14.20, the dimension entities are generally heavily denormalized. In the GEOGRAPHY DIMENSION entity, for example, the REGION ID and REGION NAME attributes will be repeated for each instance of the entity that represents smaller geographical zones, like states and zip codes. The denormalization is intentional and done in order to minimize the number of lookups and joins required when facts from mixed geographic zones are analyzed.

As can be expected, the fact entity ORDER FACT is related in one-to-many relationships to each dimension entity. This expresses the fact that, in general,

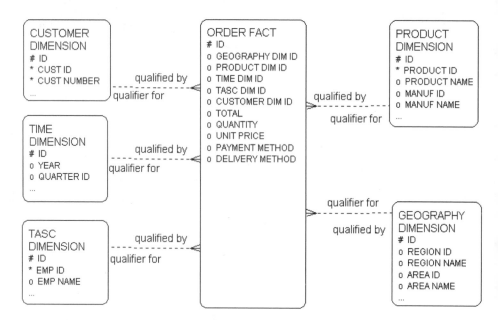

FIGURE 14.20 Dimension entities and attributes and their relationships to measures in the TASC Sales Analysis System.

multiple fact records may exist for each dimension. For example, for a given geography dimension (Region = 'East Coast,' Area = 'Mid-Atlantic,' State = 'Virginia,' and ZIP = '22201'), many facts records may exist, due to all the other instances of the other dimensions, such as customers and time periods.

The fact and dimension entities may be viewed as a vector space of the data analyzed by a corporation. Each dimension entity serves as a coordinate axis in this space. Different instances of these entities are points on the axes. The fact entity represents all the points in the space. An instance of this entity is defined by instances of dimension entities, just like a point in the vector space is defined by its projections in the coordinate axes. For this reason, the data model of an OLAP system and the data schema of a data warehouse are often called multi-dimensional data cubes or multi-dimensional data spaces. Figure 14.21 graphically presents a two-dimensional subset of the multi-dimensional data cube of the TASC Sales Analysis System, in which GEOGRAPHY DIMENSION and TIME DIMENSION serve as the coordinate axes, and different points in the plane represent instances from the fact entity ORDER FACT.

14.6.4 ORGANIZING DIMENSIONS IN HIERARCHIES

The bulk of the work for defining the data model of an OLAP system is to find all the necessary measures and facts, as well as all the dimension entities and attributes. However, organizing the dimension attributes into hierarchical data structures is often beneficial. Consider, for example, the entity TIME DIMENSION shown in Figure 14.20. Explaining to the users of your OLAP application the meaning and the elements of this dimension will be much easier if the entity is

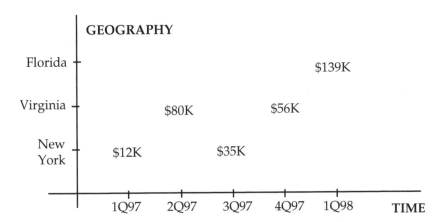

FIGURE 14.21   Visual representation of a two-dimensional data cube as a two-dimensional vector space.

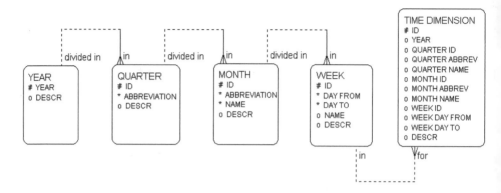

FIGURE 14.22   A hierarchy for the entity TIME DIMENSION in the
TASC Sales Analysis System.

complemented by entities YEAR, QUARTER, MONTH, and WEEK, as in Figure
14.22. Another benefit of organizing dimensions into hierarchies is that it simplifies the interface of applications used to analyze the data by these dimensions.
Browsers and navigator tools can help users drill down a dimension much more
easily if the data is organized hierarchically.

14.7   MAINTAINING MULTIPLE DATA MODELS

Previous sections discussed the importance of data normalization in general, and
bringing the data model into the Third Normal Form in particular. I recommend
that for each business area in the enterprise, you create the data model with all
the entities in the Third Normal Form. This data model should be stored in the
Designer/2000 Repository as a separate application system, independent from
any other application you may use to gather and document the requirements and
design of individual systems. This setup allows you to always go back and reference the fully normalized version of the data model, explain it to newcomers un-
familiar with the business, and use it as a starting point for every system data
modeling effort. Experience has shown that a polished 3NF data model is stable,
has a relatively long life span, and requires little maintenance. The benefits you
can draw from such a model offset significantly the cost of maintaining it.

The companion CD-ROM includes the following application systems, which you can load in your Designer/2000 Repository:

❑ **TASC 3NF.** This contains the data model of TASC's order management business area in the Third Normal Form. This data model serves as the foundation for the data model of every other system developed for and used by the business area. In particular, it is the starting point for the application systems TASC OMS (Order Management System) and TASC SAS (Sales Analyzing System) discussed below. This application system is archived in the Oracle Export file TASC3NF.DMP. You can reach from the Web pages of the CD-ROM by following the links *Software*, and *TASC 3NF Data Model*.

❑ **TASC OMS (REQ).** This application system contains the requirements for the Order Management System of TASC. It was initially created as a copy of TASC 3NF, in order to inherit the normalized data model of the business area. The data model then was customized to facilitate the design and development of an online transaction processing (OLTP) system, like OMS. By comparing the data model of this application with the fully normalized model shown of the TASC 3NF, you can notice a few differences, such as the merge of entities ADDRESS and ZIP CODE through denormalization, or the introduction of the pseudo-attribute ID as the primary unique identifier for entities like PRODUCT or EMPLOYEE, whose unique identifiers are one or more string attributes. Nevertheless, the OMS data model continues to be a highly normalized data model, a characteristic for all the OLTP systems, whose bulk transactions are made up of DML operations. TASC OMS (REQ) application system is provided in the archive OMSREQ.DMP. You can access this file by following the links *Software* and *Order Management System Requirements*.

❑ **TASC SAS (REQ).** This application system contains the data model for TASC's Sales Analysis System. While the OMS system serves as the data store for up-to-the-minute order transactions, the SAS system allows TASC executives to access and mine the data warehouse of ordering data. Like the OMS system, this system originated from TASC 3NF, and the data model was modified to fit the needs of an online analytical processing (OLAP) like TASC's SAS. By looking at the data model of this system, you can immediately tell that, unlike the data models of the previous two application systems, the data model of SAS is highly denormalized with many attributes derived, summarized, or otherwise computed from other attributes. The advantage of creating this model from the 3NF model is that in the process of denormalizing the entities, the easier approach is to identify the relationships between the original attributes and the new, denormalized ones. These relationships are captured in the form of transformations and business rules that will be implemented by the system. The export file of this application system is called SASREQ.DMP. You can get it by following the links *Software* and *Sales Analysis System Data Model*.

14.8 SUMMARY

Data modeling is an essential part of the requirements definition and the analysis of an information system. Two major techniques used in this process, entity modeling and data normalization, were the subject of this chapter. A list of the most important topics discussed in this chapter follows:

- ❏ **Techniques and Approaches to Data Modeling**
- ❏ **Entity Modeling**
    - ❏ Collecting Data about Data
    - ❏ Creating and Maintaining Entities
    - ❏ Creating and Maintaining Attributes
    - ❏ Maintaining Detailed Properties for Attributes
    - ❏ Specifying Allowable Values for Attributes
- ❏ **Domains in Designer/2000**
    - ❏ Creating Domains
    - ❏ Maintaining Properties of Domains
    - ❏ Allowed Values of a Domain
    - ❏ Maintaining Domains in the Design Editor
    - ❏ Updating Properties Inherited from Domains
- ❏ **Relationship Modeling**
    - ❏ Resolving Many-to-Many Relationships
    - ❏ Including Relationships in Unique Identifiers
- ❏ **Normalization and Denormalization of Data**
    - ❏ Unnormalized Data
    - ❏ First Normal Form
    - ❏ Second Normal Form
    - ❏ Third Normal Form
    - ❏ Denormalization
- ❏ **Data Modeling for Data Warehouses**
    - ❏ Defining the Questions
    - ❏ Defining the Measures and Facts
    - ❏ Defining the Dimensions
    - ❏ Organizing Dimensions in Hierarchies
- ❏ **Maintaining Multiple Data Models**

Chapter 15

BUSINESS RULES MODELING

- ♦ Function Data Usages
- ♦ Business Rules
- ♦ Data Definition Rules
- ♦ Data Manipulation Rules
- ♦ Access Privilege Rules
- ♦ Summary

Chapters 13 and 14 discussed the activities performed during the requirements analysis stage of a system in general and focused in particular on using Designer/2000 to capture user interface requirements and to create the logical data model of the system. Once the system's data model is in place and the screens and reports of the future system are documented in the form of functions, Designer/2000 can be used to model the data elements that each of these functions will contain. In addition, Designer/2000 can be used to capture and document the business rules that the system will implement in a novel way that is different from the way requirements of a system are defined in traditional systems. Creating and maintaining data usages of functions and using Designer/2000 to document the business rules that the system will implement are the major topics of this chapter.

15.1 FUNCTION DATA USAGES

Recall from Chapter 13 that one of the principal goals of function modeling in the Function Hierarchy Diagrammer is to define the functions that make up the user interface of the system. Of particular interest among these functions, are the elementary functions, which will ultimately be implemented as screens and reports of the system. After identifying the elementary functions of the user interface, define which entities and attributes are used by each of these functions. The associations between functions and entities are called function entity usages; those between functions and attributes are known as function attribute usages. These usages essentially track which functions create, retrieve, update, or delete which entities or attributes. These usages are also referred to as CRUD usages of functions, from the combination of the initials of the actions (Create, Retrieve, Update, or Delete) they describe. The Function Hierarchy Diagrammer and the Matrix Diagrammer are two Designer/2000 tools most commonly used to create and maintain data usages of functions. Their use is discussed in the following sections.

15.1.1 CREATING AND MAINTAINING DATA USAGES IN THE FUNCTION HIERARCHY DIAGRAMMER

The CRUD usages for individual functions are created and maintained in the Entity Usages and Attribute Usages property tabs of the Edit Function dialog box. You can access this dialog box by double-clicking the desired function in the diagram. Recall from Chapter 13 that the function OMSUI11–Create Order allows users to create a new order, the line items associated with it, and the payment information for the order. Besides entering information directly related to the order, they can associate it with other data, such as customer, product, and delivery information. Figure 15.1 shows the settings of the Entity Usages property tab for the function OMSUI11. As you can see from this figure, this function creates,

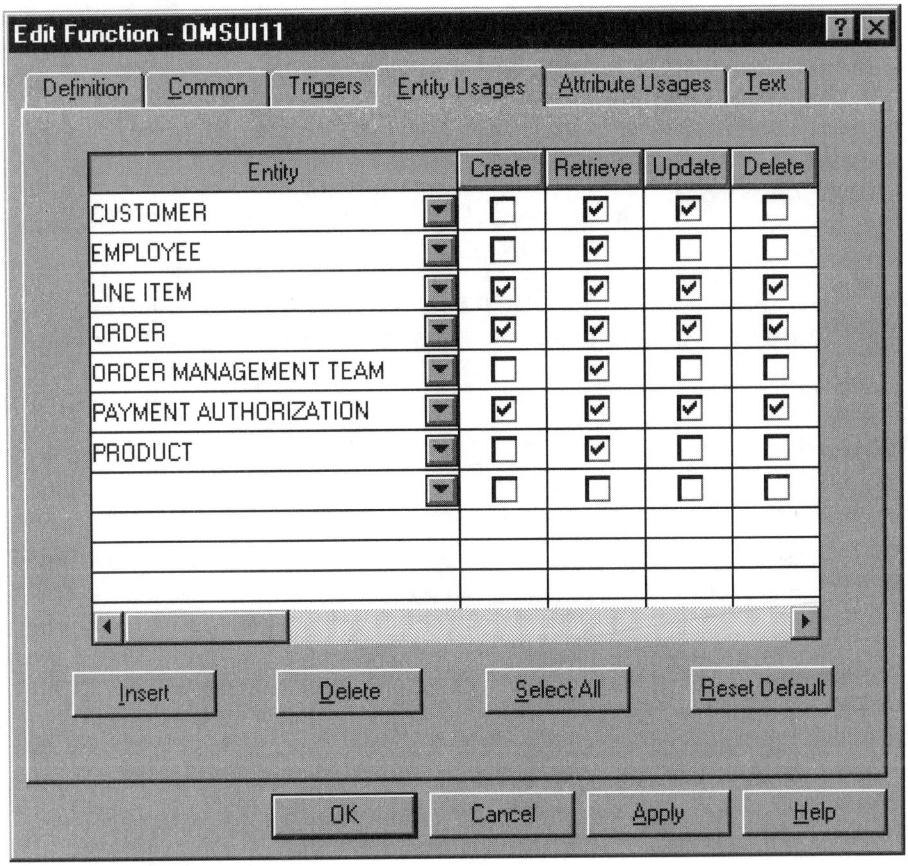

FIGURE 15.1 The Entity Usages property tab of the Edit Function dialog box.

retrieves, updates, and deletes the entities ORDER, LINE ITEM, and PAYMENT AUTHORIZATION. However, from the definition of the function OMSUI11, you can see that this function has to access other entities as well. For example, it needs to retrieve the product ordered in each line item or the customers that place, receive, or pay for the order. Therefore, the entities CUSTOMER and PRODUCT appear in the list of entities, and the check box Retrieve is marked for them. In order to allow the order entry users to quickly update information about the customer placing the order, the Update usage for the entity CUSTOMER is also checked. Similarly, the member of the Order Management Teams that creates the order should be associated with the order, a necessity that explains why the entities EMPLOYEE and ORDER MANAGEMENT TEAM are in the list of entity usages for this function with the Retrieve usage checked. (Entities like PRODUCT

❑ Some functions may also archive data from an entity. In this case, the Archive option of the function entity usage must be checked. Archiving data means deleting a record from the operational tables and moving the data into journal tables. Therefore, whenever the Archive option is set, the Delete option must be set as well.

❑ Obviously, for user interface functions that represent reports, the only meaningful usage that can be set is Retrieve.

and EMPLOYEE, which are simply retrieved by a screen function, are also called lookup entities.)

The Attribute Usages property tab is used similarly. For each entity specified in the Entity Usages tab, you can select the attributes that the function is using. For each attribute, you can indicate whether or not the function can insert, retrieve, update, nullify, or archive the attribute. The usage of attributes and entities by a function are related. If, for example, a function can update an entity, then by default, the Update flag is checked for each attribute you include from that entity. The settings of these flags are also influenced by the properties of the attributes in the data model. For example, setting the option Nullify for an attribute that is defined as mandatory in the data model does not have any effect because it does not allow the function to set this attribute to null and store it to the database. Figure 15.2 shows an example of the Attribute Usages property tab.

Two schools of thought exist regarding the amount of details you enter in the entity and attribute usages of a function. The first one recommends that you clarify in your mind the picture of the function in as much detail as possible. If it will be implemented as a screen, you identify all the entities and all the attributes that the screen module will use, even if not all of them will be displayed. If the function will be implemented as a report, identify all the data items that the report will contain. The second approach is not to spend too much time trying to identify all the data elements that will be part of the user interface module at this level in the system development life cycle. Since you will have a chance to refine and define more precisely the items of a module in the system design and development stage, you can limit the work to defining the usages of the main entities for a function. In the example of function OMSUI11, the main entities are ORDER, LINE ITEM, and PAYMENT AUTHORIZATION, but not the lookup entities PRODUCT, EMPLOYEE, and ORDER MANAGEMENT TEAM. You may use the approach that you find more appropriate for your situation. One thing to keep in mind, though, is that you should define the data usages consistently for any given function. If you decide to identify a lookup entity used by the function,

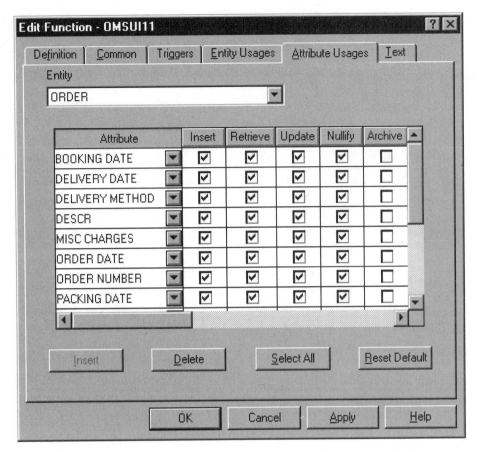

FIGURE 15.2 The Attribute Usages property tab of the Edit Function dialog box.

identify all of them; if defining detailed attribute usages for an entity, do the same for the other entities as well.

15.1.2 CREATING AND MAINTAINING DATA USAGES IN THE MATRIX DIAGRAMMER

A global method for creating, viewing, and maintaining function entity usages is offered by the Matrix Diagrammer. The matrix you create in this context is called the CRUD matrix of the system. A simple and useful CRUD diagram is shown in Figure 15.3. This matrix displays the entity names in the rows and the function label and short description in the columns. The intersection cells display the settings of *Create, Retrieve, Update, Delete,* and *Archive* properties. A similar matrix

OMS ENTITY USAGES OF UI FUNCTIONS:1				_ □ ×
Business Functions	OMSUI11	OMSUI12	OMSUI131	OMSUI132
Entities	Create Order	Maintain Existing Order	Orders by Customer	Orders per Time Window
DELIVERY TERM				
REGION				
ORDER MANAGEMENT	R			
EMPLOYEE	R			
CUSTOMER	RU	C	R	R
PRODUCT CATEGORY				
PRODUCT	R	C	R	R
LINE ITEM	CRUD	RUD	R	R
WAREHOUSE UNIT				
ZIP				
SALES UNIT				
MANUFACTURER				

FIGURE 15.3   An example of a CRUD matrix.

can be created for the usage of attributes by functions. For detailed instructions on creating matrix diagrams, refer to Chapter 7.

In a CRUD matrix for the user interface, such as the one shown in Figure 15.3, you are interested only in elementary functions that will ultimately be converted into screens and reports that users will see. To restrict the matrix to only these functions, you can apply different filtering criteria in the Settings dialog box of the matrix. Consider, for example, the Order Management System, where by convention, the labels of the all user interface functions begin with the characters OMSUI. Then to limit the functions in the matrix, you would do the following:

1. Select Edit I Settings… from the Matrix Diagrammer's menu to display the Settings dialog box.
2. Click the property tab for Business Functions. Depending on the layout of the matrix, this could be either the row or the column tab.
3. Set the Filter field for the property *Label* to *OMSUI%*. This setting limits the functions in the matrix to those whose label begins with OMSUI.
4. Set the Order list box for the property *Label* to *A*. This will order the functions in ascending order.
5. Set the Filter field for property *Elementary?* to ='Y.' Such a setting further restricts the pool of functions displayed by the matrix to the elementary functions.
6. Click OK to apply the settings to the matrix.

The CRUD matrix is a very useful tool for verifying the quality of the requirements identified for the system. By presenting a global view of the usage of data by functions, the CRUD matrix allows you to identify areas that need further examination. For example, if an elementary function does not act upon any data, requirements for that function are very likely not complete. On the other hand, an entity that is created, retrieved, or updated, but not deleted by any function, may lead you to identify requirements for a data maintenance utility function that purges the entity periodically.

15.2 BUSINESS RULES

Traditionally, analysts have defined the requirements of systems in two steps. One step involved data requirements, which included definitions of entities, attributes, and relationships, and ultimately resulted in the data model for the system. This set of requirements addressed the needs for data manipulation services and how the system would satisfy them. The second step identified the business rules that the system would implement and the types of screens and reports to be presented to the users. The outcome of this step was the functional requirements document. Whereas the data model was the starting point for the database design, the functional requirements document was a starting point for the design of programmatic structures, screens, and reports.

Chapter 14 discussed how to use Designer/2000 to build the system's data model and Chapter 13 explained how you can enter the user interface requirements in the Repository. This section will explain why you need to part from the tradition and separate the user interface requirements from the business rules that the system will implement. Then it will explain how to use Designer/2000 to document these business rules.

15.2.1 SEPARATING BUSINESS RULES FROM INTERFACE REQUIREMENTS

Looking into the history of database systems and considering what is in store for them in the future, you can identify four categories of systems.

❑ **Mainframe systems.** In these systems, all the data management and implementation of business rules was performed in large mainframe computers. Dumb terminals connected to these computers provided the data presentation services.

❑ **Early client/server systems.** These systems separated the enforcement of business rules from data management services and attached it to presentation services. The data management services now were running on separate database servers. The other two services resided on client PCs, connected to the server through Local Area Networks (LANs) and, occasionally, Wide Area Networks (WANs).

❑ **Mature client/server systems.** These systems are distinguished from earlier ones in that the enforcement of business rules in them is partitioned between the client application and the database server. These systems are related principally to the development of robust RDBMS products, such as Oracle7. Whereas database servers in earlier client/server systems provided limited support for business rules, such as referential integrity, database products like Oracle7 provide full support for implementation of application logic in the form of stored program units and database triggers.

❑ **Internet/intranet systems.** These systems reintroduce the mainframe systems paradigm into the new reality of Internet. In these systems, the data management services are stored in database servers networked together. The presentation services are offered by Web browsers running on PCs or Network Computers (NCs) connected to the corporate intranet and to the worldwide Internet. The business rules are implemented in the form of canned units of code—applets, which, upon demand, are transferred from the servers to the presentation devices, where they are executed.

Clearly, for the first two types of systems, the traditional way to define requirements (data model and functional requirements) was sufficient. In these systems, computers that hosted the data played a distinct role from that of terminals or PCs through which the system was accessed. In either case, the boundaries between these roles were very well defined. Because the implementation of business rules fell either on one side or on the other side of the border, no need existed to articulate them distinctly.

In mature client/server systems, the border mentioned above becomes fuzzy and unstable. These systems may start out with a certain configuration and partition of functionality between clients and database servers that optimize this configuration. However, as the components of the system change (newer client PCs, more RAM on the server, faster network, and so on), the configuration of the system changes. In order to maintain the performance at an optimal level, you need to repartition the application logic so that it takes advantage of the new configuration. For example, suppose that you need to compute the sum of all orders placed with the company in one day. Initially, the function will be used by five analysts sitting next to each other; you are a little short in database server memory, as well. For these reasons, in the initial release of the client/server system, you implement the function in the client application. Each time the sum is calculated, the records are retrieved from the database, and passed through the LAN to the client, which performs the calculation. Eight months later, your application has become wildly popular. Although the transfer of records from the server to the client was not a problem initially, now it has become a performance bottleneck. At the same time, you have received the money to double the memory of your database server. You can fix the problem very easily if you can move the function that calculates the sum from the client application to the database server.

How easily this move can be achieved depends on how you defined the requirements, as well as on how you designed and developed the system. If you followed the traditional way, you did not distinguish between user interface requirements and business rule implementation requirements. For this reason, the designers and developers wired the function in the code that draws the screens or manages the windows. In order to move this function from the client over to the server, you need to go through the code, dissect the function, customize, and even rewrite it so that it can be stored in the database.

On the other hand, if you identified the business rules separately, designers designed it as a separate module, and developers implemented it as a component in a PL/SQL library that was attached to the Oracle Forms client application. To transfer the function in this case, all you need to do is drag the library object and drop it in the database server. Developer/2000 components, such as Forms, Reports, and Graphics, allow you to literally drag PL/SQL libraries or components of them and drop them in the Oracle database schema. This flexibility that they provide in partitioning the application logic is why they are often referred to as second-generation client/server tools.

The need to separate the business rules from presentation services is even more acute when developing Web-based systems. As mentioned earlier, the paradigm of these applications is to store the functionality in servers and provide it to clients when they need it. This is quite different from the client/server paradigm, where a good part of the functionality is bundled and stored in the client PC, even if only a subset of it may be used at any one moment. In order to store this functionality in a clean format, you need to formulate the requirements for implementing business rules independently of the way the data will be presented to the users.

15.2.2 CATEGORIES OF BUSINESS RULES

Data elements are stored in databases in a persistent matter. In order to achieve the persistency, the database must be constructed and the system implemented to meet a number of criteria, such as the format of each data element, the identifier and relationships between instances of entities, allowable values, and so on. The business rules that identify these criteria are called data definition rules, since they essentially define the way data will be stored in the database system. Because these rules apply to persistent instances of data at any point in the life of the database system, these rules are also called static rules.

Database systems, on the other hand, are dynamic systems where a number of events cause the data to change from one persistent state to another. Processes like creating, updating, and deleting data in these systems are constrained by and subject to business rules identified during the requirements definition phase of the system. Business rules that express criteria that must be met in order to create, update, or delete data in a database system are called data manipulation rules.

For systems with a homogeneous users' community, a combination of data definition rules and data manipulation rules forms the set of all the business rules these systems implement. However, when multiple groups of users need to access different functions of the system at different levels, you need to record these requirements as a separate category of business rules. Rules that describe which users are allowed to access what functions and what entities in the system are called access privilege rules.

Thus, business rules captured during the requirements analysis and implemented by the system can be classified as follows:

❑ Data definition rules
❑ Data manipulation rules
❑ Access privileges rules

Designer/2000 allows you to specify several business rules, especially data definition rules, in a declarative way while you build the data model for the system. Other rules, primarily access privileges rules, may be modeled as associations between objects stored in the Repository. The business rules in these two categories usually are implemented automatically and are included in the system by the Designer/2000 Transformers and generators. Rules that require programmatic efforts to be implemented are modeled as functions. During the design phase, this last group of functions will help define application logic objects and stored PL/SQL modules, such as packages, functions, procedures, and database triggers. In an Oracle-based development, these modules will be implemented using PL/SQL and then deployed on the front-end client application or the Oracle Server database, depending on the architecture of the system. The following sections provide guidelines for using Designer/2000 to document business rules from these three categories.

15.3 DATA DEFINITION RULES

Data definition rules are rules with which the data will have to conform in order to be stored in the database structures. Depending on the number of data elements that they affect, the data definition rules may be classified as follows:

❑ **Rules for individual attributes.** These rules are defined for one attribute within an entity.
❑ **Rules for multiple attributes of the same entity.** These rules combine two or more attributes from the same entity and are also known as tuple rules.
❑ **Rules for individual entities.** These rules apply to all the instances of an entity.

❏ **Rules for multiple entities.** These rules combine attributes from different entities or relationships among two or more entities. They are also known as inter-entity rules.

The following sections describe these rules in more detail and provide instructions on how to store them in the Designer/2000 Repository. Examples from the TASC OMS application system are used throughout these sections. In order to follow these examples more easily, consult with the entity relationship diagrams provided in the application system TASC OMS (REQ). As I mentioned at the end of the previous chapter, the archived version of this application system can be accessed from the Web pages of the companion CD-ROM by following the links *Software* and *Order Management System Requirements*.

15.3.1 ATTRIBUTE RULES

Attribute rules are criteria that data represented by an attribute must always satisfy. A good number of these rules are also known as metadata about the attribute and include properties such as the format, data type, length, and allowable values of an attribute, as well as whether the attribute is required or optional, and whether the attribute is part of the unique identifier for the entity.

Attribute rules are often represented in the form of tables like the one shown in Figure 15.4 for the case of entity ORDER. Each table contains the list of attributes for an entity. For each attribute, analysts identify and store the name, data type or format, size, the optionality, and whether the attribute is part of a key. A description column for the attribute is used to explain the functionality of the attribute, and also to record allowable values, as in the case of the attribute DELIVERY METHOD, or any other condition or rule for the attribute, as in the case of the attribute ORDER NUMBER.

ATTRIBUTE NAME	DATA TYPE, LENGTH, AND PRECISION	OPTIONAL?	COMMENT
ORDER NUMBER	INTEGER	No	The unique identifier for the order.
CUSTOMER	VARCHAR2(100)	No	The name of the customer placing the order.
ORDER DATE	DATE	No	The date when order was placed.
DELIVERY DATE	DATE	Yes	The date by which the order must be delivered.
DESCRIPTION	VARCHAR2(240)	Yes	Instructions and other information about the order.

FIGURE 15.4 A tabular representation of attribute rules.

You have three ways to record attribute rules in Designer/2000. Each of them is described below:

❑ **Record attribute rules as properties of attributes.** Recall from Chapter 14 that the easiest way to set and manage these properties is through the property tabs Attributes, Att Detail, and Att Values of the Edit Entity dialog box in the Entity Relationship Diagrammer. The rules defined this way will be transferred automatically into properties of columns by the Database Design Transformer and will be implemented declaratively by the Server Generator and the front-end generators of Designer/2000.

❑ **Record attribute rules as domain objects.** From Chapter 14 recall also that the best way to manage format properties and allowable values of attributes is to inherit them from domain objects. As in the first case, these rules will be transferred into properties of columns by the Database Design Transformer and will be implemented declaratively by the Server Generator and the front-end generators of Designer/2000.

❑ **Record attribute rules in free-text format.** You would use this method to record rules that cannot be implemented with one of the previous two methods. The text properties of the attribute or the entity may be used to enter a clear and concise description of the rule. This description will be transferred into the respective properties of the column or the table by the Database Design Transformer. During the system design phase, you will implement the rule as check constraints for the table in question. Based on the properties of these constraints, you may implement the rule at the presentation layer (for example, in the form of validation triggers in Oracle Forms applications modules), at the data management layer in the form of table constraints, or in both the layers.

15.3.2 INTER-ATTRIBUTE RULES

Inter-attribute or tuple rules are constraints that two or more attributes from the same entity instance must fulfill. They usually control the value of an attribute based on values of one or more attributes from the same instance. Examples of such rules in the entities of the OMS system are listed below:

❑ For each order, the requested delivery date must be either NULL or later than the order date.

❑ For each line item, the total cost is given by the formula:
ITEM TOTAL = QUANTITY * UNIT MSRP * (1 − DISCOUNT)

❑ For each payment, the credit card type, cardholder name, account number, and expiration date must either all be NULL or all have a value.

❑ For a credit card payment authorization, the payment date must be on or before the expiration date.

Inter-attribute rules are recorded in free-text format in the entity's text properties *Description* or *Notes*. Like special attribute rules, they are designed as check constraints associated with the corresponding table and implemented by the Designer/2000 generators.

From the discussion in this and the previous sections, you can see that all the rules that cannot be defined and implemented declaratively are entered in free-text format. Besides these rules, you may want to associate other textual information with attributes and entities. This includes the business meaning and purpose of these objects. In order to ease the work of those who will read the information stored in these properties, following some system-wide standard is helpful. A standard commonly used is to enter the business meaning of attributes and entities in the property *Description* of these objects. The descriptions of all the business rules that will be implemented as check constraints are entered in the *Notes* property of the entity. Figure 15.5 shows how you could record the last two inter-attributes from the list above in the *Notes* property of the entity PAYMENT AUTHORIZATION.

Observe in this figure the headings DATA DEFINITION RULES and TUPLE RULES, which clearly identify the purpose of the content that follows, and the labeling convention followed to identify each rule.

```
DATA DEFINITION RULES

   TUPLE RULES

     PA01
       IF PA TYPE = CREDIT CARD THEN
          CREDIT CARD TYPE, CREDIT CARD NUMBER, EXPIRATION
          DATE, and CARD HOLDER NAME must be NOT NULL
       ELSE
          CREDIT CARD TYPE, CREDIT CARD NUMBER, EXPIRATION
          DATE, and CARD HOLDER NAME must ALL be NULL
       END IF

     PA02
       IF PA TYPE = CREDIT CARD THEN
          PAYMENT DATE < EXPIRATION DATE
       END IF
```

FIGURE 15.5 An example of recording inter-attribute business rules in the property Notes of the entity.

15.3.3 ENTITY RULES

Entity rules constrain the value of an attribute based on values of one or more attributes from the same entity, but from different instances of the entity. The most typical example of entity rules is the unique identifiers of an entity. They are stored declaratively on the UID property tab of the Edit Entity dialog box. The Database Design Transformer transfers these rules into primary and unique key constraints of the table. The Server Generator and the front-end generators take them into account when creating DDL statements and user interface software modules.

Other entity rules may require some intricate programming logic to implement. Consider, for example, the entity EMPLOYEE with the recursive relationship shown in Figure 15.6. This relationship can be expressed as follows:

❏ Each EMPLOYEE may be manager for one or more EMPLOYEEs.
❏ Each EMPLOYEE may be managed by one and only one EMPLOYEE.

A system that contains a table with such a relationship may compromise the data integrity in a serious way by allowing circular references to exist in the data. Figure 15.6 contains the example of a circular reference in which John King is manager for Julie Allen, who is manager for Mike Turner, who is manager for John King. With such data in your database, a program that displays all the employees under the supervision of a given employee will inevitably fall into an infinite loop when used for John King. In order to prevent this anomaly, implement programmatically a rule that checks the assignment of an employee to a manager and prevents circular loops.

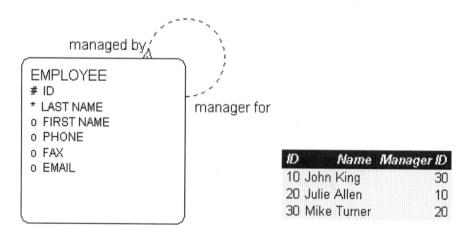

FIGURE 15.6 A recursive relationship that may lead to circular references.

The best way to enter these rules in the Repository is in the form of functions in the Function Hierarchy Diagrammer. Recall from Chapter 13 that you need to maintain at least one functional hierarchy tree to describe the user interface requirements of the system. In order to clearly separate these requirements from the business rules, maintain a separate hierarchy tree dedicated exclusively to the business functions that will be implemented by the system. In the case of the TASC Order Management System, the root of this hierarchy is the function OMSBR – OMS Business Rules, a group of all the requirements of the system.

Figure 15.7 shows the decomposition of the function OMSBR–OMS Business Rules. As you can see, the first level of children of this function are OMSBR1–Data Definition Rules and OMSBR2–Data Manipulation Rules. Then each of these functions is decomposed into further functions. For example, OMSBR1 is decomposed into the following functions: OMSBR11–Attribute and Tuple Rules, OMSBR12–Entity Rules, and OMSBR13–Inter-Entity Rules. The actual data definition rules go under one of these three functions, as shown in Figure 15.7. For systems with a large number of rules, you may need to further group the rules into additional layers, such as by subsystems, or by groups of data entities.

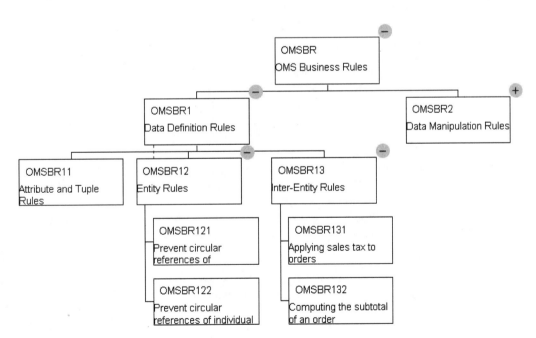

FIGURE 15.7 A function hierarchy diagram that represents the business rules of the Order Management System.

15.3.4 INTER-ENTITY RULES

Inter-entity rules describe conditions and dependencies that exist among attributes owned by two or more entities. Rules in this category that are most easily identified are relationship rules. Discovering and documenting relationships between entities is an important part of data modeling efforts, as discussed in Chapter 14. Designer/2000 allows you to maintain relationships as separate objects stored in the Repository. Recall from that chapter that among the most important properties of a relationship are the optionality and cardinality of each of its ends. Based on the properties of relationships, the Database Design Transformer implements entity relationship rules as foreign key constraints.

As I explained in Chapters 9 and 14, when the cardinality of a relationship end is set to 'Many,' this means that several instances from that entity may (or must, depending on the optionality) be associated with one instance of the entity on the other end of the relationship. Many relationships are sufficiently described by these properties. An example of such a relationship is the one between entities PRODUCT and LINE ITEM. However, some relationships may exist only under special conditions. Consider, for example, the relationship between entities PACKAGE and ORDER. A package must be for one order, however not for any arbitrary order. The following restrictions apply:

❑ The delivery method of the package must be the same or similar to the delivery method requested in the order.

❑ The delivery date of the package must be on or before the requested delivery date for the order.

Because of these restrictions, the relationship between entities PACKAGE and ORDER is a restricted relationship. In order to record a restricted relationship, you need to follow these steps:

1. Create the relationship in the Entity Relationship Diagrammer as if it were unrestricted.
2. Create a function under the Inter-Entity Rules branch of the business rules functional hierarchy that describes the conditions that must be fulfilled in order for the relationship to be established.
3. Describe the business rule in the Description property of the restricted relationship so that it appears in the data modeling reports you will present to the users.

The Function Hierarchy Diagrammer is also used to record any other inter-entity rule that does not fall into any of the categories mentioned above. Some examples of these rules are listed below:

❑ State sales tax will be applied only to those orders for which the paying customer's address is in Virginia, the state where TASC is incorporated.

❑ The subtotal of an order is the sum of total costs for all the line items in-cluded in the order.

In order to achieve completeness in the documentation of business rules, I recommend that you enter the descriptions of these rules in the *Notes* property of the entity that is most affected by the rule.

Figure 15.8 shows how you could document the two business rules listed above in the Notes property of entity ORDER. As you can see from this example, the heading INTER-ENTITY RULES is used to separate these rules from business rules of other categories. The labels of the business functions that represent these rules are also used for cross-referencing.

15.4 DATA MANIPULATION RULES

Data manipulation rules are conditions that have to be met in order to create, up-date, and delete data from the database system. They also include the events that the system will capture and respond to, as well as the response triggered by these

```
DATA DEFINITION RULES

   TUPLE RULES

      ORD01:
         (DELIVERY DATE must be NULL) or (DELIVERY DATE >
         ORDER DATE)
      ORD02:
         TOTAL ORDER CHARGE = SUBTOTAL * (1 + SALES TAX +
         MISC CHARGES) + SHIPPING CHARGES

   INTER-ENTITY RULES

      OMSBR131
         State sales tax will be applied only to those
         orders for which the paying customer's address is
         in Virginia, the state where TASC is incorporated.
      OMSBR132
         The subtotal of an order is the sum of total costs
         for all the line items included in the order.
```

FIGURE 15.8 Documenting inter-entity rules in the Notes property.

events. The following is a description of the main categories of data manipulation rules:

❑ **Create rules.** These are conditions under which new instances for a given entity may be created.

❑ **Update rules.** These rules describe conditions under which data elements may be updated.

❑ **Delete rules.** These are criteria that must be met in order to successfully delete data from the database. An important set of rules in this group is the set that describes what happens to detail records after their master is deleted.

❑ **Events and triggers.** Events that the system will capture are caused by a user action or when a certain time is reached. The triggers capture the response that these events generate within or outside the system.

Defining the entity and attribute usages for the user interface functions is an initial effort to define data manipulation rules for a system. The following sections discuss how to identify and record other less trivial data manipulation rules.

15.4.1 CREATE RULES

Create rules are conditions that must be met in order to create new instances of an entity. Examples of create rules are:

❑ Line items can be added only to orders whose status is 'Entered.'
❑ A product item can be added only to a package whose status is 'Packed.'

These rules are documented as functions in the functional hierarchy of the business rules of the system. You may use a separate branch in the functional hierarchy to group these rules together, separately from the data definition rules discussed earlier.

15.4.2 UPDATE RULES

Update rules describe the conditions under which the attributes of an entity may be updated. Two examples of these rules are listed below:

❑ The shipping and miscellaneous charges of an order cannot be updated if the status of the order is 'Packed.'
❑ If the name of a city is updated in the ZIP entity, the denormalized CITY attributes in the entities ORDER MANAGEMENT TEAM, CUSTOMER, and BUSINESS PARTNER should be updated as well.

For attributes with an enumerated list of allowable values, you may also identify the rules under which one value changes into another, as well as values into which a given value may be modified. These rules are represented very clearly in state transition diagrams. Figure 15.9 shows the transition among allowable values of the attribute STATUS for the entity ORDER. Given the meaning of this attribute for the entity, this diagram may also be considered the state transition diagram of orders in the OMS system.

The update rules described so far are recorded in Designer/2000 as functions in the hierarchy of data manipulation rules. Also, a class of update rules exists that can be recorded and implemented declaratively. Rules in this class describe whether or not a relationship between two entity instances may be modified to replace one of the instances with another one. Examples of rules in this class include:

❑ A line item, once created for an order, cannot be transferred to another order.

❑ A product included in a product category may be moved to another product category.

In the case of the first rule, the relationship between entities ORDER and LINE ITEM is non-transferable. On the other hand, the relationship between entities PRODUCT and PRODUCT CATEGORY described in the second rule is transferable. Rules in this class are often commonly known as transfer relationship rules. You can use the property *Transferable* of a relationship end to record the transfer relationship rules. This property is located on the Definition tab of the Edit Relationship dialog box. An example of this tab is shown in Figure 15.10.

The Database Design Transformer will inherit this setting in the *Transfer* property of the foreign key that corresponds to the relationship end. The front-end generators will implement the rule on the client side according to the setting of this property. If the relationship is transferable, the item that corresponds to the foreign key will be updateable; otherwise, the item will be non-updateable. The Server Generator can also implement a non-updateable constraint for Oracle databases. As part of the table API, this generator creates database triggers to enforce a restricted transferable relationship at the database server. In such cases, a good idea is to document the business rule as a separate function as well as through the property *Transferable* of the relationship.

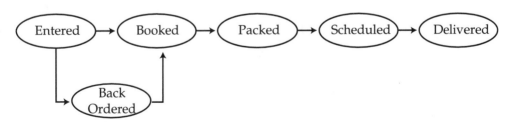

FIGURE 15.9 A state transition diagram for orders.

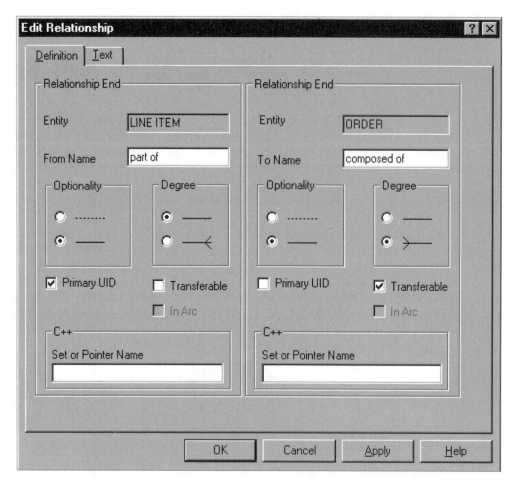

FIGURE 15.10   Recording transferable relationship rules in the Edit Relationship dialog box.

By default, all the relationship ends created in the Entity Relationship Diagrammer have the property *Transferable* set. If you unset this property, a small diamond appears across the relationship end to indicate that the relationship is non-transferable at this end. Figure 15.11 shows this indicator for the case of the non-transferable property discussed above.

15.4.3 DELETE RULES

Delete rules describe the conditions under which instances of entities may be deleted from the system. In order to ensure the integrity and consistency of data,

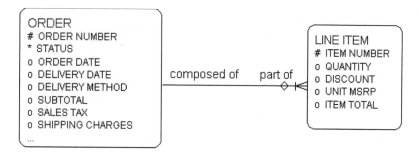

FIGURE 15.11 A visual indicator of non-transferable relationships in the Entity Relationship Diagrammer.

these rules must be clearly understood, documented, and implemented. In general, you can use one of three methods to delete data from a system:

❑ Logical delete
❑ Physical delete
❑ Archiving

As you can see from the names of these methods, each of them corresponds to a different meaning that the word "delete" may take in the business environment in which your system will be implemented. In the case of logical deletes, users do not want to physically remove the data from the database. They simply want to mark certain records as invalid, ineligible, or unavailable for certain operations. Logical deletes are usually implemented using a delete flag that can be set to indicate that the record is not available. Thus the delete rules in this case are in reality update rules. Instances deleted logically are the easiest ones to restore, since unsetting the delete flag is all that is required to make an instance available for display or other operations.

When deletes are physical, users want to remove the data from the system. This type of operation removes data without a simple way to restore them if needed. In general, deleted instances may have other instances that depend on them. An order, for example, has one or more line items related to it. Based on what happens to children records when you delete the parent, the delete can be one of the following types:

❑ **Restricted delete.** The parent record cannot be deleted if it has children records associated with it. For example, a customer record cannot be deleted if the customer represented by this record plays some role in one or more orders.
❑ **Cascade delete.** If the parent is deleted, all its children are also deleted. For

example, when an order is deleted, all its line items should be deleted. Likewise, when a product is deleted, all its product items are deleted.

❑ **Nullify delete.** In this type of delete, the parent is deleted, and the child records remain orphans but continue to exist. An example of this type of delete is when a product catalog record is deleted. The product records will no longer refer to the deleted catalog, but must still remain available in the system.

Document this type of business rule in the *Notes* property of the relationship in question. The reason is that when you create the database design based on the entity relationship model, a foreign key constraint between the master and detail tables is created based on the properties of the relationship between the corresponding entities. The Database Design Transformer transfers the settings of the property *Notes* to the new object, thus allowing you to identify the type of table constraint. You can then set the property *Delete Rule* of the foreign key constraint based on your notes from the requirements definition phase. Based on these settings, Designer/2000 generators create applications and database objects that enforce the desired delete rule.

When deletes are implemented as archiving operations, the deleted instances are removed from operational tables and stored in archive tables. Thus, the business rules that describe these operations are a combination of physical delete rules on the operational tables with insert rules in the archive tables. As you will see in coming chapters, Designer/2000 provides simple mechanisms to create journal tables as well as application logic that records insert, update, and delete operations against the operational tables. You can customize the default functionality generated by Designer/2000 to implement archiving rather effortlessly.

In addition to defining the type of delete operation you will perform on an entity, also define other rules that may restrict the delete process. These rules may require that you combine, at least conceptually, several of the delete methods discussed above. Examples of such rules are:

❑ An order cannot be deleted if its status is not 'Delivered.' However, if the status of the order is 'Delivered,' the order can be deleted together with all its line items and payment authorization information.

❑ A customer cannot be deleted if it represents a company that has placed at least one order in the last two years.

These rules must be represented as functions in the appropriate branch of the business rules functional hierarchy. As in the case of other business rules documented as functions, you may want to include their descriptions and references to the functions in the *Notes* property of the affected entity.

On a number of occasions so far, you have seen that I recommend describing the business rules associated with an entity in the *Notes* property of this entity, even if they may be represented by other objects, such as business functions. A clear advantage of this approach is that this property becomes the common storage place for most, if not all, of the business rules associated with an entity. In order to enforce this standard in your design work, you may consider setting the *Notes* property up-front for all the entities in your application system as follows:

```
DATA DEFINITION RULES

    ATTRIBUTE RULES
      N/A

    TUPLE RULES
        N/A

    ENTITY RULES
      N/A

    INTER-ENTITY RULES
        N/A

DATA MANIPULATION RULES

    CREATE RULES
        N/A

    UPDATE RULES
        N/A

    DELETE RULES
        N/A
```

Then, as you discover business rules from the categories above, you can place them in the appropriate placeholders of the template shown above. Such a template makes you more conscious about identifying and classifying the business rules. It also guarantees that the reports you generate from the definitions stored in the Repository have a consistent look and feel for all the entities.

15.4.4 EVENTS AND TRIGGERS

The events that cause a response in the system are caused either by an action of the user or at a certain time in the life of the system. You need to identify and record all the events that trigger some response from the system, together with the activity that the system performs in response to these events. Chapter 11 discussed events and functions that they trigger in the context of process modeling activities. A similar procedure is followed when event modeling is performed, to understand the events that are part of a system's life. Events are created and maintained under the group Function Event Modelling of the Repository Object Navigator using the following steps:

1. Select the node Events in the Navigator window.
2. Click the icon Create Object 🔳 on the Navigator's toolbar.
3. Switch to the Event Property Palette and enter the properties of the new event.

Figure 15.12 shows the properties settings for an event that describes a change in the entity ORDER. The property *Type* for this event is set to *'Change.'* Other settings of the *Type* property may be *'Time,' 'System,'* and *'Other.'* Depending on the type of event, additional information may be recorded in the Time or Other group of properties. Time events are those that occur at a given moment in time or periodically, at defined intervals. System events are caused by messages sent to the system by other systems, or by internal changes within the system itself. The option *Other* is a catch-all category that may be used for different purposes. You may use this type of event to capture the interactions of users with the system that you need to record explicitly.

Once an event is created in the Repository, you can associate it with business rules triggered by the event, provided that these rules already exist in the Repository in the form of functions. The following steps describe the process:

1. Expand the node that corresponds to the desired event and select the node labeled 'Triggering Functions.'
2. Click the icon Create Association 🔳 on the Navigator's toolbar.
3. Select one or more functions triggered by the event from the list displayed in the dialog box Create Event Triggers.
4. Click OK to close the dialog box Create Event Triggers.

The actions described above serve only the purpose of analyzing and documenting the events and triggers of the system. During the design and development of the system, use this information to implement the system's response to these events appropriately. Time events may be implemented using timers and

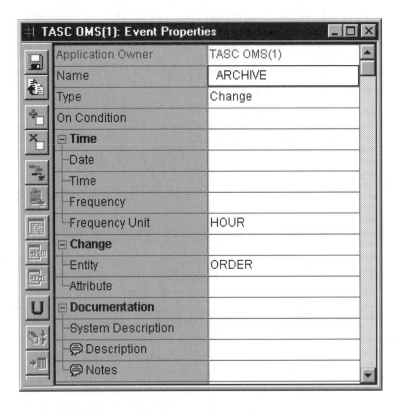

FIGURE 15.12 The Property Palette for a sample event.

other daemon processes that wake up at predefined times; change events may be implemented as triggers in the database or the front-end application that fire whenever the data is modified, and so on.

15.5 ACCESS PRIVILEGE RULES

Access privilege rules describe which users or user groups can be defined for the system, and which of them may access different parts of the system's functionality and data entities. Rules in this category include:

❑ **User group rules.** These are rules that describe which users or groups of users will access the system.

❑ **Function access rules.** These are rules that allow users to access different functions defined in the Functional Hierarchy Diagrammer. Through these rules, you may restrict access to certain screens and reports, if the functions describe the user interface of the system; or you can limit the ability of users to implement business rules defined in previous sections.

❑ **Data access rules.** The purpose of these rules is to allow a group of users to access only data that they are authorized to access. Preventing users from accessing one or more tables in the database is implemented through vertical data access rules. Horizontal data access rules are those that describe which records within a table users are allowed to access.

The following sections discuss in detail these categories of rules.

15.5.1 USER GROUP RULES

The concept of a user during the requirements analysis phase does not correspond to a system or database user, but rather to a role or group of individuals with equal privileges to access areas of the system's data and functionality. You can use business unit objects to represent these groups. Note, however, that business units in Designer/2000 are geared more towards business process reengineering activities. Therefore, during the requirements analysis for a system, you do not normally use the majority of properties of these objects. *Short Name, Name,* and *Comment* are the properties you populate when business unit objects are used to represent user groups of the system.

Note that these objects are not carried by any of the Transformers in further stages of the system's life cycle. As you will see in the coming chapters, during the physical database design, you will have to create Database Users and Roles objects to implement user security features in your system.

15.5.2 FUNCTION ACCESS RULES

Function access rules in essence list the user interface functions of the system that will be accessible for each business unit. Assuming that the business units WAREHOUSE UNIT and VENDOR are defined in the Repository, you may want to grant access to the function OMSUI41–Check Product Item Quota to both these business units, but limit the access to functions to create and approve orders to the WAREHOUSE UNIT. The Application Design Transformer takes into account these function access rules when deciding whether it should merge these modules to implement the functions into one module. The associations between business units and user interface functions can be created and maintained in the Repository Object Navigator, although the easiest place to implement this functionality is the Matrix Diagrammer. In this diagrammer, you can create a Business Units to Business Functions matrix to indicate the functions that each type of user is allowed to access.

During strategic planning and business area analysis, you may create Business Units to Functions and Business Units to Entities matrices like the ones used to record function and data access rules. However, the purpose of these matrices in those stages is to identify the organization units that have responsibility over business functions or entities. When analyzing and defining the system's requirements, these matrices describe the needs of system users to access the functionality and data of the system.

15.5.3 DATA ACCESS RULES

Data access rules describe the entities that a business unit may access. They should be identified for the purpose of achieving completeness in the system design. As in the case of function access rules, the easiest way to enter these rules in the Repository is to create a Business Units to Entities matrix that indicates which entities each group of users has privileges to access. The information you enter in these matrix diagrams is not used in any way by the Database Transformer or the Application Transformer. In the system design phase, you will have to create similar associations between database users and tables.

15.6 SUMMARY

Identifying and documenting the business rules of an information system separately from the user interface rules is an important part of the requirements analysis of the system. This activity has become increasingly more important as software engineers build mature client/server and multi-tier applications and with the explosion of the Internet technology. This chapter discusses the types of business rules to identify, and methods to record and represent them in the Designer/2000 Repository. In particular, this chapter focuses on the following topics:

- ❑ **Function Data Usages**
    - ❑ Creating and Maintaining Data Usages in the Function Hierarchy Diagrammer
    - ❑ Creating and Maintaining Data Usages in the Matrix Diagrammer
- ❑ **Business Rules**
    - ❑ Separating Business Rules from Interface Requirements
    - ❑ Categories of Business Rules

- **Data Definition Rules**
  - Attribute Rules
  - Inter-Attribute Rules
  - Entity Rules
  - Inter-Entity Rules
- **Data Manipulation Rules**
  - Create Rules
  - Update Rules
  - Delete Rules
  - Events and Triggers
- **Access Privilege Rules**
  - User Group Rules
  - Function Access Rules
  - Data Access Rules

Chapter 16

QUALITY ASSURANCE OF THE SYSTEM REQUIREMENTS

- Organizing the Diagrams
- Verifying and Reporting the Data Model
- Verifying and Reporting the Functional Model
- Summary

During strategic planning, business area analysis, and requirements definition of the systems you develop, you need to report your findings and conclusions to other interested parties on a regular basis. During these phases, keeping sponsors, executives, and other key players informed about the progress of your work is especially important. At the same time, you need to share your models and diagrams with future users of the system, to ensure that you get their input for important components of the analysis, but also to validate your conclusions and findings. Without discussing in detail the subject of deliverables and reporting in software engineering, this chapter will explain how you can use Designer/2000 to fulfill these important functions.

16.1 ORGANIZING THE DIAGRAMS

Many results of your analysis are represented in the form of diagrams, such as process flow, functional hierarchy, entity relationship, and data flow diagrams. The main purpose of these diagrams is to communicate your knowledge and understanding of the business to users in a clear and concise way. Therefore, all the diagrams you submit should be distinguished for clarity, conciseness, and precision. The following is a list of guidelines you may follow to achieve this objective in your diagrams:

❑ Establish diagramming conventions and apply them continuously and consistently.

❑ Use multiple diagrams with different levels of complexity and for different audiences.

❑ Lay out each diagram carefully by organizing its components in a way that makes the diagram readable using natural language, balancing its components, and reducing to a minimum the number of crossing lines.

❑ Minimize changes in the layout of diagrams.

❑ Use visual aids only for the purpose of adding clarity to diagrams.

❑ Associate diagrams with a legend that shows at least their title and author name.

The steps listed above may be considered guidelines to building effective diagrams or a checklist to verify the quality of the diagrams. The following sections provide additional details for each of these steps. The list is by no means exhaustive. Additional quality criteria could be applied for different types of diagrams. For example, you could search entity relationship diagrams for very rare or impossible relationships, or you could search the functional hierarchies for functions that do not operate on any data, and so on. Sections 16.2 and 16.3 discuss some of these checks and how you can use Designer/2000 matrices and reports to identify potential problems.

16.1.1 ESTABLISHING AND MAINTAINING DIAGRAMMING CONVENTIONS

Diagrams of the same type must follow an established set of conventions throughout the applications. If only one person is creating and maintaining the diagrams, these conventions are easier to follow. But in a team environment, where several analysts work with the Designer/2000 Repository tools, the potential for discrepancies and inconsistencies is greater. Every diagrammer in Designer/2000 has an established set of preferences that facilitate a great deal the task of creating consistent diagrams in a team environment. These preferences provide generic conventions that will be sufficient for most of the diagrams you will create. If you modify one of these conventions, then the whole team should be informed and follow the new convention.

When conventions are established, they should be followed continuously and consistently. The Function Hierarchy Diagrammer, for example, represents functions using their *Label* and *Short Description*, but the Process Modeller does not include the *Label*. The same labeling conventions need to be followed throughout diagrams. If you decide to add the label of process steps as an annotation in the process diagram, do so for all the steps in the diagram. Or if you decide to display the names of entities in boldface characters, this standard should be used in all the diagrams.

16.1.2 USING MULTIPLE DIAGRAMS

During the analysis of a large system, you may accumulate a vast amount of information. If you throw it in one diagram, you end up with a monolithic and cluttered representation of your knowledge about the system. Instead, try layering the information in multiple diagrams. The first diagram should contain a representation of the information at the highest level, for example the major functional areas, data subjects, or a high-level process model of the enterprise. This type of diagram is usually shown to the upper-level management and is included in executive summaries of your deliverables.

Below these high-level, context diagrams, create more detailed diagrams following a multi-tiered approach. For example, you may create a functional hierarchy diagram for each functional area, or an entity relationship diagram for each business area in the enterprise. Elements in each of these diagrams can be expanded in separate, more detailed diagrams, and so on. Usually, for functional and process diagrams, you stop when you have reached a level where each function is decomposed into elementary functions that are either executed successfully or completely rolled back. On the data side, one set of detailed diagrams contains the business area data model in the Third Normal Form. Other sets are created for each system being developed departing from the normalized version of the business area data model.

The amount of detail you present in these diagrams varies from the context. In high-level entity relationship diagrams, for example, you may want to display only the entities' names, required attributes, or those that are part of the unique identifiers or that are required. The other attributes and relationship names may be hidden from view. You may also fill entities that belong to a subsystem with the same characteristic color to give the idea that they are associated. For subsystem or lower-level diagrams, you can display all the details, including attributes and relationship names.

The display options for each diagram are maintained in the Customize dialog box, which can be accessed by choosing Option | Customize.... Figure 16.1 shows an example of the Customize dialog box for the Entity Relationship Diagrammer.

16.1.3 PLANNING THE LAYOUT OF DIAGRAMS

When building diagrams, strive for an organization and layout that helps the viewer read the diagram in a natural language rather than technical terms. Also ensure that the details you provide in the diagrams are well-balanced. In order to add clarity to the diagram, minimize the number of crossing lines in the diagram. The following paragraphs expand on these goals:

❑ **Construct diagrams that are readable using natural language.** Diagrams should be constructed such that, as the eyes flow from one object to the other, the links and the labels on the diagram get converted internally into words that make up complete sentences. This approach is especially important for entity relationship diagrams and process flow diagrams.

❑ **Create balanced diagrams.** In general, two approaches exist to decomposing high-level diagrams into lower-level, more detailed diagrams. The first one, known as the depth-first approach, expands the components of the diagram all the way down to the lowest detail. The second one, often called the breadth-first approach, expands all the components of the diagram at the same level of detail. Breadth-first diagrams are recommended since they present the information in a progressive manner, adding details with each level of decomposition included in the diagram. Depth-first diagrams, because of their nature, represent one aspect of information, whether it is a business function or data entities, in more detail than the other aspects of the same diagram. For function hierarchies for example, depth-first diagrams have a few high-level functions, and only one of them is expanded to the elementary level. The disadvantage of unbalanced diagrams is that they do not offer the large picture the senior management needs to view, and

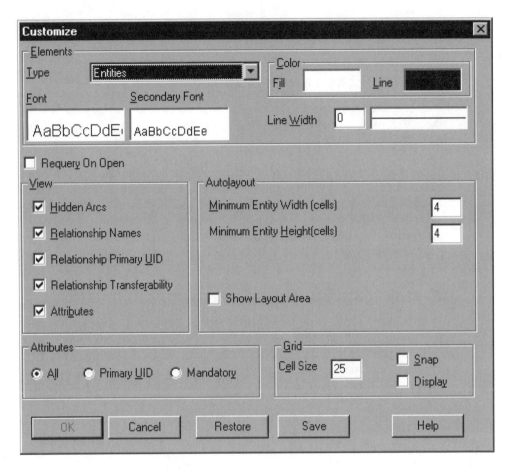

FIGURE 16.1 The Customize dialog box of the Entity Relationship Diagrammer.

they add unnecessary details to a detailed picture that users and analysts need to consider.

❑ **Minimize the number of crossing lines in the diagram.** As James Martin puts it, diagrams are aids to clear thinking about the business and the system. As such, they need to be free of congested areas, and the lines that connect their components should not intersect if possible. For some diagrams, such as functional hierarchies, the diagramming tool automatically avoids line crossings; for other diagrams, such as entity relationship or process flow diagrams, you must often adjust the diagram manually. This includes resizing objects, if possible, moving them on the diagram to more convenient positions, and modifying the extremity points or the length of lines.

16.1.4   MINIMIZING LAYOUT CHANGES

Once the diagrams are distributed to the audience, any dramatic changes in the size or relative position of their objects should be kept to a minimum. The reason is related to the way diagrams are understood and interpreted. Like any other drawing, viewers respond to the geometry, layout, and configuration of the diagrams. Rearranging objects results in a new picture that the eye has to interpret and understand, even if the objects themselves remain the same. In order to limit the modifications to your diagrams, review and test their layout carefully before publishing them. Besides finding the position and size of objects that convey more clearly the meaning of the diagram, also plan for the future introduction of other objects.

16.1.5   USING VISUAL AIDS TO ADD CLARITY TO DIAGRAMS

You can use a large variety of visual cues to add clarity to your diagrams. You can modify the fill and line colors of objects, change their font type, size, or color, embed objects from other applications using OLE technology, and so on. For process model diagrams that are demonstrated live to your audience rather than in a printed form, you can creatively use the animation features of the Process Modeller, as well as the ability to play audio and video files, or launch other applications associated with an object in the diagram.

   The other side of the token is that you do not want to burden your diagrams with unnecessary visual cues. Colors, unusual fonts, and other modifications to the diagram should be used only if they are needed to make the contents of the diagram more understandable to your audience. If they are used for unnecessary or unjustified reasons, they will have counterproductive results, since they will draw the attention away from the contents of the diagram itself.

16.1.6   ASSOCIATING DIAGRAMS WITH LEGENDS

You can also add a legend to each diagram in which you can include, among other things, the diagram's name, the application system's name, and the date when the diagram was created or last updated. These data items are maintained internally by Designer/2000. In addition, you can enter a title for the diagram and add to the legend the names of the team members who worked on the diagram. These options can be set by selecting File | Summary Information..., and checking the Show check box associated with each of them in the Summary Information dialog box. An example of the Summary Information dialog box is shown in Figure 16.2.

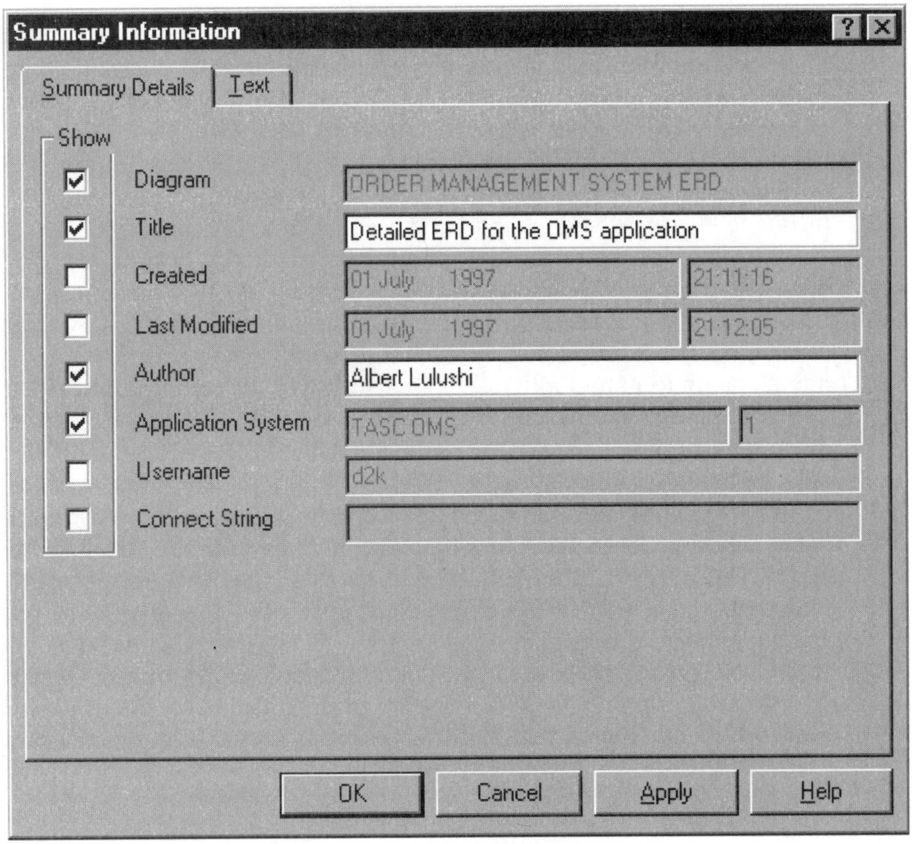

FIGURE 16.2 A Summary Information dialog box of the Entity Relationship Diagrammer.

16.2 VERIFYING AND REPORTING THE DATA MODEL

In general, the data model should be developed until all its entities are in the Third Normal Form or denormalized for justified reasons and using well documented rules. For large systems, in which several analysts work with a number of diagrams and where many entities, attributes, and relationships are identified, you can easily overlook or omit things. Therefore, you must always do some checking before giving the final touch to the diagrams. In particular, you may want to inspect the quality of relationships among entities and use several Designer/2000 reports to verify the completeness of the data model.

16.2.1 REMOVING UNCOMMON RELATIONSHIPS

The most common relationship you will create in your diagrams is the one-to-many relationship, with the many side mandatory and the one side optional. An exception to this are recursive relationships defined against the same entity to represent hierarchies. Such relationships must be optional on both sides. Recall from Chapter 15 that you want to be careful to identify a business rule to be implemented by the system that should prevent circular references in the hierarchy.

Sometimes, the one side of the relationship may also be mandatory, as in the case of entities ORDER and LINE ITEM in the OMS system. In these cases, make sure that you have defined a business rule that always associates at least one child record for each parent record. Early in the efforts to build the data model, many-to-many optional relationships will be common, but, by the end of the requirements definition stage, many of those should be resolved. Carry into the system design stage only those relationships that represent simple two-way associations between entities.

Rarely, you may also have one-to-one relationships in your diagrams, as in the example of the relationship between entities ORDER and PAYMENT AUTHORIZATION. When such relationships occur, they should be scrutinized carefully and kept only if they are needed. If both sides of a one-to-one relationship are mandatory, the entities may have been separated artificially. Figure 16.3 shows some examples of the most common relationships found in data models.

Any other relationship in the data model must be seriously questioned and transformed into one of the relationships listed above. Be especially careful to re-

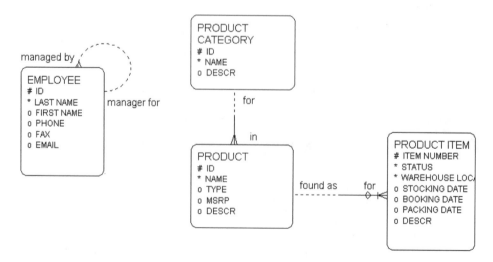

FIGURE 16.3 Entity relationships commonly encountered in entity relationship diagrams.

move relationships that cannot exist in real life, such as a recursive relationship that is mandatory on both ends.

Practice in data modeling is a good deterrent for the occurrence of such relationships in your diagrams, since an experienced eye will be able to distinguish abnormal situations in the data model. However, even the best trained data modeler may not notice an erroneous relationship, especially in the web of a complex diagram. For such cases, Designer/2000 provides a report that identifies relationships that could represent potential problems. This report is titled "Quality Checking of Relationships" and can be found under the Quality group of reports in the Repository Reports tool.

The outcome of this report is a list of uncommon or impossible relationships that currently exist in the application system. Each relationship is accompanied by a message that describes the type of problem the relationship may represent. Each of these messages is preceded by the label ERROR, which may be a little misleading in the case of rare relationships, which are nevertheless justified by your particular data model.

16.2.2 CHECKING THE QUALITY OF DATA MODEL

To help you check the quality of your data model, the report "Quality Checking of Relationships" is complemented by the report "Entity Completeness Checking." Based on the value of the parameter Entity Check Type, this second report may identify one or all of the following problems:

❑ **Entities with no Description.** With this option, the report lists all the entities for which the *Description* property is not set. This is a useful report to run before other reports, such as "Entities and their Descriptions" or "Entity Definition," which are included as appendixes to the deliverables of the requirements analysis phase.

❑ **Entities with no Relationships.** With this option, the report identifies entities that are not part of any relationship. Clearly, such entities either are overlooked or must be removed from the application system at the end of requirements analysis.

❑ **Entities with no Attributes.** With this option, the report returns entities that do not contain any attributes in their definition. Like the previous report, this one may point to areas where more analysis is required to identify the attributes that make up these entities. The only possible exceptions to such entities may be intersection entities that resolve many-to-many relationships.

❑ **Entities with no Unique Identifiers.** With this option, the report is useful to identify entities that are not analyzed to the extent required to define the unique and primary unique identifiers.

❑ **Entities not used by Functions.** With this option, the report may highlight the need for more work in the definition of the data model or the functional model. Indeed, entities may be defined properly, but the functional model may not be decomposed into the elementary level, or function entity usages are not yet created. The report may also show that the functional scope of the system is defined too narrowly. Entities and data items may have been identified, but no functions to retrieve or manipulate these data elements are included within the current boundaries of the system.

The report "Entity Completeness Checking" can be run at the application system level or for a specific diagram in the application. You can specify the values for each of these variables in the Parameters Palette of the Repository Reports tool.

16.2.3 DATA MODEL REPORTS

You can run several reports to display information about the data model stored in the Repository. These reports can be included as appendices in several deliverables that you will prepare for your audience. Their use depends on the kind of deliverable and on the type of audience for which the deliverable is intended. For high-level descriptions of the data model, which are usually directed towards senior management, you may use the following reports:

❑ **Entity Model Reference.** This report returns information about the entities defined in an application system or in an entity relationship diagram that you select. For each entity, the report displays its description, the list of attributes, and relationships in which the entity takes part. If you set the parameter Show Details, the report will also display information about the attributes defined for each entity, as well as the usages of the entity by business functions and business units. However, the information is better suited to a technical audience. The content is presented in a format that can be read and understood very easily by a person who need not be a data expert provided that the information you enter in the Repository follows conventions discussed earlier in the book. As an example, Figure 16.4 shows an excerpt from this report. A full version of this report for the OMS system is provided on the CD-ROM. You can access it by following the links *Software, Order Management System Requirements Analysis*, and *Entity Model Reference Report*.

❑ **Entity Definition.** This report returns all the information available for one or more entities in a diagram or in the whole application system. For each entity, the data are displayed in a form-like format in five sections. The first section contains properties such as the names of the entity and its synonyms. It also shows any volumetric information you have entered for the entity. The next section displays the description of the entity, followed by the list of attributes and principal properties of them, such as the *Name, Do-*

```
Entity Name : ORDER
    Short Name  : ORD
    An electronic representation of a purchase order
    placed by a customer for one or more software
    products. Order also represents the changes and
    transformations of this purchase order in the
    process of fulfilling the customer's request.

    Summary
    _____


    Attributes
    _____

      * ORDER NUMBER.............................(ORDER)
      * STATUS...................................(ORDER)
      o ORDER DATE...............................(ORDER)
      o DELIVERY DATE............................(ORDER)
```

FIGURE 16.4 An excerpt from the Entity Model Reference report.

main, Format, and *Length.* The fourth section lists all the relationships in which this entity takes part, and the last section shows any notes or remarks associated with the entity. To access a full version of this report from the Web pages of the companion CD-ROM, follow the links *Software, Order Management System Requirements Analysis,* and *Entity Definition Report.*

❏ **System Glossary.** This report returns the names and descriptions of all the entities defined in the system or in an entity relationship diagram. In addition, it returns all the synonyms defined for each entity. If the parameter Include Short Names is set to True, which is also the default setting, the report displays the short names of the entities as well. If the parameter Include Terms is set to True, the report will retrieve the business terms defined in the Repository Object Navigator. You can see a full version of this report for the OMS system by following the links *Software, Order Management System Requirements Analysis,* and *System Glossary.*

❏ **Function to Entity Matrix.** This is an important report for cross-checking the data model with the functional model, because it displays the entity usage for one or more functions in the application system. Each function is displayed on a separate page, and the entities that this function retrieves and manipulates are listed in a tabular form. Figure 16.5 shows an extract of this report for the OMS system. A full version of this report for the OMS

```
Function
------
```

```
Name      : OMSUI11
```

```
Definition: Create Order
```

Entity	Create	Retrieve	Update	Delete	Archive	Other
CUSTOMER	N	Y	Y	N	N	N
EMPLOYEE	N	Y	N	N	N	N
LINE ITEM	Y	Y	Y	Y	N	N
ORDER	Y	Y	Y	Y	N	N
ORDER MANAGEMENT TEAM	N	Y	N	N	N	N
PAYMENT AUTHORI-ZATION	Y	Y	Y	Y	N	N
PRODUCT	N	Y	N	N	N	N

FIGURE 16.5   An extract from the Function to Entity report.

system can be accessed by following the links *Software, Order Management System Requirements Analysis,* and *Function to Entity Matrix Report.*

❑ **Function to Attribute Matrix.** This report is very similar in layout to the previous function and shows the attribute usage of one or more functions. To see this report for the OMS system, follow the links *Software, Order Management System Requirements Analysis,* and *Function to Attribute Matrix Report* in the Web pages of the CD-ROM.

When the results of the requirements definition phase must be communicated to a more technical audience, or must be validated by the users community, you can include reports that return more details from the Repository in your deliverables. These reports are described in the following list:

❑ **Entities and their Attributes.** This report has a tabular format and displays the attributes defined for entities in a diagram or in the whole application system. For each attribute, properties such as *Name, Sequence, Optional, Format, Length,* and *Precision* are displayed. The results of this report serve as a quick reference to the attributes in your data model. A full version of this report for the OMS system can be accessed by following the links *Software, Order Management System Requirements Analysis,* and *Entities and their Attributes Report* in the Web pages of the CD-ROM.

❑ **Attribute Definition.** This report is the equivalent of the Entity Definition report for attributes. It displays all the information stored in the Repository for attributes of one or more entities. The information is displayed in a form layout with different sections for different groups of data. Of particular interest in this report is the section about the values that an attribute may take, if it is defined. If the attribute is within a domain, the values of the domain are listed as well. A full version of this report for the OMS system is provided on the CD-ROM. Follow the links *Software, Order Management System Requirements Analysis,* and *Attribute Definition Report.*

❑ **Attributes in a Domain.** This report is used for a quick and concise representation of all the attributes within a domain. For each attribute, the parent entity and other properties, such as *Format, Length,* and *Precision* are displayed in tabular format. Follow the links *Software, Order Management System Requirements Analysis,* and *Attributes in a Domain* to see an example of this report for all the domains in the OMS system.

16.3 VERIFYING AND REPORTING THE FUNCTIONAL MODEL

Designer/2000 provides a number of canned reports to document the functional decomposition of requirements in your application systems. These reports are grouped under the category Function Event Modelling in the Repository Reports tool. The following list provides a brief description of these reports:

❑ **Function Hierarchy.** This report is just another way of presenting the hierarchy of functions in the application system in a diagrammatic way. Although it can be considered an alternative to diagrams produced with the Function Hierarchy Diagrammer, the flexibility of these diagrams often overshadows the outcome of this report. You can see an example of this report by following the links *Software, Order Management System Requirements Analysis,* and *Function Hierarchy Report.*

❑ **Function Hierarchy Summary.** This is a useful report because it presents information about the function hierarchy in an application system in a concise tabular format. The functions in this report are listed according to a depth-first traversal of the hierarchy. The report starts from the root function and lists all the functions under one branch, all the way to the bottom of the hierarchy tree, before moving to the other branch. For each function, the report presents information such as the label, the brief description, response, and frequency requirements. The full version of this report is provided on the companion CD-ROM. Follow the links *Software, Order Management System Requirements Analysis,* and *Function Hierarchy Summary Report* to access it.

❏ **Function Definition.** The information presented by this report is focused primarily on the label and description as well as text you may have entered in the Notes properties for the report. Additional information, such as whether the function is elementary or not, decomposed or not, and its frequency and response, is part of this report as well. The information is presented in a form layout. The entity usage of a function is included in the form of a table that lists all the entities used by the function, together with the way in which the function uses these entities. You can access an example of this report for the OMS system by following the links *Software, Order Management System Requirements Analysis,* and *Function Definition Report.*

❏ **Function Data Usages Reports.** All the reports discussed earlier describe the way a function uses the data. For a more concise representation of the function entity usages, you may run the report "Function to Entity Matrix"; for a description of the function attribute usages, you may run the "Function to Attribute Matrix" report. Both these reports represent the usages in a tabular format and are discussed in Section 16.2.3.

In addition to the functions described above, you may also run reports such as "Common Functions" to present a list of all the master functions and their replicas in the functional hierarchy.

16.4 SUMMARY

One of the last activities performed during the strategic planning, business area analysis, and requirements definition of information systems is to present the findings in the form of documents and deliverables. Designer/2000 allows you to enrich these deliverables with reports and diagrams produced from the objects you have created in the Repository. This chapter discusses the types of diagrams and reports that you can produce with Designer/2000 at this stage. Important concepts explained in this chapter are:

❏ **Organizing the Diagrams**
  ❏ Establishing and Maintaining Diagramming Conventions
  ❏ Using Multiple Diagrams
  ❏ Planning the Layout of Diagrams
  ❏ Minimizing Layout Changes

       ❑ Using Visual Aids to Add Clarity to Diagrams

       ❑ Associating Diagrams with Legends

❑ **Verifying and Reporting the Data Model**

       ❑ Removing Uncommon Relationships

       ❑ Checking the Quality of Data Model

       ❑ Data Model Reports

❑ **Verifying and Reporting the Functional Model**

Part IV

SYSTEM DESIGN

Chapter 17. Creating the Initial Logical Database Design

Chapter 18. Enhancing the Logical Database Design

Chapter 19. Implementing the Physical Database Design

Chapter 20. Implementing Business Rules with Constraints

Chapter 21. Creating the Application Design

Chapter 22. Maintaining Modules in the Design Editor

Chapter 23. PL/SQL in Designer/2000

Chapter 24. Maintaining PL/SQL Objects in Designer/2000

Chapter 17

CREATING THE INITIAL LOGICAL DATABASE DESIGN

- ◆ Database Design Transformer Interface
- ◆ Creating the Logical Database Design
- ◆ Controlling the Settings of the Transformer
- ◆ How the Transformer Creates the Database Design
- ◆ Maintaining the Logical Database Design
- ◆ Mapping Supertype and Subtype Entities to Tables
- ◆ Summary

One of the major tasks in the system design phase is creating the logical and physical designs of the database. The logical design is based upon the data model created during the requirements definition phase of the system. The entities defined in this phase are mapped to tables that will store the data in the database; the attributes are mapped to table columns; unique primary identifiers yield primary keys for each table; and the relationships generate foreign key constraints. The design of the physical database is built upon the logical design by incorporating in the model information such as volumetric data, response time requirements, disk storage, and other types of requirements. As a result, additional database objects, such as indexes, tablespaces, and data files are defined in the Repository. Whereas the logical model is largely independent of implementation details, the physical model describes exactly how the logical design will be implemented in a specific environment.

Designer/2000 offers several tools to create and maintain the logical and physical design of your databases. The Database Design Transformer is an expert tool that maps the data model stored in the Repository into a logical database model. It also allows you to create elements of the physical model, such as indexes, or to set properties that are usually specified during the physical design, such as the tablespace in which database objects will be created or storage parameters for these database objects. The Design Editor is used for two purposes. The Design Navigator allows you to create elements of the physical model, such as the database, storage definitions, tablespaces, and users. Both logical and physical models are further enhanced and refined in the Data Diagrammer of the Editor. This chapter will explain the features and use of the Database Design Transformer. Chapter 18 will be dedicated to the Data Diagrammer component of this Editor. Chapter 19 will discuss how to create physical database objects in the Design Navigator of the Design Editor.

The Database Design Transformer allows you to derive the logical database model automatically from the data model stored in the Repository. This tool can be accessed independently of the Designer/2000 launch pad, or invoked from other Designer/2000 tools, such as the Entity Relationship Diagrammer or the Repository Objects Navigator. It offers a dialog box interface with several property tabs that will be explained in this section. In order to better follow the discussion in this chapter, load the application system TASC OMS (REQ) from the archive file OMSREQ.DMP into your Repository. You can find this file in the Web pages of the CD-ROM by following the links *Software* and *Order Management System Requirements Analysis.* This application system contains the requirements of the Order Management System, discussed in Part 3 of this book. Among other things, it includes the logical data model, user interface requirements, and the business rules identified for this system. After loading this application system, start the Database Design Transformer in one of the ways mentioned above, for example, by clicking the Database Design Transformer icon 🔛 in the Designer/2000 launch pad.

17.1 DATABASE DESIGN TRANSFORMER INTERFACE

The Database Design Transformer is implemented as a dialog box with multiple property tabs. This section provides an overview of these tabs. The following sections provide additional details and explain how you use each of them to create and maintain the database design.

The Database Design Transformer is built around the concept of object sets that you populate before each run. The objects in the set are processed as a group by the Transformer. You can use two modes to populate the run set of the Transformer. The default mode populates the set with all the entities and associated database objects. If you select a number of entities in the Repository Object Navigator or the Entity Relationship Diagrammer and then launch the Database Design Transformer, the default mode populates the run set with all the selected entities. The custom mode allows you to pick and choose among the available objects to include them in the run set. The tab Mode is where you select between the default and custom mode. Figure 17.1 shows an example of this tab. The other tabs of the Transformer are enabled only if the custom mode is used to populate the run set. Two of these tabs, Table Mappings and Other Mappings, allow you to explicitly populate the run set. The following paragraphs offer an overview of these tabs:

❑ **Table Mappings.** This tab allows you to include entities from the Repository in the run set. These entities may or may not be already associated with a table object. In the former case, the associated table is shown by the side of the entity.

❑ **Other Mappings.** This tab allows you to view the mappings between data model components like attributes, primary unique identifiers, and relationships to database design objects, including columns, primary keys, foreign keys, and indexes. You also use this tab to include or exclude these components from the run set.

In addition, the Database Design Transformer contains the property tab Run Options with a number of parameters that you can set and configure before running the Transformer. These parameters allow you to influence the behavior and functionality of the Transformer in the following ways:

❑ **Define the type of action performed by the Transformer.** Essentially, the Transformer performs two actions on the objects in the run set. The first one is to create database objects from definitions and properties of the data model. The second one is to modify properties of existing database objects if the data model has changed. Depending on the members of the run set and

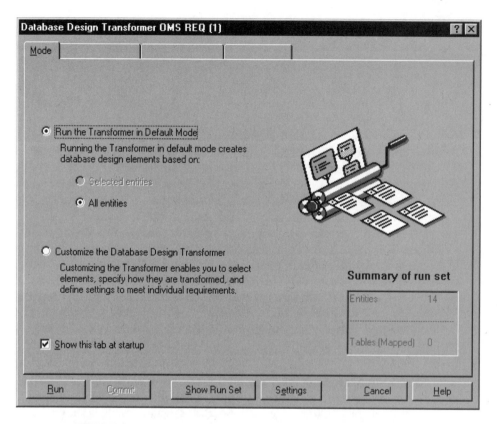

FIGURE 17.1 The Mode tab of the Database Design Transformer.

on the settings of the Run Options tab, you can create new objects and modify the properties of existing ones within the same run of the Transformer.

❏ **Define the scope of actions performed by the Transformer.** The Database Design Transformer can create and modify the properties of tables, columns, primary keys, foreign keys, and indexes. The Run Options tab allows you to control the type of objects affected by the Transformer. When you are modifying the properties of existing elements, this tab also allows you to indicate the properties that you want the Transformer to update.

At any point during the work with the Transformer you can view the elements in the run set by clicking the button Show Run Set. A dialog box similar to the one shown in Figure 17.2 will list all the elements currently included in the run set.

Finally, there is a number of physical properties that you can set for newly created database objects. These include tablespace assignments and storage parameters for tables and indexes, implementation of delete and update rules for foreign keys,

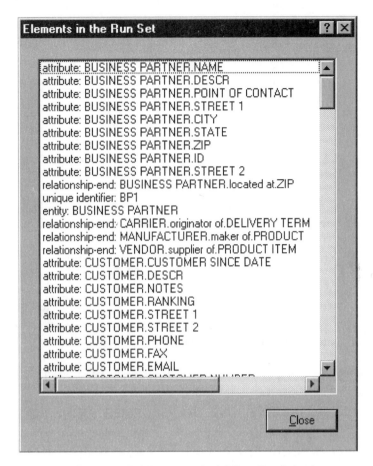

FIGURE 17.2 The Elements in the Run Set dialog box.

and implementation level for constraints. These properties are grouped in the dialog box Settings that is invoked by clicking the button with the same name in the Database Design Transformer. The upcoming sections will discuss the use of this dialog box.

17.2 CREATING THE LOGICAL DATABASE DESIGN

The logical database design is a set of database objects, including tables, primary keys, foreign keys, and indexes, that will be part of the schema of your application and that reflect its data requirements. As such, the logical database design is closely related to and derived from the data model of the application. The Database Design Transformer automates the transition from the data model to the logical database design. Using this tool, you can implement transparently the following mappings:

❑ Entities to table.
❑ Attributes to columns.
❑ Primary unique identifiers to primary keys.
❑ Unique identifiers to unique keys.
❑ Relationship ends to foreign keys. In addition, the Transformer may create indexes for each foreign key it implements.

All the mappings above can be created automatically if the Transformer is run in default mode. If you want to exercise more control in the way the Transformer works, you can use the tool as follows:

1. Populate the run set of the Database Design Transformer with the objects you want to convert.
2. Select the categories of database objects you want the Transformer to create.
3. Specify physical implementation properties, if desired.
4. Run the Database Design Transformer.

Each of these steps is discussed in the following sections.

17.2.1 POPULATING THE TRANSFORMER'S RUN SET

The process of populating the run set with data model objects for an initial mapping to database objects is very simple. By default, the Transformer will include in the set all the entities of the application system. Even if you switch to custom mode, the entities remain selected. However, the tab Table Mappings is enabled and allows you to remove some of the entities from the set. Simply clear the check box In Set to achieve this.

The Table Mappings tab, shown in Figure 17.3, lists all the entities available in the current application system. Subtype entities are listed immediately after their supertypes, indented to the right, as shown in Figure 17.3 for the case of entities BUSINESS PARTNER, CARRIER, MANUFACTURER, and VENDOR. For each entity, the text box Map Type shows whether or not the entity is mapped to a table. For entities that are not mapped to database tables, this field is set to No Mapping. When an entity is mapped to a table, the field contains Mapped, and the Table list box shows the name of the table associated with the entity, as shown in Figure 17.3 for the case of entity EMPLOYEE. For subtype entities, the Map Type text box is always set to Included.

The properties tab Table Mappings, like the entire Database Design Transformer, is designed for iterative use. You could include different entities in the

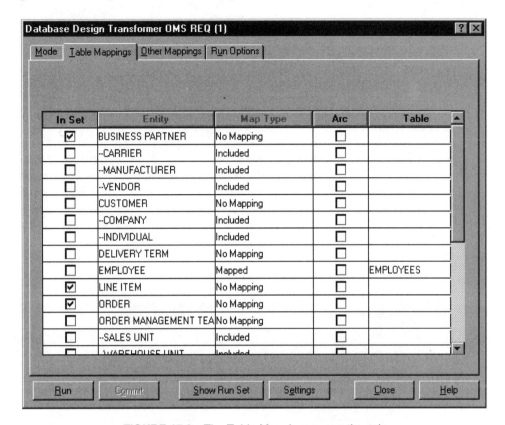

FIGURE 17.3 The Table Mappings properties tab.

run set of the Transformer each time you run it. When dealing with an environment where some entities are already mapped to tables but others are not, be careful when selecting from the drop-down list box Table. This control contains all the tables that are currently defined in the application system Repository. The current selection is the table associated with the entity, if one exists. Normally, you should let the Transformer create these associations. By accidentally picking

The only objects you need to include in the Transformer's run set are entities. Implicitly, the attributes, unique keys, and all the applicable relationship ends with other entities are added to the set.

another table from the list, you may break the association established by the Transformer.

17.2.2 SETTING THE SCOPE OF THE TRANSFORMER

After populating the run set with entities, switch to the properties tab Run Options, where you can specify what categories of database objects you want to create. An example of this tab is shown in Figure 17.4.

At the top of the Run Options tab, you see four check boxes labeled Tables, Columns, Keys, and Indexes. By default, all of them are checked, meaning that for each unmapped entity you include in the run set, the Database Design Transformer will create the corresponding table, columns, primary, unique, and foreign keys, and indexes for the foreign keys. If you want to limit the type of objects created, simply clear the appropriate check box.

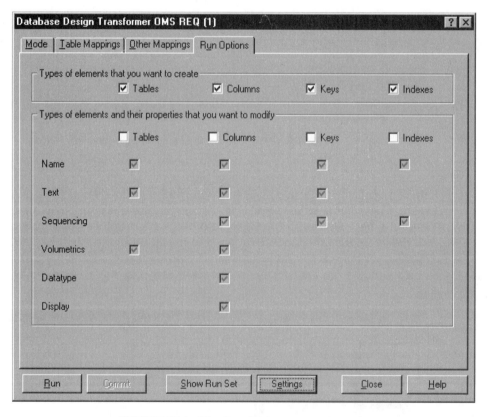

FIGURE 17.4 The Run Options properties tab.

17.3 CONTROLLING THE SETTINGS OF THE TRANSFORMER

The previous section showed how you populate the run set with data model objects and decide what database objects to derive from them. The outcome of running the Transformer with these settings is a number of table and index definitions and dependent objects. In addition, the Database Design Transformer also allows you to create implementation objects of these definitions for a particular database schema in the Repository. The Settings dialog box of the Transformer allows you to control the process of creating these implementation objects. In addition, this dialog box is used to set several other properties that influence the way the Transformer maps the data model objects to database design objects. To invoke the Settings dialog box click the button Settings in the Database Design Transformer dialog box. This dialog is composed of three tabs whose functionality will be discussed in the following sections.

17.3.1 CREATING DATABASE IMPLEMENTATION OBJECTS

The Database tab allows you to create implementation objects for tables and indexes that will be created by the Transformer. An implementation object is a physical instantiation of a logical database object, such as a table or index in a particular database schema. Creating an implementation table or index requires that you specify at least the database and user for which this object will be created. Properties of the physical object, like the tablespace or storage definition, may be specified as well. To provide settings for these properties in the Database tab, follow these steps:

1. Select the database from the list box Database. By default no database is selected, which means that the Transformer does not create the physical implementations of logical database objects.
2. Select a user from the list box Database User. This control is populated dynamically with the users of the database selected in the previous step.
3. Select the tablespace and storage definition parameters for the tables and indexes from the list boxes in the central area of the Database tab.

Figure 17.5 shows an example of this tab. Note that the objects that populate the list controls mentioned earlier must already exist in the Repository. When the logical database design is initially created, these options are not normally used, since Repository objects like databases, database users, tablespaces, and storage definitions are not added to the application system until you engage in the physical design of the database. However, in case these objects exist in the Repository, the Database Design Transformer gives you the flexibility to create tables and in-

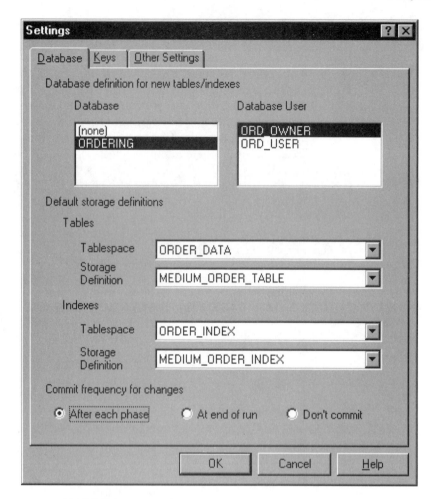

FIGURE 17.5   The Database tab of the Settings dialog box.

dexes, and, at the same time, associate them with the objects mentioned above. Chapters 18 and 19 provide more details on implementing the physical design of the database.

17.3.2   CONTROLLING THE COMMIT FREQUENCY OF THE TRANSFORMER

The work that the Transformer performs is ultimately a set of DML statements, such as inserts and updates against the Repository tables. Internally, these statements are grouped together in phases. For example, if you create tables and columns from the definitions of an entity, the Transformer executes the job in two distinct steps. First, it creates the table, and then it creates columns for each attribute defined in the entity. The radio group Commit frequency for changes at the bottom of the Database tab allows you to set the point during the run when the Database Design Transformer will commit changes to the Repository.

If the radio button After each phase is selected, the Transformer will commit the changes at the end of each step. In the example above, two commits would occur: the first after the table is created and the second after all the columns are created. If the option At end of run is set, only one commit will occur, at the end of the whole process. If the radio button Don't commit is selected, the Transformer simply posts the changes to the database. You are responsible for committing them by clicking the button Commit at the bottom of the Database Design Transformer dialog box. If you dismiss the Transformer without explicitly committing, the changes will be lost.

By default, the Transformer commits changes after each phase. This option may be especially useful when the run set includes a large number of objects, because it gives the Transformer a chance to commit the changes to the Repository after each step. In particular circumstances, especially when many objects are included in the running set of the Transformer, the amount of data posted may be significant. Since all these data are written in the rollback segments of the database that holds the Designer/2000 Repository, these segments must be large enough to accommodate them. Otherwise, the whole transaction will fail and the changes will be canceled.

17.3.3 SETTING PROPERTIES FOR KEY CONSTRAINTS

The tab Keys of the Settings dialog box allows you to set a number of properties of the referential integrity keys created by the Transformer. The following paragraphs describe the most important usages of this tab:

❑ **Set foreign key cascade rules.** For the foreign keys created by the Transformer, you can set the cascade delete and update rules ahead of time by selecting from the list boxes On Delete and On Update in the group Cascade rules for new foreign keys. However, since deciding how to implement these rules requires a careful analysis of all the options and issues involved, I recommend that you create the foreign keys with the default settings for the rules (Restricted) and return to them during the maintenance of the database design. Chapter 20 will discuss the different ways to implement the delete and update rules of foreign keys as well.

❑ **Set the implementation level of constraints.** As you will see from the following chapters, constraints serve as important tools to implement business rules identified during the analysis of the system's requirements. They can be enforced at the database level, at the client application level, or at both levels. You can ask the Transformer to set this property for the constraints it creates by selecting the options Server, Client, or Both from the list box Implementation level for constraints. By default, Both is selected to allow you to take advantage of the ability of front-end application generators to implement constraints at the client level. Chapter 20 will discuss in more detail the implementation level of constraints.

Figure 17.6 shows an example of the Keys tab. In this tab, you can see a property that has influence on the names of columns created by the Transformer. This is the control Maximum identifier length. By default, this property is set to

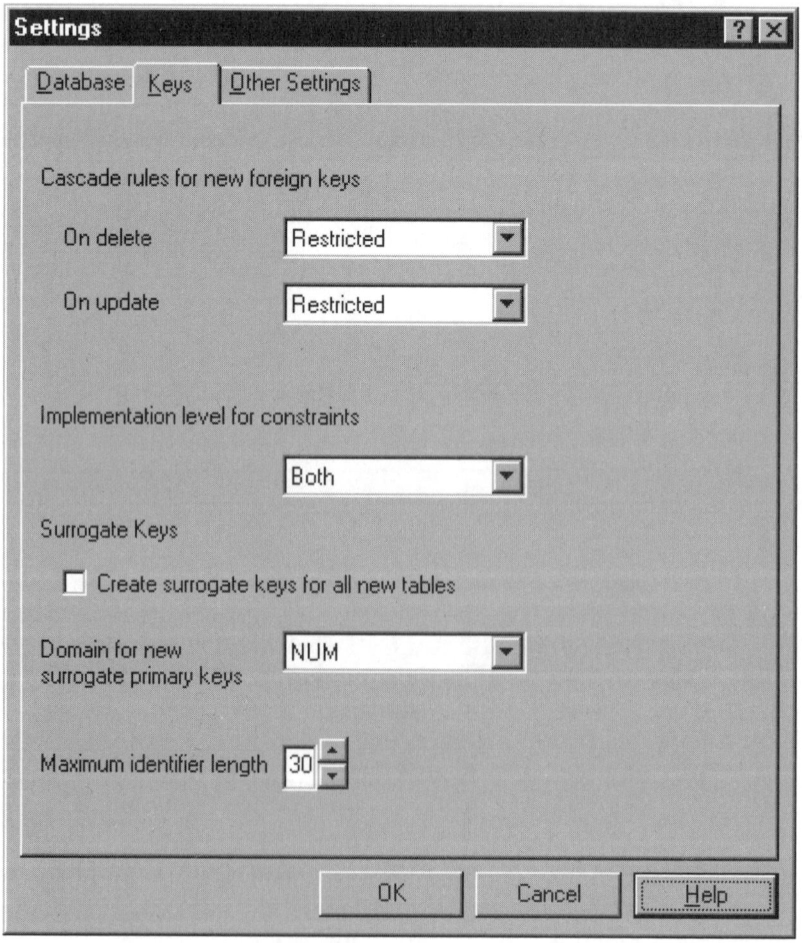

FIGURE 17.6 The Keys properties tab of the Settings dialog box.

30, which means that the Transformer guarantees the uniqueness of the first 30 characters of any names it generates. Two controls on this tab are used to implement surrogate keys for tables. These controls—Create surrogate keys for all new tables and Domain for new surrogate primary keys—and the concept of surrogate keys are discussed in Section 17.4.3.

17.3.4 SETTING MISCELLANEOUS PROPERTIES

The tab Other Settings contains a number of controls that influence the names of the tables and columns created by the Transformer. They include the text item Table prefix and the check boxes Foreign key columns, Surrogate key columns, and Columns. The text item Table prefix is usually set to an acronym for the application system, such as OMS. This will make the name of every table created by the Transformer begin with this acronym, as in OMS_CUSTOMERS or OMS_ORDERS. This feature may be helpful to avoid naming conflicts when the tables are implemented in a database schema, especially if that schema holds tables from more than one application. However, if each application uses its own database schema for its objects, prefixing the table names with the application's initials adds little value to the database design.

The column names can also be prefixed by a set of characters derived from the *Alias* property of the table. When the Transformer creates the table, it inherits this property from the property *Short Name* of the corresponding entity. If any of the check boxes listed earlier is set, the table alias will precede the name of each column in the respective category. Very little, if any, value is added to the database design by prefixing the table alias to each column in the table; therefore, this option should never be set.

Setting the check box Foreign key columns is desired and often necessary; therefore, it is set by default. Indeed, consider the case of the entity PRODUCT ITEM, which contains an attribute named ITEM NUMBER and a relationship to entity LINE ITEM, whose primary unique identifier contains a column also named ITEM NUMBER. In order to implement this relationship as a foreign key constraint on the table PRODUCT_ITEMS, the Transformer needs to include in this table a column that references LINE_ITEMS.ITEM_NUMBER. If the check box Foreign key columns is not set, this column will be called ITEM_NUMBER, thus conflicting with another LINE_NUMBER column associated with the proper attribute LINE ITEM of the entity.

An example of the tab Other Settings is shown in Figure 17.7. Notice in the lower half of this tab a list of criteria used by the Transformer to create the columns of table objects. Figure 17.7 displays the default priority of these criteria. You can lower or increase the priority level by selecting a criterion in the list and clicking the icons ▲ or ▼, respectively. However, occasions in which changes in the default priority of the Transformer are needed and justified are extremely rare. Finally, the Other Settings tab contains the check box Allow instantiable super-types, which is used to map subtype and supertype entities to tables. Section 17.6 will discuss this option.

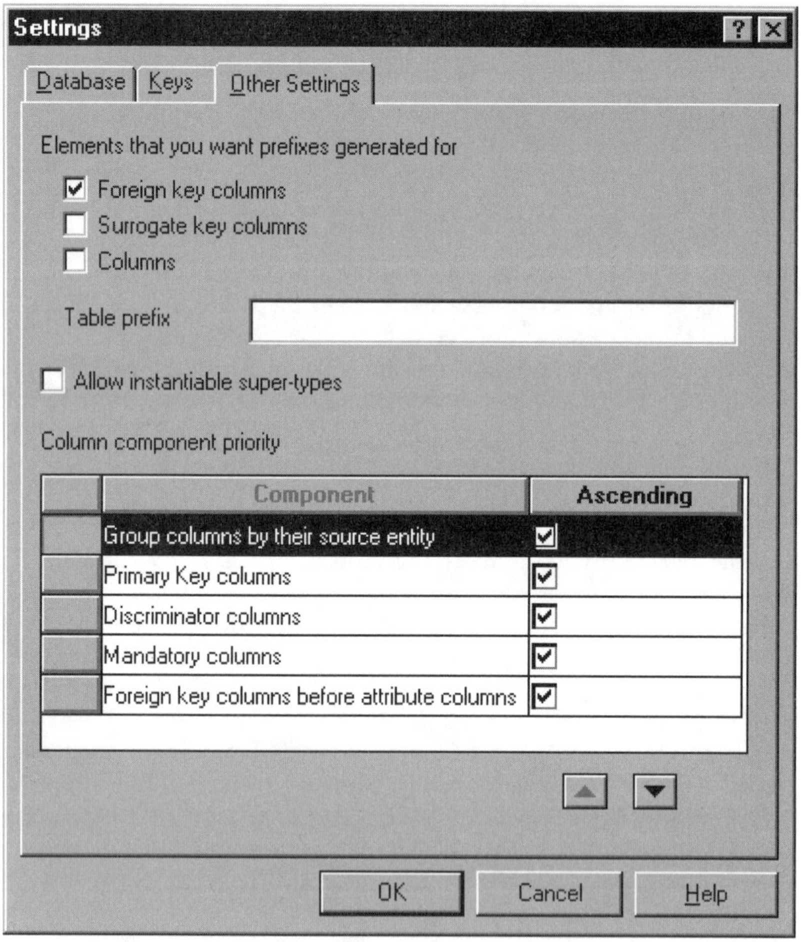

FIGURE 17.7   The Other Settings tab of the Settings dialog box.

17.4 HOW THE TRANSFORMER CREATES THE DATABASE DESIGN

The previous section discussed how you can populate the run set of the Database Design Transformer with objects and how you can control the type of objects it creates and several of their properties. The following section will provide details on how this Transformer actually converts data model objects to database objects and which properties are carried over in the process. In particular, it focuses on these topics:

❑ How the Transformer creates tables from entities definitions and properties
❑ How the Transformer creates columns from attributes and their properties
❑ How the Transformer creates primary and unique key constraints from unique identifiers
❑ How the Transformer creates foreign key constraints from entity relationships

17.4.1 CREATING TABLES

Tables are database objects that store physical instances of an entity. Therefore, a close connection exists between the entities you define during data modeling and their properties, on one hand, and the tables and their properties, on the other. In three situations, the Database Design Transformer creates tables from entities in the data model:

❑ Tables correspond to "regular" entities. The term "regular" means that the entities are not subtype of or supertype for another entity. In such cases, a straightforward mapping occurs between the entity and the table. A majority of the tables created by the Transformer fall into this category.
❑ Tables correspond to subtype and supertype entities. In four ways, subtype entities and their corresponding supertype can be converted into database tables by the Transformer. Section 17.6 discusses each of these ways.
❑ Tables do not correspond directly to an entity but are created by the Transformer to resolve many-to-many relationships. Although these cases may occur, they should be rare. In fact, if your data model contains many-to-many relationships, the data model is probably not complete nor ready to be moved to the logical database design level.

Tables that are created to implement entities inherit the majority of their properties from these entities. Figure 17.8 contains a listing of all the entity properties that the Transformer transfers to the table objects it creates.

17.4.2 CREATING COLUMNS

The Database Design Transformer draws information necessary to create columns from four sources:

❑ **Attributes.** For each attribute in the run set, the Transformer will create a column and an association between the attribute and the column. In the process, a number of attribute properties are inherited by the column. Figure 17.9 lists the attribute properties that provide the source for setting the corresponding column properties. As you can see from this figure, the number of these properties is quite large. This means that a careful collection of

ENTITY PROPERTY	TABLE PROPERTY
Plural	Name
Short Name	Alias
Name	Display Title
Initial	Start Rows
Maximum	End Rows
Description	Description, User Help Text
Notes	Notes

FIGURE 17.8   Entity properties that are mapped to table properties by the Database Design Transformer.

metadata and documentation of the data model gives you a head start in having a complete logical design of the database.

❑ **Foreign keys.** For each foreign key it creates in a table, the Transformer also creates component columns that are identical to the primary key columns of the table referenced by the foreign key. If the check box Foreign key columns on the Other Settings tab of the Settings dialog box is checked, all the foreign key columns are prefixed with the alias of the referenced table. I will say more on creating foreign keys in Section 17.4.4.

❑ **Surrogate keys.** Section 17.4.3 will show when the Database Design Transformer creates surrogate primary keys. Note that these keys are imple-

ATTRIBUTE PROPERTY	COLUMN PROPERTY
Name	Column Name, Prompt
Optional	Optional
Domain	Domain
Format	Datatype
Maximum Length	Maximum Length
Average Length	Average Length
Decimal Places	Decimal Places
Percent Used–Initial	Initial Volume
Percent Used–Final	Final Volume
Comment	Hint, Comment
Default	Default Value
Sequence in Entity	Sequence in Table
Description	Description, User Help Text
Notes	Notes

FIGURE 17.9   Attribute properties that are mapped to column properties by the Database Design Transformer.

In addition to inheriting the properties shown in Figure 17.9, a column also inherits any allowable values that may have been defined for the attribute. Recall, however, from Chapter 14 that if allowable values exist for an attribute, a more suitable approach is to create them in a domain object and to include the attribute in the domain.

mented by an extra column added to the table. The name of this column is ID, but if the check box Surrogate key columns in the Other Settings tab of the Settings dialog box is checked, the name of the column is prefixed by the table alias, as in EMP_ID or ORD_ID. This column is of NUMBER data type by default, although you can assign it to an existing domain by selecting the name of the domain from the list box Domain for new surrogate primary keys. This list is part of the Keys tab of the Settings dialog box.

❑ **Multiple entities mapped to the same table.** This situation occurs with several mappings of subtype and supertype entities. Each of these mappings is discussed in Section 17.6. Figure 17.10 shows the example of the entity PAYMENT AUTHORIZATION and its subtypes CREDIT CARD, MONEY ORDER, and CHECK implemented as one table, PAYMENT_AUTHORIZATIONS. The Transformer has added the mandatory column PA_TYPE

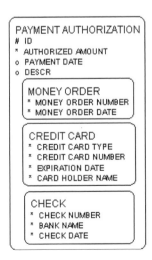

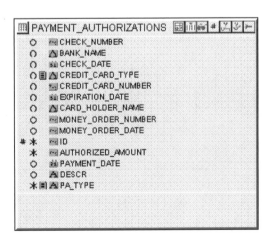

FIGURE 17.10 A column created to differentiate among physical instances of different entities stored in the same table.

with three allowable values (CC—Credit Card, MO—Money Order, and CHE—Check). For each record inserted in the table PAYMENT_AUTHO-RIZATIONS, the value of the column PA_TYPE will indicate the kind of payment authorization this record represents.

17.4.3 CREATING PRIMARY AND UNIQUE KEYS

When you run the Database Design Transformer with the option to create keys, it will create a unique key constraint for each unique identifier (UID) defined for the entity. The UID with the property *Primary* set to 'Y' yields the primary key constraint of the table. The naming convention that the Transformer uses for the constraints it generates is as follows:

❏ Primary key names are formed by concatenating the property *Alias* of the table with the string '_PK.' Examples of such names are EMP_PK, ORD_PK, LI_PK, PI_PK, and so on.

❏ Unique key names are formed by concatenating the property *Alias* of the table with the name of the unique identifier, with the string '_UQ.' Examples of such names are EMP_EMP2_UQ and PI_PI3_UQ.

Recall from Chapter 14 that unique identifiers may be composed of relation-ships as well as attributes. For example, the primary unique identifier of the en-tity LINE ITEM is composed of the attribute ITEM NUMBER and the relationship with the entity ORDER. In such cases, the Database Design Transformer creates columns to implement the foreign key, as explained in Section 17.4.2. In addition, these columns also become part of the primary key of the table, which now is a composite key. For the two entities mentioned above, the column ORDER_NUM-BER implements the foreign key to table ORDERS and is also part of the primary key of table LINE_ITEMS, together with the column ITEM_NUMBER.

When primary unique identifiers are composed of several attributes or rela-tionships, the Database Design Transformer will create a table with a composite primary key. Often this is not desirable, especially when the number of these components is large (over two or three), or when one of the components will need to be updated. In this case, you can create a surrogate column to serve as the primary key for the table. Often, this column is created during data modeling ac-tivities, but by adding an attribute to the entity that becomes the primary unique identifier of the entity. This attribute is often named ID; it has a numeric data type and is referred to as an internal identifier for the entity, to distinguish it from other attributes meaningful to the business. The Order Management System data model contains several entities with such an attribute, including PRODUCT, BUSINESS PARTNER, and EMPLOYEE.

Alternatively, you may use the Database Design Transformer to implement the primary key for you by adding a column called the surrogate primary key column. The Transformer will create this key if you set the check box Create surrogate keys for all new tables in the Keys tab of the Settings dialog box. The column created to implement the key may be prefixed with the table alias, and it can be included automatically in a domain. In addition, the Transformer creates a sequence object from which the values of the primary key will be generated. The name of this sequence is formed by concatenating the table alias with the characters '_SEQ,' as in ORD_SEQ or EMP_SEQ.

A case when the Database Design Transformer will always create a surrogate primary key is when its run set includes an entity for which you have not defined any unique identifiers. Note, however, that entities without unique identifiers are a sign that the data model probably is not complete and that you need to collect additional information about them before mapping them to database tables.

17.4.4 CREATING FOREIGN KEY CONSTRAINTS

Relationships between entities in the data model are translated into foreign key constraints in the logical database model. The following list describes how the three most important types of relationships are implemented as foreign keys:

❑ **One-to-many relationships.** For these relationships, the Database Design Transformer creates a foreign key constraint on the table that corresponds to the entity on the many end of the relationship. The relationship between entities ORDER and LINE ITEM, for example, causes the Transformer to add a foreign key constraint to the table LINE_ITEMS. In order to implement this constraint, the Transformer will add to the table columns whose properties are identical to those of the columns that make up the primary key of the referenced table. If the many end of the relationship is mandatory, the property *Optional?* of these columns will be set to *'False,'* which means that they will not allow NULL values in them. Otherwise, the property *Optional?* is set to *'True.'* (If the one end of the relationship is mandatory, you need to declare this as a business rule that will be implemented programmatically.)

❑ **One-to-one relationships.** If the ends of these relationships are both optional or mandatory, the Transformer will pick arbitrarily one table to store the foreign key that points to the other table. If one side of the relationship is mandatory and the other side is optional, then the foreign key will reside in the table on the mandatory side.

❑ **Many-to-many relationships.** For these relationships, the Database Design Transformer creates an intersection table to resolve the relationship. In order to do so, both entities must be already mapped to tables. The intersection table contains two foreign keys, each referencing the original tables. The columns that will compose these keys and their *Optional?* property setting are defined based on the primary keys of the original tables and the optionality of each relationship end.

When the Database Design Transformer creates foreign key columns to implement the referential integrity between tables, it sets the properties of these columns based on the properties of the primary key columns they reference. The names of these columns, by default, are prefixed by the alias of the table being referenced. Thus, if the primary key of table PRODUCTS is ID, if its alias is PROD, and if the table LINE_ITEMS references the table PRODUCTS, the foreign key column that the Transformer will add to LINE_ITEMS will be named PROD_ID. This behavior can be modified by clearing the check box Foreign key columns on the Keys tab of the Settings dialog box.

The Database Design Transformer also allows you to create indexes for each foreign key that is necessary to express a relationship in your data model. Arguments exist for and against creating indexes at this point in the design of the database. Normally, indexes are designed and created during the physical design of the database, after the data access patterns of the application are analyzed and optimal performance enhancement strategies are devised. On the other hand, indexes are almost always created on foreign keys, since the related tables are joined on these keys when information is queried from both tables. Therefore, depending on the particular situation in your application, you may decide to create the indexes on foreign keys using the Database Design Transformer, or postpone the task for a later moment.

 In cases when multiple relationships exist between two tables, the primary key columns of the referenced table will be included multiple times, once for each relationship. For example, an order may be created by an employee, booked by another employee, and packed by a third one. In order to implement these three foreign key constraints on the table ORDERS, the Transformer needs to create three columns that reference the primary key column of the table EMPLOYEES. For the first column, the same convention explained in this section is followed. Each additional column is further qualified by the name of the relationship end. Thus, the foreign key columns added in this case could be EMP_ID, EMP_ID_BOOKED_BY, and EMP_ID_PACKED_BY. In order to maintain consistent naming for these columns, you could change the name of the first one to EMP_ID_CREATED_BY. Chapter 19 will provide details on how you can maintain this and other properties of columns.

17.5 MAINTAINING THE LOGICAL DATABASE DESIGN

The previous sections discussed how you can create database objects based on the data model using the Database Design Transformer. As mentioned there, use the Transformer after the data model has reached a desired level of stability. However, a stable data model is not rigid. Changes and modifications are normal and to be expected, especially when the data model is maintained over a long period of time. The changing business needs of your environment and new requirements may demand that you modify entities, attributes, and relationships in the data model. The Database Design Transformer allows you to keep the database design synchronized with the data model over a period of time. In order to cascade the modifications of the data model to the database design, you need to perform the following steps with the Transformer:

1. Populate the run set of the Database Design Transformer with the objects you want to modify.
2. Select the categories of database objects you want the Transformer to modify.
3. Specify the types of properties that you want to modify.
4. Run the Database Design Transformer.

The actions you take to populate the run set of the Transformer when updating are very similar to those you take to populate this set when creating objects. In fact, to include the entities and their associations in the set, you perform the same steps described in Section 17.2.1 and work with the property tab Table Mappings shown in Figure 17.3.

When entities and their associated tables are included in the run set, the Transformer automatically includes the columns, primary, unique, and foreign keys, and the indexes on foreign keys. You can use the properties tab Other Mappings. The following sections describe the functionality and use of this tab in the Database Design Transformer.

17.5.1 MAINTAINING COLUMN MAPPINGS

The mapping of attributes of an entity to columns in the corresponding table can be viewed and maintained on the tab Other Mappings of the Transformer, by selecting the radio button Columns as shown in Figure 17.11.

With this layout of the Other Mappings tab, you can select a table from the list box Table in the upper left-hand corner. When you do this, the Transformer shows the entities that this table implements in the list control Entities imple-

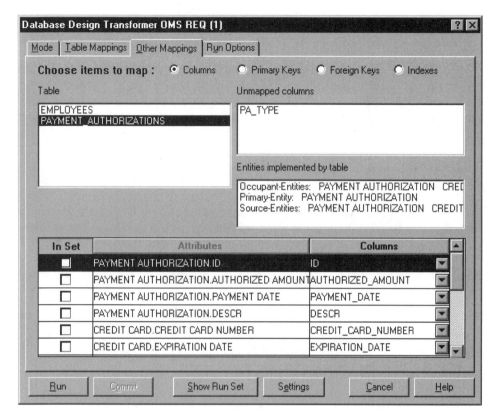

FIGURE 17.11 Displaying column mappings in the Other Mappings
properties tab.

mented by table. The multi-record control on the lower half of the tab shows all
the attributes of the entities that this table implements and their associated
columns. If attributes in the entity are not mapped to a column, you can check the
option In Set to include them in the next run of the Transformer. You may encounter this situation if you revise the data model by adding attributes to an entity and want the logical database model to reflect the changes.

The upper right-hand corner of the properties tab contains a list box titled
Unmapped columns. This list contains all the columns from the selected table
that are not mapped to an attribute. In the case shown in Figure 17.11, the unmapped column PA_TYPE represents the discriminating column introduced by
the Transformer to implement the supertype entity PAYMENT AUTHORIZA-
TION and its subtypes MONEY ORDER, CREDIT CARD, and CHECK. This column is created by the Transformer and does not have a corresponding attribute
in the data model. On the other hand, if the database design is modified by
adding one or more columns to the table, the Unmapped columns list will serve

After the initial mapping of an entity to a table and its attributes to columns, you may have to modify the data model. The Database Design Transformer will pick up new attributes added to the entity since the last run and allow you to map them to columns on the table. On the other hand, if an attribute is removed, the Transformer will not delete its corresponding column from the table. You will have to remove this column manually from the Design Editor or the Repository Object Navigator. The extra work required is another reason why the Database Design Transformer must be used after the data model is stabilized.

as a reminder that you need to update the data model with a new attribute that corresponds to this entity.

17.5.2 MAINTAINING MAPPINGS OF KEY CONSTRAINTS

The tab Other Mappings with the radio button Primary Keys selected shows how the unique identifiers defined for an entity are mapped to primary and unique keys in the corresponding table. When the radio group Foreign Keys is selected, the tab shows the mapping between relationship ends and foreign key constraints. The layout and use of the tab in both cases is very similar to the layout and use of the tab when the option Columns is selected.

The list box Table in the upper left-hand corner allows you to select one of the tables defined in the Repository. All the entities implemented by this table are listed in the Implements control. The lower half of the tab contains the unique identifiers of the entity and their associated primary or unique keys. You can modify the properties of any of these keys by checking the check box In Set. If the table contains primary or unique key constraints that do not correspond to a unique identifier, they are all listed in the list Unmapped primary/unique keys.

17.5.3 CREATING INDEXES FOR FOREIGN KEYS

The Database Design Transformer also allows you to create indexes for each foreign key necessary to express a relationship in your data model. The default settings of the Transformer are such that indexes are created automatically when the entities are mapped to tables. You can maintain the associations between foreign keys and indexes by selecting the radio button Indexes on the Other Mappings properties tab of the Database Design Transformer. The layout and use of the tab are similar for the case of indexes and columns, primary keys, or foreign keys discussed earlier.

17.5.4 SETTING THE SCOPE OF THE TRANSFORMER

You can control the types of objects in the run set that the Database Design Transformer can modify in the same way that you can control the objects that the Transformer can create. Recall from Section 17.2.2 that the Run Options tab is where you can control the scope of changes performed by the Transformer. For your convenience, this tab is shown again in Figure 17.12.

This tab contains a group of check boxes that allow you to select the type of elements and their properties that the Transformer will modify. By setting the check box Tables, Columns, Keys, or Indexes in this group, you instruct the Transformer to work with the corresponding types of objects included in the run set. For each check box selected, the appropriate check boxes below it are enabled. These check boxes allow you to specify which properties of the objects in the run set the Transformer will modify in the next run. By default, all the options are checked, however. As you can see from Figure 17.12, not all categories of properties apply to every object that can be included in the set. For example, if

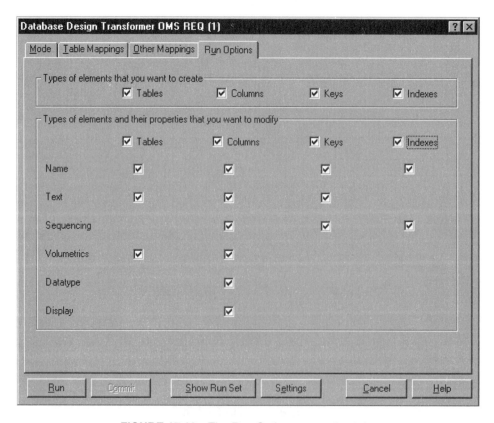

FIGURE 17.12   The Run Options properties tab.

the set contains tables, the Transformer will modify their name, volumetric properties, and text properties. But if the set contains columns, then the datatype, display properties, and sequencing properties may be modified as well.

17.6 MAPPING SUPERTYPE AND SUBTYPE ENTITIES TO TABLES

As you saw in Section 17.4.1, the way the Database Design Transformer maps entities to tables is simple and straightforward. However, for implementing subtype and supertype entities, you can choose several alternatives. Consider, for example, the subtypes CREDIT CARD, CHECK, and MONEY ORDER of supertype PAYMENT AUTHORIZATION shown in Figure 17.13.

These four entities may be mapped to tables in one of the following four ways:

❑ All the entities are mapped to a single table, PAYMENT_AUTHORIZA-TIONS, which will contain instances for each entity. This implementation is also known as supertype implementation.

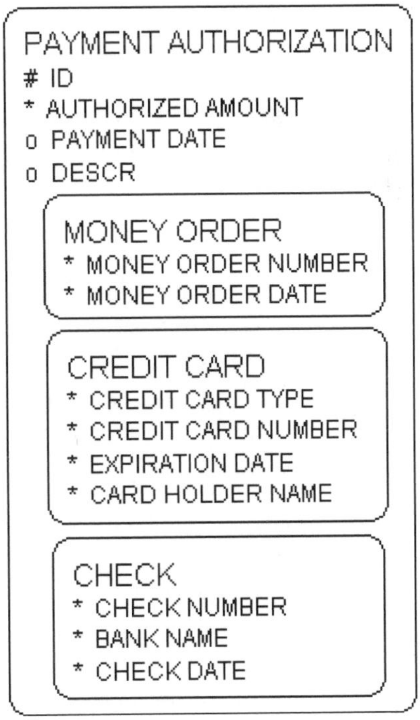

PAYMENT AUTHORIZATION
\# ID
* AUTHORIZED AMOUNT
o PAYMENT DATE
o DESCR

MONEY ORDER
* MONEY ORDER NUMBER
* MONEY ORDER DATE

CREDIT CARD
* CREDIT CARD TYPE
* CREDIT CARD NUMBER
* EXPIRATION DATE
* CARD HOLDER NAME

CHECK
* CHECK NUMBER
* BANK NAME
* CHECK DATE

FIGURE 17.13 Subtype and supertype entities.

❑   Only subtype entities are mapped to tables. The proper attributes of PAY-
MENT AUTHORIZATION, such as AUTHORIZED AMOUNT and PAY-
MENT DATE, will be replicated in each of the tables. This is called Explicit
subtype implementation.

❑   A separate table exists for the supertype and each subtype entity. As in the
case above, the proper attributes of PAYMENT AUTHORIZATION, such as
AUTHORIZED AMOUNT and PAYMENT DATE, will be replicated in each
of the subtype tables and, in addition, in the PAYMENT_AUTHORIZA-
TION table as well. This is known as the Implicit subtype implementation.

❑   A separate table exists for the supertype and each subtype entity. However,
unlike the two previous cases, the columns from the supertype table are not
replicated in the subtype tables. Instead, foreign keys are created in the supertype table that reference each subtype table. This is known as the Arc implementation.

The following sections will show the outcome of each implementation with
examples from the Order Management System. Advantages and disadvantages
of each method are also listed.

17.6.1   SUPERTYPE IMPLEMENTATION

One way to implement subtype and supertype entities in the
database is to create one table that will represent all the entities.
This table will store records that represent instances from each
entity; therefore, it will contain columns based on the attributes of
each entity. In addition, the Database Design Transformer creates
an extra column to distinguish records of one subtype from those
of other subtypes. The Transformer sets the properties of this table as follows:

❑   The *Column Name* property setting is formed by concatenating the supertype table alias with the characters '_TYPE,' as in 'PA_TYPE.'

❑   Datatype is set to 'VARCHAR2'; Average Length and Maximum Length are
set to '10.'

❑   The Optional property is set to 'False' to indicate that each record in this
table should contain a value from this column to indicate the subtype.

In addition, the Transformer creates an allowable value for each subtype of the
supertype. The *Value* and *Abbreviation* properties of each value are set to the *Short
Name* property of the subtype entity this value represents. Examples of such settings
are 'CC' for CREDIT CARD, 'MO' for MONEY ORDER, and 'CHE' for CHECK. The
Meaning property of each allowable value is set to the Name of the entity.

You can accomplish the supertype implementation of subtype and supertype entities by including only the supertype entity in the run set of the Database

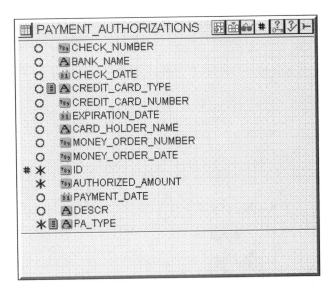

FIGURE 17.14 Results of mapping supertype and subtype entities into one table.

Design Transformer. Figure 17.14 shows the outcome of such an implementation for the PAYMENT AUTHORIZATION entity.

Some advantages of mapping supertypes and subtypes to a single table are:

❑ The database schema is simplified and the number of database objects to maintain is minimal.

❑ Accessing data for the supertype or each subtype is easier, since only one table is involved.

Disadvantages of this approach include:

❑ All the columns derived from subtype attributes must allow NULL values so that records from different subtypes may be stored in the table. This requirement means that if one of the subtype attributes is required, then you have to create a business rule that ensures that the corresponding column contains a value for the right type of record and is NULL for the other types. Recall from Chapter 15 that tuple business rules were identified to document such requirements for the case of the entity PAYMENT AUTHORIZATION and its subtypes.

❑ Data manipulation statements may have to be tailored for different sets of columns, depending on whether they implement business rules that apply to the supertype entity or any if its subtypes. This situation may be improved by creating views that contain only those columns that apply to each entity. Chapter 19 will discuss views in detail.

❑ Because some columns will always be NULL in the records of the table, some inefficient use of disk space may occur.

The supertype implementation is advantageous when the subtypes do not contain a great number of attributes that set them apart. Particularly good candidates for such an implementation are entities in which subtypes are introduced to clearly distinguish the type of instances in the data model. In the Order Management System, such cases are BUSINESS PARTNER and its subtypes (MANUFACTURER, VENDOR, CARRIER), and ORDER MANAGEMENT UNIT and its subtypes (SALES UNIT, WAREHOUSE UNIT).

17.6.2 EXPLICIT SUBTYPE IMPLEMENTATION

Another way to implement supertype and subtype entities as tables is to merge the columns derived from the supertype with columns derived from subtypes in separate tables. This method yields as many tables as the number of subtypes. Each table will contain the columns from the subtype entity and, in addition, the columns associated with attributes of the supertype entity. Thus, these columns are replicated for each table created with this method.

In order to accomplish explicit subtype implementation of entities in the Database Design Transformer, you must select the check boxes In Set for each subtype entity you want to implement—for example CREDIT CARD, MONEY ORDER, and CHECK—and clear it for the supertype entity. Figure 17.15 shows the tables created by the Transformer in the case of the entity PAYMENT AUTHORIZATION and its subtypes.

The explicit subtype implementation has the following advantages:

❑ Required attributes of subtypes are mapped to columns that do not allow NULL values. Thus, you no longer have to implement this rule programmatically.

❑ You no longer have to differentiate subtypes programmatically or by creating views.

Disadvantages include:

❑ Supertype records cannot be maintained independently. They have to be created or maintained as one of their subtypes.

❑ Queries on supertype attributes will have to be executed against separate tables and the record sets merged with a UNION operation. For example, in order to compute the sum of payments authorized on a given date, you will have to perform the computation on each individual table and then merge the results. This may result in poor performance of these queries.

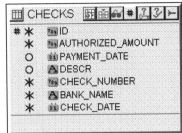

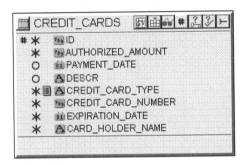

FIGURE 17.15 Results of mapping supertype and subtype entities into one table for each distinct subtype.

❑ Because one table exists for each subtype, the number of database objects to maintain and application modules to develop is generally larger than in the first case.

17.6.3 IMPLICIT SUBTYPE IMPLEMENTATION

The implicit subtype implementation addresses the deficiencies of the previous method with regard to supertype entities, by creating a separate table for the supertype entity and a table for each subtype. As in the previous method, supertype attributes are replicated in each subtype table. In order to implement this method using the Database Design Transformer, set the check box In Set for the supertype and all the subtype entities. Figure 17.16 shows the tables that you would create as a result of this approach.

The implicit subtype implementation method has the following advantages:

❑ Unlike the explicit subtype implementation, instances of the supertype entity can be accessed directly and independently of its subtypes.
❑ Unlike the supertype implementation, required attributes of subtypes are

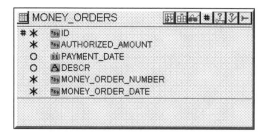

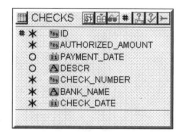

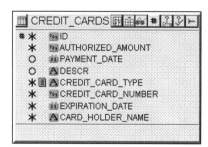

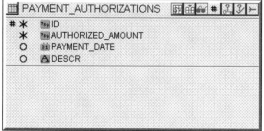

FIGURE 17.16   Mapping supertype and subtype entities using the
implicit subtype implementation method.

mapped to columns that do not allow NULL values. Thus, you no longer
have to implement this rule programmatically.

❑   You no longer need to differentiate subtypes programmatically or by creating views. At the same time, UNION operations are not required to select
supertype attributes

The disadvantages are as follows:

❑   Inserting and deleting data from the subtype tables will result in duplicate
transactions against the supertype and the appropriate subtype entities.
Similarly, updates of supertype attributes will require updates of the same
attributes in all the subtype tables. Locking problems are generally more severe in these situations.

❑   The number of database objects to maintain will be larger than for any of
the previous methods. This may lead to additional modules that will need
to be developed and maintained.

❑   Repeating columns attributes in multiple tables result in a waste of storage
space.

17.6.4 ARC IMPLEMENTATION

Finally, supertype and subtype entities may be mapped to database tables in a fourth way, known as the arc implementation method. Like the implicit subtype implementation, this method maps each supertype and subtype entity to its own table. But unlike the previous approach, the supertype columns in the arc implementation are not replicated in the subtype tables. Instead, foreign key columns related to the primary keys of each subtype are added to the supertype table.

You take a two-phase approach to implementing this kind of mapping in the Database Design Transformer. First, you create *only* the tables that correspond to each entity. In order to do so, follow these steps:

1. Set the In Set check box for the supertype and all the subtype entities.
2. Switch to the Run Options properties tab and clear the check boxes Columns, Keys, and Indexes. The intention here is to create just the tables and their associations with entities, without any of the other objects associated with these tables.
3. Click the Run button to create the tables for the entities included in the set.

After creating the tables, you need to run the Transformer one more time to create the columns and foreign keys needed to implement the arc relationship between the new tables. The following steps allow you to achieve this:

1. Switch to the Table Mappings properties tab and make sure that the check box In Set is set for the supertype and all the subtype entities you included in the Transformer's set for the initial run.
2. Set the Arc checkbox for the subtype entities. Notice how the Map Type setting changes to Arc.
3. Switch to the Run Options properties tab and select the check boxes Columns, Keys, and, optionally, Indexes.
4. Click the Run button to create the columns and arc foreign key relationships for the tables in the set.

Figure 17.17 shows the outcome of these actions for the entities PAYMENT AUTHORIZATION, CREDIT CARD, MONEY ORDER, and CHECK. Given the nature of attributes entered for subtype entities—complementary to attributes of the supertype— in most of the cases, these entities are not likely to have unique identifiers defined explicitly. As discussed in Section 17.4.3, the Transformer will create surrogate primary keys for the subtype tables. Therefore, setting the properties of these keys using the controls provided in the property tab Options of the Transformer is a good idea. In particular, I recommend that you uncheck the

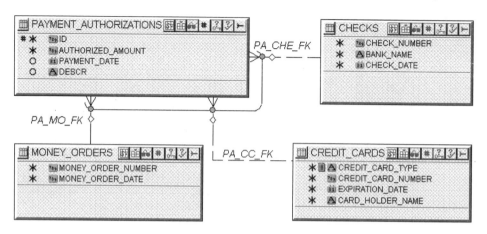

FIGURE 17.17   An example of arc implementation of supertype and subtype entities.

check box Prefix Surrogate Key Columns, and include the key column in a domain that you can select from the list box Surrogate Primary Key Domain.

The arc implementation of supertype and subtype entities has the following advantages over the previous approach:

❑   It addresses its data manipulation deficiencies because data need to be inserted or updated in only one place.

❑   It uses the disk space more efficiently.

On the other hand, the foreign key relationships between supertype and subtype tables create the following disadvantages:

❑   The existence of a mandatory arc on the foreign keys of the supertype table means that each record in this table must be associated with one record from one of the subtype tables.

❑   Queries for attributes from the supertype and the subtype tables will require a JOIN operation, which may degrade the performance under certain circumstances.

You can see from the discussion of the different methods for mapping supertype and subtype entities to tables, that each of them has its advantages and disadvantages. In any given situation, you will need to weigh the advantages and disadvantages of each approach and choose the one that best meets the needs of your system.

17.7 SUMMARY

One of the first activities performed during the system design is to create the logical database design for the application. A careful data model prepared during the requirements definition phase is the best starting point for a robust database design. The Database Design Transformer is the Designer/2000 tool that allows you to convert data model components of an application system, such as entities, attributes, unique identifiers, and relationships, into database objects like tables, columns, primary, unique and foreign key constraints, and indexes. This chapter discusses how you can use the Database Design Transformer to create the logical design of your database in the most efficient way. The most important topics presented in this chapter include:

- ❏ **Database Design Transformer Interface**
- ❏ **Creating the Logical Database Design**
  - ❏ Populating the Transformer's Run Set
  - ❏ Setting the Scope of the Transformer
- ❏ **Controlling the Settings of the Transformer**
  - ❏ Creating Database Implementation Objects
  - ❏ Controlling the Commit Frequency of the Transformer
  - ❏ Setting Properties for Key Constraints
  - ❏ Setting Miscellaneous Properties
- ❏ **How the Transformer Creates the Database Design**
  - ❏ Creating Tables
  - ❏ Creating Columns
  - ❏ Creating Primary and Unique Keys
  - ❏ Creating Foreign Key Constraints
- ❏ **Maintaining the Logical Database Design**
  - ❏ Maintaining Column Mappings
  - ❏ Maintaining Mappings of Key Constraints
  - ❏ Creating Indexes for Foreign Keys
  - ❏ Setting the Scope of the Transformer
- ❏ **Mapping Supertype and Subtype Entities to Tables**
  - ❏ Supertype Implementation
  - ❏ Explicit Subtype Implementation
  - ❏ Implicit Subtype Implementation
  - ❏ Arc Implementation

Chapter 18

ENHANCING THE LOGICAL DATABASE DESIGN

♦ Maintaining Data Diagrams

♦ Maintaining Tables

♦ Providing for Data Auditing and Journaling

♦ Creating and Maintaining Indexes

♦ Maintaining Views

♦ Maintaining Snapshots

♦ Creating and Maintaining Sequences

♦ Using the Database Object Guide

♦ Summary

As a transition step from the requirements analysis to the system design phase, you use the Database Design Transformer to convert the data model into the initial logical database design. After that, as more information becomes available, you will need to refine and enhance this model. Some of the enhancements you can add in this phase are diagramming the database objects, maintaining their properties, and implementing these objects for given databases and users. The Design Editor is the primary Designer/2000 tool you can use to enhance and maintain the data model. Its Design Navigator and Data Diagrammer components are used to perform important database design tasks such as the following:

❑ Maintain definitions of objects generated by the Database Design Transformer
❑ Associate logical design objects with physical design objects
❑ Create new tables, views, indexes, and snapshots
❑ Assign and maintain access privileges on objects for database users and roles

This chapter will show you how to use the Design Editor to complete these and other tasks.

18.1   MAINTAINING DATA DIAGRAMS

Whereas the data model of the system is documented in the form of entity relationship diagrams, the database design is documented in data diagrams created and maintained in the Data Diagrammer component of the Design Editor. Data diagrams are created after the Database Design Transformer generates tables from definitions of entities, and they usually correspond to the entity relationship diagrams. This correspondence means that if an entity relationship diagram is defined for entities involved in the process of entering orders, you will normally create a data diagram that includes the tables that correspond to these entities. You can create a new data diagram by selecting File | New Diagram from the menu.

After creating a diagram, you can populate it either by including objects already defined in the Repository, or by creating new objects in the diagram. The objects that are presented graphically and can be manipulated in a data diagram include tables, views, and snapshots, or foreign keys that represent the relationships between them.

18.1.1   INCLUDING OBJECTS IN DATA DIAGRAMS

In order to include tables, views, or snapshots in a diagram, select Edit | Include | Table/View/Snapshot… from the diagrammer's menu. This action displays the dialog box Include Tables/Views/Snapshots/Foreign Keys, shown in Figure 18.1.

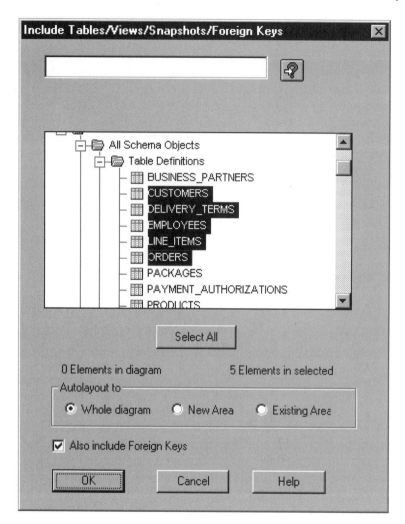

FIGURE 18.1 The Include Tables/Views/Snapshots/Foreign Keys
dialog box.

The central area of this dialog box consists of a hierarchy tree control that allows you to browse the Repository objects that you can include in the diagram—Tables, Views, Snapshots, and Clusters. These objects can be either definition objects or their implementations for the databases and database users defined in the Repository. In order to include one or more of these objects in the diagram, simply select them from the list and click OK. Standard Windows techniques, such as control-clicking and shift-clicking, can be used. In rare cases when you want to include all the objects in the list, click the button Select All. Two text labels in the dialog box indicate the number of elements currently in the diagram and the number of elements selected. (In the case shown in Figure 18.1, the diagram does not contain any elements and there are 5 elements currently selected in the list.)

The options in the radio group Autolayout to allow you to control how the new objects will be included in the diagram. By default, they will be laid out in the whole diagram, but you can choose to place the objects in a new area, or in an existing layout area. When the New Area radio button is selected and the button OK is clicked to include the objects in the diagram, the cursor changes to a cross-hair icon as an indicator that you should draw on the diagram a rectangle large enough to contain all the selected elements.

Together with the selected objects, you may also include in the diagram the foreign key constraints that exist among them. In such a case, the check box Also include Foreign Keys should be set. Although this check box is set by default, on several occasions, having it unchecked is preferable when including objects in a diagram. Two of the most common situations when I recommend including objects without foreign keys are listed below:

❑ The data diagram is initially laid out. Including the foreign keys together with the objects from the beginning complicates the task of rearranging the diagram. Including just the objects first is easier. After these objects are positioned and sized in the diagram to a satisfactory layout, you may include the foreign keys.

❑ Multiple foreign keys are defined among tables, but the context of the diagram requires only one of them. For example, in the Order Management System, two foreign keys exist between tables CUSTOMERS and ORDERS—one representing the customer who places the order, the other one representing the customer who will receive the ordered products. In a diagram of objects related to packing and scheduling deliveries, you want to

The Design Editor offers several elegant ways to create a new data diagram and populate it with database objects, or to include additional objects in an existing diagram. To include objects in a new data diagram, select them in the Design Navigator, then right-click and pick the option Show On Diagram from the popup menu. To include the objects in an existing diagram that is opened and displayed in the Design Editor, select these objects from in the Design Navigator, than drag and drop them in the diagram. If you drop the objects in an area outside the Design Navigator and any data diagram window, the Editor will display the objects in a new diagram.

show only the second of these keys. Therefore, include the tables first, and then include the appropriate key in the diagram.

In order to include foreign keys in the diagram, expand the node Missing Foreign Keys in the hierarchy tree. This node contains any foreign keys defined between objects in the Repository, but that are not included in the data diagram.

18.1.2 CREATING OBJECTS IN DATA DIAGRAMS

As I explained in Chapter 17, the Database Design Transformer maps, among other things, entities to tables and relationships to foreign key constraints, which you include in data diagrams. However, during the system design phase, you may discover that you need to create new objects in the Data Diagrammer besides the ones created by the Transformer. The following are three possible scenarios that may require you to do so:

❏ You want to include in the database design tables or constraints that were not identified in the data model.
❏ Based on the design of the application and data access patterns, you may need to create one or more views based on tables already created.
❏ Based on the system architecture requirements, you may need to define snapshots of data that will be replicated in different nodes of your distributed database environment.

 In the Data Diagrammer, you can create a table, a view, a snapshot, a cluster, a mandatory or optional foreign key constraint, or a primary key constraint. The procedure for creating any of these objects is similar. For example, to create a table, you would take these steps:

1. Click the iconic button Table 🖼 on the diagrammer's drawing toolbar. The mouse cursor changes shape to an iconic representation of the table.
2. Click and drag the cursor on the diagram to draw the new table to the desired size. After you release the mouse button, the dialog box Create Table appears if the Design Editor is set to use dialogs rather than Property Palette windows for displaying the properties of objects.
3. Enter the properties of the new object in the Create Table dialog box.
4. Click OK to complete the action.

Figure 18.2 shows a list of icons in the Data Diagrammer's toolbar and the corresponding object you create by clicking each icon. The only property you are required to specify when creating an object is its name. However, new objects created in this manner are just empty shells. In order to turn them into useful com-

ICONIC BUTTON	NAME
	Table
	View
	Snapshot
	Cluster
	Mandatory Foreign Key
	Optional Foreign Key
	Primary Key

FIGURE 18.2 Iconic buttons for different types of objects created in the Data Diagrammer.

ponents of your design, you need to edit their properties and associate additional information with them. For example, you need to create column and constraint definitions for the tables you create. The remainder of this chapter will show how you can edit the properties of different types of objects in the Data Diagrammer.

18.1.3 MAINTAINING THE LAYOUT OF DATA DIAGRAMS

 Data diagrams should convey clearly and precisely the designer's understanding of the logical model of the database. The layout of the diagram, the dimensions and position of the objects, and the lines that represent the foreign key constraints may have a signifi- cant influence on the person reviewing the diagram. This section presents some tips that can make your diagrams easier to read and understand.

The default fill colors used by the diagrammer to represent tables, views, snapshots, and clusters are intended to help you distinguish objects on the dia- gram more easily. If you want to turn these colors off and display the objects in a simple white background, you should take the following actions:

1. Select the objects in the diagram.
2. Click the icon Fill Color . The dialog box Color appears.
3. Select the box that represents the white color in the lower, right-hand corner of the dialog box.
4. Click OK.

You can also set the options of the diagram so that every object included or created in the diagram will have the same fill color or other display properties. By changing these properties appropriately, you can give a similar feel and look to data diagrams created in the Entity Relationship Diagrammer or in the Data Diagrammer.

Specifically, before creating any diagram in the Data Diagrammer, consider performing the following steps:

1. Select Options | Color/Font/Style… from the menu.
2. Select the element Table Definition from the Type drop-down list.
3. Set the Fill Color property to white and the color of the Secondary Font to black. Note that different colors should not be applied to diagram elements solely based on their type. The Data Diagrammer displays the characteristic icon of each object in the upper, left-hand corner of the object, thus making it often unnecessary to add the fill color as another distinguishing characteristic.
4. Repeat the previous step for the elements View Definition, Snapshot Definition, and Cluster Definition.
5. Click Save to store the preferences for subsequent diagrams or sessions.
6. Click OK to dismiss the dialog box.

Another thing to consider is the position and dimensions of objects in the diagram. When you create objects in the Data Diagrammer, you can determine these properties yourself, but when you include an object from the Repository, the diagrammer uses its internal algorithm for sizing and especially for positioning the objects on the diagram. You may move and resize the objects at this point; however, if you have accepted the default option to include foreign keys with the tables, the lines that represent these constraints may make this process even more cumbersome. Besides the tables, you will have to move the extremities and connection points of their constraints. The following steps simplify the process of laying out the diagram:

1. Create a new diagram in the Data Diagrammer.
2. Include the tables, views, or snapshots that you want to represent in this diagram, *without* including the foreign keys.
3. Create any new objects that will be part of the diagram.
4. Size and position the objects in a way that will enable users to grasp the meaning and contents of the diagram easily and quickly. You may have several subjective criteria upon which the diagram is laid out; however, in general, you would place tables that represent key information in the center of the diagram and in larger dimensions. Other tables, such as lookup or secondary tables, are smaller and usually reside on the sides of the diagram.
5. Include any foreign key constraints that already exist in the Repository or create new ones, if necessary. The diagrammer will introduce the lines that represent the constraints minimizing the intersections and wrapping around existing tables, if necessary.

When foreign key constraints are created on a diagram, the Data Diagrammer simply connects the two related tables with a straight line, without wrapping around any tables in its path or trying to minimize the intersections with other lines. However, if you select the constraint, cut it from the diagram, and include it right back, the diagrammer will apply the wrapping and intersection algorithms, thus allowing you to maintain the same consistent look in your diagram.

Examples of diagrams created following the suggestions discussed here are included in the application system TASC OMS (DES), provided on the companion CD-ROM in the form of the archive file OMSDES.DMP. You can easily navigate to this file in the Web pages of the CD-ROM by following the links *Software* and *Order Management System Design.*

18.2 MAINTAINING TABLES

Whether you include a table from the Repository or create it from scratch in the Data Diagrammer, you will need to edit and maintain its properties. You can view and modify the properties of a table in its Edit Table dialog box, which may be accessed by double-clicking the table on the diagram or on the Design Navigator. This dialog box is made up of several properties tabs, which are the subject of the following sections.

18.2.1 NAME PROPERTIES

Name properties of a table are maintained on the Name tab. Figure 18.3 shows an example of this tab.

The first three properties in this tab are inherited directly from the properties of the entity associated with the table. A list of these properties was presented in Chapter 17. The following paragraphs briefly describe these properties:

❑ **Table name.** This property is derived from the *Plural* property of the entity. It defines the name with which the table will be created in the database.

❑ **Display title.** This property is derived from the *Plural* property of the entity, as well. It defines the label that will represent the table in user interface modules.

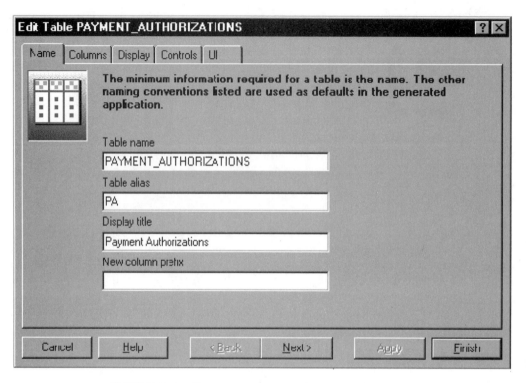

FIGURE 18.3   The Name tab of the Edit Table dialog box.

❑ **Table alias.** This property comes from the entity's *Short Name* and is used by different generators to create references to the table. For example, Developer/2000 Forms blocks based on the table are named after the table's alias by default.

❑ **New column prefix.** This property is rarely used and, when set, is used by the Database Design Transformer to prefix the new columns it creates with the characters (up to 4) entered in this field.

As you can see, most of these properties are derived from properties of their associated entities. For tables created in the Data Diagrammer, these properties must be set manually.

18.2.2   COLUMN DEFINITION PROPERTIES

You can view and maintain the database-oriented properties of columns on the Columns tab, shown in Figure 18.4. All the columns of the table are listed in the control to the left of the box. Mandatory columns in this list are displayed in red

Two important properties for a table object are *Start Rows* and *End Rows*. These properties are derived from the *Initial* and *Maximum* volume properties of the entity. The first property contains the estimated number of rows the table will contain upon creation; the second property contains an upper limit of this number upon the lifetime of the system. The settings of these two properties, together with other properties, are used by the Repository report "Database Table and Index Size Estimates" to compute the size estimated for the table and its indexes. You can access these properties in the Property Palette window.

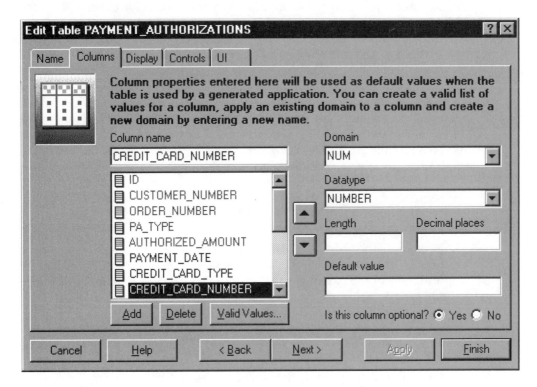

FIGURE 18.4 The Columns properties tab of the Edit Table dialog box.

characters to set them apart from the other optional columns. When you select a column in the list, all the other controls in the tab are populated with the properties for that column. These properties primarily affect the physical structure of the table in the database. Most of them are directly carried over by the Database Design Transformer from the attribute properties defined in the data model. In particular, properties such as *Domain, Datatype, Length, Decimal place* precision for a numeric column, *Optional,* and *Default value* for a column have the same settings as their counterparts in the corresponding attribute. Therefore, a detailed and completed data model may save you significant efforts in the design phase. If, on the other hand, the data model is built quickly, or if the tables are created from scratch in the Data Diagrammer, take some time to analyze carefully and properly set these properties.

There are two more properties that you may change in this tab. They are discussed in the following paragraphs:

❑ **Column Name.** For columns associated with an attribute in the data model, their name is derived from the attribute and should not be changed. Cases in which you may need to rename columns are those in which these columns are added to the table by the Database Design Transformer in order to implement a foreign key or as a discriminator column for subtypes mapped to the same table. Consider, for example, the table ORDERS as it was created by the Database Design Transformer (see Figure 18.5). Five columns in this table are added by the Transformer to implement the foreign key constraints to the tables CUSTOMERS and EMPLOYEES. The first thing you could change in these columns is to remove the prefix 'CUS_' from the columns that reference the CUSTOMERS table. The names of these columns (CUSTOMER_NUMBER and CUSTOMER_NUMBER_PLACED_ BY) clearly express this fact. The second change is to add consistency to the names of columns that implement multiple foreign keys referencing the same table. In other words, you could rename the column CUSTOMER_ NUMBER to CUSTOMER_NUMBER_SENT_TO, and EMP_ID to EMP_ID_ BOOKED_BY, as shown in Figure 18.6.

❑ **Sequence.** The order in which the columns appear in the list box of the tab defines the order of columns in the table. It is derived from the order of the attributes of the parent entity. You can change the position of a column in the table by selecting it in the list and then clicking the icons ▲ and ▼ to move the column up or down until you find the desired position.

One of the main reasons to change the order of columns in a table is storage efficiency of data in the database. Given the way Oracle stores records in its blocks, the amount of space for each record is minimized if all the required columns in the record are stored first, followed by columns that allow NULL values. Often this rule is compromised for the sake of design clarity. A customary approach, for example, is to list all the columns

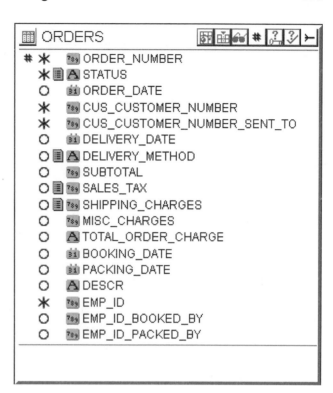

FIGURE 18.5 The table ORDERS as it is created by the Database Design Transformer.

that make up the primary key first, followed by the unique keys, followed by the foreign keys. Then the other attributes are ordered based on their affinity with each other. Columns that contain address information, for example, stay together in the usual order (Street, City, State, Zip), although the last column may be required whereas the previous three may not be. Figure 18.6 shows how the table ORDERS would look after its columns are resequenced.

I mentioned above that several properties on the Columns properties tab are inherited from similar attribute properties. But what if you revise the settings of these properties for columns in the database design model? Unfortunately, you cannot transfer these changes to the properties of the existing attributes. Thus, the inheritance of properties occurs in one direction only, from attributes to columns (and from entities to tables), and is managed by the Database Design Transformer. So if you want to keep the database design model synchronized with the data model, modify shared attributes at the data model level and then use the Transformer to forward the changes to the database design model. If you take shortcuts and apply changes only to tables and columns, be aware that you may

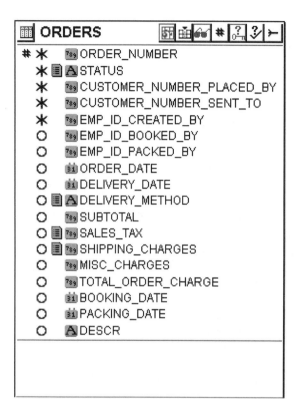

FIGURE 18.6   The table ORDERS
after modifying its properties.

lose these changes if in the next run of the Database Design Transformer, the non-synchronized entities or attributes are included in the working set.

The tab Columns also allows you to create a new column or to remove an existing one from the table. The buttons Add and Delete at the bottom of the list control are used to invoke these functions. Furthermore, you can record the allowed values of a column by clicking the button Valid Values.... If the column is a date or alphanumeric column, the Valid Values dialog box shown in Figure 18.7 appears. In this dialog you can enter the allowed values and their meanings. Select the radio buttons Query or Hard Code to have the front-end generators create code that queries the valid values from the database at runtime or to hard code these values in the body of the generated modules. Select the radio button Yes if you want the valid values to be a list of suggested values in the front-end application, which users may ignore at runtime if they need to do so. To prevent the users from entering values other than the allowed values in the column, select the radio button No.

If the column is a numeric column, the Valid Values dialog box is reduced to only two fields where you can specify the lower and upper bounds for the

Using the property tab Columns is probably not the easiest way to rename and resequence the columns of a table. The Data Diagrammer component of the Design Editor offers two features that allow you to accomplish these tasks on the diagram, without having to display the Edit Table dialog box of the table. To rename a column, click the column on the diagram twice. (Make sure that the action is not a double-click.) When the cursor lands inside the text item that contains the name of the column, simply type the new name of the column. Press ENTER or click elsewhere on the diagram to save the changes.

To resequence the columns of a table, right-click the area where the columns are displayed and then select the item Resequence Columns... from the popup menu that appears. This action invokes the dialog box Resequence Columns, which displays all the columns in the table ordered based on their sequence. To modify the order of a column, select it in the list and click the icons ▲ and ▼ as appropriate.

range of values that can be entered in the column. Recall however, that the best solution to record valid values for a column is to use a domain and include the column in that domain.

18.2.3 DISPLAY PROPERTIES

The properties accessed and maintained on the property tabs Display, Controls and UI of the Edit Tables dialog box are not directly related with the database design of your application. They allow you to specify how data items based on these columns will be formatted and displayed in the front-end applications that you generate. These properties are very important in achieving the following two goals:

❑ **Reuse of efforts.** Column-level display properties become the source for setting the properties of column usages in front-end modules. Since, in general, a column may appear in several of these modules, the effort you put into defining the display properties at the column level can pay back a high dividend. By carefully setting these properties, you minimize the amount of work required to define similar properties at the module level.

❑ **Standard interfaces across the application.** Because the display properties of column usages in front-end modules are derived from the same source—

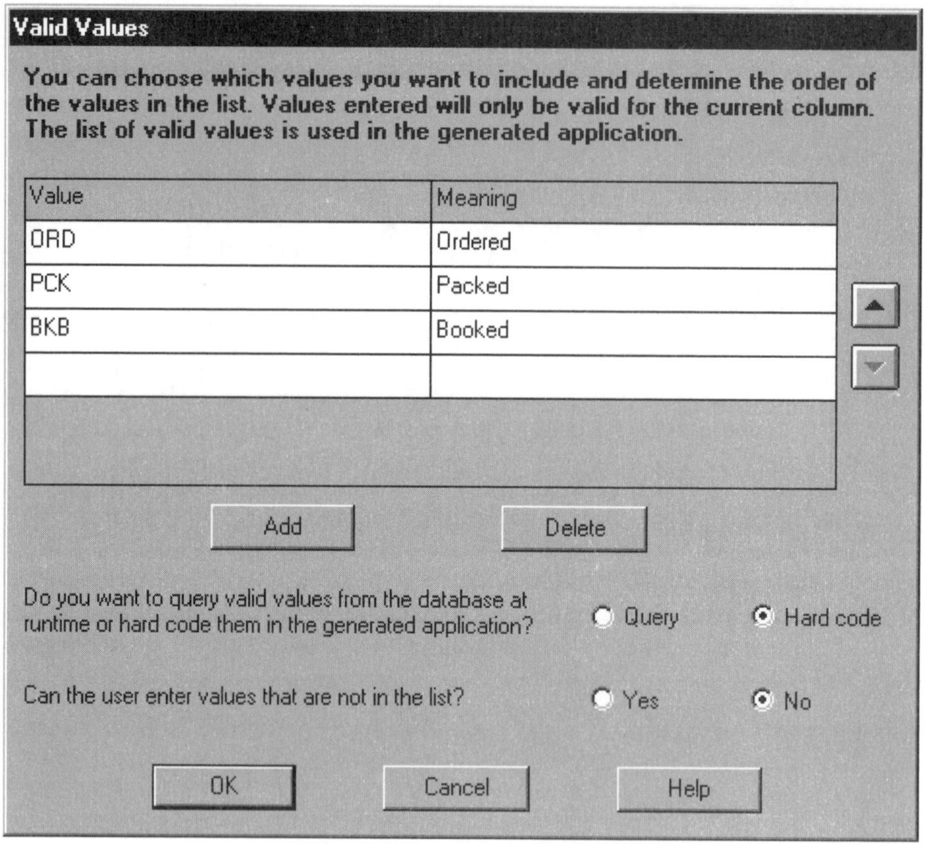

Valid Values

You can choose which values you want to include and determine the order of the values in the list. Values entered will only be valid for the current column. The list of valid values is used in the generated application.

Value	Meaning
ORD	Ordered
PCK	Packed
BKB	Booked

Add   Delete

Do you want to query valid values from the database at runtime or hard code them in the generated application?   ○ Query   ◉ Hard code

Can the user enter values that are not in the list?   ○ Yes   ◉ No

OK   Cancel   Help

FIGURE 18.7   The Valid Values dialog box.

the display properties of columns—your user interface modules will have a common interface.

The Display tab is used define which columns are displayed in the user interface modules and which ones are hidden. For the displayed columns, you can also define the order in which these columns are displayed, which may not necessarily be the same as the order in which the columns are stored in the database table.

Figure 18.8 shows an example of this property tab. Using the icons ▣ and ▣ you can exchange selected columns between the list controls Columns not displayed and Columns displayed. The icons ▣ and ▣ can be used to transfer all the columns from one control to the other. The order in which the columns are displayed in the list Columns displayed may be changed using the icons ▲ and ▼.

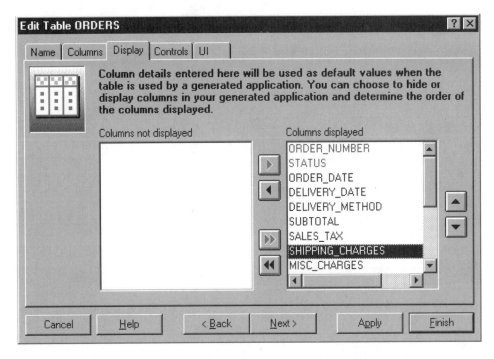

FIGURE 18.8 The Display tab of the Edit Table dialog box.

18.2.4 GUI CONTROL PROPERTIES

The tab Controls allows you to set properties that influence the type of GUI item that will be used to implement the column in the user interface modules. An example of this tab is shown in Figure 18.9. The properties set in this tab are explained in the following paragraphs.

In general, the columns that do not represent any information that is related to the users' business are not displayed in the user interface modules. Note, however, that by hiding the column in the Display tab, you exclude the column from *all* screens and reports. If the column will be displayed in some and will not be displayed in some others, leave the property set. Then when defining the properties of each module, you can decide whether to display the column or not.

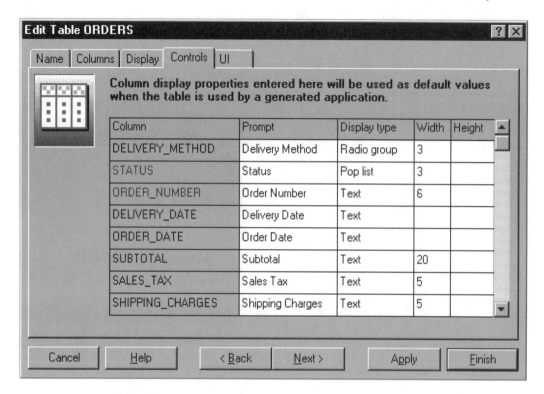

FIGURE 18.9   The Controls tab of the Edit Table dialog box.

❏ **Display type.** This property allows you to pick the GUI type that will be used to display the column on the screen or in a report. There are essentially two choices. You may display a column as a text item by setting the Display type to Text. Or you may display it as a GUI control by setting this property to the type of control that is most appropriate for the data stored in the column. In addition, Developer/2000 Forms allow you to embed OLE containers, OCX controls, VBX controls and image items in their modules.

❏ **Width and Height.** These properties control the dimensions of the item on the screen or report. For alphanumeric columns created by the Database Design Transformer, Width is set to the same value as the *Maximum Length* property of the column or '70,' whichever is less. Therefore, the property *Width* of several columns may require resetting in order to reduce the amount of space they occupy in the layout of a screen or report.

❏ **Prompt.** By setting this property, you can specify what will become a text label associated with the field on the screen or report page. Based on the column name, the Database Design Transformer generates a value for this property when it creates the column. You can modify its contents by over-riding the generated value with a more descriptive label.

18.2.5 USER INTERFACE PROPERTIES

The tab UI is used to maintain properties that influence the layout and user inter-face of the module. An example of this tab is shown in Figure 18.10. The follow-ing paragraphs discuss the properties you can set in this tab.

❑ **Hint.** This property contains information that is usually displayed in the message line of applications when the focus of the application is on the field. When the column is created by the Database Design Transformer, the setting of this property is derived from the *Comment* property of its asso-ciated attribute. Depending on the settings of your preferences, the contents of *Hint* may also be used to generate Microsoft Help files as well.

❑ **Uppercase.** This property can be set for columns that store case-insensitive data for the purpose of data consistency and standardization. When the

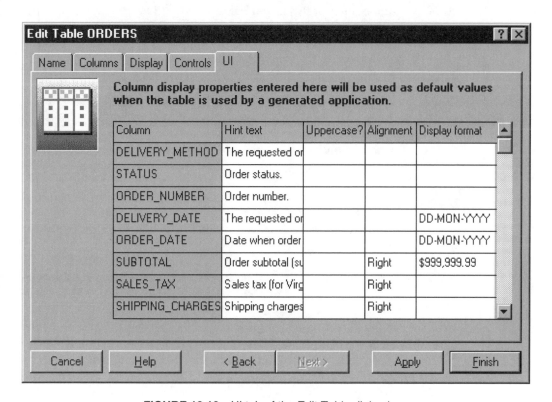

FIGURE 18.10   UI tab of the Edit Table dialog box.

property is set, front-end applications that use this column will be generated to accept and maintain the data for the column in uppercase characters. This setup will avoid storing values in the database such as 'Virginia' or 'VIRGINIA,' which are considered different values by database packages although, from a user perspective, they represent the same state. Note, however, that this property influences only the front-end application generators, such as Developer/2000 Form and Report Generators. If you want to enforce the rule at the database level, you may create a check constraint that will reject all invalid records or a database trigger that converts the value of the column to uppercase characters.

❑ **Alignment.** This property is usually set for numeric items, and especially for items that represent currency values, as in the case of the three items at the bottom of the list in Figure 18.10.

❑ **Display format.** This property allows you to define a format mask used to display data from the column in a front-end application. For example, the format mask of a field that represents the telephone numbers in the United States can be '"("999")"999"-"9999."' This allows the application to display these numbers in the familiar format, while the database stores only the digits of the number but not the additional formatting characters, thus conserving space. When setting the *Format* property, revise the setting of the *Width* property as well, to ensure that the item on the screen will allow users to view the data as well as the formatting characters.

18.3 PROVIDING FOR DATA AUDITING AND JOURNALING

You can implement two levels of data auditing very easily using Designer/2000. The first one consists of recording the user who made the last modification to a record and the time when this occurred. More explicitly, this means maintaining for each record the date the record was created or last updated and the user accounts that created or last updated the record. In order to add this level of auditing to a table, follow these steps:

1. Add columns to the table that will be used to record the auditing information. Examples of such columns are CREATE_ID, CREATE_DATE, UPDATE_ID, and UPDATE_DATE.

2. Set the properties of these columns according to the type of information they will record. If you have defined domains like DATES or SHORT_NAME in the application system, you can accomplish this step by including the columns CREATE_DATE and UPDATE_DATE in the first domain; CREATE_ID and UPDATE_ID are included in the second domain.

3. Set the property *AutoGen Type* for each column to *'Created By,' 'Date Created,' 'Date Modified,'* and *'Modified By,'* according to the purpose of the column. This property is found in the Property Palette of the column object.

The front-end application generators will create the necessary code to populate and maintain these columns without you having to worry about the implementation.

A more sophisticated level of data auditing is to record the change history of a record in a table. For a simple and quick implementation of this type of auditing, you can set the property *Journal* on the Table properties tab of the Edit Table dialog box. For tables with this property set to a value other than *'None,'* the Server Generator creates a journaling table, which contains the same columns as the parent table. In addition, this table contains the following columns:

❑ **JN_OPERATION.** This column records the type of operation that modifies the table (insert, update, or delete).

Another possible setting for the property *AutoGen Type* is *'Seq in Parent.'* This setting becomes very handy in situations where you want all the values of a column to follow each other in a sequence for a given parent record. For example, in the LINE_ITEMS table, you want the item numbers of all the line items within the same order to be sequential. Rather than implementing the functionality yourself, you can make the application generators create it for you by setting the property *AutoGen Type* for the column ITEM_NUMBER to *'Seq in Parent.'*

When the Database Design Transformer encounters an entity for which the primary unique identifier includes only one relationship end and only one numeric attribute from the entity, it automatically sets the property *AutoGen Type* to *'Seq in Parent'* for the column associated with the numeric attribute. In the Order Management System, for example, the primary unique identifier of the entity LINE ITEM is composed of the attribute ITEM NUMBER and the relationship end 'LINE ITEM must be part of one and only one ORDER.' The table LINE_ITEMS created by the Transformer has a primary key composed of columns ORDER_NUMBER and ITEM_NUMBER. The property *AutoGen Type* of ITEM_NUMBER is set automatically to *'Seq in Parent'* by the Transformer.

❑ **JN_ORACLE_USER.** This column records the Oracle user account that performed the operation.

❑ **JN_DATETIME.** This column records the date and time the modification
occurred.

❑ **JN_NOTES.** This column records any notes that users may want to record
to describe the modification.

❑ **JN_APPLN.** This column records the name of the application that initiated
the modification.

❑ **JN_SESSION.** This column records an identifier for the session that initiated the modification.

Figure 18.11 shows the DDL created by the Server Generator to implement
the PRODUCT_CATEGORIES table and its corresponding journaling table in the
Order Management System.

Obviously, the journal table must be populated with data as the parent table
is being used. When the property *Journal* is set to *'Client,'* the front-end generators
will create code such that when records from the table are being inserted, updated, or deleted, a text box appears where users can enter the notes for the particular operation. Then, the change record is inserted in the journal table. The
client-side population of the journal table has the following pitfalls:

❑ **Increased network traffic.** Each transaction that changes the parent table
must include an extra statement that records the change in the journal table.
On certain occasions, this may even double the flow of data between the
client and the database server.

❑ **Unreliable journaling implementation.** By relying only on the front-end
application to record changes in the parent table, you may create gaps in the
auditing scheme. A transaction that accesses the same table from a different
interface may not necessarily enforce your auditing scheme.

In order to address these two pitfalls, the auditing should be implemented
on the database server using database triggers. When you set the property *Journal*
to *'Server,'* the utility Generate Table API can be used to create, among other
things, triggers and PL/SQL stored procedures that log the change in the journal
table. When the property is set to *'Client calls server procedure,'* the Generate Table
API is still used to generate the stored procedure that logs the change when in the
journal table. However, with this option, it is the front-end application and not
the database triggers that call this procedure.

In cases where your journaling needs are not met by what Designer/2000
offers, you can still use its tools to help you implement your customized version

```
PROMPT
PROMPT Creating Table PRODUCT_CATEGORIES
CREATE TABLE product_categories(
   id                      NUMBER              NOT NULL,
   name                    VARCHAR2(80)        NOT NULL,
   descr                   VARCHAR2(240)       NULL
);

REM
REM     Journal table for product_categories
REM
CREATE TABLE PRODUCT_CATEGORIES_JN  (
     JN_OPERATION              CHAR(3)           NOT NULL,
     JN_ORACLE_USER            VARCHAR2(30)      NOT NULL,
     JN_DATETIME               DATE              NOT NULL,
     JN_NOTES                  VARCHAR2(240)     NULL    ,
     JN_APPLN                  VARCHAR2(30)      NULL    ,
     JN_SESSION                NUMBER(38)        NULL    ,
   id                         NUMBER                    ,
   name                       VARCHAR2(80)              ,
   descr                      VARCHAR2(240)
)
   PCTUSED 5
   PCTFREE 60;
```

FIGURE 18.11 DDL statements that create a table and its corresponding journaling table.

of the journaling scheme. The general guidelines for the implementation of a customized data auditing scheme are as follows:

1. Set the property *Journal* for the table that needs to be audited to any of the
   options discussed earlier.
2. Use the Server Generator to create the journal table in a temporary database
   schema.
3. Use the Generate Table API utility to generate the procedure that performs
   the insert in the journal table and, depending on the setting of *Journal*, the
   server-side triggers that invoke this procedure.

4. Unset the property *Journal*, so that front-end application generators may not be influenced by it.

5. Reverse engineer the newly created table and PL/SQL program units in your application system and modify them, if necessary.

As you continue reading this book, you will become familiar with the necessary information to complete the steps discussed above.

18.4 CREATING AND MAINTAINING INDEXES

Indexes are important objects in an Oracle database that must be carefully designed and integrated into the overall model of the database. They are built on one or more columns of a given table in order to improve the response time of queries against that table. However, indexes provide their benefits at a certain cost.

An important cost factor associated with indexes is the overhead for transactions that insert or delete records in the indexed table, or that update any of the indexed columns. The additional disk space required to store the index data may be a significant cost factor as well. In a successful database design, benefits provided by indexes outweigh the cost associated with them. An optimal equilibrium is not always easy to achieve, and several trials may be needed to identify the application areas that would be affected the most. A well implemented indexing strategy requires as much talent and familiarity with the application as it requires knowledge of the database architecture and of the Oracle kernel. Designer/2000 allows you to create and maintain index objects in the Repository using the Design Editor or the Repository Object Navigator.

In the Design Editor, indexes for a particular table are located on the DB Objects tab of the Design Navigator. They are grouped under the node Indexes of a given table. Double-clicking the index object displays the Edit Index dialog box. In the Name tab of the dialog, shown in Figure 18.12, you can maintain the name of the index and indicate the type of index by selecting one of the radio buttons Unique, Not unique, or Bitmap. If the index is for a foreign key, select the radio button Yes at the bottom of the tab; otherwise click No.

If the index is for a foreign key, the second tab of the Edit Index dialog box is titled Foreign Keys. The sole purpose of this tab is to allow you to select from the list of foreign keys defined on the table the one for which the index is created. If the index not associated with a foreign key, the title of the second tab is Columns. This tab lists to the left all the columns of the table that are not in the index; the columns already included in the index are displayed to the right. You can move the columns from one list to the other by using the iconic buttons provided in the tab.

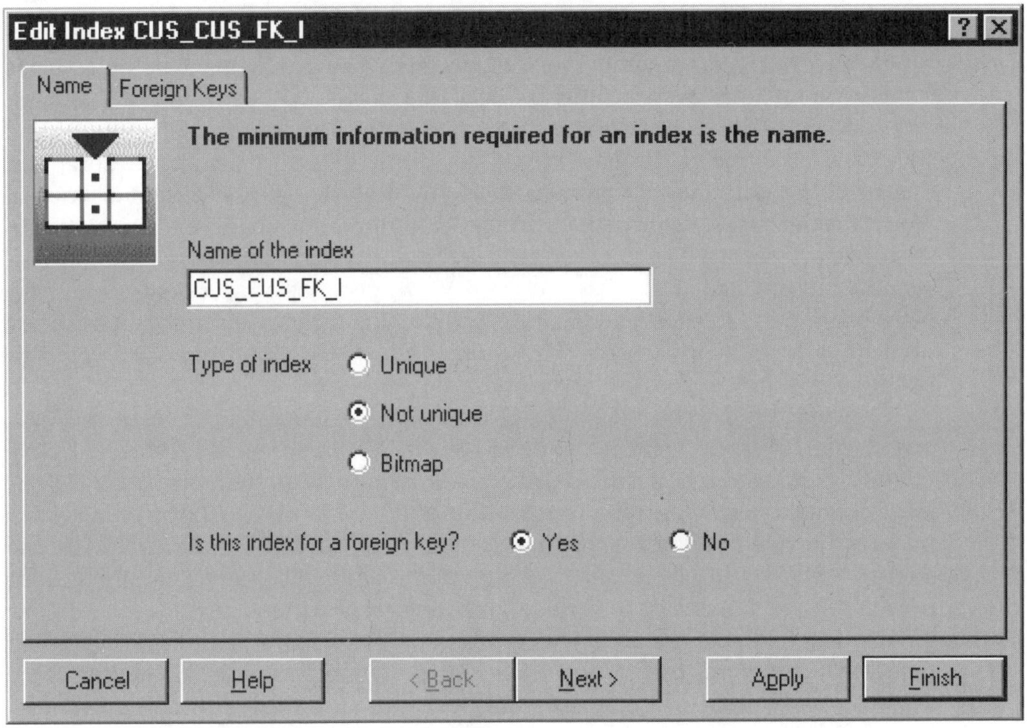

FIGURE 18.12 The Name properties tab of the Edit Index dialog box.

18.5 MAINTAINING VIEWS

Views in databases are canned queries stored in the database catalog as objects of their own. Each view is defined by a SELECT statement against one or more table or view objects. These objects are known as the base tables of the view. You have two main reasons for using views in database applications:

❏ Implementing business views of data
❏ Enforcing data access and security rules

The following sections will discuss each of these topics, as well as how to maintain the properties of views.

18.5.1   IMPLEMENTING BUSINESS VIEWS OF DATA

When you analyze and define the data model of a system, your main objective is robustness and flexibility of this model. Therefore, you begin with a business- and user-oriented view of data, incorporated in the form of reports, forms, screen shots, and other views. To these views, you apply data normalization techniques. The resulting data model serves as the foundation for all the different ways in which the data must be presented. However, a common experience is to realize in the design phase that the data model may require complex joins of tables to present data in the format that users expect. Views serve as a layer between the implementation of tables in the database and the way users see the data items they need to perform their business. Thus, views allow you hide from users complex relationships that may exist between data elements.

A similar goal can be achieved through the denormalization of the data model. However, differences exist between the two approaches. When the data model is denormalized, business views are implemented in the form of *physical* objects. Changes in business requirements that result in changes in the business views may require massive updates of data. A denormalized data model, because of the data redundancy it introduces, takes its toll on storage space and on the cost of maintaining and updating the data. Views, on the other hand, present a *logical* implementation of business data. The records they contain are assembled only when requested; therefore, they are not associated with any storage or maintenance costs. On the other hand, because their record set is created at runtime, using views affects the response time of the application. Like other decisions in the process of designing the database, your decisions on using views should be based upon a solid understanding of the application, its transactions, and users' priorities.

18.5.2   ENFORCING DATA ACCESS AND SECURITY RULES

Since views are based on SELECT statements, different filtering criteria can be used to create extracts of data from database tables for users with different access privileges. By choosing the columns to include in the SELECT statement that creates the view, you can remove from the picture columns that a group of users is not allowed to see or access. For example, in the Order Management System, outside users that represent different vendors need to select from the table PRODUCT_ITEMS in order to monitor the level of product items in a warehouse. You may want to allow them access to columns like SERIAL_NUMBER or STATUS, but you want to hide from them columns that store information internal to TASC, such as the WAREHOUSE_LOCATION. You can accomplish this goal with a view on table PRODUCT_ITEMS in which the column WAREHOUSE_LOCATION is not selected. Rules such as the one described here are also known as vertical partitioning rules.

By entering different query criteria in the WHERE clause of the statement, you can limit the set of records that a group of users may view and manipulate.

This last option is used to implement horizontal partitioning rules. Suppose, for example, that you want to partition the table PRODUCT_ITEMS in a way that a vendor may select only those records that represent product items supplied to TASC by the vendor. You can define a view for each vendor that selects the columns from PRODUCT_ITEMS where the business partner identifier (BP_ID) matches the identifier of the particular vendor. Users from each vendor then are given access to the appropriate view but not to the base table itself.

18.5.3 SETTING PROPERTIES OF VIEWS

The process of creating a view object in the Data Diagrammer was discussed in Section 18.1.2. However, simply following the steps described in that section creates an object whose properties must be set in order to become a useful view. The properties of views are maintained in the Edit View dialog box, which can be accessed by double-clicking the view object on the diagram. This dialog is composed of several property tabs. Four of them, titled Name, Display, Controls, and UI, resemble in form and functionality the same tabs in the Edit Table dialog box. I discussed them earlier in the chapter, therefore, in this section, I will focus on the tabs that are specific to the views.

An important component in the definition of a view are the base objects upon which the view is founded. These objects can be tables, snapshots, or even other views, and are maintained in the tab Table Selection. An example of this tab is shown in Figure 18.13. The list Available objects contains all the tables, views, and snapshots you have defined in the Repository. You can select one or more of these objects and click ▶ to add them to the list Objects in the view. An object may be included multiple times in the list.

After picking the base objects of a view, choose the columns that will be part of the view definition. The process of selecting these columns is performed on the Columns properties tab of the Edit View dialog box. On this tab, you select the columns you want to include from the list box Columns not in the view and click the icon ▶ to move them to the list box Columns in the view. You can also include or exclude all the columns in the view by clicking the icons ◀ and ▶. Once the columns are included in the view, you can adjust their order using the icons ▼ and ▲. Figure 18.14 shows an example of the Columns tab of the Edit View dialog box. Notice that, as in other similar tabs, the mandatory columns are displayed in red to distinguish them from the optional ones. Characteristic icons are also displayed for columns that are part of the primary key or foreign keys defined on the base objects.

When a column is included in the view, its name is formed by concatenating the alias of the base object with the name of the original column. In the tab Column Alias you can modify the name if you need to do so. With the actions discussed so far, you define the columns of the view. In order to restrict the record set of the view, you need to add selection criteria to the properties of the object.

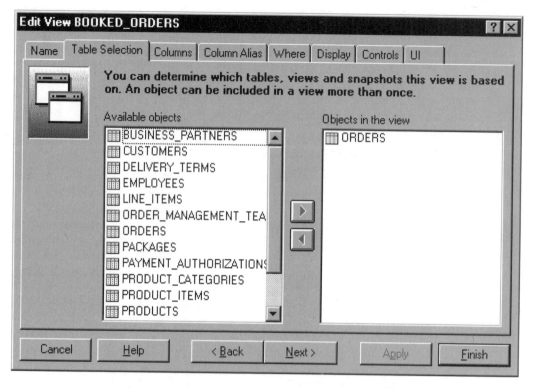

FIGURE 18.13 The Table Selection tab of the Edit View dialog box.

These criteria are entered in the Where tab of the Edit View dialog box. An example of this tab is shown in Figure 18.15. The text box in the upper part of the tab displays the SELECT statement compiled using the base objects and columns you selected in the two previous tabs. You can enter the WHERE clause of this statement in the second text box in the tab.

Everything you enter in this text box will be appended to the end of the SELECT statement that creates the view. So you can enter other clauses of a statement that syntactically follow the WHERE clause. For example, if you want to create the view with the check option, you can enter the clause WITH CHECK OPTION as the last line in the text box.

In general, the statement that populates the view with data can be as simple as a list of base columns selected from a table, or as complicated as an intricate SELECT clause for a complex query. The Edit View dialog box allows you to create this statement declaratively and works well for simple views. For more complex views, such as the ones that contain nested queries or that perform calcula-

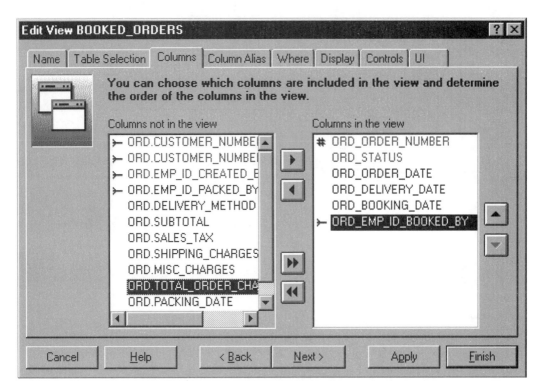

FIGURE 18.14 The Columns tab of the Edit View dialog box.

tions and group operations on the data, you can enter their specification in free format by following these steps:

1. Display the Property Palette for the view object.
2. Set the property *Free Format Select Text* to 'Yes.' Notice that the text property *Select Text* is enabled when you change the setting of this property.
3. Enter the statement that will select the data. Be sure to remove the keyword SELECT from the beginning of the text, since the Server Generator adds it automatically.
4. Click the property Select Text to display the text editor and specify any valid SQL expression that you need to apply to your data. Normally, the expression will use the base column, but this is not required.
5. Save the changes to the Repository.

When the Server Generator compiles a CREATE VIEW statement for the view, it will take the contents of the property *Select Text* and plug them into the

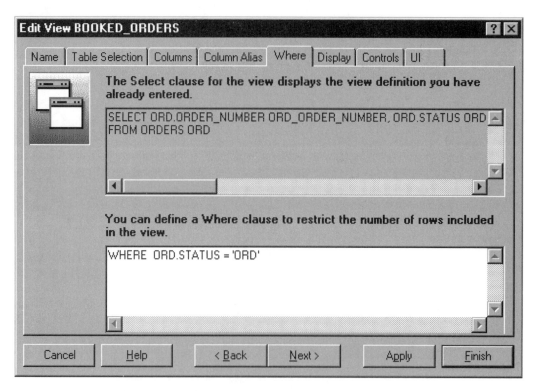

FIGURE 18.15   The Where tab of the Edit View dialog box.

SELECT clause of the statement. The contents of the *Where/Validation Condition* property will be used to populate the WHERE clause of this statement. Keep in mind that the Server Generator simply assembles the contents of these properties into one statement without checking their syntax or validity. You are responsible for ensuring that the setting of these properties will conform with the rules of the SQL language implemented in the database.

The following paragraphs contain a few examples of how you could set the Select Text property for free format views:

When the setting of the property *Free Format Select Text* is changed from *'Yes'* to *'No,'* the contents of the property *Select Text* are cleared away. In order not to lose valuable work, decide up front whether you want to create the view declaratively or in free format.

❑ Suppose that the unit of measurement used to store the weight of packages in the table PACKAGES is pounds and you want to present the data in Metric System units, such as kilograms. Knowing the relationship '1 lb = 0.453 kg,' you can use the expression 'PACKAGES.WEIGHT*0.453' in a view rather than the base column PACKAGES.WEIGHT.

❑ Suppose that in another view you want to present the code of products not as they are stored in the database (TAX, BUS, GAM, and OTH), but with more meaningful and descriptive terms, such as 'Tax Software,' 'Business Software,' 'Games,' and 'Other.' In order to achieve this goal, you may replace the base column PRODUCTS.PRO_TYPE in the *Select Text* property with the following expression:

```
DECODE(PRODUCTS.PRO_TYPE, 'TAX', 'Tax Software', 'BUS',
     'Business Software', 'GAM', 'Games', 'Other')
```

❑ Suppose that the names of employees are stored in uppercase letters in the columns LAST_NAME followed by FIRST_NAME of the table EMPLOYEES. In a view that presents employee data, you want to show the names in the familiar format used in everyday life—first name followed by last name and initial letters capitalized. You could enter the following expression in the *Select Text* property:

```
INITCAP(EMPLOYEES.FIRST_NAME)||' '||
     INITCAP(EMPLOYEES.LAST_NAME)
```

The properties discussed so far are specific to view objects. Other properties of views that can be maintained in the Edit View dialog box are similar to those of tables. These properties influence the front-end application generators, therefore they must be set for views as carefully as for tables. When setting these properties, keep in mind the final version of data that a column in the view will contain. For example, in one of the cases discussed above, the column that will present the product type in descriptive form must be large enough to contain the description of each type.

18.6 MAINTAINING SNAPSHOTS

An important factor that must be considered during the design of a database system is the physical location of data. For group and department types of applications, which serve communities of users located in local or campus area networks, all the tables, indexes and other related components are typically stored in a single database. When database applications are scaled up to enterprise-wide applications accessed from users in different geographic locations across wide area networks, centralized databases yield acceptable performance levels only at high connectivity costs. A careful analysis of data entities, business functions, and user profiles allows you to identify clusters of data items that are more important to users in one location than in others. A natural inclination then is to divide the data into multiple databases. Data elements that users in one location own and are responsible for maintaining are stored in a database in that location. The principal users can access the data from their local networks, thus resulting in better performing and cost-effective applications. The partitioning lines between data and databases are not always clear, though. To one extent or another, every distributed database system must deal with the problem of data sharing. As an example, although each location of TASC may maintain its data in local databases, the headquarters needs a global picture that unifies the information from these locations. This global picture is achieved through distributed transactions, which retrieve and access tables and other objects from remote databases.

In order for distributed transactions to succeed, databases must communicate with each other. Depending on how and when data is transferred from one database to another, the communication mode can be synchronous and asynchronous. A synchronous distributed transaction is one that uses the most up-to-date version of data from remote databases in the case of queries, or that modifies the data instantaneously in all the remote databases in the case of inserts, updates, or deletes. Although theoretically every remote transaction should be done synchronously, in practice two serious limitations exist to such transactions. The first limitation is that their performance is significantly poorer than that of similar non-distributed transactions. The second limitation is that the success of synchronous transactions depends on each remote node being operational and the link between them being available. The failure of any of these components causes the failure of the whole transaction. Clearly, then, the probability of failure is higher for distributed transactions than for non-distributed ones.

Asynchronous transactions address these two limitations of synchronous ones. They rely on versions of data from remote databases valid at a certain moment in time that are stored in the *local* database. The assumption here is that the time window between two versions of the remote data is such that asynchronous transactions still represent valid business views or implement business functions correctly. In an Oracle database, local views of remote data are maintained in distinct objects known as snapshots.

Fundamentally, snapshots come in two flavors: read-only and updateable. Read-only snapshots are those in which data is created and updated in one location, but it is copied over to remote locations where it is read like any other table by the applications in those locations. The database that hosts the updateable data is called the master site. In addition to maintaining the master version of data, this database maintains a log for each snapshot defined at remote databases. The log contains all the modifications to the master table since the last refresh of the remote snapshot. Updateable snapshots extend the concept of replicating data across remote databases because they allow each version of data to be updated locally. Oracle's symmetric replication facility distributes the changes made to one instance of data to all the other copies. In addition, with symmetric replication, you can make modifications to the table structure in any local database and propagate these modifications to all its versions in the other nodes of the distributed database environment. Figure 18.16 contains a graphical representation of snapshot and snapshot logs.

Designer/2000 allows you to create snapshot objects in the Repository and maintain their properties in the Design Editor or Repository Object Navigator. The Server Generator compiles the appropriate DDL statements based on the properties of these objects. Section 18.1.2 discussed how you can create snapshots in the Design Editor. Their properties are maintained in the Edit Snapshot dialog box, which appears when you double-click the snapshot object in the diagram. Figure 18.17 shows the Name tab of this dialog box.

Conceptually, snapshots are something in between database tables and views. Like tables, they store the data physically. Their structure, though, is defined in the same way the structure of views is defined. Indeed, you could follow exactly the same steps described in Section 18.5.3 to build the SELECT statement associated with the snapshot declaratively or in the free text form. The properties on the tabs Table Selection, Columns, Column Alias, and Where, as well as text properties such as *Select Text* or *Where/Validation Condition,* are used for this purpose. These are the only properties that influence the physical implementation of the snapshot.

From the application design perspective, properties on the other tabs, including Display, Controls, and UI, may be set to influence the front-end application generators. When setting properties on these tabs, follow the same guidelines presented in Section 18.2 for the case of tables.

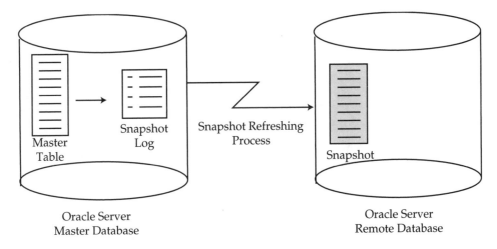

FIGURE 18.16 A graphical representation of snapshots and snapshot logs.

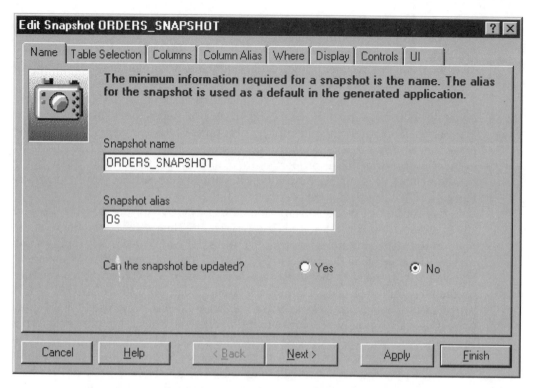

FIGURE 18.17   The Name properties tab of the Edit Snapshot dialog box.

Depending on the kind of query that creates the set of records stored in a snapshot, these objects are classified as simple and complex. Simple snapshots are based on straightforward SELECT statements on a single base table. These statements do not use any of the SQL group functions, such as COUNT, SUM, or AVG. Their WHERE clause does not contain any subqueries and, since they query only one table, they cannot contain any joins. These statements cannot return rows in hierarchical order, and therefore cannot contain the CONNECT BY clause. Finally, they cannot contain any set operations, such as UNION, INTERSECT, and MINUS.

Complex snapshots, on the other hand, can be created based on any SELECT statement, no matter how complex it is. They can be snapshots for more than one master table or view, which may not all be in the same database. All the clauses, functions, and options that are not allowed for simple snapshots can be used for complex ones.

18.7 CREATING AND MAINTAINING SEQUENCES

Chapter 17 explained how the Database Design Transformer introduces surrogate keys to map primary unique identifiers to primary keys. These keys are created based on your request or because the Transformer determines that they are needed. In order to populate the surrogate keys with values, the Transformer creates a Sequence object in the Repository for each key. Other data elements in the system may need to be populated with sequence numbers. For these columns, you may want to create and maintain the sequence objects yourself. Definitions of sequence objects are created and maintained in the DB Objects tab of the Design Navigator. Figure 18.18 shows sample properties of a sequence in the Edit Sequence dialog box.

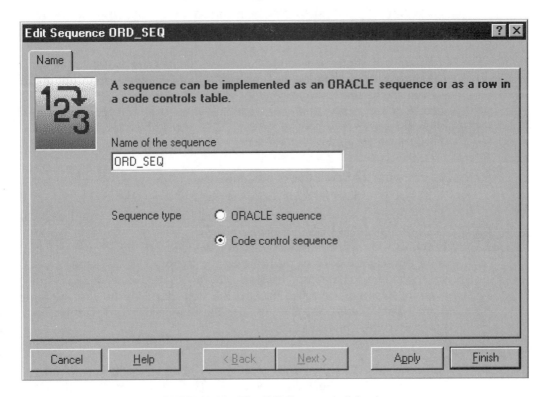

FIGURE 18.18   The Edit Sequence dialog box.

All sequences will generate unique numbers to populate your keys. However, based on the origin of these numbers, you can distinguish two types of sequences:

❑ **ORACLE sequences.** These are numbers generated by the Oracle database and used in the majority of cases, because they provide high performance and efficiency.

The Oracle sequences are the most efficient ones; however, they do not guarantee that no gaps will exist between the generated numbers. Once a number is generated from the sequence, it must be used for the intended purpose; otherwise it cannot be regenerated from that sequence. Consider, for example, a transaction that generates a sequence number for the primary key of each new record. When a record is created in the front-end application, the sequence returns a number. If the transaction that inserts the record completes successfully, the sequence number will used as intended. However, if the transaction is canceled, the sequence number is lost forever. Furthermore, each time the database server is shut down, all the sequence values currently cached are lost. Sequences that do not allow gaps between the values they generate can be implemented using code control tables, as explained below.

❑ **Code control sequences.** Code control sequences are two-column tables that are part of your database. The first column contains the name of the sequence; the second column contains the last value allocated from this sequence. A transaction that requires a new value from this sequence should follow these steps:

1. Retrieve the current value for the desired sequence from the code control table.
2. Compute the new value of the sequence.
3. Insert or update the database using the new sequence number.
4. Update the sequence record in the code control table by replacing the current number with the new number.

As you can see, when these steps are followed, generating the new sequence value and using it are part of the same transaction. Like any other transaction in the Oracle database, this transaction will be completed successfully, or all its steps will be rolled back. If the step that uses the new sequence number fails, the process that updates the sequence record is rolled back, thus preserving the sequence number.

Fortunately, the Designer/2000 generators will do all the hard work for you when it comes to using code control sequences. They will create the code control table with the appropriate record in it and generate all the necessary code to use and maintain the sequence. The generators can create a generic code control table

You can instruct the generators to choose one implementation over the others by setting the database administration (DBA) preference 'Scope of control code tables,' abbreviated as CCTABL, to APPSYS, GENERIC, or TABLE. The group of DBA preferences can be accessed under the Application Preferences node of the Preferences Navigator. Chapter 27 will discuss this navigator in detail.

that is used by all the application systems in the Repository, or a separate table for each application, or a separate table for each table object that needs such a sequence. In the first case, a table with the name *application_system*_CODE_CONTROLS, as in OMS_CODE_CONTROLS, contains a record for each code control sequence in the application; in the second case, a record for each such sequence in the Repository is created in the table CG_CODE_CONTROLS; in the third case, a single row table is created for each code control sequence.

For columns that derive their values from sequences, you can set the property *Sequence* for the column to the desired sequence object. Recall from Chapter 17 that when the Database Design Transformer creates a surrogate primary key for a table, it also creates a sequence that will be used to populate the primary key column. In these cases, the *Sequence* property of this column is set to the name of the sequence. This property can be accessed in the Property Palette of the column object.

18.8 USING THE DATABASE OBJECT GUIDE

The Design Editor offers an excellent tool that helps you organize the work you have to do during the logical database design phase. This is the Database Object Guide and you can access it by selecting Tools | Database Object Guide... from the menu. This guide helps you navigate the hierarchy of database objects that are part of your application system and helps you visualize their relationships and dependencies. When you invoke the Database Object Guide, you initially see the entry screen of the tool shown in Figure 18.19. From this screen you can embark on one of the two paths available to create database objects in your application system:

❑ Create and edit database objects in the application system
❑ Retrieve the properties of objects from an existing database by running the Design Recovery utility

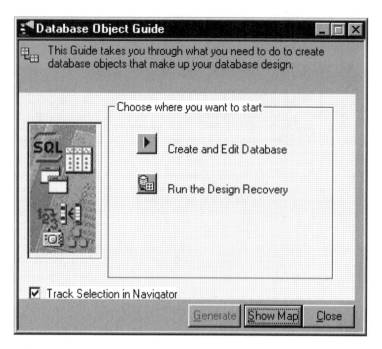

FIGURE 18.19 The entry screen of the Database Object Guide.

If you click the icon , the entry screen is replaced with a screen that lists the five categories of database objects you create and maintain during the logical database design: Tables and Columns, Domains, Sequences, Advanced Objects (including Views, Snapshots, and Clusters), and PL/SQL Objects. Each category on this second screen is preceded by the icon . Clicking the icon takes you one level further in the process of selecting the action you want to perform. The title of each category except Advanced Objects is a hyper-link to the Designer/2000 online help for the category.

Figure 18.20 shows the screen that is displayed if you choose to drill down the Tables and Columns path. The list control in the center of the screen displays all the tables defined in the repository. The following is a list of the major actions you can take from this screen:

❑ To create a new table, click Create…. The Create Table dialog box appears.
❑ To view the properties of a table object, select it in the list and click Edit…. This command brings up the Edit Table dialog box. Double-clicking the object on the list displays this dialog as well.
❑ To display one or more tables in a data diagram, select them and click Diagram….

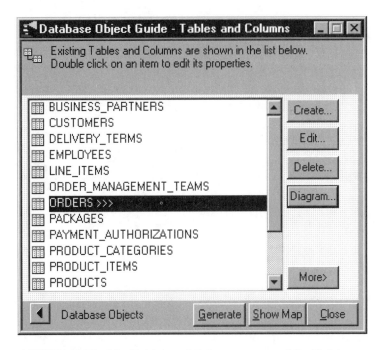

FIGURE 18.20   The Tables and Columns screen of the Database Object Guide.

❑ To delete one or more tables, select them in the list and click Delete....
❑ To invoke the Server Generator for one or more tables, select them and click Generate.

Similar actions may be performed in other screens where instances of objects are displayed. Notice that the selected table in Figure 18.20 is shown as ORDERS >>> on the list. The characters >>> are visual indicators that the object may contain additional objects as its dependents. To view the categories of these objects click the button More>. Now the Database Design Guide screen displays the menu for Constraints, Indexes, and Triggers. You can drill down one of these paths to create and edit the object of the selected category. To return to the previous screen of the Guide, click the icon ◀.

As you can see, the Database Object Guide is a very effective tool to navigate up and down the hierarchy of objects in your application system following a given path. However, you may also need to jump from one area of the hierarchy onto another, for example, from the properties of a table index to the definition of a sequence. The Map component of the Database Object Guide complements the functionality of the Guide with exactly this functionality. In order to display the map, click the button Show Map on the Database Object Guide dialog box. You

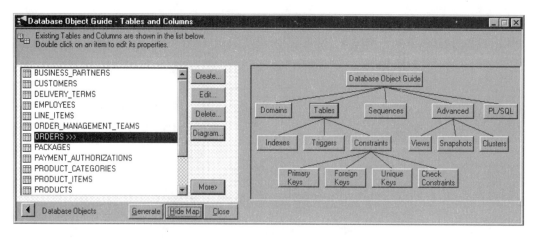

FIGURE 18.21   The Database Object Guide with the map.

will see that the dialog box will be expanded to the right to include a hierarchy tree representation of the database objects you can create and maintain in Designer/2000 application systems (see Figure 18.21). Each push button on the map represents a screen of the Database Object Guide. If the button is enabled, you can navigate to its associated screen immediately, by clicking the button. If the button is not enabled, this means that you cannot navigate to its associated screen from the screen where you are currently. The buttons under Tables, for example, are enabled only if your current screen is the Tables and Columns screen and you have selected a table object on it, as shown in Figure 18.21. They are enabled under these conditions because you can access index, trigger, or constraint objects only in the context of their parent table.

Click the button Hide Map on the Database Object Guide screen when you no longer need to display the map.

18.9   SUMMARY

The Database Design Transformer allows you to create the first-cut design of your database. After that, you need to maintain and enhance this design in order to achieve the desired functionality of your system. This process includes creating and maintaining data diagrams, tables, views, and snapshots. This chapter discusses how you can use the Data Diagrammer to maintain key parts of the database design for your system. The most important topics of this chapter are listed below:

- ❑ **Maintaining Data Diagrams**
  - ❑ Including Objects in Data Diagrams
  - ❑ Creating Objects in Data Diagrams
  - ❑ Maintaining the Layout of Data Diagrams
- ❑ **Maintaining Tables**
  - ❑ Name Properties
  - ❑ Column Definition Properties
  - ❑ Display Properties
  - ❑ GUI Control Properties
  - ❑ User Interface Properties
- ❑ **Providing for Data Auditing and Journaling**
- ❑ **Creating and Maintaining Indexes**
- ❑ **Maintaining Views**
  - ❑ Implementing Business Views of Data
  - ❑ Enforcing Data Access and Security Rules
  - ❑ Setting Properties of Views
- ❑ **Maintaining Snapshots**
- ❑ **Creating and Maintaining Sequences**
- ❑ **Using the Database Object Guide**

IMPLEMENTING THE PHYSICAL DATABASE DESIGN

♦ Documenting the System's Foundations

♦ Defining Database Components

♦ Defining Database Users

♦ Implementing Logical Design Objects in a Database Schema

♦ Using the Database Administrator Guide

♦ Preserving the Physical Database Design Flexibility

♦ Summary

After creating the logical design of your database, you need to define how its objects will be implemented physically. This process includes deciding whether these objects will be distributed among different nodes and databases on the network, how each database will be organized, and what its physical components will be, such as tablespaces, rollback segments, users, and storage parameters of an Oracle database. Ultimately, your decisions will be converted into SQL statements that will create these objects in a database environment such as the Oracle Server. Designer/2000 provides for ways to avoid the tedious process of typing "raw" SQL code to implement the database objects you will need in your application. In the Repository Object Navigator and in the Design Editor, you can create objects such as databases, tablespaces, or storage definitions, and set their properties declaratively. These objects then are associated with database object definitions to produce the physical implementations of these objects. For example, a table may be associated with a database, a database user, a tablespace, and a storage definition object, thus specifying precisely where the table should reside physically, who will own it, and how it will store the data. After the physical database design is completed, you can invoke the Designer/2000 Server Generator to automatically prepare the SQL scripts that create the database objects according to your definitions. In this chapter, you will see how you can use the Design Editor to define important components of the physical database model and maintain their properties over time.

19.1 DOCUMENTING THE SYSTEM'S FOUNDATIONS

Creating the physical model of the database is part of the larger task of designing the technical architecture of the system. The technical architecture is an important factor that directly affects the success or the failure of the new system. A carefully prepared technical architecture should provide answers for questions such as:

❑ What are the major hardware and software components required to implement the system?

❑ How will the data and the functionality of the system be spread among the components of the system in order to maximize its performance and reliability?

❑ How should the system's components be sized in order to satisfy capacity requirements for the system?

In particular, the technical architecture design should produce a system diagram that shows the major hardware nodes, the user communities, and the distribution of databases in the network. The following sections explain how to enter in the Designer/2000 Repository the information contained in such a diagram.

19.1.1 NODES

A node in the system's network is any hardware component of importance in the configuration of the system. A node can be a database server, an application server, a network interchange machine, and so on. A node may not necessarily be a single machine. It can represent a group of hardware components that share common characteristics. For example, if your network contains 100 user PCs configured similarly, only one node may be sufficient to represent them all in the network diagram.

To create a node in the Design Navigator window of the Design Editor switch to the Distribution tab, select Nodes, click Create , and then specify its properties. To view and edit the properties of an existing node, double-click the node in the Design Navigator. If the Design Editor is set to use dialog boxes, the dialog box Create Node or Edit Node appears, depending on the action you are performing. By stepping through the tabs of this dialog you can set the properties of the node and create associations between it and other objects in the Repository, like other nodes and databases. If the Design Editor is not set to use dialog boxes, the properties of the node are set and maintained in the Property Palette for the object. Figure 19.1 shows an example of this Property Palette for the node TIGER, which represents the database server used to develop the Order Management System.

As you can see from Figure 19.1, the properties of Node allow you to record its name, type, and primary usages, as well as important hardware information, such as manufacturer, model, number of CPUs, amount of RAM, and disk capacity. In addition, you can record information about the persons responsible for this node, availability requirements, and other data that you deem important for this component.

In order to describe whether and how two nodes interact with each other, you can create Network Connections objects. For example, to document the link that exists between the development database server TIGER and the development application server LION, you would take the following actions:

Recall that the Design Editor will use dialog boxes to help you create and maintain properties of objects if the icon Use dialogs is in pushed state, the Property Palette is used instead.

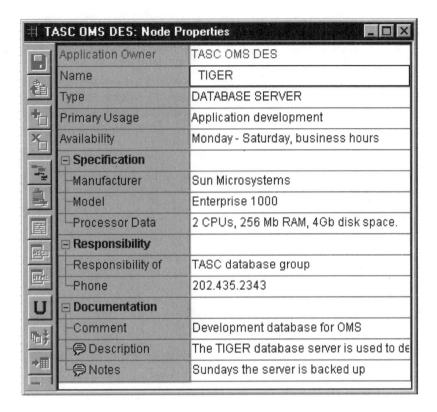

FIGURE 19.1   Sample properties of nodes.

1. Double-click the node TIGER in the Design Navigator to display the Edit Node dialog box.
2. Switch to the tab Network and click the button Add. The dialog box Nodes in Application System appears.
3. Select the node LION from the list and click OK to close the dialog box.
4. Set the properties such that they describe the network protocol and the line speed as shown in Figure 19.2.
5. Click Finish.

In the Property Palette of the network connection object you can also document the availability of the connection between the two nodes.

After the nodes for the system are defined, you may proceed with tasks related to the database and application design. During these activities, you decide how to distribute the data and the modules of the system across its nodes. Associations of application modules with a node are represented as objects of the type

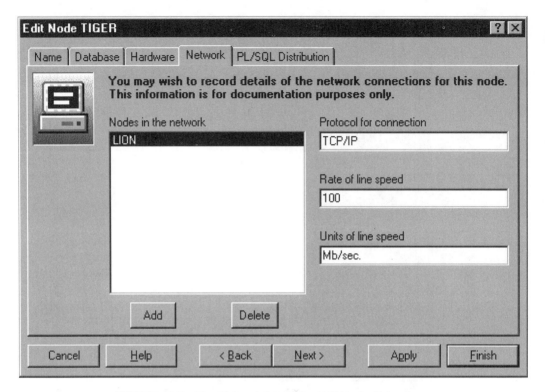

FIGURE 19.2   The Network tab of the Edit Node dialog box.

Distributed Module Processing. They are created and maintained in the tab PL/SQL Distribution of the Edit Node dialog box. Furthermore, to describe the fact that a node may host one or more databases, you can create associations between the node and the database objects. The following section describes how to associate a database with a node.

19.1.2   DATABASES

You can quickly create objects that represent Oracle databases by following these steps:

1. Select the node Databases (Oracle) in the Distribution tab of the Design Navigator.
2. Click the button Create ▪. The dialog box Create Database appears.

3. Set properties of the database object in the tabs Name, Connection, Instances, Data Files, and Log Files.
4. Click Finish.

Figure 19.3 shows an example of the properties that you can set for a database in the Property Palette. The meaning of parameters like Archive Redo Files, Max Log Files, or Max Data Files is widely documented in the documentation of the Oracle Server. The property tabs of the Edit Database dialog box also describe the meaning of these properties. Therefore I will not discuss it here. I will point

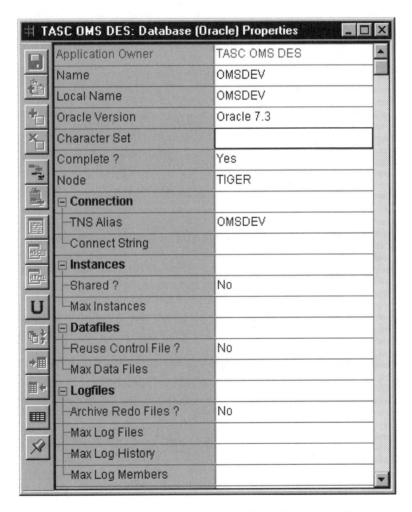

FIGURE 19.3 Setting database properties in the Repository Object Navigator.

out that the association between this database and the node where it resides is created by setting the property *Node* to the name of a node object defined in the Repository. After creating the database objects, add to the Repository definitions of components of an Oracle database such as tablespaces, operating system files, rollback segments, and so on. Section 19.2 will explain how you create such objects for a database.

Designer/2000 allows you to create and maintain the properties of a number of non-Oracle databases, including Informix, Sybase, DB2, SQL Server, Rdb, as well as ANSI standard databases. The following steps describe the process of creating a non-Oracle database object:

1. Switch to the DB Admin tab of the Design Navigator and select the node Databases (Non Oracle).
2. Click Create 🔳.
3. Enter the name and the type of the database.
4. Click Finish.

The properties you can set and maintain for non-Oracle databases are limited in number. Figure 19.4 shows the Create Database dialog box for a non-Oracle database.

19.1.3 COMMUNITIES

Besides the information entered above, the Repository Object Navigator allows you to create objects that represent user communities, organized by the type of protocol they use in their network environment. These communities are defined primarily to help the network and database administrators set up and configure Oracle's SQL*Net, which allows users to communicate with the Oracle database server. In order to create a community object, follow these steps:

1. Select the node Communities in the Repository Object Navigator.
2. Click the button Create Object 🔳 on the toolbar.
3. Switch to the Property Palette of the new community and set the property *Community Name*.
4. Set the property *Protocol* to the network protocol—for example, TCP/IP or SPX/IPX—that is used in that particular community.

In order to associate a database with a community, do the following:

1. Expand the node that represents the desired community and select the node Community Databases.

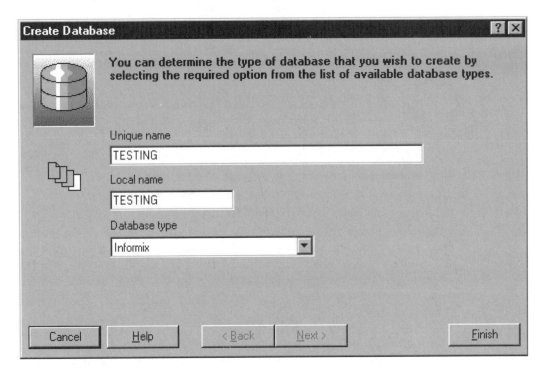

FIGURE 19.4   The Create Database dialog box for a non-Oracle database.

2. Click the button Create Association 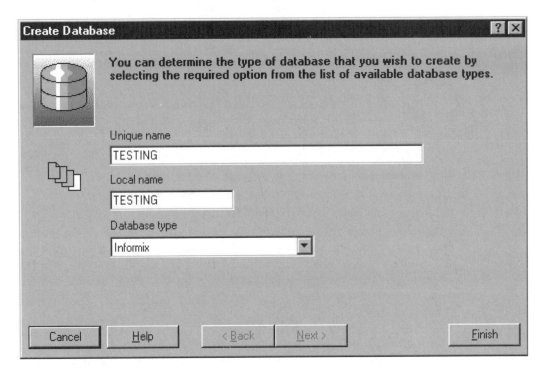 on the toolbar to create the new association.

3. In the dialog box Create Community Databases, select the database that you want to include in this community and click OK.

19.2   DEFINING DATABASE COMPONENTS

The user view of an Oracle database is a set of tablespaces where objects such as tables and indexes can be created to store and manipulate data. Physically, an Oracle database consists of a set of control files, redo log files, and data files. Control files contain information about the structure of the database, such as the names of the data files that make up the database. Redo log files contain information about every transaction that occurs in the database. Data files are the operating system physical files that implement each tablespace.

When creating a database, you need to consider both the physical and the logical aspects of its implementation. The following sections discuss how you can store information about physical files and logical structures of an Oracle database in the Designer/2000 Repository.

19.2.1 FILES

In the Design Navigator, you can create objects that represent the data files of a database by switching to the tab DB Admin, and then by following these steps:

1. Expand the node that represents the desired database.
2. Expand the node Storage and select the Datafiles in the Navigator.
3. Click the icon Create 🔳 on the toolbar.
4. In the dialog box Create File that appears, enter the logical name of the file, its physical name and location, and its size. Figure 19.5 shows the properties for a data file. The name of the file is used to identify the object in the Repository; however, the setting you enter in the text box Pathname of file is what the Server Generator will use as the name of the file in the operating system.
5. Click Next and specify whether the data file can be extended automatically as it becomes full with data. If the file is autoextendable, you can also specify the amount by which the file will be extended or the maximum size to which the file can grow during its life time.
6. Click Finish.

The actions of defining log files for the database are very similar. The only difference is that for these files the concept of autoextendibility does not apply, since all the log files are of the same size.

The names of the database files in your system, like the file shown in Figure 19.5, should follow the Oracle Flexible Architecture (OFA) standards. These standards were defined by Cary Millsap, director of The Advanced Technologies Group at the Oracle Corporation. They were first published as an Oracle Corporation white paper in 1990. You may find the complete version of this paper in *Oracle Magazine*, volume VII, number 1 (Winter 1993), under the title "An Optimal Flexible Architecture for a Growing Oracle Database."

Create File ☐ **?** ☒

To create a file quickly with minimal details, enter the name and click Finish. Further details may be entered on this and the following tab. You may choose to create a new file on the database by entering a new name or create an existing file on the database by browsing the file systems for the required file.

File name

| Order Data |

Pathname of file

| D:\ORAWIN95\Database\orddata.ora | Browse...

Size of file

| 10486272 | | bytes ▼ |

| Cancel | | Help | | < Back | Next > | | Finish |

FIGURE 19.5   The Create File dialog box for an Oracle database data file.

After the objects that represent the data files are created, you need to associate them with the appropriate tablespaces. Section 19.2.4 will discuss the process of associating data files with tablespaces.

19.2.2 STORAGE DEFINITION

As I said above, objects in an Oracle database can be created and maintained in tablespaces. The Oracle kernel is responsible for their implementation as operating system files, but this activity is transparent to the users of the database. The objects in the tablespace are made up of one or more *extents*. When the object is first created, a certain amount of free space is set aside for the object in the tablespace. This is called the first extent of the object, and its size is determined by the value of the parameter INITIAL in the STORAGE clause of the SQL statement that creates the object. If during the use of the object, the initial extent is filled up with data, another chunk of space is carved out of the tablespace and allocated to the object. This is called the next extent of the object, and its size is determined by the value of the parameter NEXT in the same STORAGE clause. As the database object continues to grow, additional extents are allocated for it. The size of these extents is determined by the value of another parameter in the STORAGE clause, PCTINCREASE, also known as Percent Increase. If this parameter is set to 0, each additional extent will be the same size as Next Extent. If the parameter is set to a number greater than zero, the sizes of the consecutive extents will increase gradually. For example, if this parameter is set to 50, the third extent will be 50 percent larger than the second, the fourth 50 percent larger than the third, and so on.

Designer/2000 allows you to maintain these profiles in the form of objects of the Storage Definition type. You can create and maintain these objects in the DB Admin tab of the Design Navigator. Figure 19.6 shows an example of the Name tab of the Edit Storage Definition dialog box where the most important properties of such an object are located.

19.2.3 SETTING STORAGE PARAMETERS TO AVOID FRAGMENTATION

Think for a moment of a large piece of land that is up for sale. As land is sold, new landlords start moving in and each of them is given a lot. As time goes by, if they need more land, they can purchase additional lots, not necessarily adjacent

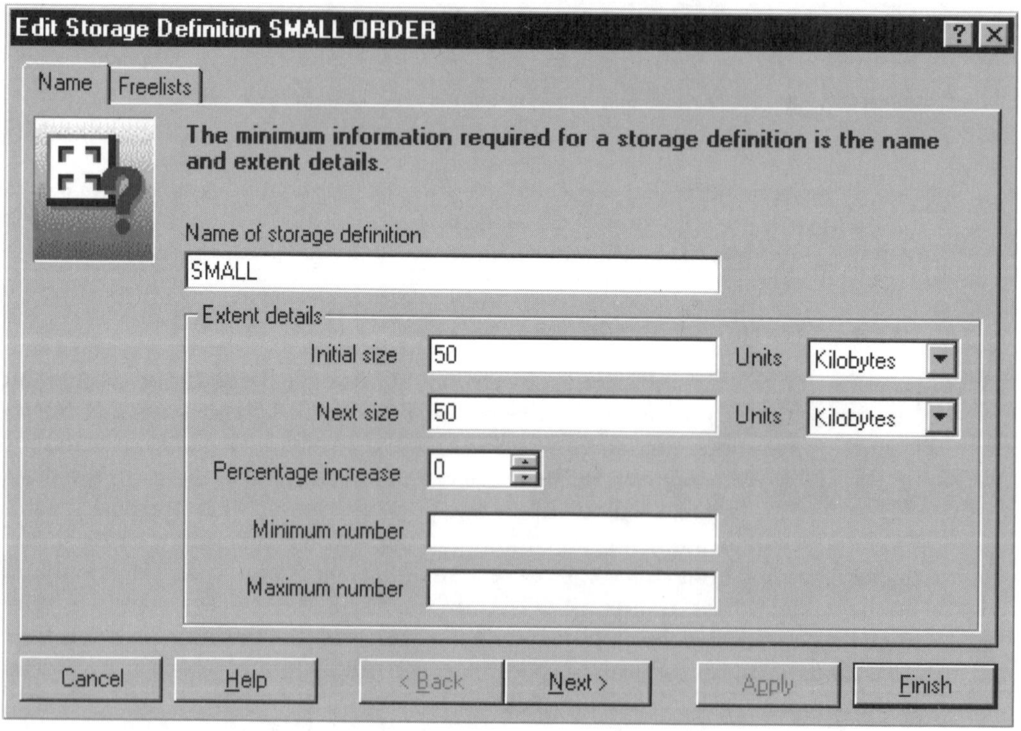

FIGURE 19.6   The Name tab of the Edit Storage Definition dialog box.

to their original one. Also, some of these landlords are evicted. At that point, they release the lot they occupy and move out of the property. The problem is that the lot they release may be an island of free space surrounded by occupied territories. The lot can be sold again only to someone looking to buy a piece of land as big as or smaller than this lot. The problem becomes more acute if many of these non-contiguous free lots exist. In such situations, a buyer who wants to purchase a lot larger than the biggest contiguous free lot will be turned away, even if the combined free space of all the vacant lots may be many times larger than the requested size. When this situation happens, the lot is fragmented. One way to fix the fragmentation is to move the tenants into adjacent lots and transform the free lots into a big contiguous piece of unoccupied land again. This process is called defragmentation. Obviously, this is costly, since heavy negotiation must occur, and almost everybody will have to relocate their belongings to a new lot. However, the most important fact is that after the land is defragmented, nothing can guarantee that the unwanted fragmentation will not occur again. As in other matters, even here, an ounce of prevention is worth more than a pound of cure. Indeed, a simple way to avoid the fragmentation problem from ever occurring is to agree from the beginning that all the lots in the property will be of equal size. If this agreement is followed consistently, a vacant lot can always be assigned to a prospective purchaser, even if it is surrounded by occupied lots.

The previous paragraph describes to a great extent, although metaphorically, the way space is used in Oracle databases. The tablespace can be viewed as the large piece of land that can be partitioned into lots and allocated to database objects, such as tables, indexes, rollback segments, and other segments. If no restrictions are placed upon the size of space that objects can reclaim, a heavily used tablespace may soon become fragmented. On the other hand, if each object in the tablespace is allocated space in extents of the same size, the fragmentation can easily be avoided. The question, of course, is to determine what this size should be. In practice, to determine a single extent size that could fit the needs of all the objects in the database is often impossible. Setting the size of the extent too high may result in waste of space, since objects that require a small amount of storage space, such as a table with a few dozen small records, will not fill out the extent allocated to them. On the other hand, setting the size too low may require a large object, such as a table with millions of records, to allocate its data in several extents, which has its detrimental effects on the performance of the system.

The best way to solve this problem is to group the objects in the Oracle database according to their storage requirements. For example, all the objects that require around 50Kb of disk space in Group 1, those that require around 100Kb in Group 2, and so on. For each of these groups, a storage profile is created such that it accommodates all the objects in the group. All these objects now will inherit their storage parameters from the group profile, meaning that even if Table A is expected to hold 30Kb worth of data and Table B 75Kb, their initial extent will be 50Kb, derived from the value of this parameter for their group.

19.2.4 TABLESPACES

I mentioned earlier that tablespaces are the way the Oracle database logically groups objects. Although only one tablespace is required for a database to exist, a well performing, easy-to-maintain database is made up of several tablespaces. Each tablespace contains database objects that have similar characteristics and requirements. You should try to meet three major goals when assigning database objects to different tablespaces:

❑ **Minimize tablespace fragmentation.** The problem of fragmentation was discussed in the previous section. One way to avoid it is to set the storage parameters at the tablespace level and allocate to the tablespace only those objects that have the same storage profile. Furthermore, you can group objects with similar life expectancy in one tablespace. For example, rollback segments, which are created during the execution of a transaction and dropped when the transaction is committed or rolled back, place continuous demands on the tablespace to allocate and deallocate extents to them. They should be assigned to a separate tablespace dedicated exclusively to them. The Oracle dictionary segments, on the other hand, are never dropped; therefore, the SYSTEM tablespace where they are created should not contain any segments that can be dropped, such as user-created tables, indexes, or rollback segments.

❑ **Minimize I/O contention.** Although database objects exist in tablespaces, these tablespaces are made up of a set of operating system files, which are stored on one or more disks in the database server. I/O contention exists when database activities require that the same disk be accessed at the same time in different locations. This situation is not desirable since it generally means that one activity will have to be idle and wait until the others complete before proceeding. The distribution of objects in tablespaces and, therefore, in physical disks, may significantly improve or deteriorate the I/O contention. For example, if a table and one of its indexes are allocated to the same tablespace, each time a record is inserted, a write operation must be performed against the table and the index objects, which physically are located in different sectors of the same disk. If, however, the index is allocated to a different tablespace, whose data files are stored in a different disk, the two write operations may proceed in parallel, since they no longer require access to the same resource.

❑ **Minimize administrative effort.** Consider a tablespace that contains objects used by two distinct communities of users. If the tablespace will have to be taken offline for maintenance, both communities will not be able to access their data. If, on the other hand, the data is partitioned into a separate tablespace for each community, the impact of tablespace maintenance is localized and minimized.

In order to achieve these goals, then, you have to create several tablespaces for your database. At a minimum, have a separate tablespace for data dictionary segments (SYSTEM), one for rollback segments (RBS), one for temporary segments (TEMP), and one for miscellaneous activities by users (USERS). Then, for each application, have at least one tablespace for tables, for example OMS_DATA, and a separate one for indexes, for example OMS_IDX. Obviously, depending on fragmentation considerations and access patterns of data, the application may require more tablespaces for its objects.

The following steps describe the process of creating a tablespace in the DB Admin tab of the Design Navigator:

1. Expand the database for which you want to create the tablespace, expand the node Storage of this database, and select the node Tablespaces.
2. Click Create ⬛ to invoke the dialog box Create Tablespace.
3. Enter the name of the tablespace in the Name tab. Other properties you can set in this tab are instruct the Server Generator to create DDL statements that bring the tablespace online upon creation, that make the tablespace read-only or read-write, and that create a normal or a temporary tablespace. Figure 19.7 shows an example of this tab as it appears in the Edit Tablespace dialog box for the tablespace ORDER_DATA.
4. Click Next and set the storage properties of the tablespace. In the Storage tab you can choose to associate the tablespace with a storage definition object created earlier, or create one such object on the fly, by clicking the button Create Storage Definition…. You can also let the tablespace use the default storage definition defined by the Oracle Server.
5. Click Next and allocate an amount of space to each user of the tablespace in the tab Quotas. The user quotas on tablespaces are discussed in detail in Section 19.3.
6. Click Finish.

Figure 19.7 shows the Property Palette for a tablespace object.

The name of the tablespace should be such that it describes its purpose, as in SYSTEM, TEMP, OMS_DATA and so on. According to OFA standards, choose names with eight characters or less.

Naming the data files with the name of the tablespace followed by a two-digit sequence number is another OFA standard that facilitates the maintenance and administration of the database when followed consistently.

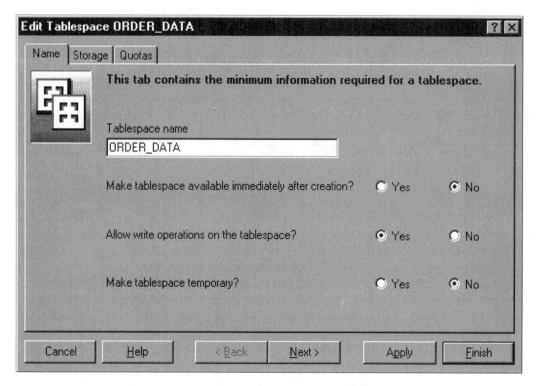

FIGURE 19.7 The Edit Tablespace dialog box.

After creating the tablespace, you need to add the data files that implement it physically. The process is the same as the one described in Section 19.2.1, therefore I will not discuss it here.

19.2.5 ROLLBACK SEGMENTS

Rollback segments are database objects where Oracle writes information necessary to reverse changes made to data files by transactions that are canceled. I recommend that all the rollback segments be created and maintained in a separate tablespace, since they acquire and release extents very frequently during their lifetime and, therefore, may interfere with the storage of other database objects like tables and indexes. The size of rollback segments depends on the type of transactions performed against the database. Short inserts, deletes, or updates generate a small amount of rollback information and require small segments. Long-running, batch-type transactions require larger rollback segments. The number of rollback segments is proportional to the number of concurrent transactions that the database will execute. Therefore, in order to define the number and the size of the rollback segments correctly, you need to have a good understanding of the types of transactions that your application will generate, as well as the frequency of these transactions.

Properties of rollback segment objects can be created and maintained in the Design Navigator. In the hierarchy tree of the Navigator, rollback segments are located under the node Storage for a given database. The most important properties for these objects are grouped in the tab Storage of the Edit Rollback Segment dialog box. Figure 19.8 shows an example of this tab. Through these properties, you can assign the rollback segment to a tablespace within that database and associate it with a predefined storage definition object.

The storage properties of a rollback segment are similar to those of other objects in the database, with the exception of the property *Optimal Size*, which is unique to rollback segments. This property determines the amount of extents that should be allocated to the rollback segments even if the segment is not in use. As said earlier, when a rollback segment is being used, especially for long-running transactions, the segment may request and the tablespace may allocate several extents. These extents are deallocated when the transaction is committed or rolled back. If another long-running transaction uses the same segment, the extents will

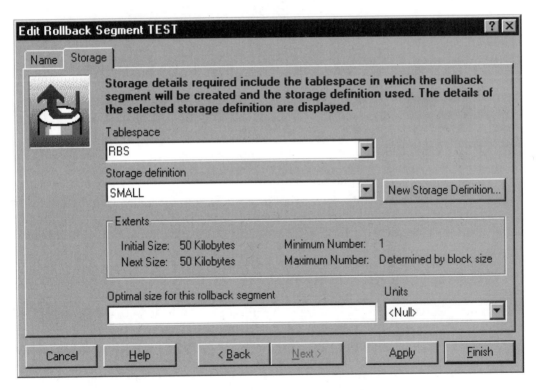

FIGURE 19.8   Sample properties of a rollback segment.

have to be reallocated and deallocated again. To avoid the overhead associated with allocating and deallocating extents to the rollback segments, Oracle allows you to specify the number of extents that should always be associated with a rollback segment. In Designer/2000, you can do so by setting the property *Optimal Size*. Based on this property, the Server Generator adds the clause OPTIMAL to the statement that creates the segment.

19.3 DEFINING DATABASE USERS

The Design Editor allows you to record information about the database schemas of your system. As with other objects, the properties you set declaratively, by pointing and clicking in the dialog boxes or Property Palettes are translated by the Server Generator into SQL statements that create or update these objects in the database. Database users are the most basic schema of an Oracle database. Although you could maintain their privileges and grants individually, for large systems with many users, a more feasible approach is to administer users through groups or, as they are known in Oracle databases, roles.

19.3.1 DATABASE ROLES

A group or role in an Oracle database is a named set of system and object privileges that can be assigned to users or other groups. Group objects are created using standard commands of the Design Navigator. Their properties are maintained in the Edit Role dialog box, composed of three tabs: Name, Roles, and System Privileges. The tab Name allows you to maintain the name of the role and an initial password for all the users granted the role. The tab Roles is used to grant the current role other roles defined in the Repository. Figure 19.9 shows an example of this tab.

In order to grant a role to the current role, select its name from the list Roles not performed to the left and click the icon ▣. The role now appears in the list box Roles performed. To give the current role the ability to grant a role assigned to it to other roles, select the role in the list box Roles performed and click the button +Grant. To revoke this ability from the role, select the role and click -Grant. In the example shown in the Figure 19.9, the role CONNECT is granted to the role VENDOR with the grant option; the role RESOURCE is not granted with this option. To revoke a role grant from the current role, select the role you want to revoke in the list Roles performed and click the icon ▣.

Besides granting a role other roles, you can also grant individual system privileges to the role. Granting a system privilege to a role means that the role is authorized to perform a given database operation. For example, granting CREATE TABLE to a role will enable every database user who has that role to create

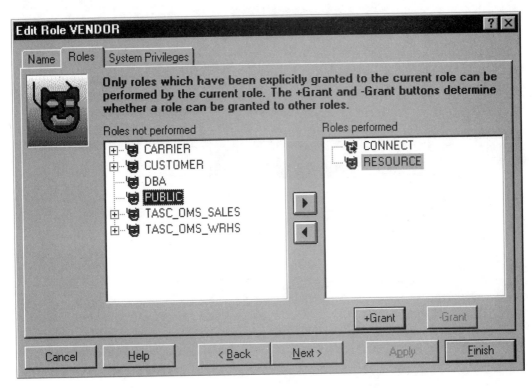

FIGURE 19.9   The Roles tab of the Edit Role dialog box.

tables in his or her schema. System privileges granted to a role are maintained in the tab System Privileges of the Edit Role dialog box. The layout of this tab is similar to that of the tab Roles. Figure 19.10 shows an example of this tab. In order to grant a system privilege to the role, select it from the list box Privileges not granted and click ▶. To grant all the system privileges to the role, click the icon ▶. The icons ◀ and ◀ are used to remove the granted privileges individually or as a group.

Often, creating at least three groups of users for each application is common. The first group includes a few users who will administer the database, the second group includes the application developers who will create all the objects required for the database, and the third group will include the users, who normally are given only CONNECT privileges.

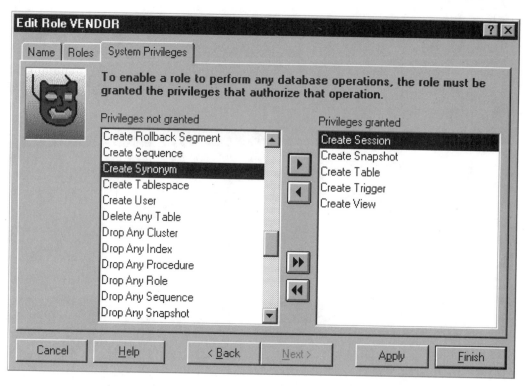

FIGURE 19.10   The System Privileges tab of the Edit Role dialog box.

In addition to system privileges, you can grant groups privileges to database objects as well, including tables, views, snapshots, and sequences. Chapter 20 will show you how to do this. Finally, groups can be given access to several modules of the application interface. In the case of Developer/2000 Form modules, this information is used to implement access control rules in your application.

19.3.2 DATABASE USERS

User accounts are the most basic component of database security in an Oracle database. In the Design Navigator, they are maintained under the node Users of a database object. The tabs of the dialog box Edit Database User are used to set the properties of a user when you create it and to maintain them during the life of the application system. The tabs Name, System Privileges, and Roles of this dialog are identical to the same tabs in the Edit Role dialog box discussed in the previous section. They allow you to define the name and an initial

In a well managed database with several individual user accounts, the best way to maintain and administer the privileges of users is to group them in database roles, assign the system or object privileges to the roles, and grant the roles to individual users.

password for the user. Furthermore, they are used to grant any system privileges or predefined roles to the database user.

The tab Tablespaces allows you to set the properties *Default Tablespace* and *Temporary Tablespace* of the current user. These properties must be set carefully, since they may have a significant impact on the application performance. The first one is where Oracle will place the objects that the user creates if she has not set the property TABLESPACE for them. The second tablespace will be used by Oracle to complete user requests that require temporary segments to be written, such as large sorts. If none of these properties is set, Oracle will use the SYSTEM tablespace for the above operations. This is a situation that must be avoided at any cost, since it may quickly fragment the SYSTEM tablespace. Good practice involves assigning a special tablespace, such as USERS, to serve as the default tablespace for all the database users, and another one, TEMP, to serve as the temporary tablespace for every user.

Users who will create objects in the database, primarily developers, should be granted the privilege Resource, or the appropriate system privileges, such as CREATE TABLE, CREATE SEQUENCE, and so on. However, in order to be able to actually create any tables or indexes, users must be granted quotas for one or more tablespaces in the database where these objects will be located. The quota levels of a user on tablespaces defined in the Repository are maintained in the tab Quotas of the Edit Database User dialog box. In the example shown in Figure 19.11, the user OMS_OWNER has unlimited space quota for tablespaces ORDER_DATA and ORDER_IDX, a quota of 500Kb on the tablespace USER, and no quota whatsoever on tablespaces RBS and TEMP.

The tab Quotas of the Edit Database User dialog allows you to create and maintain quota levels that one user has on several tablespaces. If you want to consider the other side of the relationship, that is, the quota that several users have on one tablespace, use the Quotas tab of the Edit Tablespace dialog box for the given tablespace.

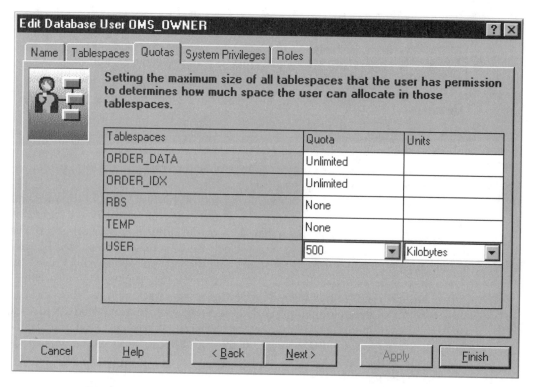

FIGURE 19.11   The Quotas tab of the Edit Database User dialog box.

19.3.3   DATABASE PROFILES

The database profiles allow you to control the amount of database resources consumed by users during their interaction with an Oracle database. In the Design Editor you can create profile objects with the following commands:

1. Switch to the tab DB Admin of the Design Navigator and expand the Oracle database to which you want to add the profile.
2. Select the node Profiles and click Create 🔢.
3. Specify the properties of the new profile in the Property Palette.

Figure 19.12 shows an example of the properties for a profile object. As you can see from this example, this profile limits to 12 the number of simultaneous database sessions a user may create. It also sets the idle time of a user connection to 30 minutes. The user with this profile will the logged out of the database if she does not perform any database activities for this interval of time.

In order to assign a profile to an Oracle database user, display the properties

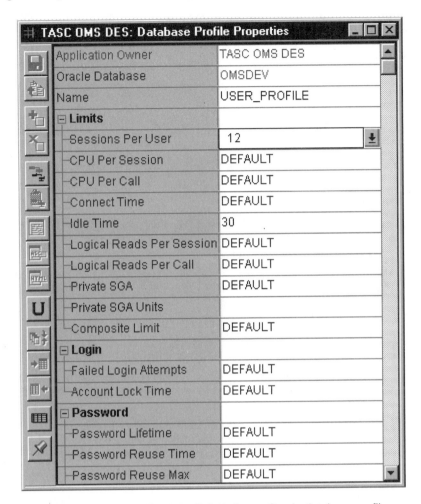

FIGURE 19.12 The Property Palette for an Oracle database profile.

of the user in the Property Palette and set the property *Database Profile* to the desired object.

19.4 IMPLEMENTING LOGICAL DESIGN OBJECTS IN A DATABASE SCHEMA

When you work on the logical design of your database, you define properties of objects like tables, indexes, views, and snapshots, to meet the needs of your application. Implementation details, such as the database and database schema that will own these objects, the storage of the objects in the databases, and so on, are not considered in this phase. During the physical design of the database, these details are analyzed and the logical database structures are implemented in the schema of one or more database users. The following sections will discuss how you create and maintain implementation objects tables, indexes, views, snapshots, and sequences.

19.4.1 CREATING IMPLEMENTATION OBJECTS

The implementation objects are created in the Design Navigator window of the Design Editor. The process of creating them is similar no matter what type of object you are implementing. The following are the steps you take to implement a table object:

1. Switch to the DB Admin tab of the Design Navigator.
2. Expand the node Databases (Oracle) or Databases (Non Oracle) and select the database in which you want to create the implementation objects.
3. Expand the node that represents the desired database, then expand the database account that will contain the objects in its schema.
4. Expand the node Schema Objects and select the category of object implementation you want to create, for example Table Implementation.
5. Click Create ⊞ on the toolbar. A dialog box that allows you to create implementations for the object type you selected appears. Figure 19.13 shows the Create Table Implementation for User dialog box. The list control in the center of the dialog contains all the objects of the selected type for which there is no implementation created in the user schema.
6. Select the object for which you want to create an implementation and click Next.
7. Enter the properties of the implementation objects in the sequence of property tabs. These tabs depend on the type of object you are implementing. They are identical with the tabs you see when you edit the object implementations and are discussed in the following sections.
8. Click Finish to complete the process.

19.4.2 MAINTAINING TABLE IMPLEMENTATIONS

In order to view and maintain the properties of a table implementation object, select the object in the DB Admin tab of the Design Navigator and double-click. The dialog box Edit Table Implementation that appears contains several property tabs, which are discussed in the following paragraphs:

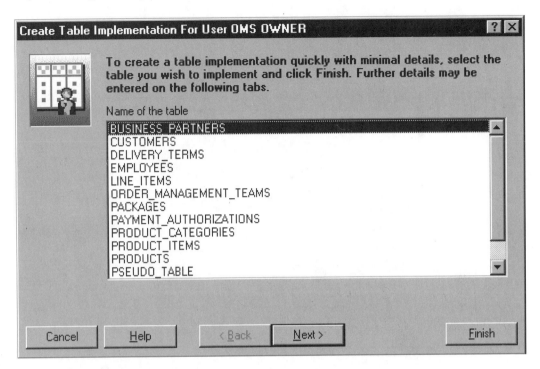

FIGURE 19.13 The Create Table Implementation for User dialog box.

❑ **Storage tab.** In this tab you can assign the table to a tablespace and define an appropriate storage definition object for the table. The list boxes Tablespace and Storage definition help you set these properties. The objects with which these lists are populated must already exist in the Repository and are created as discussed earlier in the chapter. If none of the existing storage definition objects satisfies the needs of the current table, you can click the button New Storage Definition... to define a new object. Figure 19.14 shows an example of the Storage tab of the Edit Table Implementation dialog box.

❑ **Data Blocks tab.** This tab allows you to set two important parameters that influence the way the space of the data blocks is used. The first one is the percentage of each data block that is reserved for future updates of records. This parameter corresponds to the PCTFREE clause of the CREATE TABLE statements created by the Server Generator. The default value of PCTFREE is 10, which means that each block of the table will store records until it is 90 percent full. The remaining 10 percent is reserved for expanding records in the block due to update operations. The value of this parameter should be set to minimize the number of records stored in more than one database block. This phenomenon, known as row chaining, deteriorates the perfor-

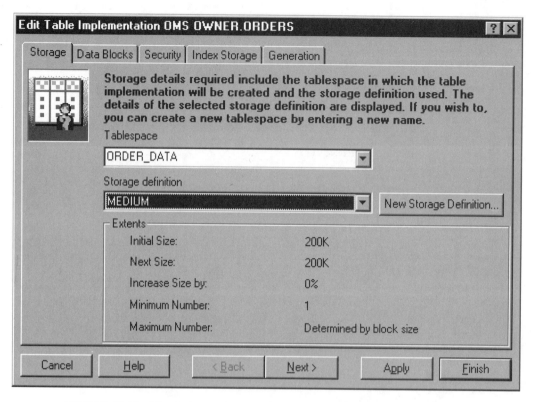

FIGURE 19.14 The Storage tab of the Edit Table Implementation dialog box.

mance of the application. A read-only table does not need any space reserved for updates; therefore, its PCTFREE should be set to 0. On the other hand, if the records will have up to 50 percent of the data specified after their insertion, the table must have PCTFREE set to 50, so that each block has enough room to accommodate the expanding records.

The second property specifies a minimal threshold of space usage that the database attempts to maintain for each block. It corresponds to the clause PCTUSED of the CREATE TABLE statement. Its default value is 40, which means that if the amount of space filled with data falls below 40 percent of the block size, Oracle may insert new data in the block.

❑ **Security tab.** This tab is used to grant privileges on the table to the users and roles defined for the database. In the example shown in Figure 19.15, the radio button Roles is selected and the tab contains all the roles defined in the database. The columns of the table control in the center of the tab represent all the object privileges that exist in an Oracle database. Those that do not apply to the current context of the table are disabled. In Figure 19.15, for

When a block is allocated to the table, Oracle will insert records in it as long as the space usage remains below (100–PCTFREE). For the default value of PCTFREE, the block will receive records as long as the space usage is below 100 – 10 = 90. When 90 percent or more of the block's space is used up, the block stops receiving new records. Due to deletes, the space usage for the block may drop below this level. However, as long as the space usage does not fall below PCTUSED, Oracle will not insert new records in the block. As soon as the PCTUSED threshold is surpassed, though, the block becomes eligible to receive new records.

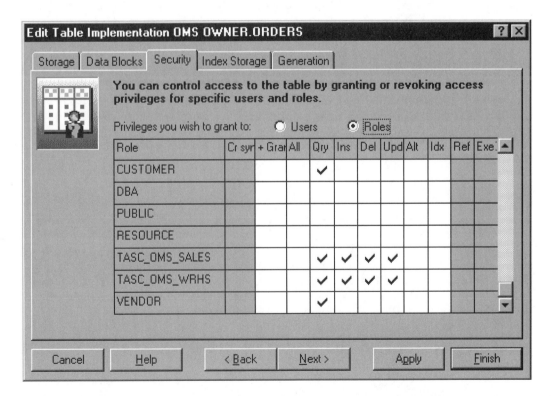

FIGURE 19.15 The Security tab of the Edit Table Implementation dialog box.

example, the column Cr syn, which represents the privilege CREATE SYN-
ONYM, is disabled because such object privilege cannot be granted to a
role. The last column Exe, which represents the privilege EXECUTE, is also
disabled, but, in this case, because this privilege does not apply to tables. To
grant a privilege to a user or role, simply click the intersection cell in the
table to place a check mark in the cell.

❑ **Index Storage tab.** This tab lists all the indexes that are associated with the
table. Some of these indexes are defined explicitly by you during the logical
database design; the others are created automatically to support a primary
or unique key constraint. If you do not specify storage characteristics for
these indexes, the default storage properties will be used. The indexes will
be created in the default tablespace of the account that owns them and the
storage parameters of this tablespace will become the storage parameters
for the index. In the general case, the default storage should not be used. Instead, the location and space usage of the indexes should be carefully analyzed and their storage properties explicitly set. Figure 19.16 shows an example of the Index Storage tab.

To set the storage properties of an index, select it in the Index Storage
tab and click Index Storage Dialog…. The first time you invoke the dialog,
its title is Create Index Storage for User. When the storage for the index is
created and you invoke the dialog, the title of the dialog will be Edit Index
Storage for User. The Index Storage dialog box allows you to assign the
index to a tablespace and to specify a storage clause for the index. The tab
Storage is used to perform these actions. This tab is identical to the Storage
tab of the Edit Table Implementation dialog shown in Figure 19.14. The second tab of this tab, titled Data Blocks, is used to set the property PCTFREE
of indexes the same way as it is used in the case of table implementation objects. Index storage objects can be created and maintained independently in
the Design Navigator by expanding the node that represents the table and
then the node Index Storage.

❑ **Generation tab.** This tab allows you to achieve two goals. First, by setting the
Yes button in the first radio group, you enable the Server Generator to generate a CREATE TABLE statement that caches the data block of a table in the
Server memory. This option may improve the performance of your system if
it is set for lookup tables with relatively few records that are queried often.
The radio button Yes in the second group should be set only if the table is the
master table in a snapshot and you want to generate a snapshot log for the refresh of this snapshot. When you set this option, two more tabs, Snapshot Log
Storage and Snapshot Log Data Blocks appear in the Edit Table Implementation dialog box. These tabs are for the snapshot log what the tabs Storage and
Data Blocks are for table objects. They allow you to assign the snapshot log to
a tablespace and to define its STORAGE, PCTFREE, and PCTUSED clauses.
Figure 19.17 shows an example of this tab.

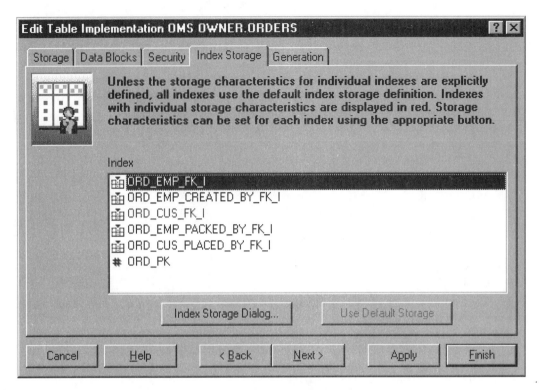

FIGURE 19.16 The Index Storage tab of the Edit Table Implementation dialog box.

19.4.3 MAINTAINING VIEW IMPLEMENTATIONS

As I explained earlier, views are logical database objects that compile their content at runtime, when needed. Because they do not store the data in the database, many storage properties that you need to worry about for other implementation objects, do not exist for view implementations. In fact, the only properties you need to maintain for a view are the privileges you grant to other users or roles.

In order to help you distinguish indexes for which the storage properties are set explicitly, the property tab Index Storage displays these indexes in red characters. Selecting one of these indexes in the list and clicking the button Use Default Storage removes the index storage object from the Repository.

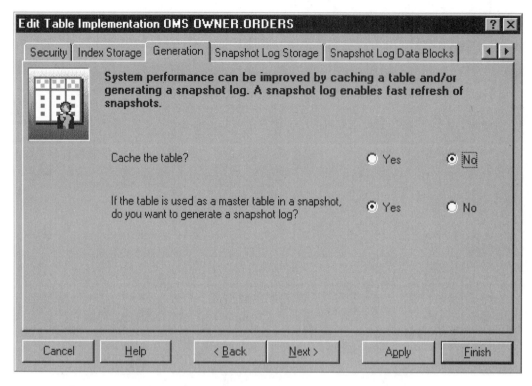

FIGURE 19.17   The Generation tab of the Edit Table Implementation dialog box.

These properties are maintained in the tab Security which was discussed in the previous section.

19.4.4   MAINTAINING SNAPSHOT IMPLEMENTATIONS

Recall that snapshots are tables in a local database that contain a copy of data elements from a remote database. So physical properties of snapshots must be defined following the same criteria that are used for table objects. The tabs Storage, Data Blocks, and Security of the Edit Snapshot Implementation contain the same properties as the tabs with the same name in the Edit Table Implementation dialog. Refer to Section 19.4.2 for a discussion about these tabs.

A fourth tab in the Edit Snapshot Implementation dialog box is the Refresh tab. This tab contains an important group of properties that influence the way Oracle refreshes the contents of the snapshot when the master data is updated. Figure 19.18 shows an example of the Refresh tab of the Edit Snapshot Implementation dialog box.

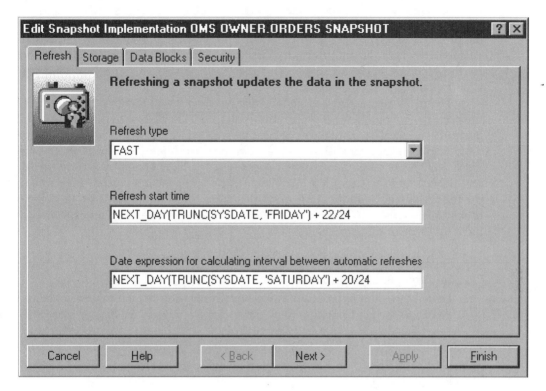

FIGURE 19.18 The Refresh tab of the Edit Snapshot Implementation dialog box.

The text box Refresh start time is set to the first time the snapshot is refreshed; the text box below specifies the next time the snapshot will be refreshed. These text boxes correspond to the properties *Refresh Start Time* and *Next Refresh Clause* of the snapshot implementation object. They are usually set to expressions that evaluate dates. SYSDATE and different SQL functions are normally used to construct these expressions. These properties need to be set to times after the cre-

Avoid setting these properties to hard-coded values as much as you can, since they hurt the flexibility of the SQL statements that can be created from the Repository. In the event that you specify a hard-coded date and time value, enclose it in quotes like any other literal in SQL statements.

ation of the snapshot object in the database. Figure 19.18 shows how you can set the property *Refresh Start Time* so that the first refresh of the snapshot happens at 10 p.m. on the first Friday after the snapshot is created. It also contains the setting for the property *Next Refresh Clause* so that each subsequent refresh of the snapshot occurs at 8 p.m. every Saturday.

The properties discussed above specify when the snapshot data will be refreshed. The list box Refresh type allows you to tell Oracle *how* to refresh the data. Basically, a snapshot can be refreshed in two ways. One is to replace all the records in the snapshot with a new set of records freshly queried from the master database. This is called a complete refresh and can be obtained by setting the list box Refresh type to Complete. Another way is to create a snapshot log table in the master database that records all the changes to this table, and use this log to refresh the snapshot. The following is a list of steps to follow in order to implement this type of refresh:

1. Set the list box Refresh type to Fast in the Refresh tab of the Edit Snapshot Implementation dialog box.
2. Display the dialog box Edit Table Implementation for the master table and switch to the tab Generate. Remember that physically, the master table is located in a database that is different from the database where the snapshot is implemented.
3. Set the radio button Yes in the second radio group to generate a snapshot log (see Figure 19.17).
4. Set the storage properties of the snapshot log in the tabs Snapshot Log Storage and Snapshot Log Data Blocks.

Depending on the amount of updates that occur in the master table between two refreshes, one refresh method may be more advantageous than the other. If only a few modifications have occurred, a fast refresh will obviously be more efficient. But if a good number of master records have been updated, simply replacing all the records of the snapshot with new records may yield better performance. The update frequency of data should be kept in mind when setting this property. In the cases when this frequency is not predictable or fluctuates signifi-

Not every snapshot can be refreshed using the fast method. Simple snapshots can be refreshed with any of the three methods described above. Complex snapshots, on the other hand, can be refreshed only with the Complete method.

cantly, you can let Oracle choose the most efficient refresh by setting the property *Refresh Type* to '*Force.*' This is also the default option that Oracle will use if you do not set this property.

19.4.5 MAINTAINING SEQUENCE IMPLEMENTATIONS

The dialog box Edit Sequence Implementation is used to view and maintain the properties of sequence objects implemented in a database schema. The first tab of this dialog, Security, allows you to grant privileges on the sequence objects to other database users. The property tab Options is used to specify whether or not the sequence numbers should be reused when the sequence reaches its threshold and whether the numbers generated by the sequence should be in the order in which they are requested. For Oracle sequences, you can also specify the number of sequence numbers to be cached in memory in order to improve the performance of the number generation process. Figure 19.19 shows an example of the Options tab.

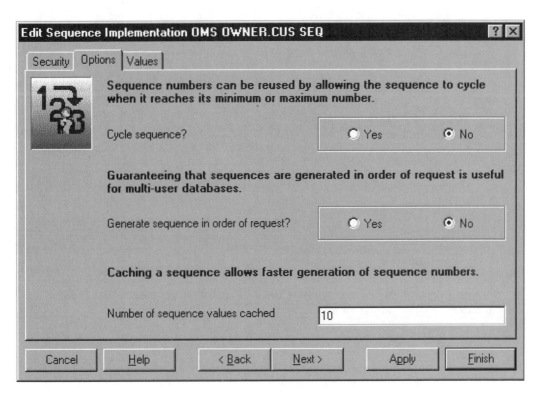

FIGURE 19.19 The Options tab of the Edit Sequence Implementation dialog box.

The property tab Values allows you to set properties that control the numbers generated by the sequence. Setting the text boxes in this tab, you can create the following types of sequences:

❑ **Increasing sequences.** These are sequences whose numbers increase starting from a lower bound, at a certain rate, until they reach an upper bound if defined, or ad infinitum if no upper bound is defined. For these sequences, you need to specify the first sequence number to be generated and the value with which the numbers will be incremented. The Increment value field must be set to a positive number such as 1. If the sequence will have an upper bound, set Maximum value to a number larger than the origin of the sequence. In the example shown in Figure 19.20, the sequence will start generating numbers starting from 1 and incrementing each subsequent value by 2. The upper bound of this sequence is the number 100000.

❑ **Decreasing sequences.** If you want the sequence to start at an upper bound and decrease, set the Increment value to a negative number, for example –1. If

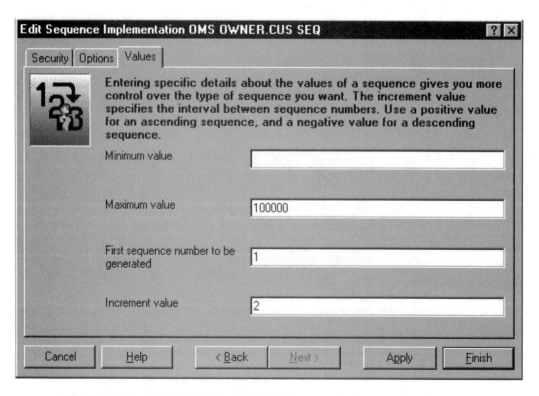

FIGURE 19.20 The Values tab of the Edit Sequence Implementation dialog box.

you want to define a lower bound for the sequence, set the property Minimum value to a number smaller than First sequence number to be generated.

19.5 USING THE DATABASE ADMINISTRATOR GUIDE

The Database Administrator Guide is the tool that the Design Editor offers to assist you with the physical database design activities. You can access it by selecting Tools | Database Administrator Guide... from the menu. The purpose of this guide is to help you navigate the hierarchy of Repository objects that are part of the physical structure of your system's database. When you invoke the Database Administrator Guide, you initially see the entry screen of the tool shown in Figure 19.21. This screen allows you to choose one of the two available options:

❑ Create and edit databases
❑ Retrieve the properties of objects from an existing database by running the Design Recovery utility

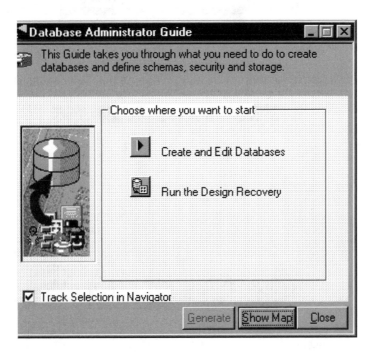

FIGURE 19.21 The entry screen of the Database Administrator Guide.

If you click the icon 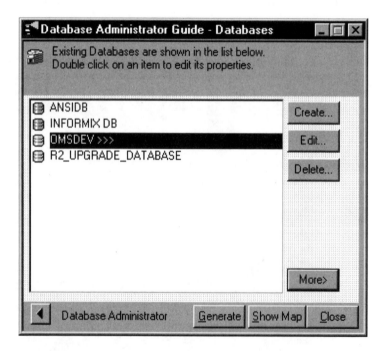, the entry screen of the guide is replaced with a screen that lists all the databases defined in the application system (see Figure 19.22). From this screen you can perform the following actions:

❑ To create a new database, click Create.... The Create Database dialog box appears.
❑ To view the properties of a database, select it in the list and click Edit.... This command brings up the Edit Database dialog box.
❑ To delete one or more database objects, select them in the list and click Delete....
❑ To invoke the Server Generator for one or more tables, select them and click Generate.

Similar actions are performed from all the other screens similar to the Databases screen that list instances of object types. The characters >>> that are appended to the currently selected object are a visual indicator that the object may contain additional objects as its dependents. To view the categories of these ob-

FIGURE 19.22   The Databases screen of the Database Administrator Guide.

jects click the button More>. If you click this button for a selected database object, you will see the categories of database objects you create and maintain during the physical database design: Storage Definition, Users, Roles, and Storage Options. Each category on this second screen is preceded by the icon ▣. Clicking the icon takes you one level further in the process of selecting the action you want to do. The titles of all the categories except Storage Options are hyper-links to the Designer/2000 online help. Storage Options itself is further broken down into Tablespaces, Datafiles, Logfiles, and Rollback Segments. You can drill down one of these paths to create and edit the object of the selected category. To return to the previous screen of the Guide, click the icon ◀.

Like the Database Object Guide, the Database Administrator Guide provides a map of the physical design object hierarchy that allows you to jump from one area of the hierarchy onto another. In order to display the map, click the button Show Map on the Database Administrator Guide dialog box. You will see that the dialog box will be expanded to the right to include a hierarchy tree representation of the objects you can create and maintain in Designer/2000 application systems (see Figure 19.23). Each push button on the map represents a screen of the Database Administrator Guide. If the button is enabled, you can navigate to its associated screen immediately, by clicking the button. If the button is not enabled, this means that you cannot navigate to its associated screen from the screen where you are currently. In the example shown in Figure 19.23, the current screen is Databases. From this screen, you can see Storage Definitions, Users, Roles, and Storage objects of any type, but you cannot see schema object implementations like tables, views, and sequences. In order to enable the buttons that represent these categories of objects, you need to display the screen Users and select a user from this screen.

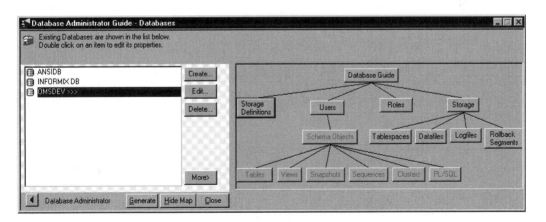

FIGURE 19.23 The Database Administrator Guide with the map.

19.6   PRESERVING THE PHYSICAL DATABASE DESIGN FLEXIBILITY

Simply entering the physical database objects into the application system Repository may not provide sufficient flexibility and portability to your database. In fact, several properties of the objects discussed in the previous sections, when set literally, may tie down your database to a very specific physical configuration, which cannot be easily ported to different environments or customized for different customer profiles. You may use two techniques to build a flexible and configurable database design:

❑ **Parametrizing properties of database objects.** This technique consists of preparing installation scripts that take a number of parameters as arguments and use them as settings for properties like tablespace names, name and location of database files, user names, and passwords. This way, users will specify the actual values for these properties at installation time, according to their specific needs.

❑ **Preparing different database sizing models.** This technique consists of calculating different storage parameters and sizing properties in cases when your installation base is so diverse that you cannot reliably predict the size of database objects.

The following sections provide details for each of these techniques.

19.6.1   PARAMETRIZING PROPERTIES OF DATABASE OBJECTS

Several properties of database objects, when set to their actual values, may restrict the flexibility of your database. The following list identifies some properties and the problems that may arise from setting them in a straightforward manner:

❑ **Tablespace name.** When you have control over the database environment, you can decide on how to set these names. As I mentioned earlier, even in this case I recommend that you follow established standards, such as the OFA standard. However, if you are developing an application to be deployed in any database, you may not always have the luxury of knowing ahead of time the name of tablespaces, such as the user, rollback segments, and temporary tablespaces. Furthermore, you may not want to give flexibility to the database administrators to install the objects of your application in any tablespace they see fit for their environment, not necessarily the ones defined by you.

❑ **Location and names of database files.** The portability of your database design is affected significantly if you hard-code the location and name of the database files. In the simplest case, this may require special hardware configuration steps to accommodate these files. The problem becomes more severe if your database will need to be deployed on a different operating system, such as UNIX or NT, that follows different naming conventions.

❏ **Oracle user names and passwords.** If you are designing an open database system, you cannot predict at design time who its users will be. Therefore, mechanisms should be provided to allow for the creation of new users and their grant of privileges on the appropriate database objects. Furthermore, hard-coded user passwords may compromise the application database security. These passwords should be specified at installation time, when the user accounts are created.

In order to avoid problems like the one described above, set these properties to values that are considered parameters by the utility used to run the installation script of your database. SQL*Plus, for example, the tool most often used to create the objects in an Oracle database, considers substitution variables to be any string that starts with one or two ampersand (&) characters. If your SQL command contains such a variable, SQL*Plus will prompt you for its value and execute the statement with the input you provide at runtime. The following steps show how to take advantage of this functionality and define the template for an Oracle user object in the Repository. This template can than be used to create a number of actual database users. Examples from the Order Management System are used.

1. Create two tablespace objects and set their property *Name* to '&&USER_TA-BLESPACE' and '&&TEMP_TABLESPACE,' respectively. These will represent the default and temporary tablespaces for each database account, which may be different from database to database.
2. Create an Oracle database user object and set its properties as shown in Figure 19.24. Note the parametric settings for properties like *Name* and *Initial Password*.

When the Server Generator is invoked for this object, it will create a SQL command like the one shown in Figure 19.25.

When you execute this file, SQL*Plus will prompt you for values as it encounters each variable in the script. Figure 19.26 shows the log produced when this command is executed in SQL*Plus.

As I mentioned above, substitution variables in SQL*Plus can be preceded by one or two ampersand characters. The difference between them is that a variable preceded by && maintains its value throughout the script, even if the variable appears multiple times in the script; a variable preceded by & maintains the value only for one occurrence.

In a script like the one shown in Figure 19.25, for example, you will be prompted for the value of &&oms_user only once, at the first occurrence of the

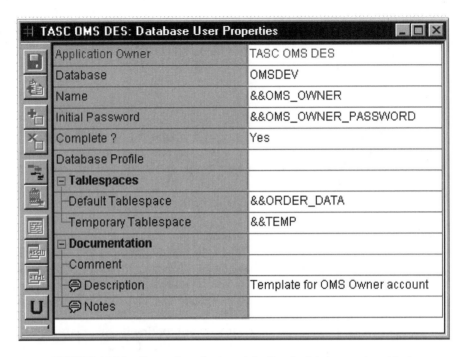

FIGURE 19.24 Properties of a template Oracle database user object.

```
REM
PROMPT Creating User &&OMS_USER
CREATE USER &&oms_user IDENTIFIED BY
&&OMS_USER_PASSWORD;

REM
PROMPT Granting Role To User &&OMS_USER
GRANT CONNECT ,RESOURCE TO &&oms_user;

REM
PROMPT Granting Default Tablespace To &&OMS_USER
ALTER USER  &&oms_user
DEFAULT TABLESPACE &&user_tablespace
TEMPORARY TABLESPACE &&temp_tablespace
DEFAULT ROLE ALL;
```

FIGURE 19.25 SQL statements created by the Server Generator
based on the properties of the database user object.

```
Enter value for oms_user: jking
Creating User jking
Enter value for oms_user_password: johnny
old   1: CREATE USER &&oms_user IDENTIFIED BY
&&OMS_USER_PASSWORD
new   1: CREATE USER jking IDENTIFIED BY johnny

User created.

Granting Role To User jking
old   1: GRANT CONNECT ,RESOURCE TO &&oms_user
new   1: GRANT CONNECT ,RESOURCE TO jking

Grant succeeded.

Granting Default Tablespace To jking
old   1: ALTER USER  &&oms_user
new   1: ALTER USER  jking
Enter value for user_tablespace: users
old   2:  DEFAULT TABLESPACE &&user_tablespace
new   2:  DEFAULT TABLESPACE users
Enter value for temp_tablespace: temp
old   3:  TEMPORARY TABLESPACE &&temp_tablespace
new   3:  TEMPORARY TABLESPACE temp

User altered.
```

FIGURE 19.26 Log that shows how parametric properties can be substituted with user-defined values during the execution of the DDL statements.

variable. This value then is used to substitute the variable in each occurrence in the script. If the variable is defined as &oms_user, you will be prompted for its value each time SQL*Plus encounters it. Clearly, setting properties of database objects to begin with && will minimize the number of arguments passed to the script.

19.6.2 PREPARING DIFFERENT DATABASE SIZING MODELS

In some cases, you may be able to predict with a fair amount of accuracy the number of records that will be stored in the database structures. In some cases, though, you may not be able to come up with a firm estimate of the resources required to implement the database objects of the application systems. These cases occur especially when your application is intended to be distributed to a number of customer sites, each with different business requirements. Since defining properties like the storage parameters of the size of data files for your database is impossible or impractical, the next best thing to do is to prepare different configuration and sizing models. These models are distributed to the customers who select the one that best fits their needs. The steps required to prepare these models are as follows:

1. Identify the core database objects that drive the sizing requirements of the entire database.
2. Identify different sizing scenarios and compute the initial and maximum number of rows that will be stored in the core objects for each scenario.
3. Run the Designer/2000 report "Database Table and Index Size Estimate," and, based on the data computed by the report, decide the storage parameters and size of data files for each scenario.
4. Set the properties of database objects, like storage definitions and database files, to reflect the analysis performed in the previous step. Create new objects of these and other categories if necessary.

By looking at the database tables of the Order Management System, you can easily see that the tables that will contain the largest number of records and therefore drive the capacity needs of the database, include ORDER, PAYMENT_AUTHORIZATIONS, PACKAGES, LINE_ITEMS, PRODUCT_ITEMS, and ZIPS. In order to prepare different sizing models for this database, then, you can focus only on these tables. For a database configuration to support 10,000 orders initially, and up to 50,000 orders, Figure 19.27 shows the properties Start Rows and End Rows of these tables and the assumptions made for these settings.

For the remaining tables in the Order Management System, you can set these properties *a priori*, to a number high enough to include every table, or you can perform a more detailed analysis and set them table by table.

After setting these properties, you can run the report "Database Table and Index Size Estimate" from the Database Design node of the Repository Reports tool. When you initially run the report, make sure that the parameter Include Help? is set to 'Yes.' With this setting, the report includes several pages of instructions on how the storage parameters are computed. By reading and understanding these pages, you will better appreciate the importance of table properties in the design of your database.

The report will process the table implementation objects for database users defined in a database object. The layout of the report will always include estimated database size summaries. If the parameter Detail Level of the report is set to 'Database only,' these summaries are the only information produced by the re-

TABLE	START ROWS	END ROWS	ASSUMPTION
ORDERS	10,000	50,000	Working assumption
LINE_ITEMS	30,000	170,000	Three line items exist per order.
PAYMENT_AUTHORIZATIONS	10,000	50,000	One payment authorization covers one and only one order.
PACKAGES	10,000	50,000	One package is for one and only one order.
PRODUCT_ITEMS	40,000	200,000	Most of the line items are for one product item. A small number of them are for more than one product item.
ZIP	40,000	40,000	U.S. Postal Service is not planning any major overhaul of the ZIP areas.

FIGURE 19.27   Sizing assumptions for the Order Management System.

port. If this parameter is set to 'Database, Tables, and Keys' or 'Database, Tables, Keys and Columns,' the report will also include a breakdown of sizing estimates for each tablespace and for each object in the tablespace. Running the report with these options provides the greatest benefit, since it allows you to view the suggested storage parameters for each table and index. Based on these suggested values and keeping in mind issues discussed in previous sections of this chapter, you can decide to create a few storage definition objects, associate them with the tables and indexes, and distribute these objects in tablespaces to minimize the fragmentation and I/O contention.

The report "Database Table and Index Size Estimate" for the case of the application Order Management System is provided on the companion CD-ROM. You can view this report by following the links *Software, Order Management System Design*, and *Database Table and Index Size Estimate*.

19.7 SUMMARY

After the initial database design is created by the Database Design Transformer, you should create and configure the objects that make up the physical infrastructure of the database. Prior to doing so, you need to design and document the overall architecture of the system. This chapter shows how you can use the Repository Object Navigator to create and maintain a number of objects that represent the physical design of your system. The principal areas covered by this chapter are:

- ❑ **Documenting the System's Foundations**
  - ❑ Nodes
  - ❑ Databases
  - ❑ Communities
- ❑ **Defining Database Components**
  - ❑ Files
  - ❑ Storage Definition
  - ❑ Setting Storage Parameters to Avoid Fragmentation
  - ❑ Tablespaces
  - ❑ Rollback Segments
- ❑ **Defining Database Users**
  - ❑ Database Roles
  - ❑ Database Users
  - ❑ Database Profiles
- ❑ **Implementing Logical Design Objects in a Database Schema**
  - ❑ Creating Implementation Objects
  - ❑ Maintaining Table Implementations
  - ❑ Maintaining View Implementations
  - ❑ Maintaining Snapshot Implementations
  - ❑ Maintaining Sequence Implementations
- ❑ **Using the Database Administrator Guide**
- ❑ **Preserving the Physical Database Design Flexibility**
  - ❑ Parametrizing Properties of Database Objects
  - ❑ Preparing Different Database Sizing Models

Chapter 20

IMPLEMENTING BUSINESS RULES WITH CONSTRAINTS

- ◆ Business Rules Reviewed

- ◆ Implementing Business Rules

- ◆ Creating and Maintaining Constraints

- ◆ Primary and Unique Key Constraints

- ◆ Foreign Key Constraint Properties

- ◆ Check Constraint Properties

- ◆ Deriving Column Values in Front-End Applications

- ◆ Summary

An important part of the requirements analysis is identifying the business rules that the application must enforce. During the application design, you plan the implementation of these rules, which occurs when the application is developed. When using Designer/2000, most of the development is performed by the generators—Server Generator and a number of front-end generators. These generators will implement business rules based on properties of design objects, such as tables, modules, and data usages. Because it directly affects the enforcement of business rules, careful setting of these properties becomes one of the most important tasks during system design activities.

As I mentioned in Chapter 15, business rules may be implemented and enforced in the client module, at the database server, or in both environments. This chapter shows what you have to do in order to implement business rules using constraints.

20.1 BUSINESS RULES REVIEWED

The following sections summarize the categories of business rules that you can identify in your application development efforts, and they describe how they are documented in the Designer/2000 Repository during the requirements analysis.

20.1.1 DATA DEFINITION RULES

Data definition rules are rules with which the data will have to conform in order to be stored in the database structures. Depending on the number of data elements that they affect, the data definition rules may be classified as follows:

❑ **Rules for individual attributes.** These are rules that data values of an attribute must conform with in order to be considered valid from the business perspective. The most important rules in this category are those that describe the data format, such as the data type and length, the optionality of an attribute, and the allowed values of the attribute. These rules are recorded using the properties of an attribute. In cases when the attribute contains allowed values, the recommended way to record these values is to define them in a domain and include the attribute in the domain.

❑ **Rules for multiple attributes of the same entity.** These rules combine two or more attributes from the same entity and are also known as tuple rules. The recommended way to document these rules is to describe them in the *Notes* property of the entity that owns the attribute.

❑ **Rules for individual entities.** These rules apply to all the instances of an entity. The most common example of such a rule is the definition of unique identifiers for an entity. This kind of rule is recorded in the UID properties of the entity. Other rules, which require complex checking and verification, are documented as functions in the business rules hierarchy and cross-referenced in the *Notes* property of the entity.

❑ **Rules for multiple entities.** These rules combine attributes from different entities or relationships among two or more entities. They are also known as inter-entity rules. The most common occurrence of inter-entity rules is documented in the form of relationships among entities. Other more complex occurrences, such as those that restrict relationships among instances of entities, or those that express complex dependencies of an attribute from other attributes in other entities, are documented as functions in the business rules hierarchy and cross-referenced in the *Notes* property of the entity.

20.1.2 DATA MANIPULATION RULES

Data manipulation rules are conditions that have to be met in order to create, update, and delete data from the system. They also include the events that the system will capture and respond to, as well as the response triggered by these events. The following is a description of the main categories of data manipulation rules:

❑ **Create rules.** These are conditions under which new instances for a given entity may be created. They are recorded as functions in the business rules hierarchy and cross-referenced in the *Notes* property of the entity.

❑ **Update rules.** These rules describe conditions under which data elements may be updated, transition of data from one state into another, and transferability of relationships. Most of the rules in this category are recorded as functions in the business rule hierarchy and cross-referenced in the *Notes* property of the entity. Those that are classified as transfer relationship rules are documented by setting the property *Transferable* of the relationship end.

❑ **Delete rules.** These are criteria that must be met in order to successfully delete data from the database. An important set of rules in this group are those that describe what happens to detail records when their master is deleted. These rules are documented in the *Notes* property of the entity.

20.1.3 ACCESS PRIVILEGE RULES

Access privilege rules describe which users or user groups can be defined for the system, and which of them may access different parts of the system's functionality and data entities. Rules in this category include:

❑ **User group rules.** These are rules that describe which users or groups of users will access the system. They are documented in the form of business units in the Designer/2000 Repository.

❑ **Function access rules.** These are rules that allow users to access different user interface functions defined in the Functional Hierarchy Diagrammer.

They are documented as associations between the functions and business units.

❑ **Data access rules.** The purpose of these rules is to allow a group of users to access only data that they are authorized to access. Preventing users from accessing one or more tables in the database is implemented through vertical data access rules. They are documented as associations between business units and entities. Horizontal data access rules are those that describe which records within a table users are allowed to access.

20.2 IMPLEMENTING BUSINESS RULES

A good number of data definition rules are implemented declaratively, by setting properties of columns and tables in the Design Editor or the Repository Object Navigator. When these objects are created by the Database Design Transformer, many of the properties in question are inherited by similar properties of data model objects. So careful work to define the requirements and properties of your data model can significantly reduce the amount of work required to implement these requirements in database objects. (Refer to Chapter 17 for more details on the correspondence between properties in data model and database design objects that this Transformer establishes and maintains.)

20.2.1 METHODS FOR IMPLEMENTING BUSINESS RULES

Designer/2000 provides two methods of implementing business rules. The first one relies on properties of objects that make up the data schema of your application. Such properties include column definition properties, primary, unique, and foreign key constraints, check constraints, and object privileges granted to database users and roles. Business rules most frequently implemented with this method include attribute rules, tuple rules, and vertical or horizontal access security rules; other rules implemented with the method include entity rules that describe unique identifiers of an entity, inter-entity rules that describe relationships among entities, and delete rules. This method is often referred to as the declarative implementation of business rules. The steps required to implement a business rule with the declarative method are as follows:

1. Set the properties of appropriate database objects according to the definition of the business rule.
2. Identify where appropriate the implementation level of the business rule.
3. Run the Designer/2000 Generators to convert these properties into SQL statements or front-end modules that enforce the rule.

As you can see, the declarative method is powerful, yet simple to implement. Therefore, whenever possible, follow it. Some business rules, however, either cannot be implemented using this method, or limit the flexibility of the application system. Business rules that cannot be implemented declaratively typically include those that perform complex calculations to check the validity of data and most of the data manipulation rules. The implementation of allowed values of an attribute, also known as domain rules, is an example of business rules that can be implemented easily with the declarative method but that hinders the application flexibility and growth. Such business rules are implemented programmatically, using program units stored in the database servers or application logic in the front-end modules.

When the business rule is implemented in the database server, its associated program units are invoked from database triggers associated with the table where the business rule should be implemented. The steps required to implement a business rule programmatically in the database server are as follows:

1. Identify the tables where the business rule should be implemented.
2. Add a database trigger object to this table. Choose the event that fires the trigger to reflect the requirements of the rules.
3. Define a PL/SQL module that performs the bulk of the work to implement the business rule. This module will be implemented as a stored program unit in the database server.
4. Call the program unit defined in step 3 from the body of the trigger defined in step 2.
5. Run the Server Generator to generate SQL statements that create the database objects that enforce the rule.

The matrix shown in Figure 20.1 maps each category of business rules to the Designer/2000 objects that may be used to implement it. The last column in this matrix represents the programmatic implementation method, whereas all the other columns represent the declarative implementation of the business rules. The following sections describe the implementation of business rules from each category using examples from the Order Management System. In order to better follow the discussion in these sections, work with the application system TASC OMS (DES) provided in the archive file OMSDES.DMP on the companion CD-ROM. You can access this file by following the links *Software and Order Management System Design* in the HTML pages of the CD-ROM.

20.2.2 ATTRIBUTE RULES

You have to do little work to implement attribute rules like the data type, length, optionality, or the default value of a data element, provided that the following two conditions are met:

	Column Definition Properties	Domains	Primary and Unique Key Table Constraints	Foreign Key Table Constraints	Check Table Constraints	Database Users and Groups	Views	Database Triggers, Stored Program Units
Data Definition Rules								
Attribute	√√	√√			√√			√√
Tuple					√√			√√
Entity			√√					√√
Inter-Entity				√√				√√
Data Manipulation Rules								
Create								√√
Update							√√	√√
Delete				√√			√√	√√
Data Access Rules								
Vertical						√√	√√	
Horizontal							√√	√√

FIGURE 20.1 A matrix that shows the database objects required to implement business rules in the database server.

❑ These requirements are documented in the settings of the attribute properties in the data model of the application system.

❑ The Database Design Transformer is used to map these properties into those of the associated columns.

Using the Design Editor as explained in Chapter 18, you can view and maintain these properties in the Columns tab of the Edit Table dialog box. I mentioned on other occasions that one of the best methods to record properties of attributes is to include them in domains, especially if attributes contain allowed values. When the Database Design Transformer creates a column associated with an attribute, it includes the new column in the same domain as the domain of the attribute. When it comes to implementing this rule in the database server, you have the following three choices:

❑ **Let the Server Generator implement it as an implicit (inline) check constraint.** This approach is the easiest way to enforce an allowed values rule, albeit the most restricting and inflexible one. All you have to do in this case is to run the Server Generator with the option Valid Value Constraints set for the table that owns the column in question. (More details about the Server Generator are provided in Chapter 26.) Figure 20.2 shows the CREATE TABLE statement produced by the Server Generator for the case of the table PRODUCT. The problem with this implementation is that modifying the constraint once it is created is very hard. In fact, even addressing these constraints after they are created is very difficult, if not impossible. The reason is that the Oracle Server names implicit constraints with system generated names, like 'SYS_C001716' or 'SYS_C001717.' In a table with multiple implicit constraints like the one shown in Figure 20.2—NOT NULL constraints count as implicit constraints as well—you would have a hard time deciding which of the system-generated names corresponds to the constraint that checks the allowed values of a column.

❑ **Handle it yourself through an explicit check constraint.** You can add a check constraint to the table PRODUCTS above, which essentially performs the same check of values of a column against its allowed values. Details on how to create a check constraint are provided in Section 20.6. The advantage this approach gives you compared with the previous one is that since you create the constraint explicitly, you decide and control its name. Therefore, you can address it more easily when you need to. Nevertheless, this approach, like the first one, has the fundamental flaw of every database constraint. It reflects a *static* rule with which data must conform throughout the life of the system. If, for example, TASC wants to group products under two new types—DB 'Database Product' and WP 'Word Processing'—you will have to drop the initial constraint, and recreate a new one with the updated list of allowed values for the column PRO_TYPE. This, of course, adds over-

```
CREATE TABLE products(
 id                     NUMBER            NOT NULL,
 manuf_id               NUMBER            NOT NULL,
 pca_id                 NUMBER            NOT NULL,
 name                   VARCHAR2(80)      NOT NULL,
 pro_type               VARCHAR2(3)       NULL
   CHECK ( pro_type IN ( 'TAX', 'BUS', 'GAM', 'OTH' )),
 msrp                   NUMBER            NULL,
 descr                  VARCHAR2(240)     NULL
)
;
```

FIGURE 20.2 An implicit constraint created by the Server Generator to enforce allowed values rule.

head in the system administration costs and limits the flexibility of the application as a whole. On some occasions, recreating the constraint may not even be possible. Indeed, if TASC wants to replace its old BUS 'Business Product' type with the two new product types described above, the new constraint will fail when it encounters old records classified as business products, which no longer comply with the new check criterion. In these conditions, Oracle Server will not allow the constraint to be created.

❑ **Procedurally validate the value against the allowed values.** The most flexible way to implement allowed values rules for an attribute is to store these values in a database table and implement a stored function that checks whether a given value is allowed for the given column or not. This function is invoked each time a new record is created or the constrained column is updated from a database trigger. Note that a similar approach is taken by the front-end generators to implement allowed values rules on the client side. These values, recorded against a column or domain in the Designer/2000 Repository, are stored in a table called CG_REF_CODES by default. The front-end generators create code that validates the values entered in the screen modules against this table.

The Designer/2000 utility Generate Table API generates a package for each table you include in its run set. One of the procedures in this table, called VALIDATE_DOMAIN, checks the values of the columns in a table against the allowed values recorded for this column. This utility also creates database triggers fired when the record is inserted or updated that invoke the procedure VALIDATE_DOMAIN. All you have to do in order to implement domain validation rules programmatically is to create these objects in the schema of the your application system. Chapter 26 will discuss the Generate Table API in more details.

20.2.3 TUPLE RULES

Tuple rules are recorded in the *Notes* property of the entity that owns the attributes and are transferred to the *Notes* property of the associated table by the Database Design Transformer. When it comes to implementing these rules in the database server, divide them in two groups:

❑ **Rules that are implemented declaratively as table check constraints.** These rules are static in nature, will apply throughout the life of a system, and do not depend on any dynamic or variable data values. An example of such a rule is one that describes how to compute the total charge for the line item of an order. This rule is shown below as it is documented in the *Notes* property of the table LINE_ITEMS:

```
TUPLE RULE
  LI01
    ITEM TOTAL = QUANTITY * UNIT MSRP * (1 - DISCOUNT)
```

These rules are implemented as check constraints added to the table that owns the columns involved. Section 20.6 discusses how you can create check constraints in the Design Editor.

❑ **Rules that are implemented programmatically.** In cases when tuple rules depend on variable data, are dynamic in nature, or are too complex to be implemented as a table check constraint, they are implemented in the form of a program unit that validates the rule. This program unit may reside in the database server or in the front-end module and is invoked from a trigger fired when a new record is inserted in the table or when an existing record is updated. Check constraints of a table in Designer/2000 do not represent only table constraints in the database sense of the word. They are used to influence the code generated by front-end generators as well. Therefore, even if tuple rules will be implemented programmatically in the database server, you should still represent them as check constraints.

20.2.4 ENTITY RULES

Entity rules that are recorded in the form of unique identifiers for the entity are automatically converted into primary and unique key constraints by the Database Design Transformer. You can view and maintain the properties of these constraints in the Design Editor. Other entity rules that do not fall into the category of unique identifier rules are documented as functions and described in the *Notes* property of the entity and its associated table. The example below shows one of these rules for the entity EMPLOYEE:

```
ENTITY RULES
  OMSBR121
    Prevent circular references of employees by other
    employees.
```

These rules are implemented programmatically in the form of a function that verifies the rule. This program unit is called when an insert or update event occurs. In order to direct the front-end generators to implement these rules, they are entered as check constraints pointing at the function referenced above. More details on this type of constraint are provided in Section 20.6.

20.2.5 INTER-ENTITY RULES

The rules that express relationships between entities are converted into foreign key constraints by the Database Design Transformer. The properties of these rules can be maintained on the Constraints properties tab of the Edit Tables dialog box. Other rules that fall into this category, whether they are restricted relationship rules or other types of rules, are documented as functions in the business rule hierarchy of the application system and cross-referenced in the *Notes* property of the appropriate entities. They are implemented programmatically through a function that validates the rule. For a complete implementation of the rule, one or more events may be required to invoke that function when records are added or modified. Consider, for example, the business rules described in the *Notes* property of ORDERS table, as follows:

```
INTER-ENTITY RULES
  OMSBR131
    State sales tax will be applied only to those orders
    for which the paying customer's address is in
    Virginia, the state where TASC is incorporated.
  OMSBR132
    The subtotal of an order is the sum of total costs
    for all the line items included in the order.
```

Whereas the first rule requires validation only in the ORDERS table, the second rule must be validated each time a line item is added or modified in an order. As in the cases above, in order to help the front-end generators implement these rules on the client side, they should be added as check constraints to the definition of the table.

20.2.6 DATA MANIPULATION RULES

Data manipulation rules are in general implemented programmatically. Triggers are defined for the events that trigger the rules (create, update, or delete). These triggers either implement the steps required by the rule, or invoke a program unit that performs these steps. One case when these rules can be implemented declaratively is when a delete operation is defined to fail if one of the following conditions is true:

❏ The record being deleted owns detail records. This kind of delete is called a restricted delete.
❏ All the detail records are deleted together with the master record. This type of delete is called a cascade delete.

The property *Delete Rule* of the foreign key constraint that represents the relationship may be set to one of these types of deletes. The Server Generator, then, creates the foreign key in a way that the rule is enforced automatically by the Oracle Server. More details on this property are provided in Section 20.5.

20.2.7 ACCESS PRIVILEGE RULES

The cornerstone of implementing access privilege rules in the database server is the database users and groups of users, or roles, that you create for an application system. Chapter 19 discussed the process of creating and maintaining roles and database users in the Design Editor. The roles correspond generally to the business units that you identify during the requirements analysis as needing access to the objects of the application systems. Database users are created for each Oracle user who will have access to these objects. Although you can grant access to the objects in your system to individual users, a common practice is to group users with similar access needs in database roles. The object privileges are granted on the role, which in turn is granted to each user. Thus, the privileges are maintained in a common fashion and transferred to each user who needs them.

You can grant object privileges two ways to database users and roles. The first one grants the necessary privileges on a single table, view, or snapshot to all the users or roles that need to have that privilege. This approach is achieved through the Security tab of the dialog box for the implementation object in the Design Editor. The procedure is simple and was discussed in Chapter 19.

The second way is to grant the object privileges one user or role at a time. In an application with a few roles or users who require common privileges on a number of database objects, this is the fastest way to accomplish the task. The following are the steps required to add Select, Insert, Update, and Delete privileges to all the tables of the Order Management System application to the user TASC_OMS_USER:

1. Switch to the tab DB Admin of the Design Navigator.
2. Expand the nodes under Databases (Oracle) until you find the user TASC_OMS_USER.
3. Select the node Object Privileges and click Create 🔲. The dialog box Database Object Grants for Database User appears.
4. Select all the tables owned by the user OMS_OWNER and click the icon 🔲 to move them to the list box of objects on which the user has privileges.
5. Click OK. The dialog box is closed, and all the selected tables are inserted under the node Object Privileges.
6. Switch to the Properties Palette for all the selected objects and set the properties Select, Insert, Update, and Delete to 'Yes.'
7. Save the changes to the Repository.

Using object grants to database roles and users, you can limit the access of users at the table level. If you want to restrict this access at a lower level of granularity, either to a set of columns or to a set of rows from the table, define views on the table and then grant privileges on these views rather than the underlying tables. Refer to Chapter 19 for further details on how views can help you enforce vertical and horizontal access privileges rules.

20.3 CREATING AND MAINTAINING CONSTRAINTS

Constraints defined against tables are conditions that data elements must fulfill in order to reside in the database table. Four types of constraints exist in an Oracle database: primary key, foreign key, unique key, and check constraints. Designer/2000 uses the concept of constraints as a method to implement certain categories of business rules. The following sections will discuss how to use the Design Editor to create and maintain constraint objects in your application system.

20.3.1 CREATING CONSTRAINTS

There are several ways in which you can create a constraint in the Design Editor. The following steps describe the process of creating them in the Design Navigator:

1. Switch to the DB Objects tab of the Design Navigator.
2. Expand the node Table Definitions, select and expand the node that represents the table where you want to add the constraint.

3. Select the category of constraint you want to create from the following: Primary Key Constraint, Unique Key Constraint, Foreign Key Constraint, and Check Constraint.

4. Click Create ▦.

5. Set the properties of the new constraints in the sequence of tabs that are provided by the dialog box that appears. These tabs are also accessed when you edit the properties of the constraint. The similarities and differences between these tabs for the different types of constraints are discussed in the following sections.

6. Click Finish to complete the process.

You can add constraints to a table in the Data Diagrammer component of the Design Editor by displaying the table in a data diagram and selecting it. Then, to add a primary key constraint click the icon ▦; to add a foreign key click the icon ▦ if the key is mandatory or the icon ▦ if the key is optional. The tool palette of the Data Diagrammer does not provide for ways to create unique key or check constraints. But the icons that appear in the toolbar of each table on the data diagram allow you to create each of these constraints. In this toolbar, ▦ represents primary keys, ▦ represents unique keys, ▭ represents foreign keys, and ▦ represents check constraints. Follow these steps to create a constraint:

1. Move the cursor over the icon that represents the type of constraint and right-click. A popup menu item appears that allows you to invoke the dialog box where you can set the properties of the new constraint.

2. Select the menu item.

3. Set the properties of the new constraints in the dialog box that appears. This is the same dialog box that appears when you create the constraint from the Design Navigator.

4. Click Finish to complete the process.

20.3.2 EDITING CONSTRAINTS

During the life of the application system, you may have to edit and maintain the properties of constraints. As with the process of creating them, you can access the dialog box with the properties of constraints from the Design Navigator or from the Data Diagrammer components of the Design Editor. To display this dialog from the Design Editor, expand the hierarchy of objects until you see the desired constraint and then double-click the constraint. When a table is displayed in a data diagram, you can click and set in pushed state the icons that represent each type of constraint. Figure 20.3 shows the table ORDERS where the icons ▦, ▦, ▭, and ▦ are clicked. As a result, the primary key, unique keys,

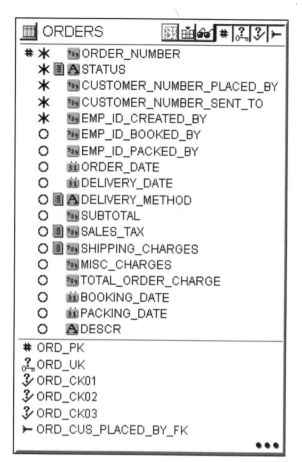

FIGURE 20.3 Representing constraints together with a table in the data diagram.

foreign keys, and check constraints of the table are shown in the diagram, at the bottom of the table. To edit the properties of one of these constraints, simply double-click it in the diagram and work in the dialog box that appears.

20.3.3 SETTING VALIDATION PROPERTIES OF CONSTRAINTS

The dialog box of each constraint type contains a tab, called Validation, with properties that define how the constraint is enforced. The settings of these properties influence the Server Generator and the front-end application generators. Figure 20.4 shows the Validation tab of the Edit Check Constraint dialog box.

The principal property in this category is used to set the level where the property is validated. By selecting the option On the server, you implement the constraint at the database level only. The front-end application generators ignore this constraint. So the generated applications will allow records that violate the

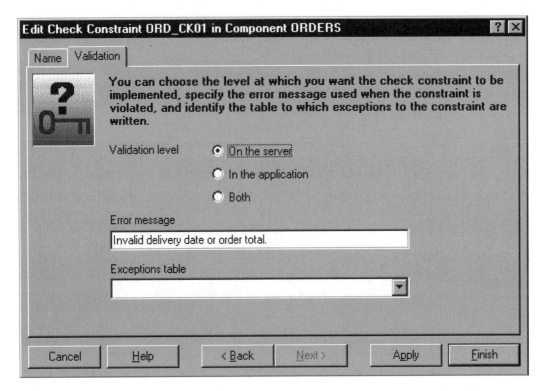

FIGURE 20.4   The Validation property tab of the Edit Check Constraint dialog box.

constraint to be sent to the database. When transactions are committed, the constraint defined at the database server will reject the violating records, thus causing the rollback of the entire transaction. When the option In the application is chosen, the Server Generator will ignore the constraint, which, for this reason, is not created at the database. The application generators, on the other hand, will create front-end applications that send to the database only valid transactions. This setting is very useful when the constraint is defined in a non-table object, for example a view, because it allows you to influence the code created by front-end generators. However, if the object is a table and it will be accessed from other applications, the possibility exists that records violating the constraint are stored to the table. Clearly from what I said above, these two types of validation complement each other. Selecting the option Both for the validation level of the constraint, ensures that all the generators involved create code that implements the constraint globally, at the database level, and in a user-friendly fashion, at the front-end application level.

The properties *Error Message* and *Exceptions Table* may be used to specify what should be done if a record that violates the constraint is sent to the database.

When *Error Message* is set, the application generators create code that displays the message to the users when the violation occurs. The property *Exceptions Table* may be set to the name of a table where violating records are inserted. This table must contain at least the same columns as the base table and must not have the same constraint defined and enabled. A quick way to create this table is to make a copy of the base table in the Repository Object Navigator without copying the constraint in question.

20.3.4 HANDLING FAILURES OF CONSTRAINTS

The first response to the question "How do I handle the failure of a constraint?" may be to enter an error message in the constraint's property *Error Message*. However, once you do this action, the contents of the message are wired into the definition of the constraint and in the code generated by the front-end application generators. This may complicate the maintenance of the generated modules, especially if they are customized manually. Consider, for example, a scenario in which three months after the delivery of the system, you discover that the contents of an error message need modifying. If the message was entered in the *Error Message* property of the constraint, you will need to modify the property, regenerate all the modules that use the table, and reapply all the customizations to the new modules; or you can edit the statement that contains the message in each of these modules yourself. In both cases, you will need to regenerate and redeploy the modules. Given all the work involved, you will probably opt for the "Do nothing" solution, thus compromising the quality of the system. I recommend then that you resist the lure of specifying error messages in the definition of the constraints.

This scenario emphasizes the need for a more robust error-handling strategy. The following are the steps required to implement one such strategy:

1. Create a system-wide table of errors, in which codes, messages, and severity levels of errors are recorded.
2. For each constraint, create a record in the error table and enter the error code as entered in the *Error Message* property of the constraint.
3. Integrate a generic routine with the front-end application generators that does not return the contents of the *Error Message* property to the user, as in the default case, but uses these contents to retrieve the message from the errors table.

If such a strategy is implemented, the scenario above requires that you update a single record in the errors table without touching any other Repository object or application module.

20.4 PRIMARY AND UNIQUE KEY CONSTRAINTS

The Database Design Transformer creates unique key and primary key constraints based on definitions of unique identifiers and primary unique identifiers of entities. Therefore, if the database design is derived from a complete data model, you are unlikely to need to create new key constraints. Nevertheless, in order to ensure an optimal design of the database, be sure to set the properties of these constraints carefully. Given the similarities between these properties for primary and unique keys, I will discuss them jointly in this section.

The dialog box with the properties of these constraints contains two tabs. The first one, called Primary Key Mandatory or Unique Key Mandatory is used to maintain primarily the name of the constraint and the columns that are part of the constraint. Figure 20.5 shows an example of the Primary Key Mandatory tab.

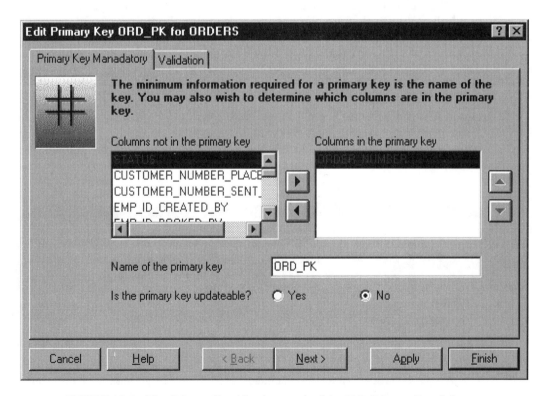

FIGURE 20.5 The Primary Key Mandatory tab of the Edit Primary Key dialog box.

The name of the constraint is used to identify the constraint among other database constraints. The Database Design Transformer follows standard naming conventions when it creates these constraints. For example, the name of primary key constraints is formed by concatenating the alias of the table with '_PK,' whereas the name of a unique identifier is formed by concatenating the alias with the name of the unique identifier and the characters '_UK.' When you create your own keys, I recommend that you follow similar standards in order to obtain a consistent naming scheme.

Each primary or unique key is defined by the columns that are part of it. Keys with more than one column in their definition are called concatenated keys. The following steps allow you to add a column to the key definition:

1. Select the column from the list to the left. This list box contains all the columns of the current table that are not part of the key.
2. Click the icon ▣ to include the selected column in the key definition.
3. Arrange the order of the columns in the key using the icons ▼ and ▲.

The radio buttons below the constraint name allow you to indicate whether or not the columns that are part of the constraint's definition can be updated. By default, the radio button No is set for primary key constraints because updating the values of primary keys requires that all their references in other tables be updated as well. The performance degradation may be significant when this occurs; therefore, updateable columns must not be part of primary keys. For unique keys, the radio button Yes may be set; however, if the columns that are part of these keys are replicated in other tables, the effects of updating them are the same as for primary keys and must be evaluated carefully. The update requirements must be an important factor in the decision whether to replicate unique key columns.

By default the Server Generator compiles SQL statements that create and enable the constraints. In some instances, you may want constraints to be defined in the data dictionary but not enabled initially. For example, if upon table creation you will perform massive loads of data that are consistent with the constraint's definition, you may significantly reduce the time required to load the data by creating this constraint disabled, load the data, and then enable the constraint. To create a constraint in a disabled mode, set the property *Enable* to *'No.'* This property can be accessed in the Property Palette of the constraint.

A distinction between primary and unique key constraints is that all the columns of the former are required to contain a value, whereas some unique key columns may not be mandatory. Therefore, the Unique Key Mandatory tab contains a second radio group that allows you to specify whether the key is mandatory or not.

20.5 FOREIGN KEY CONSTRAINT PROPERTIES

Foreign key constraints are generated by the Database Design Transformer based on properties of relationships among entities. You can view and maintain their properties in the Edit Foreign Key dialog box, composed of tabs Foreign Key Mandatory, Cascade Rules, Validation, and Foreign Key Column. The Foreign Key Mandatory tab is where you maintain the name of the constraint and specify whether the constraint is optional or mandatory. In this tab you can also view the join table of the constraint. The columns that are part of the constraint and their corresponding columns in the join table are maintained in the tab Foreign Key Column. Figure 20.6 shows an example of this tab.

The tab Cascade Rules allows you to maintain two important properties of the foreign key: Delete Rule and Update Rule. An example of this tab is shown in Figure 20.7. Each of these properties is discussed in the following paragraphs.

❑ **Delete Rule.** This property defines the actions of the application or database when a record from the join table is deleted. The default setting, 'Restricted,' prevents the parent record from being deleted if children exist. When the property is set to 'Cascades,' deleting the parent record will cause an automatic deletion of all its children. These two settings can be enforced on the server as well as on the client. The other two settings, 'Nullifies' and 'Defaults,' are ignored by the Server Generator but influence the application generators. With these settings of *Delete Rule*, when the parent record is deleted, the value in the foreign key column of the child records is set to NULL in the first case, or replaced with the default value of the column in the second case. This property is set based on the notes collected during the requirements analysis.

❑ **Update Rule.** The settings of this property are the same as the settings for *Delete Rule*. However, the default setting, 'Restricted,' which prevents the primary key column of a table from being updated if this record has children, should be used in almost every situation. As explained in the previous section, updateable primary key columns are very rare exceptions, which may be and should be avoided.

When the Database Design Transformer maps relationships to foreign keys, properties of relationship ends such as *Transferability* and Arc properties are con-

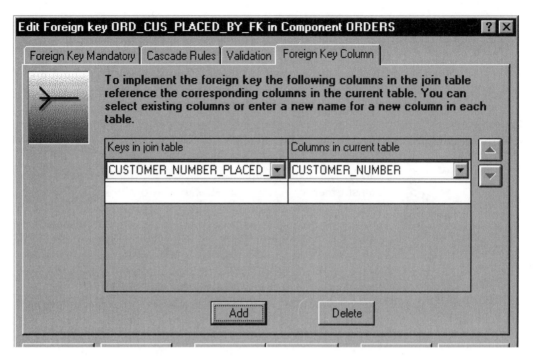

FIGURE 20.6 The Foreign Key Column tab of the Edit Foreign Key dialog box.

verted into foreign key properties. However, the meaning of these properties remains the same. Therefore, the following list will only briefly describe these properties, focusing mainly on the impact they have on the DDL and front-end application generators. These properties are accessed in the Property Palette of the relationship.

❑ **Transferable.** When this property is set, the parent of a record in the current table can be replaced by another parent. In database design terms, this replacement means that the foreign key columns may be updated. For example, since a product item may be transferred from one order line item to another, its *Transferable* property is set to *'Yes.'* When application generators create code based on this property, the column that represents the foreign key will be updateable. On the other hand, since a line item cannot be transferred to another order, the *Transferable* property for its foreign key is set to *'No'* and front-end generators will create code that does not allow updates of the corresponding column.

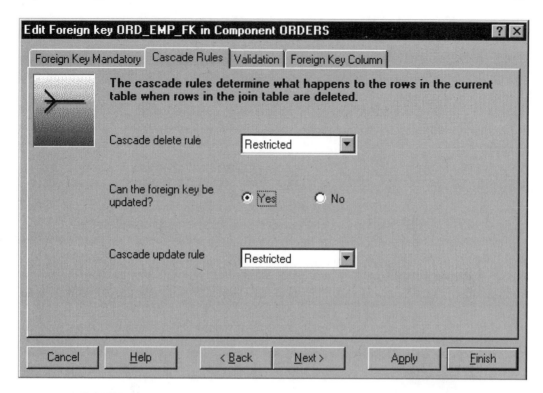

FIGURE 20.7 The Cascade Rules tab of the Edit Foreign Key dialog box.

❑ **Arc properties.** Like relationships, or rather as a direct reflection of them, foreign keys may be part of one or more arcs. On the Data Diagrammer component of the Design Editor, you can use the commands Utilities | Create Arc, Utilities | Add To Arc, and Utilities | Remove From Arc, to create and maintain table arcs. On the Property Palette you can view and maintain the number of the arc, if the table is part of more than one arc, and whether the arc is mandatory or not.

Recall that the Data Diagrammer displays foreign keys graphically in the form of connecting lines between related tables. By double-clicking the line that represents a foreign key, you can display the Edit Foreign Key dialog box, which offers another way to maintain the properties of a foreign key. Different symbols associated with the lines indicate the settings for properties like Delete Rule and Transferability. Figure 20.8 shows examples of these symbols.

Cascade

Restrict

Nullify

Default

Non Transferable

FIGURE 20.8 Symbolic representation of foreign key relationships on a data diagram.

20.6 CHECK CONSTRAINT PROPERTIES

Check constraints are used to implement business rules that can be expressed as conditions that data from one or more columns in the record must satisfy. When the database design is derived from the data model, the Database Design Transformer creates most of the primary, unique, and foreign key constraints. With check constraints, though, you are responsible for their creation as well as maintenance. The main properties of check constraints are maintained on the Name tab of the Edit Check Constraint dialog box. An example of this tab appears in Figure 20.9. Besides providing access to the name of the constraint, this tab also contains a text box where you can enter the condition of the check constraint. This text box corresponds to the property *Where/Validation Condition* of the constraint. The Validation tab has the same meaning and use for check constraints as for the other constraints.

The check constraints can be used by the Server Generator to create a database check constraint for the table in question. The conditions of these constraints, specified in the *Where/Validation Condition* property, must be a Boolean expression that evaluates to TRUE if the business rule is satisfied. In addition, they can reference only columns from the base table and cannot contain subqueries. So that the front-end application generators and the Server Generator create code that enforces these constraints, you must set the validation level of the constraint to *'Both.'*

These constraints can implement fairly complex combinations of business rules. Consider, for example, the following tuple rules recorded in the *Notes* property of the table ORDERS:

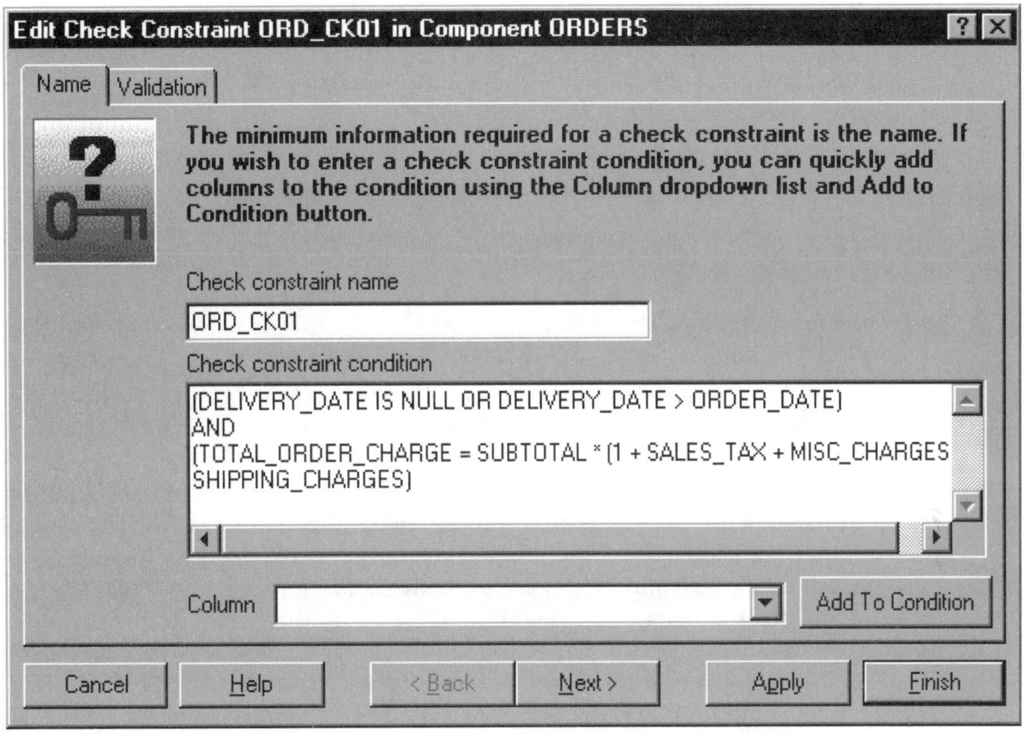

FIGURE 20.9 The Name tab of the Edit Check Constraint dialog box.

```
TUPLE RULES
  ORD01:
    (DELIVERY DATE must be NULL) or (DELIVERY DATE >
    ORDER DATE)
  ORD02:
    TOTAL ORDER CHARGE = SUBTOTAL * (1 + SALES TAX + MISC
    CHARGES) + SHIPPING CHARGES
```

In the Order Management System, this rule is implemented by the constraint ORD_CK01, whose properties are shown in Figure 20.9. The setting of the *Where/Validation Condition* property looks as follows:

```
(DELIVERY_DATE IS NULL OR DELIVERY_DATE > ORDER_DATE)
AND
(TOTAL_ORDER_CHARGE = SUBTOTAL * (1 + SALES_TAX +
MISC_CHARGES) + SHIPPING_CHARGES)
```

As you can see, several tuple rules are often combined to form one constraint. This results in a simpler interface for your applications. However, since multiple causes may exist for the violation of the constraint, you should revise your error messages to include all of them.

20.7 DERIVING COLUMN VALUES IN FRONT-END APPLICATIONS

Section 20.6 discussed how you can implement multiple business rules in the form of check constraints associated with a table. As you saw from that section, these constraints can be grouped and organized in different ways and based on different criteria. Nevertheless, the implementation of these rules in the *Where/Validation Criteria* property simply checks the validity of data. In order to build user-friendly applications, you also need to provide ways to derive values of certain data elements based on the business rules defined for them.

A number of column properties in the Derivation group allow you to place instructions for the front-end generators to create modules that derive the value of the column. The property *Derivation Expression* of a column is where you can place instructions for the front-end. The property *Derivation Expression Type* indicates whether the derivation is performed by a SQL expression or by a function call. The property *Server Derived,* when set to *'Yes'* indicates that the derivation will be performed at the server; when it is set to *'No'* it indicates that the derivation will be performed at the client. These properties are maintained in the Property Palette of the column.

If the code that derives the value of a column references only columns from the same table, then you can implement this code directly in the *Derivation Expression* property. Consider, for example, the column ITEM_TOTAL in the table LINE_ITEMS. A tuple rule defined in the *Notes* property of this table is shown below:

```
TUPLE RULES
   LI01
      ITEM TOTAL = QUANTITY * UNIT MSRP * (1 - DISCOUNT)
```

In order to implement this rule, you could set the *Derivation Expression* property of ITEM_TOTAL as follows:

```
QUANTITY * UNIT_MSRP * (1 - DISCOUNT)
```

In addition, you need to set the property *Derivation Expression Type* to *'SQL Expression.'* In this case, you can use any valid SQL operation or function to compute the value, as long as the columns referenced are defined in the table. Note, however, that the following restrictions apply:

❑ You cannot include in the expression any column that itself contains a derivation expression. In the table ORDERS, for example, if the column SUBTOTAL is derived, you cannot include this column in the calculation of another column such as TOTAL_ORDER_CHARGE.

❑ The value of a column cannot be derived from more than one source. If, for example, you have set the property *AutoGen Type* for a column, the application generators will ignore any derivation expression set for this column.

In cases when the derivation of a column requires access to columns from other tables, the derivation logic is implemented as a function and the *Derivation Expression* property is set to call this function. The property *Derivation Expression Type* in this case is set to *'Function Call.'* For example, to calculate the value of SUBTOTAL for an order, you need access values of the column ITEM_TOTAL in the table LINE_ITEMS. In such a case, you can create a PL/SQL function that takes as an argument the value of ORDER_NUMBER and returns the sum of totals for all the line items associated with this order. In the Order Management System, this function is called GET_ORDER_SUBTOTAL. The property *Derivation Expression* of the column SUBTOTAL then could be set to:

```
GET_ORDER_SUBTOTAL(ORDER_NUMBER)
```

In this case, the application generator will create code that invokes this function and sets the value of SUBTOTAL to the value returned by the function. Store the function in the database or, if developing an Oracle Forms application, place it in a PL/SQL library and attach the library to the generated form.

20.8 SUMMARY

Business rules identified during the requirements analysis need to be implemented in the system design structures. The transition between data models and database design performed by the Database Design Transformer, implements a number of these rules, such as attribute, unique identifier, and entity relationship rules. Other rules need to be implemented manually. This chapter discussed how you can accomplish this implementation, focusing primarily on the implementation of business rules at the database server. Important topics discussed in this chapter include:

❑ **Business Rules Reviewed**
   ❑ Data Definition Rules

❑   Data Manipulation Rules
❑   Access Privilege Rules

❑   **Implementing Business Rules**
    ❑   Methods for Implementing Business Rules
    ❑   Attribute Rules
    ❑   Tuple Rules
    ❑   Entity Rules
    ❑   Inter-Entity Rules
    ❑   Data Manipulation Rules
    ❑   Access Privilege Rules

❑   **Creating and Maintaining Constraints**
    ❑   Creating Constraints
    ❑   Editing Constraints
    ❑   Setting Validation Properties of Constraints
    ❑   Handling Failures of Constraints

❑   **Primary and Unique Key Constraints**

❑   **Foreign Key Constraint Properties**

❑   **Check Constraint Properties**

❑   **Deriving Column Values in Front-End Applications**

CREATING THE APPLICATION DESIGN

♦ The Purpose of the Application Design Transformer

♦ Generating Presentation Layer Modules

♦ Accepting and Rejecting Candidate Modules

♦ Generating Menu Modules

♦ Summary

The Application Design Transformer is the tool that allows you to convert the functional model created during the requirements analysis into a set of modules used to design the front-end applications. It is similar to the Database Design Transformer in that it automates the transition from analysis to design by taking into account several properties and associations between objects stored in the repository. In particular, it relies on the definition and properties of functions and the way they use the data as expressed by their entity and attribute usages. However, rather than using the properties of entities and attributes, the Application Design Transformer uses the properties of their corresponding tables and columns. Therefore, this Transformer must be used when the design of the database is complete and all the data-related business rules are implemented, as discussed in Chapter 20. This point is important to emphasize since the Application Design Transformer is a tool that is not run iteratively. Once a module is created, it cannot be re-created to update the properties of its data usages.

21.1 THE PURPOSE OF THE APPLICATION DESIGN TRANSFORMER

The Application Design Transformer is a utility that reads the definitions of business functions and related elements from the repository and creates candidate software modules that you can accept and use in your application. You can invoke this Transformer from the Utilities menu of the Function Hierarchy Diagrammer and the Repository Object Navigator or directly from the Designer/2000 launch pad by clicking the Application Transformer button 🦞. The Application Design Transformer is used for two major purposes:

❑ To generate screen and report modules that implement the presentation layer of the application
❑ To generate menu modules

A careful organization of the user interface requirements and business rules into separate hierarchies is very important for the quality of modules created by the Transformer. Refer to Chapters 13 and 15 for guidelines on how to build these hierarchies.

21.2 GENERATING PRESENTATION LAYER MODULES

During the requirements analysis phase, the presentation services of the application are separated from the application logic and the database services in order to allow for a more flexible design, more robust development, and more rapid deployment of the whole system. Define the functions in presentation services keeping in mind that ultimately they will be implemented in the form of one or more windows displayed to the users. The hierarchy of these functions should not be very complicated. The number of levels between a function and the root of the hierarchy is usually the number of distinct steps users must follow in order to access the screen or report that implements that function. In GUI platforms, this hierarchy is implemented in the form of menus. Since, according to a well-known GUI principle, the menus must not be more than two to three levels deep, the functional hierarchy of the presentation layer must have a comparable number of levels.

21.2.1 STEPS OF THE MODULE CREATION PROCESS

To generate candidate modules for the presentation layer of the system, follow these steps:

1. Invoke the Application Design Transformer in one of the ways described earlier.

2. In order to select the place in the function hierarchy from which to generate the modules, select the label of the function from the list Start Function.

3. Enter a string of six or fewer characters in the Module Prefix field. The string you enter here will serve as a prefix for the short names of all the generated modules. If no string is specified, the Transformer uses the short name of the application as a prefix. When generating interface modules, choose a prefix that will help you distinguish them from other types of modules. For example, in the case of the Order Management System, you could use the prefix OMSD2K for Developer/2000 modules, OMSOWS for Oracle Web Server modules, OMSVB for Visual Basic modules, and so on.

4. In order to choose the application environment in which screens and reports will be implemented, select from the list boxes Screen and Report in the Language group. By default, these controls are set to 'Developer/2000 Forms' and 'Developer/2000 Reports,' respectively.

5. Choose the appropriate option from the Merge Granularity group. More details on each option are provided later in this section.

6. Click the Generate button.

If you do not select a function from the Start list, the Transformer will process all the functions defined in the application system.

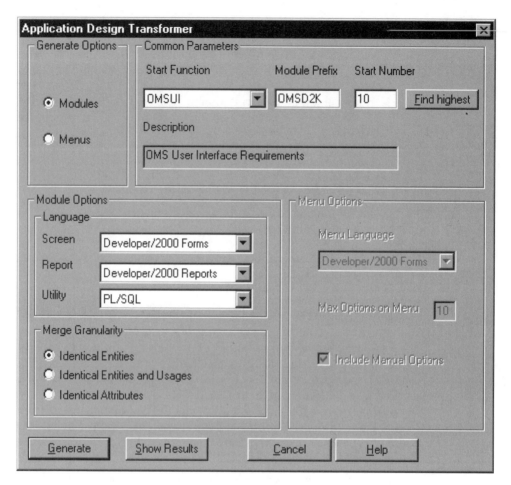

FIGURE 21.1   The Application Design Transformer dialog box.

Figure 21.1 shows an example of the Application Design Transformer dialog box.

As the Transformer performs its work, it displays the status of its activities in the dialog box shown in Figure 21.2. If any errors occur during the process, an alert box is displayed and the transformation stops. When the process of creating modules stops, either successfully or unsuccessfully, click Copy to copy the processing log into the Windows Clipboard in order to paste and save it into a text file.

After the Transformer is finished, click Close to return to the Application Design Transformer dialog box. Here you may click the Show Results button to view a report of the actions performed in a text file. Any errors encountered in

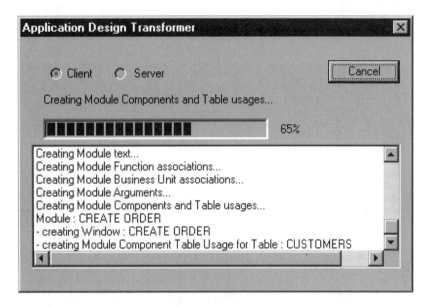

FIGURE 21.2 The Application Design Transformer activities dialog box.

the process are recorded in the report as well. Figure 21.3 shows an excerpt from a report produced by the Application Design Transformer.

21.2.2 HOW THE APPLICATION DESIGN TRANSFORMER CREATES MODULES

When you click the Generate button, the Transformer traverses the functional hierarchy tree and inspects each function that is a descendant of the one you specify in the list box *Start Function*. The Transformer will create candidate modules for the following functions:

❑ Functions with the property *Elementary* set to 'True,' no matter where they are encountered in the hierarchy. If other functions depend on an elementary function, they will be ignored by the Transformer.

❑ Functions with the property *Atomic* set to 'True.' Recall that these are leaf functions at the bottom of the hierarchy that are not decomposed into other functions.

❑ Functions that are defined as masters of other copy functions.

When the Application Design Transformer generates modules, it relies not only on the definitions of the functions but also on the data usages defined for

```
ShortName : OMSD2K0010
Name      : CREATE ORDER                    Type : SCREEN
Notes     :
Developed by Application Design Transformer from
Function OMSUI11. Candidate Module because it is an
elementary Function. Identified as a screen because
response required is immediate.
Desc      :
This function allows users to create new orders in the
database. The steps through which users create an order
in this function are:
1. Retrieve the customer that is placing the order.
   Update any information about the customer, if
   necessary.
2. Create the order based on information in the purchase
   order.
3. Associate the order with the customer who is
   receiving the products.
4. Enter each line item of the order.
5. Enter payment information about the order.
```

FIGURE 21.3 Excerpt from a report produced by the Application Design Transformer.

these functions and on the database design of the application. In order to create the data usages for a module, the Transformer starts from the entity and attribute usages of the function. Actions that the module must perform, such as select, insert, or delete, are defined based on these usages. The Transformer then uses the tables and columns mapped to the entities and attributes to create the data usage of the module. If no data usages are defined for the function, or if no tables are created for the entities, the module is created without any data usage and its type is set to 'Manual.' If the function will perform data manipulation actions, the type of the module is set to 'Screen' or 'Utility.' In order to generate screen modules, the property *Response* of the data manipulating functions must be set to 'Immediate.' If this property is set to 'Overnight' and the functions perform data manipulation actions, the Transformer will generate modules of type 'Utility.' If the only action defined for all the entities in a function entity usage is Select, the type of the generated module is 'Report.' Figure 21.4 shows in a table how the Application Design Transformer determines the type of modules it generates from the properties of the functions.

FUNCTION PROPERTIES	MODULE TYPE CREATED BY THE TRANSFORMER
No entity usages or no associations between entities and tables	Manual
Function performs data manipulation activities and the expected response is 'Immediate'	Screen
Function performs data manipulation activities and the expected response is 'Overnight'	Utility
Function only selects data	Report
Any other situation	Screen

FIGURE 21.4 A chart that shows how the Application Design Transformer determines the type of module.

21.2.3 HOW THE APPLICATION DESIGN TRANSFORMER MERGES FUNCTIONS

Another functionality provided by the Application Design Transformer is merging similar functions into one module under certain conditions. The options in the Merge Granularity radio group of the Transformer allow you to define the similarity between two functions. Here is a brief description of each option:

❑ **Identical Entities.** If this option is selected, two or more functions that have the same entities associated with them are considered similar and will yield one module. This option is the default of the Transformer. It is satisfactory as long as the generated modules will be data manipulation screens, such as

The Application Design Transformer is intended primarily as a tool to create the initial design for user interface (screens and reports) modules. From the description of how the Transformer creates the first-cut module design of your application, you can see why separating the user interface functions from other functional requirements of the application, such as business rules, is so important. If you mix functions from these two areas in the same functional hierarchy, the Transformer will create a number of screen and report modules that may not correspond to the requirements that the users have expressed. You will have to sift through these modules and decide which of them should be deleted and which of them should be further enhanced and maintained.

Developer/2000 Forms modules. Consider, however, the case of a function that inserts, retrieves, updates, and deletes instances of an entity, and another function that just retrieves data from that entity. You want to generate a Developer/2000 Forms screen to implement the first function and a Developer/2000 Reports module for the second one. With the Identical Entities option of the Merge Granularity parameter, the Application Design Transformer will consider the two functions similar and will create only one *report* module.

❑ **Identical Entities and Usages.** In order to resolve the situation above, you need to set the Merge Granularity parameter to this option. This is more restrictive than the previous option because it considers two functions to be similar if they use the same entities in the same manner.

❑ **Identical Attributes.** The default setting of the Merge Granularity parameter may restrict you in another way. Consider, for example, two functions in the Order Management System, the first of which is used to create and maintain individual customers and the second of which is used to create and maintain corporate customers. Both these functions use the same entity (CUSTOMER) in the same way (create, retrieve, update, and delete). However, the attributes used by the first function are limited only to those that are specific for persons, such as LAST NAME and FIRST NAME, whereas the attributes used by the second function apply to corporations and business organizations, such as EMPLOYEE COUNT, INDUSTRY, and FOUNDED DATE. For clarity reasons, you would prefer to have different screen modules that implement these functions. If you set the Merge Granularity parameter to any of the previous two options, the Application Design Transformer will generate only one module. However, by setting this option to Identical Attributes, you instruct the Transformer not to merge functions unless they use the same attributes.

 So how do you use the Application Design Transformer to generate modules if situations such as the ones described above do occur? One way is to use the Transformer incrementally, with small branches of the functional hierarchy. These branches should be chosen such that all the functions they contain may be generated under one Merge Granularity option. You may facilitate your job here by modifying the functional tree in the Function Hierarchy Diagrammer so that branches contain only one group of functions under the criteria defined above. After the Transformer creates the desired modules, you may set the hierarchy back to the original structure.

The Merge Granularity options guide the Application Design Transformer in the process of creating modules for similar functions. Other properties and associations you may set for these functions play a role here as well. For example, the Transformer will always create different modules for functions identical in all aspects, except for the *Response* property ('*Immediate*' or '*Overnight*'). Furthermore, if the same function is associated with more than one business unit in the repository, the Transformer will create a separate module for each such association. The Transformer appends the short name of the business unit to the module name in order to guarantee its uniqueness within the application system.

21.2.4 HOW THE TRANSFORMER CREATES MODULE ELEMENTS

I presented in Chapter 3 an overview of the major elements of modules in Designer/2000. I will discuss these elements in more detail in the next two chapters. In this section, I discuss how the Application Design Transformer creates some of these elements. The following is a list of the major categories of module elements generated by the Transformer:

❑ For every screen and report module, the Transformer creates a module component for each entity usage of the function, provided that the entity has a corresponding table in the database design. Together with the module component, the Transformer also creates a module component table usage for that table.

❑ The Transformer creates a bound item for every attribute usage of the function, provided a column in the database design is associated with this attribute.

❑ The Transformer creates bound items for surrogate columns created by the Database Design Transformer to implement primary key constraints, foreign key constraints, or supertype entities, although these columns may not have a corresponding attribute in the data model.

❑ The Transformer creates a window object that contains all the module components.

Understanding how the Application Design Transformer generates candidate modules may help you appreciate the importance and impact of the database design in the application design. Recall from the discussion about the logical database design in Chapter 18 that a good number of properties of database objects influence the front-end application generators. In particular, the properties on the property tabs Display, Controls, and UI of tables, views, and snapshots are inherited directly by the bound items of the generated modules. However, the link between these properties is not dynamic. If you edit the properties of a column and change the settings of user interface properties such as the *Width* or *Hint*, the changes will not be reflected in the module items that are bound to this

The Application Design Transformer will generate modules of different flavors, for example Developer/2000 and Visual Basic, only for different functions. If you need to develop the application, or some functions of it, in multiple flavors, you may follow two approaches:

❑ Create different versions of the modules in the Repository. Each copy is used to create modules for one user interface environment. An important step is to create these versions after the database design is completed so that the Application Design Transformer may take advantage of the settings of display properties.

❑ Generate the modules in one environment, and then use the Design Editor Copy with the New Language utility to create copies of them in the other environments.

column. In order to incorporate the new changes in the application design, you have to either edit the properties of all the module items based on the column, or delete and recreate all the modules that use this column. In both cases, these operations may be costly and require a lot of work. Therefore, use the Application Design Transformer only when the database model has matured and definitions of properties on the tabs Display, Controls, and UI for columns have stabilized.

Another similarity between the Database Design Transformer and the Application Design Transformer is that both tools allow you to transition from a logical model of the system to physical implementation details, such as the type of RDBMS where the database will reside or the environment where the front-end application will be created. The principal programming environments in which you can implement presentation services are Developer/2000, Oracle WebServer, Oracle PowerObjects and Microsoft Visual Basic. According to the environment you have selected, screen and report modules can be generated for a variety of tools and languages, such as Developer/2000 Forms, Developer/2000 Reports, Developer/2000 Graphics, Oracle WebServer, Oracle PowerObjects, and Visual Basic. Usually, all the modules will be generated for one environment, although you can mix and match if necessary.

21.3 ACCEPTING AND REJECTING CANDIDATE MODULES

 The outcome of the Application Design Transformer is a set of candidate modules that you can either accept as components of the application or reject. Accepting a module ultimately means setting its property *Candidate* from 'Yes' to 'No.' Rejecting a module means deleting it from the repository. You can accept or reject modules in the Repository Object Navigator or the Design Navigator component of the Design Editor. The following is a list of steps that allows you to achieve this goal:

1. Expand the node Modules. You can find this node under the Module Design group in the Repository Object Navigator or on the Modules tab of the Design Editor.
2. Select one or more modules you want to accept or reject.
3. To accept the selected modules, switch to the Property Palette and set the property *Candidate* to 'No.'
4. To reject the selected modules, simply delete them. Notice that because a module created by the Application Design Transformer normally contains a window object and at least one module component, you need to use the Force Delete mechanism to remove it from the Repository.

The Repository Object Navigator uses different icons to indicate candidate modules from those that are accepted. In the example shown in Figure 21.5, the

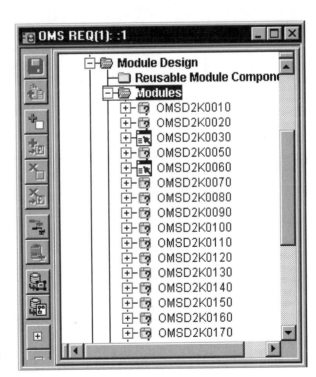

FIGURE 21.5 A listing of candidate and accepted modules in the Repository Object Navigator.

Although I list the activities related to accepting or rejecting modules in this chapter, you do not have to perform them after creating your modules with the Transformer. In fact, you can continue with the design and enhancement of a candidate module just as you would with an accepted module. However, at some point in time between the creation of the module by the Transformer and its generation by the front-end generator, you will need to accept the candidate module. The front-end generators work only with modules whose *Candidate* property is set to *'No.'*

modules OMSD2K0030 and OMSD2K0060 have been accepted and therefore are shown in the Developer/2000 Forms characteristic icon. The other modules on the list are still candidate modules.

21.4 GENERATING MENU MODULES

Besides generating screen and report modules for the user interface, the Application Design Transformer allows you to generate candidate menu modules for use in the application. The following two sections describe the process of creating candidate menus and how the Application Design Transformer creates these menus.

21.4.1 STEPS OF THE MENU CREATION PROCESS

The process of creating the first-cut menu design of your application is simple and can be summarized in the following steps:

1. Invoke the Application Design Transformer and select the radio button Menus from the group Generate Options. Notice that the controls under the group Module Options are disabled; on the other hand, the options under the group Menu Options are enabled.
2. Choose the starting function for which menu modules will be generated.
3. Enter a simple string six characters or fewer in the Module Prefix field. As in other cases, this prefix should allow you to identify the menu modules just by looking at their names. In the case of the Order Management System, for example, you could use the prefix OMSMNU.

4. Choose the language in which the menu will be implemented. This depends on the software environment you have chosen for your application. For Developer/2000 applications, it is Developer/2000 Forms.

5. Keep the default setting of the property *Max Options on Menu*, which controls the maximum number of items a menu can have.

6. Keep the default setting for the property *Include Manual Options*. If you have defined the user interface functional requirements carefully, you should not have any manual functions in the hierarchy. Therefore, the setting of this property should not matter.

7. Click Generate to complete the process.

As in other cases, the Transformer creates a set of candidate menu modules. You need to accept or reject them as described in the previous section.

21.4.2 HOW THE APPLICATION DESIGN TRANSFORMER CREATES MENUS

You need to be aware of an important constraint when generating menu modules. The Application Design Transformer will not create any menu modules unless other types of non-candidate, or accepted, modules exist in the repository. The hierarchy of menu modules created by the Application Design Transformer may be different from the hierarchy of business functions upon which the menu is based. At the root of the hierarchy, the Transformer places the main menu. A submenu for each business unit associated with functions follows. For those functions not associated with any business unit, the Transformer creates a submenu at the same level, called MISCELLANEOUS. Each of these submenus can be further organized into other submenus, based on the type of modules that the business

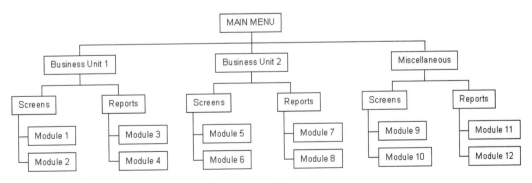

FIGURE 21.6 A visual representation of the structure of a menu created by the Application Design Transformer.

unit can access, such as screens and reports. The actual modules are placed under these submenus. Figure 21.6 shows the structure of a menu created by the Application Design Transformer. Keep in mind that this is just a first cut of the menu of your application that can be modified and enhanced afterwards. Chapter 22 shows how you can modify the relationship between modules in your system using the Design Editor.

21.5 SUMMARY

The Application Design Transformer is the Designer/2000 utility that allows you to create a first-cut design of the software modules that will make up your application. This Transformer sets the properties of modules based on properties of a number of objects, including functions, data usages of functions, tables, and columns. In order to take full advantage of the power of this Transformer, be sure to use it after the properties of database objects have stabilized and business rules have been documented. This chapter provides instructions on how to use the Application Design Transformer. Among other things, this chapter discusses the following topics:

- ❏ **The Purpose of the Application Design Transformer**
- ❏ **Generating Presentation Layer Modules**
    - ❏ Steps of the Module Creation Process
    - ❏ How the Application Design Transformer Creates Modules
    - ❏ How the Application Design Transformer Merges Functions
    - ❏ How the Transformer Creates Module Elements
- ❏ **Accepting and Rejecting Candidate Modules**
- ❏ **Generating Menu Modules**
    - ❏ Steps of the Menu Creation Process
    - ❏ How the Application Design Transformer Creates Menus

Chapter 22

MAINTAINING MODULES IN THE DESIGN EDITOR

- Modules in Designer/2000
- Structure of Modules
- Working with Modules
- Creating and Maintaining Module Elements
- Module Wizards
- Reusable Components
- Summary

During the requirements analysis, the Function Hierarchy Diagrammer is the principal tool for modeling the requirements of your system. The Application Design Transformer converts the user interface requirements into modules, thus providing you with an initial design of your application. The Design Editor allows you to enhance and expand this initial design and to bring it to a level where you can generate fully functional software modules, ready for deployment and use. This chapter will discuss the concept and structure of modules in Designer/2000, as well as some of the major activities you perform with modules in the Design Editor.

22.1 MODULES IN DESIGNER/2000

Modules represent information about a front-end application recorded in the Designer/2000 Repository. The ultimate purpose of modules is to generate a software application that meets one or more user interface requirements of your system. In the following sections, I discuss the major types of modules in Designer/2000 and methods used to populate the Repository with modules.

22.1.1 TYPES OF MODULES

The most popular way to classify modules in Designer/2000 is to group them by the language in which they will implement the user requirements of the application system. The Repository Object Navigator and the Design Navigator use a characteristic icon to denote each module type in the hierarchy tree of objects. Figure 22.1 shows a list of the principal types of modules in Designer/2000, together with their characteristic icons.

The modules listed in Figure 22.1 represent screen or report modules. Designer/2000 also allows you to maintain menu modules and libraries of application logic objects. These modules are intended primarily for use in Developer/2000 applications, although they can be implemented in other languages as

CHARACTERISTIC ICON	MODULE TYPE
	Developer/2000 Forms
	Developer/2000 Reports
	Developer/2000 Graphics
	Oracle WebServer
	Visual Basic

FIGURE 22.1 Characteristic icons for the principal categories of Designer/2000 modules.

well. In any case, Designer/2000 uses different icons for these modules, independent of the implementation language. Menus are represented by the icon ⁼ and libraries are represented by the icon ◆.

22.1.2 POPULATING THE REPOSITORY WITH MODULES

Chapter 21 discussed one of the methods used to populate the Designer/2000 Repository with module objects. With this method, user interface requirements and information about the data model of your application system are used by the Application Design Transformer to create an initial list of candidate modules. The following steps summarize this method:

1. Capture the user interface requirements of the application.
2. Perform data modeling activities to identify the data requirements and data-related business rules of the application system.
3. Define data usages for the user interface functions.
4. Generate an initial logical database design using the Database Design Transformer.
5. Enhance and expand the logical database design in the Design Editor.
6. Create an initial module design using the Application Design Transformer.
7. Accept or reject the candidate modules according to the needs of your application.

The method described above works well in cases when you are developing a new system from scratch. Often information systems are developed to replace existing systems that are outdated and no longer meet the requirements of the business community. In such situations, you can recover the design of these front-end software components into application modules stored in the Repository using the Designer/2000 Recover Module Design utility. This utility allows you to convert and store in the Repository the definitions of Developer/2000 Forms and Reports modules from the file system or a database, as well as Visual Basic project files. Combined with the Recover Database Design tool, this utility provides full support for capturing the state of an application system and modifying and redesigning it. The following are the steps required to recover the design of a Developer/2000 Forms module in the Design Editor:

1. Select Utilities | Recover Design of | Form. The Forms Design Recovery dialog box appears.
2. In the list box Location, select the environment where the module is currently located. Since Developer/2000 Forms modules are maintained mostly in the file system, the option selected in this list is normally File.
3. Enter the name and the location of the module in the file system. You can

also click Browse… to display a standard Microsoft Windows dialog box that allows you to browse the directory structure of your PC and select the module.

4. Select one of the options in the Recovery Mode radio group. By default, Recover ONLY module design is selected. If you want to also recover any program units or triggers you have built into the module, select the option Recover BOTH module design and application logic.

5. If you selected one of the first two options in the Recovery Mode radio group, enter the name of a new module in the text box Destination Module. If you are updating the application logic of an existing module in the Repository, enter the name of this module in Destination Module.

6. Set the check box Create on Diagram after Recovery if you want to display the module in a module diagram after the recovery process is completed.

Now the dialog box Forms Design Recovery should be similar to the one shown in Figure 22.2. In order to set the options of the process, click the button

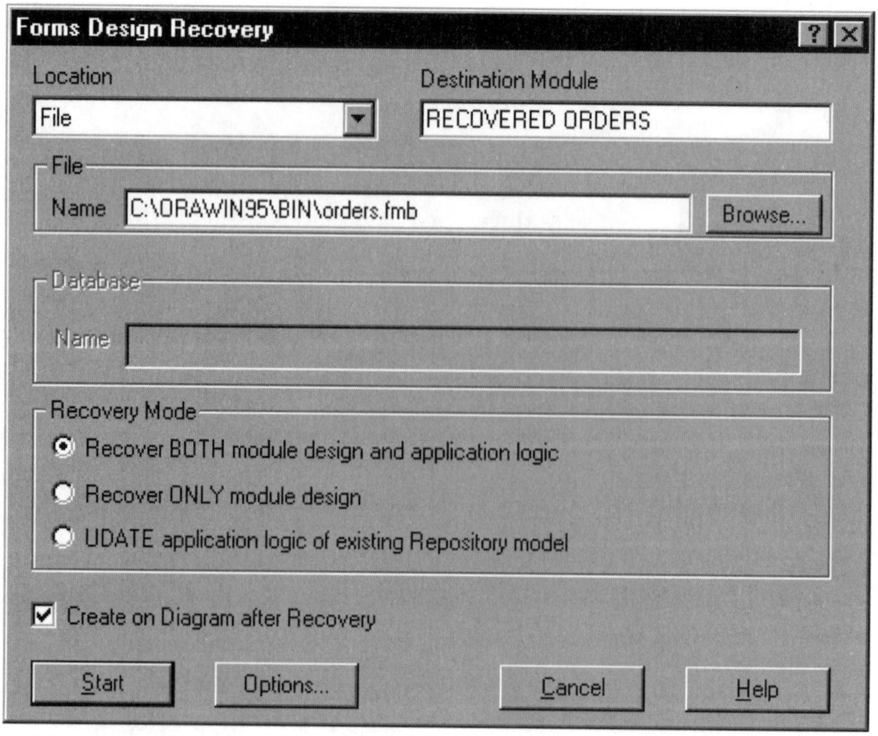

FIGURE 22.2 The Forms Design Recovery dialog box.

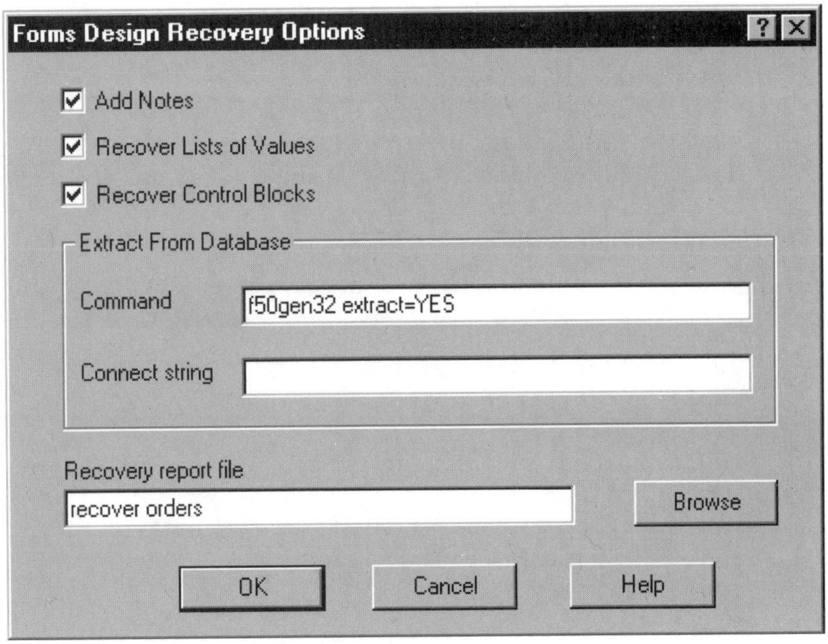

FIGURE 22.3   The Forms Design Recovery Options dialog box.

Options… to display the dialog box Forms Design Recovery Options, shown in Figure 22.3. By setting the appropriate checkboxes in this dialog box, you can add notes to different module elements, you can instruct the utility to create lookup table usages for the list of values defined in the module, and you can recover the design of control blocks in addition to the design of base table blocks. In this dialog box, you can also enter the name and location of a file where the utility writes a report of activities performed during the design recovery process.

After you have set the options of the recovery tool, click Start to begin the process of recovering the design of the selected module in the Repository. The Message Window of the Design Editor will display the messages generated by the process, as well as any errors or warnings encountered. When the recovery is complete, you are prompted to save the new module in the repository, to revert the changes, or to go to the Design Editor and review the changes individually. If you set the option to generate a report, you may also review this report to see a log of all the actions performed. Excerpts from such a report are shown in Figure 22.4.

Figure 22.4 shows some of the elements of a module that the Design Recovery utility creates in the Repository, based on the properties of the recovered

```
CREATE WINDOW - ROOT_WINDOW from
Title:Order Maintenance Form

CREATE MODULE COMPONENT - ORD1 from
Insert:True  Update:True  Query:True  Delete:True

CREATE MODULE DETAILED TABLE USAGE - ORD1 from
Table:ORDERS Type:BASE

CREATE ITEM - ORDER_NUMBER from
Column:ORDER_NUMBER Type:BASE
Display:True  Insert:True  Update:False  Query:True
Nullify:False
Display Datatype: Display Width:6 Display Height:1
Prompt:Order Number
Hint Text:The unique identifier for an order.
Order By Sequence:1
Justification:2

CREATE ITEM - CUSTOMER from
Column:CUSTOMER Type:UNBOUND
Display:True  Insert:True  Update:True  Query:True
Nullify:False
Display Datatype: Display Width:48 Display Height:1
Prompt:Customer
Hint Text:The name of the customer placing the order.
Order By Sequence:1
Justification:1
```

FIGURE 22.4 Excerpts from a report of the Forms Design Recovery utility.

module. These elements include the module definition itself, module components, windows, bound and unbound items, and so on. Section 22.2 provides more details about these elements.

So far, I have presented two methods of populating the Repository with modules that are automated to a good degree by Designer/2000 utilities. When everything else fails, you can always create the modules manually in the Design Editor. Section 22.3 discusses this process.

22.2 STRUCTURE OF MODULES

You can look at the structure of a module in two ways:

❑ **Data view.** The elements that are part of the data view of a module describe the interaction of the modules with sources of data, such as database objects.

❑ **Display view.** The elements that make up the display view of a module describe the layout of the user and how the users will interact with the data elements of the module.

The Module Diagrammer component of the Design Wizard allows you to represent visually the data and display views of a module. The Design Navigator, on the other hand, maintains the objects that are part of each view under separate nodes in the hierarchy of a module. The names of these nodes are Data View and Display View. The following sections describe the module elements that are parts of each view.

22.2.1 THE DATA VIEW OF A MODULE

The data view of a module, as the name implies, represents the module elements as they appear from the database interaction perspective, without any consideration of the layout or the position of these elements. Figure 22.5 shows the major elements of this view. Each of these elements is described in the following paragraphs:

❑ **Module component.** Module components are groupings of data items that can be maintained, addressed, and used independently in Designer/2000 modules. A module component is characterized by the types of operations it performs on its data elements and by the way these elements are organized in the user interface. The power of the module components as design elements resides in the fact that they bundle together data items, data relationships, application logic, and layout properties. With respect to their use in modules, you can divide module components into reusable and specific module components. Reusable module components extend the concept of software reusability into reusability of design. They are module components that are designed, stored, and maintained independently of any module. When needed, these components can be included in any module that requires the functionality they offer. When the module component is used in the context of a given module, it is called a specific module component. As you progress in the design efforts of your application system, carefully identify those mod-

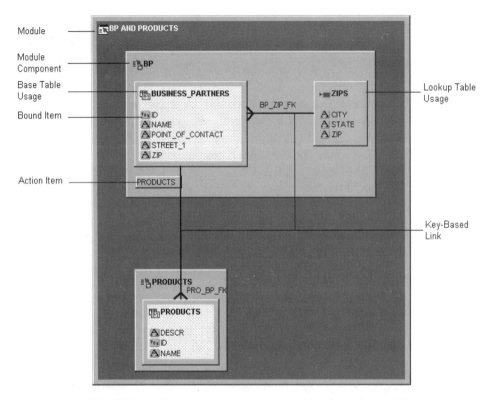

FIGURE 22.5 The major elements in the data view of a module.

ule components that have potential for reuse and store them as reusable components. If you do this process consistently and to a reasonable extent, you will reach a point where you will be able to create new modules by simply assembling components used by other modules, without having to go though the pain of building everything from the scratch.

❑ **Module component table usages.** Table usages represent the items from a database table used within a module component. A module component is not required to contain a table usage, in which case it is known as a *control module component.* However, when the module component contains table usages, one of them must be a base table usage, which shapes the characteristics of the module components. It is complemented by lookup table usages, which are another popular type of table usages. Occasionally and in certain types of report modules, like the Developer/2000 Reports modules, you may encounter table usages that represent nested SELECT statements or computations of SQL group functions, like SUM, COUNT, MIN, and MAX, for each record of the base table usage.

❏ **Module component links.** These links represent associations that module components inherit because of associations that exist between their base table usages. They are divided into key-based links and shared-data links. Key-based links are very common and occur in every type of module. They can be established between two module components as long as a foreign key constraint is defined between the underlying base table usages of these components. Shared-data links are encountered only in Developer/2000 Forms and Developer/2000 Reports modules that contain a chart component embedded in them. If the module components pass data to the chart component for graphical display, the relationship is represented by a shared-data link.

❏ **Items.** Items represent containers of data used in the application system. When the items correspond to a database column, they are called *bound items.* An item whose value is not directly associated with a database column is called an *unbound item.* A third category of items, *action items,* represents push buttons that allow users to perform some action implemented by the application logic associated with the item. They can also be used to implement navigational buttons to components within the module or to different modules. Bound items are owned by a module component table usage. Graphically, they are presented within the boundaries of the parent table usage. Unbound and action items on the other hand, are owned by the module component. Therefore, they are shown on data diagrams within the boundaries of the module component but outside any table usage.

22.2.2 THE DISPLAY VIEW OF A MODULE

The display view of a module shows the elements of a module from the layout and user interface perspective. Two module elements shared between the display and data views are the module component and the items. Figure 22.6 shows the display view of the same module shown in Figure 22.5 in its data view. By comparing these two figures, you can easily identify the modules and the common

 The data view of module diagrams also displays links between modules, like the one shown in Figure 22.5. These links are intended to visually represent the calling relationship that exists between modules in your application system. They are very typical for menu modules and less common in other types of modules. The example in Figure 22.5 shows a menu item calling a screen module.

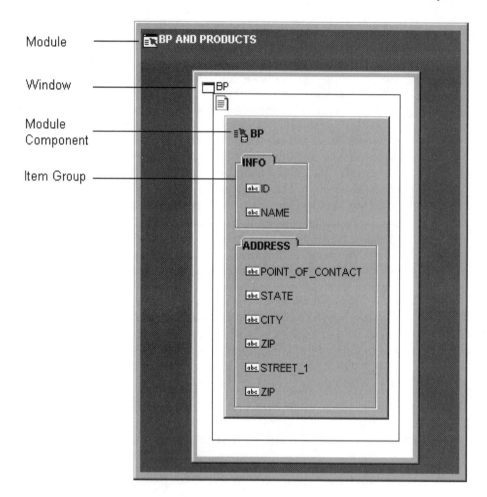

Module

Window

Module
Component

Item Group

FIGURE 22.6   The major elements in display view of a module.

items between the two views. Note, however, the following difference in the way items are represented in the display view:

❑ Table usages of module components are not shown in display mode.
❑ No distinction exists between bound or unbound items in display view.
❑ Only the items that are displayable are shown in display view.
❑ The characteristic icon of each item in data view represents its data type, such as alphanumeric, number, or date; the characteristic icon of the same item in display view represents the display type of the item, such as text item, list box, or radio group.

Two important elements of a module are present in the display view of the module. They are windows and item groups. The following paragraphs describe these elements:

❑ **Windows.** Windows are the GUI containers of all the displayed items of a module. A module may contain multiple windows, and a window may contain multiple module components in it. Windows represent different objects for different types of modules. They represent windows in Developer/2000 Forms, the entire report in Developer/2000 Reports, layers in Developer/2000 Graphics, forms in Visual Basic applications, and HTML pages in WebServer modules.

❑ **Item groups.** As the name implies, item groups are a way to group together different displayed items of a module component. The main purpose for bundling items in a group is so that they are considered as one layout item by the front-end generator. They serve the purpose of displaying logically-related data items. Item groups can be laid out individually in the window, or can be stacked in the same area of the window. In the case of stacked item groups, only one group can be visible at any one moment. The principal use of stacked items is to implement tabbed property controls in your Developer/2000 Forms and Visual Basic modules.

22.2.3 MODULE APPLICATION LOGIC

Important components of a module are application logic elements that can be associated with the entire module or with elements of the module. *Application logic* is the term that encompasses the code generated by the front-end generators and the code that you associate with different elements of the module. Events and named routines are two categories of application logic objects maintained in the Design Editor. The front-end generators create events and named routines based on the properties of the modules defined in the Repository and on a number of other sources, like object libraries and templates. You have the opportunity to add your own specific programmatic structures to the ones created by the generators, by associating the code with events and named routines in the Repository. For environments like Developer/2000 Forms, Reports, and Graphics, events correspond to triggers, and named routines correspond to program units.

22.3 WORKING WITH MODULES

Section 22.1.2 provided an overview of the three methods used to populate the Designer/2000 Repository with modules and provided the general steps for performing two of them: creating modules using the Application Design Transformer and recovering the design of existing modules using the Module Design

Recovery utility. In the following sections, I will discuss the process of creating and maintaining modules in the Design Editor.

22.3.1 THE MODULE APPLICATION GUIDE

Chapters 18 and 19 introduced the Database Object Guide and the Database Administrator Guide as two powerful tools that can help you organize and track the work you perform during logical and physical database design activities. The Module Application Guide is the counterpart of these guides that leads you through the process of creating and maintaining the design of your modules. To access this guide in the Design Editor, select Tools | Module Application Guide.... The entry screen of the tool is shown in Figure 22.7. From this screen, you perform one of the following actions:

❑ Create and edit modules in the application system
❑ Recover the design of existing modules by running the Module Design Recovery utility

FIGURE 22.7 The entry screen of the Module Application Guide.

If you click the icon 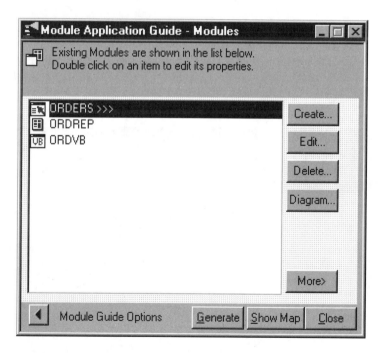, the entry screen of the guide is replaced with a screen that lists the three categories of module elements you can create and maintain in the Design Editor: Modules, Module Components, and Menus. By clicking the icon , you can move to the next level of action you can perform in this guide. As in the other guides of Design Editor, the titles of the categories of objects are hyperlinks to the Designer/2000 online help for the category.

Figure 22.8 shows the screen that is displayed if you choose to proceed with the process of creating and editing modules. The list control in the center of the screen displays all the modules defined in the repository. From this screen, you can perform one of the following actions:

❑ Create a new module by clicking Create....

❑ Display the properties of a module by selecting it in the list and clicking Edit.... You can also double-click to bring up the Edit Module dialog box, where these properties are maintained.

❑ Display a module in its module diagram by selecting it in the list and clicking Diagram....

❑ Delete one or more modules by selecting them in the list and clicking Delete....

FIGURE 22.8 The Modules screen of the Module Application Guide.

❑ Invoke the appropriate front-end generator for a module by selecting it and clicking Generate.

Similar actions may be performed in other screens where elements of modules are displayed. Buttons like Diagram or Generate will be disabled where the context does not allow you to perform the functions that they represent. If the currently selected object contains other categories of objects within its definition, its name is followed by the characters >>>, as shown in Figure 22.8 for the case of the module ORDERS. To view the categories of these objects, click the button More>. In each screen, you can click the icon ◄▌ to return to the previous screen of the guide.

Like the other guides, the Module Application Guide is a very effective tool to navigate up and down the hierarchy module elements. It also provides a Map component that allows you to jump from one area of the hierarchy onto another. In order to display the map, click the button Show Map on the screen. Figure 22.9 shows the hierarchy tree representation of the module elements you can maintain in the Design Editor. Each push button on the map represents a screen of the Module Application Guide. If the button is enabled, you can navigate to its associated screen immediately, by clicking the button. If the button is not enabled, the context of the current screen is such that it does not allow navigation to that particular element. In the example shown in Figure 22.9, the nodes Data, Items, and Groups under the Reusable Component button are not enabled because the context of the guide is the modules defined in the Repository. If you switch the context to the reusable components of the application system and select one such object from the list, the nodes mentioned earlier will be enabled.

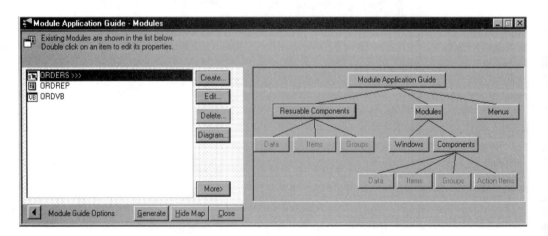

FIGURE 22.9   The Module Application Guide with the map.

22.3.2 CREATING AND MAINTAINING MODULES

The process of creating modules is simple and, despite some differences between different types of modules, can be summarized as follows:

1. Invoke the Create Module dialog box. You can invoke this dialog by using the Module Application Guide as explained in the previous section or in a more conventional way by selecting the node Modules on the tab with the same name of the Design Navigator and then clicking the icon Create 🖼 .
2. Set the properties of the new module on the first tab of the dialog. Among the most important properties you set in this step are the short name and the implementation language of the module. Figure 22.10 shows an example of the settings on this tab.
3. Click Finish to complete the process.

You could also click Next to enter other properties of the new module; however, I recommend that you quickly create the modules you need to add in the

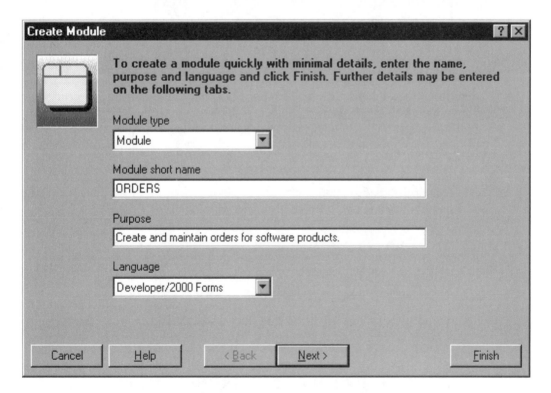

FIGURE 22.10 The Create Module dialog box.

application system, and then complete the definition of their properties in the Edit Module dialog box. You can invoke this dialog box by double-clicking the module in the Design Navigator, provided that the Design Editor is in the 'Show Dialogs' mode. If the module is presented in a data diagram, you can display its property dialog box by double-clicking the module frame on the diagram.

The Edit Module dialog box is composed of multiple property tabs. The number of these tabs depends on the language selected to implement the module. The first tab of the Edit Module dialog box for every module type is the tab Name with the same properties and layout as Figure 22.10. In addition, every module contains a tab that allows you to associate user help about the module, and another one that allows you to associate the current module with other modules. Where appropriate, some modules, like Developer/2000 Reports and Graphics, contain a tab to enter parameters; some other modules contain a tab that allows you to maintain the title for the module, which may become the title of the report in the case of Developer/2000 Reports, the title of the HTML page in the case of Oracle WebServer, or the title of the generated form in the case of Visual Basic modules. The following sections discuss the most important properties you maintain for modules.

22.3.3 MAINTAINING HELP CONTENTS

For software modules that will be deployed on Microsoft Windows platforms, such as Developer/2000 Forms, Visual Basic, and Oracle Power Objects modules, the best method to provide user help is to compile it in the form of Microsoft Help files integrated with the applications. In order to prepare for the generation of such files, you need to enter the help content as you refine the design of your application modules. The Help tab in the Edit Module dialog box allows you to associate help information with the module. Figure 22.11 shows an example of this tab.

As you can see from Figure 22.11, you enter two types of text in the Help text item of this tab. First you enter a description of the module that the users will see when they request help for the module. Then you enter the keywords to enable the search of this help page. Each keyword or phrase must be in a separate line and preceded by the characters '@@' to be recognized. In addition, you may also specify an image file that will be included in the help page for the module.

22.3.4 CREATING AND MAINTAINING MODULE ASSOCIATIONS

Various modules in the application system you develop may be associated to form what is called a module network. Menu modules, for example, may call screen or report modules, screen modules may invoke other screen or report modules, a library module may be linked to a Developer/2000 Forms module, and so on. The tab Module Network allows you to create and maintain associations of the current module with other modules. Figure 22.12 shows an example

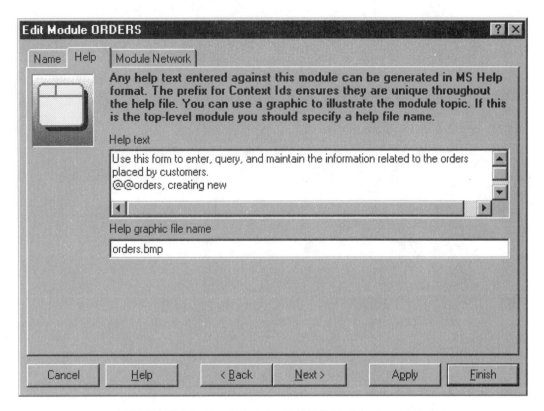

FIGURE 22.11 The Help tab of the Edit Module dialog box.

of this tab in which the library ORD_APPL_LOGIC is associated with the module ORDERS.

To create an association between the current module and an existing module, click Select Modules… and choose the desired module to link from the dialog box that appears. You can also type the name of a new module in the text item Called Modules to create a new module and association at the same time.

 In certain circumstances, you may find very useful the ability to create new modules and associate them with the current module on the Module Network tab of the Edit Module dialog box. For example, you could use it to build the menu structure of your application with all the submenus and menu items that call the appropriate screen or report modules.

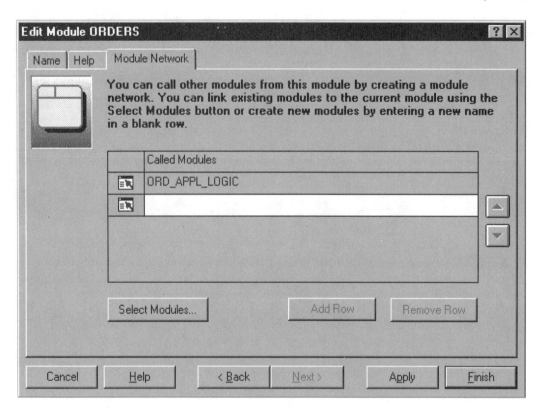

FIGURE 22.12 The Module Network tab of the Edit Module dialog box.

22.3.5 MAINTAINING MODULE ARGUMENTS

In general, you can create arguments for any of the Developer/2000 modules; however, they are mostly used in Developer/2000 Reports and Developer/2000 Graphics modules, where they are called *parameters*. The Parameters tab of the Edit Module dialog is where you can create and maintain the parameters of a report or chart module. Figure 22.13 shows an example of this tab.

To create a new parameter, click Add, and then place the cursor inside the text box Name and type the name of the parameter. In the controls to the right, you can enter the label that users will see for this parameter, pick its data type, and set the maximum length when applicable. You can inherit these last two properties from a domain already defined in your Repository. To select the domain, click the button Domain..., and choose it from the list of domains that appears.

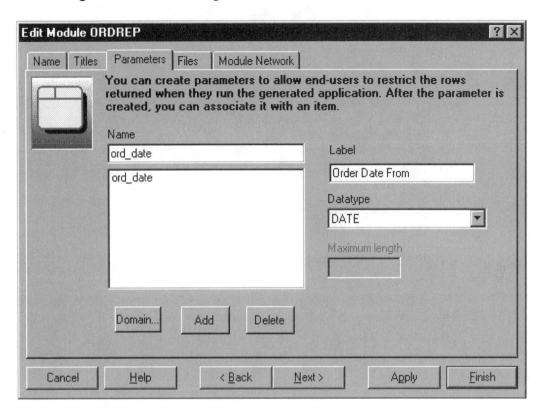

FIGURE 22.13 The Parameters tab of the Edit Module dialog box.

22.3.6 COPYING MODULES

Yet another way to expand the module portfolio of your application system with new modules is to copy existing modules. In order to copy a module in the Design Editor, you need to select it in the Design Navigator and then choose Utilities | Copy. This operation brings up the Copy Objects dialog box, whose functionality was discussed in Chapter 5. In the case of modules, the Design Editor offers a twist to the copy procedure that allows you to recast a module implemented in one language into modules of other languages. For example, you could copy a Developer/2000 Forms module into an Oracle WebServer or Visual Basic module, and vice versa. The following are the steps you need to follow to accomplish this task:

1. Select the source module in the Design Navigator.
2. Select Utilities | Copy with New Language…. The dialog box Create As Copy appears.

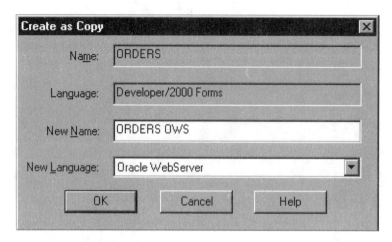

FIGURE 22.14 The Create As Copy dialog box.

3. Enter the new name of the module and select the implementation language for the new module as shown in Figure 22.14.
4. Click OK.

The process of copying a module with a new language is really advantageous in the following cases:

❑ When you are required to implement the module in multiple environments, for example Developer/2000 and Visual Basic. In this case, you could analyze the user requirements in a unified way and use the Application Design Transformer to create the initial module design for one language. Using the utility described above, you could then create the modules for the second implementation language with minimal effort.
❑ When you are required to implement an existing application system into a new environment. In this situation, you could recover the design of the current modules, for example Developer/2000 modules, copy these modules

Be sure to understand that when you copy a module from one language implementation to another, inevitably, details will be lost. If, for example, you have recorded application logic in a Developer/2000 Forms module and copy it as a WebServer module, the application logic will not be carried over, due to the different event models of these tools.

with the new language implementation, for example Oracle WebServer, and then generate the modules in the new environment. This approach is followed quite often to Web-enable a number of client/server applications.

22.3.7 DEVELOPER/2000 MODULE SECURITY

When designing Developer/2000 applications, you can combine the Developer/2000 Menus security roles with the Oracle database users and roles to control the access to modules invoked by the menu items. The following steps allow you to grant access for a module to a database user:

1. Expand the node that represents the user and select the node Security.
2. Click the icon Create ▣ . The dialog box Oracle User Module Accesses for Module appears (see Figure 22.15). In this dialog, the list to the left represents the Oracle database users who do not have access to the module; the list to the right represents those users who already have access.
3. Perform the familiar operations to move a database user from the list to the left, to the list to the right, thus effectively granting her access to the module.
4. Click OK.

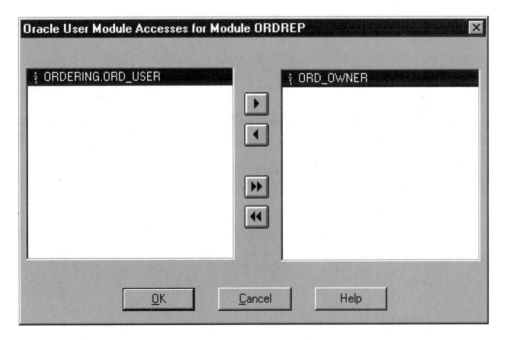

FIGURE 22.15 The Oracle User Module Accesses for Module dialog box.

The method described in this section works well when you grant access to users one module at a time. For more complicated scenarios, you could create a matrix diagram that maps modules to database users or roles. In order to limit the modules included in the matrix, set the Filter of the *Language* property to *'Dev%.'* Refer to Chapter 7 for details on creating and setting filters for matrix diagrams.

Similar actions can be performed to grant access to a role. I mentioned that a condition for implementing user security rules with the method described above is that the modules should be Developer/2000 modules. In fact, modules of other types do not even have a node called Security under their hierarchy. Even for Developer/2000 modules, the following two conditions must be met in order for the generators to implement these rules:

❑   The module should be invoked from a menu module.
❑   The database user or role associations should be created not only for the module in question, but also for all the ancestor menu modules that are used to access the module.

22.4   CREATING AND MAINTAINING MODULE ELEMENTS

During the design of your application system, you will need to add new elements to modules or maintain the properties of existing ones. Like every other activity required during the application design, you can perform these actions in the Design Navigator. However, displaying the modules in the Data Diagrammer component of the Design Editor and accessing these functions from its interface is more intuitive. The following sections discuss ways and methods to perform these tasks efficiently in module diagrams. In particular, they focus on these topics:

❑   Displaying modules in module diagrams.
❑   Creating module elements in the module diagram.
❑   Maintaining the properties of module elements in the module diagram.

22.4.1 DISPLAYING MODULES IN DIAGRAMS

One way to create a module diagram is to select File | New | Module Diagram... from the Design Editor's menu. The dialog box that comes up as a result of this action contains a list of all the modules defined in the Repository. To complete the action, select one of them and click OK. Another method is to expand the hierarchy tree of the Design Navigator until you see the desired module, and then right-click the module. From the popup menu that appears, select the item Show On Diagram.

Module diagrams in the Design Editor come in two flavors. They can show the data view or the display view of the elements of a module. In data view, the module diagram allows you to create, view, and edit module components, their table usages, including base and lookup usages, the bound items that are part of the table usages, and the unbound and action items that are part of the component. In the diagram's data view, you can also see the key-based links, the shared-data links, or the module links of a module. In order to display the data view of a module diagram, select View | Data View or click the icon Switch to Data View.

The diagram in display view is used to maintain the layout elements of the module. Although you can use it to access and maintain the properties of module components and items, the display view is used primarily to create and maintain properties of windows and item groups. To show a module diagram in display view, select View | Display View or click the icon Switch to Display View.

22.4.2 CREATING MODULE ELEMENTS

The tool palette of the Module Diagrammer offers a number of iconic tools that can be used to create the different elements that make up the module. The following paragraphs describe the steps to create each of these elements. These paragraphs will list only the minimal properties you need to set in order to create the element. The remaining properties are discussed in Sections 22.4.3 through 22.4.8.

The following elements can be created in the data view of the module diagram:

❑ **Module components.** To create a new module component, select the icon Create Specific Component and click the module on the diagram. In the Create Module Component dialog box that appears, enter the name and language implementation of the component. Optionally, you may also enter a title that will be used to identify the component on the screen or the report. Click Next to move to the other tabs where you can set additional properties of the module component, or click Finish to complete the process. If you want to include a reusable component in the module, select the icon Include Reusable Component and click the module object on

When you select one of the icons on the tool palette, you will notice that the mouse cursor will indicate the areas on the diagram where you can and cannot create the new element.

the diagram. In the dialog box Include Module Component that appears, select the desired component and click OK.

❏ **Table usages.** To create a new module component table usage, select the icon Create Table Usage and click inside the module component that will own this table. If the module component does not contain any table usages, this action will invoke the Create Base Table Usage dialog box. In this dialog, select the name of the base object for the component from the list of tables, views, and snapshots in the Repository, and click Finish. If the component has a base table usage defined already, the action above will invoke the Create Table Lookup Usage dialog box. This dialog box displays a list of the database objects that are referenced by a foreign key of the base table usage of the component. Select one of the objects from the list and click Finish.

❏ **Key-based links.** If two base table usages share a foreign key constraint, you can implement that constraint in the form of a key-based link between these usages. To create such a link, select the icon Create Links and click the parent table first and then the detail table. The link is automatically shown on the diagram.

❏ **Items.** To create a bound item, select the icon Create Item and click a table usage on the diagram. In the dialog box Create Bound Item that appears, select the column on which the bound item will be based and provide the name of the new item. To create an unbound item, select the icon Create Item and click inside the module component, but outside any table usage of this component. Provide the item name and type in the dialog box Create

The link may not necessarily go from the 'One' end to the 'Many' end of the foreign key constraint. You can have a link whose source is the detail record and the destination the parent record, identified by the value of the primary key that is recorded in the foreign key column of the detail record.

Unbound Item and click Finish. Finally, action items can be created by selecting the icon Create Action Item and clicking the module component that will own this item. In the dialog box Create Navigation Action Item that appears, choose the type of action that the action will perform and click Finish.

The following elements are created in the display view of the module diagram:

❑ **Windows.** To create a window, select the icon Window ▣ and then click the module on the diagram. In order to place one or more module components in the new window, draw a rectangle on the diagram that includes these components.

❑ **Item groups.** To create a group of items and populate it with elements at the same time, select the items on the diagram and click the icon Create Group ▦. In the dialog box Create Item Group that appears, enter the name and label of the item group and choose whether the item group is stacked or not.

As I mentioned earlier, the procedures described in this section allow you to simply create the elements of the module, without worrying much about properties other than what is absolutely required to insert the element in the Repository. Sections 22.4.3 through 22.4.8 describe the most important properties of these objects.

22.4.3 MAINTAINING MODULE COMPONENTS

The properties of modules components are maintained in the Edit Module Component dialog box displayed when you double-click the object in the diagram or in the Design Navigator. Except for a few differences, modules implemented in different languages have common property tabs, some of which are discussed in the following paragraphs:

❑ **Operations.** The purpose of this tab is to allow you to specify whether the base table usage of this module will allow users to perform the four basic operations: Insert, Update, Delete, and Query. This tab is common for all the modules that are used to implement screens. For modules implemented with tools like Developer/2000 Reports and Developer/2000 Graphics, the only operation is Select, therefore this tab is not present. Figure 22.16 shows an example of the Operations tab for a Developer/2000 Forms module. Notice that for this type of module, the source and destination of data may be objects other than database tables. To populate the data block that corresponds to the module component, Developer/2000 allows you to query a table, or to use a stored procedure or a transactional trigger. Likewise, the changes and modifications to the data may be sent directly to the table or through a stored procedure or transactional triggers. The list boxes Data-source type and Datatarget type in Figure 22.16 allow you to specify these behaviors of the data block that will be created by the Developer/2000 Forms Generator.

❑ **Display.** This property tab is used primarily to define the number of records that the generated module component will accommodate on the screen or report. Usually, components with a form layout display the data one record at a time. Components that display multiple records should not display more than 5–8 records at a time, unless they occupy the entire window. Another important control on this tab is the list box Overflow Style. The setting of this control provides instructions to the front-end generators about the layout of the items they create. Two options in this list are most often used: Wrap line is used to give the data block in the generated module a form layout; Spread table is used to present the data block in tabular format, in the form of a spread table. Figure 22.17 shows an example of the Display tab.

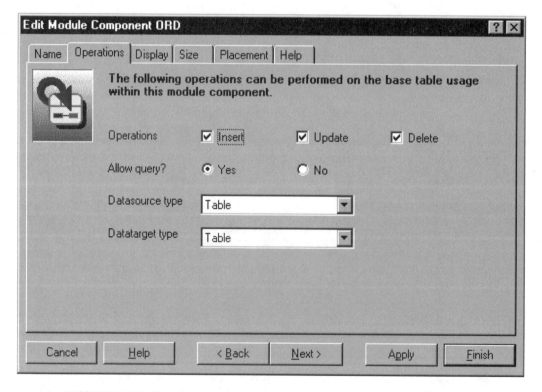

FIGURE 22.16   The Operations tab of the Edit Module Component dialog box.

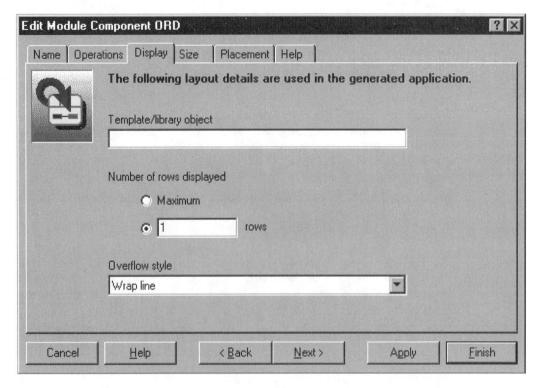

FIGURE 22.17   The Display tab of the Edit Module Component dialog box.

❑ **Placement.** This tab essentially allows you to control what you already see in the diagram of a module: whether a module component is placed in a new window or in the same window as its predecessor. For certain environments, you can also specify the size that the module items should occupy on the screen, although letting the generators compute the values and set these properties is better.

❑ **Help.** This tab is used to associate context-sensitive help with the module component. What I said in Section 22.3.3 for the case of modules applies for their components as well.

22.4.4   MAINTAINING TABLE USAGES

Despite its name, the dialog box with the properties of a module component table usage is used primarily to maintain the properties of the bound items within the table. Different tabs in this dialog box allow you to include columns in the list of bound items for the table and to maintain a number of their properties, like allowed operations, display order, optionality, and so on. The following paragraphs provide some details for the most important tabs in the Edit Base Table Usage dialog box.

❑ **Where.** This tab is used in cases where you want to restrict the records returned to the table usage by a query. The conditions you specify in the text box become the WHERE clause of the SELECT statement that retrieves these records. If, for example, you enter *STATUS = 'A'* on the Where tab of table usage ORDERS, the generated block will retrieve only active orders from the database. When set for lookup table usages, this property may also restrict the options that users may have available for setting an item.

❑ **Items.** The purpose of this tab is to allow you to maintain the list of items that you want to include in the table usage. You can include an item by moving it from the list Available columns into the list Selected items. For the items already included in the table usage, you can indicate whether or not you want them displayed to the users by setting or clearing the check box associated with each element in the list. By arranging the ranking of items in the list Selected items, you can also set their display order in the front-end module. Figure 22.18 shows an example of this tab.

❑ **Item Names.** This tab allows you to maintain the names of the items included in the tab module. By default, these items are named as the corresponding columns.

❑ **Operations.** This tab is where you check those items in the table usage that will be used to enter query criteria, that will accept data when a new record is created, and that will be updateable. By default, the usages are set based on the properties of the database columns. Columns that are part of primary keys, for example, are not updateable.

❑ **Optional.** The main purpose of this tab is to identify the items for which users will have to enter data in the generated module. By default, the list Mandatory items on the right-hand side of this tab is populated with items that correspond to NOT NULL database columns. You can add to this list items from the list Optional items if the situation requires you to do so.

❑ **Display.** This tab captures some of the display properties of each item in the table usage, including Prompt, Display Type, Width, and Height. Like other item properties, properties of items on this tab are inherited from their corresponding columns.

❑ **Context.** This tab is used to identify those data items within a table usage that identify a record of data from the business and user perspective rather than from the system or database perspective. In the example shown in Figure 22.19, for example, the item NAME is the context item for the CUSTOMER table because a user identifies customers by their name. The value of their CUSTOMER_NUMBER, which is what the database uses to uniquely identify customers, may be meaningless to the users. Context

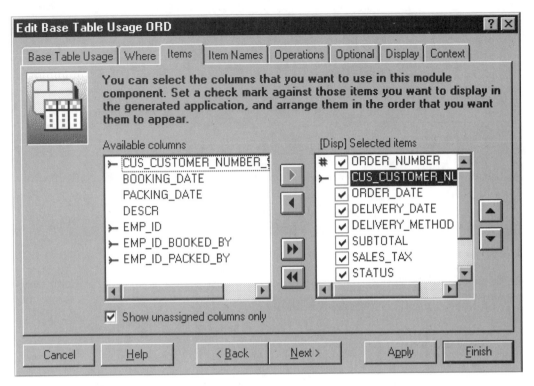

FIGURE 22.18 The Items tab of the Edit Base Table Usage dialog box.

items are very useful in cases where the layout of the module component is a spread table and not all the data items can be displayed simultaneously. In such a case, users may scroll to the right to view the hidden data items but still keep in front of them the context items for the record.

The dialog box for lookup table usages contains all the tabs described in the previous paragraphs. In addition, this dialog contains the tab LOV, which is specific for this type of table usage. Figure 22.20 shows an example of this dialog box. As you can see from the example, the LOV tab allows you to pick the items that will be displayed in the list of values—hence the abbreviation LOV. It also allows you to enter a title for the dialog box in which the list will be displayed.

22.4.5 MAINTAINING BOUND ITEMS

From the description of the property tabs of table usages presented in Section 22.4.4, you can easily see that most of the properties of bound items are maintained in the dialog box of the par-

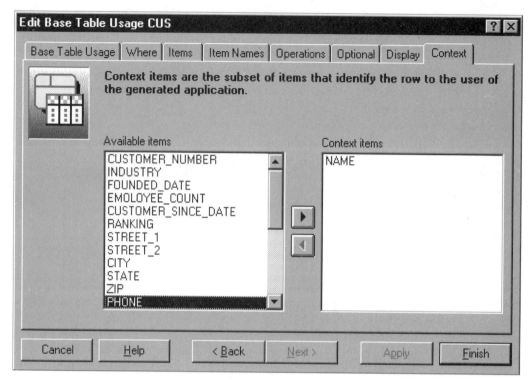

FIGURE 22.19   The Context tab of the Edit Base Table Usage dialog box.

ent table usage. However, you may need to access the properties of items on an individual basis, especially for the purpose of fine-tuning those properties that control the GUI implementation of the item. The dialog box Edit Bound Item contains five property tabs, which are described briefly below:

❏ **Column.** This tab is used to maintain the name of the item, associate it with a base table column, and set the *Display* property of the item to 'Yes' or 'No.'

❏ **Operations.** On this tab you select the operations (Insert, Update, and Select) that may be performed against the item. If the module is an Oracle WebServer module, you can also indicate that the item is indexed by a policy of the Oracle ConText Cartridge. When the WebServer Generator encounters an item with the property Context set to 'Yes,' it customizes the query form of the module component so that it includes controls to specify full-text search criteria.

❏ **Definition.** This tab is used to set the data type of the item, any default values you may want to associate with the item, and whether the item is required or optional.

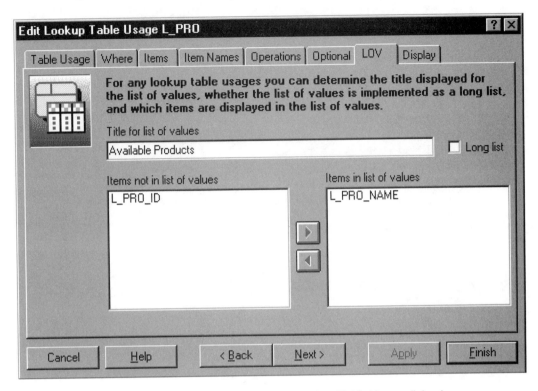

FIGURE 22.20   The LOV tab of the Edit Lookup Table Usage dialog box.

❑ **Display.** This is probably the tab you will access and modify the most, since, as the name suggests, it contains the display properties of the item. Figure 22.21 shows an example of this tab. Among the properties most frequently accessed on this tab are *Display Type,* which defines the type of GUI control that will represent the item; *Alignment*; and *Format Mask.* Closely related with the Display Type list box is the list box Show Meaning. This list box is set when the display type is a list box or radio group. Its setting defines the value used to represent the elements of the list or the radio buttons of the radio group. In the example shown in Figure 22.21, the item STATUS will be displayed as a drop-down list (also known as a popup list), and its elements will display the meaning associated with each allowed value registered against the column or the domain.

❑ **Help.** On this tab you can view and maintain the Hint property of the item, as well as help content that will be incorporated by the Microsoft Help Generator in the help files of the application.

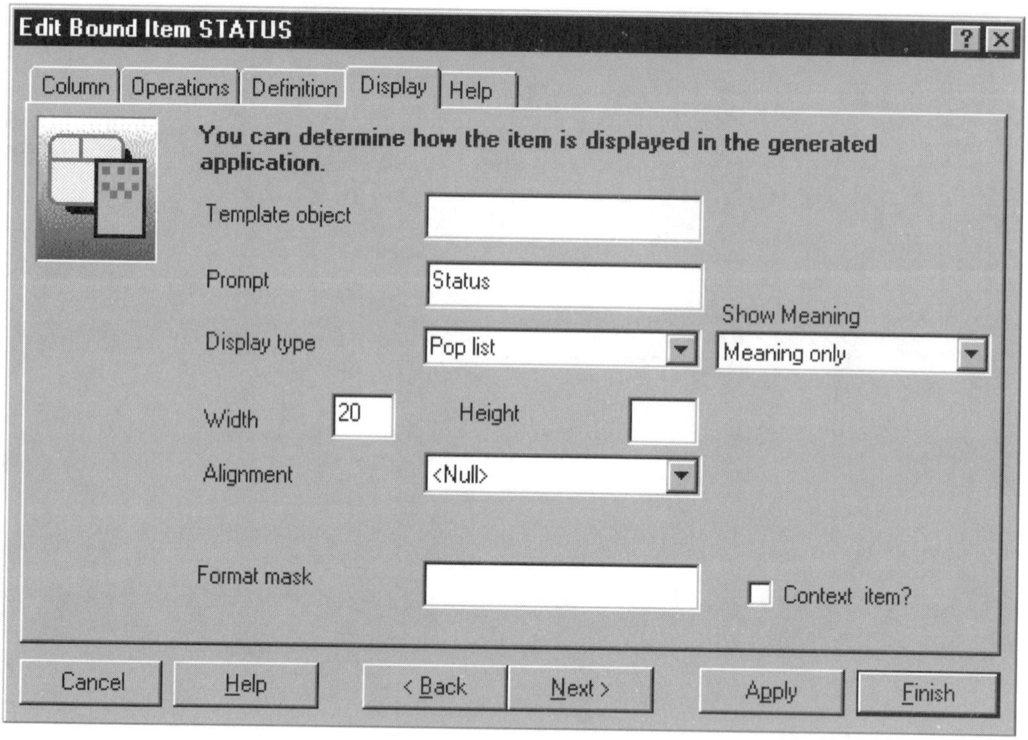

FIGURE 22.21 The Display tab of the Edit Bound Item dialog box.

22.4.6 MAINTAINING UNBOUND ITEMS

A lot of overlap exists between the bound and unbound items when it comes to the organization of their properties on the tabs. The Edit Unbound Item dialog box in fact contains the property tabs Operations, Definition, Display, and Help, which are similar in content and layout to the corresponding tabs in the Edit Bound Item dialog box. Differences exist as well, such as the fact that unbound items are not associated with any database column. Furthermore, each type of unbound item contains properties that are specific to the functionality covered by the type. The type of an unbound item is set and maintained on the Name tab, together with the name of the item. Modules implemented in different languages may contain unbound items of different types. The following paragraphs describe the types of unbound items used in Developer/2000 Forms modules and the properties associated with them.

❑ **Client Side Function.** These items derive their value from a function implemented in the front-end application. The statement that calls this function and passes the necessary arguments is added and maintained on the tab Client Side Function.

❑ **Computed.** These items derive their value from a bound item in the table usage, using one of the standard SQL group functions, like AVG, SUM, MIN, and MAX. The function and the item used to compute this value are maintained on the tab Computed.

❑ **Custom.** Custom items are implemented as push buttons or menu items in the generated Developer/2000 Forms module. You can enter and edit the application logic that is associated with these items on the Custom tab.

❑ **SQL Expression.** An unbound item of this type derives its value from the SQL expression defined on the tab with the same name. This expression may use values from one or more bound items and one or more scalar SQL functions. The difference between a SQL Expression unbound item and a computed one resides in the type of SQL functions used to derive the values (scalar versus group). When you create an unbound item, its type is by default SQL Expression. Figure 22.22 shows an example of such an item that

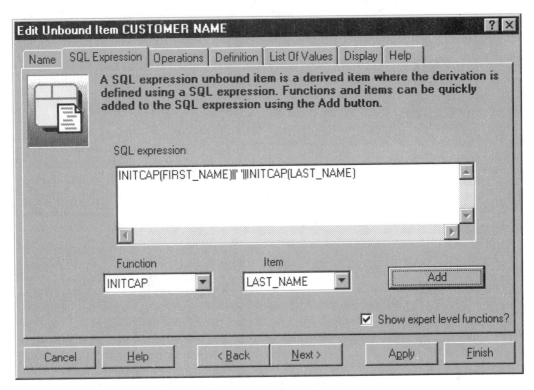

FIGURE 22.22   The SQL Expression tab of the Edit Unbound Item dialog box.

displays the name of the customer in a friendly format. Notice at the bottom of this tab a feature that is available on other tabs as well. The list box Function allows you to select the function you want to use, and the list item contains all the bound items in the current table usage. When you set these lists, you can click Add to paste the usage of the function in the text box SQL expression, thus saving yourself some typing efforts.

❑ **Server Side Implementation.** Items of this type derive their value from a PL/SQL function stored in the database server. You can maintain the name and arguments passed to this function on the tab Sever Side Implementation.

Action items are a special case of unbound items that allow you to navigate to different module components within the module or to a different module, as well as to perform any user-defined action. These items are ultimately implemented as buttons; therefore their properties that require customization are very limited. Besides the properties Name and Prompt, for navigation action items, you may need to maintain the target of their navigation. The property tab Navigation serves this purpose. As you can see from the example shown in Figure 22.23, all you need to do to set the target of the navigation is to select an object from the list of candidates and click Apply.

22.4.7 MAINTAINING ITEM GROUPS

As I explained earlier, you can create and view item groups only if the module diagram is in display mode. To bring up the dialog box of the properties for an item group, double-click the item group in the diagram or in the Design Navigator. The Edit Item Group dialog box is composed of two tabs. The first one, called Name maintains the name and prompt of the item group. The most important property on this tab is Stacked. Recall that in Developer/2000 Forms and Visual Basic, stacked item groups implement tabbed dialog boxes in the generated module.

The members of the item group are maintained on the Items tab of the Edit Item Group dialog, shown in Figure 22.24. On this tab you can add or remove items from a group and arrange their display sequence within the group.

22.4.8 MAINTAINING WINDOWS

The number of properties of a window object are very limited, and they are grouped in two tabs of the Edit Window dialog box. The property you would edit the most on the tab Name is Window Title. As part of your goal to create user-friendly applications, carefully set the title of each window to reflect the functionality of the module components that the window contains.

The second property tab, Size, sets the position and size of the window object in the generated module. For each module and possibly across all the mod-

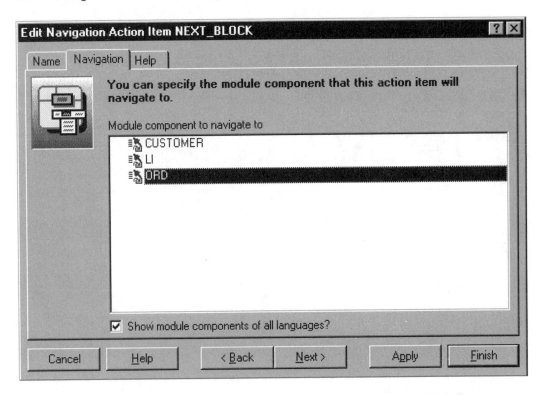

FIGURE 22.23   The Navigation tab of the Edit Navigation Action Item dialog
box.

ules, try to minimize the variance in the dimensions of the window objects. Furthermore, if a module contains multiple windows, set the X-Position and Y-Position of these properties in such a way that when the windows are opened initially, they are cascaded. To achieve this effect, you may set these properties to multiples of a certain number for the window objects of the module. If, for example, your module contains three windows, then the coordinates of the first window could be (0, 0), those of the second window (3, 3), and those of the last window (6, 6). Figure 22.25 shows an example of the Size tab of the Edit Window dialog box.

22.5 MODULE WIZARDS

The previous sections of this chapter described the different elements that form the architecture of a module and provided information about how you can set and maintain their properties in the Design Editor. From the information pre-

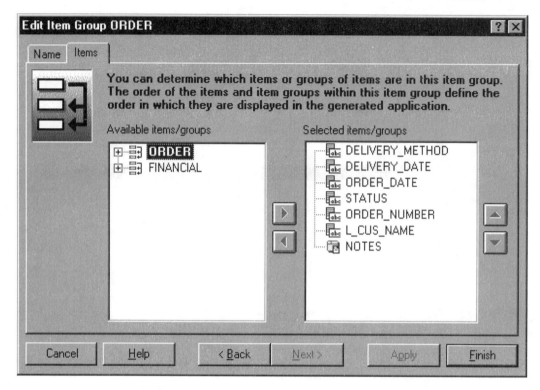

FIGURE 22.24   The Items tab of the Edit Item Group dialog box.

sented there, you can easily identify the following steps required to add a new component to your module:

1. Create and set the properties of the module component.
2. Add the table usages (base and lookup) to the module component.
3. Set the properties of items within the module component.
4. Define the layout and visual attributes of the module objects.

These steps may be performed by accessing the properties of the module elements in the dialog boxes and property tabs discussed in Section 22.4. Given the number of dialog boxes and tabs involved, clearly some guidance through the process is required. As in similar situations, the Design Editor provides tools and utilities that you can use to simplify and streamline the creation of new module components. These tools are:

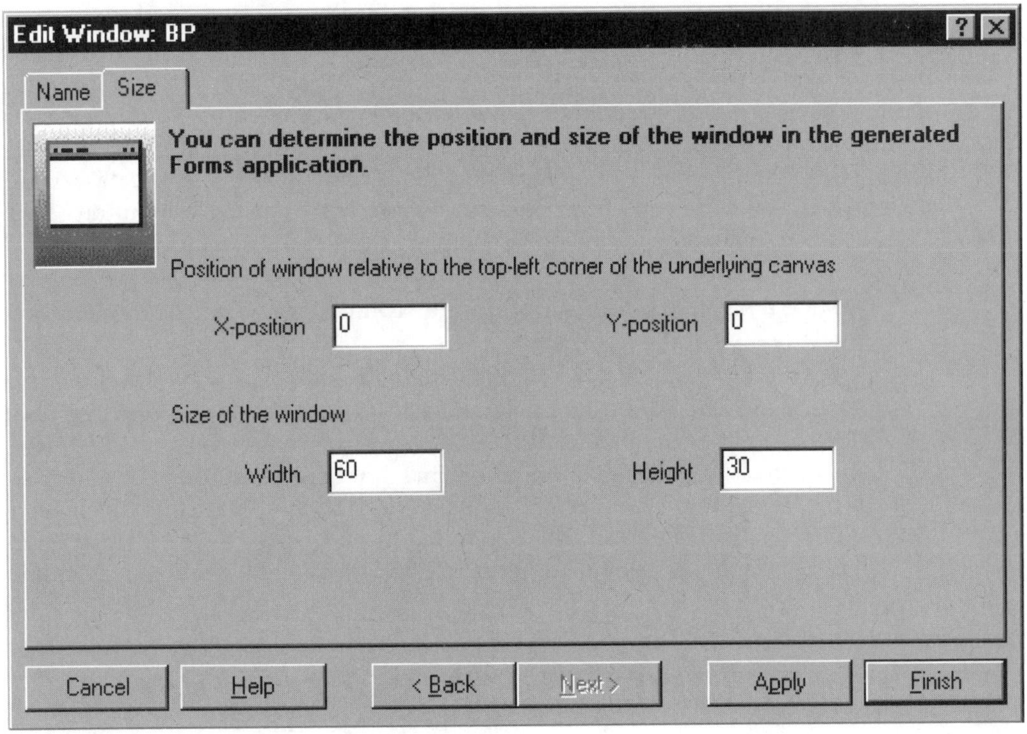

Edit Window: BP ? X

Name | Size

You can determine the position and size of the window in the generated Forms application.

Position of window relative to the top-left corner of the underlying canvas

X-position |0| Y-position |0|

Size of the window

Width |60| Height |30|

Cancel | Help | < Back | Next > | Apply | Finish

FIGURE 22.25 The Size tab of the Edit Window dialog box.

- ❏ **Module Component Data Wizard.** This tool provides a road map for the process of creating table usages and bound items of a module component.
- ❏ **Module Component Display Wizard.** You can use this Wizard to define the interface layout of the module components.
- ❏ **Chart Wizard.** This is a utility that walks you through the steps of creating a Developer/2000 Graphics chart.

The following sections will highlight the functionality of each of these wizards.

22.5.1 THE MODULE COMPONENT DATA WIZARD

This wizard combines together steps from the process of creating module components, table usages, and bound items into one activity that allows you to create a new module component and populate it with the necessary data elements. To invoke it from anywhere in the Design Editor, select Tools | Module Component Data Wizard. If the context of the Editor is a module, the Wizard will create a module component for that particular module; otherwise, the Wizard will create a reusable module component. The following is a list of steps you can follow to create a module component with the Module Component Data Wizard. Each of these steps is implemented as a separate tab in the Module Component Data Wizard dialog box. You can move from one step to another by using the buttons Back and Next and, when you are ready to complete the activity, click Finish.

1. Provide a name and title for the module component; select the implementation language of this component.
2. Select the table object that will become the base table usage of the module component. The tab on which you select the table has a useful feature that allows you to create lookup table usages together with the base table usage. The control Lookup table usages on this tab displays all the tables defined in the Repository that reference the table selected in the list box Base table usage. You can expand each node in the list to display the tables that reference the table, as shown in Figure 22.26. To include a table as a lookup

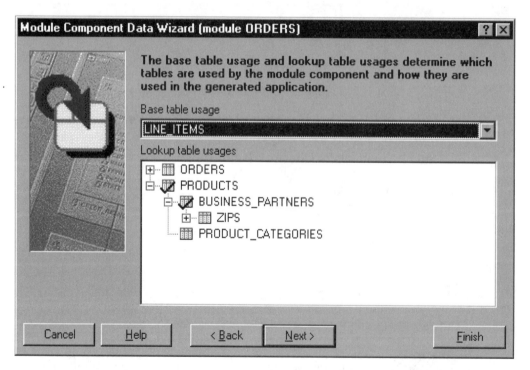

FIGURE 22.26   The Table Usage tab of the Module Component Data Wizard.

usage, click the icon associated with the table name to place a check mark across this icon.

The advantage that this tab provides is that it allows you to define nested lookup table usages. For example, with the settings of Figure 22.26, the module component will contain the base table usage LINE_ITEMS, the lookup table usage PRODUCTS that complements ORDERS, and the lookup table usage BUSINESS_PARTNERS that complements PRODUCTS. Such a combination of table usages may be useful if you want to display the name of the product and its manufacturer for each line item in an order.

3. Define the operations that users will be allowed to perform on the base table of the module component.

4. Select the columns that will be included in the base table usage. Mark those items that you want to display to the users and arrange the display order of the items.

5. Accept the default names of the items derived from the corresponding column names or provide new names.

6. Specify whether users will be able to insert, update, or query the items included in the base table usages.

7. Define which items will be optional and which ones will be mandatory in the generated module.

8. Click Finish to complete the process.

22.5.2   THE MODULE COMPONENT DISPLAY WIZARD

Whereas the Module Component Data Wizard helps you define the data elements that will become part of a module component, the Module Component Display Wizard is a power tool used to enhance the layout of the component. You can invoke this Wizard by selecting a module component and then choosing Tools | Module Component Display Wizard. The dialog box that appears is composed of property tabs that correspond to the steps you may take to define layout and visual properties of the module component using this Wizard. These steps are listed below:

1. On the Display tab, set the number of rows displayed by the module component and the overflow style of its data items.

2. On the tab Displayed Items, maintain the list of the displayed items and their order.

3. On the tab Item Details, maintain the prompt and display type of each item. To view properties of the database column upon which an item is based, select this item and click the button Column Details. The dialog box that appears displays properties such as Column Name, Datatype, and Length.

4. On the tab Item Groups, maintain item group properties like Name, Prompt, and Stacked. You can also create a new item group on this tab.

5. On the tab Items and Groups, maintain membership properties of items in items groups. Figure 22.27 shows an example of this tab. The icons ▲ and ▼ on this tab are used to move items in and out of groups, to arrange the order of items within a group, and to arrange the order of items and item groups in the layout of the module component.

6. On the tab Context, identify the items that define the business context of the data items.

7. Click Finish to complete the process.

22.5.3 THE CHART WIZARD

The Chart Wizard allows you to create module components whose implementation language is Developer/2000 Graphics. Like the other wizards discussed in the previous two sections, this wizard combines property tabs from different edit

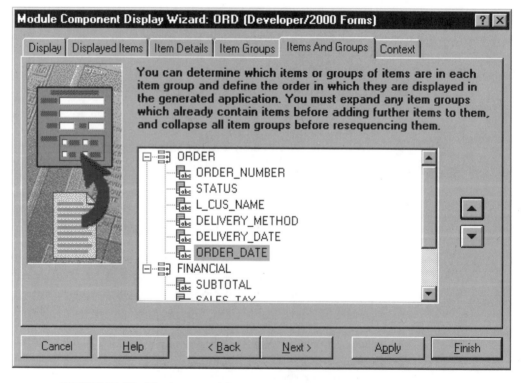

FIGURE 22.27   The Items and Groups tab of the Module Component Display Wizard.

If the component is a specific component for a given module, you need to specify the name of the container module component and the chart item; whether this item will appear in an existing module window or in a window of its own; and whether you want to create a new chart from scratch, create a new chart that shares data with other module components, or incorporate a reusable chart component.

dialog boxes into one sequence of steps that facilitates the process of creating chart module components. The steps through which the Chart Wizard guides you are as follows:

1. Define the name of the new module component. Specify whether the component is a reusable component or attached to a specific module.
2. Select the base table and any lookup tables that will be required by the chart. The property tab that allows you to select the table usages is the same as the one discussed in Section 22.5.1 and shown in Figure 22.26.
3. Select the columns from the base and lookup tables that will be used by the chart.
4. Create any unbound items the chart will need to display the data.
5. Select the chart style.
6. Click Finish to complete the process.

22.6 REUSABLE COMPONENTS

In many areas of the economy, assembling existing objects or components into higher-level objects or products is typical. In recent years this concept has found wide acceptance in software engineering as well. The component-based development paradigm essentially means building application systems by assembling reusable components. The popularity of ActiveX and COM on one hand and JavaBeans and CORBA technologies on the other has pushed the component-based development into the mainstream. The Gartner Group recently predicted with 0.7 probability that by the end of 1999, component software will be the dominant method of new application development.

While software component technologies focus on the development and reuse of software, a higher level of thinking of components is to come up with reusable design objects—encapsulations of data structures and software module layouts that can be reused over and over in new applications. The reusable module components are the technology provided by Designer/2000 to allow you to componentize important design concepts in such a way that you can easily reuse them in different modules. You have two ways to create a reusable module component in the Design Editor:

❑ Use the Module Component Data Wizard. Make sure that the context is not a module when you invoke the tool.

❑ In the Design Navigator, switch to the tab Modules, select the node Reusable Module Components, and click the icon Create 🔳.

Reusable module components and specific components are no different as far as the way the properties are set and the elements included in them. What sets apart these two types of modules is the property *Module Component Type*, which is set to *'Re-usable'* or *'Specific.'* You can access this property in the Property Palette of a module component. In order to include a reusable component in an existing module, you can take one of the following actions:

❑ In the Design Navigator, drag the reusable module component and drop it on the module where you want to add it.

❑ If the module is shown already in the Data Diagrammer, click the icon Include Reusable Component 🔳, and click the module in the diagram. From the list of reusable module components defined in the repository, select the component you want to add and click OK.

The properties of reusable module components included in a particular module cannot be modified. Technically speaking, these components are read-only references of the source component in the body of the module. So if you have included the same reusable module component in multiple modules, you need to modify and maintain the properties in only one place. The reference mechanism implemented by Designer/2000 will ensure that the properties are propagated at each instance. Thus, reusable module components extend the inheritance concept of object-oriented programming into the design world.

In order to break the link between a reusable module component and its use in a module, you need to switch the property *Module Component Type* from *'Re-usable'* to *'Specific.'* To be able to do so, the reusable component must be used by only one module. When the property setting is modified, the component becomes an element of the module. Conversely, you can promote any specific module component to a reusable component by setting the property *Module Component Type* to *'Re-usable.'*

As I explained earlier in the chapter, the data diagram of a module is very helpful for understanding and visualizing the elements and layout of modules.

The Design Editor allows you to display reusable module components in module diagrams although these components do not represent complete modules. To display a reusable component in the Module Diagrammer, select it in the Design Editor and issue one of the following commands:

❑ Select Tools | Reusable Component Graphical Editor.
❑ Right-click the component and select the item Show On Diagram from the popup menu that appears.

The Diagrammer window for a reusable module component is the same as the Diagrammer for regular modules in all aspects, except that it lacks all the tools that are meaningful for modules but not for reusable components, such as the ability to create new module components or windows.

22.7 SUMMARY

The Design Editor is the environment in which you perform all the activities related to the creation, maintenance, and design of the modules in your application system. This chapter discusses how to use this Editor to perform a number of activities related to modules. The major topics of the chapter include:

❑ **Modules in Designer/2000**
  ❑ Types of Modules
  ❑ Populating the Repository with Modules
❑ **Structure of Modules**
  ❑ The Data View of a Module
  ❑ The Display View of a Module
  ❑ Module Application Logic
❑ **Working with Modules**
  ❑ The Module Application Guide
  ❑ Creating and Maintaining Modules
  ❑ Maintaining Help Contents
  ❑ Creating and Maintaining Module Associations
  ❑ Maintaining Module Arguments
  ❑ Copying Modules
  ❑ Developer/2000 Module Security
❑ **Creating and Maintaining Module Elements**
  ❑ Displaying Modules in Diagrams
  ❑ Creating Module Elements
  ❑ Maintaining Module Components
  ❑ Maintaining Table Usages

❑ Maintaining Bound Items
❑ Maintaining Unbound Items
❑ Maintaining Item Groups
❑ Maintaining Windows

❑ **Module Wizards**
  ❑ The Module Component Data Wizard
  ❑ The Module Component Display Wizard
  ❑ The Chart Wizard

❑ **Reusable Components**

Chapter 23

PL/SQL IN DESIGNER/2000

♦ Overview of PL/SQL

♦ Procedural Constructs of PL/SQL

♦ Data Types and Variables

♦ Cursors in PL/SQL

♦ PL/SQL Program Units

♦ Exception Handling

♦ Summary

PL/SQL is the Oracle Corporation's procedural language (PL) that extends the Structured Query Language (SQL) with procedural capabilities such as program units, loops, and conditional statements. If your applications are being developed using Oracle's development tools, such as Developer/2000 Forms, Developer/2000 Reports, and WebServer, PL/SQL is the main programming language you will use to implement the business logic. However, even if the applications will be developed using other tools, such as Visual Basic, the business logic implemented in the Oracle Server will be programmed in PL/SQL.

Designer/2000 allows you to define software modules that will be implemented in the form of PL/SQL program units stored in the database server. These software modules include packages, functions, procedures, and database triggers. Designer/2000 also allows you to associate PL/SQL application logic with front-end modules. This chapter offers an overview of the major features and constructs of PL/SQL that you will encounter in your work with Designer/2000 tools.

23.1 OVERVIEW OF PL/SQL

In the following four sections I present a brief history of the PL/SQL language, an overview of the functionality of the PL/SQL engine in the Developer/2000 Forms and the Oracle Server, the major structural components of PL/SQL blocks, and the most important manipulation statements used in PL/SQL Blocks.

23.1.1 BRIEF HISTORY OF THE PL/SQL LANGUAGE

The major innovation of SQL as a programming language is its simple syntax, which allows users to focus on the data they need without worrying about how to access the data or how to process them after they are retrieved from the database. However, by design, SQL lacks features of other programming languages such as language control structures, subroutines, arguments, and so on. From the early days of relational databases, the fact became clear that the advantages of SQL as a result-oriented language would be increased by incorporating these features into extensions to the language.

A solution offered initially was to open up existing procedural languages such as C, COBOL, FORTRAN, and others to syntactic structures of SQL. This marked the birth of embedded SQL and pre-compilers. Early development tools, such as SQL*Forms V2, used a rudimentary scripting language, which was tedious to program and did not support much functionality. The increasing needs of data processing systems could be met only with a full-fledged programming language that would combine all the benefits of procedural languages with the non-procedural characteristics of the SQL language.

The response of Oracle Corporation to this need was PL/SQL (Procedural Language/Structured Query Language). Its first version was introduced in 1990 with Oracle products such as SQL*Forms Version 3.0 and Oracle RDBMS Version 6.0. Every subsequent release of these products included enhanced versions of PL/SQL. A series of development tools, such as Developer/2000 Forms, Graphics, Reports, and Procedure Builder, are built with PL/SQL engines embedded in them. The Oracle7 Server with Procedural Option contains its own PL/SQL engine to process and execute programming constructs stored in the database server.

The fact that PL/SQL is a language shared by the Oracle database server and all the tools in the Developer/2000 suite, including Developer/2000 Forms, Reports, and Graphics, has several advantages. First, mastering programming in PL/SQL in any of these environments enables you to become proficient in all the other areas of systems development where PL/SQL is used. Second, the sharing of code between the database server and the front-end tools becomes a trivial task. The same PL/SQL procedure can be called from a form, report, or graphic. It can also be stored in the database and be used by other front-end development tools. Finally, the application code can be tuned and distributed easily between client and server to maximize performance.

23.1.2 FUNCTIONALITY OF PL/SQL ENGINES

Despite the differences in the implementation of PL/SQL in the development tools and the database server, the PL/SQL engines contain similar functionality. Figure 23.1 presents graphically the workflow of the PL/SQL engine in one of the front-end development tools, such as Developer/2000 Forms.

This engine breaks up objects that contain PL/SQL code, such as triggers, functions, and procedures, into smaller units called PL/SQL blocks. Each of these PL/SQL blocks is processed separately. Its statements are divided into three major categories. Procedural statements such as IF ... ELSE, or LOOP statements, are handled internally by the Procedural Statement Executor. SQL statements such as SELECT, INSERT, UPDATE, and DELETE statements are stripped out and sent to the Oracle Server's SQL Statements Executor. Any calls to functions and procedures stored in database structures, also known as stored program units, are sent to the PL/SQL engine of the Oracle Server.

The PL/SQL engine in the Oracle Server proceeds in a similar fashion. Its functionality is presented in Figure 23.2.

If the database server receives a call for one of its stored program units, the called object is retrieved and handed out for processing to the PL/SQL engine. Like its counterpart in Developer/2000 Forms, this engine breaks up the stored unit into PL/SQL blocks, which then are processed individually. For each block, procedural statements are separated from SQL statements. The former are sent to the Procedural Statement Executor, the latter to the SQL Statement Executor. SQL statements from Developer/2000 Forms pass through this engine as well.

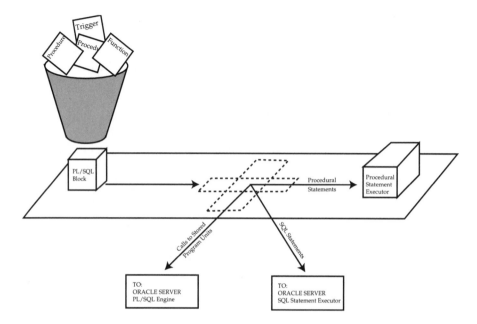

FIGURE 23.1   A graphical representation of the PL/SQL engine in Developer/2000 Forms.

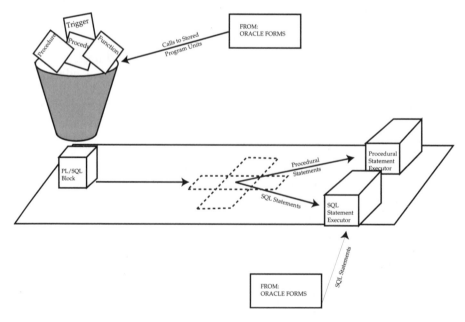

FIGURE 23.2   A graphical representation of the PL/SQL engine in Oracle Server.

23.1.3 STRUCTURAL ELEMENTS OF PL/SQL BLOCKS

As the discussion in the previous paragraph showed, no matter how complicated a PL/SQL program unit is, it is ultimately broken up into units of code called PL/SQL blocks. Figure 23.3 represents a typical PL/SQL block used in Developer/2000 Forms applications.

Following the SQL language conventions, each statement in a PL/SQL block must be terminated by a semicolon (;). The statement may be on one line or span multiple lines. The PL/SQL parser will process all the lines up to the semicolon as one statement. Multiple statements can reside on one line as well.

A PL/SQL block may have up to three distinct sections: declaration, execution, and exception. The declaration section begins with the keyword DECLARE. Variables that will be used in the block are declared and initialized here. Con-

```
DECLARE
   f_name VARCHAR2(30);
   l_name VARCHAR2(30);
BEGIN
   SELECT first_name, last_name
   INTO f_name, l_name
   FROM customers
   WHERE customer_number = :ORD.CUSTOMER_NUMBER;

   IF (f_name IS NULL) AND (l_name IS NULL) THEN
      :ORD.CUSTOMER_NAME := 'Missing Name';
   ELSE
      f_name := UPPER(f_name);
      l_name := UPPER(l_name);
      :ORD.CUSTOMER_NAME := f_name ||' '||l_name;
   END IF;
EXCEPTION
   WHEN TOO_MANY_ROWS THEN
      MESSAGE('Duplicate customer records.');
      RAISE FORM_TRIGGER_FAILURE;
   WHEN OTHERS THEN
      MESSAGE('Error retrieving Customer Name.');
      RAISE FORM_TRIGGER_FAILURE;
END;
```

FIGURE 23.3 A typical PL/SQL block used in Developer/2000 Forms applications.

stants and other PL/SQL constructs such as cursors and user-defined exceptions are defined in this section as well.

The execution section contains statements that perform the core functionality of the PL/SQL block. Here is where all the data are selected and manipulated. In general, the execution section is preceded by the declaration section and followed by the exception section. The keyword BEGIN separates the declaration section from the execution section, as shown in Figure 23.3.

The exception section protects the application from unexpected events or failures. In the example presented in Figure 23.3, the SELECT statement retrieves the first name and last name of the customers based on the CUSTOMER_ID stored in the ORD block. Many things can go wrong during the execution of this statement. In the example of Figure 23.3, you explicitly handle the situation where the query returns no records. If any other error occurs, a generic message is displayed. The exception section is optional, but I strongly suggest it. The keyword EXCEPTION marks the beginning of this section. The keyword END marks the end of the PL/SQL block. The keywords BEGIN and END must always be in matching pairs.

In every application development environment, documenting the code is important. A program unit that is well documented is much easier to maintain or modify without adversely affecting the rest of the application. PL/SQL allows you to write comments on one line or across multiple lines. The symbol '—'comments out everything until the end of the line. The symbols '/* ... */' comment out everything enclosed between them, even if it spans several lines.

23.1.4 MANIPULATING DATA IN PL/SQL BLOCKS

Data in PL/SQL blocks can be selected and manipulated using the following SQL language statements: SELECT, INSERT, UPDATE, DELETE, COMMIT, and ROLLBACK. These are also the only SQL commands that can be used in a PL/SQL block. DDL statements such as CREATE and DROP or DCL statements such as GRANT and REVOKE cannot be used directly.

Structurally, SELECT statements in PL/SQL are similar to their counterparts in the SQL language. They may contain clauses like SELECT, FROM, WHERE, GROUP BY, and ORDER BY. A new clause that is always required for PL/SQL SELECT statements is the INTO clause, which follows immediately the SELECT clause. The reason for this clause is simple and reflects one of the main reasons for the existence of PL/SQL as a supplement of SQL. SQL is an interactive language. You type a statement at the command prompt and wait to see the results on the screen. You have no need to redirect the data, except probably to a spooled file. PL/SQL, though, being a procedural language, aims at not just displaying the data, but also processing the information and making decisions based on its content. This task is greatly facilitated if data retrieved from the database is stored in memory locations that can be easily accessed and manipulated. These memory locations are represented by PL/SQL variables, and the redirection is done by the INTO clause.

The PL/SQL block shown in Figure 23.3 contains the example of a SELECT statement in a PL/SQL program. This example shows that for each column or expression in the SELECT clause, a PL/SQL variable must be in the INTO clause to store the value returned from the SELECT statement.

In general, the SELECT statement may return zero, one, or more rows from the database. In SQL, this behavior does not cause any problems. However, in PL/SQL, queries must be tailored so that they return one record, at most. The normal outcome of a SELECT statement in PL/SQL is to return only one row. If the query retrieves no rows, the exception NO_DATA_FOUND is raised; if more than one row is returned, the exception TOO_MANY_ROWS is raised.

Little difference exists between SQL INSERT, UPDATE, and DELETE statements and their counterparts in PL/SQL blocks. The only novelty is that PL/SQL variables can be used to supply the values and expressions required by each statement. An example will be provided for each statement.

The following PL/SQL statement inserts a record into the table PRODUCTS.

```
INSERT INTO products(id, name, descr)
VALUES (vn_prod_id, vc_prod_name, vc_prod_descr);
```

The fact that the SELECT ... INTO statement should raise an exception if more than one row is found is an ANSI standard. To conform with this standard, whenever the first row of a query is returned, the PL/SQL engine makes another trip to the database to see whether the query returned more rows. If not, everything is fine; otherwise, the TOO_MANY_ROWS exception is raised. In any event, the second trip is superfluous. In the best case, it returns little needed information (additional records are returned by the query but not retrieved by the PL/SQL engine); in the worst case, it is a waste of computing time and resources (the extra trip to the database just to find out that the row you have already is the only one retrieved by the query). To remedy this behavior of the SELECT ... INTO statement, PL/SQL cursors are used. Section 23.4 discusses the structure and functionality of PL/SQL cursors.

The following statement updates the description of a record in PRODUCTS:

```
UPDATE products
SET descr= vc_new_prod_descr
WHERE id = vn_prod_id;
```

The following statement deletes the record from the table PRODUCTS:

```
DELETE FROM products
WHERE id = vc_prod_id;
```

23.2 PROCEDURAL CONSTRUCTS OF PL/SQL

Procedural statements allow PL/SQL to control the flow of program execution. They include conditional branching statements such as the IF ... ELSE clause, loop statements such as LOOP, WHILE, or FOR clause, and the unconditional branching statement GOTO.

23.2.1 IF STATEMENT

The simplest form of this statement is shown here:

```
IF <condition> THEN
  <PL/SQL statements>;
ELSE
  <PL/SQL statements>;
END IF;
```

When this statement is executed, the logical condition <condition> between the keywords IF and THEN is first evaluated. If its value is TRUE, then the statements in the IF clause are executed. If it is FALSE or UNKNOWN, then statements in the ELSE clause are executed. The ELSE clause is not required, and it can be omitted if no action should be taken when the condition is not fulfilled. Multiple IF statements can be nested inside each clause. A typical nested IF statement follows:

```
IF <condition> THEN
  <PL/SQL statements>;
  IF <condition> THEN
    <PL/SQL statements>;
  END IF;
ELSE
  <PL/SQL statements>;
END IF;
```

When the condition may have more than just a TRUE/FALSE outcome, the IF ... ELSE statements can be nested. The following template can be used to check for a three-values condition:

```
IF <condition> THEN
  <PL/SQL statements>;
ELSE
  IF <condition> THEN
    <PL/SQL statements>;
  ELSE
    <PL/SQL statements>;
  END IF;
END IF;
```

This representation can be tedious and difficult to understand, especially when multiple conditions are evaluated. To simplify this situation, PL/SQL allows the use of the ELSIF keyword. Now the previous construct is simplified as follows:

```
IF <condition> THEN
  <PL/SQL statements>;
ELSIF condition THEN
  <PL/SQL statements>;
ELSE
  <PL/SQL statements>;
END IF;
```

Multiple ELSIF clauses can be specified if necessary. However, only one ELSE clause and only one END IF statement are needed.

23.2.2 LOOPING STATEMENTS

Loops perform actions repetitively. The iteration they control continues until a certain condition evaluates to TRUE, or while a certain condition holds TRUE, or a specific number of times. Based on these three different situations, you can distinguish three types of loops.

The first type repeats the loop statements until the exit condition evaluates to TRUE. Its general syntax is:

```
LOOP
  <PL/SQL statements>;
  EXIT WHEN <condition>;
END LOOP;
```

The PL/SQL statements within this loop are executed at least once. If the exit condition evaluates to FALSE or NULL, the loop will repeat its iteration. Only when the exit condition evaluates to TRUE, the loop stops and control is passed to the rest of the statements outside the loop.

The second type of loop executes the statements only if and while the entry loop condition is TRUE. Its general syntax is:

```
WHILE <condition> LOOP
  <PL/SQL statements>;
END LOOP;
```

In this loop, the PL/SQL statements may be executed zero or more times. The execution will occur only if the loop entry condition evaluates to TRUE and stops as soon as the condition evaluates to FALSE or NULL.

The third type of loop is used when the iterations will be performed a certain number of times. Its general syntax is:

```
FOR <counter> IN <lower_bound>..<upper_bound> LOOP
  <PL/SQL statements>;
END LOOP;
```

The loop counter is declared internally as an integer, meaning that you do not need to declare it explicitly. The value of the counter can be assigned to other variables inside the loop. However, because the counter is maintained internally, you cannot assign a value to it or change its existing value. Therefore, the counter will faithfully increment by one unit, starting from the lower bound of its range values all the way up to the upper bound.

The implicit handling of the loop counter by the PL/SQL engine protects the loop from accidentally becoming an infinite loop. You do not have to worry about incrementing the loop counter in each iteration. PL/SQL will make sure that the loop executes exactly the number of times allowed by its range.

23.2.3 UNCONDITIONAL BRANCHING

For backward compatibility and traditional reasons, more than for its usefulness, PL/SQL continues to support unconditional jumps to labels in the code using the command GOTO. This command does not provide any functionality that is not already implemented better and more elegantly by other constructs. Therefore, I will not discuss it to any extent.

23.3 DATA TYPES AND VARIABLES

Like any other programming language, PL/SQL uses variables as placeholders of information needed by program units. The data stored in variables are transient in nature. They exist as long as the scope of the execution remains within the block in which the variables are declared, but are wiped out of memory as soon as the execution of the program moves out of the block. This section will discuss how to declare and use variables in PL/SQL programs.

23.3.1 PL/SQL DATA TYPES

An important characteristic of variables is their data type. PL/SQL comes with a large number of predefined data types, which can be grouped in three categories: scalar, composite, and reference data types. Scalar data types allow you to manipulate numeric, alphanumeric, date, and Boolean variables. The first release of PL/SQL provided support only for a limited number of scalar data types, such as NUMBER, CHAR, VARCHAR2, DATE, and BOOLEAN. The next major upgrade of the language (version 2.0) introduced a number of new data types, such as BINARY_INTEGER, and PLS_INTEGER. In addition, it extended the language to include two composite data types, RECORD and TABLE, whose behavior and functionality are similar to structures and arrays in C or PASCAL. Version 2.3 of the language, released with Oracle7 Server version 7.3, introduced in PL/SQL the concept of pointers through the first reference data type, REF CURSOR.

The data types in PL/SQL can also be classified into base types and subtypes. All the data types mentioned above are base types. Subtypes derive their properties from a base data type, but add a restriction to the base type. For example, NATURAL is a predefined PL/SQL subtype whose base type is BINARY_INTEGER. NATURAL variables allow you to manipulate only nonnegative BINARY_INTEGER values. In addition to predefined subtypes, PL/SQL allows you to define your own subtype data types. The following statement defines a new subtype based on the scalar base type NATURAL:

```
DECLARE
   SUBTYPE LoopCounter IS NATURAL;
   k LoopCounter;
BEGIN
   ...
END;
```

The following statement defines a new data type as a VARCHAR2 base type that can hold up to 240 bytes of data:

```
DECLARE
   vc_descr                 VARCHAR2(240);
   SUBTYPE Description IS vc_descr%TYPE;
   product_description  Description;
BEGIN
   ...
END;
```

23.3.2 PL/SQL VARIABLES

As I mentioned above, variables are declared in the declaration section of a PL/SQL block. Each variable must be assigned a data type upon declaration. At the same time, an initial value may be assigned to the variable. If the variable is not initialized explicitly, PL/SQL initializes it to NULL, which represents the absence of data. The following statements represent several examples of declaring and initializing scalar data type variables:

```
DECLARE
   vn_prod_id     PLS_INTEGER;
   vc_prod_descr  VARCHAR2(240);
   vn_score       NUMBER := 0;
   vn_revenue     NUMBER(8,2) NOT NULL := 0.0;
   vb_discount    BOOLEAN DEFAULT TRUE;
BEGIN
   ...
END;
```

From the statements above, two remarks can be made about the declaration and initialization of variables. First, to assign an initial value to a variable, you can use the standard assignment operator ':=' or the keyword DEFAULT. Note, however, that this place is the only one in a PL/SQL program where DEFAULT can be used to assign a value to a variable. Second, you can declare a variable to be a required one in the program by specifying the keywords NOT NULL after the data type. A required variable must always be initialized.

Another way to specify the data type of a variable is to reference the %TYPE attribute of another variable that is already defined. In the following example, the first line defines a variable named `price`. The second line then defines a second variable, `discount_price` of the same type as `price`.

```
DECLARE
  price            NUMBER;
  discount_price price%TYPE;
BEGIN
  ...
END;
```

This type definition has a clear advantage. If the definition of `price` changes in the future, the change will automatically propagate to the variable `discount_price`, or any other variable defined based on the type of `price`. You do not have to change the type definition of the derived variables. The technique is especially useful when variables are declared based on the data type of a table column in the database. In the following example, both `price` and `discount_price` are declared using the definition of the column MSRP in the table PRODUCTS.

```
DECLARE
  price            PRODUCTS.MSRP%TYPE;
  discount_price PRODUCTS.MSRP%TYPE;
BEGIN
  ...
END;
```

Defining the data type of variables as shown here assures that the database structure will always be synchronized with the application code. If the requirements change in the future, the only place where you need to change the type definition is the database. The application will automatically reflect the change.

23.3.3 PL/SQL CONSTANTS

Variables can be assigned values throughout the life of the PL/SQL program. Constants, on the other hand, may be assigned values only during the initialization phase. During the execution of the program unit, the constants preserve this value and cannot be assigned a different value. When you are declaring a constant, you must specify the keyword CONSTANT immediately before the data type. The following statements provide an example of how to declare and use a PL/SQL constant.

```
DECLARE
  VA_TAX                      CONSTANT NUMBER := 0.045;
                              /*Virginia state tax*/
  vn_subtotal                 NUMBER(8,2) := 100.00;
  vn_taxed_subtotal           NUMBER(8,2);
BEGIN
  vn_taxed_subtotal := vn_subtotal(1 + VA_TAX);
END;
```

23.3.4 PL/SQL RECORDS

PL/SQL records are used to create record-like data types in PL/SQL program
units. They allow you to bundle together a number of fields of different data
types. The RECORD data type extends the functionality of the attribute %ROW-
TYPE of database tables, which has existed in PL/SQL since the early versions of
the language. Records created using the %ROWTYPE attribute are bound to the
structure of the corresponding table. Their elements contain exactly the same
fields and data types as the columns in that table. Using the RECORD data type,
you are not bound to one table anymore. Columns from different tables can be
combined with non-database fields in one structure. Furthermore, records can be
nested into definitions of more complex record structures.

    In order to use records in your program units, you must first declare a user-
defined data type for the record and then declare an object of that data type. The
following statements contain examples of declaring RECORD data types:

```
DECLARE
  TYPE LocationType IS RECORD (
    region        VARCHAR2(80),
    area          VARCHAR2(80),
    name          VARCHAR2(80));

  TYPE SalesDataType IS RECORD (
    order_total   ORDERS.TOTAL_ORDER_CHARGE%TYPE := 0.0,
    industry      CUSTOMERS.INDUSTRY%TYPE,
    location      LocationType);

  city            LocationType;
  daily_sales     SalesDataType;
  daily_total     ORDERS.TOTAL_ORDER_CHARGE%TYPE;

BEGIN
  ...
END;
```

The first record type groups data used to describe a geographic location, including the region, area, and name of that location. The second record type expands the first one by adding to the location placeholders for the total revenue generated by orders from customers of a particular industry. As you can see from this example, the components of a record can be initialized upon declaration.

Structures of the RECORD data type can be referenced using the usual dot notation. The following two statements are examples of how you can assign a value to, or retrieve a value from, a field of a record. These statements use the variables defined above and could reside in the execution part of the PL/SQL block shown above.

```
city.name := 'Washington D.C.';
city.region := 'East Coast';
city.area := 'Mid-Atlantic';
daily_total := 10000.00;

daily_sales.location := city;
daily_sales.order_total := daily_total;
daily_sales.industry := 'Small Business';
```

You can also assign values to several or all fields of a record, by making them part of the INTO clause of a SELECT … INTO statement that retrieves data that match these fields. Cursors can be used as well.

23.3.5 PL/SQL TABLES

The PL/SQL data type TABLE is a composite data type that allows you to implement in PL/SQL programs functionality similar to that of arrays in other programming languages. Like arrays, PL/SQL tables are indexed by a number, in this case a number of data type BINARY_INTEGER. In addition, each indexed position in the table allows you to store and access data of another data type. The components of PL/SQL tables are often referred to as the primary key and the columns, for analogy with the terminology that describes regular tables.

The data stored in PL/SQL tables may be of scalar data type, declared using any of the base data types, pre-defined subtypes, or user-defined subtypes, as discussed earlier in the chapter. The following statements show two examples of PL/SQL tables with elements of scalar data types:

```
DECLARE
  TYPE CustNameType IS TABLE OF VARCHAR2(80) NOT NULL
  INDEX BY BINARY_INTEGER;

  TYPE ProdCategType IS TABLE OF PRODUCT_CATEGORIES.NAME%TYPE
  INDEX BY BINARY_INTEGER;

  customer_names        CustNameType;
  prod_categories       ProdCategType;
BEGIN
  ...
END;
```

The first table type `CustNameType` will store alphanumeric strings up to 80 characters long and will not allow NULL elements in the table. The second table inherits the data type properties for its element from those of the column NAME in the table PRODUCT_CATEGORIES.

PL/SQL also allows you to store in tables elements of RECORD data types. The definition of these records may be derived from database tables or specified by you in a user-defined data type. However, the components of these records must be of scalar data type. Examples of tables with elements of RECORD data types appear below:

```
DECLARE
  TYPE CustomerType IS TABLE OF CUSTOMERS%ROWTYPE
  INDEX BY BINARY_INTEGER;

  TYPE LocationType IS RECORD (
    region      VARCHAR2(80),
    area        VARCHAR2(80),
    name        VARCHAR2(80));

  TYPE LocationTableType IS TABLE OF LocationType
  INDEX BY BINARY_INTEGER;

  customers_tab  CustomerType;
  cities_tab     LocationTableType;
BEGIN
  ...
END;
```

The first table type `CustomerType` will hold records whose properties are inherited from the columns of the database table CUSTOMERS. The second table type `LocationTableType` will contain elements whose data type is determined by the user-defined record `LocationType`.

After a table is declared, its elements can be populated or accessed through the index of the table, like usual arrays. For example, to store the name `'Michelle Johnson'` in the fifth position of the table `customer_names` of data type `CustNameType` defined earlier, you would use this statement:

```
customer_names(5) := 'Michelle Johnson';
```

The index of the table can be any integer in the range of a BINARY_INDEX data type, including negative numbers. So if the name `'John Michael'` is stored in position –5 of the table `customer_names`, the following statement assigns its value to the pre-declared variable `current_customer`, which has the same data type as the element of the table.

```
current_customer := customer_names(-5);
```

The structure of the table does not enforce any bounds or cohesion between its indices. So the table can contain elements in positions –2, 5, and 155, and these can be the only three elements of it. If the program references any other table elements, the exception NO_DATA_FOUND will be raised. In order to prevent the exception from being raised, you can use the PL/SQL table method EXISTS, as in the following example:

```
IF customer_names.EXISTS(-5) THEN
  current_customer := customer_names(-5);
ELSE
  current_customer := NULL:
END IF;
```

PL/SQL defines additional methods for table objects that enhance the features and functionality of PL/SQL tables and make them truly useful data types for your program units. The methods FIRST and LAST allow you to get the index of the first and last entries in the table; the method COUNT returns the number of entries in the table; the methods NEXT and PRIOR return the index of the next or previous row in the table from a given position within the table, if they exist. In addition, the method DELETE can remove a single entry, a range of entries, or all the entries from a table.

23.4 CURSORS IN PL/SQL

When the Oracle Server receives a SQL statement for execution, it makes sure that it is a valid SQL statement and that the user issuing it has the appropriate privileges to issue that statement. If both these checks are successful, a chunk from the database server memory, called the *private SQL area,* is allocated to the statement. If this time is the first that the statement has been issued against the database, Oracle will parse the statement and store its parsed version in another memory structure, called the *shared SQL area.* The shared SQL area will also contain the plan that Oracle will follow in order to execute the statement. Finally, the statement will be executed.

This division of the information contained within the SQL statements allows Oracle to bypass the parsing phase the next time the same statement is issued. In such a case, the private SQL area for the statement is still created, but when Oracle realizes that a parsed version of the statement is present in the library cache of the shared SQL area, it proceeds directly with the execution of this parsed representation. This chain of events will hold true even if the statement is issued by a different connection in the database established by a different user of your application.

The private SQL area contains information about the statement that can be divided into two categories. The first one is static and permanently attached to the statement. This includes, for example, the table and column names that the statement affects and the binding information between them and the bind variables in the statement. The second category is dynamic, and its size changes, depending on the actual values of the bind variables when the statement is issued. This part of the private SQL area is known as *runtime area,* because it expands and shrinks in size and content as the statement is executed. If, for example, the statement is a SELECT that returns 20 rows, the runtime area will be expanded to accommodate those records. Figure 23.4 shows graphically how the SQL Statement Executor manages the SQL statements.

This figure assumes that Statement A is sent prior to Statement B. When Statement A is received, Oracle binds the value '01-SEP-94' for FOUNDED_DATE to the bind argument :1, and records the column names in the private SQL area of this statement—in its permanent part, to be exact. Then the statement is parsed and stored in the library cache in the shared SQL area. The execution plan that Oracle will follow is stored here as well. Finally the statement is sent to the RDBMS to retrieve the data. When Statement B is received, the process is similar, except that the statement is not parsed again. After binding, Statement A and Statement B are the same. Therefore, the SQL Statement Executor proceeds directly with the retrieval of data. The data returned from each query are stored in the runtime part of each statement's private SQL area.

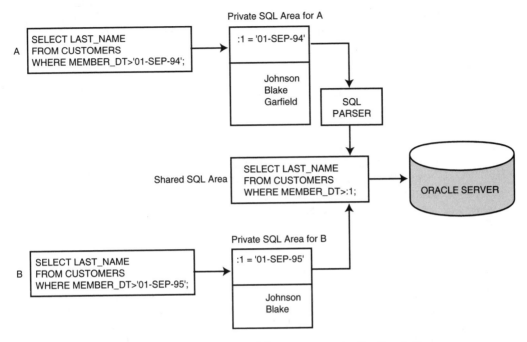

FIGURE 23.4 The execution of SQL statements by the Oracle Server.

A cursor is nothing but a name, or a *handle,* for the memory location of the private SQL area of a statement that allows you to access the information stored there from within PL/SQL blocks.

23.4.1 DECLARING EXPLICIT CURSORS

Explicit cursors are PL/SQL objects built upon SELECT statements that allow you to better manipulate records returned by queries. They can also be used to create complex queries in a more procedural fashion, and in certain instances improve the performance of the application. Cursors are declared in the DECLARE part of a PL/SQL block following the syntax:

```
CURSOR <cursor_name> IS <select_statement>;
```

The SELECT statement in a cursor declaration should not contain the INTO clause that is normally used in PL/SQL. As you will see in Section 23.4.2, the storage of the retrieved data into PL/SQL variables is done as a separate step with cursors. However, this statement defines the number and data type of the columns that each record returned by the query in the cursor's runtime area will have. The following statements contain two examples of cursor declaration:

```
DECLARE
  CURSOR c_line_items_101 IS
    SELECT LI.ORDER_NUMBER, LI.ITEM_NUMBER, LI.ITEM_TOTAL
    FROM LINE_ITEMS LI
    WHERE LI.ORDER_NUMBER = 101;

  CURSOR c_line_items (ord_num NUMBER) IS
    SELECT LI.ORDER_NUMBER, LI.ITEM_NUMBER, LI.ITEM_TOTAL
    FROM LINE_ITEMS LI
    WHERE LI.ORDER_NUMBER = ord_num;
BEGIN
  ...
END;
```

In both these examples, the runtime area will contain records with fields of the same data type as the columns ORDER_NUMBER, ITEM_NUMBER, and ITEM_TOTAL of table LINE_ITEMS. The cursor presented in the first example is not very useful because of the static nature of its SELECT statement. The cursor will contain only those records from the table LINE_ITEMS that correspond to the order with a specific value of ORDER_NUMBER. The cursor becomes really effective and usable if its SELECT statement is free of any hard-coded values, as in the second example. In this case, the cursor uses an argument in its statement much the same way a procedure or a function would use it.

23.4.2 METHODS AND ATTRIBUTES OF EXPLICIT CURSORS

Explicit cursors, being names of a particular memory location allocated to the SELECT statement, are considered a special kind of object in PL/SQL. As such, they have their attributes and methods to access and manipulate them.

After the cursor is declared, you can use the statement OPEN cursor_name to execute the query contained in the cursor, and store the records in the runtime part of the private SQL area. If the declaration of the cursor contains parameters, the value of these parameters is specified in the OPEN statement. So the statements that open the cursors shown in the previous section will be:

```
OPEN c_line_items;
OPEN c_line_items (order_num);
```

The attribute %ISOPEN keeps track of the state of the cursor. If the cursor is opened, this attribute evaluates to TRUE; otherwise, its value will be FALSE.

Since the predefined exception CURSOR_ALREADY_OPEN will be raised if the OPEN statement is issued against a cursor that is already open, checking for the state of the cursor before opening it is always a good idea.

Opening the cursor only identifies the records that the query will return. However, none of these records is returned to the calling environment until the FETCH command is issued explicitly. When the cursor is opened, a pointer is placed on the first record retrieved by the query. When the first FETCH statement is issued, this record is returned to the calling environment, and the pointer is advanced to the next record. This process will continue until all the records in the runtime area are returned. The pointer to the current record can only be advanced by one record at a time. So, for example, the second FETCH will return only the second record, if it exists. No way exists to advance the pointer so that the fifth record is returned before its predecessors, or to set it back so that the first record is returned again.

When you use the FETCH statement, you must always follow it with an INTO clause, which will place the data from the fetched record into the variables of the routine that will use them. To avoid any runtime errors, these variables must have the same data type and size as the data being fetched. One way to ensure this is to declare the data type of these variables using the %TYPE attribute of the corresponding table columns.

The number of the records fetched is stored in another attribute of the cursor, called %ROWCOUNT. Whenever the cursor is opened, this attribute is set to zero; after the first record is fetched, it is set to one; and after each FETCH operation, it is incremented by one unit. The value of this attribute can be useful if you want to retrieve only a certain number of records from the set of all the records that the cursor may contain. For example, to retrieve only the first three records, the FETCH command is issued within a loop until the %ROWCOUNT evaluates to three.

As I said earlier, the FETCH statement returns the current record of the cursor to the calling environment. But what happens if the last record is fetched and another FETCH is issued? Or when the cursor contains no records and the first FETCH is issued? To help you deal with these situations, cursors are equipped with two more attributes: %FOUND and %NOTFOUND. They are Boolean attributes that complement each other. They are both set to NULL when the cursor is opened. Then, after each FETCH, the values of these attributes are set according to the outcome of the statement. If the record was fetched successfully, %FOUND is set to TRUE and %NOTFOUND is set to FALSE. If all the records of the cursor are fetched, the next fetch will not return a valid row, %FOUND will be set to FALSE, and %NOTFOUND to TRUE.

These attributes are used as exit conditions for loops that should retrieve all the records of a cursor and stop safely after the last one is fetched. For these loops, the exit condition should be tested immediately after the FETCH statements and should follow this format:

```
EXIT WHEN cursor_name%NOTFOUND;
```

In this case, during the iteration after the one that fetches the last record, the FETCH statement will fail, thus setting the %NOTFOUND attribute to TRUE. This result causes the iteration to stop and the control of the program to jump outside the loop.

Note, however, that this exit condition relies on the cursor to contain at least one record. If the query that populates the cursor returns no records, the FETCH statement is not executed. Therefore, the attribute %NOTFOUND remains set to the original value NULL. Because the exit condition of the loop does not evaluate to TRUE, its iterations will continue forever. In order to handle the case when the cursor may not have records to fetch, you can add an additional check in the exit condition of the loop for NULL values of the attributes %FOUND and %NOT-FOUND. Two examples of using each of these attributes follow:

```
LOOP
  FETCH c_line_items INTO ord_num, li_num, li_total;
  EXIT WHEN (c_line_items%NOTFOUND
  OR c_line_items%NOTFOUND IS NULL);
  ...
END LOOP;
```

```
LOOP
  FETCH c_line_items INTO ord_num, li_num, li_total;
  IF c_line_items%FOUND
  OR c_line_items%FOUND IS NULL THEN
    ...
  ELSE
    EXIT;
  END IF;
END LOOP;
```

After the record is opened and used, you must close it to release the database resources it occupies. For this action, you issue the CLOSE statement followed by the name of the cursor to close, as in :

```
CLOSE c_line_items;
```

When you have to process some of the records from the set of all the records that are returned by a query, you must construct your code around the statements described above. In order to avoid runtime errors that may occur if the statements are not issued in the proper context, follow the steps below:

1. Declare the cursor in the DECLARE part of the PL/SQL block or program unit.

2. Open the cursor.
3. Create a loop with the appropriate EXIT condition that will scroll sequentially through the records of the cursor and process each record according to your needs.
4. Close the cursor.

Figure 23.5 shows an example of a PL/SQL block that manipulates a cursor following these steps.

23.4.3 USING THE FOR LOOP WITH EXPLICIT CURSORS

Many of the steps described in the previous section, and the possibility of mixing them up, can be avoided by using the FOR loop with the cursor. The PL/SQL block shown in Figure 23.6 contains the same functionality as the one in Figure 23.5.

No comments are needed to point out the significant gains in simplicity that this technique represents. You do not have to explicitly open the cursor, fetch the rows in variables declared previously, and close it when finished. The FOR loop will inherently open the cursor with the appropriate input variables that you

```
DECLARE
  CURSOR c_line_items (ord_number LINE_ITEMS.ORDER_NUMBER%TYPE) IS
    SELECT ORDER_NUMBER, ITEM_NUMBER, ITEM_TOTAL
    FROM LINE_ITEMS
    WHERE ORDER_NUMBER = ord_number;
  ord_num      LINE_ITEMS.ORDER_NUMBER%TYPE;
  li_num       LINE_ITEMS.ITEM_NUMBER%TYPE;
  li_total     LINE_ITEMS.ITEM_TOTAL%TYPE;
BEGIN
  OPEN c_line_items (121);
  LOOP
    FETCH c_line_items INTO ord_num, li_num, li_total;
    EXIT WHEN c_line_items%NOTFOUND
      OR c_line_items%NOTFOUND IS NULL;
      /* Processing statements go here. */
    END LOOP;
  CLOSE c_line_items;
END;
```

FIGURE 23.5   An example of correct usage of cursors.

```
DECLARE
  CURSOR c_line_items (ord_number LINE_ITEMS.ORDER_NUMBER%TYPE) IS
    SELECT ORDER_NUMBER , ITEM_NUMBER, ITEM_TOTAL
    FROM LINE_ITEMS
    WHERE ORDER_NUMBER = ord_number;
  ord_num   LINE_ITEMS.ORDER_NUMBER%TYPE;
  li_num    LINE_ITEMS.ITEM_NUMBER%TYPE;
  li_total LINE_ITEMS.ORDER_NUMBER%TYPE
BEGIN
  FOR current_li IN c_line_items (121) LOOP
    ord_num       := current_li.ORDER_NUMBER;
    li_num        := current_li.ITEM_NUMBER;
    li_total      := current_li.ORDER_TOTAL;
    /* Processing statements go here.     */
  END LOOP;
END;
```

FIGURE 23.6   An explicit cursor in a FOR loop.

specify. The index of the loop will be automatically declared of the same data type as the records that the cursor contains. The FOR loop will fetch in this index each record until the last one, unless you exit before the last record is fetched. For each iteration, you can access the data fetched by referencing the fields of the record that is also the iterator of the loop. Finally, when the loop is exited, either because the last record was retrieved or because you chose to terminate it, the cursor is closed automatically.

Using the cursor FOR loop, you can even declare the cursor on the fly. For example, you could write the following statement, which inherently declares a cursor, opens it, fetches each record in the index current_order, and closes the cursor at the end of the loop.

```
FOR current_order IN (SELECT * from ORDERS) LOOP
  /* Processing statements go here.*/
END LOOP;
```

23.4.4 CURSOR VARIABLES

In the examples used so far, the SELECT statement that populates a cursor with data is specified when the cursor is declared, meaning that if two or more program units need to manipulate data from the same cursor, each of them will have to declare, open, fetch, and close the cursor. Starting from version 2.2 of PL/SQL, released with Oracle7 RDBMS version 7.2, cursors can be declared and manipulated like any other PL/SQL variable. The cursor variables are references or handles to static cursors. They allow you to pass references to the same cursor among all the program units that need access to that cursor. With cursor variables, the SELECT statement is bound to the cursor dynamically, at runtime. The same cursor variable can be bound to more than one SELECT statement, thus adding flexibility to your PL/SQL programs. Figure 23.7 shows an example of how you could use cursor variables in PL/SQL programs. In general, follow these steps:

1. Declare a composite data type for the cursor variable of type REF CURSOR. You may, but are not required to, provide the structure of the records that will be returned by cursor variables of this cursor data type. Not providing the structure is especially useful when the cursors will return records of different structure, as in the case shown in Figure 23.7.
2. Declare one or more cursor variables of the reference cursor data type declared in the previous step.

```
DECLARE
  TYPE custCursorType IS REF CURSOR;
  TYPE custShortRecType IS RECORD (
    id            CUSTOMERS.CUSTOMER_NUMBER%TYPE,
    name          VARCHAR2(80));

  custCursor      custCursorType;
  custShortRec    custShortRecType;
  custFullRec     CUSTOMERS%ROWTYPE;
BEGIN
  OPEN custCursor FOR SELECT CUSTOMER_NUMBER, NAME FROM CUSTOMERS;
  FETCH custCursor INTO custShortRec;
  CLOSE custCursor;

  OPEN custCursor FOR SELECT * FROM CUSTOMERS;
  FETCH custCursor INTO custFullRec;
  CLOSE custCursor;
    /*Processing data in custShortRec and custFullRec.*/
END;
```

FIGURE 23.7 An example of the use of cursor variables in PL/SQL.

3. Instantiate each cursor variable using the method OPEN. In this step, the SELECT statement is bound to the cursor variable and executed in the database server. From this point, until the cursor variable is instantiated as another cursor, it can be used as a regular cursor.
4. Fetch the data from the cursor in local variables.
5. Close the cursor when finished.

23.4.5 IMPLICIT CURSORS

Oracle uses a cursor for every SELECT ... INTO statement that is not referenced by an explicit cursor. It also uses cursors for all INSERT, UPDATE, or DELETE statements that it processes. These are called *implicit cursors* to distinguish them from the ones you declare and manipulate explicitly. Although they are created and managed internally by the RDBMS, you do have a way to check the attributes of the last implicit cursor used by Oracle. This cursor can be addressed with the name SQL, and its attributes can be accessed like any other explicit cursor you create.

Of the four cursor attributes discussed in Section 23.4.2, %ISOPEN is what you will probably never use for implicit cursors. The simple reason is that when the control returns from the DML statement that used the cursor to the line where you may want to check the value of %ISOPEN, the cursor is already closed by the RDBMS. Therefore, this attribute for implicit cursors will always be FALSE.

The attributes %FOUND and %NOTFOUND find out whether the DML statement affected any records at all. The example shown in Figure 23.8 inserts a record in the table PRODUCTS_CATEGORIES. Then it inserts a product that is classified under that category in the table PRODUCTS. Clearly, if the first INSERT fails, the second statement should not be issued, because the referential integrity of the data will be violated. The attribute %FOUND checks the outcome

```
BEGIN
  INSERT INTO PRODUCT_CATEGORIES(ID, NAME)
  VALUES(12, 'Sport Trivia');
  IF SQL%FOUND THEN
    INSERT INTO PRODUCTS(ID, MANUF_ID, PCA_ID, NAME)
    VALUES(121, 34, 12, 'Baseball Trivia CD-ROM');
    COMMIT;
  END IF;
END;
```

FIGURE 23.8 Checking the attributes of the SQL cursor.

Recall that if a SELECT ... INTO statement returns no records, the predefined exception NO_DATA_FOUND is raised. If the statement returns more than one record, the exception TOO_MANY_ROWS is raised. You can use these exceptions instead of directly checking the %FOUND, %NOTFOUND, or %ROWCOUNT attributes of the implicit cursor associated with that statement.

In fact, in the second case, the %ROWCOUNT attribute will not contain the number of the records returned by the query. Oracle raises the exception TOO_MANY_ROWS and sets this attribute to 1 whenever the query returns more than one record.

of the first statement and, depending on this outcome, either proceeds with the second one or not.

The attribute %ROWCOUNT returns the number of rows affected by the DML statement. Structuring your code in a fashion similar to Figure 23.8, you can use the value stored in SQL%ROWCOUNT to take certain actions that depend on the number of the records affected by your statement.

23.5 PL/SQL PROGRAM UNITS

The material presented so far has discussed concepts and features of PL/SQL language in the context of anonymous blocks. These blocks may be executed interactively from the SQL*Plus prompt or stored in Developer/2000 development tools components, such as in Developer/2000 Forms triggers. However, whenever some functionality will be executed more than once and across development environments, the code can be organized into PL/SQL program units such as functions and procedures. Logically related functions and procedures can be grouped together with related data in larger PL/SQL objects called *packages*. This section will provide an overview of functions, procedures, and packages in PL/SQL.

23.5.1 COMPONENTS OF PROGRAM UNITS

In PL/SQL, as in other programming languages, procedures are defined as objects that perform certain actions, whereas functions are objects that must return a value. The syntax rules of PL/SQL do not prohibit procedures from returning values to the calling environment, or functions from performing tasks. However, the code is more clear if these two criteria are followed. In order to discuss the

```
FUNCTION Days_Between(first_dt IN DATE, second_dt IN DATE)
RETURN NUMBER IS
  dt_one NUMBER;
  dt_two NUMBER;
BEGIN
  dt_one := TO_NUMBER(TO_CHAR(first_dt, 'DDD'));
  dt_two := TO_NUMBER(TO_CHAR(second_dt, 'DDD'));

  RETURN(dt_two - dt_one);
END;
```

FIGURE 23.9   An example of a function.

components of functions and procedures, a typical function and procedure are provided. Figure 23.9 contains the definition of the function `Days_Between`. Figure 23.10 contains the definition of the procedure `Set_Cust_Phone`.

Each program unit has a specification part and a body. The specification for a procedure is made up of the keyword PROCEDURE, the name of the procedure, and the argument list enclosed in parentheses. The specification for a function is made up of the keyword FUNCTION, the name of the function, the argument list enclosed in parentheses, and the RETURN clause, which defines the data type of the value returned by the function. The argument definition list contains the name, mode, and data type of each argument.

```
PROCEDURE Set_Cust_Phone (cust_id IN OUT NUMBER,
                  cust_phone IN OUT VARCHAR2) IS
BEGIN
  UPDATE customers
  SET phone = cust_phone
  WHERE customer_number = cust_id;
EXCEPTION
 WHEN OTHERS THEN
  RAISE_APPLICATION_ERROR(-20001, 'Internal error occurred.');
END;
```

FIGURE 23.10   An example of a procedure.

The body of the program unit begins with the keyword IS. If local variables will be used, they must be declared between this keyword and the keyword BEGIN, as in the case of function `Days_Between`. Named program units do not use the keyword DECLARE to indicate the beginning of the declaration section. The executable statements followed by the EXCEPTION section are placed between the keywords BEGIN and END, which are mandatory for named functions and procedures.

23.5.2 ARGUMENTS IN PROGRAM UNITS

The arguments defined in the header of a program unit and used in its body are called *formal arguments*. For example, the arguments `first_dt` in Figure 23.9 and `cust_id` in Figure 23.10 are formal arguments. The values passed to the program unit when it is called are called *actual arguments*. The actual arguments can be passed using the positional notation or the named notation. The following statements show how you can use the function and procedure discussed here with arguments in the positional notation:

```
days := Days_Between(order_dt, delivery_dt);
Set_Cust_Phone(cust_id, new_phone);
```

The following statements show how you can use the same program units to obtain the same results, but this time using arguments in the named notation. In the named notation, the association operator => associates the formal variable to the left with the actual variable to the right. As you can see from the second of these statements, the order in which arguments are passed to a program unit is not important when the named notation is used:

```
days := Days_Between(first_dt => rent_dt, second_dt =>
return_dt);
Set_Cust_Phone(cust_phone => new_phone, cust_id =>
customer_id);
```

The mode of arguments can be IN, OUT, or IN OUT. It defines the way the program unit handles the data passed to it through these arguments. IN arguments are used to pass a value that should not be changed by the program unit. In the program unit's body, an IN argument behaves like a constant whose value cannot be modified by assignment statements. If not specified otherwise, an argument is by default an IN mode argument. OUT arguments modify the value of the actual argument in the calling environment. The value of an OUT actual argument before the call, is no longer available when the control returns back to the calling environment. The program unit must assign a value to all its OUT arguments; otherwise, their value after the unit's execution completes is undetermined. Assignments are the only operations in which OUT arguments can be used inside the program unit. IN OUT arguments allow the calling environment to pass values to a program unit. In its body, they are treated like normal variables. The program unit may modify the value of the argument, and this modification is visible to the outside environment.

23.5.3 PL/SQL PACKAGES

Functions and procedures are important PL/SQL objects that allow you to group together and modularize the PL/SQL statements that are necessary to perform the functionality of the application. Packages are PL/SQL objects that take this process one step further. They bundle together in one object data and program units that access and modify the data.

Packages provide the PL/SQL implementation of several fundamental concepts of object-oriented programming, such as encapsulation of data with the operations performed on the data, code reusability, dynamic binding of data types, and data hiding. They are a close equivalent of the concept of classes in object-oriented programming languages, such as C++ or Java.

Structurally, a package is divided in two parts: the specification and the body. The specification part holds the data, functions, and procedures that will be freely accessible by all the other routines that will use the package. This part also contains the specification for those program units that other programs may call but that they do not need to see implemented. Thus, in a sense, the specification of a package is the communication protocol of the package with the outside environment.

The body part of the package contains private information that cannot be seen or accessed by the routines outside the package. The functions and procedures in the body are a direct implementation of the program units declared in the specification part of the package. But the body part may also contain functions and procedures that are not declared in the specification part. They will not be accessible by program units other than those within the body. Figure 23.11 shows a graphical representation of the package object. It is also known as the Booch diagram of the packages, after Grady Booch, one of the founders of object-oriented programming.

In the example shown in Figure 23.11, the pseudo-package PACKAGE contains some data declaration Data, a function specification Function A, and a procedure specification Procedure B. The body of the package, represented by the shaded area, contains some data declarations that are strictly local to the body, and the implementation for Function A and Procedure B. Function A in its body calls Function C, and Procedure B calls Procedure D and Function C. The definitions for both these program units are within the package body.

The programs outside can access and use only what is available in the specification part. The program unit shown in the box to the right can access the public

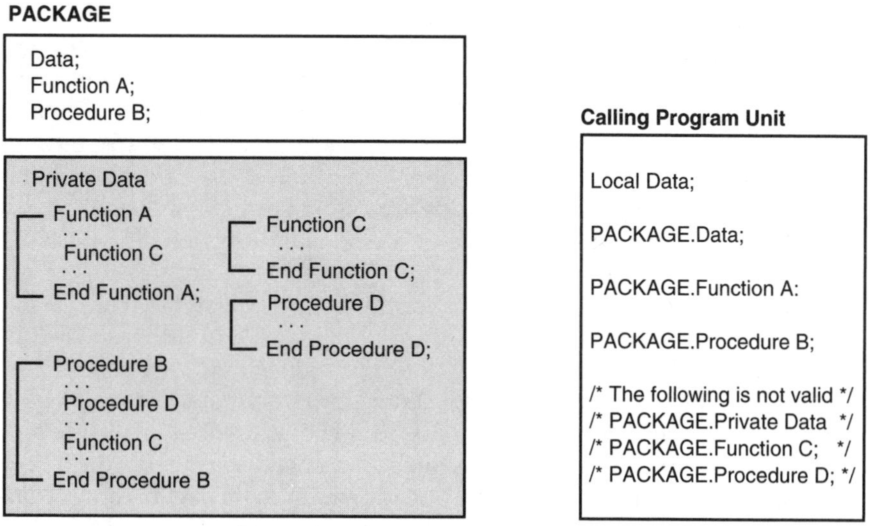

PACKAGE

FIGURE 23.11   A graphical representation of a package.

data and functions using the syntax PACKAGE.Data, PACKAGE.Function A, or
PACKAGE.Procedure B. Implicitly, through this interface, this program unit is
using Function C or Procedure D only because these program units are used
by Function A or Procedure B. However, it cannot access these objects directly. In fact, if Function A inside the package's body is modified to implement
a different algorithm, or data structure, the calling program would have no way
of knowing about the modification.

23.5.4   BENEFITS OF PACKAGES

Even from this graphical presentation, packages clearly encapsulate in one object
the data elements and the operations or methods that manipulate them. The advantage of this approach versus the more traditional one is that it represents the
world that the application describes more naturally, as a continuum of objects
that interact with each other.

Also, Figure 23.11 very clearly shows how a package can achieve the hiding
of code and implementation details. The benefit of hiding the code from the outside routines is that the application becomes more robust as a whole. Because the
outside routines do not know how the internals of the public components of the
package are implemented, no risk exists that they will become wired into the details of this package. As long as the interface, or specification, of the package remains unchanged, modifications inside the body will not force the calling routines to change their behavior or have to be recompiled.

Another great usage of the information-hiding capability of packages is when designing and prototyping the application. In the top-down design approach, you define the high-level objects and routines first, and then move on to the detailed implementation. When you are still at the high-level phase, you can place all the functions and procedures declarations in the specification of a package. Then the rest of the application can continue to be developed independently. The calls to the package are made according to its specification. They will compile and execute successfully, although not much functionality exists behind them. Meanwhile, as the implementation of the package progresses, the rest of the development team does not have to modify and constantly change their code. All this work happens in the gray area of Figure 23.11, which, as I said, is invisible to the rest of the world.

Finally, the other object-oriented programming feature of packages is the dynamic binding of data types, also known as *overloading*. Inside a package, you can create functions and procedures that have the same name but take arguments of different data types. For the outside routines, the fact becomes transparent that different program units are executed when different arguments of different data types are used. The package intelligently selects which routine to invoke when it receives a call, thus removing the burden of the programmers to make that selection themselves, based on the data type of the arguments.

When cursors are declared in packages, you have the choice of dividing the SELECT statement of the cursor definition from its body. In the package specification, you could place statements like these:

```
/* Specifications of other public package components may
go here.    */
CURSOR c_line_items_total (ord_number
LINE_ITEMS.ORDER_NUMBER%TYPE)
RETURN LINE_ITEMS.ITEM_TOTAL%TYPE;
/* Specifications of other public package components may
go here.    */
```

As you can see, you must provide the data types and the number of data elements of records that the SELECT statements of the cursor will return. Then in the package body you specify the actual SELECT statement, as shown in the following example:

```
/* Body of other package components may go here.       */
CURSOR c_line_items_total (ord_number
LINE_ITEMS.ORDER_NUMBER%TYPE) IS
    SELECT ORDER_NUMBER , ITEM_NUMBER, ITEM_TOTAL
    FROM LINE_ITEMS
    WHERE ORDER_NUMBER = ord_number;
/* Body of other package components may go here.       */
```

Implementing cursors this way draws all the benefits that packages bring into PL/SQL programming, as I discussed above. In particular, it allows you to change the WHERE clause of the select statement, if need be, without affecting the programs that will use the cursor.

23.5.5 PL/SQL LIBRARIES

PL/SQL Library (PLL) modules are a special type of module in the Developer/2000 environment that serves the purpose of grouping related program units of an application for ease of maintenance. The major advantage of PLL modules is that they allow reuse of the code over and over across all the Oracle application development tools. You may store in a library PL/SQL objects that can be accessed from and used in any form or menu module, but also in reports and displays developed with Developer/2000 Reports and Oracle Graphics. For more information on how to create, save, compile PLL modules, populate them with objects, and attach them to a form or menu module, refer to *Developing Oracle Forms Applications* (Prentice Hall, 1996).

23.5.6 DATABASE TRIGGERS

With each table in the Oracle Server database, you can associate methods of PL/SQL code that will be executed when the event for which the method is defined occurs. Using database triggers enforces a business rule about the data at the database level. It ensures that all the applications that access the database objects follow the rule consistently and precisely as it is defined in the object itself. Database triggers associate the flexibility of the relational model with the advantages of object-oriented programming. If the data should follow certain rules, you attach these rules to the table that will hold the data. This place is the only one where the method is coded. Each application that uses the table, from that moment on, will not need to recode the rule. The method associated with the table will wait patiently until one of these applications sends the message that causes its event to occur. When this happens, the method, or trigger, will fire and execute its statements. This process is the only way the method will become active.

Based on the events that cause the triggers to fire, they can be classified into three categories: Insert, Update, and Delete triggers. Triggers from each of these categories can be further divided into two groups. *Before triggers* are those that fire before the statement is executed by the Oracle Server. *After triggers* fire after the Oracle Server executes the triggering statement. Finally, based on the granularity of action performed by the triggers, they can be grouped into two more categories. Table-level triggers will fire only once, when the event occurs; row-level triggers will be executed for each record affected by the triggering statement. Figure 23.12 summarizes the different types of database triggers that can be defined. When defining a trigger, you should specify a value from each of the categories in

CATEGORIES	VALUES
Event Type	Insert, Update, Delete
Trigger Timing	Before, After
Trigger Execution Level	Table, Row

FIGURE 23.12 Categories for different types of database triggers.

this figure. The result then is that only 12 discrete types of database triggers can exist (3 event types x 2 timings x 2 execution levels).

When triggers fire for each row, Oracle keeps two copies of each record affected by the statement. The state of the record in the database, before the statement is executed, is referred to as OLD. The version of that record after the statement is executed can be referenced as the NEW record. Understandably, when a record is being inserted, its OLD version contains NULL values for all the columns. The reason is that the record does not exist in the database until the INSERT statement is executed, and the snapshot that creates OLD is taken before this event. For a similar reason, the NEW version of a deleted record contains NULL columns. (After the DELETE is completed, the record no longer exists in the table.) If the statement is UPDATE, both NEW and OLD versions of the record will contain some values.

Both versions of the record are accessible in all the triggers. However, you cannot set the columns of the NEW record in an After trigger. Recall that this trigger will fire after the triggering statement is executed. Therefore, the NEW version of the record is created and set before the trigger enters into the action. OLD and NEW are also called *correlation names*.

With the settings I've discussed so far, the triggers can fire only in two extreme cases: only once or for every single row affected by the system. On some occasions, a trigger should fire only for a particular set of the records affected by the statement. Imagine, for example, that another application besides yours using the same database. While you are implementing the generation of identification numbers at the database, the developers of the other application are using a fancy algorithm to come up with a unique number, based on some biographical data provided by the customer. By creating a database trigger, you are enforcing the rule globally. In other words, when a record is about to be inserted in the table CUSTOMERS, the trigger will not check to see which application is sending it— yours or theirs. It will simply enforce your rule and override the value placed in the column ID by the other application. In order to restrict the number of records that a record-level trigger will affect when fired, a Boolean condition can be specified in the definition of the trigger. The trigger will be fired only for those records that evaluate the condition to TRUE.

23.6 EXCEPTION HANDLING

When discussing the components of a PL/SQL block, I also mentioned the purpose and usage of exceptions in PL/SQL code. They are abnormal conditions in the PL/SQL environment, associated with a warning or error of which the user of the application must be aware. When any of these abnormal conditions occur, an exception is raised. The execution flow of the program is interrupted. The control jumps to the EXCEPTION part of the block, which the programmer should be careful to include. The exception section of the PL/SQL block is where you write the code that gracefully handles the error condition, or takes measures to correct it.

Two types of exceptions can occur in an Oracle application. The first category includes all the exceptions that the PL/SQL engine raises automatically when the abnormal condition occurs. These are called *internal exceptions*. The second category includes *user-specified exceptions*. They are not Oracle processing errors, but rather situations in the application to which the user's attention must be attracted.

23.6.1 INTERNAL EXCEPTIONS

Each internal exception is associated with an Oracle Server error number. The group of internal exceptions is further divided into *named* and *unnamed exceptions*. The named internal exceptions are a number of exceptions that occur most frequently and are defined in the PL/SQL engine. Figure 23.13 lists some of these exceptions that you are likely to encounter the most in your development practice.

EXCEPTION NAME	ORACLE ERROR	DESCRIPTION
NO_DATA_FOUND	ORA-01403	SELECT ... INTO statement returns no rows
TOO_MANY_ROWS	ORA-01427	SELECT ... INTO statement returns more than one row
ZERO_DIVIDE	ORA-01476	Numeric value is divided by zero
VALUE_ERROR	ORA-01403	Error occurred during a computation or data conversion
STORAGE_ERROR	ORA-06500	No sufficient memory available, or memory is corrupted
PROGRAM_ERROR	ORA-06501	Internal error of PL/SQL

FIGURE 23.13 Examples of named internal exceptions.

Examples provided in this chapter, such as the PL/SQL block in Figure 23.3, show how to handle these exceptions. The majority of internal errors are not named explicitly, although they automatically raise an exception when they occur. However, in order to trap and handle them appropriately, the code of these errors must be associated with an exception that you have declared ahead of time. The pragma EXCEPTION_INIT associates an error number with the user-defined exception. In PL/SQL, a *pragma* is a directive that instructs the PL/SQL compiler to bind the internal error number to the specified exception name. Whenever the error occurs, the name can handle the exception.

Figure 23.14 shows how to handle an unnamed internal exception. In this case, you assume that a check constraint in the table LINE_ITEMS does not allow the discount for a product to be above 70 percent. If the record sent for INSERT to the database contains a higher value for the column DISCOUNT, the statement will violate the check constraint defined in the table LINE_ITEMS. The error raised by the database server will be ORA-02290. The internal value of this error and all other internal Oracle errors has a negative sign. In the PL/SQL block

```
DECLARE
- Declare a name for the constraint
  check_constraint_violated  EXCEPTION;
- Bind the constraint to an Oracle error code
  PRAGMA EXCEPTION_INIT (check_constraint_violated,
-2290);
  vn_discount NUMBER := 0.75;
BEGIN
  INSERT INTO line_items (order_number, item_number,
pro_id, quantity, discount, unit_msrp)
  VALUES (101, 1, 14, 2, vn_discount, 49.99)
 - INSERT fails if discount > 70 percent (0.70)
 - Violation of check constraint raises ORA-02290
 - In such 'case control jumps to EXCEPTION section
  COMMIT;
EXCEPTION
  WHEN check_constraint_violated THEN
    RAISE_APPLICATION_ERROR(-20002, 'Excessive discount.')
  WHEN OTHERS THEN
    RAISE_APPLICATION_ERROR(-20001, 'Internal error
occurred.');
END;
```

FIGURE 23.14 Using unnamed internal exceptions.

shown in Figure 23.14, this error is associated with the user-declared exception check_constraint_violated using the pragma EXCEPTION_INIT.

23.6.2 USER-DEFINED EXCEPTIONS

Some abnormal situations in an application are not due to a failure or error of the database engine, but to a violation of the requirements or logic of the application. In that case, a user-specified exception may be used to trap and handle the situation. Figure 23.15 shows an improvement on the previous code, because it does check the value of DISCOUNT before the record is sent for insertion into the database.

The difference between unnamed internal exceptions and user-named exceptions is that the second type must be raised explicitly when the abnormal condition occurs. The RAISE statement in a sense serves as a GOTO statement, because the program execution is interrupted and the flow jumps to the exception. However, using the RAISE command makes the code more uniform and consistent with other situations.

```
DECLARE
— Declare a name for the constraint
  check_constraint_violated  EXCEPTION;
  vn_discount NUMBER := 0.75;
BEGIN
  IF (vn_discount > 3) THEN
    RAISE check_constraint_violated;
  END IF;

— If control comes here, discount is less then 70 percent
  INSERT INTO line_items (order_number, item_number,
pro_id, quantity, discount, unit_msrp)
  VALUES (101, 1, 14, 2, 0.75, 49.99)
  COMMIT;
EXCEPTION
  WHEN check_constraint_violated THEN
    RAISE_APPLICATION_ERROR(-20002, 'Excessive discount.')
  WHEN OTHERS THEN
    RAISE_APPLICATION_ERROR(-20001, 'Internal error
occurred.');
END;
```

FIGURE 23.15 An example of a user-named exception.

In order to return an application-specific error number and a description of the error, you can use the built-in procedure RAISE_APPLICATION_ERROR with user-defined exceptions. When the calling application receives an exception raised with this procedure, it will treat it like any other Oracle Server error raised internally.

The procedure RAISE_APPLICATION_ERROR is defined in the DBMS_STANDARD package that comes with the Oracle Server. It takes two arguments, the first of which is the error number and the second of which is the message text that will be associated with this number. The error number is always negative and between −20999 and −20000. This range of numbers is reserved by the Oracle RDBMS software for user-defined errors. If you specify a number outside this range, the routine will compile successfully, but at runtime you will get an error message.

23.6.3 ERROR-REPORTING FUNCTIONS

A known fact in the information technology environment is that the number of things that could potentially go wrong with an application is proportional to the functionality of the application. However, a recognized trend is that the systems developed today are more robust and protected than systems developed in the past, due to great improvements in hardware and software development tools and to better preparation of programmers to handle different situations that a system can face. But expecting an application to handle every error that can occur is unrealistic. The developer must decide which errors can and must be corrected when they occur, and which ones may simply be reported and taken care of later.

In PL/SQL programs, a good place to put error-reporting code is in the OTHER clause of the EXCEPTION section. Whenever an error occurs, Oracle provides the number of that error and a brief descriptive message. They can both be retrieved and further manipulated by the functions SQLCODE and SQLERRM. These are PL/SQL-specific functions that cannot be used in a SQL statement. SQLCODE returns the error number, and SQLERRM returns the error message. Figure 23.16 expands the functionality of the PL/SQL block in Figure 23.15 by adding error-reporting functionality.

23.6.4 PROPAGATION OF EXCEPTIONS

When an exception is raised, Developer/2000 Forms looks for a handler clause for that exception in the PL/SQL block where the exception occurs. If one is found, the instructions contained in that handler are executed. If no handler exists, then the exception is passed to the parent block, if it exists. The same check for an exception handler occurs here. The exception continues to propagate upward until it reaches the upper programmatic layer. Figure 23.17 represents the diagram of a database trigger that contains a call to Procedure_A and Function_B in its body. Procedure_A in turn issues a call to Function_C, and

```
DECLARE
  err_code NUMBER;
  err_text VARCHAR2(255);
— Declare a name for the constraint
  check_constraint_violated  EXCEPTION;
  vn_discount NUMBER := 0.75;
BEGIN
  IF (vn_discount > 3) THEN
    RAISE check_constraint_violated;
  END IF;

— If control comes here, discount is less then 70 percent
  INSERT INTO line_items (order_number, item_number,
pro_id, quantity, discount, unit_msrp)
  VALUES (101, 1, 14, 2, 0.75, 49.99)
  COMMIT;
EXCEPTION
  WHEN check_constraint_violated THEN
    RAISE_APPLICATION_ERROR(-20002, 'Excessive amount')
  WHEN OTHERS THEN
    err_code := SQLCODE;
    err_text := SQLERRM;
    RAISE_APPLICATION_ERROR(-2000, 'Error '||
TO_CHAR(err_code)||' - '|| err_text);
END;
```

FIGURE 23.16   Using the functions SQLCODE and SQLERRM.

Function_B to Procedure_D. The diagram identifies the checkpoints an exception has to pass through when raised.

Any exception raised in Function_C can be handled in the EXCEPTION part of this function. If it is not trapped here, the exception will propagate to Procedure_A, where it can be handled by its EXCEPTION section, labeled as Trap 3 in the figure. If no handler is defined in Procedure_A, the exception will be propagated to the body of the calling trigger. The EXCEPTION section of this trigger, Trap 5, is the last chance to handle the raised exception. If it is not handled even here, the trigger will fail. If in any of these steps, a handler for the exception OTHERS is used, none of the exceptions raised in the block and all its enclosing blocks will be propagated outside the block. For example, if you place the WHEN OTHERS clause in Trap 4, all the exceptions that can be raised by Proce-

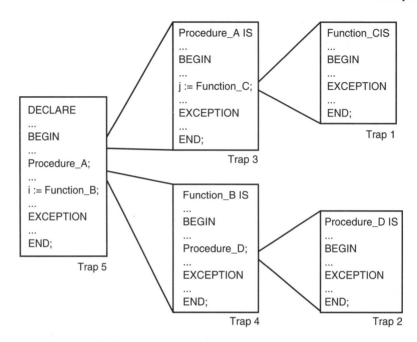

FIGURE 23.17 Trapping exceptions in a database trigger.

dure_D or Function_B that are not handled by explicit handlers will be trapped and handled by the statements in this clause.

23.7 SUMMARY

PL/SQL is the programming language used by a number of development tools produced by the Oracle Corporation, including Developer/2000 and Oracle Web-Server. In addition, all the business units implemented in the Oracle Server in the form of stored program units and database triggers are programmed in PL/SQL. This chapter is an overview of the major syntactic structures and concepts of PL/SQL. Major topics of this chapter include:

- ❑ **Overview of PL/SQL**
  - ❑ Brief History of the PL/SQL Language
  - ❑ Functionality of PL/SQL Engines
  - ❑ Structural Elements of PL/SQL Blocks
  - ❑ Manipulating Data in PL/SQL Blocks

- ❏ **Procedural Constructs of PL/SQL**
  - ❏ IF Statement
  - ❏ Looping Statements
  - ❏ Unconditional Branching
- ❏ **Data Types and Variables**
  - ❏ PL/SQL Data Types
  - ❏ PL/SQL Variables
  - ❏ PL/SQL Constants
  - ❏ PL/SQL Records
  - ❏ PL/SQL Tables
- ❏ **Cursors in PL/SQL**
  - ❏ Declaring Explicit Cursors
  - ❏ Methods and Attributes of Explicit Cursors
  - ❏ Using the FOR Loop with Explicit Cursors
  - ❏ Cursor Variables
  - ❏ Implicit Cursors
- ❏ **PL/SQL Program Units**
  - ❏ Components of Program Units
  - ❏ Arguments in Program Units
  - ❏ PL/SQL Packages
  - ❏ Benefits of Packages
  - ❏ PL/SQL Libraries
  - ❏ Database Triggers
- ❏ **Exception Handling**
  - ❏ Internal Exceptions
  - ❏ User-Defined Exceptions
  - ❏ Error-Reporting Functions
  - ❏ Propagation of Exceptions

Chapter 24

MAINTAINING PL/SQL OBJECTS IN DESIGNER/2000

♦ Maintaining Server Side PL/SQL Objects

♦ Understanding and Maintaining the Server API

♦ Maintaining Application Logic Objects

♦ The Logic Editor

♦ Working with the Logic Editor

♦ Summary

PL/SQL objects are an important part of the software assets of an application system that you can define and maintain in Designer/2000. They are important because they implement in the application logic or the Oracle Server database the business rules identified during the analysis of the system's requirements. Among PL/SQL objects you define in the Designer/2000 Repository are functions, procedures, packages, database triggers and application events, cursors, complex data types, and so on.

Like other components that are part of the design of your application system, PL/SQL objects are created and maintained in the Design Editor. The DB Objects tab of the Design Navigator allows you to create and maintain definitions of objects that will be stored in the Oracle Server database; the DB Admin tab implements these objects in the schema of a selected user from a given database. PL/SQL objects that are part of the application logic are maintained in the context of individual modules, associated with different components of these modules. They can also be bundled together in library modules. This chapter will discuss the process of creating and maintaining PL/SQL objects in the application system.

24.1 MAINTAINING SERVER SIDE PL/SQL OBJECTS

A good number of PL/SQL objects you maintain in the Repository will be ultimately implemented in the Oracle Server database as stored program units. The sections under Section 24.1 will discuss the process of creating these objects and the three available methods for defining their properties in Designer/2000.

24.1.1 CREATING PL/SQL DEFINITIONS

Designer/2000 allows you to implement the following stored program units: functions, procedures, packages, cursors, and trigger logic. The definitions of these objects are maintained on the DB Objects tab of the Design Navigator, under the node PL/SQL Definitions. The following are the steps required to create a new PL/SQL definition object:

1. Select the node that represents the type of PL/SQL object you want to create, for example, Function Definition.
2. Click the icon Create ⚏ to invoke the Create PL/SQL Function dialog box.
3. Enter the short name and the name of the new object. Optionally provide a brief description of the purpose of this object, as shown in Figure 24.1.
4. Click Next to move to the tab Type, which allows you to set the type of the PL/SQL object definition, the method used to define it, the return data type, whether the object is a function, and the scope of the object. Figure 24.2 shows

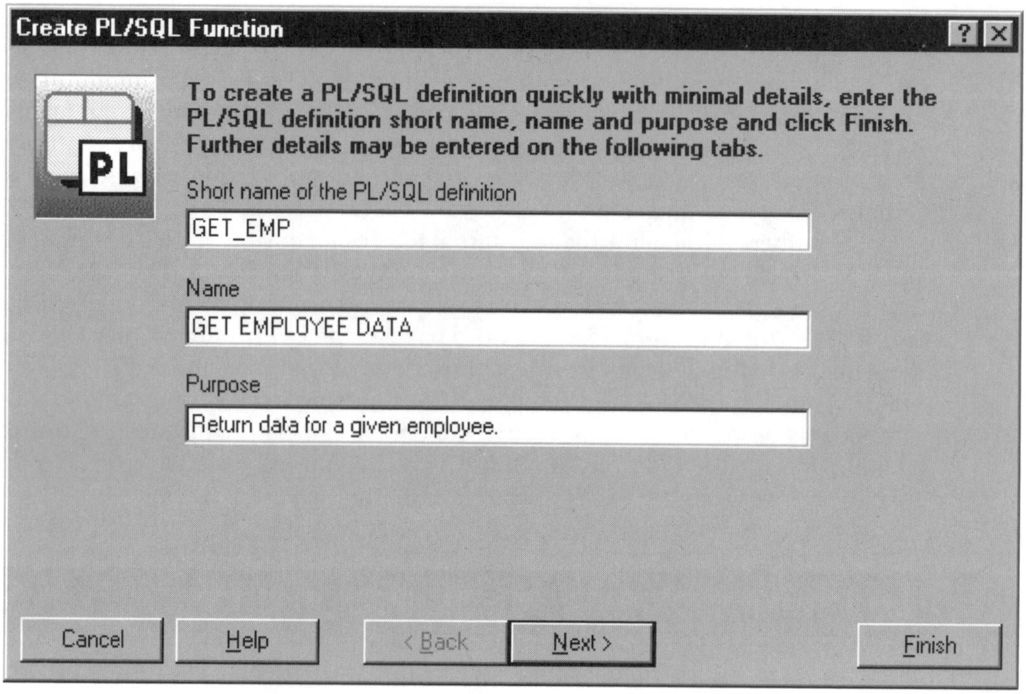

FIGURE 24.1   The Create PL/SQL Function dialog box.

an example of settings for the tab Type. The tabs that follow depend on the option you select for the implementation method of the PL/SQL object.

5. Click Finish to complete the process.

You can use three methods for defining PL/SQL objects in Designer/2000:

❑ Operating System File
❑ Free Format
❑ Declarative

Sections 24.1.2–24.1.5 explain each of the methods.

24.1.2   DEFINING PL/SQL OBJECTS WITH THE OPERATING SYSTEM FILE METHOD

This method is the most trivial, but also the least used for defining a PL/SQL object. It consists of storing the structure and contents of the module in a text file in the file system, outside the Designer/2000 Repository. In order to define an object with this method, set the list box How the PL/SQL will be defined, located on the

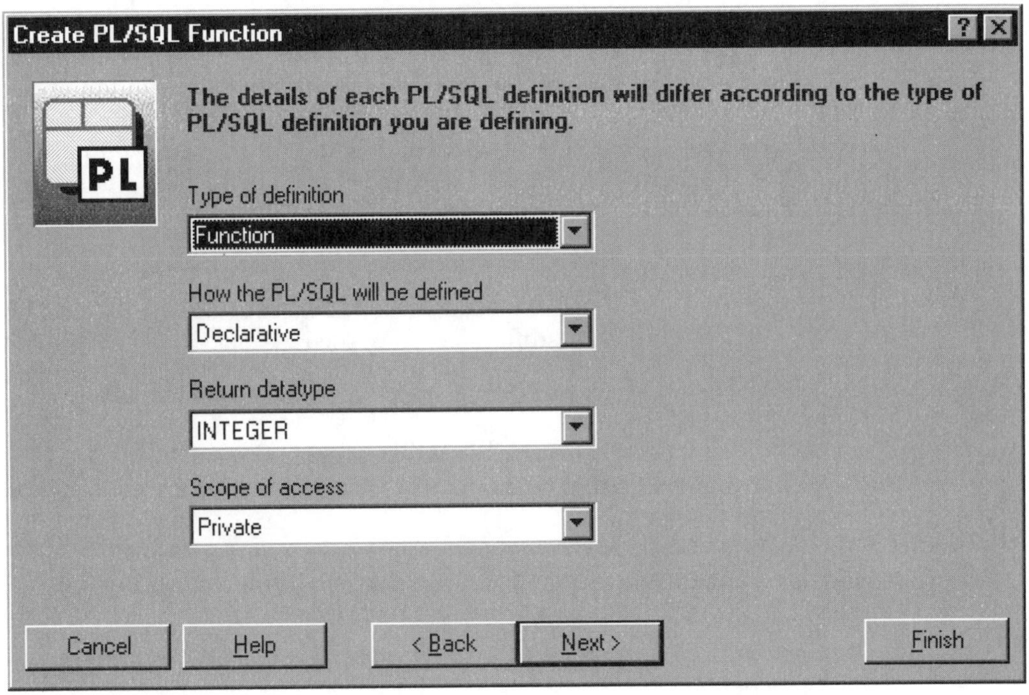

FIGURE 24.2 The tab Type of the Create PL/SQL Function dialog box.

tab Type, to Operating System File. When you do, the dialog box of properties for this object contains a third tab, called File, in which you can set the path and name of the file that contains the source for the object.

When the Server Generator is asked to generate the appropriate SQL syntax to create the module in the Oracle database, the only statement it generates is a call to this file. For PL/SQL objects defined with the source file method, any information you may enter in the other properties of the module are ignored by the generator.

Because the useful information maintained by the Repository for this type of modules is minimal, this method is rarely used. However, when it is used, the Logic Editor component of the Design Editor facilitates the editing of the source file that contains the contents of the module. As Section 24.5.2 explains, you can import the contents of this file into the Editor, use the Editor's features to edit and check the syntax of the module, and export it back to the file system.

24.1.3 DEFINING PL/SQL OBJECTS USING THE FREE FORMAT METHOD

With this method, the definition and contents of PL/SQL objects are stored in the Designer/2000 Repository. This setup allows you to inherit all the benefits of the repository-driven development. In particular, you can apply to PL/SQL objects the same version control strategy that you would apply to the entire application system and use the editing- and syntax-checking capabilities of the Logic Editor.

To implement a PL/SQL object with the free format method, you need to select the option Free Format on the tab Type. When you do, the dialog box of the object is populated with a third property tab, called Parameters. Recall from Chapter 23 that each PL/SQL program unit is composed of the header, the declaration section, the execution section, and the exception section. When a PL/SQL object is defined using the free format method, the Server Generator creates the header part of the object using module properties, such as *Name, Type,* and *Return Type* in the case of functions. The arguments of the object, if any, are derived from properties set on the Parameters tab. Arguments can be specified only for functions, procedures, or cursors. In general, an argument is created following these steps:

1. Click the button Add to create an empty record on the tab Parameters and place the cursor inside the text field Parameters.
2. Type the name of the parameter.
3. Use icons ▼ and ▲ to arrange the order of the arguments, if multiple arguments are defined.
4. Specify the data type of the argument by selecting the appropriate option from the list box Parameter datatype.
5. Specify the mode of the argument by selecting from the Parameter type list one of the following options: 'Input,' 'Output,' or 'Modify.'
6. Provide a default value for the parameter, if applicable, by entering it in the text field Default value.

Figure 24.3 shows the settings of the Parameters tab of the Edit PL/SQL Function dialog box.

The free format method creates the header of the PL/SQL object using the properties you set as described above. The declaration, execution, and exception sections of the PL/SQL object are usually created and maintained in the Logic Editor and stored in the property *PL/SQL Block* of the object.

Technically speaking, the free format method can be used to implement any type of PL/SQL object. But given the fact that only the header of the object is generated from its properties, this method is usually used for cursors or functions and procedures that do not contain variable declarations. Functions or procedures with significant code in the declaration section are usually defined using the declarative method. PL/SQL packages are defined almost exclusively with the declarative method as well.

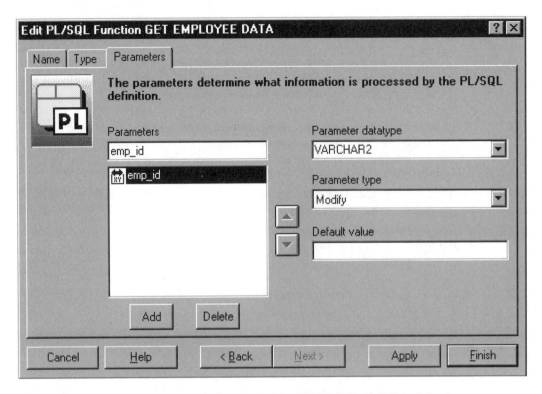

FIGURE 24.3   The Parameters tab of the Edit PL/SQL Function dialog box.

24.1.4 DEFINING PL/SQL OBJECTS USING
THE DECLARATIVE METHOD

When functions and procedures are defined with the declarative method, the Server Generator can generate the header and declaration section of the program unit based on properties set in the Edit Module dialog box. The execution and exception sections of the module are stored in the *PL/SQL Body* property. For objects defined with this method, the Server Generator creates the header of the program unit by using all the properties used when the free format method is applied. In addition, it uses properties on the tabs Exceptions and Data to create the declaration section of the PL/SQL object. These tabs are present only for objects defined with the declarative method.

The tab Exceptions is used to record declaratively the user-defined exceptions and the code that handles them when they are raised. The following is how you record a constraint on this tab.

1. Click the button Add to create a new record and place the cursor inside the text field Exception name.
2. Type the name of the new exception.
3. Click in the text box Code for the exception and enter the statements that will be executed when the exception is raised.

An example of the Exceptions tab appears in Figure 24.4.

You use the properties tab Data to declare any local variables or constants that will be used by a program unit. The generic procedure to follow is this:

1. Click the button Add to create an empty record on the tab Data and place the cursor inside the text field Declaration name.
2. Type the name of the new declaration object.
3. Specify the data type of the argument by selecting the appropriate option from the list box Datatype.

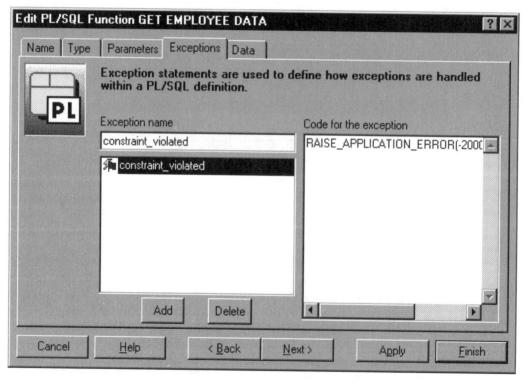

FIGURE 24.4 The Exceptions tab of the Edit PL/SQL Function dialog box.

4. Provide a default value for the declaration, if applicable, by entering it in the text field Default value.
5. Define the type of the declaration by selecting either the button Variable or the button Constant from the radio group Type.
6. Specify the maximum length of the variable or constant if it is applicable.

Figure 24.5 shows an example of the Data tab.

24.1.5 ADVANTAGES OF THE DECLARATIVE METHOD

The real advantage of the declarative method is evident when the same PL/SQL object is needed in several program units. Consider, for example, a database cursor that selects all the employees who work for a given type of order management team—either SALES UNIT or WAREHOUSE UNIT. Assume also that this cursor is used by the function COMPUTE_BENEFITS and the procedure

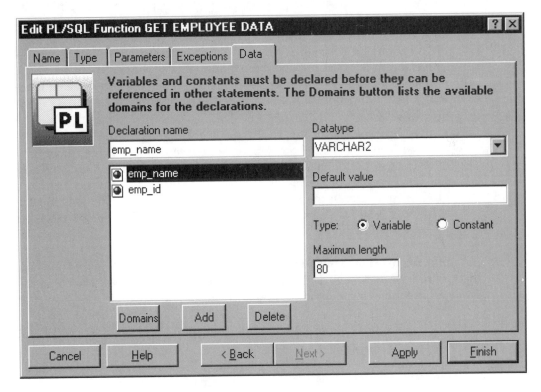

FIGURE 24.5　The Data tab of the Edit PL/SQL Function dialog box.

You may inherit properties like Datatype and Maximum length by clicking the button Domain and selecting the appropriate domain from the dialog box that appears.

TRANSFER_EMPLOYEE, both defined as PL/SQL objects in the Designer/2000 Repository. You can implement this functionality in three ways:

❑ Implement the cursor for each of these program units. When the Server Generator runs, it includes the definition of the cursor in each object. Clearly, with this approach, the work to define the cursor in function COMPUTE_BENEFITS will have to be repeated in procedure TRANSFER_EMPLOYEE.

❑ Define the cursor as an independent PL/SQL object and include it in the definition of the other two modules. In this case, the declarative method allows you to define the cursor once and include it in the definition of both the function and procedure. The approach discussed above reuses the design object, but it does not avoid the redundancy of the generated code. The statement that defines the cursor C_EMP_BY_OMT_TYPE is repeated identically in the function COMPUTE_BENEFITS and the procedure TRANSFER_EMPLOYEE.

❑ Define the cursor, function, and procedure as components of a PL/SQL package. The optimal implementation is to design and code the cursor only once and use it as often as needed. This can be achieved by defining the cursor, function, and procedure as independent objects and placing them in a PL/SQL package. In the case discussed here, you can define the package MANAGE_EMPLOYEES. Then create include associations between the package and the three PL/SQL objects in question.

In order to achieve this functionality, you need to create a module network that defines the inclusion of the cursor, function, and procedure objects in the package. The following steps allow you to create such a network.

1. Expand the node that represents the package MANAGE_EMPLOYEES in the Design Navigator.
2. Select the node Included PL/SQL, and click Create ▣. The dialog box Module Networks for PL/SQL Definition appears.
3. Transfer the cursor, function, and procedure to the list box to the right, as

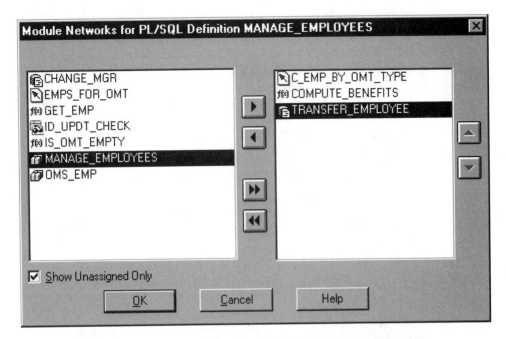

FIGURE 24.6 The Module Networks for PL/SQL Definition dialog box.

shown in Figure 24.6. This list box represents the PL/SQL definitions included in the package.

4. Click OK.

In order to expose only the function and procedure to the calling environment, but hide the cursor itself, set the property *Scope* to '*Private*' for the cursor and to '*Public*' for the function and the procedure. This property is located on property tab Type of the Edit dialog box for each object. In these conditions, the Server Generator creates the specification and body for the package without requiring you to enter a single line of code. Because of this simplicity, the declarative method is the preferred method for implementing packages in Designer/2000.

24.1.6 IMPLEMENTING PL/SQL OBJECTS

The PL/SQL program units you define in the Repository, like other objects that are part of your database design, are implemented in the schema of one or more Oracle database users. The implementation process is very simple, as the following steps describe:

1. Switch to the DB Admin tab of the Design Navigator.
2. Expand the node Databases (Oracle), and then expand the hierarchy tree of database instances and users until you select the user for whom you want to create the implementation object.
3. Expand the node Schema Objects for this user and select the node Package Implementation, Function Implementation, or Procedure Implementation, depending on the type of PL/SQL object you want to implement.
4. Click the icon Create 🔲 . The dialog box Create PL/SQL Module Implementation for User appears.
5. Select the PL/SQL object you want to implement from the list and click Next.
6. Assign privileges on the implementation object to other users. Typically, the EXECUTE privilege is the one you would assign more frequently.
7. Click Finish.

24.1.7 DATABASE TRIGGERS

Database triggers are PL/SQL methods attached to tables that are invoked when a triggering event occurs in the table. Unlike other PL/SQL objects, which can stand as independent objects, triggers are always attached to a table. In the Design Editor, triggers can be created with the following commands:

1. Switch to the DB Objects tab of the Design Navigator and expand the table object.
2. Select the node Triggers and click Create 🔲 . This command invokes the Create Trigger dialog box.
3. Enter the name of the trigger and a brief description of its purpose.
4. Click Next to move to the other property tabs and specify the remaining properties of the trigger. These tabs are accessed in the Edit Triggers dialog box and will be discussed next.
5. Click Finish.

Notice that as a by-product of the process of creating the trigger, a PL/SQL object that represents the logic of this trigger is created as well. This statement will be executed when the trigger is activated.

Important properties of a trigger are those that define the event that activates the trigger and the timing of the trigger. These properties are maintained on the tab Fires of the Edit Trigger dialog box. Figure 24.7 shows an example of this tab. As you can see, by setting the controls on this tab, you can define which events will activate the trigger, whether the trigger will be fired for every affected

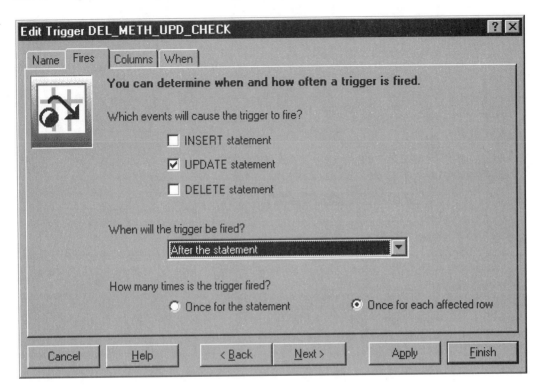

FIGURE 24.7 The tab Fires of the Edit Trigger dialog box.

row or once for the entire statement, and whether the triggers will fire before, after, or instead of the triggering statement.

When the trigger fires on UPDATE statements, you have the option to specify one or more columns whose update activates the trigger. The tab Columns is used for this purpose. In the example shown in Figure 24.8, the trigger will fire only when DELIVERY_METHOD is updated.

In general, the number of rows that a record-level trigger affects when fired can be restricted by specifying a Boolean condition in the *Trigger When Condition* property of the trigger. The trigger will fire only for those records for which this Boolean condition evaluates to TRUE. This property can be accessed on the tab When of the Edit Trigger dialog box.

The actual text of the PL/SQL statements that form the body of the trigger are maintained in the PL/SQL object of type TRG-LOGIC that is associated with the particular trigger. Thus, in order to complete the process of creating a trigger, you must specify the contents of this module. Like other PL/SQL objects discussed here, the Logic Editor component of the Design Editor is the tool of choice for editing the content of trigger logic modules.

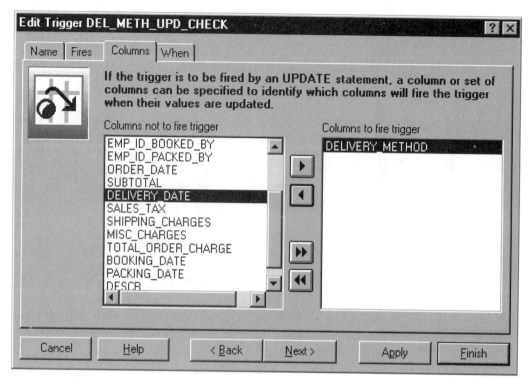

FIGURE 24.8   The tab Columns of the Edit Trigger dialog box for an update trigger.

24.2   UNDERSTANDING AND MAINTAINING THE SERVER API

When the back end of your application system is implemented in the Oracle Server database, you may take advantage of support that Designer/2000 provides for implementing a number of business rules and constraints in the form of a series of PL/SQL program units known commonly as the *Server Application Programmatic Interface (API)*. Implementing the business rules at the database level

The body of a database trigger is always an anonymous PL/SQL block, the size of which should be kept to a minimum. If complicated checks or computations must be performed, the functionality is normally extracted in the form of a stored function or procedure that is then called from the trigger body.

provides certain advantages, highlighted especially in a thin-client, fat-server application architecture. Some of these advantages are listed below:

❑ The business rules are implemented consistently and independently of the particular application system.

❑ The business rules are maintained centrally. Modifications and updates of these rules do not require massive updates of the applications installed on the client machines.

❑ The business rules are enforced consistently, and the front-end application is no longer responsible for ensuring that they are implemented.

❑ The level of code reuse is increased significantly. The business rule is implemented once; its implementation is reused by any application system that needs it. The advantage is even greater when a power tool like Designer/ 2000 ensures a consistent implementation of similar business rules.

The Server API components generated by Designer/2000 are grouped into three categories:

❑ **Table API.** For each database table, Designer/2000 generates a package and a set of database triggers that may be installed in the database when the table object is created. The methods of this package may be invoked by any application environment that supports calls of PL/SQL stored procedures, including Developer/2000 tools, Visual Basic, and Oracle WebServer.

❑ **Database triggers.** For each table, Designer/2000 may also generate a set of 12 database triggers, which are used to enforce the business rules implemented by the table API when records are manipulated by an external application.

❑ **Module Component API.** This API is used only for Developer/2000 Forms modules. It allows you to implement query and data manipulation statements through PL/SQL procedures, rather than through the regular Developer/2000 Forms interface. The module APIs generate module components with the properties Datasource Type and Datatarget Type set to *'View'* or *'PL/SQL Procedure.'*

Sections 24.2.1–24.2.3 provide details on the APIs in each category and show how you can customize them to add your programmatic logic structures.

24.2.1 TABLE API

For each table in your Repository, Designer/2000 allows you to generate an application programmatic interface (API) composed of methods that allow you to interact with these tables programmatically rather than from a SQL interface. These methods are encapsulated in packages, also known as *table handlers.* One package is available for each table, and its name is cg$<table_name>, as in cg$ORDERS or cg$LINE_ITEMS. The following is a list of the major methods supported by this package:

❑ **INS.** Insert a record into the table.
❑ **UPD.** Update a record identified by the primary key value.
❑ **DEL.** Delete a record identified by the primary key value.
❑ **LCK.** Lock a record.
❑ **SLCT.** Select a record based on the value of its primary key.

In addition, based on the properties defined for the table object in the Repository, this package provides methods to validate constraints, to populate columns associated with sequences with values from those sequences, and to populate columns for which you have set the property *Autogen Type.* If you have requested that journaling be performed for the table, methods to populate the journal tables are part of this package as well.

Designer/2000 allows you to define in the Repository your own processing instructions that are executed before or after the generated part of the methods INS, UPD, DEL, and LCK. The Generate Table API utility combines, into the body of the procedure, the user-defined application logic with the statements created based on the properties of the table. Figure 24.9 shows the typical structure of these procedures. In this figure, EVENT stands for one of the event names: Insert, Update, Delete, or Lock.

The following are the steps required to add your own application logic to the table API procedures.

```
BEGIN
—  Application_logic Pre-<EVENT> <<Start>>
     — User-defined logic
—  Application_logic Pre-<EVENT> << End >>

—  Designer/2000 generated logic

—  Application_logic Post-<EVENT> <<Start>>
     — User-defined logic
—  Application_logic Post-<EVENT> << End >>
END;
```

FIGURE 24.9 A typical structure of a table API method.

1. Switch to the tab DB Objects of the Design Navigator and expand the table to which you want to add the programming logic.

2. Select the node Table API/Trigger Logic, and click Create. The dialog box Create Trigger/API Code appears (see Figure 24.10).

3. Select the event to which you want to add programmatic logic, and click Next. The events whose programmatic statements are inserted in the table API procedures are the last eight events at the bottom of the list.

4. Enter a brief description of the programmatic logic you are about to add to this event in the text field Name. A longer description may be entered in the text box Comment.

5. Click Finish to complete the process.

As in the other cases discussed in this section, the actual statements that make up the logic must be implemented in the Logic Editor.

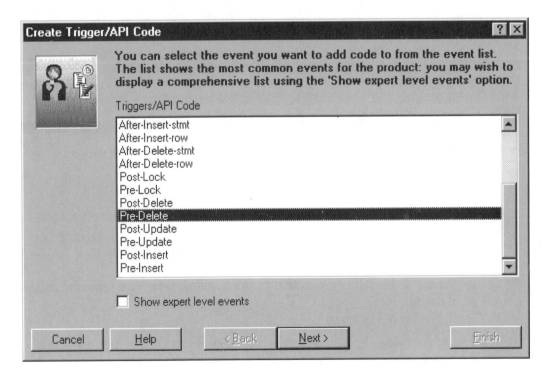

FIGURE 24.10 The Create Trigger/API Code dialog box.

24.2.2 DATABASE TRIGGERS

In combination with the characteristic package, the Generate Table API utility creates a set of 12 database triggers that cover all the possible events for which a trigger may be defined. In a number of these triggers, Designer/2000 creates its own programmatic logic. For example, the triggers Before Insert Row, Before Update Row, and Before Delete Row invoke the procedures INS, UPD, and DEL from the table handler, as well as a number of other methods through which the triggers validate arc constraints, foreign key constraints, and domain rules defined for the table.

All the triggers allow you to add your own logic to them. The Generate Table API utility coordinates your statements with those it generates based on the properties of the table. The steps to add a user-defined logic object to the table triggers are similar to those described in the previous section. The only difference resides in the type of event you select in the dialog box Create Trigger/API. For the case of triggers, select one of the first 12 events in the list.

Because the database triggers that are part of the Table API invoke the table handler procedures and because you can place user-defined logic in the triggers and procedures, be careful not to replicate the logic in these objects. You can avoid the replication if you understand well the flow of execution of the statements in the generated triggers and procedures. To help form this understanding, I present in Figure 24.11 a diagram of the code segments that may be executed when the event Before Insert Row occurs. This event is handled by the table API trigger CG$BIR_<TABLE>, which contains a set of statements defined by you and another set generated by Designer/2000. Part of the second set of statements

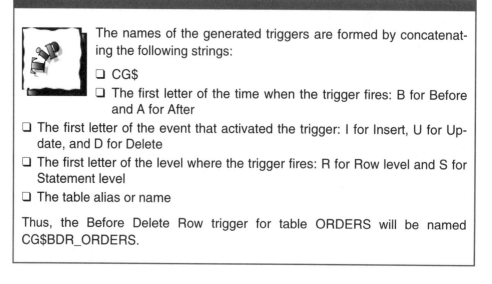

The names of the generated triggers are formed by concatenating the following strings:

❑ CG$

❑ The first letter of the time when the trigger fires: B for Before and A for After

❑ The first letter of the event that activated the trigger: I for Insert, U for Update, and D for Delete

❑ The first letter of the level where the trigger fires: R for Row level and S for Statement level

❑ The table alias or name

Thus, the Before Delete Row trigger for table ORDERS will be named CG$BDR_ORDERS.

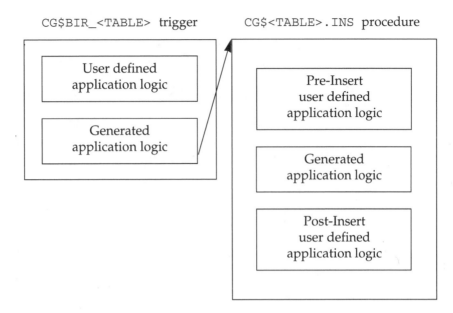

CG$BIR_<TABLE> trigger   CG$<TABLE>.INS procedure

User defined
application logic

Generated
application logic

Pre-Insert
user defined
application logic

Generated
application logic

Post-Insert
user defined
application logic

FIGURE 24.11 A diagram of code segments executed during a typical Before Insert Row event.

is a call to the table handler procedure CG$<TABLE>.INS. This procedure contains application logic generated by Designer/2000 and around it, the statements defined by you in the Pre-Insert and Post-Insert event. As you can see from this diagram, you may define up to three distinct units of logic for this event. You need to make sure that the statements in these units do not conflict or replicate statements in the other units, generated by you or Designer/2000.

From the discussion in this section, you may be left with the question: "What is the relationship between triggers defined explicitly as dependents of the table and trigger logic defined as part of the table API?" The answer to this question is that these objects should be viewed as two mutually exclusive alternatives to adding database triggers to your tables. Early on in the design, decide whether or not you will create the API for the tables in your application. If you will, then the trigger logic objects are used to implement the functionality. If not, you need to define explicit triggers as part of the design of your tables.

24.2.3 MODULE COMPONENT API

 The module component API is a package characteristic for the module component that provides methods to query a table and return the data in a PL/SQL table, or insert, update, delete, and lock the records in the base table of the module component. For similarity with the table API, this package is often called the *module component handler*. As in the case of the table API, you may specify your own application logic to be executed before or after the operations Insert, Update, Delete, and Lock take place. The following is the procedure to create these objects:

1. Switch to the tab Modules and find the module component to which you want to add the programming logic. This may be a reusable component or a specific one, implemented in a module.
2. Expand the node that represents the module and select API Logic.
3. Click Create ⬜. The dialog box Create Module Component API Code appears.
4. Select the event to which you want to add programmatic logic and click Next.
5. Enter a brief description of the programmatic logic you are about to add to this event in the text field Name. A longer description may be entered in the text box Comment.
6. Click Finish to complete the process.

The module component API is built on top of the table API for the base table of the module component. The methods for inserting, updating, deleting, and locking the module component handler perform these operations by invoking the corresponding methods from the table handler. As in the case of database triggers, know the execution sequence of your logic objects and those created by Designer/2000. Take careful steps to avoid conflicting statements in these handlers.

24.3 MAINTAINING APPLICATION LOGIC OBJECTS

The Designer/2000 front-end generators create fairly complex software modules based on the information you record in the Repository during the database design and application design activities. They also have the ability to incorporate in the generated modules objects and property settings from object libraries and template modules. Nevertheless, some business rules and situations require programming logic to be associated with the entire module or elements of it. To help you record this information in the Repository, Designer/2000 provides the following objects:

❑ Events

❑ Named Routines

❑ Library Modules

Sections 24.3.1–24.3.3 describe each of these categories of application logic objects and provide instructions on their use.

24.3.1 EVENTS

Some of the programming environments you use to implement modules in the application system have a well-defined event model that is supported by the Designer/2000 Repository. Examples of these environments are Developer/2000 Forms, Oracle WebServer, and Developer/2000 Graphics. In these cases, you can associate your own programming logic to any event that is available in a specific context. The steps required to populate an event with content are simple and apply to all situations and environments. The following is a list of such steps.

1. Select the module for which you want to add an event logic.
2. Expand the node Application Logic at the level where you want to add the event. Event handlers may be typically added at the module level, at the module component level, and at each individual item level.
3. Select the node Event and click Create ❚. The dialog box Create Application Logic appears. This dialog box initially displays the tab Event, shown in Figure 24.12. By default, this tab lists the most important events that may be handled in the context in which you are creating the user-defined event. In order to see the entire list of events applicable to the context, place a checkmark in the check box Show expert level events.
4. Select the event to which you want to add programmatic logic and click Next. Now you are presented with the tab Logic of the Create Application Logic dialog box (see Figure 24.13). This tab lists a description of all the program units that are defined for the selected event. The ones that will be implemented by the front-end generator are distinguished by the characteristic icon ▣ .
5. Enter a brief description of the programmatic logic you are about to add to this event in the text field Name. A longer description may be entered in the text box Comment.
6. Adjust the sequence in which the generator-implemented code and your code will fire.
7. Click Finish to complete the process.

At this point, you have created the specification for the event. You can use the Logic Editor to add the actual statements that implement the desired functionality.

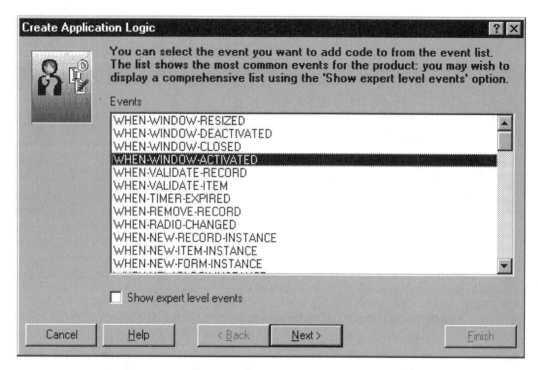

FIGURE 24.12   The tab Event of the Create Application Logic dialog box.

24.3.2 NAMED ROUTINES

 Often the programming logic may be complex and extensive. It may also be reused in other events or situations. In these cases, I recommend that you save this logic as a named routine associated with the module. Then you can invoke the routine from any event where you want to perform the functionality encapsulated by the routine. In order to create a named routine, perform the following steps:

1. Select the module to which you want to add the named routine.
2. Expand the node Application Logic at the level at which you want to add the routine.
3. Select the node Named Routines and click Create ⊞ . The dialog box Create Application Logic appears.
4. Enter the name of the routine and its type—Function, Procedure, Package Specification, or Package Body.
5. Click Finish.

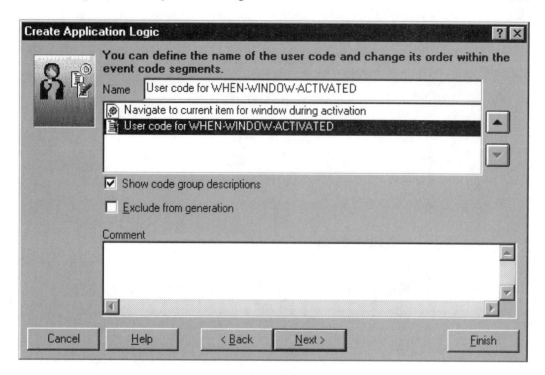

FIGURE 24.13 The tab Logic of the Create Application Logic dialog box.

As with events, you need to specify the contents of the routine in the Logic Editor.

24.3.3 LIBRARY MODULES

As you develop more and more complex named routines, you will realize that more than one module may use the same routine. In such cases, you implement the routines in library modules that are attached to the modules that require access to the functionality these routines offer. Creating a library is very similar to creating any module in the Design Editor. Only be careful to set the *Module Type* property of the new module to *'Library.'* Named routines are the only types of objects that libraries may contain. Adding a named routine to a library is the same as adding the routine to a regular module. Follow the instructions in the previous section to perform this activity.

In the Developer/2000 Forms environment, libraries correspond to PL/SQL library (PLL) modules. So that the generated Forms module can access the program unit stored in a library, this library must be attached to the form. The Forms Generator of Designer/2000 can generate the PLL module and attach it to the

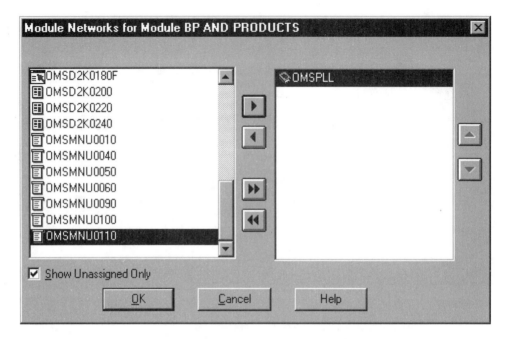

FIGURE 24.14   The Module Networks for Module dialog box.

form module, provided you have linked the two modules in a module network. The following actions allow you to create this link in the Design Editor.

1. Select the Developer/2000 Forms module and right-click.
2. Choose the item Called Modules... from the popup menu that appears. This action displays the dialog box Module Networks for Module.
3. Select the library module from this list and move it to the list box on the right-hand side of the dialog box (see Figure 24.14).
4. Click OK.

24.4   THE LOGIC EDITOR

The Logic Editor component of the Design Editor specifies the PL/SQL statements that will make up the body of PL/SQL definitions and application logic objects. The Logic Editor is implemented as a window where the contents of a particular object are displayed and maintained. This window contains two panes: the Outline pane and the Editor pane. The Outline pane to the left represents the contents of the PL/SQL object schematically. The Editor pane to the right is where the actual PL/SQL statements of the module are entered, viewed, and modified. In addition, the Logic Editor keeps open by default the Selection Tree window. This window contains all the syntactic structures of PL/SQL and programming elements that you may drag and drop into the Editor pane during development. Sections 24.4.1–24.4.3 discuss the components and functionality of the Logic Editor.

24.4.1 THE OUTLINE PANE

The Outline pane uses a structured approach to represent the contents of the PL/SQL object. The statements that form the body of the object are grouped in the appropriate hierarchy levels, indented for ease of view. The structured representation of program units in the Outline pane has several advantages, which are identified in the following list:

❑ Each programmatic structure is clearly marked and nested in the appropriate level of code hierarchy. This arrangement makes the process of debugging large and complex program units easier.

❑ Because the beginning and the end of each program token is clearly marked, identifying the missing semi-colons or misplaced terminating statements is much easier, such as END, ENDIF, and END LOOP, which often complicate the life of a programmer.

❑ The structured tree of the PL/SQL object components facilitates the navigation between these components. Indeed, by clicking a tree node in the Outline pane, the statement represented by that node in the Editor pane will be highlighted for ease of view.

By default, a program unit is represented in Outline mode, as shown in Figure 24.15. This mode represents the statements in the module and the category in which they fit, such as Select and IF...THEN...ELSE. On some occasions, you may want more information shown in the module tree. You can switch from Outline mode to Detail mode by selecting View | Detail check item. To switch the representation of the PL/SQL object from Detail to Outline mode, select View | Outline check item.

The default representation of the program structure follows the familiar metaphor of Windows Explorer. Each node in the tree is preceded by the Closed Folder icon ⊞▢ if the node is collapsed or does not contain any children, and by the Open Folder icon ⊟▤ if the node is expanded. Besides these generic icons, the Logic Editor comes with a set of icons that represent all the different types of nodes in the tree. In order to view the Logic Editor's icons in the structure tree, select View | Iconic check item. To toggle back to the regular mode of the Outline pane, deselect View | Iconic check item.

You can customize the structure tree of PL/SQL statements in the Outline pane in other ways. For example, the comments embedded in the module are by

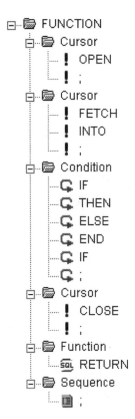

FIGURE 24.15   The Outline pane of the Logic Editor window.

default shown as nodes in the tree. To hide them, uncheck the menu item View |
Comments from the Navigator menu. Especially for heavily commented program
units, this option may significantly reduce the size of the tree.

You may also have statements in your program units in which function calls
are nested several levels deep. As an example, consider the following statement
which converts the last five characters of a string into uppercase:

```
uc_str := UPPER(SUBSTR(str, LENGTH(str) -5));
```

In such instances, you can easily end up with unbalanced parentheses, which result in compiling errors often difficult to debug. To avoid such situations, you
may view the structure tree with parameters by selecting View | Parameters
from the Navigator menu. In this mode, you can easily see the beginning and end
of each parameter, which correspond to left and right parentheses in the PL/SQL
statement.

Finally, the Logic Editor allows you to embed pseudo-code in your program units together with valid PL/SQL syntax. This capability is important especially in the early stages of application development, when you may describe in natural language the functionality of the program unit before actually implementing it. If you describe the steps that the program unit will perform according to an established convention, you will be able to see these descriptions in the structure tree of the program unit in the Outline pane. The convention is very simple and is presented below:

```
/*_Enter your description here_*/
```

The enclosure of the description in the PL/SQL comment tokens "/* ... */" ensures that what you enter there will not affect the syntax checker of the Navigator. The character '_' immediately before and after the description allows the Navigator to distinguish it from regular comments in the body of the program. These descriptions are known as To Do statements by the Navigator. By default, they are displayed in the hierarchy tree of the Outline pane. If you want to hide them, uncheck the menu item View | ToDo Statements from the Navigator's menu.

The default settings of the Outline pane are defined in the Logic Editor Options dialog box, which you can invoke by selecting Options | Logic Editor Options.... This dialog box contains two properties tabs, labeled Outliner and Editor, which allow you to view and set properties such as the font and color of the pane, and the level of indentation of the hierarchy tree. Other properties you can set here define whether the hierarchy tree will display the outline or the details of the program unit; whether the Navigator's icons will be used or not; and whether comments, To Do statements, and parameters will be displayed or not. Figure 24.16 shows the Outliner properties tab of the Logic Editor Options dialog box.

24.4.2 THE EDITOR PANE

The Editor pane is where the actual code of the PL/SQL object is viewed and edited. This pane is tightly coupled with the Outline pane. The content of the Outline pane is defined by what is entered in the Editor pane. A nice feature of the Editor pane, which greatly improves the quality of code, is the capitalization of Oracle and PL/SQL reserved words as you type them. This allows you to enforce this programming standard for all the PL/SQL objects you develop using Designer/2000. By distinguishing them from the rest of the code, this standard also prevents you from accidentally using any of these reserved words to label your own variables.

The Logic Editor Options dialog box of the Logic Editor contains the tab labeled Editor, where you can maintain properties that control the level of indentation and the length of lines in the Editor pane. In addition, this tab contains a se-

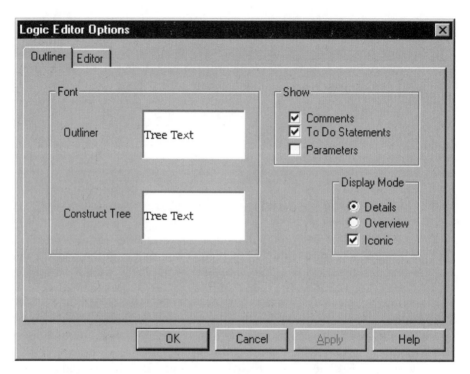

FIGURE 24.16   The Outliner properties tab of the Logic Editor Options dialog box.

ries of check boxes that, among other things, allow you to turn on and off the ability of the Editor pane to perform the following functions automatically:

- ❑ Recognize and capitalize Oracle and PL/SQL keywords
- ❑ Indent the PL/SQL statements you enter
- ❑ Format the text entered in the Editor
- ❑ Display line numbers

Figure 24.17 shows the Editor properties tab of the Logic Editor Options dialog box.

24.4.3 SELECTION TREE WINDOW

The Selection Tree window serves as a reference card that you can consult during development efforts. It contains all the PL/SQL constructs, syntax elements, functions, and data types that you will need in your applications. Like the Out-

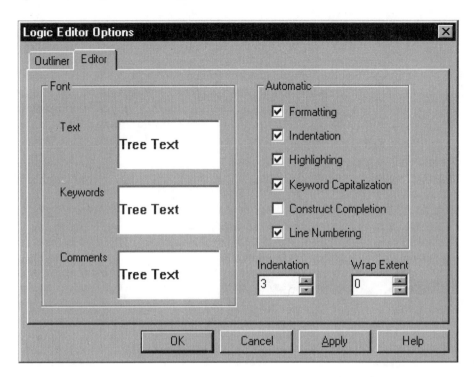

FIGURE 24.17 The Editor properties tab of the Logic Editor Options dialog box.

line pane, the Selection Tree is built around the Windows Explorer metaphor, which means that you can expand and collapse the nodes in the hierarchy tree of objects. The highest level of the hierarchy contains three nodes: Constructs, Statements, and Static Data. The following paragraphs provide details on each of them:

❑ **Constructs.** The nodes under this hierarchy contain templates for defining the headers of PL/SQL programs; the declaration, execution, and exception sections of a PL/SQL block; iterations; conditional statements; and terminators. These nodes can be used to build the framework of the program unit.

❑ **Statements.** The nodes under this part of the tree represent the syntax of the PL/SQL statements you may use in the program unit. They include statements used to declare variables, manipulate data, handle cursors, manage transactions, and lock and handle exceptions.

❑ **Static Data.** The children of this node represent the PL/SQL program units built in the Oracle Server database. These program units are organized into the following groups: error reporting, numeric, character, conversion, date, and miscellaneous.

Figure 24.18 shows two levels of the hierarchy of nodes in the Selection Tree.

The main usage of the Selection Tree is to search for, find, and include a syntactic component of PL/SQL in your program. Its drag-and-drop functionality simplifies the task of adding any of the programming tokens contained in the tree to your program unit. To perform this task, follow the steps below:

1. Place the cursor at the location where you want to insert the new component in the Editor pane of the module you are editing.
2. Select the desired component in the Select Tree window. Expand the appropriate nodes to find the object, if necessary.

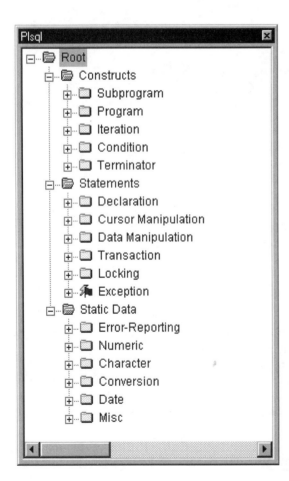

FIGURE 24.18   PL/SQL syntax components of the Selection Tree.

3. Drag the object from the Selection Tree and drop it in the Editor pane. The Logic Editor will add the new component at the insertion point you defined in step 1.

The components inserted into the program unit using this method are normally templates of code. You need to provide specific arguments or data to transform them into fully functional PL/SQL statements. In these cases, the Navigator provides placeholders where these details should be added. The format of these placeholders is such that they appear as To Do Statements in the Outline pane. For example, if you drag and drop from the Select Tree the WHILE loop iteration, the Navigator will create the following statements in the Editor pane:

```
WHILE /*_condition_*/ LOOP
   /*_actions_*/
END LOOP;
```

You can fill this template with the conditions and actions that are specific to the program unit in question.

24.5 WORKING WITH THE LOGIC EDITOR

The discussion about the components of the Logic Editor in the previous sections inevitably touched on some important uses of this tool, such as adding PL/SQL constructs to your module and viewing it in different modes. In addition, the Logic Editor allows you to check the syntax of the PL/SQL objects you create and to exchange the contents of these objects with other environments using the import and export utilities. These two functions are discussed in the following sections.

24.5.1 CHECKING THE SYNTAX OF PL/SQL OBJECTS

The Logic Editor has built-in functionality that allows you to check the syntax of the PL/SQL statements you enter in the Editor pane. You can invoke the syntax checker by select Utilities | Check Syntax....

A prerequisite to running the syntax checker is that the changes in the module contents must be saved. If changes are pending and the utility is invoked, you will be prompted to save the changes. The syntax checker analyzes the contents of the Editor pane for correctness and validity. If it finds errors, they are displayed in a message window.

Be sure to understand the difference between the syntax checker embedded in the Logic Editor and the PL/SQL engine incorporated in the Oracle Server or the Developer/2000 tools. The former relies on definitions of database objects as they exist in the Designer/2000 Repository, whereas the latter uses the properties of objects stored in the database or in the application modules. If a PL/SQL object depends on one or more database objects that are defined in the Repository but are not created in the target database, the module will pass successfully the scrutiny of the syntax checker, but it will fail when created in the target database, unless all the other objects referenced by this object are created as well.

24.5.2 IMPORTING AND EXPORTING THE CONTENTS OF PL/SQL OBJECTS

The Logic Editor allows you to import text from operating system files into the Editor pane and to export text from this pane into files. This functionality is especially important for PL/SQL objects defined with the source file method. By bringing the contents of these files into the Editor pane, you can benefit from all the features of this component, even if you are not maintaining the PL/SQL object in the Designer/2000 Repository. In particular, you can:

❑ Facilitate the development process using the Select Tree and Outline pane
❑ Organize the code in a consistent fashion through the support of the Editor for indentation and keyword recognition
❑ Develop code that uses database objects defined in the Repository without having to create them in a database schema
❑ Ensure that the code you develop is syntactically correct

In order to import text from an operating system file, follow these steps:

1. Select Edit | Import Text... from the Navigator menu. The standard Windows Open dialog box appears.
2. Select the file you want to import.
3. Click OK. The contents of the file are inserted into the Editor pane.

In order to export the contents of the Editor pane to a text file, follow these steps:

1. Select Edit | Export Text... from the Navigator menu. The standard Windows Save As dialog box appears.
2. Select the folder where you want to store the file.
3. Specify the name of the file. Note that the Navigator will by default assign the extension .mod to the file.
4. Click OK. The contents of the Editor pane will be written to the file you selected.

By default, the dialog boxes mentioned above will initially display the folder BIN of the ORACLE_HOME directory of your environment (for example, C:\ORAWIN95\BIN or C:\ORANT\BIN). Using standard Windows commands, you can navigate to a different folder and select the file you want.

24.6 SUMMARY

PL/SQL objects are an important part of the applications you design and develop using Designer/2000. The structure and properties of these objects are maintained in the Design Editor. The content of the PL/SQL objects may be maintained in the Logic Editor component of this diagrammer. This chapter focuses on how the Design Editor and the Logic Editor help you define the content of PL/SQL objects. The major topics of this chapter are:

- ❑ **Maintaining Server Side PL/SQL Objects**
  - ❑ Creating PL/SQL Definitions
  - ❑ Defining PL/SQL Objects with the Operating System File Method
  - ❑ Defining PL/SQL Objects Using the Free Format Method
  - ❑ Defining PL/SQL Objects Using the Declarative Method
  - ❑ Advantages of the Declarative Method
  - ❑ Implementing PL/SQL Objects
  - ❑ Database Triggers
- ❑ **Understanding and Maintaining the Server API**
  - ❑ Table API
  - ❑ Database Triggers
  - ❑ Module Component API
- ❑ **Maintaining Application Logic Objects**
  - ❑ Events
  - ❑ Named Routines
  - ❑ Library Modules
- ❑ **The Logic Editor**
  - ❑ The Outline Pane
  - ❑ The Editor Pane
  - ❑ Selection Tree Window
- ❑ **Working with the Logic Editor**
  - ❑ Checking the Syntax of PL/SQL Objects
  - ❑ Importing and Exporting the Contents of PL/SQL Objects

Part V

SOFTWARE GENERATION AND DEVELOPMENT

Chapter 25. Generating Database Server Objects

Chapter 26. Generating Front-End Software Modules

Chapter 27. Introduction to Generating Developer/2000 Forms Modules

Chapter 28. Advanced Developer/2000 Forms Generation

Chapter 29. C++ Object Layer Generator

GENERATING DATABASE SERVER OBJECTS

- ◆ Preparing for Generation
- ◆ Designer/2000 Server Generator
- ◆ Post-Generation Tasks
- ◆ Different Scenarios of Using the Server Generator
- ◆ Recovering the Design of Databases
- ◆ Summary

After the elaborate work you do to analyze the data model and design the database objects of your application, the point comes when you want to create these objects in a database server. The Server Generator is the Designer/2000 tool that reads the definitions of the database objects stored in the Repository and generates the SQL statements that create these objects. Because of the category of statements it creates (Data Definition Language, or DDL statements), this generator is also known as the DDL Generator. Running the Server Generator is an iterative process. As the design and development process progresses, parts and components of the data model become mature and ready to be implemented. The Server Generator is run to generate each of these components. Also, as the development effort evolves, the data model may need additions and modifications. The Server Generator in these cases generates the statements that reconcile the properties of database objects stored in the Repository with the objects that reside in the actual database.

25.1 PREPARING FOR GENERATION

Before invoking the Server Generator, you need to complete the following two tasks:

❑ Perform a quality check for the objects that will be generated.
❑ Take any steps necessary to prepare the target database for the new objects.

Sections 25.1.1 and 25.1.2 discuss each of these pre-generation steps in detail.

25.1.1 CHECKING THE QUALITY OF GENERATED OBJECTS

Consider two aspects when checking the quality of database objects that you are about to generate. First, ensure that these objects fulfill the business requirements of your application by performing a final review of the analysis and design work that led to the creation of these objects in the Designer/2000 Repository. Second, ensure that these objects are sound from a technical perspective. For example, check that the storage parameters of tables and indexes are set at appropriate levels, or that PL/SQL module names do not use reserved keywords.

Designer/2000 provides a series of reports that you can run in order to check the quality of database objects before you invoke the Server Generator. These reports can be accessed by expanding the nodes Database Object Definition, Database and Network Design, and Quality in the Repository Reports hierarchy tree. The following paragraphs describe some of these reports:

❑ **Table Definition.** This report displays general attributes of tables, such as name, description, and volume properties. It also displays a summary of column definitions; information about the primary, unique, and foreign key constraints; and the validation clause of the check constraints defined against the table.

❑ **Database Object Implementation Definition.** This report displays details about the implementation of database objects. For each database, the report returns the users and properties of objects implemented for these users, like tables and indexes.

❑ **Database Objects.** This report presents a listing of all the objects defined for a database. The database administration objects are presented first, followed by the database users and the schema objects assigned to these users.

❑ **Database User Definition.** This report displays detailed information about the users defined in the Repository. Properties like Default Tablespace and Temporary Tablespace, as well as the objects implemented for the user, are listed in the report.

❑ **Database Definition.** This report displays properties about databases defined in the Repository. All the parameters that go in the CREATE DATABASE statement are listed in this report.

❑ **Constraint Definition.** This report displays detailed information about all the primary key, unique key, foreign key, and check constraints defined against the tables of your application system. Properties of columns that are part of the key constraints are presented as well.

❑ **PL/SQL Module Definition.** This report retrieves information about the functions, procedures, and packages you have defined in the Repository. For each program unit, the report also displays the content of its body.

Running and analyzing the reports discussed here is certainly not a goal in itself, but an activity that may lead to the revision and enhancement of the physical data model for your application. The process of discovering discrepancies and inconsistencies in the database objects and the PL/SQL program units defined in the Repository and eliminating them is a recursive process that must continue after the initial run of the Server Generator utility.

The companion CD-ROM contains these and other reports for the TASC OMS application system. You can navigate to them by following the links *Software*, *Order Management System Design*, and *Repository Reports*.

25.1.2 PREPARING THE TARGET DATABASE

In order to use the output of the Server Generator, you need to run the SQL scripts it produces against an Oracle database. You need to prepare the environment so that the statements contained in these scripts complete successfully. You may take different measures, depending on the kind of objects you will be creating. If, for example, you are creating the database or some tablespace, you may have to take several steps to set up the appropriate hardware and software environment, such as:

❑ Install the appropriate Oracle Server software on the target database server. This includes not just the kernel RDBMS software, but also its extensions, such as SQL*Net, which will allow you to access the database server from your Designer/2000 or any client workstation. You may need to create a new database instance as well, if no appropriate database exists to host the new objects.

❑ Install and configure the disks and file systems that will contain the data files. If RAID technology will be used, you need to decide which kind of RAID you will use and how to configure the available disks.

If, on the other hand, you are simply adding some objects to an existing database instance, you must ensure that no conflicts will arise as a result of applying the changes. Furthermore, when upgrades to an existing application are deployed, a good practice is to define a strategy to fall back to the database state prior to the upgrade. This may come in very handy in case the system upgrade is aborted.

Although I discuss the issue of preparing the target database prior to discussing the Server Generator, this order does not imply a temporal dependency of these two tasks. In fact, as you will see in the following section, you can run the Server Generator and create a series of SQL script files that implement the database schema of your application without interacting with any database. Then you can prepare the hardware and software environment for the new database and, finally, run the scripts generated earlier in the new environment.

25.2 DESIGNER/2000 SERVER GENERATOR

Sections 25.2.1 through 25.2.6 discuss the features of the Server Generator and how you can use them to generate SQL code that implements the database objects and PL/SQL modules you have defined in the Designer/2000 Repository for a given application system.

25.2.1 PURPOSE OF THE SERVER GENERATOR

The Server Generator is the Designer/2000 tool that reads the properties of database objects from the Repository and generates SQL statements to create these objects in an Oracle database or in other database environments, such as an Informix, DB2, Sybase, or a generic ANSI-compliant database. It also reads the definitions of PL/SQL modules and generates statements that implement these modules as stored program units in the Oracle Server database.

The Server Generator can be accessed as a utility from the Design Editor by selecting the objects you want to generate and then issuing one of these commands:

❑   Click the icon Generate 🖳 on the Editor's toolbar.
❑   Select Utilities | Generate….

The Server Generator is materialized in the form of two utilities implemented in separate dialog boxes. The first one, Generate Database Administration Objects, generates scripts that create structural objects of the database, such as the database itself, users, roles, tablespaces, and rollback segments. The second utility, Generate Database Objects, generates the implementations of database objects for a particular schema. Depending on the object you choose prior to invoking the Generate utility, the Design Editor will launch one utility or the other.

Typically, the process of creating the database objects in your application system goes through two steps. First you create the structure of the database; then you create the database objects required by the application. The two utilities of the Server Generator help you create the scripts required to implement each of these steps. Although they are used for different purposes, functionally the two dialog boxes that implement these utilities are similar. The following two sections will discuss each of them.

25.2.2 GENERATING THE DATABASE STRUCTURE OBJECTS

In order to generate the structural objects of your database, you need to select one of the objects that falls into this category—for example, the database you want to create—and then invoke the Server Generator as explained in the previous section. The Generate Database Administration Objects is composed of two tabs: Target and Objects. The properties located on the tab Target allow you to define the location where the generated files will be created and the options of the generation process. Figure 25.1 shows an example of this tab.

The main options that you set on this tab are the prefix string, which serves as a common name for all the output files that the Server Generator will create, and the directory where these files will be written. On this tab, you can also select the type of the RDBMS for which the objects will be created. By default, all the check boxes in the Generation Options group are set. If you do not want to generate one of the objects controlled by these options, simply clear the appropriate check box.

The second tab of the dialog box, titled Objects, populates the working set of the generator with objects for which it will create the DDL scripts. The list box to

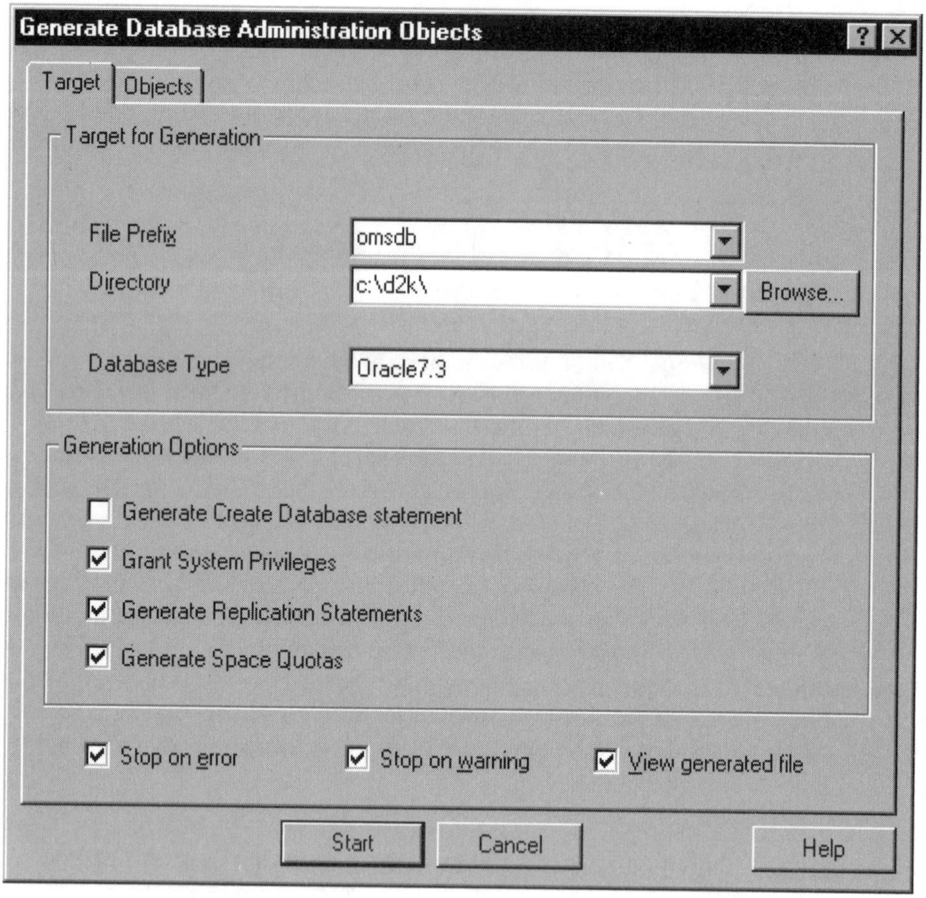

FIGURE 25.1 The Target tab of the Generate Database Administration Objects dialog box.

the left displays available objects, whereas the list box to the right represents objects already in the set. The iconic buttons between the list boxes transfer individual objects or groups of objects from one set to the other. Figure 25.2 shows an example of the Objects tab.

When you have populated the run set of the Generator with the desired objects, click Start. The Generator creates one script file for each type of objects it processes. The name of each file is the prefix string you provided; the extension of each file represents the type of objects the file contains. For example, <file>.DB contains the CREATE DATABASE statement, <file>.TBS contains the statements to create tablespaces, <file>.USR contains the statements to create the database users, and so on.

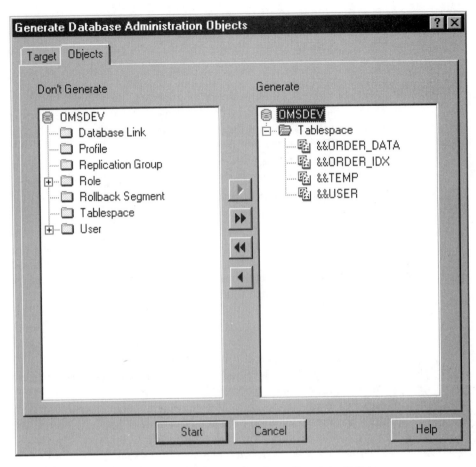

FIGURE 25.2 The Objects tab of the Generate Database Administration Objects dialog box.

25.2.3 GENERATING DATABASE OBJECTS

The process of generating database objects is very similar to that of generating database administration objects. It may be described as follows:

1. Select one or more database implementation objects and invoke the Server Generator. The dialog box Generate Database Objects opens.
2. Set the target of the generation on the tab Target.
3. Refine the members of the run set on the Objects tab.
4. Click Start.

One important difference between generating database administration objects and database objects is the target of the statements produced by the Server Generator. The Generate Database Objects utility allows you to generate the objects to three targets:

❑ **Operating system files.** In order to generate the statements to script files, select the radio button File on the tab Target. Then specify the prefix and the directory of the generated files and the type of database for which you want to generate the scripts.

❑ **Online Oracle database.** To create the database objects to an Oracle database, select the radio button Oracle on the tab Target and provide the database user name, password, and connect string.

❑ **Online ODBC database.** In order to create the database objects to an online non-Oracle database using an ODBC connection, you must first select the radio button ODBC. Then select the ODBC data source from the list box Source. This data source must be set to connect to a target database prior to running the Generate Database Objects with the ODBC target. Select the type of the data source from the list box Type.

Figure 25.3 shows an example of the Target property tab of the Generate Database Objects dialog box.

You can configure several options before running the Generate Database Objects utility. They are maintained in the dialog box Database Generation Options, shown in Figure 25.4. To access this dialog box, click Options... in the Generate Database Objects dialog box. The options in this dialog are organized into two groups. The group General contains options that apply to all the target databases; the group Oracle specific contains options that influence the generator only when the target database is an Oracle Server database. To prevent the generator from creating objects from one of the categories listed in this dialog box, clear the check box that corresponds to that category.

When the check box Generate Valid Value Constraints is set, the Server Generator will implement an implicit check constraint for every column that has a list of allowed values defined and that has the property *Dynamic List* set to '*No.*' Recall from the discussion in Chapter 20 that the enforcement of allowed values of columns through implicit or explicit check constraints should be a conscious decision made after you understand the implications this may have on the flexibility of your database architecture. Consider clearing this check box to avoid creating such constraints accidentally.

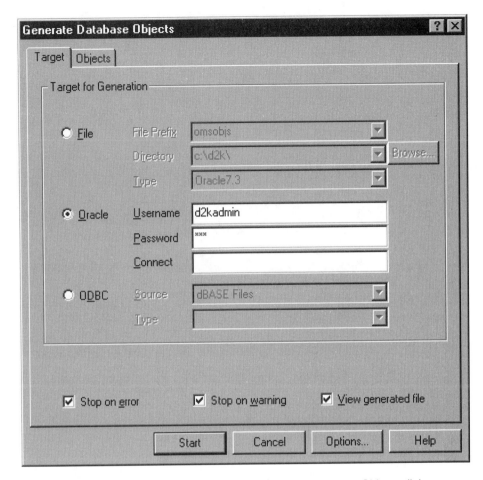

FIGURE 25.3   The Target tab of the Generate Database Objects dialog box.

25.2.4   THE OUTPUT OF THE SERVER GENERATOR

As I discussed in the previous section, the objects in the working set of the Generator belong to different categories of database objects, such as tables, indexes, packages, procedures, users, and so on. When the target database is an Oracle Server database, the Server Generation preserves this organization in the output files it produces. All these files share the same name defined by the prefix you specify on the Target tab. The statements that create each type of object are grouped in a file with a characteristic extension. A 'root' file with extension .SQL contains SQL calls to each of these files. When the target database is a non-Oracle database, all the generated statements are written in one file with the extension .SQL.

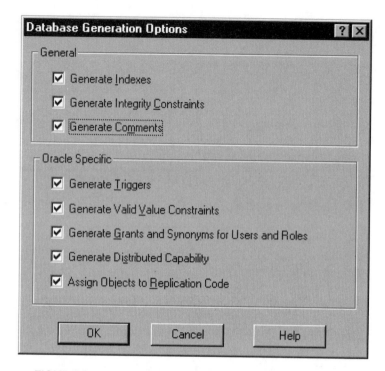

FIGURE 25.4   The Database Generation Options dialog box.

25.2.5   GENERATING TABLE API AND MODULE API

As I explained in Chapter 24, the table and module application programmatic interface (API) is composed of PL/SQL packages and database triggers. The process of generating and installing them is, therefore, very similar to the process of generating PL/SQL program units using the Generate Database Objects utility. You can invoke the Generate Table API utility by selecting the table object in the Design Editor and then choosing Utilities I Generate Table API.... Selecting a module and choosing Utilities I Generate Module Component API... activates the second utility.

25.2.6   GENERATING CODE CONTROL AND REFERENCE
          CODE TABLES

When your application requires sequence generators that return numbers while preserving the order of these numbers, Designer/2000 generators use tabular structures rather than Oracle sequences as the source for these numbers. These tables are known as *code control tables*. Depending on how you set the scope of the generators, there can be a global code control table called CG_CODE_CON-TROLS, an application-specific table called <application name>_CODE_CON-TROLS, or even a code control table for each table that needs it, called <table_name>_CODE_CONTROLS.

Similarly, the generators use a reference code table to retrieve the allowed values of columns and domains. Depending on the scope, a global reference code table can exist, called CG_REF_CODES, or an application-specific one called <application name>_REF_CODES.

The scope of code control and reference code tables is maintained in the General Generator Options dialog box that appears if you select Options | Generator Options | General... from the Design Editor menu. This dialog box appears in Figure 25.5.

When you run the Server Generator with tables in the working set, the generator also provides the statements required to create and populate these tables. The table script with the extension .TAB contains the CREATE TABLE statements for these tables; the sequence script .CCS contains the statements to populate the code control table with a record for each sequence of this type in the run set; the 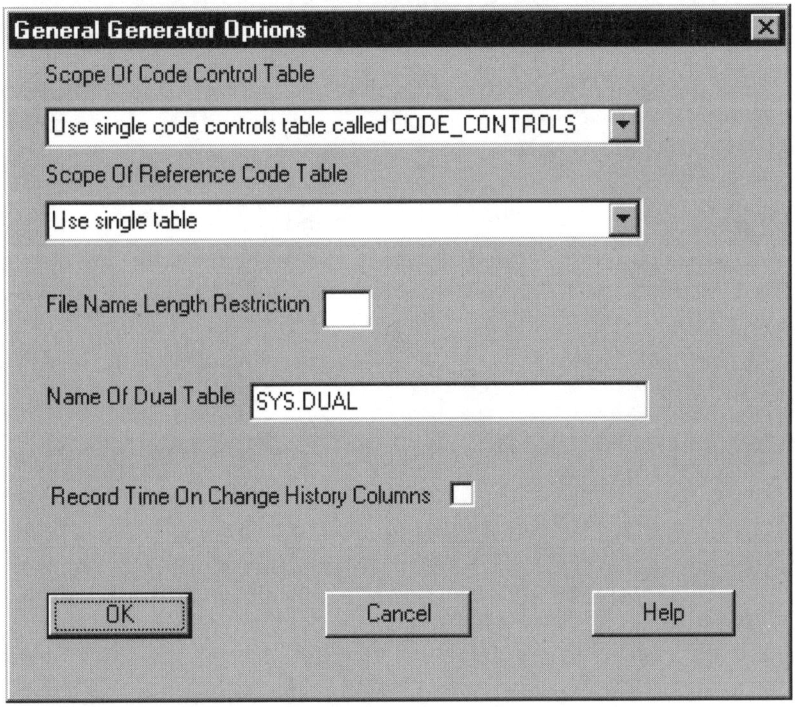

FIGURE 25.5 The General Generator Options dialog box.

allowed values script with extension .AVT contain the statements that populate the code reference table with allowed values for the columns included in the run set.

You can also create the reference code table and the statements that update the values stored in them for modules or database objects that use this table. The following steps allow you to create these statements:

1. Select Utilities | Generate Reference Code Tables... to invoke the dialog box with the same name.
2. Set the target of the generation on the Target tab, just as you would do it in the Generate Database Objects dialog box discussed in Section 25.2.3.
3. Select the objects for which you want to generate the reference code table on the tab Objects. This tab works exactly like its counterpart in the Generate Database Objects dialog box. The only difference is that the objects that populate the hierarchy trees in the Generate Reference Code Tables dialog box are limited to modules, tables, snapshots, and views.
4. Click Start to initiate the process.

25.3 POST-GENERATION TASKS

After the Server Generator writes the DDL statements in the output files, you can take a few more steps to complete the work that started with the data analysis and modeling efforts at the beginning of the project. In particular you want to:

❑ Review the generated statements and regenerate if necessary.
❑ Deploy the generated objects to the target database.
❑ Test the deployed objects. Regenerate and re-deploy if necessary.

Sections 25.3.1, 25.3.2, and 25.3.3 provide additional details on each of these tasks.

25.3.1 REVIEWING THE GENERATED DDL STATEMENTS

I mentioned that assuring the quality of the data models and database design is an important step in preparation for generating DDL statements. However, errors and inconsistencies may pass undetected even after careful reviews of data diagrams and Designer/2000 Repository reports. The output files of the Server Generator offer a last chance to discover such problems before objects are actually created in the database. You can view the contents of these files when they are created by the Server Generator. Or you can access these files using any ASCII text editor at any point in time after the Server Generator has completed its job.

You can resolve any problems discovered during the review of the generated files by modifying the properties of the appropriate objects and regenerating them. Depending on the type of object and the kind of problem, you may use different components of the Design Editor to reset the violating property. For example, if the problem is with the exit condition of the WHILE loop in the body of a function, the Logic Editor would be the preferred tool. If, on the other hand, the wrong procedure is included in a package, the module network and the associations of that package are more easily modified in the Design Navigator.

After editing the properties of objects that are not set accurately, you may regenerate the objects and review the output files. The process of generating, reviewing, debugging, fixing, and regenerating is an iterative process that should continue until you are satisfied with the quality of the DDL statements you are about to run against the database.

25.3.2 DEPLOYING THE GENERATED OBJECTS

Deploying the generated objects is equivalent to running the DDL statements generated by the Server Generator against a particular database. You can run the generated scripts immediately after their generation if the generation target is set to an Oracle or non-Oracle database connected via ODBC. However, in the light of the discussion in the previous section, first ensure the quality of the generated statements before using them to modify the database schema.

Before executing the DDL statements, you must also make sure that the target database is ready to accept the new objects. If you are installing a new application, make sure that the owner schema of the application is created in the database with the necessary privileges and resources to execute all the generated DDL statements. You can achieve this if you have set the properties of database structural objects in the Repository and have executed the scripts produced by the Generate Database Administration Objects utility.

If you are upgrading an existing application, make sure that the tablespaces contain enough contiguous free space to create new segments or that objects with conflicting names do not exist in the schema. When you are ready to execute the DDL statements, connect to the target database as the application owner schema and execute the file *FileName*.SQL.

25.3.3 TESTING THE DEPLOYED OBJECTS

Once the DDL statements are executed successfully, it is time for one more verification to make sure that they implement the intended business rules and data stores. Loading data in tables and indexes allows you to verify that their properties are properly defined. For PL/SQL modules, a more rigorous testing process should be implemented. Check that every function, procedure, package, and database trigger displays the desired functionality. If any inconsistencies are discovered, the problems can be fixed in one of the following ways:

❏ Fix the problem in the Repository. In order to apply the changes to the database schema, run the Generate Database Objects by setting the target to the online database. With this option, the utility will generate any ALTER statements that are necessary. In cases when the utility needs to drop the old objects from the application schema, it will create the DROP statements, regenerate new DDL statements, and create new objects using these statements.

❏ Fix the problem in the database. In order to reflect the changes in the Designer/2000 Repository, use the Recover Database Design utility to identify the differences and update the Repository definitions based on the target database data dictionary.

❏ Fix the problem in the Repository and apply the same fix to the appropriate object in the database. Although this option requires you to duplicate efforts, it is very appealing, especially when the fixes in question are minor and do not justify running the Reconcile utility.

25.4 DIFFERENT SCENARIOS OF USING THE SERVER GENERATOR

Following the discussion so far allows you to easily generate the DDL statements that implement the database schema of a new application in a particular database. The following sections show how you can use the Server Generator to solve some typical needs of the application development life cycle. In particular, they focus on the following issues:

❏ Generating database schemas for different software environments, such as a development, testing, and production database, with minimal changes to the Designer/2000 Repository

❏ Generating upgrades of an existing database schema for new versions of the application

❏ Generating database schemas for multiple independent production sites

25.4.1 GENERATING THE SAME DATABASE SCHEMA FOR DIFFERENT ENVIRONMENTS

In a typical application development environment, you start with a development database against which the application modules are developed and tested. This database is created using the DDL statements generated by the Server Generator. The objects in this database must be such that they meet the application requirements. Therefore, as new requirements are identified, changes and modifications to the properties of these objects may be needed. The development database and the contents of the Designer/2000 Repository need to be synchronized during the development phase. Any of the methods discussed in Section 25.3.3 may be used to synchronize the database and the Repository. Database configuration issues such as the distribution of tables and indexes across multiple tablespaces to minimize I/O, or an appropriate number of rollback segments to minimize contention, are usually not a concern for the administrator of the development database. The amount of data stored in the development database is usually minimal and the content of the data itself is not important.

At a certain point in the project's life, a checkpoint occurs at which all the developers submit the software modules for integration testing. After the modules are successfully integrated and any communication issues are resolved, the application moves to the testing phase. In preparation for this phase, the customary approach is to create a testing database, separate from the development database, against which the testers run the application. The structure of this database is again created using the output of the Server Generator. The testing database will obviously resemble the development database in that it contains the same schema objects with the same properties. It should also contain the same tablespaces as the production database, and the distribution of database segments in these tablespaces should be identical for both databases. Thus, the testing and production databases are structurally equivalent. In an ideal situation, they are identical; however, in most cases, a testing database contains only a fraction of the data for which the production database is designed and sized. Therefore, storage properties of certain objects are different in the testing and production environment. The testing phase may reveal the need to modify properties of database objects. When such modifications are needed, they must be applied to the Designer/2000 Repository, the development database, and the testing database. At the end of this phase, all these three environments must be fully synchronized.

When the testing is successfully completed, the system is ready to be deployed. The Server Generator is used again to generate the scripts that create all the necessary objects of the database. These scripts are part of and should be installed together with other software deliverables for the first release of the project. At this point, the current version of the application system is frozen in the Designer/2000 Repository.

From the discussion so far, clearly, the Server Generator needs to be used more than once at different points in the life of the software project. However, each time, the output of the tool must be slightly different to accommodate differences among development, testing, and production environments. A careful choice of the objects to include in the Generator's working set and different ways to set the properties of these objects allow you to use the Server Generator multiple times with the same Designer/2000 application system and create the DDL statements that implement the development, testing, or production database. Some recommendations for generating the database schema for each environment follow:

❏ **Development database.** Include in the working set of the Server Generator only those categories of objects used by the software modules. Such categories are Tables, Views, Sequences, Database Triggers, Functions, Procedures, and Packages. Indexes may be included, although many of them may be left out as well. Database administration objects, such as tablespaces, rollback segments, database roles, and users, are rarely needed at this point. For objects, such as tables and indexes, that require storage parameters, to leave these properties unset is better so that they inherit the storage parameters of the development tablespaces.

❏ **Testing database.** Objects from all the categories must be included in the Generator's working set. You need to test the scripts that define the structure of the database, as well as those that define the database objects required by your application. If the testing will not stress the capacity or throughput of the system, you may not need to set storage parameters of tables and indexes when you implement them. In every other aspect, the testing environment must mirror the production one.

❏ **Production database.** In preparation for the generation of the production database scripts, be careful to set the storage parameters of all the objects that require them. The Repository report 'Database Table and Index Size Estimates' may be used to help you decide how to set these properties.

25.4.2 IMPLEMENTING DATABASE UPGRADES

The actions described above work well in the case of the initial installation and setup of databases. But for subsequent releases of the software, take a different approach. For these releases, you cannot create all the objects of the database from scratch. CREATE DDL statements apply only to those objects that are added in the new release. For other objects whose properties change, appropriate statements must be generated to update the schema.

When a release of the software is rolled out, the application system that was used to implement that release must be frozen in the Repository. By freezing a particular version of an application system, you can recreate it in a consistent manner at any point in time. Any new development work must be performed either against a new version of the application system or against a copy of it. Thus, when the first release of an application is deployed, you create a new copy of its corresponding application system in the Designer/2000 Repository. The original application system is frozen for later reference.

From that point on, all the new design and development work must be performed against the newly created application system. As this work progresses, the information contained in this system will in general differ from the information contained in the previous version of the application and in the production database.

When the moment of testing and deploying the second release of the software arrives, you need to create a set of scripts that upgrade the database from the previous state to the new state. Designer/2000 helps you automate the task of creating these scripts. The Generate Database Objects utility can be run against a replica of the production environment to identify the differences between this database and the new version of the application system in the Repository. Based on these differences, the utility generates the appropriate ALTER statements required to upgrade the database. If any objects need to be dropped, the DROP statements are placed in a separate file. All these files are placed in the Oracle home directory, for example C:\ORAWIN95\BIN or C:\ORANT\BIN.

Depending on the amount and type of changes, some of these modifications may have to be implemented manually, as well. Ultimately, the generated scripts and those created manually become part of the next release of the software. Running these scripts during the installation of the release rolls the database forward from the previous version to the new version.

When upgrading the database, you must keep in mind that dependencies among objects in the schema may force you to work with more objects than the ones you are updating. If for example, a PL/SQL stored procedure uses an object, such as a table or a view, and the definition of this object is changed, Oracle will flag the procedure for recompilation. Any other program unit or database trigger that calls that procedure will also be set in an uncompiled state. Although Oracle will compile at runtime any PL/SQL object that is not in a compiled state, this situation must be avoided at any cost. The runtime compilation may require considerable resources and degrade the application performance significantly. In addition, errors may slip undetected until they interrupt the work of your application users. The easiest way to avoid this situation is to use the Server Generator to create or replace all the PL/SQL modules of your application after every major mod-

When the Generate Database Objects runs against an online database, its processing is divided into two phases. In the first phase, the objects in the online database are reconciled with those in the Repository. A byproduct of the reconciliation phase is a set of scripts that create any new objects or alter existing ones so that the Repository and the database objects are synchronized. In the second phase, the Generate Database Objects executes these scripts against the online database to apply the upgrade. In order to protect the production environment, I recommend that you run the utility against a replica of the production database, for example, the testing database. After reviewing and finalizing these scripts, you can run them to upgrade the production environment at the appropriate time.

ification of the schema. The scripts generated by the utility become components of the database upgrade script and are invoked after the scripts that alter the database objects.

Some of the DDL statements created during the cross-referencing phase of the Generate Database Objects utility may not run successfully in your environment, even if they are syntactically correct. For example, you cannot add a NOT NULL column to a table that already contains one or more rows, even if they do not violate the constraint. Similarly, you cannot modify the data type or the size of a column if at least one record with a non-NULL value is in that column. The following is a generic list of actions you can take to remove a column from a table or to modify the properties of columns in a table when the regular DDL statements will not execute successfully:

1. Rename the existing table.
2. Create a new table with the desired columns and properties.
3. Load the data from the renamed table to the newly created table. Ensure that the data will not violate any of the properties of the new table. Often, this step is performed simultaneously with the previous step if the new table is created with the command CREATE TABLE <TableName> AS <SubQuery>.
4. Drop the old table from the database.

Thus, the scripts generated during the cross-referencing phase of the Generate Database Objects utility should be viewed only as the starting point for creating the scripts that upgrade the database of an application from one version to another. Careful work is needed to supplement these scripts with the appropriate DDL commands that prepare the database to support the requirements of the new version of the application.

25.4.3 GENERATING DATABASE SCHEMAS FOR MULTIPLE SITES

The underlying assumption in the previous two sections is that your application will be deployed in one production site. In a general case, the software you develop may be distributed to multiple sites that are not related or dependent on each other. Figure 25.6 represents such a scenario.

In the situation shown in this figure, the first release of the software goes into production in January and is installed on Site A. At this point, you need the Release 1 Database Installation scripts produced using the Server Generator, as explained in Section 25.4.1. The second release of the software goes into production in May and Site B decides to install it. At the same time, Site A decides to upgrade its software to the newest release. At this point, you need the Release 2 Database Installation scripts for Site B and the Release 1 to 2 Database Upgrade scripts produced, as explained in Section 25.4.2. Finally, in December, you release the third

	JANUARY—RELEASE 1	MAY—RELEASE 2	DECEMBER—RELEASE 3
Site A	DBInstall.SQL, Version 1	DBUpgrade.SQL, Version 1 to 2	DBUpgrade.SQL, Version 2 to 3
Site B		DBInstall.SQL, Version 2	DBUpgrade.SQL, Version 2 to 3
Site C			DBInstall.SQL, Version 3

FIGURE 25.6 A typical scenario of a software product installed at different independent sites.

version of your application and Site C joins the list of sites where the application is installed. The utilities needed now are Release 3 Database Installation scripts for Site C, and Release 2 to 3 Database Upgrade scripts for Site A and Site B.

Thus, when moving from one version of the application to the other, simply creating the database upgrade scripts may not be sufficient. Together with them, you may also need scripts that generate the entire database schema from scratch. The management of database versions should be considered part of the larger issue of configuration management and software control for your software applications.

25.5 RECOVERING THE DESIGN OF DATABASES

Whereas the Server Generator allows you to create database objects out of the definitions of these objects in the Repository, the Recover Database Design Utility is intended to perform the opposite task. This utility reads the definitions of objects in the database dictionary or DDL script files and creates Repository objects based on these definitions.

An important use of the utility is as an aid to requirements definition and analysis in the early stages of the project. If the goal of the project is to build upon or improve an existing application system, you can start by creating in the Designer/2000 Repository a copy of the database objects in the existing database. The scrutiny and critique of the properties of these objects may be a good starting point for the analysis and design effort. In this case, the tables created by the Recover Database Design utility do not have corresponding entities in the Designer/2000 Repository. The Table to Entity Retrofit utility can be used to create entities for any tables in the Repository that are not already mapped to entities. The Recover Database Design and Table to Entity Retrofit utilities will be discussed in the following sections.

25.5.1 THE RECOVER DATABASE DESIGN UTILITY

The Recover Database Design utility brings in the Designer/2000 Repository definitions of objects and their properties. These definitions may come from the data
dictionary of a database or from a SQL script file that creates these objects. You
can invoke it from the Design Editor by selecting Utilities | Recover Design of |
Database…. This action displays the Design Recover Database dialog box.

The Recover Database Design utility operates on a working set of objects
whose definitions are brought over in the Repository. It contains two property
tabs, titled Source and Objects. The Source tab, shown in Figure 25.7, is where
you provide information about the location of the objects whose design you want
to recover and set other options that control the scope and the activities of the
utility.

The group of controls Source of Design Recovery instructs the utility where
to find the objects that will be included in the run set. You can set the source of
the tool to be one of the following categories:

❑ **Operating system file.** To achieve this, select the radio button File and provide the name and location of the file. Specify the type of the database objects contained in the file, as well. When reading specifications from a file,
   the tab Objects is removed, since you can dynamically populate the run set
   only when the source is an online Oracle or non-Oracle database.

❑ **Oracle database.** To read the definitions of an online Oracle database, set
   the radio button Oracle and provide the database user name, password, and
   connect string.

❑ **Non-Oracle database accessed via an ODBC connection.** To establish this
   connection, select the ODBC radio button and then choose the data source
   and the connection type.

Besides specifying information about the source of objects to recover, the
Source tab also assigns the database schema where these objects will be created
when recovered in the Repository. The list box Recover Object Into contains all
the database users that exist in the Repository.

By setting the appropriate check boxes on the Source tab, you may ask the
utility to recover the constraints, indexes, and database triggers together with the
properties of their parent table. In addition, if the objects you are about to recover
may be displayed on a data diagram, you can set the check box Show Results on
new Data Diagram to create a new data diagram with the recovered objects.

The Objects property tab is used to populate the working set with the objects that will be recovered. This tab is displayed only if the source of the recovery
is an online database. Figure 25.8 shows an example of this tab. The hierarchy
tree to the left displays all the available objects in the database schema to which
you are connected. The hierarchy tree to the right contains the objects currently

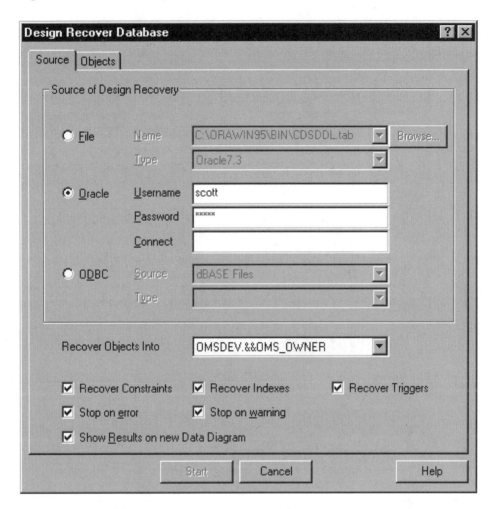

FIGURE 25.7 The Source property tab of the Design Recover Database dialog box.

included in the run set. Using the icons between the two controls, you can populate this set with the objects whose design you want to recover.

When the working set is constructed, you can click Start to initiate the process of recovering the design of the selected objects. As the utility performs its actions, the Message pane of the Design Editor displays any warnings or errors that may be encountered. At the end of this process, the utility displays a message box informing you that the design recovery is complete. The changes identified by the utility are inserted into the Repository but are not saved yet. You may save or revert these changes by clicking the buttons with the same names in the

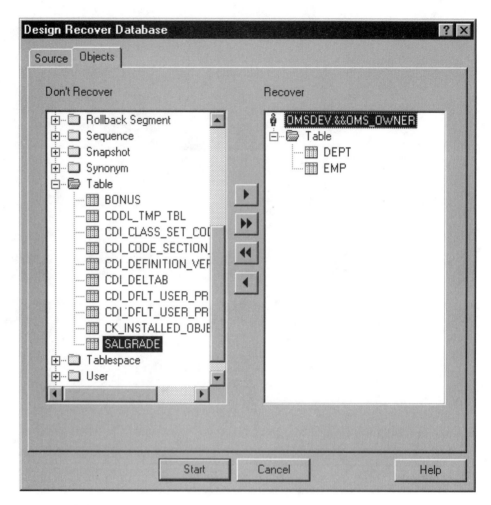

FIGURE 25.8 The Objects tab of the Design Recover Database dialog box.

message box. You can also click Browse/Edit to close the message box and return to the Design Editor.

The background of the Design Navigator is now gray to indicate that unsaved objects are in the hierarchy tree. Any objects inserted by the Recover Database Design utility are displayed in red to help you easily identify them. Figure 25.9 displays an example of the Design Navigator window where the tables EMP and DEPT are the ones recovered from the schema of the Oracle user SCOTT.

After reviewing and editing the new objects created by this utility, you can save the changes to the Repository.

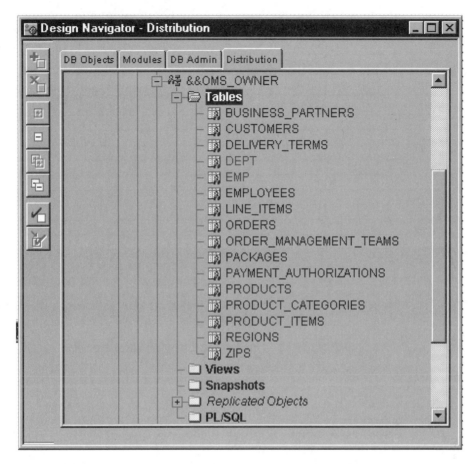

FIGURE 25.9 Sample output of the Recover Database Design utility.

25.5.2 THE TABLE TO ENTITY RETROFIT UTILITY

If tables exist in the Repository that are not associated with an entity, you can use the Table to Entities Retrofit utility to create entities based on the properties of these tables. This utility is used primarily when the database of an existing application is recovered, as described in the previous section, and you want to create a logical data model from the definition of the physical tables and database constraints.

The Table to Entity Retrofit utility can be accessed from several Designer/2000 tools such as the Repository Object Navigator, Entity Relationship Diagrammer, and Data Schema Diagrammer by selecting Utilities | Table to En-

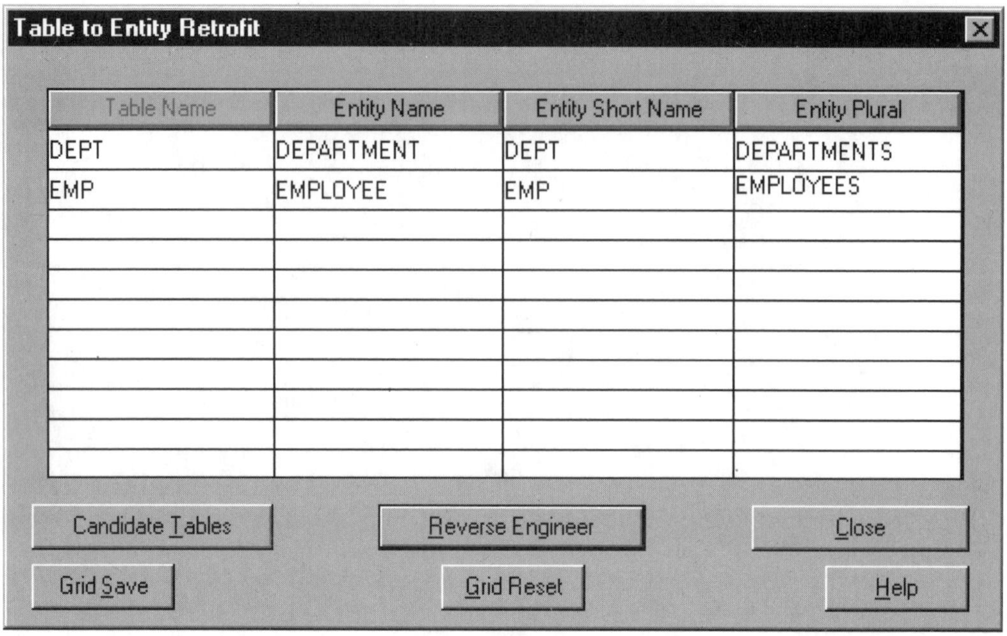

FIGURE 25.10   The Table to Entity Retrofit dialog box.

tity Retrofit.... It is made up of the dialog box Table to Entity Retrofit shown in Figure 25.10.

When the Table to Entity Retrofit dialog box is initially displayed, it is empty. Clicking the button Candidate Tables displays a dialog box with all the tables defined in the application system that are not associated with entities. In this dialog box, you can select the tables you want to retrofit and click OK to have them listed in the dialog box Table to Entity Retrofit, as shown in Figure 25.10. The utility creates the names of the new entities based on the names of the tables. You can overwrite the proposed names, as well as specify the short name and plural names for an entity, by typing in the appropriate field in the dialog box. When you are ready to start the retrofit process, click the button Reverse Engineer. Depending on the tables you have selected to retrofit and their properties, the utility may perform some or all of the following tasks:

1. Create entities based on table definitions. Each new entity will have a comment in the Comment property that explains its origin.

2. Create associations between entities and tables.

3. Create relationships between entities based on referential integrity constraints of the tables.

4. Create attributes for entities based on the column properties of the corresponding tables.

5. Create unique identifiers for entities based on primary and unique key definitions of the corresponding tables.

When the utility completes its work, you can refine the properties of the new objects and create diagrams based on them using the Entity Relationship Diagrammer.

25.6 SUMMARY

The Server Generator is the Designer/2000 utility that converts definitions and properties of database objects stored in the application system's Repository into a set of DDL statements that can be used to implement these objects in your environment. In addition, this tool can synchronize the schema of a database instance with the specifications of that schema in the Designer/2000 Repository. This chapter discusses the functionality of the Server Generator and ways of working with it. Major items covered in this chapter are listed below:

❑ **Preparing for Generation**
  ❑ Checking the Quality of Generated Objects
  ❑ Preparing the Target Database
❑ **Designer/2000 Server Generator**
  ❑ Purpose of the Server Generator
  ❑ Generating the Database Structure Objects
  ❑ Generating Database Objects
  ❑ The Output of the Server Generator
  ❑ Generating Table API and Module API
  ❑ Generating Code Control and Reference Code Tables
❑ **Post-Generation Tasks**
  ❑ Reviewing the Generated DDL Statements
  ❑ Deploying the Generated Objects
  ❑ Testing the Deployed Objects
❑ **Different Scenarios of Using the Server Generator**
  ❑ Generating the Same Database Schema for Different Environments

❑ Implementing Database Upgrades
❑ Generating Database Schemas for Multiple Sites

❑ **Recovering the Design of Databases**
  ❑ The Recover Database Design Utility
  ❑ The Table to Entity Retrofit Utility

GENERATING FRONT-END SOFTWARE MODULES

- Repository-Based Software Development
- Maintaining Preferences
- Object Class Libraries
- Generator Templates
- Designer/2000 Front-End Generators
- Summary

One of the major advantages of using Designer/2000 in the software development process is its ability to generate modules based on the analysis and design
information stored in the Repository. Provided that the right objects are stored in
the Repository and the appropriate sequence of steps is followed, you can create
functional software components from the early stages of the application design.
This capability allows you to build prototype models that you can use to refine
the requirements and the design of your application. As new information is gathered, the properties of objects in the Repository are updated and new and more
refined modules are generated to reflect these properties. The cyclic and evolu-
tionary approach to software development enabled by the Designer/2000 generators ultimately allows you to create applications whose functionality meets the
real needs of your users. This chapter will discuss the use of Designer/2000 generators in software development projects. In particular, it focuses on the following topics:

- Repository-based software development
- The influence of preferences in the generation process
- The role of object libraries and template software modules in the generation
  process
- Properties of different Designer/2000 generators
- Iterative development and regeneration

26.1 REPOSITORY-BASED SOFTWARE DEVELOPMENT

In a traditional software development environment, a very clear line divides requirements analysis and application design from application development. The
approach, methods, and tools used to perform the tasks in the first two categories
are different from those used to complete tasks of the last category. The people
who analyze requirements and design systems are often different from those who
develop the software modules. The picture is quite different in an environment
where Repository-based tools such as Designer/2000 are used. These tools store
the information about the application in a common Repository so that it can be
shared by multiple users and accessed at different stages of the software life
cycle. The distinctions among analysis, design, and development are blurred.
When a software engineer works on defining the properties of a function in a tool
such as the Function Hierarchy Diagrammer, she is not only analyzing and documenting the properties of that function but also laying the foundations for the design of the module that will be created by the Application Design Transformer.
Similarly, when she defines the data usages and other properties of the module,
she is also accomplishing a good part of the development of the modules in the
target software package. Whereas a developer would build the module from

scratch by manually creating each object, the Designer/2000 engineer simply sets a few properties of these objects in the graphical interface provided by the tools. In order to create actual software modules, she uses the Designer/2000 generator for the target environment.

All the front-end application generators of Designer/2000 work based on the same principles. They create code based on the properties of objects defined in the Repository and on a number of other sources. The following list describes the components used by these generators to create the software modules of your application:

❏ Definitions in the Repository of the data model, including tables, columns, and related properties.

❏ Definitions in the Repository of modules and their properties.

❏ Definitions in the Repository of module components, table usages, items—including bound, unbound, and action items.

❏ Settings of generation preferences for the particular generator. The Generator Preferences component of the Design Editor manages and accesses these settings in the Repository.

❏ Libraries of objects from which generated applications may inherit their properties and template modules with objects that will be included in or used by the generated modules. These are software modules usually stored as operating system files outside the Designer/2000 Repository.

❏ Database objects in an accessible database. These objects should be created based on the definition of Repository objects. They are not required to generate the modules, but they are required to compile them, where applicable, and execute them so that you can view and test their functionality.

So far in this book, you have seen how to create the data model of an application in the Repository and how to implement it in a database, how to create modules, and how to set the properties of their data usages. Sections 26.2, 26.3, and 26.4 will discuss the role of preferences, object libraries, and templates in the generation of software modules.

26.2 MAINTAINING PREFERENCES

As I explained in Section 26.1, each Designer/2000 front-end generator needs, among other things, a set of preferences to create software modules from definitions of objects stored in the Repository. Designer/2000 provides default values for these preferences, which are also known as *factory settings.* They enable you to create software modules without having to set a single preference manually. In fact, during prototyping efforts, modules are often generated with the default factory preferences. However, after finalizing on the elements that will be part of a module and after establishing their properties, you can enhance the look and feel of the front-end application you develop by setting the preferences of the generator. The Design Editor provides the Generator Preferences as the tool to view and maintain preferences of its generators. The following sections will discuss properties of this tool and the different functions you can perform with it.

26.2.1 THE GENERATOR PREFERENCES

One of the following commands may be used to access the Generator Preferences:

- ❏ Click the Generator Preferences 🖾 on the toolbar.
- ❏ Right-click the module in the Design Navigator and select Generator Preferences from the popup menu that appears.

At any moment in time, the Generator Preferences allows you to view and set the preferences of an application system for a particular product. To work with the preferences of a different product, select it from the list box Product. Figure 26.1 shows an example of the Generator Preferences for the Developer/2000 Forms Generator.

The Generator Preferences shares many common functions with other navigators in Designer/2000. The main area of its window is taken up by a hierarchy tree where all the preferences are displayed. The nodes in the tree can be expanded to display their children or collapsed to hide the details. These nodes fall into one of the following two categories:

- ❏ **Preference Type.** A preference type node serves the purpose of grouping together related preferences in order to simplify the process of viewing and accessing them. In Figure 26.1, for example, Action Item is a preference type that groups together several preferences that govern the way the generator creates action items in the modules it generates.
- ❏ **Preference.** A preference node represents the actual preference that you set and that influences the way the front-end generator creates the software modules. Preferences always belong to a preference type. Examples of preferences for the Action Item type are Action Item Button Width and Action Item Button Bar Order.

By default, the preferences displayed in the Generator Preferences window are coordinated with the objects selected in the Design Navigator. The title bar of this window always indicates the context in which the preferences are set. In the case shown in Figure 26.1, the preferences are for the module ORDERS. The check menu item Palette | Track Selection allows you to turn on or off the ability

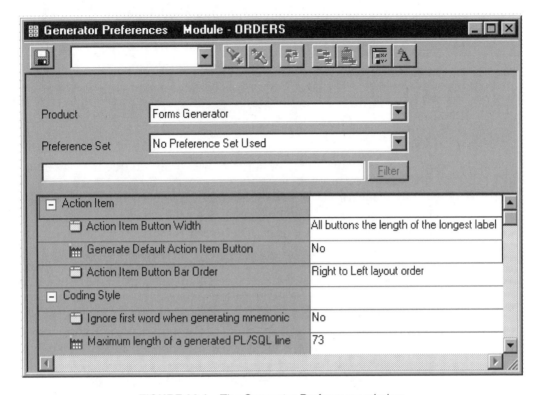

FIGURE 26.1   The Generator Preferences window.

of the Generator Window to update its preferences when the focus on the Design Navigator changes.

26.2.2 MANAGING THE GENERATOR PREFERENCES

The number of individual preferences displayed in the Generator Preferences window is large. To help you locate a preference quickly, the Generator Preferences provides all the standard browsing tools found in other hierarchy tree navigators, such as expanding and collapsing the hierarchy or searching the tree for a node based on its name.

In addition to the search features described above, the Generator Preferences provides you with multiple ways to display the nodes in the hierarchy tree. The different configurations that the hierarchy tree can take allow you to view the preferences in different, more descriptive formats and to reduce the number of nodes that the tree contains. By default, the Generator Preferences displays the preferences using their name, a six-character string, which is not very mnemonic or descriptive. Indeed, names like LOVMWD and DFTLED are very difficult to associate with a meaningful preference. Therefore, you will often display the descriptions of preferences rather than their names. To do so, select View | Show Description from the menu.

By default, the Generator Preferences displays all these nodes, although in some circumstances, hiding some of the branches of the tree may be advantageous. Different options under the submenu View allow you to hide different parts of the Preferences Hierarchy window. A description of some of these options follows:

❑ **Hide Default Values.** This option removes from the tree the preferences with default or factory settings. Given the fact that the majority of your preferences will inherit the factory settings, you can reduce the number of nodes in the tree significantly with this option.

❑ **Hide Application Level Values.** This option removes from the tree all the preferences that are set at the application level, including those that maintain the factory settings. As you will see in Section 26.2.3, in most cases, you will set the preferences at this level. Therefore, this option may reduce the number of nodes in the tree significantly, as well.

❑ **Show Modified Values.** This option will keep in the hierarchy tree only those preferences whose factory setting is overwritten. Thus, the outcome of selecting this option is the same as that of selecting the option Hide Default Values discussed above.

❑ **Show All Values.** This option returns the display of preferences to its default setting by displaying all the values.

26.2.3 WORKING WITH PREFERENCES

Section 26.2.2 discussed how to search for and manage the display of preferences. In this section, you will see how to set preferences and what is involved in this process. The process of setting a preference is simple and can be performed with the following steps:

1. Select the preference in the Generator Preferences window.
2. Select a setting from the list of allowed values for the preference. Most of the preferences are set this way. For a few of them, you have to type the setting in the text box rather than pick it from a list.

As I mentioned earlier, each preference comes with a default value known as its factory setting. You can always revert to the factory setting of a preference that has been modified manually by selecting the preference in the hierarchy tree and clicking the icon Inherit 🔡 on the Generator Preferences toolbar.

The preference may be set for different objects in the Design Navigator. For example, the preference PLSMAX—Maximum number of items in a popup list,

When you set a preference, the navigator precedes its label in the hierarchy tree with an icon that indicates the level where the setting occurs. The icons are the characteristic icons of the objects used by the Repository Object Navigator.

can be set at several levels, including Application, Module, Table, and Item. The level where you set a preference is closely related to the impact of its setting on the generated code. Setting the preference at the Item level will affect only one particular item instance; setting the property at the Module level will affect all the items within that module that will be displayed as list boxes; and setting the property at the application level will affect all the list boxes in all the modules of that application.

Setting preferences for different objects also implies an order of precedence used by the generators to retrieve the settings of these preferences. When creating an object, the generators use the first applicable setting of the preferences they can find. The search starts from the lowest level where the preference may be set. This can be Item when generating a text item, Item Group when generating an item group, Module Component when generating a Developer/2000 Forms block, and so on. If a preference is set at that level, the generator uses it to create the object. Otherwise, it looks at the same preference in the next level. If the preference is not set in any level, including the application level, the factory setting is used. The order in which generators look at preference settings leads to the following guidelines for setting preferences:

❑ Set a preference at the highest level possible in order to ensure that the generators will create applications with a consistent look and feel.

❑ When a preference is set at multiple levels, understand the precedence order, scope, and implications of each setting.

❑ Consider the process of setting preferences as an important part of the application development effort and not as a byproduct of module design efforts.

❑ Consider preference settings like coding standards for the software modules you generate. Document them, make them available to the development team, and override them only for well founded reasons.

26.2.4 CREATING AND MAINTAINING NAMED PREFERENCE SETS

The order in which the generators evaluate the preference settings helps you create software modules with consistent interface and functionality. Like coding standards, preference settings should apply across applications whenever possible. Using the same preferences for multiple applications will provide you with software modules with the same look and feel across the enterprise. To facilitate the process of sharing preference settings among different application systems, Designer/2000 provides a special type of object, called a *preference set*. A preference set is a group of preferences whose settings can be applied to one or more objects in one or more applications. In the Generator Preferences, you can create a preference set by following these steps:

1. Select an object in the Design Navigator and display its preferences in the Generator Preferences.
2. Select Edit | Create As Preference Set....
3. Enter the name of the new set in the dialog box Create Set As.
4. Click OK.

I prefer to create preference sets using the method described above because you can inherit all the settings and the product flavor of the preferences as you create the set. However, another method is described below:

1. Switch to the Modules tab of the Design Navigator and expand the node Preference Sets.
2. Select the node that represents the flavor for which you want to create the set.
3. Click Create ![icon].
4. Provide the name of the set in the Property Palette.
5. All the preferences in the set created with this method have the factory settings. To modify these settings, select the set in the Navigator, invoke the Generator Preferences, and set the desired preferences as described in Section 26.2.3.

26.2.5 IMPLEMENTING PREFERENCES SECURITY

Preferences are a way of enforcing coding standards in the software modules you create. Therefore, you naturally want some way of enforcing these standards by protecting preferences set at a certain level. The Generator Preferences provides two methods of preserving preference settings. The first one is intended primarily to protect users from accidentally modifying preferences of one or more instances in the Generator Preferences. In order to achieve this, follow these steps:

1. Select the object whose preferences you want to protect in the Design Navigator and switch to the Generator Preferences window.
2. Select Security | Lock Preferences.

At this point, the icon 🏛 is displayed to the left of each preference to indicate that it is protected from changes. To remove the protection of preferences for an object, select the object and choose Security | Unlock Preferences. To remove the preference protections set by a user for all the objects in the application system with one command, choose Utilities | Remove Locks. Objects protected by a user remain protected for other users as well. To these users, the Generator Preferences displays the characteristic lock icon in a yellow background.

Any application user may set and remove his or her own locks on preferences. The application owner or any user with administration privileges on the application can remove the protections from object instances set by other users by selecting Security | Remove All User Locks.

Another method to protect preference settings is to freeze them. This method is available only to application owners or users with administration privileges. Preferences set in frozen state cannot be modified by other users of the application system. The steps below allow you to freeze preferences of one or more objects in the Generator Preferences:

1. Select an object whose preferences you want to freeze in the Design Navigator and switch to the Generator Preferences window.
2. Select Security | Freeze.

The navigator displays the icon ♣ to the left of each instance to indicate that the objects are protected from changes. To unfreeze the preferences of an object, select it, switch to the Generator Preferences window, and choose Security | Unfreeze. To remove the protection from all the objects in the application system with one command, choose Security | Unfreeze All.

I mentioned that one of the differences between locking and freezing preferences is that any user can lock but only application administrators or owners can freeze preferences of an object. Another difference is that when freezing preferences of an object that contains dependent objects, you freeze the preferences of the dependents as well. Freezing the preferences of a module, for example, will freeze the preferences of all its components, items, and item groups. If, on the other hand, you lock the preferences of the module, you will prevent users from modifying its preferences, but they can still modify the preferences of its components and items.

26.3   OBJECT CLASS LIBRARIES

Object class libraries are special Developer/2000 modules that contain one or more objects and simplify the use of these objects in other modules. When the Developer/2000 Forms Generator creates the new software module, it subclasses or copies objects from the libraries. The following sections will focus on these topics:

❑   Subclassing, objects, and object libraries
❑   Types of objects in an object library
❑   Object libraries supplied by Designer/2000

26.3.1   SUBCLASSING, OBJECTS, AND OBJECT LIBRARIES

Subclassing is an object-oriented concept that represents the coexistence and co-operation of inheritance and specialization in the object world. Subclassing is like inheritance because it allows you to create an object based on the properties of another object and maintain the link between these objects throughout their lives. Because of this inheritance, when you modify the properties of the base object, the changes are propagated to every object inherited from the base object. Sub-classing, while using inheritance to set the properties of derived objects, also al-lows you to override the inheritance. In particular, you can expand the inherited object by adding new features and properties to it.

The concept of subclassing was introduced with version 2 of Devel-oper/2000 as an expansion of the reference mechanism offered by earlier versions of the product. Whereas referencing allowed you to create a replica of the refer-enced object, the properties of which you could not modify, subclassing allows you to inherit an object and extend it without losing its inheritance ties to the original object. Together with the concept of subclassing, Developer/2000 intro-duced object libraries as a container for storing objects that then can be sub-classed by the application modules. These libraries serve as centralized sources of objects for your application, since they allow any number of modules to subclass from them and they are the place to go to when the properties of a source object need to be modified. Because of these features, the object libraries are important tools that help boost code reusability and enforce standard in your application system.

26.3.2   TYPES OF OBJECTS IN AN OBJECT LIBRARY

Object libraries are an important source of information used by the Devel-oper/2000 Forms Generator to create software modules. Based on the settings of the preference OLBSOC—Object Library Subclass or Copy, the generator will subclass or copy the objects included in the library. An object library used by the generator contains two major categories of objects from which the generator inherits new objects. The following paragraphs describe these categories.

❑ **Standard source objects.** These are special objects that you create in the object library according to predefined conventions and that are understood by the generator. These objects create objects of a particular type in the generated module.

The name of each object tells the generator whether it is dealing with a standard source object or an implementation source. Conventionally, all the standard source objects are named according to this pattern:

```
CGSO$<RecognizedKeyword>
```

If the generator encounters an object whose name begins with CGSO$ but is not followed by a recognized keyword, this object is ignored altogether. Standard source objects allow you to subclass or copy all the objects of a given category from the same object. If, for example, you create an item named CGSO$DATE in the object library, all the generated items of data type DATE in the target form will inherit their properties from this item. In most cases, you can refine the inheritance of properties for the same type of object by creating new items whose name contains predefined suffixes recognized by the generator. For example, the item CGSO$DATE_MR inherits date items in multi-record blocks, CGSO$DATE_CT is used for date items in control blocks, CGSO$DATE_DO displays items, and CGSO$DATE_MD is used for mandatory date items. A combination of these suffixes may be used as well. CGSO$DATE_MR_DO, for example, is used by display date items in multi-record blocks.

A predefined hierarchy of source objects is used by the generator to inherit the properties of the objects it creates. Figure 26.2 shows this hierarchy for the case of date items. When the generator is about to create a date item

```
CGSO$DEFAULT_ITEM
    CGSO$CHAR
        CGSO$DATE
                CGSO$DATE_MR
                CGSO$DATE_CT
                CGSO$DATE_DO
                CGSO$DATE_MD
```

FIGURE 26.2 A hierarchy of visual attributes recognized by the Developer/2000 Forms generator.

in a multi-record block, it looks in the object library for an item titled CGSO$DATE_MR. If it finds the item, it uses the item to copy or subclass the generated item. If it does not find one, it navigates up the tree shown in Figure 26.2 until it finds a source object.

❏ **Implementation source objects.** These are objects that are used instead of standard source objects when an object is generated. The property *Template/Library Object* of the element in the Repository must be set to the name of the implementation source object in the library.

The standard object library provided with Designer/2000 contains a number of implementation source objects. The names of these objects begin with CGAI$, to distinguish them from implementation objects you may create. You can use these objects to create buttons that invoke the built-in Developer/2000 Forms functionality. They are used for action items and unbound items that will be displayed as buttons. The number of generator items in this category is quite large. Figure 26.3 contains only a few of these objects.

26.3.3 OBJECT LIBRARIES SHIPPED WITH DESIGNER/2000

Designer/2000 provides a library of objects you can use in the generation of Developer/2000 Forms modules. The name of this library is OLGSTND1.OLB. By default, the library is located in the ADMIN folder of the Developer/2000 Forms Generator, for example C:\ORAWIN95\CGENF50\ADMIN or C:\ORANT\ CGENF50\ADMIN. This library contains all the standard source objects used by the generator and the implementation source objects discussed in the previous section. The objects are organized into six tab folders, as shown in Figure 26.4. The first five tabs organize the standard source objects (CGSO$) into groups of parent objects, those used in multi-row and data blocks, and those that correspond to display and mandatory objects. The last tab lists the implementation source objects (CGAI$).

During the development of your application, you will find the need to customize the default object library. I recommend that you work with a copy of the

GENERATOR OBJECT NAME	DEVELOPER/2000 FORMS BUILT-IN FUNCTIONALITY
CGAI$COMMIT	Commit
CGAI$EXIT	Exit
CGAI$ENTER_QUERY	Enter Query
CGAI$EXECUTE_QUERY	Execute Query
CGAI$COUNT_HITS	Count Query Hits
CGAI$INSERT_RECORD	Insert Record

FIGURE 26.3 Generator objects that implement Developer/2000 Forms built-in functions.

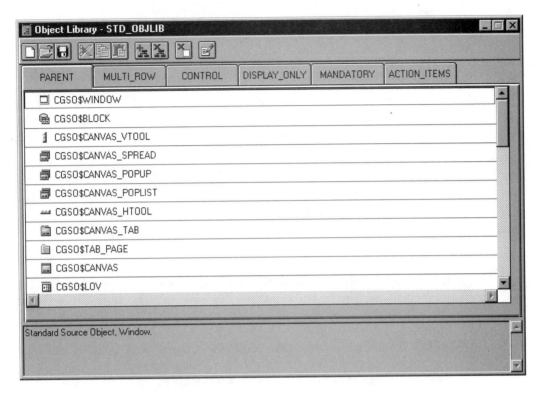

FIGURE 26.4 The Designer/2000 shipped object library.

library supplied by Designer/2000. If you need to modify the properties of an existing object, perform the following actions:

1. Open the object library in the Developer/2000 Form Builder and create a new Form module.
2. Drag the object you want to modify and drop it in the appropriate location in the Form module. Notice that you need to respect the hierarchy in which the objects are stored in a Developer/2000 Forms module. For example, to be able to drop the object CGSO$DEFAULT_ITEM, a block must already exist in the module.
3. Copy the object to the new module when the Form Builder prompts whether to copy or subclass it.
4. Modify the properties of the object according to your needs.
5. Drag the object from the Form module onto the object library.
6. Choose the option to replace the existing object when prompted whether you want to replace it or not.
7. Save the object library.

If you want to add new objects to the library, I recommend that you create one or more separate tab folders and drag the new objects into these folders.

26.3.4 USING OBJECT LIBRARIES DURING GENERATION

A few preferences are set in order to point the Developer/2000 Forms Generator to the appropriate object library during the generation of your modules. These preferences are located in the Standards group and are described in the following paragraphs:

❏ **STOOLB—Name of Object Library for Generation.** This preference is set to OFGSTND1.OLB, which is the object library shipped with Designer/2000. If you are using a different object library, specify its name in this preference. Note also that you can override the setting of the preference when you invoke the Developer/2000 Forms Generator, by specifying the name and location of the object library.

❏ **OLBSOC—Object Library Subclass or Copy.** By default, this preference is set to subclass objects. I recommend that you keep this setting in order to take advantage of the benefits that subclassing provides in Developer/2000 Forms.

❏ **OLBOLD—Library Keep Old Preferences.** As I mentioned earlier, the concept of object libraries was introduced with version 2.0 of Developer/2000. The Developer/2000 Forms Generator included with version 2.0 of Designer/2000 takes advantage of these libraries to generate the modules. A number of properties that in version 2.0 are inherited from library objects were set using preferences in earlier versions of Designer/2000. For example, all the properties of window objects were maintained through preferences in versions of Designer/2000 prior to version 2.0. Although these preferences are considered obsolete, Designer/2000 allows you to use them for backward compatibility reasons. In order to do so, set the preference OLBOLD—Library Keep Old Preferences to Yes.

I recommend that you maintain the preference OLBOLD—Library Keep Old Preferences set to No and use the object libraries to implement the functionality offered by the obsolete preferences. As such, the support for these preferences will eventually be discontinued.

26.4 GENERATOR TEMPLATES

For software modules created with Developer/2000 tools, an important source of information that Designer/2000 generators use is template modules. These are Developer/2000 Forms and Developer/2000 Reports modules that reside in the file system and have a number of properties and objects that may be used in the modules you are generating. In the case of Developer/2000 Forms modules, the generator derives the names of templates from the setting of the preference STFFMB— The name of the template form, in the Standards group of preferences. In the case of Developer/2000 Reports modules, the template names are maintained in the preferences DETREP—Detail Report Template and LAYREP—Layout template. Both of these preferences are located in the Templates group of preferences.

Sections 26.4.1–26.4.4 will focus on the purpose and use of templates, the types of objects in a template, the Designer/2000 supplied templates, and how to customize these templates for the special needs of your applications.

26.4.1 PURPOSE AND USE OF TEMPLATES

Templates used in the generation of Developer/2000 Forms or Developer/2000 Reports modules serve primarily two purposes:

❏ To add objects to your modules that you cannot or do not want to specify in the Designer/2000 Repository. In this case, templates allow you to expand and customize the functionality of the generated modules. Such objects are known as *user objects.*

❏ To modify form-level properties.

Among the objects that you can include in the generated modules, the most important are:

❏ Control blocks in Developer/2000 Forms modules. A particular case of control blocks is iconic toolbars that you can attach to the MDI frame or to individual windows of your application.

❏ Form-level triggers common across all modules.

❏ Parameter forms for Developer/2000 Reports modules.

❏ Headers and footers in Developer/2000 Reports modules.

❏ Boilerplate items, such as logos or background images.

One way in which you can influence the look and feel of generated modules is to define the coordinate system and cell size for the generated modules.

For versions of Designer/2000 prior to release 2.0, templates were a very important source of objects and properties for the Developer/2000 Forms Generator.

They enforced application development standards and allowed you to include objects recognized by the Generator and objects defined by the users, to include triggers and module-specific program units, and to specify PL/SQL library attachments. Expanded features of Designer/2000 version 2.0 have greatly diminished the role of templates in the generation of Developer/2000 Forms modules. These features include the support for control module components, the ability to attach application logic in the form of events and named routines, and the ability to define library attachments using module networks. Due to the use of object libraries by the Developer/2000 Forms Generator, the templates have also lost their role as tools to enforce standards and include user-defined objects in the generated modules.

26.4.2 TYPES OF TEMPLATE OBJECTS

Although template objects are Developer/2000 Forms and Reports modules, they are not in general functional modules that can be used independently. Their main purpose is to serve as containers for objects that are included in or influence the properties of generated modules. These objects are classified into two groups:

❑ **User objects.** These are objects for which the generator creates an identical copy in the generated module. In Developer/2000 Forms templates, they include blocks, items within blocks, triggers defined at any level, program units, attached PLL libraries, windows, and canvases. In the template module, these objects may be defined as references to other modules. In the case of Developer/2000 Reports, user objects include any objects defined in the header, trailer, or margin areas of the template module.

❑ **Generator objects.** These are special objects that you create in the template module according to predefined conventions and that are understood by the generator. These objects are not merely copied over to the generated module. In a general sense, they serve as a set of instructions or directives for the generator. For each of these objects that the generator encounters in the template, the generator takes a well-defined list of actions. These may include creating objects in the generated module, creating PL/SQL code, creating boilerplate text, or any combination of these.

The name of each object tells the generator whether it is dealing with a user object or a generator object. Conventionally, all the generator objects are named according to this pattern:

```
CG$<RecognizedKeyword>
```

If the generator encounters an object whose name begins with CG$ but is not followed by a recognized keyword, this object is ignored altogether. An exception to this rule is when multiple generator objects of the same type need to be created in different areas of the module. Since the object names must be unique, add some unique characters *after* the recognized keyword, to avoid any naming conflict that may arise. Generally, a sequence number, as in CG$AT_1 and CG$AT_2, refers to two instances of the generator item that store the application title. In the case of canvas generator objects in Developer/2000 Forms, the sequence appended after the recognized keyword implies an association with another object generated in the module. For example, the generator object CG$HORIZONTAL_TOOLBAR represents a toolbar canvas that will be associated with all the windows that do not have an explicit toolbar assigned to them. The generator object CG$HORI-ZONTAL_TOOLBAR_0 represents the toolbar associated with the first window created by the generator. The generator objects can be grouped into the following categories:

❏ **Objects whose content is populated from Repository information.** These generator objects when included in your modules will inherit their settings from properties of the application system and the current module stored in the Repository. These objects are usually used as boilerplate items or used to set the title bar of windows dynamically at runtime. Figure 26.5 contains some of the most common generator objects in this category. They can be used in both Developer/2000 Forms and Reports modules.

❏ **Objects that implement standard built-in Developer/2000 Forms functions.** These objects may create buttons that invoke the built-in Developer/2000 Forms directives. The functionality of objects in this category has been superseded by the implementation source objects in the object library supplied by Designer/2000 (CGAI$ objects).

❏ **Objects that serve as boilerplate text.** These objects can display information such as the date, the Oracle user running the module, the current page, and the total number of pages. Some of them, like the first two, can be used equally well in Developer/2000 Forms and Developer/2000 Reports modules. Some others, like the last two objects, are more suitable for reports than forms. Figure 26.6 shows the most representative objects in this category.

GENERATOR OBJECT NAME	SOURCE OF CONTENT
CG$AN	Application system name
CG$AT	Application title
CG$MN	Module name
CG$MP	Module purpose

FIGURE 26.5 Generator objects that derive their content from Repository information.

GENERATOR OBJECT NAME	TYPE OF TEXT GENERATED IN THE BOILERPLATE
CG$DT	Current date
CG$US	User of the module
CG$PN	Current page number
CG$PT	Total number of pages
CG$PM	Page n of m, where n is the current page number and m is the total number of pages.

FIGURE 26.6   Generator objects that implement Developer/2000 Forms built-in functions.

❑ **Visual attribute objects.** These objects allow you to set the visual attributes of objects in Developer/2000 Forms at the object category level. This functionality has been superseded by the concept of standard source objects. Use these objects to set not only the visual attribute properties, but also every other property of the objects.

In order to define visual attributes of Developer/2000 Reports modules, you create text objects in the body area of the template report. The names of these objects correspond to categories of Reports objects for which you can control visual attributes. By setting the visual attributes of these objects, you instruct the Developer/2000 Reports generator to apply the same settings to the objects in the generated module. Figure 26.7 lists all the generator objects you can create in the body area of the template report and the categories of objects that inherit their visual attribute properties.

26.4.3   TEMPLATES SUPPLIED BY DESIGNER/2000

Developer/2000 Forms and Developer/2000 Reports generators come with a number of templates that allow you to generate modules without having to define any of your own templates. The functionality they provide is often sufficient

GENERATOR OBJECT NAME	OBJECTS THAT INHERIT VISUAL ATTRIBUTE PROPERTIES
CG$PROMPT	Field prompt
CG$FIELD	Field
CG$HEADER	Frame title
CG$PARAMETER	Parameter prompt
CG$SIZING	Font, font size, and font weight

FIGURE 26.7   Visual attribute generator objects used in Developer/2000 Forms.

for the needs of the modules you develop. These templates are especially important for prototyping efforts and in rapid application development environments. The following paragraphs offer a brief description of the major templates used by the Developer/2000 Forms Generator.

❑ **OFG4PC1T.FMB.** This is the default template that the Developer/2000 Forms generator uses. It is customized for modules generated for Microsoft Windows platforms. This template includes a toolbar with some of the major Developer/2000 Forms built-ins implemented as icons on a horizontal toolbar canvas. The forms generated with this template use a real coordinate system with the inch as the unit. The MDI frame title of these forms is set to the name of the application system defined in the Repository.

❑ **OFG4PC2T.FMB.** This template may be used to generate modules that call other modules. Based on the network modules defined in the Design Editor, the Developer/2000 Forms generator will create buttons to navigate between forms if the OFG2PC2T.FMB template is used. In addition, modules generated with this template will inherit all the functionality of modules generated with OFG2PC1T.FMB.

❑ **OF4GUIT.FMB.** This template is used to generate Developer/2000 Forms modules with character coordinates intended to run primarily on non-GUI environments.

26.4.4 CREATING CUSTOMIZED TEMPLATES

As I discussed in the previous sections, generator templates are Developer/2000 Forms and Reports modules with objects that can be included in the generated modules. Therefore, the process of creating a customized template is no more complicated than that of creating and editing a regular form or report. A copy of any of the provided templates can serve as a starting point for your custom-developed templates. You can modify them in any of the following ways:

❑ Add generator objects according to naming standards discussed in Section 26.4.2.

The best way to handle navigation among modules is to use navigation action items in the module component from which the navigation occurs.

❑ Add user-defined objects to the template, including items, blocks, windows, and canvases.

❑ Add PL/SQL objects to the template, including triggers and program units.

26.5 DESIGNER/2000 FRONT-END GENERATORS

Designer/2000 provides a series of generators that allow you to create front-end software modules for different programming environments. These include generators for a series of Oracle programming tools, such as Developer/2000 Forms, Developer/2000 Reports, Developer/2000 Graphics, and Oracle WebServer. In addition, Designer/2000 allows you to generate Microsoft Help files associated with your modules, and provides a generator for MS Visual Basic projects. The process of invoking and setting the options of these generators is discussed in Sections 26.5.1–26.5.7.

26.5.1 INVOKING AND USING FRONT-END GENERATORS

In order to invoke a front-end generator, you need to select the module you want to generate in the Design Editor and perform one of the following actions:

❑ Select Utilities | Generate....
❑ Click the icon Generate 🖳 on the Editor's toolbar.

Based on the implementation language of the module you selected, Designer/2000 launches the appropriate generator. In some cases, you may want to generate a module defined in one language into a different implementation language. This may be helpful, for example, in cases where you have requirements to produce data entry screens and reports with similar layout. In such cases, you can design one Developer/2000 Forms module and generate it in its native environment and as a Developer/2000 Reports module. The following actions allow you to generate a module for an implementation environment different from the one used by the module:

1. Select the module in the Design Navigator.
2. Select Utilities | Generate As... from the Editor's menu.
3. Select the target generator from the dialog box Generate Module As that appears (see Figure 26.8).
4. Click OK to invoke the selected generator.

As you will see in Sections 26.5.2–26.5.7, each generator has its own characteristic dialog box that allows you to set its properties. In principle, however, all

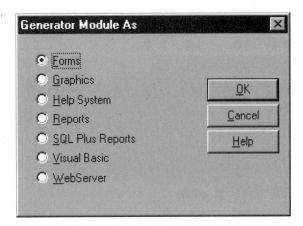

FIGURE 26.8 The Generate Module As dialog box.

the generators work alike. After setting the properties and options of the generator, you click Start to initiate the generation process. At this point, the Design Editor displays the Messages pane, where the principal activities of the generator are listed. Warnings issued by the generator or errors encountered in the process are listed in this pane, in blue and red letters, respectively. During the generation process, the generator may apply default settings to properties you have not set explicitly or prompt you to modify conflicting settings of other properties. If the generation is successful, you have the option to save these settings to the Repository, revert them, or view the changes and edit them individually.

If the generation process is not successful, you can use the information listed in the Messages pane to see what caused the failure and identify the module object that is responsible for it. The following actions can be performed after you place the cursor in a message line:

❑ Click ▧ or select Messages | Show Help on Message to get an explanation about the message.
❑ Click ▧ or select Messages | Go to Source of Error to place the focus in the Design Navigator on the violating object.

 In order to generate Microsoft Help files for Developer/2000 Forms and Visual Basic modules, generate these modules using the Help System generator.

Other icons on the Messages pane toolbar and their corresponding items on the menu Messages may be used to copy all the contents of the pane to the Windows Clipboard, to navigate to the next or previous message, and to clear the messages from the pane.

Finally, when you set the generator options, you may decide to queue some actions of the generator in an action list. For example, you may decide to generate a Developer/2000 Forms module, and place in the queue the processes of compiling and executing the generation module. To view the contents of the queue, click ▣ on the toolbar of the Messages pane or select Messages | List Actions.... In the Build Action dialog box that appears, you can see all the processes placed in the queue. To execute one of these processes, select it and click Run. Figure 26.9 shows an example of this dialog box.

26.5.2   DEVELOPER/2000 FORMS GENERATOR

Developer/2000 Forms Generator is the most sophisticated Designer/2000 generator that creates Developer/2000 Forms, Menus, and PL/SQL library modules from properties of modules stored in the Repository. Its interface is implemented via a dialog box, called Generate Form, shown in Figure 26.10. The properties in this dialog box serve primarily the following purposes:

❑ **Defining the generation option.** The list box at the top of the Generation Option group of properties instructs the generator to create only forms, menus, or libraries. The check boxes in this group control whether or not the generator ignores the application logic defined in the Repository, generates the menu and any PL/SQL modules associated with the module, or generates other Forms or Reports modules that may be called from the current

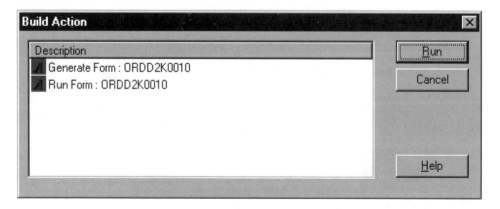

FIGURE 26.9   The Build Action dialog box.

All the generators allow you to compile, where appropriate, and execute the generated modules right after their generation. In order for these processes to succeed, all the database objects required by the module must be installed in the development database schema. These objects include the obvious ones, like tables, views, and sequences, but also the less obvious ones, like the code control tables, the reference code tables, the table API, and the module API.

module. Furthermore, in cases when the module has been previously generated, you can use the check box Preserve Layout to instruct the generator to preserve or override the layout of the previously generated module.

❑ **Specifying which generation preferences to use.** By selecting one of the radio buttons in the Use Preferences radio group, you can direct the generator on which preferences to use. By default, the generator will use the module preferences as defined in the Generator Preferences. In order to enforce coding standards across multiple modules in your application, you may also use the preferences that a specific module or a named preference set. In this case, you must select the radio button Other Module or Named Set, and pick the name of the module or named set from the list box Module/Named Set. One option of generating modules, although very rarely used, is not to use any preference settings. You can achieve this by selecting the radio button None in the Use Preferences group.

❑ **Specifying the object library and module template used during the generation.** The options in the group Standards allow you to use the default object library and template module, as specified by the Generator preferences, or to click Browse and select a specific file yourself.

A number of options you can set to influence the way the generator runs are maintained in the Forms Generator Options dialog box. To invoke this dialog box, click the button Options… in the Generate Form dialog box. This dialog box is composed of multiple property tabs, which will be described in the following paragraphs.

The property tabs File Option, Menu Option, and Library Option are similar in form and functionality. They are used primarily to define the location of the generated software modules of the corresponding type. By default, these modules are stored in the file system, in the subdirectory BIN of your ORACLE_HOME directory. You can specify your own directory by setting the property Destination, as shown in Figure 26.11 for the case of Forms. You may use the Browse button to navigate the directory tree and pick the desired location

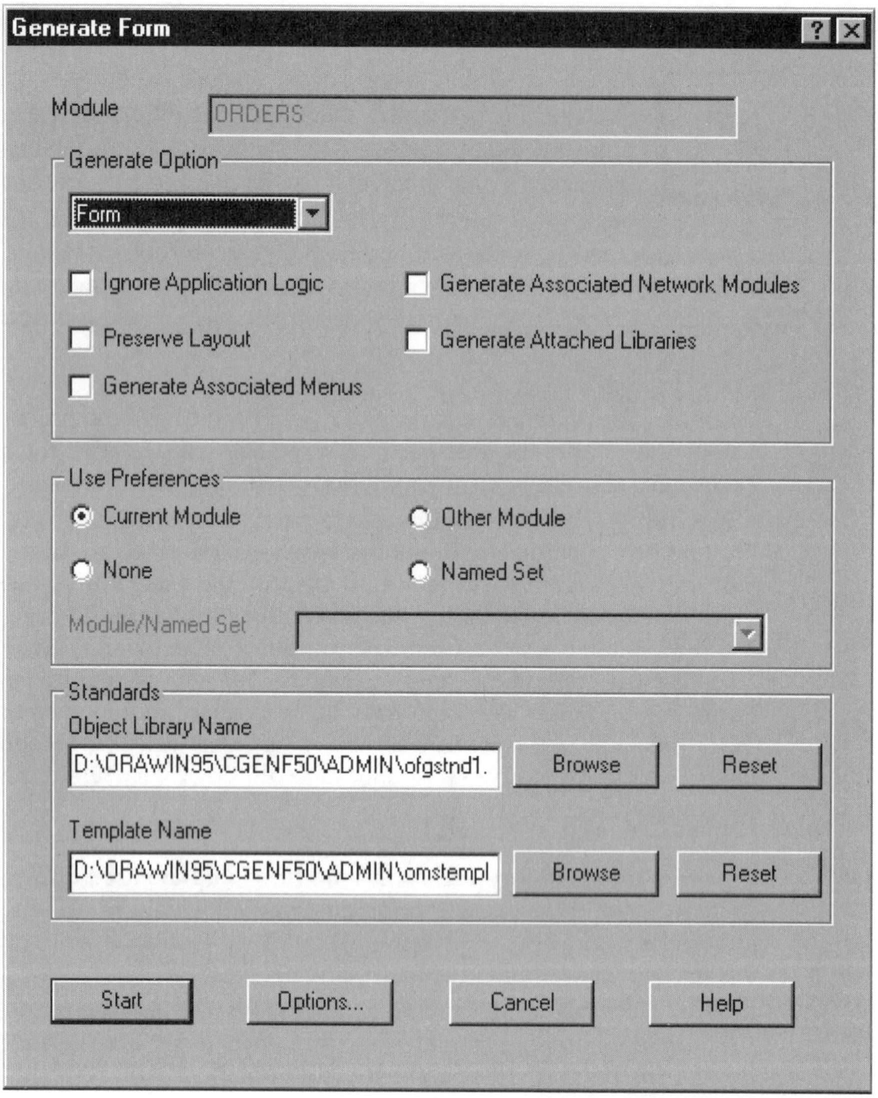

FIGURE 26.10 The Generate Form dialog box.

more easily. Developer/2000 Forms and Menus modules may be stored in an Oracle database as well. If they are, the list box Location is set to Local Database—the database where the Repository resides, or Other Database. The text box Connect String contains the user name, password, and connect string used to establish a connection to a remote database. The text items in the Commands

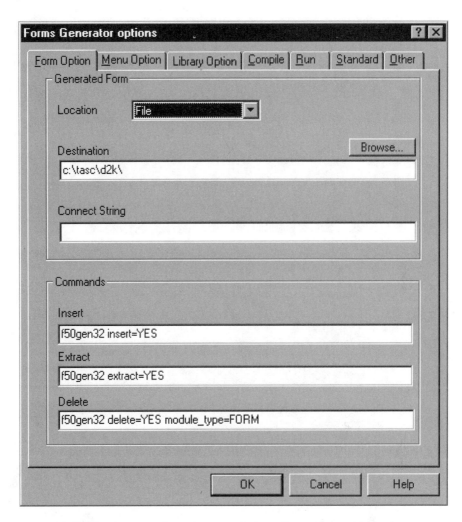

FIGURE 26.11 The Form Option tab of the Forms Generator Options dialog box.

group specify the commands for inserting, extracting, and deleting the modules from the database.

The process of developing modules is often an iterative one, in which the design of the module is modified and the new module is generated, compiled, and executed in order to validate the changes. The Developer/2000 Forms generator provides a smooth transition among these three stages by allowing you to compile and execute a module that is successfully generated. The generator creates the software modules in binary format (.FMB or .MMB) and can compile

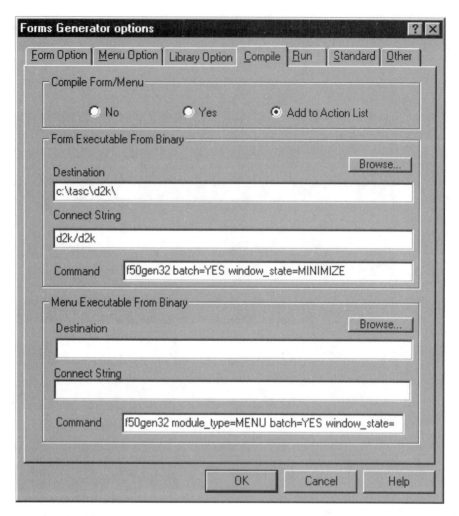

FIGURE 26.12   The Compile tab of the Forms Generator Options dialog box.

them in executable modules (.FMX and .MMX). The Compile tab, shown in Figure 26.12, is where you set the preferences that control this process. By setting the properties in the Compile Form/Menu radio group, you can direct the generator to compile the binary module, not to compile it, or to add the compilation task to the action list. Obviously, the compiling process can initiate only if the module is generated successfully.

If modules will be compiled, you can specify the directory where the executables will be stored by setting the text box Destination. When generating Developer/2000 Forms modules that access database objects, these objects must exist in a given schema, and the Developer/2000 Forms Generator must have access to this schema. By default, the generator looks for these objects in the schema of the current Repository user. In general, though, this schema must not contain objects used by an application. You can use the Connect String as shown in Figure 26.12 to specify the user name, password, and connect string for the schema that contains the objects used by the application system.

Once a Forms module is successfully generated and compiled, you may choose to run its executable. The Run tab allows you to set properties that control how the generator executes the module. Depending on the selection of the radio group Run Form, the generator will stop after the generation is complete, it will run it without prompting, or it will queue the task in the action list. The generator can run a module only if it compiles it successfully. You need to provide the user name, password, and database string in the property Connect String to allow the user to connect to a database schema where all the objects used by the module exist. Figure 26.13 shows an example of the Run tab.

Figure 26.14 shows the Standard tab, used to specify the location of the template module that will be used during the generation. In general, you access this tab if you are storing the templates in a location different from the default directory. If it is another directory, its name is specified in the Path text box. If the template module is stored in the database, the properties Location, Command, and Connect String have meanings similar to the same properties on the Form Option of Menu Option tab. Be sure to note that although this tab allows you to specify the location of the template module, the name of the module itself is controlled by the preference STFFMB—The name of the template form, specified in the Standards group of preferences.

The property tab Other contains a miscellaneous group of generation properties, the most important of which is the property PLL Files Path. When set, this property instructs the generator where to find the PL/SQL modules that contain program units invoked by the generated forms. However, do not use this property, since the libraries will be attached with the hard-coded path, possibly resulting in problems when the software is deployed. The best way to specify the location of these libraries is to set the variable FORMS50_PATH in the client's Registry.

Despite the number of properties that can be set in the Forms Generator Options dialog box, you don't usually need to set them each time you run the generator. A number of properties, such as the destination of generated and compiled modules, location of templates, and the necessary information to connect to the appropriate database schema, reflect the software environment of your application. Assuming that you have set up this environment correctly, you will have to specify these properties only once.

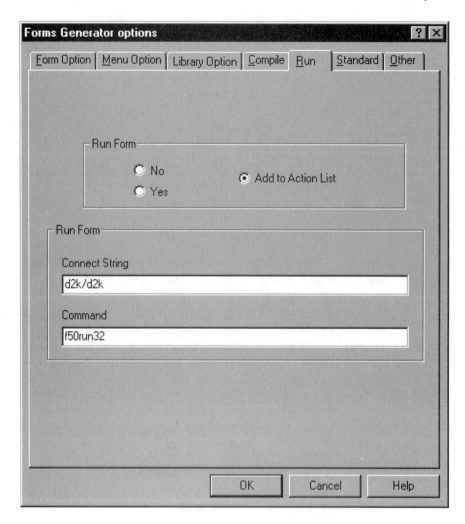

FIGURE 26.13   The Run tab of the Forms Generator Options dialog box.

If the Developer/2000 Forms modules you are generating contain module components that require the module API packages, you need to create and install them before compiling and executing the generated module.

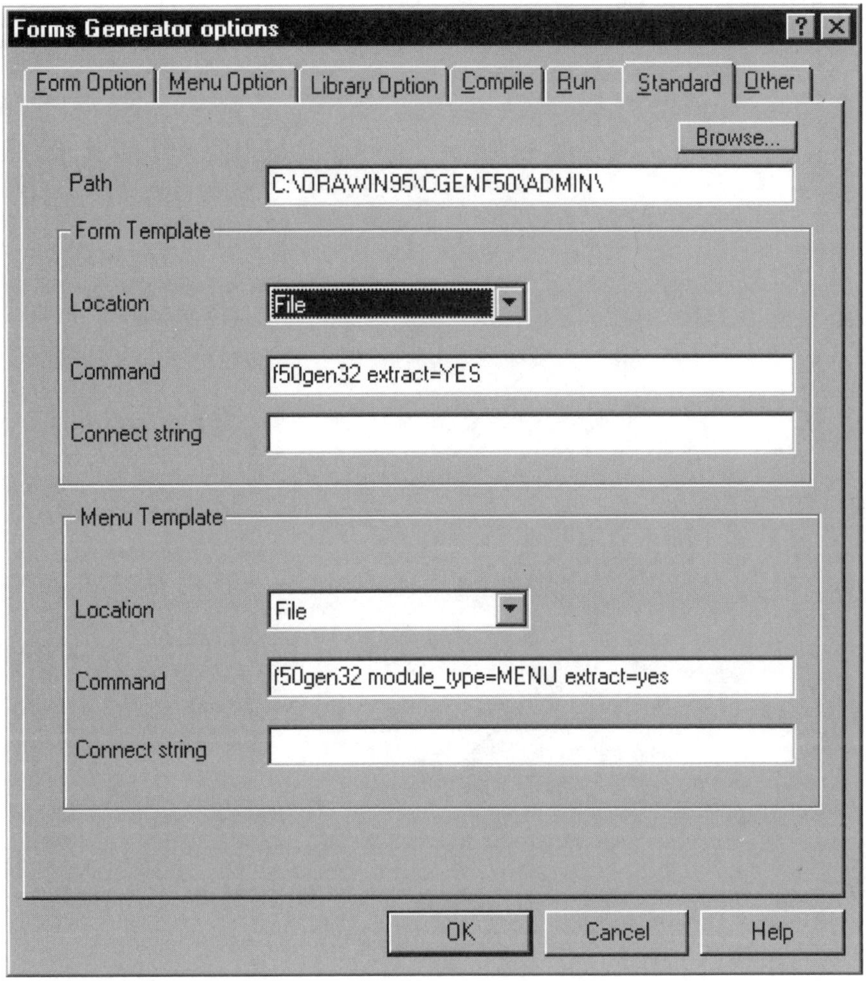

FIGURE 26.14 The Standard tab of the Forms Generator Options dialog box.

26.5.3 DEVELOPER/2000 REPORTS GENERATOR

The Developer/2000 Reports Generator is implemented in the form of the Generate Report dialog box shown in Figure 26.15. This dialog box is similar to the Generate Form dialog box discussed in Section 26.5.2. It allows you to specify the preferences and the template that the Generator will use. The check box Generate reports linked to this one, when set, instructs the generator to create modules linked to the selected module.

Generate Report	? X

Module
ORDERS BY CUSTOMER(D2K)

Use Preferences

◉ Current Module

○ None

○ Other Module

○ Named Set

Module/Named Set

Template

Browse...

Name

corp1.tdf

Password

☐ Generate reports linked to this one

| Start | Options... | Cancel | Help |

FIGURE 26.15 The Generate Report dialog box.

 The text box Password in the Generate Report dialog box is enabled only if you have set the runtime database user name and password in the Reports Generate Options dialog box. Splitting the information required to establish a database connection into two dialog boxes helps you define the user name and connect string once, when the options are defined. The password, on the other hand, is not stored anywhere, but it is provided each time you run the generator.

The Reports Generate Options dialog box—invoked by clicking the button Options... — contains only a few properties that specify the location of the generated modules and database connection information to run the generated report. As in the case of the Developer/2000 Forms generator, these properties reflect the software configuration environment of your application and are set normally only the first time the Reports Generator is invoked.

26.5.4 DEVELOPER/2000 GRAPHICS GENERATOR

The Developer/2000 Graphics Generator is implemented in the form of the dialog box Generate Graphics, which is almost identical to the Generate Reports dialog box shown in Figure 26.15. The Graphics Generate Options dialog box is also identical in layout and functionality to the Reports Generate Options dialog box (Figure 26.16 shows an example). Its properties allow you to define where the

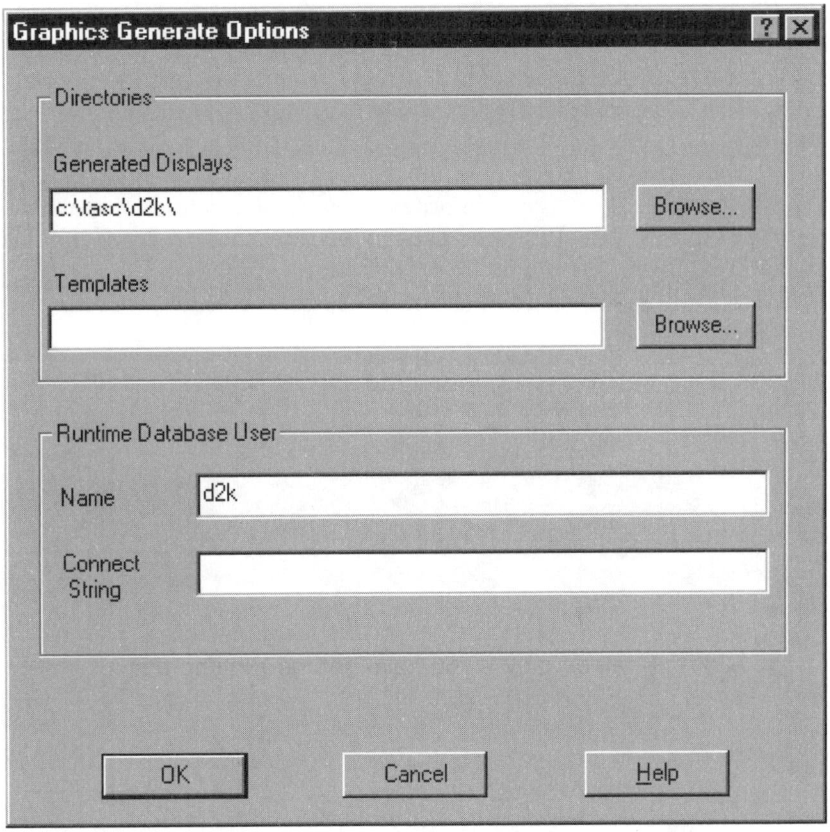

FIGURE 26.16   The Graphics Generate Options dialog box.

generated display will be stored, the template that the Generator will use, and database connection information used when the generated module is executed.

26.5.5 ORACLE WEBSERVER GENERATOR

The WebServer Generator's interface is implemented in the dialog box Generate WebServer. This dialog box, shown in Figure 26.17, contains only two properties you can set. The first one is a check box that allows you to include the module network in the generation process. The call associations among modules are implemented in the form of HTML hyperlinks. The second property is a text field where you supply the password used to connect to the database and install the PL/SQL packages created by the Generator. As in the case of Reports and Graphics generators, this field is enabled only if you have entered the database user name and connect string information in the Generate WebServer dialog box.

As in other generators, clicking the button Options... displays the Web-Server Generate Options dialog box. The properties of this dialog box are used to specify the destination where the generated PL/SQL program units will be created. In order to install the generated program units in a database user schema, use the text fields Name and Connect String to specify the information required to access the database. By setting the check box Auto-install after Generation, you instruct the Generator to install the PL/SQL program units in the database after it creates them. The WebServer modules generated by Designer/2000 are executed by the Oracle Web Agent. In order to run these modules after they are generated, enter the Uniform Resource Locator (URL) of this agent in the list Web Agent URL. Populate the text box Browser with the path and file name of your favorite Web browser. Figure 26.18 shows an example of how properties on this tab may be set.

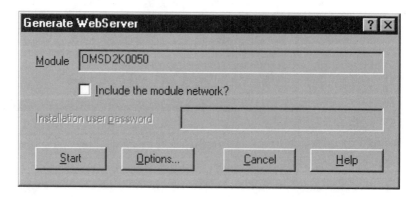

FIGURE 26.17   The Generate WebServer dialog box.

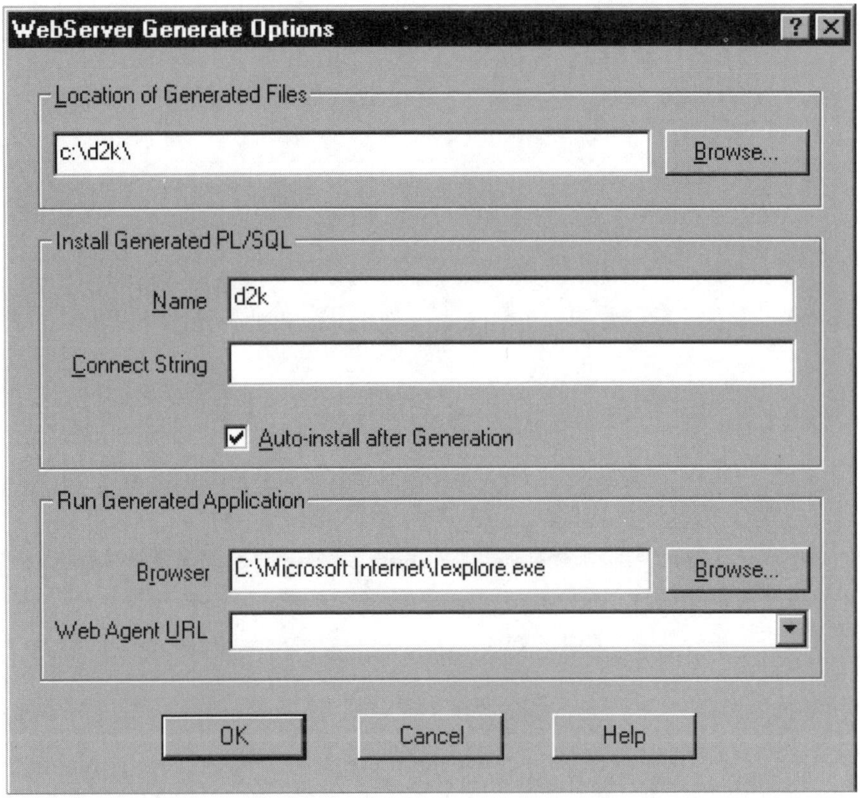

WebServer Generate Options   ? X

Location of Generated Files

c:\d2k\   Browse...

Install Generated PL/SQL

Name   d2k

Connect String

☑ Auto-install after Generation

Run Generated Application

Browser   C:\Microsoft Internet\Iexplore.exe   Browse...

Web Agent URL

OK   Cancel   Help

FIGURE 26.18 The Options tab of the Generate WebServer dialog box.

26.5.6 VISUAL BASIC GENERATOR

This generator is implemented in the Generate Visual Basic dialog box shown in Figure 26.19. Depending on the radio button you select in the Generate Options group, the generator follows one of the following scenarios:

The Oracle WebServer uses the Table API triggers and packages to implement the functionality of its modules. Before installing and executing the WebServer modules, you need to generate and install this API for all the tables used by the modules.

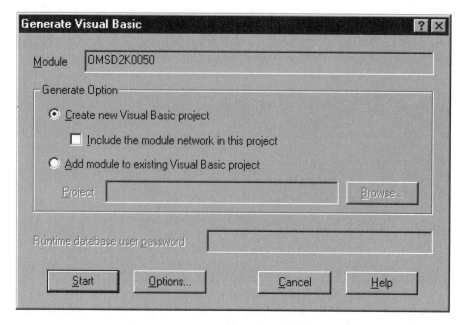

FIGURE 26.19 The Generate Visual Basic dialog box.

❑ **Create a new project for the module.** This project may include only the selected module. Or, if you set the check box associated with the first radio button, the project will include all the modules in the network of the selected module.

❑ **Add the selected module to an existing Visual Basic project.** You need to specify the name and location of this project in the Project text field. You may use the Browse button to help locate the project file.

The Visual Basic Generate Options dialog box contains properties that are similar to the options dialog boxes used by other generators. A special option you need to set for this generator is the Data Access Method. By selecting one of the buttons in the radio group with the same name, you instruct the Generator to create a module that connects to the database using Oracle's Objects for OLE or Microsoft's Data Access Objects. Figure 26.20 shows an example of this dialog box.

26.5.7 MICROSOFT HELP GENERATOR

Designer/2000 allows you to generate Microsoft Help projects for modules in your application system based on information you enter for modules, module components, table usages, and items at design time. Despite different types of

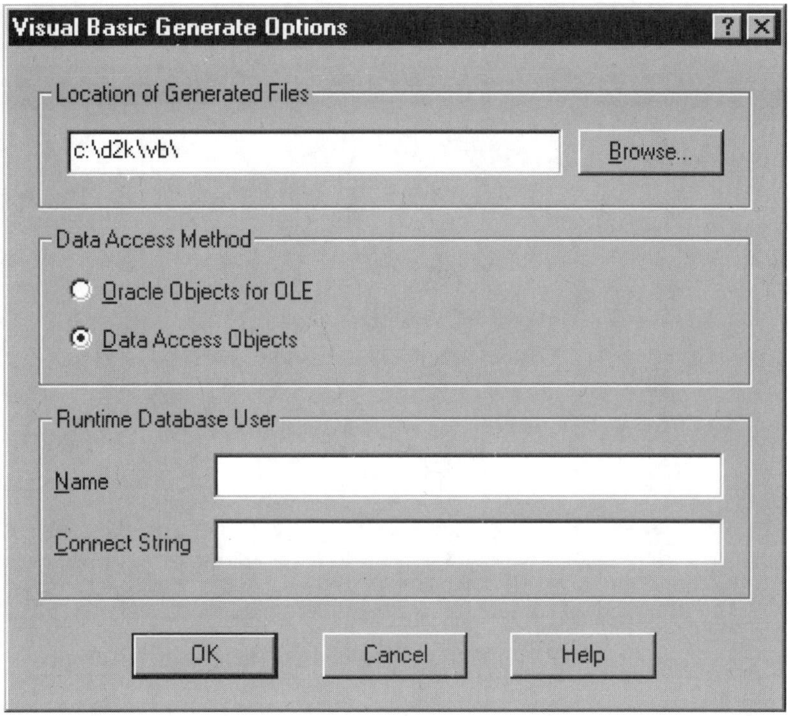

FIGURE 26.20 The Visual Basic Generate Options dialog box.

modules you can create and maintain in Designer/2000, help implemented with the Microsoft Help engine is useful only for those environments that can use it, such as Developer/2000 Forms and Visual Basic modules. These Help projects are generated using the Designer/2000 Help Generator. The properties that control the behavior of this generator are grouped in the dialog box Generate Help System, shown in Figure 26.21.

How the Help project is generated depends on the radio button selected from the group Generate Options in this dialog box. Based on the selected option, the generator will perform one of the following actions:

❑ **Generate all the source files required to build the Help project for a given module.** If the check box associated with the first radio button is set, the generator will create the Help project for the selected modules and for all the modules that are below it in the module network. This option is used the most when the Microsoft Help Generator is invoked.

❑ **Generate only the topic and the mapping files for the selected module.** This option is typically used when the help contents for a module have been

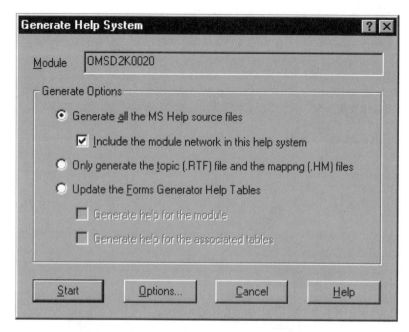

FIGURE 26.21   The Generate Help System dialog box.

modified and you want to update the contents of your Help project without
having to recreate it from scratch.

❑ **Update Forms Generator help tables.** This is the least used option and will
not result in any Microsoft Help files. The generator will instead update internal Developer/2000 Forms tables, which are used in an alternative implementation of context-sensitive help. The implementation was used in earlier
versions of Designer/2000. It is implemented in the form of a Devel-
oper/2000 Forms module that is invoked by a given form through a trigger.
Based on the parameters passed from the calling form, the help form would
query tables where help information is stored and present this information
to the user.

Be sure to note that the output of the Microsoft Help generator is not a Help
file, but rather a set of files that can be used to produce the Help file. In order to
create the final Help file that will be used in the application, you have to pass
these source files through a utility that builds Help projects. The location where
all the generated files will be stored, as well as the path and location of the Help
Compiler and the Help Executable, is specified in the Help System Generate Options dialog box, shown in Figure 26.22.

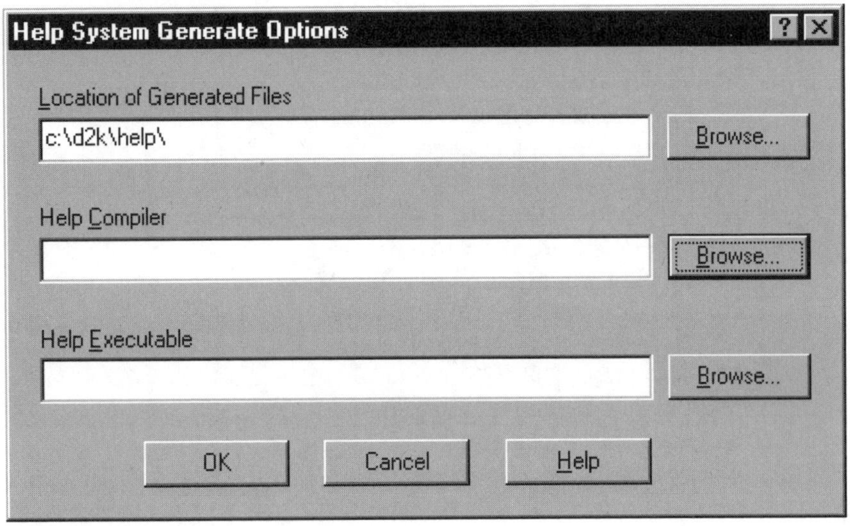

FIGURE 26.22   The Help System Generate Options dialog box.

26.6 SUMMARY

Designer/2000 provides a number of tools that generate software modules to implement the user interface of your applications in different products and flavors, such as Developer/2000 Forms, Developer/2000 Reports, and Oracle WebServer. These tools are commonly known as front-end generators. The software modules they produce are defined by a number of components, including the properties of modules in the application system Repository, settings of preferences, and template modules. This chapter explains the relationship among these components, as well as the major properties of each front-end generator. The major topics of this chapter are:

❏ **Repository-Based Software Development**
❏ **Maintaining Preferences**
   ❏ The Generator Preferences
   ❏ Managing the Generator Preferences
   ❏ Working with Preferences
   ❏ Creating and Maintaining Named Preference Sets
   ❏ Implementing Preferences Security
❏ **Object Class Libraries**
   ❏ Subclassing, Objects, and Object Libraries
   ❏ Types of Objects in an Object Library

❑ Object Libraries Shipped with Designer/2000
❑ Using Object Libraries During Generation

❑ **Generator Templates**
  ❑ Purpose and Use of Templates
  ❑ Types of Template Objects
  ❑ Templates Supplied by Designer/2000
  ❑ Creating Customized Templates

❑ **Designer/2000 Front-End Generators**
  ❑ Invoking and Using Front-End Generators
  ❑ Developer/2000 Forms Generator
  ❑ Developer/2000 Reports Generator
  ❑ Developer/2000 Graphics Generator
  ❑ Oracle WebServer Generator
  ❑ Visual Basic Generator
  ❑ Microsoft Help Generator

INTRODUCTION TO GENERATING DEVELOPER/2000 FORMS MODULES

- Preparing for Generation
- Enforcing Application-wide GUI Standards
- Implementing a Flexible Messaging Strategy
- Generating Developer/2000 Forms Modules
- Summary

As I discussed in the previous chapters, the process of generating front-end software involves a number of tools and techniques. These chapters offered a general overview of such tools and techniques. Now, this chapter and the ones to follow will guide you through the actual steps of generating front-end modules. These chapters have a workshop format that requires that you practice the instructions presented here. To assist you in the process, the companion CD-ROM contains the file OMSDEV.DMP, which contains the archived application system TASC OMS (DEV). As a preliminary step, import this file and restore the application system in your Designer/2000 Repository. This chapter shows how you can implement the functionality of this application system in Developer/2000 Forms modules.

27.1 PREPARING FOR GENERATION

Before you start the process of generating modules, you must take several steps to ensure that the process will be completed successfully and its outcome will be software modules of quality. Some of these steps are listed below:

1. Finalize the database design of the application system.
2. Finalize the implementation of business rules.
3. Create the first version of front-end modules with the Application Design Transformer.
4. Reorganize and enhance the structure of the application system.
5. Generate and install in the development database the back-end part of the application system.

27.1.1 OVERVIEW OF THE SAMPLE APPLICATION SYSTEM

The application system TASC OMS (DEV) provided on the CD-ROM has already implemented the first two of these steps. In particular, it contains the database design of the application and the business rules defined in the form of constraints, table and column properties, and PL/SQL modules. In addition, this application system contains an implementation of the user interface modules as Developer/2000 Forms and Oracle Reports modules. The first draft of this implementation was prepared using the Application Design Transformer. After that, certain actions were taken to transform this initial design. The following are the major areas in which the initial design was modified:

❑   Branches of modules that correspond to CUSTOMER and VENDOR business units were removed. The Developer/2000 implementation of OMS will be used only by members of TASC's order management teams.

❏ Redundant modules created by the Transformer for each business unit were removed.

❏ The menu modules were completely reorganized and restructured to reflect an interface that is friendlier to the users and easier to understand.

In addition, a number of properties of the remaining modules, like *Name*, *Purpose*, and *Title* were modified and set to more appropriate values than those created by the Transformer. The following sections will provide instructions on how you can implement the last step in the list of preliminary activities you should take before generating modules. Chapter 25 explained in detail how you can use the DDL Generator to create and install database objects in the Oracle Server database. Therefore, Sections 27.1.2 and 27.1.3 will simply list the actions you need to take to complete this task for the TASC OMS application system.

You may create the objects of this application by invoking the DDL Generator multiple times. In the scenario discussed here, you will use the generator three times to accomplish the following objectives:

❏ Create the database objects required to implement the structure of the database. These include tablespaces, users, and roles. The files created by the Generator in this run should be executed by an account with database administration privileges, like SYSTEM.

❏ Generate and install the database objects that are part of the TASC OMS application system, including tables, indexes, user accounts, grants, and so on. The scripts created in this iteration are executed by the application owner account created in the first iteration.

❏ Create the appropriate database roles and grants to the application system objects that will enable different users to access these objects.

Each of these iterations is discussed in detail in the following two sections.

27.1.2 CREATING THE DATABASE ADMINISTRATION OBJECTS

The following steps allow you to implement the database administration objects for the TASC OMS application system:

1. Switch to the DB Admin tab of the Design Navigator, expand the node Databases (Oracle), and select the database OMSDEV.
2. Click the icon Generate 📖 to launch the Generate Database Administration Objects utility.
3. On the Target tab, choose File as the target for generation.
4. Set File Prefix to 'OMSsupp,' Directory to the location in the file system where the files will be located, and Type to the Oracle database type where the objects will be created.

5. Clear the check box Generate Create Database Statement on the Target tab. I assume here that you will create the objects for the OMS application system in an existing Oracle database.

6. Switch to the tab Objects and include the following objects in the working set of the generator: tablespaces &&ORDER_DATA and &&ORDER_IDX; role TASC_USER; and users &&OMS_OWNER and &&OMS_USER. The Generate Database Administration Objects dialog box should now look like the one shown in Figure 27.1.

7. Click Start to begin the generation process.

When the process completes, the following files are created:

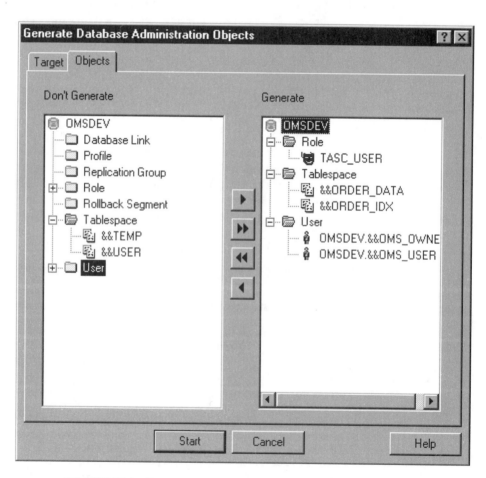

FIGURE 27.1   Settings of the Generate Database Administration Objects dialog box.

❏ **OMSsupp.tbs.** This file contains the tablespace creation commands.

❏ **OMSsupp.rle.** This file contains the command that creates the role TASC_USER.

❏ **OMSsupp.usr.** This file contains the command that creates the owner and user database accounts of TASC OMS.

❏ **OMSsupp.sql.** This file contains calls to the other files and will not be used in this iteration.

If you choose to create the tablespaces &&ORDER_DATA and &&ORDER_IDX in your development database, you should know that they are associated with the data files &&ORDER_DATA_FILE and &&ORDER_IDX_FILE. The sizes of these data files are modest (10Mb and 5Mb, respectively), and their names are set in parametric form to allow you to place them as it best fits your environment. The following steps are used to create these tablespaces:

1. Start a SQL*Plus session and connect as a database administrator.
2. Type '@<*path*>*OMSsupp.tbs*' at the SQL*Plus prompt. In this command, <path> should be replaced with the directory where the Generator created the files.
3. Provide the tablespace names of your choice and data file names and locations when prompted.

Following similar steps with the scripts OMSsupp.rle and OMSsupp.usr, you can create a new role and the users of the TASC OMS application.

27.1.3 CREATING THE DATABASE OBJECTS

After creating or identifying the tablespaces and the TASC OMS owner and user accounts, you are ready to proceed with the creation of the database objects of this application. The following steps summarize this process:

1. Expand the following nodes on the DB Admin tab of the Design Navigator: Database (Oracle), OMSDEV, Users, &&OMS_OWNER, Schema Objects, and Table Implementations.

If you decide not to create these tablespaces, you need to identify two existing tablespaces where the objects of the application system will be created and an existing database schema that will own the objects.

The scripts discussed in this section are provided ready for use in the folder on the companion CD-ROM. Follow the links *Software, Order Management System Development,* and *DDL* to access them.

2. Select all the tables under the node and click Generate 🔧 to invoke the Generate Database Objects dialog box.
3. On the Target tab, choose File as the target for generation.
4. Set File Prefix to 'OMSobjs,' Directory to the same location where you created the database administration files, and Type to the Oracle database type where the objects will be created.
5. On the Objects tab, include in the run set all the objects defined under the schema of &&OMS_OWNER.
6. Click Start.

After the Generator completes its run, install the generated scripts by following these commands:

1. Start a SQL*Plus session and connect as the OMS owner account you created in Section 27.1.2.
2. Type '@<path>\OMSobjs.sql' at the SQL*Plus prompt. In this command, <path> should be replaced with the directory where the Generator created the files.
3. Provide the tablespace names where the files and indexes will be created when prompted by the scripts.

As a result, the Order Management System objects and the appropriate grants on these objects to the user of the application are created.

27.2 ENFORCING APPLICATION-WIDE GUI STANDARDS

Several modules in the Order Management System are implemented as Developer/2000 Forms modules. Although each of them serves a different purpose and encapsulates some characteristic functionality, they all should have a common interface that is presented to the users. This section shows some steps you may take to ensure that all the modules you will generate conform with GUI standards set, maintained, and enforced at the application level.

As I explained in Chapter 26, the generator template is a Developer/2000 Forms module in which you set the properties of objects in a way that influences the modules created by the generator. Designer/2000 provides a number of templates that allow you to generate modules of different flavors and for different platforms. These templates are located in the subdirectory \CGENF50\ADMIN of the Oracle home directory (for example, C:\ORAWIN95\CGENF50\ADMIN or C:\ORANT\CGENF50\ADMIN) of your installation. By default, the generator uses the template OFG4PC1T.FMB. The module you generated in Chapter 3 of this book used this template. In larger application systems, like the Order Management System, maintaining your own template is desirable. The remainder of this section describes the process of creating this module, setting its coordinate system properties, and creating code to set the MDI frame title for each generated module. As a preliminary step, launch the Form Builder and create a new Form module. Then perform the following actions:

1. Double-click the icon that represents the template module in the Object Navigator window. This action displays the Properties window for the module.
2. Select the property *Name* in this window and set it to 'TASC_OMS_TEM-PLATE.'
3. Select the property *Coordinate Information* in the Physical group of properties and click the button More... to display the dialog box in which these properties are maintained.
4. Set the properties in this dialog box as shown in Figure 27.2.
5. Click OK to close this dialog box.

The properties in this dialog box define the coordinate system of the generated forms. The settings of the properties *Coordinate System, Real Unit, Character Cell Width,* and *Character Cell Height* shown in Figure 27.2 mean that the object dimensions, distances, and other measurements in the form's layout will be in inches, and that one cell in the layout is 0.1 inch × 0.1 inch. In other words, if the *Display Length* property of an item in the Designer/2000 Repository is set to 20, the real size of the item on the screen of the generated module is 20 × 0.2 = 2 inches.

Another modification you will make to the template is to add functionality that sets the MDI frame title of every generated module to the application system title followed by the purpose of the module. The concept of setting the MDI frame title of your application is borrowed from the default template OFG4PC1T.FMB provided by Designer/2000. This template contains a set of objects used to implement this functionality, as well as a number of other objects that will be useful to your applications. The following are the steps required to copy these objects into your template.

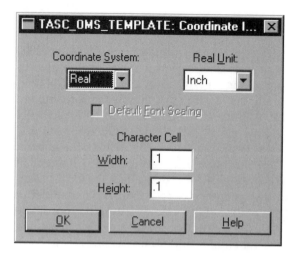

FIGURE 27.2 The TASC_OMS_TEMPLATE Coordinate Information dialog box.

1. Open the module OFG4PC1T.FMB in the Form Builder along with the module you just created.
2. Expand the node Alerts in the module OFG4PC1T.FMB.
3. Select all the alert objects under that node, drag them, and drop them under the node Alerts of the new module. When prompted, choose to copy the objects into your template.
4. Expand the node Program Units and copy the procedure MSG_ALERT in the new module. The procedure MSG_ALERT displays the messages copied in step 3.
5. Expand the node Data Blocks and copy the block CG$CTRL into your template. The following paragraph explains how you modify the items included in this block.
6. Expand the node Canvases and copy the canvas CG$STACKED_FOOTER into your template.
7. Close the module OFG4PC1T.FMB.

The following are the steps required to complete the required functionality in the template OMSTMPL.FMB:

1. Expand the node Data Block and Items in the Object Navigator.
2. Select the item CG$LB and click the icon Delete ![icon] to delete this item.
3. Select the item CG$AT and choose Edit | Duplicate.
4. Rename the new item CG$MP. The names CG$AT and CG$MP are recognized by the Forms Generator. When the module is generated using the template, the Developer/2000 Forms Generator will set the *Hint* property of

The way you created the template module for the OMS application demonstrates the typical cases when you would use a template in the generation process:

Include in the generated module objects, like alerts, that cannot be created and maintained in the repository.

Include in the generated module objects and PL/SQL code that appear consistently in all the generated modules. The block CG$CTRL and the trigger PRE-FORM fall into this category. Conceptually, you could create the block as a control module component and the triggers as an application logic object, but including it through the template is much simpler.

the item CG$AT to the property *Title* of the application system in the Designer/2000 Repository. The property *Hint* of the item CG$MP will be set to the property *Purpose* of the generated module.

5. Select the node Triggers at the module level and choose Program | Smart-Triggers | PRE-FORM from the Form Builder menu. This command creates

```
/*The following lines of code use the application system
Title property and the property Purpose for each module
to set the MDI frame window title for the generated
module.*/
DECLARE
  vc_app_title    VARCHAR2(100);
  vc_mod_purpose VARCHAR2(100);
BEGIN
  vc_app_title  :=
GET_ITEM_PROPERTY('CG$CTRL.CG$AT',HINT_TEXT);
  vc_mod_purpose:=
GET_ITEM_PROPERTY('CG$CTRL.CG$MP',HINT_TEXT);

  SET_WINDOW_PROPERTY(FORMS_MDI_WINDOW,TITLE,
    vc_app_title||' - '||vc_mod_purpose);
END;
```

FIGURE 27.3   The template form trigger that sets the MDI frame title of the generated module.

a new form-level trigger of type PRE-FORM and opens up the PL/SQL Editor window.

6. Enter the contents of the PRE-FORM trigger as shown in Figure 27.3.
7. Click Compile and Close to close the PL/SQL Editor window.
8. Save the new module under the name OMSTMPL.FMB. As a starting point, save the module in the subdirectory CGENF50\ADMIN of the Oracle Home directory.

In order for the generator to use the new template, set the preference *STFFMB— The name of the template form* to 'OMSTMPL.FMB.' Set this preference in the Design Editor for the application system TASC OMS (DEV).

27.3 IMPLEMENTING A FLEXIBLE MESSAGING STRATEGY

Recall from discussions about the properties of tables and the implementation of business rules in Chapter 20 that Designer/2000 allows you to associate error messages with several design objects, such as primary, unique, and foreign key constraints, and check constraints. When these constraints are enforced at the client side, the generators create code that validates the constraints and displays the text of the error message if the validation fails. Aim for three important goals when implementing message-handling functionality in your application:

❑ Maximize the flexibility of your application.
❑ Maximize the performance of your application.
❑ Display the messages in a user-friendly manner.

The following sections discuss different strategies you can follow to implement messages in your applications while preserving these goals.

27.3.1 HARD CODING AND SOFT CODING MESSAGES

You have two ways in which you can set the property *Error Message* of a constraint for Developer/2000 applications. In the first one, you use this property to enter the full description of the message. In this case, the generator will embed the text in the application module. This method seems the easiest and the most appealing way to implement user messages, but it has some negative impact on the application flexibility. This comes from the fact that the Developer/2000 Forms generator embeds these messages in the body of the form. If you need to modify the content of the messages displayed to the users, you need to make the modifications in the Designer/2000 Repository and regenerate the modules or edit the modules manually. In both cases, the operation may be costly and often impossible to implement.

The second way to handle error messages consists of decoupling the identification label of the message from its body. The label sets the *Error Message* property of constraints, whereas the body is stored externally. The generator embeds the label in the body just as before; however, because the actual contents of the message are retrieved from a container outside the module, these contents may be modified or replaced without requiring a regeneration of the module.

Storing the message content externally is also known as *soft coding* the message, as opposed to *hard coding* it in the body of the form. It can be implemented very easily, and the benefits you gain from the added flexibility of your application significantly offset the cost of the effort. The following list contains a summary of the actions you need to take in order to implement such a strategy in the TASC OMS application system.

1. In the Design Editor, set the preference *MSGSFT—Use Soft Coded Messages* to 'Yes' for the application system. This preference is located in the End User Interface group of preferences.

2. Copy the PL/SQL library OMSMSG.PLL from the directory \FORMS\PLL of the companion CD-ROM into the same folder as the template form. Follow the links *Software, Order Management System Development,* and *Error Messages* on the Web pages of the CD-ROM for an easy way to access this module. The library OMSMSG.PLL contains the messages that will be displayed to the users when a constraint in the OMS application is violated.

3. Open the library OFGTEL.PLL provided by Designer/2000 in the Form Builder.

4. Edit the package CG$ERRORS in this library to handle not only Designer/2000 messages, but also user-defined messages.

When you set the preference *MSGSFT—Use Soft Coded Messages* to 'Yes,' the Forms Generator does not embed the contents of these messages in the body of the generated modules, but uses the package CG$ERRORS instead to retrieve the messages from attached libraries and display them in message boxes. I explain the details of specifying the messages in the message library and the detailed components of the package CG$ERRORS in Sections 27.3.2–27.3.5.

27.3.2 CUSTOMIZING THE CG$ERRORS PACKAGE

Designer/2000 provides the PL/SQL library OFGTEL.PLL, which contains a number of program units used by the Developer/2000 Forms Generator to generate modules. One of these program units is the package CG$ERRORS. In its original form, this package performs these two functions:

❑ Retrieves a Generator message stored in the PL/SQL library OFGMES.PLL provided by Designer/2000. This library is attached automatically to the generated module when the preference *MSGSFT—Use Soft Coded Messages* is set to 'Yes.' The function MsgGetText is responsible for retrieving the contents of the message and, optionally, replacing up to four parameters, specified as <p1>, <p2>, <p3>, and <p4> with substitution strings.

❑ Displays the message in one of the alert boxes defined in the template module OFG4PC1T.FMB provided by Designer/2000.

The template OMSTMPL.FMB you created in Section 27.2 contains these alerts already. Therefore, the only modification you have to perform is to expand the package CG$ERRORS so that it handles the user-defined error messages as well as the Generator messages. The steps required to achieve this result appear below:

1. Open in the Form Builder the PL/SQL library OFGTEL.PLL.
2. Attach the library OMSMSG.PLL to the library OFGTEL.PLL. Do not store the hard-coded path to the library when prompted by the Form Builder.
3. Expand the node Program Units of the library OFGTEL.PLL.
4. Double-click the package body of CG$ERRORS to display it in the PL/SQL Editor.
5. Insert the lines shown in Figure 27.4 as the first statements in the body of the procedure Push, right after the keyword BEGIN.

As you can see from the contents of the modified Push procedure, you are taking advantage of the fact that when the Forms Generator issues a call to this procedure, it provides a number as the `msgid` argument. This number is zero for all user-defined messages, and a positive number for the internal Designer/2000-generated messages. The following two sections describe how the contents of the messages are retrieved based on this message number.

```
/* msgid is set to zero only for user messages          */
IF ( msgid = 0 ) THEN
  /* Get the message from the library for user-defined
messages */
  msg_string := Get_TASC_OMS_Message(msg_string);
END IF;
```

FIGURE 27.4   The modifications required in the procedure CG$ERRORS.Push.

27.3.3 EXTERNALIZING APPLICATION-SPECIFIC MESSAGES

The function Get_TASC_OMS_Message, called from CG$ERRORS.Push, as shown in Figure 27.4, is responsible for implementing messages that should be displayed to users in cases when the validation of a constraint fails. In principle, this function works the same as the procedure MESS_LIST provided by Designer/2000 in the library OFGMES.PLL and to be discussed in Section 27.3.4. For each message identified during the application design and stored in the *Error Message* property of constraints, an ELSIF block in the procedure sets the text corresponding to that message. This information is returned to the calling environment for further processing. Figure 27.5 shows excerpts from the function Get_TASC_OMS_Message.

Storing the messages of your application in a PL/SQL library attached to the template module is similar to storing them in message files, an approach followed by many other software applications, including all the Oracle products. The greatest benefit of this approach is that messages are separate from the application and, being stored locally, together with the other software components of the application, the performance for retrieving and displaying these messages is optimal. A down side is that when you need to modify the content of some message, you need to distribute the new message library to all the instances where the application is installed. A fully flexible way to handle messages with minimal administration cost can be achieved with the following actions:

```
FUNCTION GET_TASC_OMS_MESSAGE (
  p_msg_code    IN    VARCHAR2)
RETURN VARCHAR2
IS
  v_msg_string  VARCHAR2(200);
BEGIN
  IF (p_msg_code = 'TASC OMS 00001') THEN
    v_msg_string := 'Order with this Order Number
already exists.';
  ELSIF (p_msg_code = 'TASC OMS 00002') THEN
    v_msg_string := 'Delivery date must be after order
date.';
  /* Other messages listed here. */
  END IF;
  RETURN (v_msg_string);
END;
```

FIGURE 27.5 Excerpts from the function Get_TASC_OMS_Message.

1. Create a table as part of the application system database with columns to store the message code and text. An example of the SQL statement that creates such a table follows:

```
CREATE TABLE TASC_OMS_MESSAGES (
   msg_code          VARCHAR2 (30),
   msg_string        VARCHAR2 (200);
```

2. Insert records in this table for each message you identify during the application design.
3. Implement a function similar to Get_TASC_OMS_Message so that for a given message code, it selects the text of that message from the table. Figure 27.6 shows the contents of the database-driven version of this function, named Get_TASC_OMS_DB_Message. This function is also included in the library OMSMSG.PLL.

Although the database-driven approach shown in Figure 27.6 minimizes the administration and maintenance costs of the application messages, use it only in extreme cases. The reason is evident in the contents of the function

```
FUNCTION GET_TASC_OMS_DB_MESSAGE (
   p_msg_code      IN      VARCHAR2)
RETURN VARCHAR2
IS
   v_msg_string    VARCHAR2(200);
BEGIN
   SELECT msg_string
   INTO v_msg_string
   FROM TASC_OMS_MESSAGES
   WHERE msg_code = p_msg_code;
   RETURN (v_msg_string);
EXCEPTION
   WHEN NO_DATA_FOUND THEN
      v_msg_string := 'Message information is not
available.';
   RETURN (v_msg_string);
END;
```

FIGURE 27.6 The procedure that implements a database-driven approach to message handling.

Get_TASC_OMS_DB_Message. As you can see, for each message to be displayed to the users, the application must perform a query against the database. In applications that generate a large number of messages, that are accessed by a large number of users or distributed in slower networks, the performance may deteriorate significantly from these additional queries. In most cases, implementing the messages in PL/SQL libraries offers an acceptable flexibility of the application without taking a toll on its performance. Therefore, I recommend this approach in your applications.

27.3.4 EXTERNALIZING DESIGNER/2000 FORMS GENERATOR MESSAGES

In order to externalize the Designer/2000 internal messages, the function MsgGetText of CG$ERRORS contains a call to the procedure CG$MESSAGE.GET_MESSAGE. This procedure is part of the package CG$MESSAGE provided by Designer/2000 in the PL/SQL library OFGMES.PLL. You can find this library in the same folder (\CGENF50\ADMIN) as the other template modules that come with Designer/2000.

In order to see some examples of messages created in the modules by the Developer/2000 Forms Generator, open the library OFGMES.PLL in the Form Builder and display the body of package CG$MESSAGE in the PL/SQL Editor window. The procedure MESS_LIST in this package contains the message numbers and text used by the generator. An excerpt from this procedure is shown in Figure 27.7. If you want to modify some of the default messages produced by the generator, all you have to do is edit the contents of the procedure MESS_LIST.

27.3.5 HANDLING MESSAGES RAISED BY STORED PROGRAM UNITS

In an application that implements part of its business rules as program units stored in the database server, you need to display to users error messages triggered by these program units. Recall from the discussion on PL/SQL and stored program units in Designer/2000 that the built-in procedure RAISE_APPLICA-

Although the procedure CG$MESSAGE.GET_MESSAGE is located in the PL/SQL library OFGMES.PLL, you do not need to attach this library to the template form. When you set the preference *MSGSFT—Use Soft Coded Messages* to 'Yes,' the Developer/2000 Forms Generator automatically attaches this library to the module it creates.

```
procedure mess_list
(msgno   in   varchar2
,str     out varchar2)
IS
BEGIN

  if (msgno =  '3') then
    str := 'No row in table %s';
  elsif (msgno = '4') then
    str := 'Cannot update %s while dependent %s exists';
  elsif (msgno =  '5') then
    str := 'Cannot delete %s while dependent %s exists';
  elsif (msgno =  '6') then
    str := 'Row exists already with same %s';
  ...
  end if;
END;
```

FIGURE 27.7   An excerpt from procedure MESS_LIST, which contains the codes and text of messages produced by Designer/2000.

TION_ERROR can be used to send these messages from the database server to the front-end application. This procedure takes as arguments the number of the error, which is a negative number between −20000 and −30000, and a description of the error situation. An example of using RAISE_APPLICATION_ERROR appears below:

```
RAISE_APPLICATION_ERROR(-20000, 'Delivery date must be after
                    order date.');
```

In order to create an application with a consistent error handling interface and in order to increase the flexibility of the application, do not hard code the descriptions of these messages in the program units and database triggers. Instead, use the same labeling scheme that you follow to record the error messages raised by front-end modules. Replace the example shown above with the following statement:

```
RAISE_APPLICATION_ERROR(-20000, 'TASC OMS 00002');
```

In the PL/SQL library or database table where you record the information about the error messages, record the code and the description for these messages, just as you would for any other message identified during the design of the application. In addition to the benefits already discussed, handling messages raised from stored procedures in this manner provides another important advantage. In cases when the same business rule is implemented at the front end and back end of your application, you need to enter the message only once. For example, you can set the Error Message property of the check constraint ORD_CK1 to 'TASC OMS 00002' and enter the details for this message code as shown in Figure 27.5. In an Insert and Update trigger on the table ORDERS, which enforces the same rule, you can raise the error when the rule is violated with the following statement:

```
RAISE_APPLICATION_ERROR(-20000, 'TASC OMS 00002');
```

With a slight modification, the procedure Push, discussed in Section 27.3.2, may display the same information no matter whether the violation is trapped by the front-end module or sent by the database server. The modification required is due to the content of the message string sent to the Developer/2000 Forms module by the RAISE_APPLICATION_ERROR procedure. In the case above, the string received by the front-end application is:

```
'ORA-20000: TASC OMS 00002'
```

Clearly, the procedure Push will work as in the previous cases if, before calling the function Get_TASC_OMS_Message, you strip from this message code string the first 12 characters ('ORA-20000: '). Figure 27.8 shows only the body of

```
    /* msgid is set to zero only for user messages     */
    IF ( msgid = 0 ) THEN
       IF (SUBSTR(msg_string, 1, 9) = 'ORA-20000') THEN
          /* message is of format 'ORA-20000: TASC OMS
xxxxx' */
          msg_string := SUBSTR(msg_string, 12);
       END IF;
       /* Get the message from the library for user-defined
messages */
       msg_string := Get_TASC_OMS_Message(msg_string);
    END IF;
```

FIGURE 27.8 The message-handling function for errors raised by front-end and back-end modules.

Recall that the table handlers and database triggers created by the Server Generator as part of the table API implement all the data-related business rules at the database server. The Server Generator defines the contents of the property *Error Message* of a constraint as constants of the table-handler package. These constants are returned to the application whenever the constraints are violated. Therefore, the strategy to externalize error messages described here works equally well with the program units created by the Server Generator as part of the table API.

the procedure DISPLAY_MESSAGE, modified to handle errors raised from both front-end and back-end modules.

27.4 GENERATING DEVELOPER/2000 FORMS MODULES

At this point, you are ready to begin the process of generating the Developer/2000 Forms components of the Order Management System. The following sections will walk you through different scenarios, starting from the most simple cases to more difficult ones. By default, the generated modules will be created in the \BIN subdirectory of the ORACLE_HOME folder in your PC. In order to make it easier to find these modules, you may consider creating a separate directory where the generator will place each module it creates. Sections 27.4.1–27.4.3 will assume that this directory is C:\TASC\D2K.

27.4.1 GENERATING MODULES WITH A SINGLE-RECORD FORM LAYOUT

This section will discuss the process of generating blocks that display only one record at a time in a form layout. The module generated here will be the screen module OMSD2K0180, which is used to create and maintain business partners. In order to prepare the module for generation, start the Design Editor and create a new diagram for the module OMSD2K0180. This module has only one detailed module component, BP with BUSINESS_PARTNERS, as its base table usage. Edit the properties of this component as follows:

1. Display the module in the module diagram and switch to the display view of the diagrammer.

2. Double-click the window object on the module diagram and set the window name to *'BP'* and the window title to *'Create and Maintain Business Partners.'* Both these properties are located on the Name tab of the Edit Window dialog box.

3. Click Finish.

4. Double-click the module component, switch to the Display tab, and set the number of rows displayed to *'1.'*

5. Click Finish.

The following steps describe the process of generating the module:

1. Click the icon Generate ⬚ on the toolbar or select Utilities | Generate... to invoke the Developer/2000 Forms Generator.

2. Set the object library to point to the library OFGSTND1.OLB provided by Designer/2000.

3. Set the template to point to the template OMSTMPL.FMB that you created in Section 27.2.

4. Display the Forms Generator Options tab and set the destination of the generated modules to your preferred directory, for example, *'C:\TASCOMS\D2K.'* Specify the same destination on the Compile tab for the executable modules created by the Form Compiler.

5. Set the properties *Compile Form / Menu* on the Compile tab and *Run Form* on the Run tab to the option *'Add to Action List.'*

6. Set the property *Connect String* on the Compile and Run tabs so that the Developer/2000 Forms Generator and Developer/2000 Forms Runtime can connect to the database as a user account of the OMS application.

7. Click OK to close the Forms Generator Options dialog box. These options will be used for the generation of other modules as well.

8. Click Start to begin the generation process.

When the generation process is completed, save the changes made by the Generator to the module. Then select Messages | List Actions... to display the Build Action dialog box. Select the task to compile the newly generated form and click Run. When the compilation of the form is completed, run the form from the Build Action dialog box.

Figure 27.9 shows the first version of the module OMSD2K0180. One way to improve the layout of this module is to group the items that identify a business partner together in a tab folder and the items that provide information about the point of contact for this business partner in a second tab folder. The description of the business partner will appear under the tabs and it will be available at all moments.

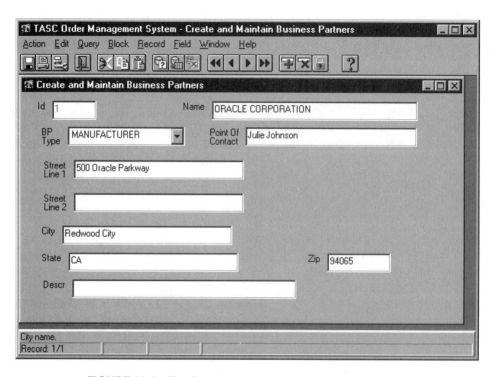

FIGURE 27.9 The first version of the OMSD2K0180 module.

The quickest way to implement this layout is to show the module diagram in display view and then follow these instructions:

1. Select the items ID, BP_TYPE , and NAME and click the icon Create Group ▩. The Create Item Group dialog box appears.
2. Enter *'ID'* in the text field Item group name, enter *'Identification'* in the Prompt field, and select the button Yes from the radio group Stacked.
3. Click Finish to create the item group.
4. Create a second stacked item group with the name POC_INFO and prompt Point of Contact. This group should include all the remaining items except for DESCR.

In order to make the item DESCR appear at the bottom of the stacked item groups, double-click the item on the diagram to display the Edit dialog box for this item. Then set the properties as follows:

1. Switch to the Display tab.
2. Set *Prompt* to *'Description,'* *Width* to *'40,'* and *'Height'* to *'3.'*

3. Click Finish to close the dialog box.
4. Arrange the display order of the module items so that item groups ID and POC_INFO are first, followed by the item DESCR.

At this point, you can invoke the Developer/2000 Forms Generator to re-generate the module with the new changes. The Generator will recognize that a version of this module is already generated and it will ask you whether you want to generate it again or not. Click Yes in the dialog box Yes/No to confirm that you want to proceed with the generation. When the generation is complete, compile and execute the module using the Build Action dialog box as explained earlier. The layout of the module ORDD2K0180 after the changes and modifications discussed here appears in Figure 27.10.

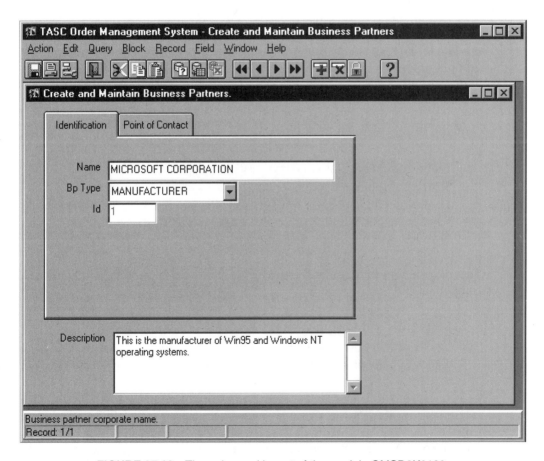

FIGURE 27.10 The enhanced layout of the module OMSD2K0180.

As a last action with this module, save the module component as a reusable module component, so that you can assemble it in any other module where your users will need to edit and maintain business partner data. Follow these actions to convert the component BP into a reusable module component:

1. Select the module component BP in the Design Navigator.
2. Display the properties of this component in the Property Palette.
3. Switch to the Property Palette and set the property Name to 'BP_REUSE.'
4. Set the property Module Component Type to 'Re-usable.'
5. Save the changes to the Repository.

27.4.2 GENERATING MODULES WITH A MULTI-RECORD TABULAR LAYOUT

This section will discuss issues related to the generation of modules that contain multi-record blocks with tabular layout. The example used in this section is the module OMSD2K0140. This module will be used to create and maintain geographic regions and zip codes. As a preliminary step, start the Module Data Diagrammer and create a new diagram for the module OMSD2K0140. Notice that this module has two components defined. Create a key-based link from the component REG to the component ZIP. Then set the properties of the module component REG and its elements as follows:

1. Set the number of rows displayed by the component to '4.'
2. Set the name of the window to 'REG' and its title to 'Regions and ZIP Codes.'
3. Display the dialog box of properties for the item DESCR. Set *Prompt* to '*Description*' and *Width* to '40,' so that the item can fit in the window of your form while remaining in the same record as the name of the region.

The following steps describe the properties you need to modify for the module component ZIP:

1. Set the title of the component to 'ZIP Codes for Selected Region.'
2. Set the number of rows displayed to '7.'
3. Check that the placement of the module component is set to '*Same page.*'

In order to achieve a tabular look and feel of the items displayed in each block, use the preference *ITMIPG—Item/prompt gap*. This preference allows you to control the space between items in the same record. By default, it is set to '2;' for multi-record groups with a tabular layout, set it to '0.' The preference is normally set at the module component level, although for modules like OMSD2K0140, where all the module components have a tabular layout, you can set it at the module level. This preference is in the Layout – Item group of preferences.

In order to distinguish the blocks REGION and ZIPS from each other, you can increase the blank space between the two blocks by setting the preference *PAGIBS—Content canvas inter-block separator* to '1.' This preference is part of the Layout – Content Can preference category. Although the title of the first block in a form is usually redundant and therefore not displayed, the title of any other subsequent blocks is displayed as a text label. In order to align this label with other controls in the form, set the preference *BLKTLM—Block title margin* to '1' in the Layout – Group category. Set both these preferences at the application system level.

27.4.3 ADDING A CURRENT RECORD INDICATOR
TO TABULAR BLOCKS

In order to make it easier for your users to identify the current record of a tabular block, you may add an item to these blocks, which will serve as an indicator that the focus of the application is on the current record. When the users click or otherwise navigate to a record, the background color of the indicator will change to distinguish this record from the remaining ones in the block. The following steps describe the process of adding a current item indicator to the REGIONS module component.

1. Click the icon Create Item and click the module component REG outside the table usage REGIONS. The Create Unbound Item dialog box appears.
2. Set the item name to 'REGIONS_IND' and select 'Custom' from the list Item type.
3. Click Next twice to navigate to the Definition tab.
4. Set Datatype to 'CHAR' and the radio button 'No' to make the item optional.
5. Click Next twice to navigate to the Display tab.
6. Set Display type to 'Current record' and Width to '1.'
7. Click Finish to complete the process.

At this point, switch to the display view of the module diagram and make the unbound item the first displayed item in the module component. The process of adding a current record indicator item to the module component ZIP is very similar. Follow the steps presented earlier for the component REG and set the name of this indication to 'ZIPS_IND.'

In order for the Generator to create functionality that changes the background color of the record indicator for the current record in the data block, the template module must contain two visual attributes named CG$CURRENT_INDICATOR and CG$OTHER_RECORD. The template OFG4PC1T.FMB shipped with Designer/2000 contains these two visual attributes. Using techniques discussed earlier in the chapter, copy these objects into your template OMSTMPL.FMB. Alternatively, define such attributes yourself, taking care to set the background color of CG$CURRENT_INDICATOR to a color that contrasts with the background of CG$OTHER_RECORD—which I recommend that you set to white. The following is a list of instructions to create these visual attributes yourself:

1. Start the Form Builder and open the module OMSTMPL.FMB.
2. Create a new visual attribute called CG$OTHER_RECORD.

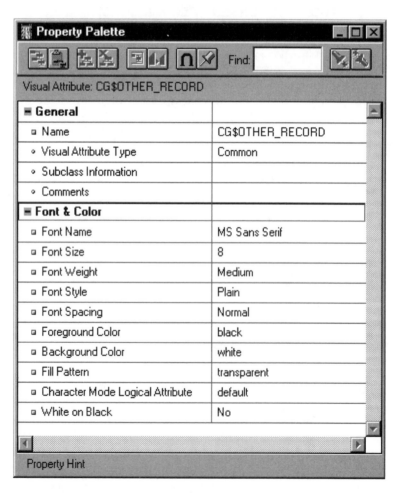

FIGURE 27.11   The properties of the visual attribute CG$OTHER_RECORD.

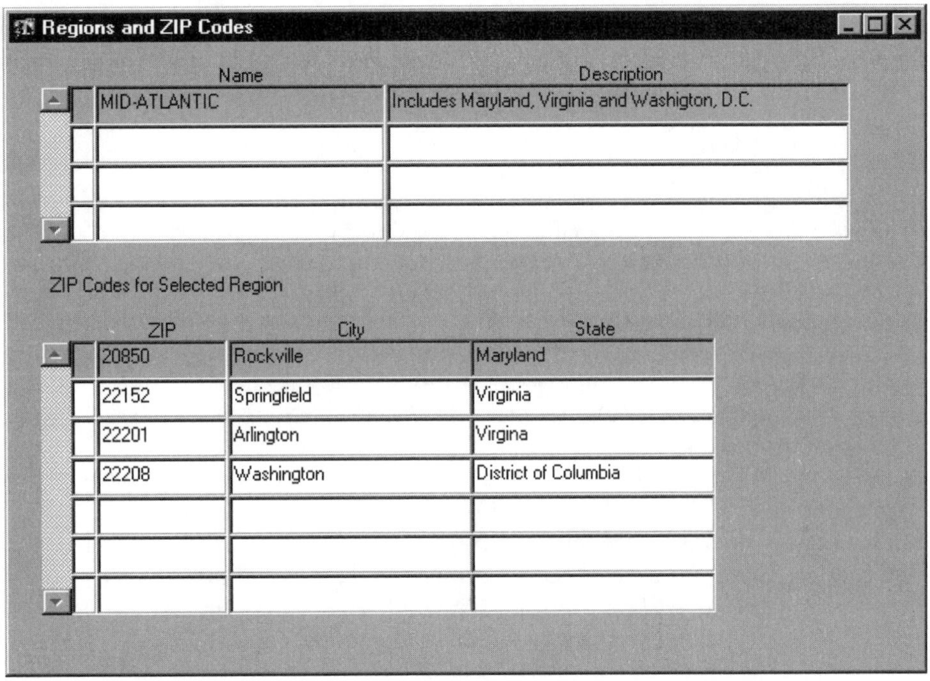

FIGURE 27.12   The layout of the generated module OMSD2K0140.

3. Set the properties of this attribute as shown in Figure 27.11.
4. Create a second visual attribute and name it CG$CURRENT_RECORD.
5. Subclass this object from CG$OTHER_RECORD to inherit its properties.
6. Set the *Background Color* property to a color different from *'white.'* I prefer to set it to *'canvas,'* so that it looks like the background canvas.
7. Save the template and exit the Form Builder.

After these changes, you are ready to generate the module OMSD2K0140. Figure 27.12 shows the generated version of this module.

27.5 SUMMARY

Developer/2000 Forms modules are among the most important front-end applications that you can generate with Designer/2000. In order to generate modules of high quality that conform to established GUI standards and that present a friendly interface to the users, you must prepare carefully and plan the generation process. This chapter discusses the major activities performed before the generation process, as well as the actual generation of modules with form and tabular layout. Major topics of this chapter include:

❏ **Preparing for Generation**
   ❏ Overview of the Sample Application System
   ❏ Creating the Database Administration Objects
   ❏ Creating the Database Objects
❏ **Enforcing Application-wide GUI Standards**
❏ **Implementing a Flexible Messaging Strategy**
   ❏ Hard Coding and Soft Coding Messages
   ❏ Customizing the CG$ERRORS Package
   ❏ Externalizing Application-Specific Messages
   ❏ Externalizing Designer/2000 Forms Generator Messages
   ❏ Handling Messages Raised by Stored Program Units
❏ **Generating Developer/2000 Forms Modules**
   ❏ Generating Modules with a Single-Record Form Layout
   ❏ Generating Modules with a Multi-Record Tabular Layout
   ❏ Adding a Current Record Indicator to Tabular Blocks

ADVANCED DEVELOPER/2000
FORMS GENERATION

- ♦ Generating Forms with Multiple Table Usages
- ♦ Item Lookups and Lists of Values
- ♦ Adding GUI Controls to Modules
- ♦ Adding Calendar Controls to Developer/2000 Forms Modules
- ♦ Summary

Chapter 27 discussed how you can lay the groundwork for generating Developer/2000 Forms modules. In this chapter you will use the information presented there and build upon it to create more complex modules. In particular, you will learn to perform the following tasks:

❑ Generate complex forms with multiple table usages.
❑ Add a calendar control to modules to facilitate the entry and maintenance of date values.
❑ Add Web browsing functionality to your modules through ActiveX technologies.

28.1 GENERATING FORMS WITH MULTIPLE TABLE USAGES

In Sections 28.1.1–28.1.3, you will generate a module with multiple table usages, both base and detail usages. This is module ORDD2K0070, which will be used to create and maintain complete information about products, including product categories and product items.

28.1.1 REARRANGING THE MODULE LAYOUT

As you have done with other modules, start by defining the layout of the module in the Design Editor. When you create a new diagram for the module, you will see that ORDD2K0070 contains five module components. The following steps show you how to rearrange the layout of these usages:

1. Delete from the diagram and Repository the module components with table usages BUSINESS_PARTNERS and ORDER_MANAGEMENT_UNITS. Your module will need to associate the remaining usages with lookups from these modules, but, as you will see in a minute, you have a much simpler way to add this information to your module.
2. Create key-based links between PRODUCT_CATEGORIES, PRODUCTS, and PRODUCT_ITEMS in such a way that PRODUCT_CATEGORIES is master of PRODUCTS, and PRODUCTS is master of PRODUCT_ITEMS.
3. Switch to the display view of the module and organize the module components so that those with table usages PRODUCT_CATEGORIES and PRODUCTS are in the first window and PRODUCT_ITEMS is in the second window.

Now you can create lookup usages that will complement the base table usages with information. The following instructions show how you add the lookup table usage BUSINESS PARTNERS to the base table usage PRODUCT.

1. Switch to the data view of the module diagram.

2. Select the icon Create Table Usage and click inside the module component PRODUCTS. The dialog box Create Lookup Table Usage appears, with the candidate tables that can become lookups of PRODUCTS.

3. Select the table BUSINESS_PARTNERS and click Next.

4. Enter *'BP_TYPE = 'MAN' ORDER BY NAME'* in the text box WHERE clause of the query and click Next. This condition restricts the business partners displayed in this component to the manufacturers of products. These manufacturers will be displayed ordered by their name.

5. Select NAME as the column that will be displayed in the list of values.

6. Click Next twice until the tab Operations is displayed. Select Query as the only operation for the new item.

7. Click Next twice to navigate to the tab LOV. Enter *'Available Manufacturers'* as the title for the list of values.

8. Click Finish to complete the process.

Perform similar actions to add BUSINESS_PARTNERS as a lookup of PRODUCT_ITEMS in the third module component. For this usage, set the WHERE clause of the query to *'BP_TYPE IN ('VEN', 'MAN') ORDER BY NAME,'* select the column NAME to display in the list of values dialog box, choose Query as the only operation that will be performed, and set the title of the list of values dialog box to *'Available Vendors.'* The need to set this property is due to the fact that the business vendors in the context of product items are the vendors who supply these items to TASC.

Finally, add a second lookup usage to PRODUCT_ITEMS, based on the table ORDER_MANAGEMENT_TEAMS. For this usage, set the WHERE clause to *'OMT_TYPE='WH' ORDER BY NAME,'* select the column NAME to display in the list of values dialog box, choose Query as the only operation that will be performed, and set the title of the list of values dialog box to *'Available Warehouses.'*

28.1.2 DEFINING THE LAYOUT OF THE PRODUCT INFORMATION WINDOW

The layout of the first window in the module ORDD2K0070 will resemble the layout of the module ORDD2K0140 which you generated in Chapter 27. The module component PRODUCT_CATEGORIES will play the role of REGIONS, whereas PRODUCTS will be in place of ZIP. Because the process of setting the properties and preferences for such a layout were discussed in detail in Chapter 27, this section will present only a summarized list of actions you have to take to apply this layout to module ORDD2K0070.

1. Set the name of the first window to *'PI'* and its title to *'Product Information.'*

2. Set the number of rows displayed to *'4'* for the module component PRODUCT_CATEGORIES.

3. Set *Prompt* to *'Description'* and *Width* to *'40'* for the bound item DESCR in the base table usage PRODUCT_CATEGORIES.

4. Set the title of the module component PRODUCTS to *'Products in the Selected Category.'*

5. Set the number of rows displayed to *'7'* for the module component PROD-UCTS.

6. Set *Prompt* to *'Description'* and *Width* to *'30'* for the bound item DESCR in the base table usage PRODUCTS.

7. Set the preference *ITMIPG – Item/prompt gap* to *'0'* for the module compo-nents PRODUCT_CATEGORIES and PRODUCTS.

8. Add a record indicator unbound item to the module component PROD-UCT_CATEGORIES.

An important difference between the modules ORDD2K0070 and ORDD2K0140 resides in the layout of the detail module components. In the case of ZIPS, all the items fit comfortably in the module's window. But in the case of PROD-UCTS, not all the items fit in this window. To solve this problem, you could attempt to reduce the display width of items in the component; however, a much simpler way is to set the property *Overflow Style* of the module component PRODUCTS. This property is located on the tab Display of the Edit Module Component dialog box. The four possible settings of this property are explained in the following paragraphs:

❏ **Wrap Line.** This is the default setting of the property. When the generator can-not fit all the items and text labels in one row, it simply wraps the remaining items in additional lines. For multi-record blocks, use this setting only when you are sure that all the items will be able to fit within the allocated space.

❏ **Spread Table.** When the *Overflow Style* is set to this option, the generator will fit in the window as many items as it can. Any remaining items are im-plemented so that they are not visible at first but can become visible if users scroll to the right. You may set aside one or more items, called *context items,* to be always visible in the table. When the module component is imple-mented as a spread table, be careful to hide from the main view only those items that are not very critical and that do not need to be constantly in front of the users. If users have to scroll each time to view data items that are not displayed, the spread table metaphor may become very irritating.

❏ **Overflow Area Below.** In cases when all the items must be visible to the users, you may choose this option as the *Overflow Style* for the module com-ponent. In this case, the generator will fit in the available space all the items that it considers to be context items. The remaining items are displayed below the multi-record region of the module component.

❏ **Overflow Area Right.** This option is very similar to the previous option for the *Overflow Style*. The only difference is that in this case, the context items will be displayed to the right of the multi-record region of the module component.

From the description of the *Overflow Style* options, you can see that the concept of context items plays an important role in the structure of spread tables and overflow areas. The Developer/2000 Forms Generator will always place in the context area the first displayed item in the module component. Then, depending on the setting of the preference *OFADFT—Overflow area table uses default context items*, the Generator may select which items to consider context items in one of the following two ways:

❑ If the preference OFADFT is set to 'Y,' the generator will consider context items those that compose the primary key of the base table as well as those that are declared as descriptor columns in the base table usage of the component. With this preference setting, for example, the module component PRODUCTS will have two context items: ID and NAME—the first one because it is the primary key of PRODUCTS and the second one because the bound item NAME has the property *Descriptor Sequence* in the Property Palette set. Given the fact that the primary keys will always be displayed as context items and that you have to go to the properties of the table in order to create additional context items, this option is usually not used.

❑ If the preference OFADFT is set to 'N,' the generator will pick the context items only among those items that have the property *Context* set. You can access this property in the Property Palette or on the Display tab of the Edit Item dialog box. The generator will make context items all the items it finds until it runs out of canvas space or until it reaches an item with the property *Context* not set. So if you set this property for the item NAME, but not for ID, and ID comes before NAME in the list of column usages, the generator will not make NAME a context item. In order to force the generator to make NAME a context item, place it before ID, and before any other item whose property *Context* is not set. Thus, while setting the preference OFADFT to 'N' allows you to pick exactly those items you want to make context items in any given situation, it also forces you to change the display order of the items in the DTU by bringing forward all those that will be context items.

The preference *OFADFT—Overflow area table uses default context items*, is part of the Layout – Overflow group of preferences and should be set at the application system level. Another preference that controls the appearance of spread tables is *SPRBEV—Spread table bevel*, in the Layout – Spread Tab category of preferences. In order to have a smooth transition between context items and non-context items, this preference should be set to 'NONE.'

At this point, you are ready to complete the layout of the window Product Information. Take the following steps to implement the module component PRODUCTS as a spread table:

1. Set the property *Overflow Style* of the module component PRODUCTS to *'Spread Table.'*
2. Set the property *Context* for the item NAME. This property is represented by the check box labeled Context item? on the Display tab of the Edit Bound Item dialog box.
3. Ensure that preferences OFADFT and SPRBEV are set as described above.

Figure 28.1 shows the layout of the Product Information window in the module ORDD2K0070.

28.1.3 DEFINING THE LAYOUT OF THE PRODUCT ITEMS WINDOW

The module component PRODUCT_ITEMS will display product items associated with a particular product in a tabbed dialog box. Unlike the module component PRODUCTS in the previous section, the *Overflow Style* of the component PROD-UCT_ITEMS will be set to *'Wrap Line.'* The following is a list of properties you need to set for this module component and its elements:

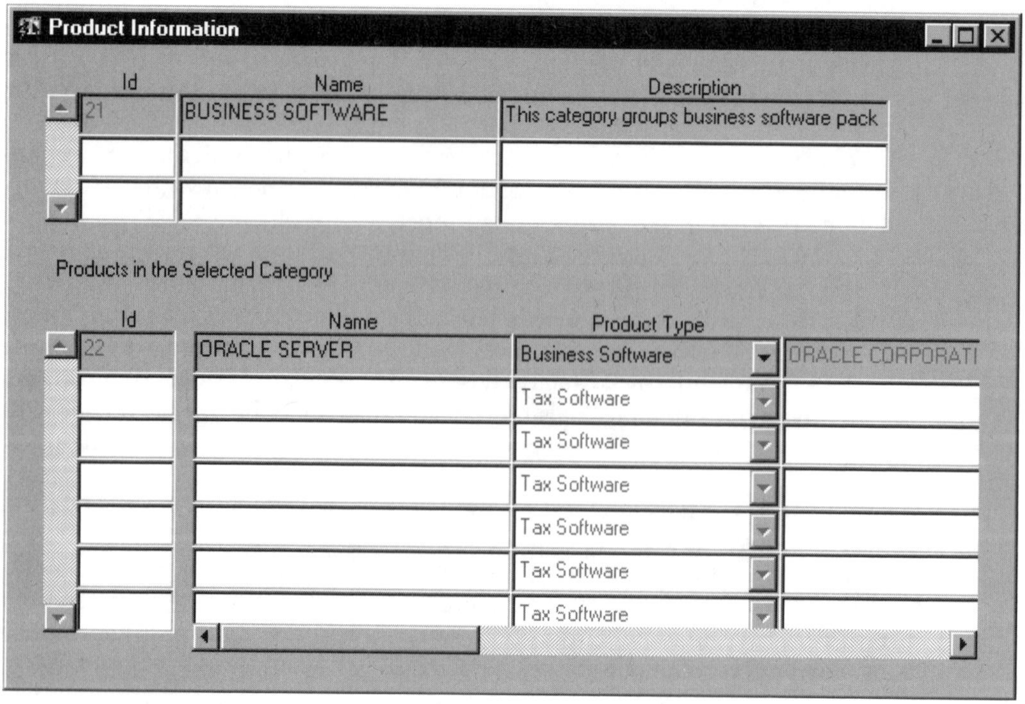

FIGURE 28.1   The final layout of the Product Information window of the ORDD2K0070 module.

1. Set the title of the window that corresponds to this module component to 'Product Item Information.'

2. Switch to the Size tab of the Edit Window dialog box and set the properties *X-position* and *Y-position* to '2.' The reason for this setting in the second window is so that it does not overlay the first window when it is first invoked. In order to preserve the cascaded look of windows, you have to set these properties according to the order of the window in the application. A third window, for example, should have these properties set to '4.'

3. In the Edit Module Component dialog box, set the number of rows displayed to '6' and the property *Overflow Style* to '*Wrap Line.*'

4. Create the stacked item group named PI_ID with *Prompt* set to '*Product Item.*' Include the following items in this group: ITEM_NUMBER, SERIAL_NUMBER, STATUS, STOCKING_DATE, BOOKING_DATE, PACKING_DATE, and SERIAL_NUMBER.

5. Set the property *Display Type* of the item STATUS to '*Pop list*' and select the option 'Meaning only' from the Show Meaning list.

6. Create an item group named 'PI_DETAILS' with *Prompt* set to '*Product Item Details.*' Include in the group the items that represent the name of the vendor of the product item and the warehouse where the item is located. Both these items are shown as NAME in the display view of the module diagram. In addition, include in the group the items WAREHOUSE_LOCATION and DESCR.

7. Set the preference *OFADEC—Overflow area decoration* to '*NONE.*' This decoration is not needed since you will surround the overflow items with the decoration of the item group. Since the layout of overflow items will be defined in this manner for all the modules, set this preference at the application system level.

The block PRODUCT_ITEMS is a detail block displayed in a separate window from its master PRODUCTS. In such situations, the generator carries over in the new window enough information to allow the users to maintain the context of information. In particular, all the items with the property *Context* set in the master block are displayed in the context area of the detail window. If space permits, the generator will bring over any descriptor items from the master block. In order to give the context group the appearance of other items in your application, set the following preferences from the Layout – Context group of preferences:

1. Set *CONDEC—Context decoration* to '*INSET RECTANGLE.*'

2. Set *CONDFT—Context uses default items* to '*N.*' The meaning of this preference is similar to that of OFADFT, discussed in Section 28.1.2.

3. Set *CONHDS—Context header separator* and *CONFTS—Context footer separator* to '*1.*' By default, these preferences are set to '*0,*' which causes the context group to be displayed too close to the top of the window and the following form items.

4. Set *CONTLM—Context title margin* and *CONTLS—Context title spacing* to '1' to match the corresponding item group preferences *GRPTLM—Item group title margin* and *GRPTLS—Item group title spacing*.

At this point, the layout of the second window of the module ORDD2K0070 is complete. When you generate the module, the tab Product Item of this window should look like the one shown in Figure 28.2.

28.2 ITEM LOOKUPS AND LISTS OF VALUES

By looking at the generated module ORDD2K0070, you will notice that the items from lookup usages are implemented as display items associated with the base foreign key columns. When your cursor lands inside an item such as the Manufacturer Id in PRODUCTS block, or Vendor Id and Warehouse Id in PRODUCT_ITEMS block, the hint in the message line contains the terms 'list of values available.' By selecting Edit | Display List... from the menu, you can view

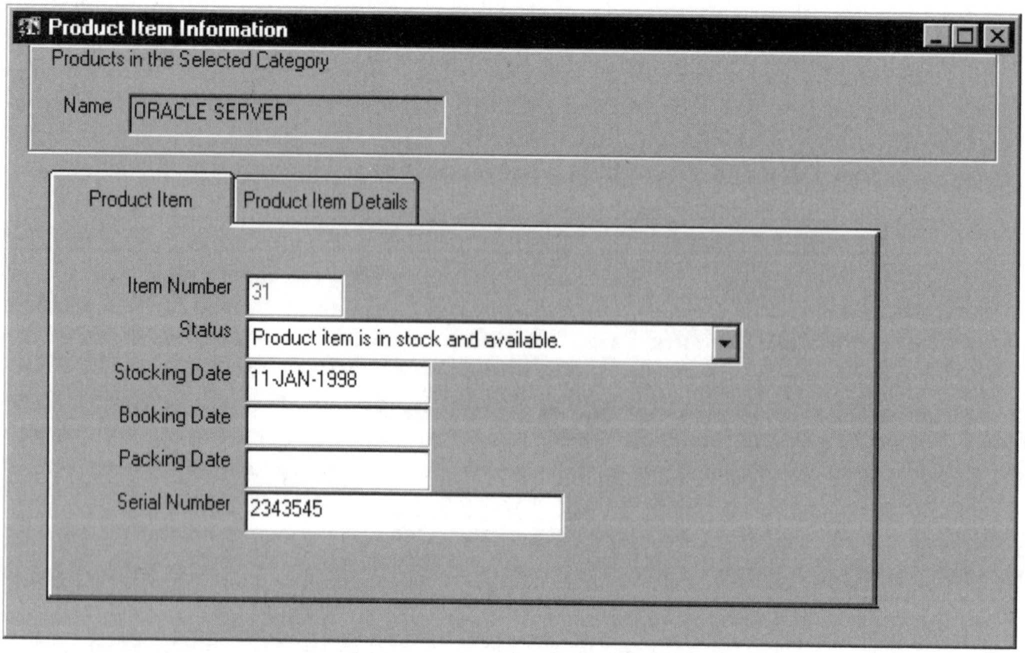

FIGURE 28.2   The final layout of the Product Item Information window of the module ORDD2K0070.

all the available values from which you can select the desired one to populate the foreign key column. An example of the list of values control appears in Figure 28.3.

Sections 28.2.1 and 28.2.2 discuss the features of Developer/2000 Forms list of values controls, and how to use them to restrict access to data and to help in the process of entering and validating data.

28.2.1 FEATURES OF LIST OF VALUES CONTROLS

The list of values in Developer/2000 Forms has two important features:

❑ **Search.** In order to search for an element in the list, you click inside the text item Find and type the search criterion. Standard SQL wildcards like '%' and '_' can be used to build the search string. When you are ready to search, click the button Find.

❑ **Auto-reduction.** This feature is especially useful when the list contains a large number of items. To activate it, you simply click inside the list control

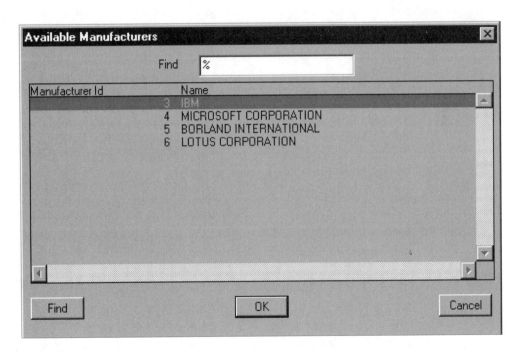

FIGURE 28.3 The Developer/2000 Forms List of Values control.

and start typing the value for which you are searching. The elements of the list are reduced as you type, to match the characters you enter.

28.2.2 USING LISTS OF VALUES TO RESTRICT DATA ACCESS

When the list of values control is invoked, by default, it presents all the records from the associated table in the order in which they are entered in the database. Often, you want to populate the list with only a subset of these records, ordered according to certain criteria. In these situations, you need to specify your WHERE and ORDER criteria on the WHERE property tab of the lookup table usage dialog box. Section 28.1.1 showed examples of how you would set these criteria.

Another modification you can make to items of lookup tables is to enable them to search using the Developer/2000 Forms search-by-example paradigm. You can achieve this by allowing the Query operation to be performed on these items. In Section 28.1.1, for example, you allowed this operation for the columns NAME in all three lookup usages of module ORDD2K0070. In these conditions, the Generator will create these items so that they are enterable when the form is in ENTER QUERY mode. In addition, the generator creates PRE-QUERY triggers that modify the query to include the criteria you enter in the item. Thus, if you enter 'ORA%' in the MANUFACTURER_NAME item of block PRODUCTS, the default WHERE statement of the block query will be appended by the following clause:

```
AND (MANUF_ID IN
    ( SELECT ID
      FROM BUSINESS_PARTNERS
      WHERE NAME LIKE 'ORA%')
```

28.2.3 ADDING A LIST OF VALUES BUTTON

I mentioned earlier that when an item is associated with a list of values, the hint message of the item indicated this fact. However, in a GUI environment, you would want to convey this information to the users without waiting until they place the focus of the application on the item. Usually, in such cases, an icon is displayed by the side of the item associated with a list of values control. The icon and functionality of this button are the same as the one shown on the application's toolbar. You can add this feature very easily into your module by setting the preference *LOVBUT—Use a button to indicate available list of values* to 'Y.' In order to offer a consistent interface and application behavior to the users, this preference should be set at the application level. This preference is part of the List of Values category of preferences. Other list of values preferences that you should consider setting are listed below. These preferences control the dimensions and the initial position of the control on the screen:

1. Set preferences *LOVHPN—Horizontal position of LOV* and *LOVVPN—Vertical position of LOV* to 'CENTER.'
2. Set *LOVMHT—List of values height* to '30' and *LOVMWD—Maximum width of LOV* to '60.' Although the list of values control is not bound to the MDI frame of your application, this control should not be wider than other windows of the application.
3. Set *LOVXCO—List of values – X co-ordinate* to '40' and *LOVYCO—List of values – Y co-ordinate* to '30.'

The settings shown here are good for a SVGA 800x600 resolution display. For different resolutions, you may use different values.

List of values controls discussed so far are used to populate foreign key with values from the lookup tables. Another use of such controls is to display the values of columns with a list of allowed values recorded in the reference code table. In order to display the product types in a list of values, for example, change the properties of the column PRO_TYPE as follows:

1. Change *Display Type* from *'Pop list'* to *'Text.'*
2. Set the property *'Display in LOV?'* to *'Yes'* in the Property Palette.

With such an implementation, the generator will create a text item where the values of the item are displayed, and a second text item associated with a list of values control. This control displays the abbreviation and meaning for the allowed values of a column as defined in the reference code table. In most cases, the users of the application are interested in the meaning of the values rather than how they are stored in the database. The GUI list controls provide them just that and, therefore, should be used instead of the Developer/2000 Forms lists of values.

28.2.4 USING A LIST OF VALUES FOR DATA ENTRY AND VALIDATION

The argument of hiding from users the complexity of key values and internal identifiers applies to lookup usages as well. When entering the manufacturer of a product or the vendor of a product item, your users should not need to specify the number that identifies these records in the database. Instead, they should be able to type the first few characters of the name of the company and move to the next item. The application internally does a search for companies whose name matches the entered string. If none are found, the focus does not leave the item; if only one item is found, the application fills in the foreign key column with the appropriate value and the name item with the full value; if more than one are found, the application brings up a list control that allows users to pick the desired value. As in the previous case, the foreign key column and the name item are filled in with the selected values. The Developer/2000 Forms list of values controls allows you to support the functionality described above with minimal effort. The following is the list of steps to implement this functionality for the manufacturer name in the module component PRODUCTS block of the module ORDD2K0070:

1. In the module data diagram, double-click the table usage BUSINESS_PARTNERS, which is a lookup for PRODUCTS.

2. Switch to the tab Operations and set the flag Insert for the item L_BP_NAME, which corresponds to the column BUSINESS_PARTNERS.NAME.

3. Open the dialog box for the base table usage PRODUCTS and unset the property Insert for the item MANUF_ID. Because the users will enter the name of the manufacturer rather than their internal identifier, there is no reason why this item should be visible to them.

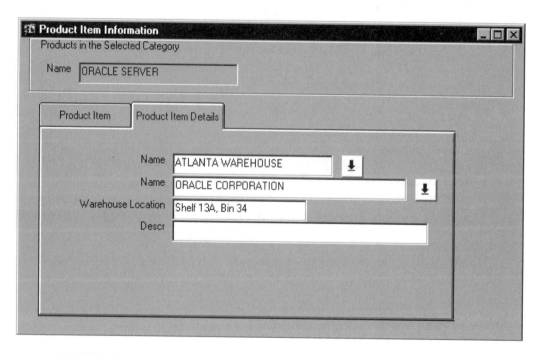

FIGURE 28.4 The simplified layout of the Product Item Information window of module ORDD2K0070.

Following these instructions with lookup usages in the second window, also make non-displayed the items VENDOR_ID and OMT_ID and allow users to enter the name of the product item's vendor and the name of the warehouse where it is located. You can use the savings in screen real estate gained from hiding the foreign key to display more product item records. Figure 28.4 shows the simplified layout of the Product Item Information window with the list of values iconic buttons by the side of Vendor Name and Warehouse Name.

28.3 ADDING GUI CONTROLS TO MODULES

In the modules discussed so far, you have seen several cases of GUI controls created by the generator. Some of these are created based on properties of items, such as Display Type set to 'Pop List,' and a list of allowed values associated with the column, or its domain. Some other controls, such as the ones on the application's toolbar, are part of the default functionality provided with each Developer/2000 Forms module. In the Sections 28.3.1–28.3.5, you will see how to convert items in your modules into GUI controls, including push buttons, text boxes, combo boxes, check boxes, and radio groups. As a case study, these sections will use module ORDD2K0030, which creates and maintains customer information.

28.3.1 OVERVIEW OF THE MODULE

To begin the discussion, open the module ORDD2K0030 in a module diagram. From this diagram, you can see that this module is made up of two components based on the same table (CUSTOMERS); however, the components play a different role. The first one, named CUSTOMERS, will be used to enter information about customers of TASC. Items in this usage are organized into the following three stacked item groups:

- ❑ **Customer.** This includes items that identify customers of both types, individuals and corporations.
- ❑ **Company.** For corporate customers, this group includes items such as INDUSTRY, FOUNDED_DATE, and EMPLOYEE_COUNT.
- ❑ **Address.** This group includes address information about the customer.

The second component, named POC, is also based on the table CUSTOMERS, but it shows information about individuals that serve as contacts for this customer. The items in this component are divided into the following stacked item groups:

- ❑ **POC Information.** This group includes the items used to record the name of the point of contact.

❑ **Address.** This group contains items about the address of the point of contact.

❑ **POC Phone and Email.** This group contains the items PHONE, FAX, and EMAIL.

In the following sections, you will enhance the layout of this module with additional GUI controls. Open the module in the Module Data Diagrammer in order to follow the instructions presented here.

28.3.2 ADDING PUSH BUTTONS

Start by adding a push button in the first block that, when clicked, will navigate to the second block. This push button can be implemented as a navigation action item. The following are the steps required to create such an item:

1. Select the icon Create Action Item and click the module component CUS-TOMERS on the diagram. The dialog box Create Navigation Action Item appears.
2. Select the radio button Navigation within the module as the type of action item to create; click Next.
3. Enter 'POC' as the item name and 'POC...' as the prompt for the new item; click Next.
4. Select POC from the list of module components where you can navigate.
5. Click Finish to complete the process.

28.3.3 ADDING CHECK BOXES

Check boxes are controls that allow you to pick one of two values by placing a check mark or by clearing the control. In the first component of module ORDD2K0030, you can implement the item CUS_TYPE as a check box. In order to achieve this, take the following steps:

1. Double-click the item CUS_TYPE to display its Edit Bound Item dialog box.
2. Switch to the Display tab.
3. Set Prompt to 'Is Company?'
4. Set Display type to 'Check Box.'
5. Set Width to '10.'
6. Click Finish.

The generator populates the values of the control with the allowed values of the column registered either directly against the column or against its domain. At most, two of such values may exist, and the first one will correspond to the

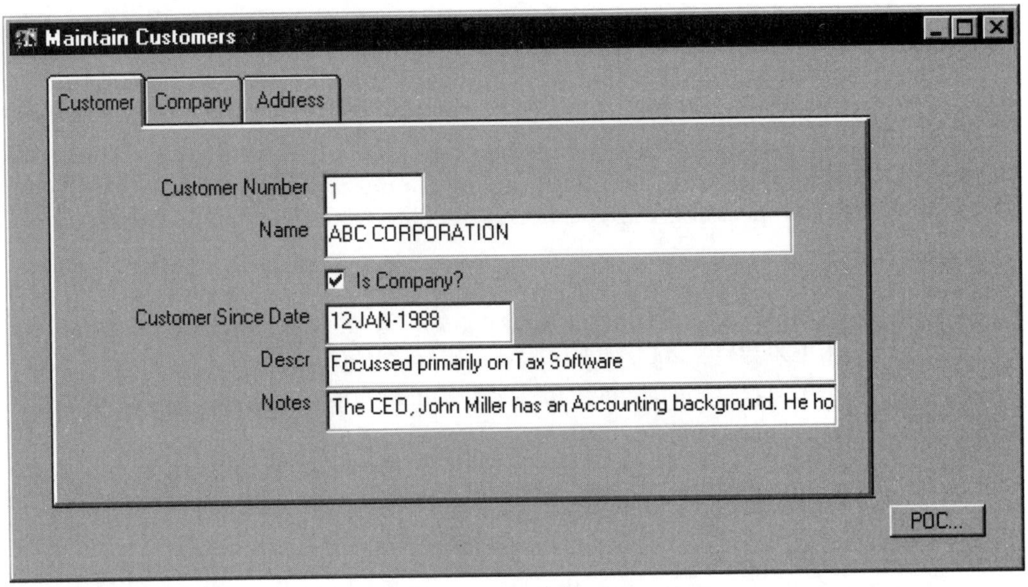

FIGURE 28.5 The tab Customer of the Maintain Customers window in module ORDD2K0030.

checked state of the control. Figure 28.5 shows the layout of this check box in the final version of module ORDD2K0030.

28.3.4 ADDING RADIO GROUPS

Radio groups present items that may take a limited number (three to five) of mutually exclusive values. The entire item is implemented as a radio group, whereas each individual value that the item may take represents a radio button within the group. In order to implement the column RANKING in the Customer Information window of module ORDD2K0030 as a radio group, you need to take the following actions:

1. Double-click the item RANKING to display its Edit dialog box.
2. Set Display type to *'Radio Group.'*
3. Set the list box Show Meaning to *'Abbreviation only'* or *'Meaning only.'* Each radio button corresponds to one of the allowed values recorded against the column or its domain. The setting of this property allows you to control

which piece of information from the allowed value serves as the label of the button on the canvas.

4. Click Finish.

The generator implements radio groups similarly to item groups you create explicitly in the module. In order to give them the same look and feel, set the following preferences at the application system level:

1. Set *RADDEC—Radio group decoration* to 'INSET RECTANGLE.'
2. Set *RADTLM—Radio group title margin* to '1.'
3. Set *RADTLP—Radio group title position* to 'ON DECORATION.'
4. Set *RADTLS—Radio group title spacing* to '1.'

Generally, radio groups display their controls aligned vertically. In rare instances, you may want to align the radio buttons horizontally. In these cases, set the preference *RADOWG—Radio group orientation within group* to 'HORI.' By default, this preference is set to 'VERT.' When implementing an item as a radio group, you must keep in mind that the item will always have a value in the database, due to the fact that one of the buttons of the radio group is always selected. Furthermore, because the radio buttons are embedded in the body of the form, the values they represent must be static and not prone to changes or modifications during the normal life of the application. Figure 28.6 shows the layout of the radio group in the final version of module ORDD2K0030.

28.3.5 ADDING LIST CONTROLS

Like radio groups, list controls allow you to select an option from a list of available ones. However, the number of options they implement can be much higher than in the case of radio groups. Furthermore, if the lists are built on columns and domains with the property *Soft LOV?* set, they can support changes and modifications in the values of these options during the application's life.

The most popular version of list boxes is the drop-down list box, also referred to as a popup list. You can implement an item as a drop-down list by setting its *Display type* property to 'Pop list' and *Show Meaning* to 'Abbreviation only,' 'Meaning only,' or 'Meaning alongside code.' You have already seen cases of such lists in the modules discussed in this chapter and Chapter 27. These items were implemented as such by the Application Design Transformer because the *Display type* had been set to 'Pop list' for all the columns with allowed values in the Order Management System.

Drop-down lists display only one option to the users and require them to expand the list in order to view the remaining options. Text lists display on the screen more than one option, thus making it easier to browse and find the desired option. However, because they occupy a larger area on the screen, they are not

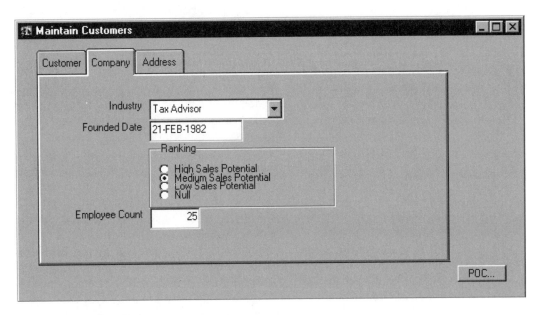

FIGURE 28.6   The tab Company of the Maintain Customers window in module ORDD2K0030.

used as often as the first type of list. You can easily implement an item with allowed values recorded against its column or domain as a text list by setting its *Display type* property to *'Text list'* and *Show Meaning* to *'Abbreviation only,'* *'Meaning only,'* or *'Meaning alongside code.'* As an example, set *Display type* to *'Text list'* and *Show Meaning* to *'Meaning only'* for the item INDUSTRY in the first component of module ORDD2K0030. Figure 28.6 shows how this item will look in the final version of this module.

A third type of list controls is the combo box. The behavior of this control is a combination of the drop-down list and the text item, hence its name. Like lists, the control displays available values associated with the item; like text items, the control allows you to type a value that is not one of the predefined options. Good candidates for implementation as combo boxes are items for which a list of values is already defined, but users may enter their own values if this list does not contain the option they want. For this reason, such controls are also known as *suggested lists of values.* Two good candidates to be implemented as suggested lists in module ORDD2K0030 are PREFIX and SUFFIX, in the second component. Here are the actions you need to take in order to turn these items into combo boxes:

1. Set *Display type* to *'Combo box.'*
2. Set the property *Suggestion List* of the columns PREFIX and SUFFIX in the table CUSTOMERS to *'Yes.'*

Note two points about the implementation of the combo boxes:

❑   As users enter new values in the combo box, you may want to add these
    values to the reference code tables. This way, your application populates the
    database with values as it is being used, and you avoid the entry of incon-
    sistent or redundant data. In order to add this functionality to the combo
    box, you need to implement programmatically a trigger fired when a new
    entry is defined, which adds this entry in the reference code table. This trig-
    ger can be implemented at the front-end module or at the database level.
    For an example of how to do this, refer to *Developing Oracle Forms Applica-
    tions* (Prentice Hall, 1996). The requirement to set the property Suggestion
    List of the column that corresponds to the DCU should be seen as an extra
    step introduced to remind you of the potential need to develop the update
    mechanism of the allowed values.

❑   When implementing drop-down or text lists, you can display the abbrevia-
    tion or the meaning of the elements, while the actual values are stored in the
    database. You can display the abbreviation or the meaning of the suggested
    values in combo boxes as well, by setting Show Meaning to *'Abbreviation
    only,' 'Meaning only,'* or *'Meaning alongside code.'* However, problems may

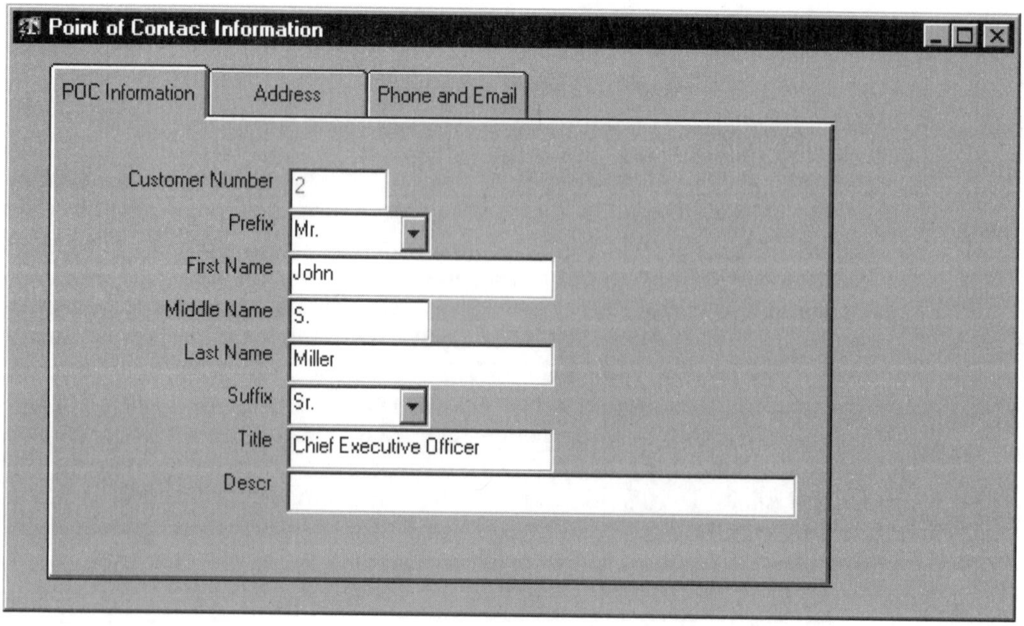

FIGURE 28.7   The final layout of the Point of Contact Information window in
module ORDD2K0030.

arise when users enter new values, especially when the column length in the database is smaller than the display length of the more descriptive abbreviation or meaning of the value. Therefore, combo boxes usually display the actual value associated with the column. Figure 28.7 shows the items PREFIX and SUFFIX implemented as combo boxes in the window Point of Contact Information of module ORDD2K0030.

28.4 ADDING CALENDAR CONTROLS TO DEVELOPER/2000 FORMS MODULES

Dates are one of the most tedious types of data to enter in applications. Even the best typists have to slow down and think before typing them. Formatting restrictions you place on the date items may render the task even more difficult. In order to solve this problem, offer your users a point-and-click interface to enter data values. You can very easily add this interface to Developer/2000 Forms modules generated with Designer/2000. The interface consists of native Developer/2000 Forms objects provided in a template module and a PL/SQL library. In this section, you will add the calendar control to the data usages in module ORDD2K0030. As a preliminary step, copy the template module you have been using so far, OMSTMPL.FMB, into a new module, OMSTMPLCAL.FMB. The new module will be modified to support the generation of the calendar control. Use it as a template only for those modules that will contain the calendar control. For modules where you do not need or want to add this control, you can still use the initial template. Perform the following actions in the Form Builder.

1. Open the template module OMSTMPLCAL.FMB.
2. Open the template form OFG4CALT.FMB. This template is provided by Designer/2000 together with the other templates and object libraries (in the subdirectory \CGENF50\ADMIN of the Oracle home directory).
3. All the objects required to implement the control are bundled in the object group STANDARD_CALENDAR in OFG4CALT.FMB.
4. In the Object Navigator, expand the node Object Groups of module OFG4CALT.FMB.
5. Drag the object group STANDARD_CALENDAR and drop it in the module OMSTMPLCAL.FMB.
6. When prompted to subtype or copy the objects, choose to copy them.
7. Attach the library OFG4CALL.PLL to the template OMSTMPLCAL.FMB. This library is provided by Designer/2000 and contains the functionality required by the calendar control.
8. Save the template module OMSTMPLCAL.FMB and exit the Form Builder.

At this point, you need to return to the Design Editor to complete the work. Start the Module Data Diagrammer and open the diagram for module ORDD2K0030.

1. Select the bound item CUSTOMER_SINCE_DATE in the Design Navigator and display its properties in the Property Palette.
2. Click the property *PL/SQL Block* to display the TextPad window and enter the following line in the text area:

CALENDAR.SHOW;

3. Repeat the first two steps for the item FOUNDED_DATE.
4. Save changes to the Repository.

With similar actions, you can edit the properties of the item CUSTOMER_SINCE_DATE for the module component POC. In order to complete the work, you need to set the following preferences:

1. Set the preference *USECAL—Add call to calendar window for date fields* to 'Y.' This preference is part of the End User Interface category. As in other cases, consider setting this preference at the application system level in order to generate applications with a common date entry mechanism.
2. Set the preference *STFFMB—The name of the template form* to 'OMSTM-

FIGURE 28.8 The Developer/2000 Forms Calendar control window.

PLCAL.FMB.' Assuming that a majority of modules in your application system will use the calendar control, set this preference at the application system level. For modules that will not need this control, you can reset the preference to the old value *'OMSTMPL.FMB'* at the module level, or you can override the setting of the preference by specifying the template name when you invoke the Generator.

At this point, you are ready to generate the new version of the module. Figure 28.8 shows an example of the Developer/2000 Forms calendar window created by the Developer/2000 Forms Generator.

28.5 SUMMARY

This chapter discusses enhancements and techniques you can use to make the generator create modules that are functional but also present a nice interface to the users. In particular, it shows how you can implement native Developer/2000 Forms list of values controls and all the basic GUI widgets, including list boxes of different kinds, check boxes, radio buttons and push buttons. In addition, the chapter shows how you can add a calendar control to the forms. Highlights of this chapter include:

- ❑ **Generating Forms with Multiple Table Usages**
  - ❑ Rearranging the Module Layout
  - ❑ Defining the Layout of the Product Information Window
  - ❑ Defining the Layout of the Product Items Window
- ❑ **Item Lookups and Lists of Values**
  - ❑ Features of List of Values Controls
  - ❑ Using Lists of Values to Restrict Data Access
  - ❑ Adding a List of Values Button
  - ❑ Using a List of Values for Data Entry and Validation
- ❑ **Adding GUI Controls to Modules**
  - ❑ Overview of the Module
  - ❑ Adding Push Buttons
  - ❑ Adding Check Boxes
  - ❑ Adding Radio Groups
  - ❑ Adding List Controls
- ❑ **Adding Calendar Controls to Developer/2000 Forms Modules**

C++ OBJECT LAYER GENERATOR

- The Purpose of the C++ Object Layer Generator
- Preparing for C++ Generation
- Using the C++ Object Layer Generator
- Understanding the Output of the C++ Object Layer Generator
- Summary

Designer/2000 comes with a number of generators responsible for converting the information you collect during analysis and design activities into software modules. Based on the type of software they produce, these generators may be classified into one of the following two groups:

❑ **Generators of back-end software modules.** This group includes the Server Generator and the Oracle WebServer Generator. The first one allows you to generate DDL statements that build the database schema of your applications. When Oracle Server is used as the back-end database server, the Server Generator also produces the PL/SQL program units stored in the server. The Oracle WebServer Generator allows you to generate applications according to the thin client/thick server paradigm. The thin client layer provides presentation services and is presented to users with a standard Web browser. The thick server layer includes all the business logic and data manipulation services and is implemented as a series of stored procedures and services handled by the database server and the Oracle Web-Server.

❑ **Generators of front-end client software modules.** The members of this group include the generators of Developer/2000 components, as well as Visual Basic and Oracle PowerObjects. These generators ultimately create two tiered client/server applications.

The C++ Object Layer Generator is a generator that has functionality from both these categories, yet does not fit exactly in one of them. This generator allows you to create a set of C++ classes to access the database objects maintained in the repository. However, the output of the generator is not a finished, visual application that you can use right away. This chapter discusses the purpose, functionality, and use of the C++ Object Layer Generator.

29.1 THE PURPOSE OF THE C++ OBJECT LAYER GENERATOR

The contents of a typical database application can be classified into one of the following layers: presentation, business logic, or database. Traditional client/server development tools, such as Developer/2000 Forms, Visual Basic, and Power-Builder, tend to place a good amount of the business logic layer in the client application, whereas the database server is responsible primarily for the storage and manipulation of data. In particular situations, as in applications developed using Developer/2000 tools and an Oracle Server database, the application architect has some flexibility in distributing the business logic between the client and the server. This is due primarily to the fact that PL/SQL is the common programming language used to develop Oracle Forms applications, Oracle stored procedures, and database triggers. Despite the different ways in which the business logic of an application may be distributed, the applications developed as described above remain fundamentally two-tiered applications with the code partitioned between the client and the server.

Two-tiered applications are typically used to solve business problems, often complex ones, that face groups and departments. The users of a typical two-tiered application are ideally all located in a local area network. In cases when the application is designed and optimized carefully, the users can be located in a campus-like environment, in which multiple local area networks are connected through a high-capacity, high-throughput backbone. However, for enterprise-wide applications, which serve hundreds of users distributed in multiple geographically remote locations, two-tiered applications are no longer a viable solution. Some of the problems that these applications face are the relatively small bandwidth of network connections, the unavailability of permanent connections for technical or economic reasons, and the high maintenance and administration costs. To overcome these problems, the business logic layer is dissociated from the presentation and data layers not just conceptually but also physically. The resulting applications have at least three and, in many cases, multiple tiers of code. Figure 29.1 shows the typical architecture of a multi-tiered application.

As you can see from this figure, the main responsibility of the User Interface tier is to allow users to formulate requests for information, to pass these requests to the Business Logic tier, to retrieve the results from this tier, and to display the information to the users. The Business Logic tier receives requests from the User Interface tier and interprets them. These requests may contain different components, such as retrieve or post data in a database, find and return an image file from a warehouse, send a message to a user, and so on. The Business Logic tier is responsible for identifying and separating these components, routing the requests to the appropriate component of the Back-End tier, retrieving the results from this tier, and merging them into one cohesive results set that is returned to the User Interface tier.

Thus, interaction with one or more database servers is one of the services that the middle tier provides in multi-tiered applications. Other services provided may be security, event logging, messaging, workload balancing, and so on. Because users never directly access the services provided by the middle tier, these services are usually implemented using 3GL programming languages, such as C or C++, whereas the User Interface tier is normally implemented in a 4GL programming tool. Java programming language is becoming a viable alternative and a popular tool to implement both layers.

The traditional way of accessing Oracle databases from C or C++ programs is to write SQL or PL/SQL statements embedded in these programs according to the rules and syntax of Oracle's Pro*C/C++ pre-compiler. The files that contain embedded SQL statements are fed to the pre-compiler, which checks the SQL and PL/SQL statements for accuracy. If the pre-compiler finds no errors, these files are converted into files that contain only native C or C++ statements. These files can be compiled and linked using the desired C or C++ compiler. Pro*C/C++

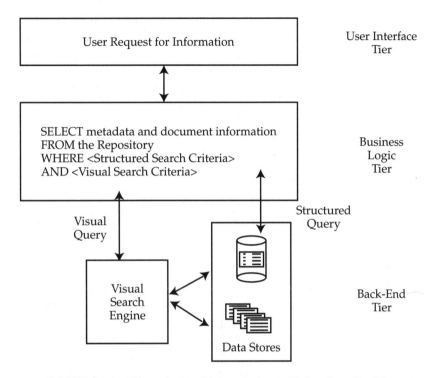

FIGURE 29.1   The typical architecture of a multi-tiered application.

programs have been used for a long time and continue to be used to interact with Oracle databases. However, despite their popularity, some problems are associated with developing applications using pre-compilers:

- ❑ Writing a Pro*C/C++ program requires developers skilled not just in C or C++, but also in SQL and PL/SQL.
- ❑ Even simple database schema modifications may result in significant manual changes of the modules.
- ❑ SQL as a results-oriented language and PL/SQL as a procedural language differ fundamentally from the object-oriented C++. Embedding statements from the first two languages in C++ programs complicates the implementations of useful features of object-oriented programming, such as inheritance, polymorphism, and encapsulation.

The C++ Object Layer Generator is the Designer/2000 tool that allows you to access Oracle databases from object-oriented applications without any of the problems described above. The main functionality of this tool is to read the definitions of entities, attributes, relationships, tables, and columns stored in the Designer/2000 repository and build a set of C++ classes based on these definitions. These classes provide the database interface for C++ applications that need to retrieve and modify data stored in Oracle databases. The functionality they provide allows you to focus on the implementation of the business logic without worrying about the details of interacting with the database.

In general, in order to develop a C++ application using the classes produced by the C++ Object Layer Generator, follow these steps:

1. Finalize the logical and physical design of the database schema in the Designer/2000 repository.
2. Use the Server Generator to create and install the schema objects in the target database environment.
3. Use the C++ Object Layer Generator to create the C++ classes that implement the interaction with the database schema in an object-oriented fashion.
4. Design and develop other components of the application, based on the business logic and user interface requirements. These components interact with the database using the classes generated in the previous step.
5. Build, test, and debug the final application.

These steps clearly show the important role that Designer/2000 plays in the process. The rewards for careful data modeling and database design efforts are the implementation of the Back-End tier and the part of the Business Logic tier concerned with database interaction in an automated and precise fashion. Creating applications using classes produced by the C++ Object Layer Generator has several advantages over the traditional method of programming using embedded SQL and pre-compilers. Some of them are listed below:

❑ The generated classes hide the complexity of database access from the applications you develop.
❑ The application developers do not need to know details of SQL or PL/SQL languages. C++ and object-oriented programming are the only required core competencies for these developers.
❑ The applications that use the generated classes can use all the object-oriented capabilities of C++.
❑ Manual changes required to synchronize the application code when the database schema is modified are minimized, since the database access layer for the modified objects can be regenerated by the tool in a matter of seconds.

The rest of the chapter will show you how to use the C++ Object Layer Generator to create the database interface layer of your applications. In particular, I will discuss the following topics:

❑ Preparing the Designer/2000 repository for generation of C++ classes
❑ Using the C++ Object Layer Generator
❑ Understanding the output of the C++ Object Layer Generator
❑ Using components created by the C++ Object Layer Generator to develop applications

29.2 PREPARING FOR C++ GENERATION

Like other generators in Designer/2000, the C++ Object Layer Generator works upon a set of objects, which are known as *class sets*. The objects that make up a class set are entities defined in the repository. The properties of these entities determine the content of the generated C++ classes. In addition, these classes also depend on other factors, such as the mapping of each entity in the set to a table in the repository, appropriate relationships between entities, and so on. In this section you will learn how to create and populate a class set in the Repository Object Navigator. You will also learn how to set the properties of objects included in a class set so that the generation of C++ classes is successful.

29.2.1 C++ GENERATOR CLASS SETS

As I mentioned above, a C++ generator class set is made up of the entities for which you want to generate C++ classes. Class sets are created and maintained in the Repository Object Navigator. To create a class set, follow these steps:

1. Select the node C++ Generator Class Sets in the hierarchy tree of the Navigator. This node is located in the group of objects with the title C++ Object Layer Generation.
2. Click the Create Object button 🔳 or select Edit | Create Object.
3. Type the name of the set in the newly created node or in the property *Name* of the Property Palette for the new object.
4. Save the changes by clicking the Save button 🔳 or selecting File | Save.

After creating a class set, you need to populate it with entities. Obviously, you need to identify first in your mind the entities that will be included in the set. Afterwards, follow these steps to create associations between them and the new C++ Generator class set:

1. Expand the node that represents the class set and select the node Set Members.
2. Click the Create Association button 🔳 or select Edit | Create Association. In the dialog box Select Type that appears, choose Entities and click OK.

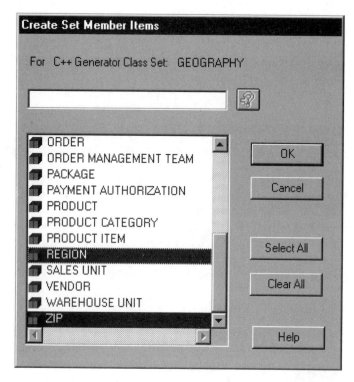

FIGURE 29.2 The Create Set Member Items dialog box.

This action displays the dialog box Create Set Member Items shown in Figure 29.2.

3. Select one or more entities from the list and click OK to include them in the C++ class set.

4. Save the changes to the class set.

Which entities to include in a C++ generator class set depends on the objects that will be accessed by the application that will use the generated classes. Include all the entities if the entire application will be developed in C++. On the other hand, if you are implementing only a functional component of the application in C++, then you need to include in the class set only those entities that are part of that component.

29.2.2 CHECKING THE PROPERTIES OF ENTITIES IN THE CLASS SET

The C++ Object Layer Generator will be able to create C++ classes based on the entities included in the class set, if the properties of these entities meet certain conditions. The following is a list of these conditions together with steps you need to take to ensure that they are met:

❑ The entities included in the class set must contain only one-to-many relationships. If one-to-one or many-to-many relationships exist between entities, the C++ Object Layer Generator will not be able to create classes for those entities. At the stage when you invoke the C++ generator, the application data model should be in a fairly stable state. Many-to-many relationships should have been resolved by the introduction of intersection entities. However, some one-to-one relationships may still occur and be valid. In these cases, change these relationships to one-to-many, in order to generate the C++ classes, and reset them to their previous state after the C++ Object Layer Generator has completed its task.

❑ Each attribute of the entities included in the class set must be assigned to a domain. The C++ Object Layer Generator can define a C++ datatype for the class element that corresponds to an attribute only if that attribute is assigned to a domain. Fulfilling this condition may require the greatest effort from you, especially if generating C++ classes based on the properties of entities comes as an afterthought, after these properties are defined in the repository. To help you in such a situation, the first time the C++ Object Layer Generator is run, it creates three domains, if they are not already defined in the repository. These domains are DATE, NUMBER, and STRING. You can use the Repository Object Navigator to assign multiple attributes from different entities to one of these domains. The condition is automatically fulfilled if you establish and follow from the beginning a design standard that requires assigning each attribute to a domain.

❑ Each domain discussed in the previous condition must be associated with an appropriate C++ data type that is used by the C++ Object Layer Generator to create the class components. The Generator library provides three basic data types that can be associated with domains. They are OLDate, OLNumber, and OLString. In order to associate a domain with a C++ data type, you must set the property *Datatype Name* of the domain to the name of the data type. This property can be accessed in the C++ group of properties from the Repository Object Navigator, or on the Definition tab of the Edit Domains dialog box. (This dialog box can be accessed by selecting Edit | Domains... from the menu of the Entity Relationship Diagrammer.)

❑ Each entity in the class must be mapped to a table in the repository. This condition is automatically fulfilled if you have used the Database Design Wizard to create table definitions from entities or the Table to Entity Retrofit utility to create entities from reverse-engineered tables.

The C++ Object Layer Generator can derive several properties of generated C++ classes from the definitions of entities, attributes, and relationships. These properties can be generated by default, or you can set them explicitly, before the C++ classes are created. The following is a list of such properties:

❑ The class name is derived from the entity name. Use the property *Class Name* to specify an explicit name for the class. In the Repository Object Navigator, this property can be accessed in the C++ group of the entity's Property Palette. You may also find it on the Definition tab of the Edit Entity dialog box in the Entity Relationship Diagrammer.

❑ The class member name is derived from the attribute name. Use the property *Member Name* to specify an explicit name for the member. This property can be accessed in the attribute's C++ group of properties in the Repository Object Navigator or on the Att Detail tab of the Edit Entity dialog box (see Figure 29.3).

❑ All class members are created as public members. To make a member protected or private for the class, set the property *Scope* to '*Protected*' or '*Private*,' respectively. This property can be accessed in the attribute's C++ group of

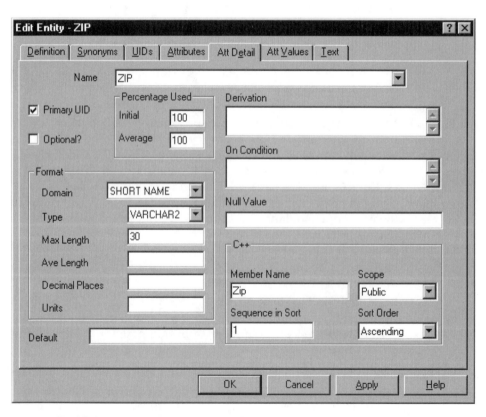

FIGURE 29.3 Explicitly setting attribute properties to influence the C++ Generator.

properties in the Repository Object Navigator or on the Att Detail tab of the Edit Entity dialog box shown in Figure 29.3.

❑ By default, the method to retrieve records from the database will not sort them. To generate code that sorts these records by attributes in a certain sequence, set the property *Sequence in Sort* for those attributes. When sorting is performed, it is in ascending order by default. To change the order to descending, set the property *Sort Order* for the desired attributes. Both these properties are located in the attribute's C++ group of properties in the Repository Object Navigator or on the Att Detail tab of the Edit Entity dialog box (see Figure 29.3).

❑ The C++ Object Layer Generator generates class members based not only on the attributes but also on the relationship ends of an entity. The names of these members are derived from the name of the relationship end, but you can override them by setting the property *Set or Pointer Name* in the relationship's C++ group of properties. This property can be accessed from the Repository Object Navigator or from the Definition tab of the Edit Relationship dialog box in the Entity Relationship Diagrammer.

29.3 USING THE C++ OBJECT LAYER GENERATOR

Section 29.2 discussed how you can define C++ class sets, populate them with entities, and ensure that these properties will not conflict with the C++ class generation process. After these steps are completed, you are ready to use the C++ Object Layer Generator. Generating C++ classes from the data model information stored in the repository in general requires the following actions:

1. Launch the C++ Object Layer Generator.
2. Load the C++ class set for which you will generate classes.
3. Remove any anomalies identified by the generator by setting the properties of objects properly. Repeat steps 2 and 3 until the objects in the C++ class set contain no errors.
4. Define the classes that the generator will create.
5. Define the distribution of generated code in files.
6. Set the options that control how the C++ Object Layer Generator creates the code.
7. Verify the quality of the generated code.
8. Generate the C++ classes.

The following sections discuss how to complete each of the steps above.

29.3.1 LAUNCHING THE C++ OBJECT LAYER GENERATOR

The C++ Object Layer Generator can be started by selecting Utilities | Generate C++ Classes... from a tool such as the Repository Object Navigator or the Entity Relationship Diagrammer. Each of these commands displays the dialog box C++ Object Layer Generator. This dialog box contains a series of properties tabs, which are used to complete several of the steps outlined at the beginning of Section 29.3.

29.3.2 LOADING C++ CLASS SETS

The first tab in the C++ Object Layer Generator dialog box allows you to view a list of all the C++ class sets defined in the repository. The generator can create code for only one class set at a time. Load this desired set in the work area of the generator by following these steps:

1. Select the C++ class set from the list of all the sets that are defined in the repository.
2. Click Load.

At this point, the generator reads the properties of objects included in the selected C++ class set and produces a list of errors and anomalies found in these properties. These anomalies are listed in the dialog box Model Anomalies. Once a class set is loaded, the list of available class sets is disabled. In order to load a different class set, you must exit and restart the C++ Object Layer Generator.

29.3.3 REMOVING ANOMALIES FROM A C++ CLASS SET

Figure 29.4 shows a list of typical anomalies displayed in the Model Anomalies dialog box. The number of messages in the list depends on the objects included in the C++ class set and the setting of their properties. The creation of C++ classes cannot proceed as long as the generator identifies anomalies in the class set. To remove an anomaly, you can take one of the following actions:

❑ Set the properties of the violating objects so that they do not conflict with the C++ Object Layer Generator.
❑ Instruct the generator to ignore the anomaly and to remove the violating object from the C++ class set.

In general, modifying the properties of violating objects requires that you go back to a particular Designer/2000 tool, such as the Entity Relationship Diagrammer or the Repository Object Navigator, to access these properties. However, the list of Model Anomalies will not be refreshed until the next time you load the class set in the generator.

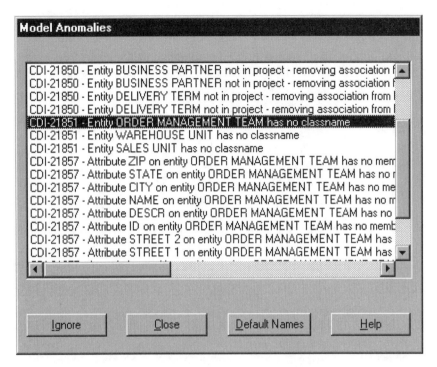

FIGURE 29.4   The Model Anomalies dialog box.

The following list groups into categories some of the messages you are most likely to encounter and provides instructions on how to remove them from the list of model anomalies:

❑ **Errors due to the definition of the C++ class set.** In general, C++ class sets may not contain all the entities that exist in the repository. As I mentioned earlier, the generator will create class members for each attribute and relationship of an entity. If an entity is related to entities that are not included in the C++ class set, the generator will not create members to represent these associations. To solve this anomaly, either include the entities on the other end of the relationship in the class set, or select the error message in the Model Anomalies dialog box and click the button Ignore.

❑ **Errors due to the fact that classes or members do not have a name assigned to them.** The easiest way to resolve these anomalies is to select all the messages in the Model Anomalies dialog box and click the button Default Names. This button is enabled only when errors of this category are selected. As I explained earlier, the default names are generated based on the names of entities, attributes, and relationships. If you are not satisfied with these names, you can assign your own names explicitly.

❑ **Errors due to violations of conditions outlined in Section 29.2.2.** These errors must be removed either by editing the violating properties in the repository or by choosing to ignore them.

29.3.4 DEFINE THE CLASSES TO BE GENERATED

The class set you load in the C++ Object Layer Generator may contain several entities. During one run of the generator, you may not want to create classes for each of these entities. The properties tab allows you to select only those entities from the class set that you want to include in the working set of the generator for the current run. An example of this tab is shown in Figure 29.5.

The functionality of this tab is really simple. You just select the classes to include in the working set from the Class List control, and move on to other tabs. However, this tab also has a nice feature. It presents in concise matrix format the generation status of each category of code for all the classes in the set. As you will see later in the chapter, for each entity, the C++ Object Layer Generator generates the definition of the mapped class, the implementation of the mapped class, definitions for support classes, and implementation of these support classes. The status of generated code for each of these categories is displayed in the columns Mapped.h, Mapped.cpp, Support.h, and Support.cpp, respectively. These columns represent only the status of the generated code and not any actual files, although their notation may lead you to believe otherwise. Figure 29.6 lists the most common statuses that a category of code may have, together with the icon used to represent them on the Classes tab.

29.3.5 DISTRIBUTING THE GENERATED CODE TO FILES

 As I mentioned in Section 29.3.4, for each entity, the C++ Object Layer Generator creates code that falls into four categories. In addition, the generator can create other code that is used either by you directly or by the generated classes. The following list summarizes each category of code created by the generator:

❑ **Mapping header.** This category contains the definition of the C++ class that is mapped to the entity. For each entity in the working set, the C++ Object Layer Generator creates one mapped C++ header.

❑ **Mapping implementation.** This category contains the implementation of the C++ class defined in the mapping header section.

❑ **Support header.** This category contains definitions of a series of additional classes that the generator creates for each entity in the working set. The classes you will use in your application are described in more detail in Sec-

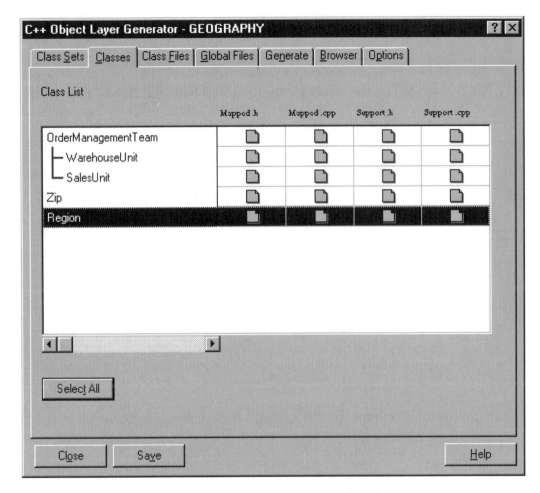

FIGURE 29.5 The Classes properties tab.

ICON	STATUS	DESCRIPTION
No icon	No assignment	The code for this category has not been assigned to a file for generation.
🗋	No generation	The code for this category is assigned to a file for generation, but has not been generated yet.
🖹	Successful generation	The code for this category has been successfully generated to a file.

FIGURE 29.6 Statuses of each category of code generated by the C++ Object Layer.

tion 29.4. This category also contains classes that are used internally by the generated code or by the support library provided with the generator.

❏ **Support implementation.** This category contains the implementation of the classes defined in the support header section.

❏ **Application model class definition and implementation.** This category contains a global class, whose members enumerate all the classes, members, and associations implemented in the previous four categories.

The C++ Object Layer Generator allows you to create the code for each of the categories described above in separate files. In your projects, you will usually have one file to store the application model class definition and another one for the application model class implementation. For the other categories, the code can be distributed in a number of ways. One way is to group together the code of each category for several or all the classes included in the set. Another way is to create two files for each entity in the class set. The first one, a header file, will contain the definitions of the mapped class and all the support classes that the generator creates for the particular entity; the second one will contain the implementation of these classes.

The properties tabs Class Files and Global Files direct the output of the generator to the desired operating system files. As a preliminary step, associate at least one source file with each category of code that can be generated. In order to achieve this association, start by selecting the category of code you want to associate with a file. On the Class Files tab, shown in Figure 29.7, the categories can be selected from the drop-down list Code Section Types; on the Global Files tab, they can be selected from the list Global Code Types. For each category of code you select, the control File List displays all the files already associated with the category. You can add a new file by following these steps:

1. Click the button Add Files. The dialog box Browse is displayed.
2. Select the location of the file in the directory tree.
3. Select the file from the list of all files in the selected directory with the appropriate extension. You may also create a new file by providing its name and extension.
4. Click OK to return to the properties tab. The new file is present in the list.
5. Click Save to commit the changes to the repository.

If you want to remove a file from the project, simply select it from the list and click Drop Files. Do not forget to commit the action to the repository.

You can use the following steps to store the generated code for one or more classes to the desired operating system file:

1. Select the desired code category from the list Code Section Types on the Class Files tab.

2. Select one or more classes from the control Class List.
3. Select a file from the control File List.
4. Click the button Assign.

When the code category of a class is assigned to a file, the characteristic icon ✳ is displayed in the column that corresponds to that category in the class list. When a particular class is selected in this list, the assignment icon appears by the name of the file in which the code for the given category will be stored. In the example shown in Figure 29.7, mapped header and implementation code of the class WarehouseUnit is assigned to a file, whereas the other two categories are not assigned. Furthermore, the mapped class header will be created in the file C:\ORAWIN95\BIN\geomap.h.

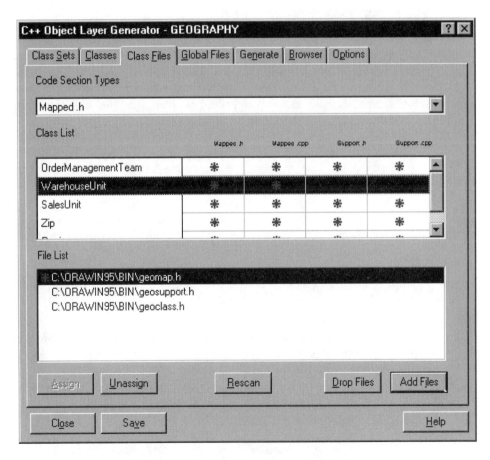

FIGURE 29.7 The Class Files properties tab.

You can also break the association between a category code and a file for a given class by performing the following actions:

1. Select the desired code category from the list Code Section Types on the Class Files tab.
2. Select one or more classes from the control Class List.
3. Click the button Unassign.

In both cases, the changes must be committed to the repository by clicking the button Save in the C++ Object Layer Generator dialog box. The associations between global code categories and operating system files are maintained in similar fashion on the properties tab Global Files. However, given the nature of this code, you use one file to store the code for the entire project.

29.3.6 SETTING GENERATION OPTIONS

The C++ Object Layer Generator has a series of options that influence the type and flavor of the code generated for each run. These options can be set on the properties tabs Generate and Options. The properties on the Generate tab allow you to generate code from one or more categories for the entities in the working set. In a typical application development environment, the process of running the C++ Object Layer Generator can be as follows:

1. Run the generator one or more times to create classes for all the entities in the class set. During these runs, only the Generate Classes check box must be checked.
2. Generate the global code after all the individual classes have been generated. All the global code can be generated in one run, by setting the check boxes Application Model Class Definition and Application Model Class Implementation on the Generate tab.
3. Develop the application that will use the generated classes.
4. If the data model changes, use the generator to synchronize the C++ classes by running it with the Regenerate Classes option set.

Figure 29.8 shows an example of the Generate tab. Note that the properties that control the generation of global code are enabled only if you have associated the code categories with files in the file system.

The properties on the Generate tab control the type of code generated during one run. The properties on the Options tab control features of the generated code. These properties allow you to do the following:

❑ Assign a name to the name space class. By default, the generator uses the name of the class set.

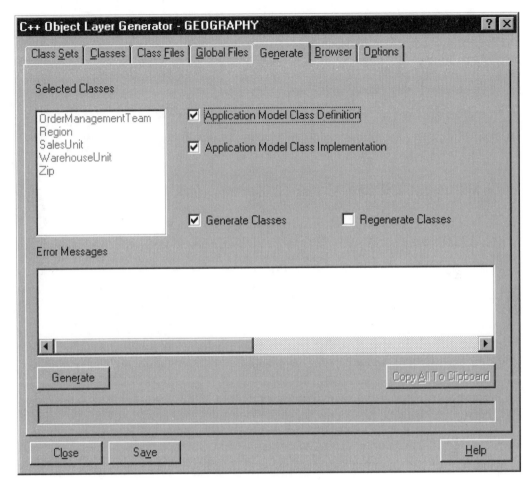

FIGURE 29.8 The Generate tab.

❑ Provide a prefix and a suffix for the class names. By default, the generator prefixes every class with the letter 'C.'

❑ Provide a prefix and a suffix for the attributes of each class. By default, the generator prefixes each member with the characters 'm_.'

❑ Generate methods that access members of a class (Get and Set) by setting the check box Generate Accessors.

❑ Generate code that marks an object as modified if that object is on the foreign key side of a relationship and the relationship is modified by the object on the other side. In order to generate the code, you need to set the property Auto Association Mark Modified.

C++ Object Layer Generator - GEOGRAPHY [?] [X]

| Class Sets | Classes | Class Files | Global Files | Generate | Browser | Options |

Name Space Class Name   Geography

Class Name Prefix   C   Suffix

Member Name Prefix   m_   Suffix

Auto Association Mark Modified ☑

Generate Accessors   ☐

| Close | Save | | Help |

FIGURE 29.9 The Options tab.

Figure 29.9 shows an example of the Options tab.

29.3.7 BROWSING THE GENERATED CLASSES

The C++ Object Layer Generator provides a utility that allows
you to browse the database using the classes defined in the C++
class set. This utility is accessible from the Browse tab of the generator's dialog box. It does not require that the classes be generated, compiled, and linked in any form, since it relies only on
properties of components of the class set stored in the De-
signer/2000 repository. However, it requires that the tables exist in an Oracle
database and that they contain some data.

The Browse utility is used mainly as a rapid prototyping tool that allows you to review the quality of the generated classes in a graphical interactive interface. Its benefits are considerable, since you can assess the functionality of these classes without having to build any user interface applications that use them, and without even generating them. In particular, the Browse utility allows you perform the following functions:

- ❏ View the instances of any object in the class set as they are stored in the database.
- ❏ Navigate from one instance of an object to instances of other objects, based on the relationships among objects.

The steps listed below describe how to achieve these functions.

1. Select the object to browse on the Classes properties tab and switch to the Browse tab.
2. Enter the user name, password, and connect string for the database where the instances of the selected object reside.
3. Click Browse. This action brings up two dialog boxes. The Object Browser dialog box displays the object you are browsing. The second dialog box displays the instances of this object one at a time.

Figure 29.10 shows an example of these two dialog boxes. As you can see from this figure, the Browse utility displays the values of each member of the object, including the relationships with other objects. By clicking the buttons Next>> and <<Previous, you can scroll the instances defined in the database for the selected object. To navigate to a related object, select the instance member that represents the relationship and click the button Goto… . This action opens a new dialog box that displays all the instances related to the instance of the initial object. The Object Browser dialog box is updated with a representation of the new

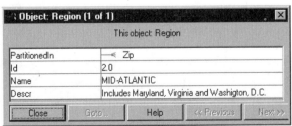

FIGURE 29.10 Sample dialog boxes displayed when the Browse utility is initially displayed.

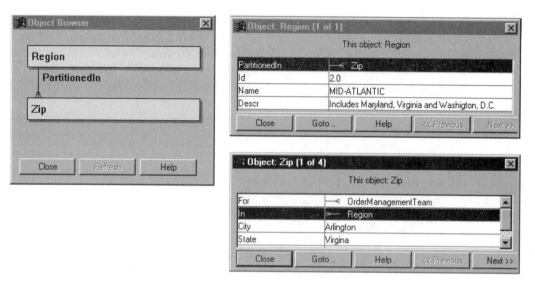

FIGURE 29.11 Sample dialog boxes after navigating through multiple levels of relationships.

object and relationship. Figure 29.11 represents the Browser dialog boxes after the user has navigated through a relationship.

29.3.8 GENERATING THE C++ CLASSES

Most of the work to generate the C++ layer that implements business objects for your environment is done when you build the data model, convert it to a database schema, create the C++ class set, and set the properties of its components as described in previous sections of this chapter. After carefully designing the C++ object layer, you should also prototype and test it with live data using the Browse utility. After performing these steps, creating the C++ code is a simple task in itself. In order to generate the C++ classes for the object in the current working set of the C++ Object Layer Generator, simply click the button Generate on the properties tab Generate. Any messages generated during the generation process are listed in the control Error Messages in the lower half of this tab.

29.4 UNDERSTANDING THE OUTPUT OF THE C++ OBJECT LAYER GENERATOR

For each object included in the C++ class set, the C++ Object Layer Generator creates code that enables your applications to retrieve its instances stored in an Oracle database and manipulate them according to the business needs. This code consists of a class that implements each object and a set of support classes that provide additional functionality. Figure 29.12 groups these classes into functional categories and provides a brief description for each category.

In addition to these classes generated for each object in the C++ class set, your applications use some of the classes provided with the runtime library of the C++ Object Layer Generator. These classes are typically used to establish or remove connections to one or more databases and to manage database transactions. Sections 29.4.1–29.4.3 discuss each of these categories in more detail.

29.4.1 MAPPING CLASS

For each entity in the working set, the C++ Object Layer Generator creates a class that represents that entity in the application environment. The name of this class is derived from the property *Class Name* of the entity. All the mapping classes contain a method to construct a new instance from scratch or from a copy of an existing instance. The constructors create new records in the database. The mapped class also provides a method to query the records from the database, a method to query and lock records, and a method to delete records from the application's memory and database.

Depending on the attributes defined for the entity, the mapped class will contain a variable number of attribute members. The name of each member is de-

FUNCTIONAL CATEGORY	CLASS NAME	DESCRIPTION
Mapping	<Entity Name>	This class represents the instances of the object <Entity Name>. It allows you to retrieve and modify instances of an object.
'Smart' referencing of object instances	Ref<Entity Name> constRef<EntityName> SetRef<Entity Name> IteratorSetRef<Entity Name>	Although the instances of an object can be referenced through physical pointers to mapped classes, the C++ Object Layer Generator creates four 'smart' classes that hide the complexity of transferring instances from the database into the application memory.
'Smart' referencing of relationships of object instances	Rel<Entity Name> SetRel<Entity Name> ECSetRel<Entity Name> IteratorSetRel<Entity Name>	These classes implement navigation from one instance to another, based on the relationships among objects. Like classes in the previous category, the classes in this category hide the complexity of database interaction from the application.

FIGURE 29.12   Generated classes divided by functionality.

rived from the property *Member Name* of the attribute. The scope of the class member can be public, private, or protected, based on the setting of the attribute property *Scope*. The data type of the member is derived from the property *Datatype Name* of the domain in which the attribute is defined.

The generated C++ class will contain a member to represent each relationship that exists between the entity and other entities in the class set. The name of this member is derived from the property *Set or Pointer Name* of the relationship. A relationship member is considered non-set valued if the cardinality of the relationship is one and set valued if the cardinality is many. Non-set valued relationship members are of data type Rel<RelatedClass>; set valued relationship members are of data type ECSetRel<RelatedClass>. Classes Rel<RelatedClass> and ECSetRel<RelatedClass> are part of the set of classes generated for the related entities and will be discussed in Section 29.4.3.

Finally, if the C++ Generator Layer is run with the option Generate Accessors on the Generate tab set, it generates Get and Set methods for each member of the class.

29.4.2 CLASSES THAT REFERENCE OBJECT INSTANCES

For each entity in the class set, the generator creates four classes used to reference instances of the entity. These entities are described below:

❑ **Ref<ClassName>.** Each instance of this class is a smart pointer to an instance of the mapped class. The pointer is more than a physical pointer, because whenever it is referenced, it checks to see if the instance is already loaded in the application's memory. If not, it issues a query against the database to bring the record instance into memory.

❑ **constRef<ClassName>.** This class is very similar in purpose and functionality to Ref<ClassName>.

❑ **SetRef<ClassName>.** This class handles multiple instances of ref classes. Among the most useful methods of this class are those that insert, return, and delete an element from the set. Furthermore, the class provides methods that allow you to copy members of a set onto another set, concatenate two sets, and compare two sets.

❑ **IteratorSetRef<ClassName>.** This class navigates through the instances of a set of ref classes. It provides methods that return ref classes to the object at which the iterator currently points.

In addition to smart pointers, your application may use regular (physical) pointers to mapped class instances. These pointers become invalid if the object instance is moved to a different memory location. In order to prevent invalid references to mapped class instances, declare physical pointers using the Pin method of the corresponding Ref class. Objects remain pinned in memory until the object is requeried or deleted, or until the method Unpin is invoked.

29.4.3 CLASSES THAT RELATED OBJECTS USE TO REFERENCE THE OBJECT INSTANCE

For each entity in the class set, the C++ Object Layer Generator creates a number of classes used by other related classes to reference instances of the class. In order to clarify the purpose of these classes, consider the entity relationship diagram shown in Figure 29.13. In this diagram, the entity COMPANY is in a one-to-many relationship with entity DEPARTMENT. For each of these entities, the generator creates a Rel<ClassName>, a SetRel<ClassName>, and a ECSetRel<ClassName> class. A description of these classes follows:

❏ **Rel<ClassName>.** This class is used as a smart pointer to a single mapped instance that represents the one side of a one-to-many relationship. In the case of Figure 29.13, the class RelCompany serves as the data type for the member m_included_in of class CDepartment that corresponds to the relationship between entities COMPANY and DEPARTMENT. Each time this member is accessed, the generated code checks to see if the related instance of CCompany is in memory and issues a query to retrieve it from the database if it is not.

❏ **ECSetRel<ClassName>.** This class serves as a smart pointer to a set of instances related to the current object instance in a many-to-one relationship. In the scenario shown in Figure 29.13, the data type of member m_composed_of of class CCompany is the class ECSetRelDepartment. When this member is accessed for the first time, the code transparently issues a query that retrieves the departments of the current company. Using methods of this class, you can check whether the set is empty or not, you can return the number of elements in the set, you can insert, retrieve, or remove an element from the set, you can populate the set with incremental fetches from the database, and so on.

❏ **SetRel<ClassName>.** This class is where the actual instances of related objects are stored. In the case discussed here, Ref objects for each department

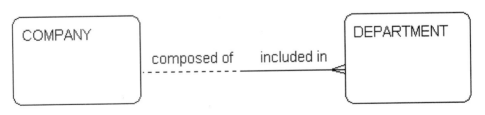

FIGURE 29.13 The entity relationship diagram used to clarify the meaning of Rel classes.

related to a company are all stored in a SetRelDepartment class. Methods of this class allow you to insert or remove Ref objects from the set.

29.5 SUMMARY

The C++ Object Generator allows you to create a transparent layer of C++ classes based on the entities defined in your data model. The mappings between these entities and tables of the physical database are implemented as methods of these classes. They minimize the amount of database knowledge an application developer must have and eliminate the SQL proficiency skills required to access and manipulate objects in the database. The principal topics of this chapter are listed below:

- ❑ **The Purpose of the C++ Object Layer Generator**
- ❑ **Preparing for C++ Generation**
    - ❑ C++ Generator Class Sets
    - ❑ Checking the Properties of Entities in the Class Set
- ❑ **Using the C++ Object Layer Generator**
    - ❑ Launching the C++ Object Layer Generator
    - ❑ Loading C++ Class Sets
    - ❑ Removing Anomalies from a C++ Class Set
    - ❑ Define the Classes to Be Generated
    - ❑ Distributing the Generated Code to Files
    - ❑ Setting Generation Options
    - ❑ Browsing the Generated Classes
    - ❑ Generating the C++ Classes
- ❑ **Understanding the Output of the C++ Object Layer Generator**
    - ❑ Mapping Class
    - ❑ Classes that Reference Object Instances
    - ❑ Classes that Related Objects Use to Reference the Object Instance

INDEX

Action Items, 73, 82
Application Design
    Transformer
    creating menu modules,
        684
    creating modules, 675
    how it creates menus, 685
    how it creates module
        elements, 681
    how it creates modules, 677
    how it merges functions,
        679
    introducing, 66
    invoking, 674
Application Design Wizard,
    445
Application Logic
    creating, 89
    events, 791
    named routines, 792–793
    types, 790
Application system
    archiving, 158
    closing, 147
    copying, 151
    creating, 9, 143

creating new version, 149
deleting, 152
freezing, 148
opening, 146
renaming, 148
restoring, 160
saving, 146
sharing objects, 163
transferring objects, 165
transferring ownership, 157
unfreezing, 148
unsharing objects, 164
user access, 154
Associations, 114
Assumptions, 282
Attributes
    allowable values, 455
    properties of, 298
Autolayout, 222
Automation, 403

Bound items, 73, 715
BPR
    activity-based costing, 390
    benchmarking, 389
    characteristics, 405

competitive index notes,
    389
critical path analysis, 394
modeling the customer,
    341
prerequisites to
    reengineering, 407
reasons for reengineering,
    406
steps to reengineer, 409
symptoms of processes that
    need BPR, 400
value added analysis, 388
value chain notes, 388
value-adding activities,
    387
Broadcast, 199
Business areas, 353
Business functions
    associating with entities, 316
    relationship with business
        processes, 329
Business process
    reengineering (BPR), 405
Business processes, 322
    criteria for defining, 326

Business processes (*cont.*)
  relationship with business
    functions, 329
Business rules
  access privilege rules, 649
  attribute rules, 495
  categories, 493
  column derivation, 670
  create rules, 502
  data access rules, 511
  data definition rules, 494,
    648
  data manipulation rules,
    501, 649
  defining, 22
  delete rules, 504
  entity rules, 498
  events, 508
  function access rules, 510
  implementation methods,
    650
  implementing access
    privilege rules, 657
  implementing attribute
    rules, 651
  implementing data manipu-
    lation rules, 657
  implementing entity rules,
    655
  implementing inter-entity
    rules, 656
  implementing tuple rules,
    655
  inter-entity rules, 500
  restricted relationships,
    500
  transferable relationships,
    503
  tuple rules, 496
  update rules, 502
  user group rules, 510
Business units
  associating with entities, 318
  associating with functions,
    295
  associating with goals, 271
  associating with problems,
    275

  creating, 256
  creating subdivisions, 258
  maintaining, 256

C++ Object Layer Generator
  advantages, 922
  class browser, 936
  classes that reference
    instances, 940
  classes used by related
    classes, 941
  creating class sets, 923
  defining classes, 930
  distributing code to files,
    930
  how it derives properties of
    entities, 925
  launching, 928
  loading class sets, 928
  mapping classes, 939
  populating class sets, 923
  removing anomalies from
    class set, 928
  setting generation options,
    934
  steps to use, 927
Candidate modules, 67
  accept, 683
  reject, 683
Cascade delete, 505
Champy, James, 405
Chart Wizard, 726
Check constraints, 56
Check in, 174
Check out, 174
Codd, Edward F., 475
Code control sequences, 598
Code control tables, 816
Collapse, 188
Collapse All, 189
Columns
  layout properties, 51
  maintaining, 50
  user interface properties, 51
Communities, 610
Constraints
  arc properties, 667
  check, 668

  creating, 658
  delete rule, 665
  editing, 659
  foreign key, 665
  handling failures, 662
  primary key, 663
  transferability of foreign
    keys, 666
  unique key, 663
  update rule, 665
  validation properties, 660
Copy, 166, 168
Copy properties, 201
Creating attributes, 16
Creating relationships, 15
Critical success factors, 276
CRUD matrix, 318
Cursors
  % FOUND, 751
  % NOTFOUND, 751
  CLOSE, 752
  FETCH, 751
  FOR loop, 753
  implicit, 756
  OPEN, 750
  REF CURSOR, 755

Data auditing
  adding audit columns, 582
  journaling, 583
Data diagrams
  creating, 45
  creating objects, 568
  including objects, 565
  populating, 45
  setting object display
    properties, 569
  steps for an optimal layout,
    570
Data Diagrammer
  maintaining column display
    properties, 577
  maintaining column proper-
    ties, 572
  maintaining GUI control
    properties, 579
  maintaining table
    properties, 571

maintaining user interface
properties, 581
setting the options, 570
Data Flow Diagrammer, creating new diagram, 441
Data requirements, 11
Data subjects, 297
Data warehouses
creating the data model, 477
data cubes, 481
dimensions, 480
facts, 479
measures, 479
Database Administrator
Guide, 637
Database Design Transformer
creating implementation objects, 539
creating indexes, 553
creating key constraints, 541
how it creates columns, 545
how it creates foreign key
constraints, 549
how it creates primary and
unique keys, 548
how it creates tables, 545
introducing, 33
maintaining column
mappings, 551
maintaining database object
properties, 551
maintaining key constraints,
553
mappings, 536
populating the run set, 536
setting commit frequency,
540
setting the scope, 538
usage steps, 536
Database Object Guide, 599
Database objects, 38
Database users, 40
Delete, 170
DeMarco, Tom, 439
Denormalization, 476
Derivation items, 81
Design Editor
creating objects, 197

filtering objects, 195
starting, 37
Design Recovery utility, 41
Designer/2000
components, 106
properties, 107
Designer/2000 diagrammers
changing application
system, 221
changing connection, 221
creating shortcuts, 111
customizing preferences,
235
menus, 212
toolbars, 214
Designer/2000 launch pad, 4
Designer/2000 Reports Generator, introducing, 98
Designer/2000 Repository
backing up, 123
checking object sizes, 127
checking object status, 126
creating, 119, 129
diagnosing, 125
optimizing, 125
extending, 132
installation steps, 116
objects, 108
preparing for creation, 118
recompiling objects, 124
recreating objects, 124
removing, 123
restoring, 124
tablespace analysis, 127
upgrading, 123
Developer/2000 Forms Generator, 94, 854
Diagrams
changing zooming levels,
221
closing, 216
conventions, 515
creating, 215
deleting, 218
expanding, 226
legends, 518
maintaining the layout, 222,
224, 514, 516

opening, 215
printing, 220
saving, 217
summary information,
219
using multiple levels of,
515
visual aids, 518
Dimensions, in data
warehousing, 480
Domains
allowed values, 460
in the Design Editor, 461
in the Entity Relationship
Diagrammer, 457
maintaining properties, 459
updating attributes in, 463
updating columns in, 463

Entities
associating with business
functions, 316
associating with business
units, 318
fact entities, 479
modeling, 448
properties of, 297
subtype, 312
supertype, 312
Entity Relationship
Diagrammer
adding to arc, 315
attribute properties, 450
creating an arc, 314
creating attributes, 450
creating entities, 300
creating relationships, 308
introducing, 13
maintaining entities, 300,
449
maintaining relationships,
310
removing from arc, 315
Entity relationship diagrams
creating, 14
saving, 14
Expand, 188
Expand All, 189

Fast Create, 197
Find utility, 190
First Normal Form, 468
Force Delete, 198
Foreign Key constraints, 53–54
Formula items, 79
Front-end generators
  Developer/2000 Forms
    Generator, 854
  Developer/2000 Graphics
    Generator, 863
  Developer/2000 Reports
    Generator, 861
  introduction, 93
  invoking, 852
  Microsoft Help Generator,
    866
  Visual Basic Generator, 865
  WebServer Generator, 864
Function
  attribute usages, 29
  creating, 24
  entity usages, 27
  maintaining, 26
Function Hierarchy
    Diagrammer
  creating a diagram, 287
  creating a function, 287
  creating attribute usages,
    488
  creating entity usages, 317,
    486
  introducing, 23
  maintaining functions, 292
  modeling user interface
    requirements, 442
  resequencing functions, 290
Functional areas, 285
Functional diagrams, 23
Functional requirements, 22
Functions
  associating with business
    units, 295
  associating with key
    performance indicators,
    296
  associating with objectives,
    295

atomic, 291, 444
common, 291
copying, 291
elementary, 291, 444
master, 291
root, 290

**Generating Developer/2000
  modules**
  calendar controls, 915
  check boxes, 910
  current record indicator, 893
  list controls, 912
  push buttons, 910
  radio groups, 911
  single record layout, 888
  tab folder layout, 890
  tabular layout, 892
Generator Preferences
  creating preference sets, 840
  freezing preferences, 841
  invoking, 836
  locking preferences, 840
  managing preferences, 837
  setting preferences, 838
  unfreezing preferences, 841
  unlocking preferences, 841
Goals
  associating with business
    units, 271
  characteristics of, 268
Goto Mark, 195

Hammer, Michael, 405

Indexes, 59, 586
Item groups, 270

Key based links, 73
Klein, Mark, 406

Load, 179
Locations, 260
Logic Editor
  checking syntax, 801
  Editor pane, 797
  exporting text, 802
  importing text, 802

introducing, 87
Outline pane, 795
Selection Tree window, 798

Manganelli, Raymond, 406
Mapping entities to tables
  arc implementation, 561
  explicit subtype
    implementation, 558
  implicit subtype
    implementation, 559
  supertype implementation,
    556
Mark, 195
Matrix Diagrammer, 435, 489
Measures, in data warehouses,
    479
Messages
  externalizing, 883
  hard coding, 881
  implementing, 880
  raised by stored program
    units, 885
  soft coding, 881
Metamodel, 115
Mission statement, 270
Module Application Guide,
    698
Module component, 76
  Data Wizard, 724
  Display Wizard, 725
  maintaining properties,
    711
  re-ordering, 73
Module diagram
  creating, 70
  data view, 70, 693
  display view, 70, 695
  elements of, 71
Module Diagrammer
  creating item groups, 711
  creating items, 710
  creating key-based links,
    710
  creating module
    components, 709
  creating table usages, 710
  creating windows, 711

Modules
  application logic, 697
  copying, 705
  copying with new language,
    705
  creating, 701
  creating associations with
    other modules, 702
  data view, 693
  display view, 695
  item groups, 697
  items, 695
  links, 695
  maintaining arguments, 704
  maintaining help, 702
  module component, 693
  table usages, 694
  types, 688
  user security with
    Developer/2000 menus,
    707
  windows, 697

Navigate, 189
Network connections, 606
Nodes, 606
Non-Oracle databases, 610
Normalization, 468
Notification, 199
Nullify delete, 506

Object libraries
  customizing, 844
  setting related preferences,
    846
  types of objects, 842
Object Navigator, 183
Object sets, 172
Objectives
  associating with functions,
    295
  in Designer/2000, 270
Objects in diagrams
  changing the colors of
    objects, 233
  changing the font of objects,
    232
  collapsing, 226

  collapsing all, 227
  copying objects, 231
  creating objects, 227
  cutting objects, 231
  deleting objects, 230
  editing properties of objects,
    233
  expanding all, 227
  hybrid layouts, 225
  moving objects, 229
  pasting objects, 231
  resizing objects, 229
  reviewing changes, 230
  selecting multiple objects, 228
  selecting objects, 228
OLAP systems, 13, 481
OLTP systems, 13, 481
Oracle database
  avoiding fragmentation, 614
  database profiles, 624
  database roles, 620
  database users, 622
  files, 612
  guidelines for object distrib-
    ution, 616
  rollback segments, 618
  storage definition, 613
  tablespaces, 617
Oracle sequences, 598
Order Management System
  Requirements, 445
Overflow style
  overflow area below, 900
  overflow area right, 900
  spread table, 900
  wrap line, 900

Pages, 73
Paste Properties, 202
Physical database design
  flexibility, 640
  parametrizing properties of
    objects, 640
PL/SQL
  benefits or packages, 761
  constants, 743
  cursors, 748
  data types, 741

  database triggers, 763
  explicit cursors, 749
  history, 732
  IF statement, 738
  library modules, 763
  looping statements, 740
  named internal exceptions,
    765
  packages, 760
  PL/SQL records, 744
  PL/SQL tables, 745
  propagation of exceptions,
    768
  SQLCODE, 768
  SQLERRM, 768
  unnamed internal
    exceptions, 766
  user-defined exceptions, 767
  variables, 742
PL/SQL blocks, 736
PL/SQL engines, 733
PL/SQL objects
  creating database triggers,
    782
  creating definitions in
    Design Editor, 773
  declarative method
    definition, 777
  file method definition, 774
  free format definition, 775
  implementing in
    Designer/2000, 781
PL/SQL program units
  arguments, 759
  components, 757
  defining, 84
  generating, 92
Planning horizon, 270
Planning items
  creating, 262–263
  maintaining, 262
Primary Access Controlled
  (PAC) elements, 113
Primary key constraints, 53
Problems
  associating with business
    units, 275
  in Designer/2000, 274

Process Modeller
 animating diagrams, 381
 calculating critical path,
  395
 configuring for multimedia,
  382
 decision points, 348
 diagrams, 330
 events, 370
 exporting process data, 392
 maintaining multimedia
  properties, 377
 new animated figures, 381
 organization units, 333, 334
 outcomes, 338
 process flows, 339, 373
 process steps, 337, 368
 roles, 365
 root processes, 331
 stores, 348, 372
 triggers, 338
 using multimedia files, 384
Property Palette
 display the properties of
  multiple objects, 204
 intersect mode, 203
 pin properties, 203
 set properties, 201
 union mode, 203

Recover Database Design
 Utility, 825–826
Recover Module Design, 689
Reference code table, 817
Referencing, 842
Relationships
 arcs, 314
 as part of unique identifiers,
  466
 cardinality, 304
 optionality, 304
 resolving many-to-many,
  464
 tools in the Entity Relationship Diagrammer, 307
 types, 305
Repository Administration
 Utility, 116

Repository Object Navigator
 creating objects, 197
 customizing Navigator
  groups, 265
 customizing Property
  Palette, 205
 deleting, 198
 filtering criteria, 193
 filtering groups of objects,
  146
 introducing, 7
 search engine, 190
Repository Reports
 attribute definition, 525
 attributes in a domain, 525
 constraint definition, 809
 database definition, 809
 database object implementation definition, 809
 database objects, 809
 database user definition,
  809
 entities and their attributes,
  524
 entity completeness
  checking, 521
 entity definition, 522
 entity model reference, 522
 function data usages
  reports, 526
 function definition, 526
 function hierarchy, 525
 function hierarchy
  summary, 525
 function to attribute matrix,
  524
 function to entity matrix,
  523
 PL/SQL module definition,
  809
 quality checking of relationships, 521
 system glossary, 523
 table definition, 808
Repository users
 creating, 130
 reconciling, 130
Requery, 198

Restricted delete, 505
Restructuring, 404
Reusable Component
  Graphical Editor, 729
Reusable module component
 creating, 728
 displaying on diagrams, 729
 including in a module, 728
Revert, 201
Rightsizing, 404

Second Normal Form, 468
Secondary Access Controlled
  (SAC) elements, 113
Selection Tree, 88–89
Sequence, 597, 635
Server API
 components, 785
 database triggers, 788
 generating, 816
 module components API,
  790
 table API, 785
Server Generator
 generating database
  administration objects,
  811
 generating database objects,
  813
 generating schema for
  different environments,
  820
 generating schemas for multiple sites, 824
 implementing database
  upgrades, 822
 introducing, 60
 invoking, 810
 output, 815
Share, 168
Sizing models, 644
Snapshot, 595, 632
Snapshot logs, 595
Software engineering, 104
Subclassing, 842
System requirements
 categories of, 429
 data requirements, 430

Designer/2000 tools for, 435
documentation
    requirements, 432
functional requirements,
    430
hardware and software
    requirements, 433
intersystem interface
    requirements, 432
reliability, availability, and
    serviceability
    requirements, 434
security requirements, 431
user interface requirements,
    429

Table implementation
    creating, 47, 626
    maintaining, 626
Table to Entity Retrofit utility,
    829
Table usages, 72, 713

Templates
    creating new, 877
    customizing, 851
    purpose, 847
    types of objects, 848
The American Software Club
    (TASC), 252
Third Normal Form, 468
Total Quality Management
    (TQM), 404

Unbound items, 73, 718
Unique constraints, 53
Unique identifiers, 17
Unload, 179
User Extensibility
    adding new properties, 134
    creating new association
        types, 137
    creating new element types,
        134
    creating new text types, 138

extracting, 140
loading, 140
procedure, 133
types, 133
User-defined sets
    creating, 173
    locking, 173
    populating, 173
    unlocking, 174

Views
    enforce data access rules,
        588
    implement business views
        of data, 588
    maintaining, 631
    set properties, 589

**Window, maintaining, 76,
    720**

Yourdon, Edward, 439

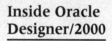

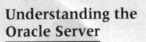

LICENSE AGREEMENT AND LIMITED WARRANTY

READ THE FOLLOWING TERMS AND CONDITIONS CAREFULLY BEFORE OPENING THIS SOFTWARE MEDIA PACKAGE. THIS LEGAL DOCUMENT IS AN AGREEMENT BETWEEN YOU AND PRENTICE-HALL, INC. (THE "COMPANY"). BY OPENING THIS SEALED SOFTWARE MEDIA PACKAGE, YOU ARE AGREEING TO BE BOUND BY THESE TERMS AND CONDITIONS. IF YOU DO NOT AGREE WITH THESE TERMS AND CONDITIONS, DO NOT OPEN THE SOFT-WARE MEDIA PACKAGE. PROMPTLY RETURN THE UNOPENED PACKAGE AND ALL AC-COMPANYING ITEMS TO THE PLACE YOU OBTAINED THEM FOR A FULL REFUND OF ANY SUMS YOU HAVE PAID.

1. **GRANT OF LICENSE:** In consideration of your payment of the license fee, which is part of the price you paid for this product, and your agreement to abide by the terms and conditions of this Agreement, the Company grants to you a nonexclusive right to use and display the copy of the enclosed software program (hereinafter the "SOFTWARE") on a single computer (i.e., with a single CPU) at a single location so long as you comply with the terms of this Agreement. The Company reserves all rights not expressly granted to you under this Agreement.

2. **OWNERSHIP OF SOFTWARE:** You own only the magnetic or physical media (the enclosed CD-ROM) on which the SOFTWARE is recorded or fixed, but the Company retains all the rights, title, and ownership to the SOFTWARE recorded on the original CD-ROM copy(ies) and all subsequent copies of the SOFTWARE, regardless of the form or media on which the original or other copies may exist. This license is not a sale of the original SOFTWARE or any copy to you.

3. **COPY RESTRICTIONS:** This SOFTWARE and the accompanying printed materials and user manual (the "Documentation") are the subject of copyright. You may not copy the Documentation or the SOFTWARE, except that you may make a single copy of the SOFTWARE for backup or archival purposes only. You may be held legally responsible for any copying or copyright infringement which is caused or encouraged by your failure to abide by the terms of this restriction.

4. **USE RESTRICTIONS:** You may not network the SOFTWARE or otherwise use it on more than one computer or computer terminal at the same time. You may physically transfer the SOFT-WARE from one computer to another provided that the SOFTWARE is used on only one computer at a time. You may not distribute copies of the SOFTWARE or Documentation to others. You may not reverse engineer, disassemble, decompile, modify, adapt, translate, or create derivative works based on the SOFTWARE or the Documentation without the prior written consent of the Company.

5. **TRANSFER RESTRICTIONS:** The enclosed SOFTWARE is licensed only to you and may not be transferred to any one else without the prior written consent of the Company. Any unauthorized transfer of the SOFTWARE shall result in the immediate termination of this Agreement.

6. **TERMINATION:** This license is effective until terminated. This license will terminate automatically without notice from the Company and become null and void if you fail to comply with any provisions or limitations of this license. Upon termination, you shall destroy the Documentation and all copies of the SOFTWARE. All provisions of this Agreement as to warranties, limitation of liability, remedies or damages, and our ownership rights shall survive termination.

7. **MISCELLANEOUS:** This Agreement shall be construed in accordance with the laws of the United States of America and the State of New York and shall benefit the Company, its affiliates, and assignees.

8. **LIMITED WARRANTY AND DISCLAIMER OF WARRANTY:** The Company warrants that the SOFTWARE, when properly used in accordance with the Documentation, will operate in substantial conformity with the description of the SOFTWARE set forth in the Documentation. The Company does not warrant that the SOFTWARE will meet your requirements or that the operation of the

SOFTWARE will be uninterrupted or error-free. The Company warrants that the media on which the SOFTWARE is delivered shall be free from defects in materials and workmanship under normal use for a period of thirty (30) days from the date of your purchase. Your only remedy and the Company's only obligation under these limited warranties is, at the Company's option, return of the warranted item for a refund of any amounts paid by you or replacement of the item. Any replacement of SOFT-WARE or media under the warranties shall not extend the original warranty period. The limited warranty set forth above shall not apply to any SOFTWARE which the Company determines in good faith has been subject to misuse, neglect, improper installation, repair, alteration, or damage by you. EX-CEPT FOR THE EXPRESSED WARRANTIES SET FORTH ABOVE, THE COMPANY DISCLAIMS ALL WARRANTIES, EXPRESS OR IMPLIED, INCLUDING WITHOUT LIMITATION, THE IMPLIED WARRANTIES OF MERCHANTABILITY AND FITNESS FOR A PARTICULAR PURPOSE. EXCEPT FOR THE EXPRESS WARRANTY SET FORTH ABOVE, THE COMPANY DOES NOT WARRANT, GUARANTEE, OR MAKE ANY REPRESENTATION REGARDING THE USE OR THE RESULTS OF THE USE OF THE SOFTWARE IN TERMS OF ITS CORRECTNESS, ACCURACY, RELIABILITY, CURRENTNESS, OR OTHERWISE.

IN NO EVENT, SHALL THE COMPANY OR ITS EMPLOYEES, AGENTS, SUPPLIERS, OR CONTRACTORS BE LIABLE FOR ANY INCIDENTAL, INDIRECT, SPECIAL, OR CONSEQUEN-TIAL DAMAGES ARISING OUT OF OR IN CONNECTION WITH THE LICENSE GRANTED UNDER THIS AGREEMENT, OR FOR LOSS OF USE, LOSS OF DATA, LOSS OF INCOME OR PROFIT, OR OTHER LOSSES, SUSTAINED AS A RESULT OF INJURY TO ANY PERSON, OR LOSS OF OR DAMAGE TO PROPERTY, OR CLAIMS OF THIRD PARTIES, EVEN IF THE COMPANY OR AN AUTHORIZED REPRESENTATIVE OF THE COMPANY HAS BEEN ADVISED OF THE POSSI-BILITY OF SUCH DAMAGES. IN NO EVENT SHALL LIABILITY OF THE COMPANY FOR DAM-AGES WITH RESPECT TO THE SOFTWARE EXCEED THE AMOUNTS ACTUALLY PAID BY YOU, IF ANY, FOR THE SOFTWARE.

SOME JURISDICTIONS DO NOT ALLOW THE LIMITATION OF IMPLIED WARRANTIES OR LIABILITY FOR INCIDENTAL, INDIRECT, SPECIAL, OR CONSEQUENTIAL DAMAGES, SO THE ABOVE LIMITATIONS MAY NOT ALWAYS APPLY. THE WARRANTIES IN THIS AGREE-MENT GIVE YOU SPECIFIC LEGAL RIGHTS AND YOU MAY ALSO HAVE OTHER RIGHTS WHICH VARY IN ACCORDANCE WITH LOCAL LAW.

ACKNOWLEDGMENT

YOU ACKNOWLEDGE THAT YOU HAVE READ THIS AGREEMENT, UNDERSTAND IT, AND AGREE TO BE BOUND BY ITS TERMS AND CONDITIONS. YOU ALSO AGREE THAT THIS AGREEMENT IS THE COMPLETE AND EXCLUSIVE STATEMENT OF THE AGREEMENT BE-TWEEN YOU AND THE COMPANY AND SUPERSEDES ALL PROPOSALS OR PRIOR AGREE-MENTS, ORAL, OR WRITTEN, AND ANY OTHER COMMUNICATIONS BETWEEN YOU AND THE COMPANY OR ANY REPRESENTATIVE OF THE COMPANY RELATING TO THE SUBJECT MATTER OF THIS AGREEMENT.

Should you have any questions concerning this Agreement or if you wish to contact the Company for any reason, please contact in writing at the address below.

Robin Short
Prentice Hall PTR
One Lake Street
Upper Saddle River, New Jersey 07458

INSIDE ORACLE DESIGNER/2000 COMPANION CD-ROM

The companion CD-ROM contains a number of application systems that you can load in your Designer/2000 Repository. This will enable you to follow the discussion of different topics in *Inside Oracle Designer/2000* by performing the activities discussed in your own environment. In addition, the CD contains a number of Lotus ScreenCam movies that illustrate the most important tasks you can accomplish with Designer/2000. For more information on the content of the CD-ROM and instructions for configuring the ScreenCam Player, refer to the section "Companion CD-ROM" in the Preface.

The software provided on the CD is configured for Microsoft Windows 95 and Windows NT (4.x) operating systems. You can browse the contents of the CD by using your Web browser. Simply point to the file DES2000.HTM on the CD and then follow the hyperlinks to different assets provided on the CD. For questions, comments, or an updated list of contents, point your Web browser to the author's page at www.alulushi.com.

TECHNICAL SUPPORT

Prentice Hall does not offer technical support for this software. However, if there is a problem with the media, you may obtain a replacement copy by emailing us with your problem at:

discexchange@phptr.com